Hoyo de Monterrey smokers have included

Presidents, Prime Ministers,

Sultans, Kings,

Barons of the business world,

Hollywood legends...

...and, of course, other notables.

www.cigarworld.com ©2008 General Cigar Co., Inc.

EVERY MAN DESERVES A HOYO
HOYO DE MONTERREY

PUNCH.
True to its name.

Perelman's Pocket Cyclopedia of Cigars

2008 edition

TABLE OF CONTENTS

TABLE OF CONTENTS

Please send comments, inquiries, questions and suggestions to the author at:

PERELMAN, PIONEER & COMPANY
POST OFFICE BOX 67548
CENTURY CITY STATION
LOS ANGELES, CALIFORNIA 90067 USA

Telephone: (213) 365-7965
Facsimile: (213) 365-7895
Internet: editor@CigarCyclopedia.com

Authoritative, on-line coverage at

≡ CigarCyclopedia .com ≡

*Daily coverage of
cigars, accessories, issues and people*

MATURITY
is the only path to **PERFECTION.**

CAMACHO.

INTRODUCTION

Here we go again.

Despite the incredibly negative environment across the U.S. for smokes of all tobacco products, the cigar industry continues to thrive and expand. If not a boom, certainly a renaissance.

The number of brands covered rose for the third straight edition, by 5.8% to 1,305. That's after receding in five consecutive editions from 2000 through 2004. Over the last four years, the total rose from 1,002 to 1,091 to 1,233 and now, 1,305, the second-highest ever. The all-time high of 1,448 came in 1999.

Here are a few tips to help users of this book, to make your exploration and research efforts more fun:

About this book:
We have provided critical details on a lot of cigars. A total of 1,305 brands are profiled, comprising more than 5,000 models. That's a lot more than the 370 brands we started with in our inaugural edition in 1995.

We note that our listing represents virtually every brand *marketed* nationally. Readers will find some brands which are not listed here, but which are available at his or her local smokeshop. These brands are very likely:

▸ Private label or unbranded cigars offered by major manu-facturers, on which store names are placed for local sale;

▸ House brands produced for individual cigar lounges, mail-order/on-line houses or retailers, which are not available at wholesale for national distribution to tobacco stores;

INTRODUCTION

- Cigars produced by small, local factories and marketed regionally, or brands which are still *available* nationally, but without any active marketing effort behind them;

- New lines introduced after this book was completed;

- Close-outs (still widely sold!) or discontinued brands no longer produced or available from manufacturers.

This should not dissuade readers from trying or enjoying these cigars. We actively encourage everyone to try new cigars and refrain from the kind of "cigar snobbery" which is so easy for premium cigar smokers to fall into. ***The best cigar you will ever smoke might be the next one you try.***

Readers looking for details on these brands may wish to consult our previous editions, which covered many brands now out of production. Please visit our *CigarCyclopedia.com* web site if you wish to purchase back issues of our *Perelman's Pocket Cyclopedia of Cigars*.

About the brands:
We have tried to list, for each handmade brand, the country of origin of the wrapper, filler and binder. While we have received wonderful cooperation from the manufacturers and distributors, more than one executive has told us something like, "This is what we would like to use, but if we can't get it, we will blend in something else."

In most cases, this should *not* be of great concern. After all, most consumers buy specific cigars based on an expectation of taste and draw, not on the ingredients. Recent history shows that

CRAFTSMANSHIP WITHOUT COMPROMISE

CREDO
www.credo.fr

master blenders have little difficulty re-configuring brands with different tobaccos to achieve the same taste and quality of construction.

About the shapes:
The major trends in brands and shapes for 2007 showed (1) fewer shapes in most brands, concentrated on bigger ring gauges. (2) more strongly-flavored blends and (3) more consumer-friendly packaging. The clearest trends are for:

- Continued introduction of new lines which are extensions of well-known brands, giving the new blends a major marketing advantage;

- More perfecto and "box-pressed" shapes with reference to old Cuban sizes and shapes and larger ring gauges;

- New packaging not only offering the smoker their favorite brands in packs of 3, 4, 5 or 10, but also sampler packs of brands with a range of sizes in a single box. For so many smokers who enjoy a variety of brands, this is a welcome (and cost-saving) development indeed!

A list of the brands which feature extra large, extra long or striped-wrapper cigars is listed in section 2.04.

Cuban cigars:
Because of our concentration on cigars available in the U.S., listings of cigars produced in Cuba are not included. Please us our companion volume, *Perelman's Pocket Cyclopedia of Havana Cigars (3rd edition),* available through your local tobacconist or by writing to us directly.

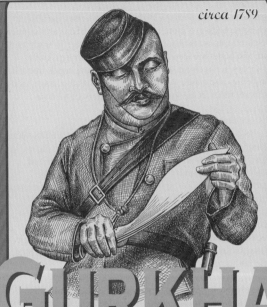

INTRODUCTION

The future:
Cigar sales are up, perhaps as smokers from the Cigar Boom have come back in a more mature way, or perhaps as a segment of cigarette smokers change to cigars. The future is bright, with more and better tobacco available, but difficult legislative challenges are keeping smokers from enjoying cigars freely in many cities and states. At some point, this has to change, as it has many times in the long and rocky history of tobacco.

With our thanks:
This book could not have been produced without a tremendous amount of help from many people in and around the cigar industry. Representatives of most every manufacturer and distributor in the country endured many telephone calls requesting information, and virtually everyone we contacted was not only forthcoming, but enthusiastic.

Special thanks to assistant editor Steve Harris, marketing director Pat Harris and Chromatic Lithographers of Glendale, California for their effort in printing. Without them, this book could not have been produced.

We're always happy to hear from you; you can contact us through *CigarCyclopedia.com* or via electronic mail at editor@CigarCyclopedia.com. I hope to see you in a smoke-filled room soon!

RICHARD B. PERELMAN
Los Angeles, California
November 2007

Premium Handmade Cigars   Savor a Tradition of Excellence

www.torano.com

NOVENTA

VIRTUOSO

SIGNATURE

EXODUS SILVER

EXODUS 1959

CAMEROON

RESERVA DECADÉNCIA

RESERVA SELECTA

CASA TORAÑO MADURO

CASA TORAÑO

1.
CIGAR BASICS

1.01 ABOUT CIGARS
The joy of smoking rolled tobacco leaves began in the Americas hundreds of years ago and was introduced to Europeans after Christopher Columbus' return from his first voyage in 1492.

In the ensuing years, the popularity and sophistication of tobacco products has grown and the 1990s has brought a significant increase in the popularity of cigars in the United States. Despite much controversy, the status of cigars as a luxury product in American culture is secure.

The important technical elements to be appreciated in cigars include their construction and the many shapes and sizes.

1.02 CONSTRUCTION
What goes into cigars? The answer to this question is the key to assessing the quality of a specific cigar. All but the thinnest cigars include three elements: (1) the filler tobacco at the center, (2) a binder leaf which holds the filler together and (3) the outer wrapper, which is rolled around the binder.

Cigars which are made by hand use "long filler" tobacco: leaves which run the length of a cigar. In a handmade, the filler, binder and wrapper are combined manually.

Machine-made cigars utilize high-speed machinery to combine "short filler" tobacco – usually scraps or pieces of tobacco leaves – or a mixed filler of long and short pieces with a binder and wrapper. Because of the tension placed on the tobacco by the machines, the binders and wrappers are often made of a "homogenized tobacco leaf" product (called "HTL" or "sheet") which is stronger than natural leaves and can be produced in a variety of flavors, strengths and textures.

A few brands combine machine-bunching (using long-filler tobacco) with hand-rolled wrappers; this practice has been very properly dubbed "hand-rolled" as opposed to handmade by cigar expert Rick Hacker in *The Ultimate Cigar Book*. And some larger cigars use "mixed" or "combination" filler of long-filler and short-filler tobaccos.

The most obvious characteristic of most cigars is the color of the exterior wrapper. While not the only factor in the taste of a cigar, it is an important element and a key in many people's purchase of specific cigars. Although manufacturers have identified more than 100 different wrapper shades, six major color classifications are used herein, as noted below:

Color	Abbrev.	Description
Double Claro	*"DC"*	Also known as "American Market Selection" [AMS] or "Candela," this is a green wrapper. Once popular, it is only occasionally found today.
Claro	*"Cl"*	This is a very light tan color, almost beige in shade; usually from Connecticut.
Colorado Claro	*"CC"*	A medium brown found on many cigars, this category covers many descriptions. The most popular are "Natural" or "English Market Selection" [EMS]. Tobaccos in this shade are grown in many countries.
Colorado	*"Co"*	This shade is instantly recognizable by the obvious reddish tint.

Ten years ago they said that our little cigar company would never make it.
Five years ago they said we'd never last.
Three years ago they started paying attention.
Today we're right where we belong: in your hand.
Against all odds!

www.rockypatel.com

Color	Abbrev.	Description
Colorado Maduro	*"CM"*	Darker than Colorado Claro in shade, this color is often associated with African tobacco, such as wrappers from Cameroon, or with Havana Seed tobacco grown in Honduras or Nicaragua.
Maduro	*"Ma"*	Very dark brown or black.Tobacco for Maduro wrappers is primarily grown in Connecticut, Mexico, Nicaragua and Brazil.
Oscuro	*"Os"*	This is black...really black. This shade of wrapper reappeared with more frequency in 2001 and is in our listings.

The listing of cigar brands in this book assumes that, unless otherwise noted, handmade cigars utilize long-filler tobacco and machine-made cigars use short-filler.

1.03 SHAPES AND SIZES

There are cigars of every shape and every size for every occasion. From tiny, cigarette-like cigarillos to giant monsters resembling pool cues, there is a wide variety to choose from.

Certain sizes and shapes which have gained popularity over the years and have become widely recognized, even by non-smokers. Cigar shape names such as "corona" or "panatela" have specific meanings to the cigar industry, although there is no formally agreed-to standard for any given size.

The following table lists 20 well-known shapes, and is adapted from Paul Garmirian's explanation of sizes in *The Gourmet Guide to Cigars.* The "classical" measurements for which this shape is known are given, along with a size and girth range for each size for classification purposes:

CUBAN CRAFTERS

BOUTIQUE PREMIUM CIGARS
RANKED AMONG THE BEST

9.1 SMOKE Rated

9.1 SMOKE Rated

9.2 SMOKE Rated

9.4 SMOKE Rated

| DON KIKI WHITE LABEL VINTAGE CHURCHILL | CUBAN CRAFTERS CHAIRMAN | CUBAN CRAFTERS CABINET SELECTION TORO | DON KIKI BROWN LABEL TORO |

BOUTIQUE PREMIUM CIGARS

Find your nearest retailer at www.cubancrafters.com
OR
ORDER TOLL FREE 1-877-244-2701

Shape	*Classical Lngth. x Ring*	*Length range*	*Ring range*
Giant	9 x 52	8 & up	50 & up
Double Corona	7¾ x 49	6¾-7¾	49 & up
Churchill	7 x 47	6¾-7⅞	46-48
Perfecto	none	all	all
Pyramid	7 x 36→54	all	flared
Torpedo	6⅛ x 52	all	tapered
Toro	6 x 50	5⅝-6⅝	48 & up
Robusto	5 x 50	3-5½	48 & up
Grand Corona	6½ x 46	5⅝-6⅝	45-47
Corona Extra	5½ x 46	4½-5½	45-47
Giant Corona	7½ x 44	7½ & up	42-45
Lonsdale	6½ x 42	6½-7¼	40-45
Long Corona	6 x 42	5⅞-6⅜	40-44
Corona	5½ x 42	5⅛-5¾	40-44
Petit Corona	5 x 42	4-5	40-44
Long Panatela	7½ x 38	7 & up	35-39
Panatela	6 x 38	5½-6⅞	35-39
Short Panatela	5 x 38	4-5⅜	35-39
Slim Panatela	6 x 34	5 & up	30-34
Small Panatela	5 x 33	4-5	30-34
Cigarillos	4 x 26	6 & less	29 & less

For the purposes of classification, the cigar models of the 1,305 brands profiled have been separated into these 20 major groups. With the great increase in shaped cigars, here are our classification criteria for *figurados:*

- Culebras, which is made up of three small cigars twisted together. This shape has returned to the U.S. market and a few manufacturers have this unique shape available (see section 2.04 for an up-to-date listing).

▸ Perfecto, which has two tapered ends. Until recently, there were just a few cigars which offered Perfecto "tips" on the foot, but true Perfectos have made their comeback. For the bold, take a look at the Puros Indios Gran Victoria (10 inches long by 60 ring) to see a true "pot-bellied" cigar.

▸ Torpedo, which was traditionally a fat cigar with two fully closed, pointed ends, but has now come to mean a cigar with an open foot and a straight body which tapers to a closed, pointed head. This "new" torpedo was popularized by the Montecristo (Havana) No. 2. The Torpedo differs from "Pyramid"-shaped cigars, which flare continuously from the head to the foot, essentially forming a triangle.

Like the Torpedo, whose meaning has changed over time, the Royal Corona or Rothschild title is seen less and less on cigars now known as "Robustos." This change has been rapid over the past 4-5 years, but some manufacturers still label their shorter, thicker cigars as Rothschilds or even as a "Rothchild" (an incorrect spelling of the famous German banking family name). A few manufacturers use both and label their 5-5½-inch, 50-ring models as "Robustos" and reserve the "Rothschild" name for shorter, but still 50-ring, cigars of 4-4¾ inches!

Many other shape names are used by manufacturers; some cigars even have multiple names. For convenience, the many types of small, very thin cigars are grouped under the "Cigarillo" title rather than distributed over a long list of names such as "Belvederes," "Demi-Tasse" and others

ESCAPE WITH

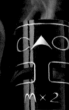

1.04 ENJOYING CIGARS

The enjoyment of cigars is a personal pleasure, which is as varied as the 1,305 brands profiled. However, there are certain matters which should be considered carefully by all smokers and which require attention.

- Foremost among these is storage and the usefulness of a humidor in proper working condition cannot be underestimated. The death of a quality cigar due to a lack of care is a sad occurrence indeed.

- For those carrying cigars on the go, travel humidors or leather cigar cases are important items to keep your cigars safe and in good smoking condition.

- Finally, the proper tools for cutting and lighting your cigar are necessary accessories for full enjoyment.

In addition, *an often under-utilized resource for the smoker is your local smokeshop.* Most are experienced, knowledgeable and have access to experts, manufacturers and the Retail Tobacco Dealers of America trade association. Use their expertise to help you!

Desflorado - not a common term, nor a common wrapper.

Our blend of tobaccos from Nicaragua, Indonesia and the Dominican Republic provides much of the distinctive flavor in La Flor de Ynclan, but the wrapper leaf gives the cigar its unique character. The Connecticut wrapper is grown in Ecuador, and following the harvest of the normal five primings, the plant is left to flower and the top leaves to grow. This extra time on the plant gives the leaf more sunlight and nourishment, providing the beautiful color and full-bodied taste. Only three out of ten of these leaves are high enough in quality to be selected. These "late harvest" leaves are referred to as *desflorado*, and you'll find them only in the finest quality of cigars – like La Flor de Ynclan.

Taste La Flor de Ynclan, and we think you'll agree it's not a common wrapper – and *not* a common cigar.

2.
THE CIGAR ALMANAC

Here are facts, figures and a little fun about the 1,305 brands (1,145 handmades, 90 machine-made and 70 small cigars) profiled in this year's edition:

2.01 BIRTHS AND DEATHS
The total number of brands in circulation increased by 72 brands overall and 71 in handmades. A total of 214 brands (201 handmades) entered (or re-entered) national distribution since the last edition, compared with 194 brands (176 handmades) last year. Of the 201 new handmades, 17 returned to the market in 2007 (marked by ■) after being out of national distribution in recent years. The new entries:

Handmade (201):

5 Vegas Cask Strength
898 Collection Tricolor
1876 Reserve
A/R Flagship
A/R Green Band
A/R Select
Adonis
Adonis Maduro
Aganorsa Leaf
Arganese
Aspira Corojo & Maduro
Astral GRV '96
Aurora Barrel Aged
Avalon
Avo 787
Bahia Icon
Bandidos
Bayamo Superiores ■
Belmore Colorado
Belmore Maduro
Black Pearl Conga ■
Black Pearl Morado
Blair ■
Blanton's
Bluntville
Bock y Ca. Edicion de Oro

Brittania Reserve
Brocatus
C.A.O. America
C.A.O. Black VR
Café Libertad
Camacho Triple Maduro
Campesino
Canimao
Carbon Copy Shorty's
Carbon Copy Wedge
Casa Torano Maduro
Carlos Torano Res. Decad,
Casa Fernandez
Casa Gomez
Chairman's Choice ■
Cisso Bourbon
Cisso Grande
Cisso Superior ■
Cisso Wine ■
Colba 1492
Colinas
Costa
Costa Brava
Cremosa Cubana
Cuba Aliados Anniversary
Cuban Honeys
Cuban Sandwich

Cumbres Gold
Daniel Marshall Red ■
Daniel Marshall White Label
Dominican ■
Defiance
Dominican Santiago Sel.
Dominicano
Don Cisso ■
Don Elias
Don Elio's
Don Gonzalez
Don Lino 1989
Don Pepin Garcia - Black
Don Pepin Garcia - Serie JJ
  Maduro
Don Priamo ■
Don Tomas Sun Grown
Double Happiness
Duque
El Botin Dominicano
El Coloso
El Duque Cognac
El Premer Mondo
El Rey del Mundo Olivados
El Titan de Bronze Gr. Res.
Erin Go Bragh
Famous Dom. Sel. No. 2000

ALMANAC

Famous Dom. Sel. No. 3000
Famous Dom. Sel. No. 4000
Famous Dom. Sel. No. 5000
Famous Hon. Sel. 3000
Famous Nic. Sel. 4000
Felipe Gregorio 1957 Series
Felipe Art of Power
Five Star 2000
The Flava
Flor de Copan ■
Flower City Cigar ■
Fonseca Habana Selection
Frank Vincent Signature
Free Cuba
Fuego del Dios
Fundacion Ancestral
The Good, Bad & Ugly
Grande de Espana ■
Guantanamera
Gurkha Centurion
Gurkha Double Maduro
Gurkha East India
Gurkha Platinum
Gurkha Regent
H. Upmann Cabinet Sel.
Habana Clasico
Habana Real
Habanos Puros Sel. Suprema
Harly
Havana Sandwich
Havana Sunrise
Hoyo de Tradicion
HuzGar
Illusione
Indian Tabac 10 Year Ann.
Indian Tabac Maduro
Isla de Cuba
Isla del Sol
J. Fuego Gran Reserva
Jack's Reserve
JML 1902
Joya de Nicaragua Serie C
Just For Retailers
Kentucky Gentlemen Cigar
King David
Kinky Friedman
La Herencia de Cuba
La Rosa Especial ■

La Vieja Habana - The Early
  Years ■
Laurato
Lazo
Legends
Le Gran Fuma
Licenciados Aniversario
Liga Privada No. 9
Magellan Dominicans
Mardo (2 lines)
Martinez N.Y. Gold Series
Mistakes
MJH
Montalvo
Monte Verde
Montecristo Cabinet Sel.
Montecristo Serie C
Mosaico
Mr. Dominic ■
Nat Sherman 489
Nestor Miranda Special Sel.
Oliva Serie V
Oliveros Cuban Spliff
Oliveros Eight Zero
Oliveros Kopi Luwak
Origins
Oro Cubano
Oxford Post-Embargo Sel.
Padilla 1948
Padilla Series '68
Palma Real
Paul Garmirian Soiree
Perdomo Habano
Personales
Pintor Dynasty
Playboy
Por Larranaga Cabinet Sel.
Pueblo Dominicano Serie II
Quadrado
Rafael Ramos
Ramon Allones Reserve
Rav
Rey Miguel
Rocky Patel Am.Mkt.Sel.
Rocky Patel Connecticut
Rocky Patel Decade
Rocky Patel Factory Selects
  Corojo & Maduro

Rocky Patel Fusion
Rocky Patel Hon. Classic
Rocky Patel Rosado
Romeo y Julieta Cabinet Sel.
Romeo y Julieta Ed. Limit.
Romeo y Julieta Hab. Res.
Romeo y Julieta Viejo
Royal Dominican
San Cristobal
Santa Rosa ■
Selecto Puro Dominicano
Sergio Master
Sol Cubano
Stixx
Stradivarius de los Maestros
Summus
Supervisor Selection
Ta Cuba
Te-Amo World Sel. Series
Ted's Made by Hand
Tobacconist Choice
Trinidad Habana Reserve
Troya Clasico
Value Line Hon. No. 500
Vega Fina
Vega Real
Villa Dominicana
Z-Gar

Machine-made (3):
Banker's Choice
La Fendrich ■
Nat Cicco's ■

Small cigars(10):
Beach Palm
Dark Horse
Djarum Spice Islands
Double Diamond
New York Minute
Premium One
Richwood
Twinkle
Vaquero
Vendetta

ALMANAC

(A few brands which are new to this book are not listed as new in this list, since they were previously in regional or occasional distribution and not actually a "new" brand. We *have* listed brands which went off the market and have now returned.)

The following 155 brands were not included in this year's listings because they have (1) been discontinued (even if still being sold as close-outs), (2) are not being marketed for national sale since: (a) they may be a regional or house brand or (b) a brand which is still available, but which is not being actively marketed on a national basis to retailers, or (c) a brand which is not sold by a U.S. distributor, or (3) when we called to find out about these brands, the telephone number of the manufacturer or distributor was disconnected, was now another business or even a residence!

Handmade (144):
A/R Epicure
Adriana's Sweets
Allegria!
American Born Cubans
Ancla y Cazador
Antico Cubano
Aquarius
Arte Cubano
Arzt de Los Reyes
Ashe
Bahia Blu
Bahia Ticos
Beethoven
Biker Boy International
Blue Label
Bogar
Bucanero Crew
C.A.O. l'Anniv. eXtreme
C.A.O. Artistry of
   Champions
C.A.O. Odyssey
C.A.O. Sixty-Fifth Anniv.
Cisso Coffee & Honey
Cisso Gordito
Cojimar Exotics

Companion Bronze Series
Companion Red Series
Companion Silver Series
Connecticut Yankee
Criollo 101856
CSB
Cuba Libre (Honduras)
Cuba Libre (Nicaragua)
Cuban Bullet
Cuban Cigar Factory
   Maestros
Cuban Heritage
Cuba Parejo
Cuban Vieja
DaGars
Diesel Fuerte
Don Antonio
Don Bernardo
Don Melo Centenario
Don Rafael Blue Edition
Don Rafael Gold Edition
Don Sergio Ramar
Dos Montes
Dos Rios
Due Mondi
Ego

Ejecutivos
El Pelotero
El Taino Vintage Cedar
Established 1844
Estates Collection
Fidalgo Negro
Famous Dom. Selection
FDP
Felipe II Reserva
Flor de Farach
Fuego de la Noche
Fuma Dominica Especial
Habana Cuba Premier Sel.
Habanos Puros Ltd. Reserve
Havana Verde
Hoja
Independencia
Inmenso
Irene
J. Donovan Leigh
Jamaican Vanilla
Joyas de Panama
Joyitas
John Aylesbury
Kahlua Especial
King David (Dom. Rep.)

La Casella	New Cuba	Sun Ripened Oscuros
La Casta	Nikki	Sweet Tip
La Estella Cubana	Nuevitas	SweeTeez
La Perfecta	Oliveros Gran Reserva	Tabacos Baez
La Primadora Select	One Off	Tadone
La Prueba	Oro de Panama	Taino
La Rica	Padilla Hybrid	Tamboril Sumatra
La Tradicion Cubana Anniv.	Padilla Maduro	Tre Sigari
Lady Jane	Perdomo Exclusivo	XXO
Las Vegas	Perdomo Reserve Moments	XXO 30 Year Oold
Le Creole	Pinar de Oro	XXO Titanium
Leoninos	Puros Indios Maxima	Ynego Montoya
L'il Sweets	Reserva Especial	
Lucky 8	Pyro	*Machine-made (5):*
M&R Pre-Embargo Ltd.Ed.	Queen City	Ballermann 6
Macabi Reserve	Quisqueya	National Cigar
Maestro Cubano	Rey Alfonso	Red Dot
Mantequilla	Rosalones	Schimmelpennick VSOP
Mantequilla Tapa Negra	Royal Jamaica	Trabucos
Medina	Royal Silk	
MiCubano	San Fernando de Omoa	*Small Cigars (6):*
Miranda	San Juan Martinez	Bliss
Mocambo	Sauza Tres Generaciones	Don Carbone
Mojo	Sherpa	Dunhill Small Cigars
Montecruz	Signet	Encore
Morro Castle	Smokin' Ass Cigars	MacBeth
Nat Sherman Cameroon	Stock 10	Remy

2.02 BRAND FACTS

Here are some entertaining facts about cigar brands and where they are produced:

Ancient brands:

Some brands have been with us since the early part of the 19th Century, originating primarily in Cuba. Some of the older brand names still being produced (or at least, available) for the U.S. market, with their original country of origin, include:

1810	Cabañas (Cuba)		1845	La Corona (Cuba)
1834	Por Larrañaga (Cuba)		1845	Partagas (Cuba)
1837	Ramon Allones (Cuba)		1848	El Rey del Mundo (Cuba)
1840	Bances (Cuba)		1850	Romeo y Julieta (Cuba)
1840	Marsh Wheeling (USA)		1867	Hoyo de Monterrey (Cuba)
1840	Punch (Cuba)		1868	Bauza (Cuba)
1844	H. Upmann (Cuba)		1871	Baccarat (USA)

1873 Dannemann (Brazil)	1903 Topstone (USA)
1876 Temple Hall (Jamaica)	1905 Bering (USA)
1881 Calixto Lopez (Cuba)	1912 Arturo Fuente (USA)
1882 Garcia y Vega (USA)	1912 Muniemaker (USA)
1884 Cuesta-Rey (USA)	1916 El Producto (USA)
1884 Judge's Cave (USA)	1922 Royal Jamaica (Jamaica)
1887 White Owl (USA)	1928 Rafael Gonzalez (Cuba)
1888 Villiger (Germany)	1935 Montecristo (Cuba)
1891 Fonseca (Cuba)	1946 Davidoff Chateau series by
1896 Topper (USA)	Hoyo de Monterrey (Cuba)
1901 Bolivar (Cuba)	1962 Montecruz (Canary Islands)
1903 La Aurora (Dom. Rep.)	1964 Don Diego (Canary Islands)

Bands on brands:

It is well established that in 1850, Gustave Bock of the Netherlands put bands on cigars for the first time, as a method of distinguishing his firm's Cuban-made cigars.

Brand production:

The Dominican Republic remains the top producer of U.S.-marketed cigars by a wide margin. In this edition, 44.9% of the handmade brands were produced there down from 43.0% in the 2007 edition, but not far from its recent high of 48.7% in 2000. Machine-made brands are starting to be produced in the Dominican as well and that total will grow.

After three years in third place, Honduras had the second-most handmade brands, some 21.5% of the total, up from 20.3% last year. Nicaragua was third with 20.2% of handmades, down from 22.4% last year.

The U.S. remained fourth with 6.4% of handmades (down from 6.9% last year), but with 13.9% of all cigars (down from 14.6% last year).

the cigar revolution has begun

POWER
to the PEOPLE!

RATED
91
Cigar Insider

Rated
EXCEPTIONAL
by Cigar Encyclopedia

Felipe Gregorio POWER

ALMANAC

Country	Handmade Cigars	Machine Made	Small Cigars	Total
Bahamas	9¼	–	–	9¼
Belgium	–	–	5	5
Brazil	3	–	4	7
Colombia	–	–	1	1
Costa Rica	4	–	–	4
Denmark	–	–	1½	1½
Dominican Republic	514¾	14½	4	533¼
Ecuador	15	–	–	15
Egypt	1	–	–	1
Germany	–	1	4	5
Honduras	246¼	–	–	246¼
India	1	–	5	6
Indonesia	5	–	1	6
Ireland	–	2	–	2
Italy	–	–	1	1
Jamaica	9	–	–	9
Mexico	10	–	–	10
Netherlands	–	½	4½	5
Nicaragua	230¾	–	–	230¾
Panama	4½	–	–	4½
Peru	3	–	–	3
Philippines	3	–	1	4
Spain	3	–	2	5
Switzerland	–	½	2	2½
United States	76½	71½	34	182
Venezuela /26/	6	–	–	6
Totals: (vs. 2007)	1,145 (+71)	90 (-4)	70 (+5)	1,305 (+72)

In classifying the origin of each brand, fractional attributions were made for cigars that are produced in more than one country

2.03 Cigars: Large and Small

Length:

The longest cigars? Here are the longest shapes:

18 inches	(x 66 ring)	Puros Indios Chief
16	(x 50)	Graycliff Big Bamboo
16	(x 50)	Graycliff Profesionale Big Bamboo
12	(x 70)	Hoja Real Grande Cedar
12	(x 192)	La Tradicion Cubana The Big One
10 inches		Cigars of this length are offered by 10 makers: Carbonell, Casa Blanca, Cibao, Dominican Original, Flor de Oliva, Gilberto Cubana, Hoja Real, King Dominican, Mendez y Lopez and Puros Indios.

A previous length leader – the Santa Clara Magnum (19 inches by 52 ring) – is still made, but the brand had no U.S. distributor as of press time.

The shortest? Cigarillos of just under three inches in length by:

$2\frac{5}{8}$	Al-Capone	$2\frac{7}{8}$	Dannemann
$2\frac{3}{4}$	Schimmelpennick	$2\frac{7}{8}$	Panter
$2\frac{3}{4}$	Twinkle	$2\frac{7}{8}$	Villiger
$2\frac{7}{8}$	Candlelight		

Readers looking for a short, handmade smoke with a more robust ring gauge might look at:

3	(x 38)	Natural Aqua Jucy Lucy
3	(x 45)	Musashi Sport
$3\frac{1}{2}$	(x 43)	Davidoff Entreacto
$3\frac{1}{2}$	(x 43)	Paul Garmirian 15th Anniversary Bombones
$3\frac{1}{2}$	(x 43)	Paul Garmirian Gourmet Series Bombones
$3\frac{1}{2}$	(x 43)	Paul Garmirian Gourmet Series Maduro Bombones
$3\frac{1}{2}$	(x 44)	Macuro Tatu
$3\frac{1}{2}$	(x 52)	San Martin Piccolo
$3\frac{1}{2}$	(x 55)	Felipe Gregorio Fat Boys
$3\frac{5}{8}$	(x 38)	Cerdan Perlas
$3\frac{3}{4}$	(x 44)	Adan y Eva Cabinet Seleccion Especial Figurado No. 1
$3\frac{3}{4}$	(x 48)	Oliva Serie G Special G
$3\frac{3}{4}$	(x 48)	Oliva Serie G Maduro Special G
$3\frac{3}{4}$	(x 48)	Pheasant Honduran Selection Fast Break
$3\frac{3}{4}$	(x 48)	Pheasant Nicaraguan Gran Reserva Fast Break

Honorable mention to the 24A69.com WBC (4 x 60) and Acid Kong Cameroon (4 x 62).

Ring gauge:

The fattest of the fat? Remembering that ring gauge is measured in 64ths of the inch, there are 33 in-production cigars of an inch (64/64) or more in diameter:

192	(x 12)	La Tradicion Cubana The Big One
96	(x 6½)	Las Memorias Cubana Especiales XXL
86	(x 5)	C.A.O. "The Sopranos" Limited Edition No. 86
82	(x 7¼)	Moore & Bode Full Brass
70	(x 12)	Hoja Real Grande Cedar
70	(x 7⅞)	Costa Toro
70	(x 6)	Bohemian Big Sur
70	(x 6)	Bohemian Black Big Sur
70	(x 5½)	Moore & Bode Brass
68	(x 8)	Carbonell Piramide Gigante
68	(x 8)	Mendez y Lopez Piramide Viajante
68	(x 6)	Quisqueyana Original Series Figurado
66	(x 18)	Puros Indios Chief
66	(x 10)	Casa Blanca Jeroboam
66	(x 10)	Dominican Original Fat Tub
66	(x 10)	Flor de Oliva Giants
66	(x 10)	Gilberto Cubana Gigante
66	(x 10)	King Dominican No. 9
66	(x 5½)	Puros Indios Corona Gordas No. 5
66	(x 5)	Casa Blanca Half Jeroboam
66	(x 5)	King Dominican No. 13
66	(x 5)	Nat Sherman Metropolitan Selection Bankers
65	(x 9)	Quisqueyana Original Series Gigante
65	(x 7)	Quisqueyana Original Series Dona Rosa
65	(x 5)	Domingold Phat
65	(x 5)	Quisqueyana Old Style Grande
64	(x 7½)	Carbonell Piramide
64	(x 7½)	Mendez y Lopez Piramide
64	(x 6¼)	Puros Indios Special Aged Piramide
64	(x 6)	Diamond Crown Figurado No. 6
64	(x 6)	Las Memorias Cubana Especiales
64	(x 5⅞)	Arturo Fuente Añejo Shark No. 77
64	(x 5)	Las Memorias Cubana Gordos

Honorable mention to the scarcely-produced Fuente Fuente Opus X BBMF and Rising X (both 64 x 6½).

The thinnest? There are a number of brands of small cigars which match the ring gauge of cigarettes, at 20 ring.

Shapes:

The leading brands by the number of shapes offered under one brand name:

45 Gurkha	27 Avalon	22 Old Fashioned
42 Flor de Gonzalez	26 El Rey del Mundo	22 Romeo y Julieta 1875
39 La Flor Dominicana	25 Macanudo	21 El Credito
33 Arturo Fuente	25 Torres	21 Paul Garmirian
32 Davidoff	24 Origins	21 Quisqueyana
31 Mosaico	24 Acid	20 Flor de Oliva
30 La Gloria Cubana	22 Flor de Consuegra	20 Montecristo
28 Lone Wolf	22 Leon Jimenes	20 Moore & Bode

2.04 CIGARS: SPECIAL MODELS

Not too long ago, flavored cigars and double-wrapped models were rarities. Today, there are lots of choices in brands which feature all kinds of special models:

Double/Triple wrapper:

Still unusual, however, are special double-wrapped cigars which emulate barber poles and culebras. Brands with "barber pole"-wrapped models include:

898 Collection Tricolor	Camacho Liberty 2007
A/R Flagship	Capas (Dos or Tres!)
Acid	Conch Republic
Aganorsa Leaf	Exquisito
Arganese	Felipe Art of Power
Arturo Fuente Hemingway Series	Kentucky Gentlemen Cigar
C.A.O. America	Little Cigar Factory
C.A.O. Bratalia	Miura Director de Fabrica

These brands have dual natural and maduro wrappers on the same shape:

Avalon	Scarface Tony Montana Series
Black Pearl Black & Tan	(three wrapper segments on one cigar!)
Kentucky Gentlemen Cigar	Torres Rey Cubano
La Flor Dominicana	Two-Tone

ALMANAC

Culebras:

Handmade brands (5):

Adan y Eva
Elogio
Habana Real
Illusione
Natural

Flavored brands, or brands with one or more flavored shapes:

Handmade (96):

Adan y Eva
Aguila Flavored
Alma Sweets
Ambrosia
American Stogies
Arango Statesman
Avalon
Baccarat "The Game" Havana
Bering
Biker's Butt
Blanton's
Bluntville
C.A.O. Flavours
Canela
Carlos Torano Reserva Decadencia
Carnaval by Cojimar
Casa Marina
Chevere Ice Cream Flavors
Cisso Bourbon
Cisso Wine
Cojimar
Coppo Flavors
Cordova
Courvoisier
Cuban Cigar Fac.Van.Sweets
Cuban Delights
Cuban Honeys (2 brands)
Cuban Pleasures
Delicioso
Dominican Delights
Dominican Sweets
Don Pablo
EZ-Duz-It
Earth Supernatural
El Duque Cognac
El Guajiro
Erin Go Bragh

Esplendido
Fittipaldi
The Flava
Gilberto Cubana
Gurkha
Harvill
Havana Dreams
Havana Honeys
Havana Sweets
Heaven
Helix Remix
Honey Delights
Hookah
Isabella
Isla del Sol
Island Amaretto
Island Collection
Island Delights
John Hay Ambassador Series
John T's Crowdpleaser
Kahlua
Kalua Sunrise
Kick Ass Sweet Cigars
La Fontana Vintage
La Luna Little Havana Blend
Las Vegas Cigar Co.
Little Cigar Factory
Maker's Mark
Montserrat Flavors
Mursuli
nu
Oliveros Flavors
Oliveros Gold
Oliveros Kopi Luwak
Oliveros Platinum
Premium Value
Principes
The Repeater
Rocky Patel Java
Rough Rider Sweets

Rum Runner
Ruy Lopez
St. Croix
Santa Ana
Savinelli Aperitifs
Scarface
Sweet Aromas by Macabi
Sweet Daddies
Swisher Sweets Prem. Sel.
T.N.J. Smokin' Spirits
Taino Sweets
Taino XO
Tatiana
Tobacconist Choice
Torres
Tropical Delights Jubilee
Tropical Treasures
Verona
West Indies Vanilla

Machine-made (27):

Alamo Sweets
Arango Sportsman
Black & Mild
Blunt Wrap Loaded
Candlelight
Cherry Blend
Chevere Small Cigars
Dutch Masters
Garcia y Vega
Gladstone
Jamaican Smalls
John Hay
King Edward
Miami Suites
Muriel
Optimo
Phillies
Prince Albert
Royal Blunts

S.F.S.
Santa Fe
Swisher Sweets
Tampa Sweet
Texas Sweets
Villazon Deluxe Aromatics
White Owl
Wolf Bros.

Small Cigars (51):
Agio
Al-Capone
Alternativos
American Made
Antonio y Cleopatra Wise
 Guys
Avanti
Backwoods
Beach Palm
Blackstone
Blunt Master

Captain Black Little Cigars
Dannemann
Dark Horse
Djarum Spice Islands
Dean's Lil' Cigars
Dockers Sweet Tip
Dona Flor
Double Diamond
Ducados
Dutch Treats
Erik
Gabriella
Gold Rush
Happy Hour
Hat's Off
Hav-A-Tampa
Henri Wintermans
Hummer
I-80
New York Minute
Omega

Panter
Parodi
Phillies Little Cigars
Pipers
Premium One
Prime Time
Racers
Red Buck
Richwood
Smoker's Choice
Smokin Joes
Super Value
Supreme Blend
Swisher Sweets Little Cigars
Torino
Twinkle
Vaquero
Vendetta
Villiger
Winchester

Celebration cigars:

If you need a cigar for a special reason, here are some of your
many, many options:

It's a Boy/It's a Girl — Handmade:

Arturo Fuente Brevas	Dom. Rep.	5½ x 42
Ashton Crystal No. 1 Tubos	Dom. Rep.	6½ x 44
Ashton Crystal Belicoso Tubos	Dom. Rep.	6 x 49 torpedo
Baccarat "The Game" Havana Selection	Honduras	6 x 43
Bering Imperial Tubos	Honduras	5½ x 42
Cusano Toro	Dom. Rep.	6 x 50
Davidoff Special R Tubos	Dom. Rep.	4⅞ x 50
Davidoff 2000 Tubos	Dom. Rep.	5 x 43
Don Rex	Honduras	5½ x 50
Exclusive Cigars Corona	Dom. Rep.	5½ x 42
Governor	Dom. Rep.	6 x 42
Humberto Mendoza	Philippines	5¾ x 42
JM's Dominican	Dom. Rep.	5½ x 42
John T's Crowdpleaser Tubo	Dom. Rep.	5¼ x 38
Miami Cigar & Co. Corona Tubos	Dom. Rep.	6½ x 42
Miami Cigar & Co. Corona Vanilla Tubos	Dom. Rep.	6½ x 42
Olympia Churchill	Dom. Rep.	7 x 48
Repeater	Honduras	5½ x 43
Romeo y Julieta Reserva Real Tubos	Dom. Rep.	5½ x 44

It's a Boy/It's a Girl — Machine-made:		
Antonio y Cleopatra Grenadiers Tubos	Puerto Rico	5⅝ x 42½
Arango Sportsman No. 200	Dom. Rep.	6¼ x 42
Bances Palmas	Dom. Rep.	6 x 42
Dutch Masters Panetela	USA	5½ x 36
Garcia y Vega English Corona Tubos	Dom. Rep.	5¼ x 41
Hav-A-Tampa Jewels	USA	4⅞ x 29
IB&G (Palma Throw-Outs)	USA	6½ x 43
J&R Famous	USA	6 x 42
King Edward Imperial	USA	5¾ x 42
Lord Beaconsfield Lindas	Dom. Rep.	6½ x 36
Muniemaker Regular	USA	4½ x 47
Rigoletto Londonaire Tubos	USA	6¼ x 44
Rigoletto Palma Grande	USA	6¼ x 41
Sam Houston Perfecto	USA	4¾ x 46 perfecto
Swisher Sweets Slims	USA	5⅜ x 36
Topper Broadleaf	USA	4⅞ x 46
White Owl Invincible	USA	5⅜ x 41
Wm. Ascot Palma	USA	6¼ x 42
Zino Classic Sumatra	Switzerland	4¾ x 41
Zino Grand Classic Sumatra	Switzerland	5½ x 46

Some celebratory cigars no longer in circulation . . . but should be:

It's Twins	by Don Tomas (Honduras)	6½ x 46 torpedo
Just Divorced	by Bering (Honduras)	7⅛ x 42
Just Married	by Bering (Honduras)	7⅛ x 42
Just Married	by Cusano (Dom. Rep.)	6 x 50
Merry Christmas and Happy New Year	by Atlantic Cigar Co. (Dom. Rep.)	6 x 50 torpedo

2.05 The Cigar Bowl

Of course there was a college bowl game named for cigars! The Cigar Bowl was played in Tampa, the hotbed of U.S. cigar-making from 1947-54, between college-division teams:

I	1947	(Jan. 1)	Delaware 21, Rollins 7	(attendance 7,500)
II	1948	(Jan. 1)	Missouri Valley 26, West Chester 7	(10,000)
III	1949	(Jan. 1)	Missouri Valley 13, St. Thomas (Mn), 13	(11,000)
IV	1950	(Jan. 2)	Florida State 19, Wofford 6	(14,000)
V	1951	(Jan. 1)	Wisconsin-La Crosse 47, Valparaiso 14	(12,000)
VI	1951	(Dec. 29)	Brooke Army Medical 20, Camp LeJeune Marines 0	(7,500)
VII	1952	(Dec. 13)	Tampa 21, Lenoir-Rhyne 12	(7,500)
VIII	1954	(Jan. 1)	Missouri Valley 12, Wisconsin-LaCrosse 12	(5,000)
IX	1954	(Dec.)	Tampa 21, Morris Harvey 0	(unknown)

ALMANAC

How about a bowl game in Havana? Absolutely! On January 1, 1937, Auburn and Villanova played to a 7-7 tie in the first and only "Bacardi Bowl," held before 12,000 spectators as a part of the Cuban National Sports Festival.

INDEX
OF ADVERTISERS

3.
HANDMADE CIGARS:
LISTINGS BY BRAND

This section provides the details on 1,145 brands of cigars, *actively marketed nationally* in the United States, a net *increase* of 71 brands from the 2007 edition. Each brand listing includes notes on country of manufacture, the origin of the tobaccos used, shapes, names, lengths, ring gauges, wrapper color and a brief description *as supplied by the manufacturers and/or distributors of these brands.* Ring gauges for some brands of cigarillos were not available.

Please note that while a cigar may be manufactured in one country, it may contain tobaccos from many nations. The designation "handmade" indicates the use of long-filler tobacco unless otherwise noted.

Although manufacturers have recognized more than 70 shades of wrapper color, six major color groupings are used here. Their abbreviations include:

- DC = Double Claro: green, also known as American Market Selection, "AMS" or Candela.
- Cl = Claro: a very light tan color.
- CC = Colorado Claro: a medium brown common to many cigars
- Co = Colorado: reddish-brown.
- CM = Colorado Maduro: dark brown.
- Ma = Maduro: very dark brown (also "double Maduro")
- Os = Oscuro: black.

Many manufacturers call their wrapper colors "Natural" or "English Market Selection." These colors cover a wide range of browns and we have generally grouped them in the "CC" range. Darker wrappers such as those from Cameroon show up most often in the "CM" category.

Shape designations are based on our shape chart in section 1.03. Careful readers will note the freedom with which manufacturers attach names of shapes to cigars which do not resemble that shape at all! For easier comparison, all lengths were rounded to the shortest eighth of an inch, although manufacturers list sizes in 16ths or even 32nds of an inch.

Although 1,145 brands are listed, house brands of cigar lounges or individual tobacco stores do not appear. To qualify for inclusion, a brand must be actively marketed (as opposed to simply available) to retailers through a wholesale distributor *in the United States*. Beginning with the 2007 edition, we have *condensed* the listings of brands we believe to be in production, but for which complete details were not provided. Brands distributed from *outside the U.S.* for import are not listed. Sorry!

Readers who would like to see their favorite listed in the 2009 edition can contact us at *www.CigarCyclopedia.com.*

3x3
Handmade in Santiago, Dominican Republic.

Wrapper: USA/Connecticut *Binder: Dom. Rep.* *Filler: Dom. Rep.*

Shape	Name		Lgth	Ring	Wrapper
Churchill	Churchill	(tubed)	6¾	48	CC
Corona	Corona	(tubed)	5½	43	CC
Robusto	Robusto	(tubed)	4⅞	50	CC

This is a bundle of nine tubed cigars, in three rows of three! It's a value-priced cigar, offering a medium body.

4x4
Handmade in Santiago, Dominican Republic.

Wrapper: USA/Connecticut *Binder: Dom. Rep.* *Filler: Dom. Rep.*

HANDMADE CIGARS: BRAND LISTINGS

Shape	Name	Lgth	Ring	Wrapper
Churchill	Churchill	6¾	48	CC
Petit Corona	Corona	5	43	CC
Torpedo	Figurado	4¾	48	CC
Long Corona	Lonsdale	6¼	43	CC
Petit Corona	Petit Corona	4½	43	CC
Robusto	Robusto	4⅞	50	CC

Introduced in 2005, this is the sister to the 3x3 tubed line, offering a 16-cigar bundle with a medium-bodied flavor presented with individual cellophane sleeves.

5 VEGAS
Handmade in Esteli, Nicaragua.

Wrapper: Indonesia   *Binder: Nicaragua*   *Filler: Dom. Rep., Nicaragua*

Shape	Name	Lgth	Ring	Wrapper
Panatela	Panatela	6	38	CM
Corona	Corona	5½	44	CM
Robusto	Robusto	5	50	CM
Toro	Double Corona	6	48	CM
Double Corona	Churchill	7	52	CM
Torpedo	Torpedo	6	54	CM

A Cigar Boom brand that died, 5 Vegas was resurrected by Keith Meier of Cigars International and is now distributed by Meier & Dutch. It's medium-to-full in body with a Sumatra wrapper and now offered in boxes of 25 except for the Torpedo, in 20s.

5 VEGAS CASK STRENGTH ★*New*★
Handmade in Santiago, Dominican Republic.

Wrapper: Dom. Rep.   *Binder: Dom. Rep.*   *Filler: Brazil, Dom. Rep., Nicaragua*

Shape	Name	Lgth	Ring	Wrapper
Toro	Toro	5¾	54	CM

Introduced in 2007, only 3,000 boxes of 20 of this cigar have been produced. It's full-bodied and offered in unique boxes that look like a whiskey cask with a pull-out bottom to open a drawer that holds the cigars!

5 VEGAS GOLD
Handmade in Danli, Honduras.

Wrapper: USA/Connecticut　　　*Binder: Honduras*　　　*Filler: Honduras*

Shape	Name	Lgth	Ring	Wrapper
Robusto	Robusto	5	50	CC
Toro	Toro	6	50	CC
Torpedo	Torpedo	6	54	CC
Double Corona	Churchill	7	50	CC
Double Corona	No. 1	7½	54	CC

This is a mild-to-medium blend introduced by Meier & Dutch into national distribution in 2006. It's offered with elegant gold bands in triangular boxes of 20.

5 VEGAS SERIE A
Handmade in Esteli, Nicaragua.

Wrapper: Costa Rica　　*Binder: Nicaragua*　　*Filler: Dom. Rep., Honduras, Nicaragua*

Shape	Name	Lgth	Ring	Wrapper
Petit Corona	Anomaly	4½	44	Ma
Robusto	Artisan	5	52	Ma
Toro	Archetype	6	50	Ma
Torpedo	Alpha	6	52	Ma
Double Corona	Apostle	7	50	Ma
Toro	Apocalypse	6	60	Ma

Meier & Dutch introduced this medium-to-full-bodied, all-maduro blend in 2006. It's offered strictly in boxes of 20.

24A69.COM
Handmade in Frankfort, New York, USA.

Wrapper: Cameroon, USA/Connecticut　　　*Binder: Ecuador or Mexico*
Filler: Dominican Republic, Mexico, Venezuela

HANDMADE CIGARS: BRAND LISTINGS

Shape	Name	Lgth	Ring	Wrapper
Double Corona	Crazy Clown	7	50	CM
Robusto	Court Jester	5	50	Ma
Pyramid	High Life Joker	5	54	CM
Corona Extra	Everything	5	46	CM
Robusto	WBC	4	60	CM

This is a part of the Lars Tetens line and is medium-to-full in body. Created in 1994, the cigars are aged from 2-4 years after rolling. All sizes are offered in boxes of 30.

420's
Handmade in Esteli, Nicaragua.

Wrapper: Brazil   Binder: Nicaragua   Filler: Nicaragua

Shape	Name	Lgth	Ring	Wrapper
Torpedo	Marley	6	54	CM
Double Corona	Shotgun	7	52	CM
Toro	Double	6	48	CM
Robusto	Toke	5	50	CM

Created by the Tabacalera Esteli, this is a mild-bodied blend named for the latitude of the factory's farms. It was introduced in 2005, offered in boxes of 24 or bundles of 25.

601
Handmade in Esteli, Nicaragua.

Wrapper: Ecuador, Nicaragua   Binder: Nicaragua   Filler: Nicaragua

Shape	Name	Lgth	Ring	Wrapper
	Connecticut and Habano series:			
Churchill	Churchill	7	48	CC-CM
Toro	Toro	6	50	CC-CM
Robusto	Robusto	5	50	CC-CM
Torpedo	Torpedo	6½	52	CC-CM
Grand Corona	Rabito	6½	46	CC-CM

	Habano series only:			
Small Panatela	Guapito	4	32	CM
	Habano Oscuro series:			
Petit Corona	Corona	5	42	CM
Robusto	Tronco	5	52	CM
Robusto	La Fuerza	5½	54	CM
Toro	Trabuco	6½	58	CM
Perfecto	La Punta	5½	52	CM
	Maduro BP series:			
Robusto	Robusto	5¼	52	Ma
Torpedo	Torpedo	6⅛	52	Ma
Toro	Toro	6¼	54	Ma
Robusto	Prominente	5½	56	Ma

This blend was introduced by United Tobacco in 2006 and is made by Don Pepin Garcia in Nicaragua. The Connecticut (Black Label) uses an Ecuadorian-grown wrapper and is mild to medium in body. The Habano (Red Label) line has a Nicaraguan wrapper and is full-bodied. The Habano Oscuro line debuted in 2007 and is full-bodied with a Nicaraguan wrapper. The Maduro (Blue Label) line was also introduced in 2007, is box-pressed and uses a Nicaraguan-grown wrapper. All sizes are offered in boxes of 20.

A special Edicion Limitada cigar (7½ x 52) was introduced in 2007, offered in special ceramic jars of 24 cigars each. It has all-Nicaraguan tobacco with a Habano wrapper.

898 COLLECTION
Handmade in Santiago, Dominican Republic.

Wrapper: USA/Connecticut   *Binder: Dom. Rep.*   *Filler: Dom. Rep.*

Shape	Name	Lgth	Ring	Wrapper
Double Corona	Churchill	7½	49	CC
Corona	Corona	5½	42	CC
Lonsdale	Lonsdale	6½	42	CC

| Torpedo | Belicoso | 6¼ | 52 | CC |
| Robusto | Robusto | 5½ | 49 | CC |

Introduced in 1991, this brand was originally made in Kingston, Jamaica. It is now made in the Dominican Republic and is uncompromising in its commitment to quality of construction and ease in smoking. These are mild-bodied cigars, offered in boxes of 25.

898 COLLECTION TRICOLOR ★New★
Handmade in Tamboril, Dominican Republic.
Wrapper: Indonesia, Nicaragua, USA/Connecticut Binder: Dom. Rep. Filler: Dom. Rep.

Shape	Name	Lgth	Ring	Wrapper
Double Corona	Churchill	7	50	Stripe
Toro	Toro	6	50	Stripe

Here is an unbelievable edition of a striped cigar, using three different wrappers: Indonesian natural, Nicaraguan candela and Connecticut Broadleaf maduro! It's medium in body, made for Mike's Cigars by Felipe Gregorio Cigars. Both sizes are offered in boxes of 10.

1876 RESERVE ★New★
Handmade in Santiago, Dominican Republic.
Wrapper: Ecuador   Binder: Dom. Rep.   Filler: Dom. Rep.

Shape	Name	Lgth	Ring	Wrapper
Robusto	Robusto	5	50	CM
Toro	Toro	6	50	CM
Torpedo	Torpedo	6½	52	CM
Double Corona	Churchill	7¼	50	CM

Here's an inexpensive, mild-to-medium cigar distributed by Meier & Dutch. It's made with a Sumatra-seed wrapper and offered in boxes of 20.

A. TURRENT
Handmade in San Andres Tuxtla, Mexico.
Wrapper: Mexico   Binder: Nicaragua   Filler: Mexico

HANDMADE CIGARS: BRAND LISTINGS

Shape	Name	Lgth	Ring	Wrapper
Corona	Corona	5½	44	CM
Robusto	Robusto	5	54	CM
Toro	Toro	6	50	CM
Torpedo	Torpedo	6⅛	52	CM
Double Corona	Churchill	7	52	CM

This is a medium-to-full-bodied blend created in 2005 to celebrate the 125th anniversary of the Turrent family as cigar makers. It's offered in an all-box-pressed series in boxes of 20.

A/R FLAGSHIP ★New★
Handmade in Guayaquil, Ecuador.

Wrapper: Ecuador   *Binder: Ecuador*   *Filler: Ecuador*

Shape	Name	Lgth	Ring	Wrapper
Robusto	Robusto	5	50	CC-CM-Ma-Stripe
Toro	Toro	6	52	CC-CM-Ma-Stripe
Double Corona	Churchill	7	50	CC-CM-Ma-Stripe
Torpedo	Belicoso	6	52	CC-CM-Ma-Stripe
Toro	Gordo	6	60	CC-CM-Ma-Stripe

Puros de Armando Ramos introduced this blend in 2007. Depending on the wrapper, the taste ranges from mild-to-medium to full-bodied. A striped wrapper is also available on all sizes. All cigars are presented in boxes of 25.

A/R GREEN BAND ★New★
Handmade in Guayaquil, Ecuador.

Wrapper: Ecuador   *Binder: Ecuador*   *Filler: Ecuador*

Shape	Name	Lgth	Ring	Wrapper
Robusto	Robusto	5	50	CC-CM-Ma

Toro	Toro	6	52	CC-CM-Ma
Double Corona	Double Corona	7½	50	CC-CM-Ma
Torpedo	Belicoso	6⅛	54	CC-CM-Ma
Toro	Gordo	6	60	CC-CM-Ma

This blend was introduced in 2007 with a choice of Ecuadorian-grown wrappers in four shapes: Connecticut, Corojo, Maduro and Rosado. All but the Corojo (medium to full) are medium in body and all are offered in boxes of 25.

A/R SELECT ★New★
Handmade in Guayaquil, Ecuador.

Wrapper: Ecuador   *Binder: Ecuador*   *Filler: Ecuador*

Shape	Name	Lgth	Ring	Wrapper
Petit Corona	Shorty	4	40	CC-CM
Corona	Corona	5½	44	CC-CM
Lonsdale	Lonsdale	6½	44	CC-CM
Robusto	Robusto	5	50	CC-CM
Toro	Toro	6	50	CC-CM
Torpedo	Torpedo	6	54	CC-CM
Toto	Gigante	6½	54	CC-CM
Double Corona	DC	7½	50	CC-CM
Giant	Prez	8½	52	CC-CM

This is a medium-bodied blend, introduced in 2007. There are three styles of wrapper: Cameroon, Criollo and Connecticut, all grown in Ecuador and offered in bundles of 20.

ABAM
Handmade in Santo Domingo, Dominican Republic.

Wrapper: Ecuador   *Binder: Indonesia*   *Filler: Dom. Rep., Nicaragua*

Shape	Name	Lgth	Ring	Wrapper
Long Panatela	Lanceros	7½	38	CC-CM
Long Corona	Corona	6	43	CC-CM

Giant	Gran Corona	9¼	47	CC-CM
Churchill	Churchill	7	48	CC-CM
Double Corona	Doble Corona	7⅞	50	CC-CM
Robusto	Robusto	5	50	CC-CM
Torpedo	Belicoso	6¼	52	CC-CM

This brand was introduced in 1996 and offers Connecticut-seed or Sumatra-seed wrappers in seven sizes. It provides a medium-bodied or medium-to-full-bodied flavor in boxes of 25.

ACID
Handmade in Esteli, Nicaragua.
Wrapper: Natural – Cameroon, Honduras, Indonesia, USA/Connecticut
Wrapper: Maduro – Ecuador, Mexico or Nicaragua
Binder: Nicaragua   Filler: Dom. Rep., Ecuador, Honduras, Mexico, Nicaragua

Shape	Name		Lgth	Ring	Wrapper
	Acid series (red):				
Robusto	Liquid		5	50	CC
Pyramid	Nasty		4	52	Ma
Pyramid	Nefasto		6	62	Ma
	Holistics series (yellow):				
Robusto	Atom Maduro		5	50	Ma
Petit Corona	Earthiness		5	42	CM
Lonsdale	Cold Infusion Tea		6¾	44	CC
	Remi series (blue):				
Short Panatela	Blondie		4	38	CC
Robusto	Deep Dish		5	58	CM
Robusto	Kuba Kuba		5	54	CM
Toro	Kuba Deluxe	*(tubed)*	6	50	CM
Robusto	1400 cc	*(tubed)*	5	50	CC
Perfecto	Kong Cameroon		4	62	CM

Robusto	Wafe	5	54	CC
	Juggernaut series (purple):			
Torpedo	Acid 1	5	54	CM
Churchill	Roam	7	48	CC
Toro	Extra Ordinary Larry	6	60	Ma
Cigarillo	C-Note	5	20	CM
Toro	Ming	6	60	CM
Torpedo	Ming Dynasty Belicoso	6	60	Stripe
	Krush Classics:			
Small Panatela	Krush Classics	4	32	CC-CM-Ma
	Limited:			
Torpedo	Def Sea	6	52	CM
	Subculture:			
Short Panatela	Ronin	4	38	CM
Robusto	Ronin Deluxe	5	54	CM
Toro	Ronin Ridikuloso	6	60	CM

This is a unique brand, introduced in 1999, that offers an herbal aromatic flavor in all of its shapes. The creative force behind this brand is artist Scott "Acid" Chester, who brings his flair for industrial design to the artisanal product and the endlessly inventive Jonathan Drew on the blending side. Acid (red band) is medium-bodied with the Liquid, Nasty and Acid One shapes finished with a pigtail head and uncut foot; Holistics (yellow) is mild-bodied with all shapes uncut at the foot; Remi (blue) is mild-to-medium in body with the Kuba Kuba shape finished in a pigtail head and Juggernaut (purple) is full-bodied with the Extra Ordinary Larry finished with a pigtail head. Connecticut Broadleaf is used for all maduro wrappers. The brand uses more than 140 botanicals, herbs and oils to impart a unique flavor.

The Krush Classic was introduced in 2003 and has a mild-to-medium body, available in tins of 10. It is offered in a choice of wrappers: Red (Cameroon), Gold (Sumatra), Blue (Connecticut) and Morado (maduro).

The Limited line (Sumatra wrapper) is distributed by Meier & Dutch and debuted in 2006. The Acid Subculture series was created in 2005 and is distributed by Alliance Cigar. The Ronin has a Cameroon wrapper while the Deluxe and Ridikuloso use Honduran Habano wrappers.

ACID 5
Handmade in Esteli, Nicaragua.

Wrapper: USA/Connecticut   *Binder: Nicaragua*   *Filler: Nicaragua*

Shape	Name	Lgth	Ring	Wrapper
Robusto	Robusto	5	52	Ma
Torpedo	Torpedo	6	54	Ma
Petit Corona	Short Corona	4	44	Ma

Created to celebrate the fifth anniversary of the Acid line in 2005, this is a medium-bodied cigar featuring a Connecticut Broadleaf wrapper. Each cigar is lined with cedar and a special silver band; all sizes are offered in boxes of 20. Actual production of these cigars (in 2001!) was limited to 2,500 boxes of two sizes and 500 of the Short Corona.

ADAN Y EVA
Handmade in Navarette, Dominican Republic.

Wrapper: Cameroon, Dominican Republic, Ecuador, Nicaragua
Binder: Dominican Republic   *Filler: Dominican Republic, Nicaragua*

Shape	Name		Lgth	Ring	Wrapper
Torpedo	Belicoso	*(porcelain jar)*	5	52	CM
Perfecto	Figurado	*(porcelain jar)*	5	52	CM
Double Corona	Double Corona		7½	50	CC-CM-Ma
Churchill	Churchill	*(tube available)*	7	48	CC-CM-Ma
Torpedo	Pyramid		6⅛	52	CC-CM-Ma
Torpedo	Belicoso		5½	50	CM-Ma
Perfecto	Figurado Perfecto		5½	52	CC-CM-Ma
Long Corona	Longsdale		6	42	CC-CM-Ma
Short Panatela	Petite Corona		4	38	CC-CM-Ma

HANDMADE CIGARS: BRAND LISTINGS

Long Panatela	Panetela		7	38	CC-CM-Ma
Robusto	Robusto XO	*(tubed)*	5	50	CM
Small Panatela	Cigarillo		4½	30	CM
Perfecto	Figurado No. 1		3¾	44	CC-CM-Ma
Perfecto	Figurado No. 2		5	50	CC-CM-Ma
Perfecto	Figurado No. 3		5½	52	CC-CM-Ma
	Cabinet Seleccion Especial: *(Belicoso, Churchill, Longsdale, Panatela, Pyramid and Robusto sizes above, plus)*				
Culebras	Pecadores		6⅝	34	Mixed

Re-introduced in 2005, "Adam and Eve" offers a choice of wrappers from Cameroon (mild to medium in body), a Connecticut-seed wrapper grown in Ecuador (mild-bodied), a Habano 2000 wrapper from Nicaragua and a maduro-shade Dominican wrapper. The Robusto XO and the Cabinet Seleccion Especial all feature a Habano 2000 wrapper from Nicaragua. Flavored versions of the Robusto XO were introduced in 2007 and are available in Champagne or Cognac. All sizes are offered in boxes of 25 except for the Robusto XO (15) and the Pecadores, offered in a box of 30.

ADDUCI JAMAICAN
Handmade in Kingston, Jamaica.
Wrapper: Jamaica   *Binder: Jamaica*   *Filler: Jamaica*

Shape	Name	Lgth	Ring	Wrapper
Double Corona	Churchill	7	49	CC
Corona	Gran Corona	5½	42	CC
Robusto	Robusto	5	50	CC-Ma
Torpedo	Torpedo	6	50	CC-Ma

Created by Joseph Adduci, this line debuted in the U.S. in 2006. These are medium-bodied cigars, made of all Jamaican tobacco, available in bundles of 25.

ADONIS ★*New*★
Handmade in Danli, Honduras.
Wrapper: USA/Connecticut   *Binder: USA/Connecticut*   *Filler: Honduras*

HANDMADE CIGARS: BRAND LISTINGS

Shape	Name	Lgth	Ring	Wrapper
Petit Corona	Orion	4	41	CC
Corona	Sphinx	5½	44	CC
Robusto	Amazon	5	50	CC
Churchill	Gorgon	7	48	CC
Toro	Titan	6	54	CC
Torpedo	Minotaur	6	54	CC

Named for the Roman god, this mild-to-medium-bodied blend was created in 2005 and introduced to national distribution in 2007. It offers a creamy flavor with shapes named for famous characters from antiquity in boxes of 25.

ADONIS MADURO ★New★
Handmade in Guayaquil, Ecuador.

Wrapper: Ecuador *Binder: Ecuador* *Filler: Ecuador*

Shape	Name	Lgth	Ring	Wrapper
Robusto	Adonis 50	5	50	Ma
Churchill	Adonis 48	7	48	Ma
Torpedo	Adonis 54	6	54	Ma
Toro	Adonis 60	6	60	Ma

Made with all Ecuadorian-grown tobaccos, this is a medium-to-full-blend which debuted in 2007. It features a Criollo Maduro wrapper and is offered in boxes of 20.

AGANORSA LEAF ★New★
Handmade in Esteli, Nicaragua.

Wrapper: Nicaragua *Binder: Nicaragua* *Filler: Nicaragua*

Shape	Name	Lgth	Ring	Wrapper
Toro	Doble Capa Toro	6½	54	Stripe
Torpedo	Doble Capa Torpedo	6⅛	52	Stripe

Tabacalera Tropical introduced this medium-to-full-bodied, striped-wrapper blend in 2007. Both sizes are offered in bundles of 25.

HANDMADE CIGARS: BRAND LISTINGS

AGUILA
Handmade in Santiago, Dominican Republic.

Wrapper: USA/Connecticut   *Binder: Dom. Rep.*   *Filler: Dom. Rep.*

Shape	Name	Lgth	Ring	Wrapper
Corona	Coronita	5½	40	CC
Lonsdale	Brevas 44	7½	44	CC
Grand Corona	Brevas 46	6½	46	CC
Double Corona	Brevas 50	7½	50	CC
Robusto	Petit Gordo	4¾	50	CC

Created in 1989, this is a mild-to-medium-bodied cigar. The Connecticut wrappers are aged for 5-7 years before production.

AGUILA FLAVORED
Handmade in Manila, the Philippines.

Wrapper: Indonesia   *Binder: Philippines*   *Filler: Philippines*

Shape	Name	Lgth	Ring	Wrapper
Small Panatela	Slim Panatela	4½	33	CM

This is a mild blend introduced by F&K Cigars in 2006. It is offered in Cherry Blossom, Chocolate Truffle, Honey Nectar, Spiced Rum or Vanilla Creme flavors (in boxes of 50), or in a Gourmet Pack with one of each flavor!

AIDA
Handmade in Cumana, Venezuela.

Wrapper: Ecuador   *Binder: Venezuela*   *Filler: Venezuela*

Introduced in 1998, this brand features two-year-aged tobacco. It has a mild body, offered in five sizes and packed in boxes of 25.

AL CAPONE
Handmade in Esteli, Nicaragua.

Wrapper: Brazil   *Binder: Nicaragua*   *Filler: Nicaragua*

Shape	Name	Lgth	Ring	Wrapper
Robusto	Robusto	4½	50	CM
Lonsdale	Corona Grande	6¾	43	CM

HANDMADE CIGARS: BRAND LISTINGS

| Toro | Toro | 6 | 50 | CM |
| Double Corona | Imperial | 7 | 49 | CM |

This is a 1996 extension of the long-time cigarillo brand produced in Germany. Named for the corpulent Chicago-based gangster of the 1920s, the brand is not surprising in its medium-bodied flavor, but it also exhibits a slightly sweet taste.

ALAMEDA
Handmade in Santiago, Dominican Republic.

Wrapper: USA/Connecticut   *Binder: Brazil*   *Filler: Dom. Rep.*

Shape	*Name*	*Lgth*	*Ring*	*Wrapper*
Churchill	Churchill	6⅞	48	CC
Toro	Toro	6	50	CC
Robusto	Wavell	5	50	CC
Corona Extra	Breva	4½	45	CC

Manuel Quesada's Alameda debuted in 2001, offering a mild-to-medium-bodied taste. You can enjoy them in value-priced boxes of 20.

ALCAZAR
Handmade in Esteli, Nicaragua.

Wrapper: Nicaragua   *Binder: Nicaragua*   *Filler: Nicaragua*

Shape	*Name*	*Lgth*	*Ring*	*Wrapper*
Giant	No. 1	8	52	Ma
Double Corona	No. 2	7	50	Ma
Toro	No. 3	6	50	Ma
Robusto	No. 4	5	52	Ma
Torpedo	No. 5	6½	52	Ma

This brand was introduced by the J.C. Newman Cigar Co. in 1998 and features a medium body in an all-maduro line. It is offered in bundles of 20 cigars each.

ALEC BRADLEY MAXX
Handmade in Danli, Honduras.

Wrapper: Nicaragua   *Binder: Costa Rica*
Filler: Colombia, Honduras, Mexico, Nicaragua

Shape	Name	Lgth	Ring	Wrapper
Robusto	Fix	5	58	CM
Toro	Culture	6½	54	CM
Toro	Freak	6⅜	60	CM
Torpedo	Curve	7	58	CM
Giant	Ego	9¼	50	CM
Corona Extra	Nano	4	46	CM
Toro	Vice	6½	62	CM

More flavor, more power and more balance was the goal of the MAXX line, introduced in 2006. It's a medium-to-full-bodied blend offered in boxes of 20, or in 100s for all but the Ego, Nano and Vice. The Ego is offered in boxes of 20, the Nano in boxes of 40 and the Vice in boxes of 50 . . . just enough for when friends drop by! The medium-bodied Nano and Vice use Dominican filler instead of Colombian leaf and the Vice is box-pressed.

ALL AMERICAS
Handmade, with mixed filler, in Esteli, Nicaragua.

Wrapper: Nicaragua   *Binder: Nicaragua*   *Filler: Nicaragua*

Shape	Name	Lgth	Ring	Wrapper
Churchill	Churchill	7	48	CM-Ma
Corona	Corona	5½	44	CM-Ma
Robusto	Robusto	4¾	50	CM-Ma
Toro	Toro	6	50	CM-Ma

Introduced by Phillips & King in 2003, this is a medium-bodied blend offered in economical bundles of 20.

ALMA SWEETS
Handmade in Tamboril, Dominican Republic.

Wrapper: Indonesia   *Binder: Dom. Rep.*   *Filler: Dom. Rep.*

HANDMADE CIGARS: BRAND LISTINGS

Shape	Name	Lgth	Ring	Wrapper
Small Panatela	Petit Panatela	4¼	32	CM
Short Panatela	Panatela	5	36	CM
Corona	Corona	5½	42	CM
Toro	Toro	6	50	CM

Introduced by the JM Tobacco Company, this is a flavored cigar with sweetness added, and offered in boxes of 25, except for the Petit Panatela, available in 50s.

ALMIRANTE
Handmade, with short filler, in Santiago, Dominican Republic.

Wrapper: Indonesia   *Binder: Dom. Rep.*   *Filler: Dom. Rep.*

Shape	Name	Lgth	Ring	Wrapper
Giant	Churchill	8	50	CM
Double Corona	Presidente	7	50	CM
Grand Corona	Doble Corona	6½	46	CM
Robusto	Robusto	5½	50	CM
Long Corona	Lonsdale	6	44	CM

This short-filler brand was introduced in 1998 and offers a mild-to-medium-bodied taste. You can find it in bundles of 25.

ALONSO MENENDEZ
Handmade in São Gonçalo de Campos, Brazil.

Wrapper: Brazil   *Binder: Brazil*   *Filler: Brazil*

Shape	Name	Lgth	Ring	Wrapper
Double Corona	Especiale	7½	50	CC-Ma
Lonsdale	No. 10	6½	44	CC-Ma
Corona	Corona	5½	44	CC-Ma
Robusto	Robusto	5	52	CC-Ma
Toro	6x60	6	60	Ma
Robusto	Box Pressed	5	52	Ma

HANDMADE CIGARS: BRAND LISTINGS

This is a full-bodied cigar from Brazil in both the natural and maduro-wrapped versions. Well-known in Brazil, it was introduced to the U.S. market in 2005 and offered in boxes of 25 or packs of five.

ALTERNATIVE BREWS
Handmade in Santiago, Dominican Republic.
Wrapper: USA/Connecticut   *Binder: Dom. Rep.*   *Filler: Dom. Rep.*

From the Cigar Factory de Yaque comes this medium-bodied cigar, introduced in 2002 and offered five sizes in boxes of 25.

AMBROSIA
Handmade in Esteli, Nicaragua.
Wrapper: Cameroon, Indonesia, USA/Connecticut

Binder: Nicaragua   *Filler: Honduras, Nicaragua*

Shape	Name	Lgth	Ring	Wrapper
Petit Corona	Nectar	5	42	CC
Robusto	Vann Reef	5	50	CM
Torpedo	Spice	5	54	CM
Toro	Mother Earth	6	50	CC
Double Corona	Triple Corona	7	50	CM
Small Panatela	Clove Tiki	4	32	CC

Here is another invention from the Drew Estate cigar folks, introduced in 2002. The band features a fierce-looking tiki god and the cigars are equally wild, with a "spiced" blend incorporating "exxotic" spices from Europe and southern Asia. All of the cigars are aged for 120 days after rolling and then cured for a final 45 days before shipment to ensure their aromatic nature. These are full-bodied cigars, produced in limited production of 6,000 boxes annually. The Clove Tiki size, introduced in 2006, actually incorporates cloves into the production process!

AMERICAN STOGIES
Handmade in Esteli, Nicaragua.
Wrapper: Nicaragua   *Binder: Nicaragua*   *Filler: Nicaragua*

Shape	Name	Lgth	Ring	Wrapper
Torpedo	Break Time	4¼	40	CM-Ma

HANDMADE CIGARS: BRAND LISTINGS

Robusto	Robusto	4¾	52	CM-Ma
Robusto	Super Robusto	5	62	CM-Ma
Long Corona	Corona	6	44	CM-Ma
Toro	Toro	6	50	CM-Ma
Torpedo	Torpedo	6¼	54	CM-Ma
Double Corona	Churchill	7	49	CM-Ma
Double Corona	Super Churchill	6¾	62	CM-Ma
Double Corona	Presidente	7½	54	CM-Ma
	Classic Cuban Corojo series:			
Petit Corona	Break Time Corojo	4½	40	CM
Robusto	Robusto Corojo	4¾	52	CM
Robusto	Super Robusto	5	62	CM
Toro	Toro Corojo	6	50	CM
Double Corona	Churchill Corojo	7	49	CM
Double Corona	Super Churchill Corojo	6¾	62	CM
Torpedo	Torpedo Corojo	6¼	52	CM
Double Corona	Presidente Corojo	7½	54	CM
	Small Cigars:			
Small Panatela	Little Braves	4¼	30	CM
Petit Corona	Petit Corona	4¼	40	CM-Ma

This box-pressed brand (except for the Break Time and Super Robusto) was introduced in 2001. It offers a medium-to-full body in a choice of Nicaraguan-grown wrappers and is recognized by a blue band. The Classic Cuban Corojo series (red band) was introduced in 2003 and offers a fuller body. You can enjoy them in boxes of 25 except for the Break Time, in 48s.

The Small Cigars were introduced in 2004 and are available in packs of ten or eight. The Little Braves are available in a natural blend, or in Amaretto or Cherry Creme flavors. The Petit Coronas are offered in a natural blend or Irish Creme flavor.

HANDMADE CIGARS: BRAND LISTINGS

ANCIENT WARRIOR
Handmade in Santiago, Dominican Republic.
Wrapper: Brazil   *Binder: Dom. Rep.*   *Filler: Dom. Rep., Honduras*

Shape	Name	Lgth	Ring	Wrapper
Robusto	Robusto	4½	52	CM
Double Corona	Churchill	7	50	CM
Torpedo	Torpedo	6	54	CM
Toro	Emperor	6	60	CM
Perfecto	Perfecto No. 2	5	56	CM
Toro	Rothchild	6	55	CM
Robusto	El Duke	4¾	60	CM

Here is a medium-bodied cigar with a pinch of spiciness from the makers of Gurkha, introduced in 2005, offered in boxes of 20.

ANDROS
Handmade in Santiago, Dominican Republic.
Wrapper: Brazil, USA/Connecticut   *Binder: Dom. Rep.*   *Filler: Dom. Rep.*

Shape	Name	Lgth	Ring	Wrapper
Double Corona	Churchill	7½	50	CC-Ma
Corona Extra	Corona	5½	46	CC-Ma
Lonsdale	Lonsdale	6¾	44	CC-Ma
Robusto	Robusto	4½	52	CC-Ma
Double Corona	Toro	6¾	50	CC-Ma

This is a bundled brand from Famous Smoke Shop, offering a mild-to-medium-bodied taste. Take your pick of a natural (Connecticut) or maduro (Brazil) wrapper in value-priced bundles of 25 cigars each.

ANDULLEROS
Handmade, with medium filler, in Santiago, Dominican Republic.
Wrapper: Indonesia   *Binder: Ecuador*   *Filler: Dom. Rep.*

HANDMADE CIGARS: BRAND LISTINGS

Shape	Name	Lgth	Ring	Wrapper
Double Corona	Churchill	7½	50	CM
Double Corona	Presidente	7	50	CM
Grand Corona	Doble Corona	6½	46	CM
Robusto	Robusto	5½	50	CM
Long Corona	Lonsdale	6	44	CM

Here is a short filler, handmade cigar which offers a mild-bodied smoke in an inexpensive bundle package of 25.

ANTELO
Handmade in Miami, Florida, USA.

Wrapper: USA/Connecticut   Binder: Mexico   Filler: Dom. Rep.

Shape	Name	Lgth	Ring	Wrapper
Double Corona	Presidente	7⅝	50	Cl-Ma
Churchill	Churchill	7	46	Cl-Ma
Lonsdale	No. 1	6¾	42	Cl-Ma
Corona	Cetros	5¾	42	Cl-Ma
Cigarillo	Senoritas	4⅝	28	Cl-Ma
Panatela	Panatela	6⅞	36	Cl-Ma
Corona Extra	Wavell	5⅛	46	Cl-Ma
Giant Corona	Double Corona	7½	42	Cl-Ma
Churchill	Super Cazadore	7½	46	Cl-Ma

These cigars are made by hand in a small factory in Miami, using imported leaf. The taste ranges from mild (Senoritas and Panatelas) to medium (No. 1 and Cetros) to heavy (all other shapes).

ANTILLIAN NICARAGUAN COROJO PREMIUM
Handmade in Esteli, Nicaragua.

Wrapper: Nicaragua   Binder: Nicaragua   Filler: Nicaragua

Shape	Name	Lgth	Ring	Wrapper
Double Corona	Presidente	7¾	52	CM

HANDMADE CIGARS: BRAND LISTINGS

Double Corona	Churchill	6⅞	50	CM
Toro	Regulares	6	50	CM
Lonsdale	No. 1	6¾	44	CM
Corona	No. 4	5½	44	CM
Torpedo	Torpedo	6	52	CM
Robusto	Rothschild	5	50	CM

Full-bodied flavor is the promise of this line of all-Nicaraguan cigars introduced in 2006. Using a Corojo wrapper and all Jalapa-grown interior leaves, all sizes are offered in economical bundles of 25.

ARANGO STATESMAN

Handmade in Danli, Honduras and Santiago, Dominican Republic.

Wrapper: Ecuador   Binder: Dom. Rep., Honduras   Filler: Dom. Rep., Honduras

Shape	Name		Lgth	Ring	Wrapper
Churchill	Barrister		7½	45	CC
Toro	Trustee		6¼	50	CC
Double Corona	Advocate		7¼	52	CC
	Machine-made:				
Corona	Counselor		5	40	CC-Ma
Petit Corona	Executor		6	42	CC-Ma
Torpedo	Belicoso		5¾	46	CC
Corona	Guardian	*(glass tube)*	5¾	43	CC
Perfecto	Solicitor		5¼	43	CC

Introduced in 1988, this a combination brand of hand and machine-made cigars. The three handmade shapes are medium-bodied, handmade cigars from Honduras, which should not be confused with its sister brand, the Arango Sportsman, which is a flavored machine-made cigar. The Statesman is quite aromatic, with just a hint of vanilla flavor to charm the smoker and an Ecuadorian wrapper and Honduran binder. The machine-made sizes are manufactured in the Dominican Republic (since 2000) and are all tobacco, with Ecuadorian wrappers, Dominican binder and blended filler.

HANDMADE CIGARS: BRAND LISTINGS

ARGANESE ★New★
Handmade in Tamboril, Dominican Republic.
Wrapper: Brazil, Cameroon, Nicaragua, USA/Connecticut
Binder: Dominican Republic, Indonesia   *Filler: Dominican Republic*

Shape	Name	Lgth	Ring	Wrapper
Corona Extra	Corona	5½	45	CC-CM-Ma
Double Corona	Churchill	7	50	CC-CM-Ma-Stripe
Torpedo	Torpedo	6⅞	52	CC-CM-Ma
Robusto	Robusto	5	50	CC-CM-Ma
Perfecto	Figurado	6¼	54	CC-CM-Ma
Petit Corona	Petit Corona	5⅛	42	CC-CM-Ma

Gene Arganese decided there was room on the market for at least one more brand: his. So in 2007, he debuted the unique Arganese phalanx of cigars, with a choice of three different blends and five different wrapper styles! The Ambassador blend is the lightest, with a choice of Nicaraguan (mild to medium) or Connecticut (mild) wrappers. The Chairman blend is medium-to-full in body, offered with a choice of Brazilian maduro, Cameroon, Connecticut or a striped wrapper (Brazilian and Connecticut) in the Churchill size. The Presidente is full-bodied and the only blend with a Dominican binder, plus a choice of Brazilian maduro, Nicaraguan or Connecticut wrappers. All are offered in boxes of 25.

ARTE CUBANO
Handmade in Santiago, Dominican Republic.
Wrapper: Ecuador   *Binder: Dom. Rep.*   *Filler: Dom. Rep., Nicaragua*

Shape	Name	Lgth	Ring	Wrapper
Torpedo	Torpedo	6	52	CC
Churchill	Churchill	7	47	CC
Robusto	Robusto	5	50	CC
Long Corona	Corona	6	44	CC

The Tabacalera Esteli commissioned this cigar from a Dominican maker in 2006. It's mild in body with a buttery note, offered in elegant boxes of 25.

HANDMADE CIGARS: BRAND LISTINGS

ARTURO FUENTE
Handmade in Santiago, Dominican Republic.
Wrapper: Ecuador or USA/Connecticut, Cameroon
Binder: Dominican Republic   Filler: Dominican Republic

Shape	Name	Lgth	Ring	Wrapper
Corona	Brevas Royale /medium filler/	5½	42	CC-Ma
Giant	Canones	8½	52	CC-Ma
Churchill	Churchill	7¼	48	DC-CC-Ma
Grand Corona	Corona Imperial	6½	46	CC-Ma
Corona Extra	Cuban Corona	5¼	45	CC-Ma
Lonsdale	Curly Head /medium filler/	6½	43	DC-CC-Ma
Lonsdale	Curly Head Deluxe /medium filler/	6½	43	CC-Ma
Long Panatela	Panatela Fina	7	38	CC-Ma
Short Panatela	Petit Corona	5	38	CC-Ma
Lonsdale	Seleccion Privada No. 1	6¾	44	DC-CM-Ma
Robusto	Rothschild	4½	50	CC-Ma
Lonsdale	Spanish Lonsdale	6½	42	DC-CM-Ma
Grand Corona	Flor Fina 8-5-8	6	47	CM-Ma
Perfecto	Short Story	4	49	CM
Small Panatela	Exquisito /medium filler/	4½	33	CM
Small Panatela	Cubanitos	4½	32	CM
	Chateau Series:			
Double Corona	Chateau Fuente Royal Salute	7⅝	54	CC-Ma
Toro	Double Chateau Fuente	6¾	50	CC-Ma
Robusto	Chateau Fuente	4½	50	CC-Ma
	Fuente Seleccion D'Oro:			
Churchill	Churchill Sel. d'Or	7¼	48	CC

HANDMADE CIGARS: BRAND LISTINGS

Grand Corona	Corona Imperial Sel. d'Or	6½	46	CC
Lonsdale	Privada No. 1 Sel. d'Or	6¾	44	CC
	Fuente Sun Grown:			
Torpedo	King B	6	55	CM
Torpedo	Cuban Belicosos	5¾	52	CM
Grand Corona	Flor Fina 8-5-8	6¼	47	CM
	Hemingway Series:			*(perfecto tips)*
Churchill	Hemingway Classic	7	48	CM-Ma
Grand Corona	Hemingway Signature	6	47	CM-Ma
Giant	Hemingway Masterpiece	9	52	CM
Robusto	Hemingway Short Story	4	49	CM
Torpedo	Hemingway Best Seller	5	55	CM
Torpedo	Hemingway Work of Art	4⅞	60	CM
Double Corona	Hemingway Untold Story	7⅝	54	Ma
Torpedo	Hemingway Between the Lines	5	54	Stripe

Arturo Fuente learned the art of growing and processing tobacco and the making of premium, handmade cigars in Cuba at the end of the 19th century, producing his own line in 1912. Today, his son Carlos and grandson, Carlos, Jr. oversee the more than 500 rollers who manufacture more than 24 million cigars every year. Their line offers a medium-to-full-bodied taste, with the celebrated Hemingway series a little mellower, thanks to an additional 140 days of aging. Many of the natural-wrapped cigars (including the Hemingway series) feature Cameroon leaves, with Connecticut leaf used for maduros. Most sizes are offered in boxes of 25.

The Cuban Belicoso, Chateau Fuente, Chateau Fuente Royal Salute and Double Chateau Fuente use either Ecuadorian sun-grown, Connecticut-seed or Connecticut wrappers. The King B, introduced in 2005, has an Ecuadorian Rosado wrapper and with three other shapes that use a sun-grown Ecuadorian wrapper make up the Fuente Sun Grown series. The Fuente Seleccion d'Oro features a Connecticut Shade wrapper in place of Cameroon.

HANDMADE CIGARS: BRAND LISTINGS

ARTURO FUENTE AÑEJO
Handmade in Santiago, Dominican Republic.

Wrapper: USA/Connecticut   Binder: Dom. Rep.   Filler: Dom. Rep.

Shape	Name	Lgth	Ring	Wrapper
Grand Corona	Reserva No. 46	5⅝	46	Ma
Churchill	Reserva No. 48	7	48	Ma
Double Corona	Reserva No. 49	7⅝	49	Ma
Robusto	Reserva No. 50	5¼	50	Ma
Torpedo	Reserva No. 55	6	55	Ma
Torpedo	Shark No. 77	5⅞	64	Ma

Introduced in 2000, this remarkable brand features the binder and filler blend used in the Fuente Fuente Opus X brand plus a Connecticut Broadleaf maduro wrapper. This provides a full-bodied taste with power and sweetness. You can enjoy these cigars in boxes of 25.

ARTURO FUENTE DON CARLOS
Handmade in Santiago, Dominican Republic.

Wrapper: Cameroon   Binder: Dom. Rep.   Filler: Dom. Rep.

Shape	Name	Lgth	Ring	Wrapper
Torpedo	No. 2	6	55	CM
Corona	No. 3	5½	44	CM
Petit Corona	No. 4	5⅛	43	CM
Robusto	Robusto	5¼	50	CM
Robusto	Double Robusto	5¾	52	CM
Toro	Presidente	6½	50	CM
Torpedo	Belicoso	5⅜	52	CM

Here is the result of careful planning and brilliant execution in the making of a new brand from the workshops of Tabacalera A. Fuente. The flawless construction and smooth taste of this medium-bodied cigar make it a rewarding experience from the beginning. All sizes are offered in boxes of 25.

HANDMADE CIGARS: BRAND LISTINGS

ARUBA
Handmade, with mixed filler, in Santiago, Dominican Republic.

Wrapper: Indonesia   *Binder: Indonesia*   *Filler: Honduras*

Introduced in 1997, this is a five-size brand that offers the medium-bodied, pleasant experience you'd enjoy if you were in Aruba! All sizes are available in boxes of 25.

ASHTON CLASSIC
Handmade in Santiago, Dominican Republic.

Wrapper: USA/Connecticut   *Binder: Dom. Rep.*   *Filler: Dom. Rep.*

Shape	Name	Lgth	Ring	Wrapper
Double Corona	Churchill	7½	52	CC
Churchill	Prime Minister	6⅞	48	CC
Lonsdale	8-9-8	6½	44	CC
Panatela	Panetela	6	36	CC
Corona	Corona	5½	44	CC
Slim Panatela	Cordial	5	30	CC
Toro	Double Magnum	6	50	CC
Robusto	Magnum	5	50	CC
Toro	Majesty	6	56	CC
Small Panatela	Esquire	4¼	32	CC-Ma
Torpedo	Sovereign	6¾	55	CC
Toro	Crystal Belicoso *(glass tube)*	6	49	CC
Lonsdale	Crystal No. 1 *(glass tube)*	6½	44	CC
Corona	Imperial *(tubed)*	5½	44	CC
Toro	Monarch *(tubed)*	6	50	CC

Robert Levin of Holt's Tobacconist of Philadelphia, Pennsylvania set out to create a great cigar in 1985 . . . and he succeeded. Ashton cigars are manufactured without compromise at the Tabacalera A. Fuente, blending six tobaccos: Dominican filler and Dominican-grown, Cuban-seed binder leaves with perfect shade-grown wrapper leaves from the Connecticut Valley for a medium-bodied taste. Most sizes are offered in boxes of 25, with the Esquire and glass-

HANDMADE CIGARS: BRAND LISTINGS

tubed shapes in 10s and Imperial and Monarchs in 24s.

ASHTON AGED CABINET SELECTION
Handmade in Santiago, Dominican Republic.

Wrapper: USA/Connecticut   *Binder: Dom. Rep.*   *Filler: Dom. Rep.*

Shape	Name	Lgth	Ring	Wrapper
Perfecto	No. 1	9	52	CC
Perfecto	No. 2	7	46	CC
Perfecto	No. 3	6	46	CC
Robusto	No. 6	5½	50	CC
Toro	No. 7	6¼	52	CC
Double Corona	No. 8	7	49	CC
Perfecto	No. 10	7½	52	CC
Pyramid	Pyramid	6	52	CC
Petit Corona	Tres Petite	4⅜	42	CC
Torpedo	Belicoso	5¼	52	CC

The medium-bodied Aged Cabinet Selection was introduced in the early 1990s and offers a unique range of sizes which are packed in all-cedar cabinets of 10 (No. 1), 20 (Nos. 2, 3, 10) or 25 (other sizes) with most sizes also available in packs of four or five. The most prominent shapes include four large perfectos, including the mighty No. 1.

ASHTON AGED MADURO
Handmade in Santiago, Dominican Republic.

Wrapper: USA/Connecticut   *Binder: Dom. Rep.*   *Filler: Dom. Rep.*

Shape	Name	Lgth	Ring	Wrapper
Double Corona	No. 60	7½	52	Ma
Churchill	No. 50	7	48	Ma
Toro	No. 40	6	50	Ma
Lonsdale	No. 30	6¾	44	Ma
Corona	No. 20	5½	44	Ma

www.CigarCyclopedia.com   - 64 -   *www.CigarCyclopedia.com*

Petit Corona	No. 15	4⅜	44	Ma
Robusto	No. 10	5	50	Ma
Pyramid	Pyramid	6	52	Ma

Only the finest Connecticut-grown Broadleaf wrapper is good enough to use for the Ashton Aged Maduro series. These are sensuous, medium-to-full-bodied cigars available in limited quantities in varnished, elegant cabinets of 25.

ASHTON ESTATE SUN GROWN
Handmade in Santiago, Dominican Republic.

Wrapper: Dom. Rep.   *Binder: Dom. Rep.*   *Filler: Dom. Rep.*

Shape	*Name*	*Lgth*	*Ring*	*Wrapper*
Double Corona	ESG No. 20	6¾	49	CM
Robusto	ESG No. 21	5¼	52	CM

The ESG was scheduled to be introduced in 2005, but was held up for a year. The No. 20 was the vanguard of a six-year program leading to the 25th anniversary of Ashton in 2010. It's especially noteworthy for the special wrapper leaf grown at the Chateau de la Fuente. Both the No. 20 and 21 are full-bodied and spicy, with only 50,000 of each to be made, offered in boxes of 25.

ASHTON HERITAGE PURO SOL
Handmade in Santiago, Dominican Republic.

Wrapper: Cameroon   *Binder: Dom. Rep.*   *Filler: Dom. Rep.*

Shape	*Name*	*Lgth*	*Ring*	*Wrapper*
Double Corona	Double Corona	7	52	CM
Robusto	Robusto	5½	50	CM
Grand Corona	Corona Gorda	5¾	46	CM
Churchill	Churchill	6¾	48	CM
Torpedo	Belicoso No. 2	4⅞	49	CM

Introduced in 2003, this line features a Cameroon wrapper and offers a medium-bodied taste with all sun-grown tobaccos in the filler, binder and wrapper. It is presented in all-wood boxes of 25.

HANDMADE CIGARS: BRAND LISTINGS

ASHTON VIRGIN SUN GROWN
Handmade in Santiago, Dominican Republic.

Wrapper: Ecuador *Binder: Dom. Rep.* *Filler: Dom. Rep.*

Shape	Name	Lgth	Ring	Wrapper
Torpedo	Belicoso No. 1	5¼	52	CM
Torpedo	Torpedo	6½	55	CM
Robusto	Robusto	5½	50	CM
Grand Corona	Corona Gorda	5¾	46	CM
Lonsdale	Illusion	6½	44	CM
Double Corona	Sorcerer	7	49	CM
Perfecto	Enchantment	4⅜	60	CM
Double Corona	Spellbound	7½	54	CM
Petit Corona	Tres Mystique	4⅜	44	CM
Toro	Wizard	6	56	CM

The Ashton Virgin Sun Grown series was introduced in November 1999 and brings a full-bodied taste to the Ashton line. It features an Ecuadorian-grown wrapper with extra ligero leaf in the blend for the maximum in flavor. The all-box-pressed series is offered in elegant boxes of 24, except for the Enchantment, offered in 22s and the Wizard, in 37s.

ASPIRA
Handmade in Danli, Honduras.

Wrapper: Nicaragua *Binder: Honduras* *Filler: Honduras, Nicaragua*

Shape	Name	Lgth	Ring	Wrapper
Lonsdale	Lonsdale	6½	42	CM
Churchill	Presidente	7	48	CM
Robusto	Robusto	4¾	50	CM
Toro	Toro	6	50	CM
Torpedo	Torpedo	6½	54	CM

Introduced in 2000, this is a full-bodied, box-pressed cigar that offers big flavor at reasonable prices. You can find it in bold-looking red, blue and gold boxes of 25.

HANDMADE CIGARS: BRAND LISTINGS

ASPIRA COROJO & MADURO ★*New*★
Handmade in Danli, Honduras.
Wrapper: Nicaragua, USA/Connecticut

Binder: Honduras   *Filler: Honduras, Nicaragua*

Shape	Name	Lgth	Ring	Wrapper
Lonsdale	Lonsdale	6½	42	CM-Ma
Churchill	Presidente	7	48	CM-Ma
Robusto	Robusto	4¾	50	CM-Ma
Toro	Toro	6	50	CM-Ma
Torpedo	Torpedo	6½	54	CM-Ma

Cigar Domain offers these medium-to-full-bodied blends, which debuted in 2007. Take your choice of an H2000 natural or Connecticut Broadleaf maduro wrapper in bundles of 25.

ASTRAL
Handmade in Danli, Honduras.
Wrapper: Ecuador, Mexico   *Binder: Dom. Rep.*   *Filler: Dom. Rep., Nicaragua*

Shape	Name	Lgth	Ring	Wrapper
Robusto	Besos	5	52	CM-Ma
Small Panatela	Favorito	4⅛	32	CM
Torpedo	Grandee	6¼	50	CM-Ma
Lonsdale	Lujos	6½	44	CM
Double Corona	Maestro	7½	52	CM
Torpedo	Perfeccion	7	48	CM
	House of Oxford series:			
Double Corona	Phoenix	7½	50	CM
Lonsdale	Candela	6½	44	DC
Torpedo	Forget Me Nots	7	48	CM

Mild-to-medium in body, the Connecticut-seed wrappers give this line, introduced in 1995, an elegant appearance, with silky expresso and cream flavors.

Two shapes were developed for the House of Oxford in 2002. The Phoenix is mild-to-medium in body with an Indonesian wrapper, but the Candela is medium in body with a special Honduran Talanga Cubano Candela wrapper, Mexican binder and Dominican and Nicaraguan fillers, offered in 25s.

ASTRAL CAMEROON
Handmade in Danli, Honduras.

Wrapper: Cameroon   Binder: Honduras   Filler: Honduras, Nicaragua

Shape	Name	Lgth	Ring	Wrapper
Robusto	Beso	5	52	CM
Churchill	Double Corona	7	48	CM
Toro	Double Robusto	6	60	CM
Torpedo	Favorita	7	48	CM
Lonsdale	Lujo	6½	44	CM
Double Corona	Maestro	7½	52	CM
Perfecto	Perfeccion	7	48	CM

This is a medium-bodied version of the Astral line, developed for Cigars by Santa Clara. Introduced in 2004, it is offered in boxes of 25.

ASTRAL GRAND RESERVE VINTAGE
Handmade in Danli, Honduras.

Wrapper: USA/Connecticut   Binder: Mexico   Filler: Brazil, Dom. Rep., Nicaragua

Shape	Name		Lgth	Ring	Wrapper
Double Corona	Maestro	*(tubed)*	7½	52	CC
Torpedo	Grandee	*(tubed)*	6¼	50	CC
Lonsdale	Lujo	*(tubed)*	6½	44	CC
Robusto	Beso	*(tubed)*	5	52	CC

Introduced in 1998, this is a medium-to-full-bodied blend with notes of sweetness and a light peppery character. It is offered in elegant glass tubes in stunning all-mahogany boxes of 10.

HANDMADE CIGARS: BRAND LISTINGS

ASTRAL GRV '96 ★*New*★
Handmade in Danli, Honduras.

Wrapper: Ecuador   *Binder: Nicaragua*   *Filler: Honduras, Nicaragua*

Shape	Name	Lgth	Ring	Wrapper
Robusto	552	5	52	CC
Torpedo	652 Belicoso	6¼	52	CC
Toro	654	6⅝	54	CC
Double Corona	752	7½	52	CC

Here is a special version of the Grand Reserve Vintage, made specially for House of Oxford Distributors. Introduced in 2007, it's medium in body and offered in boxes of 25.

ASTRAL TALANGA VALLEY SELECTION
Handmade in Danli, Honduras.

Wrapper: Honduras   *Binder: Mexico*   *Filler: Brazil, Dom. Rep., Nicaragua*

Shape	Name	Lgth	Ring	Wrapper
Robusto	Robusto	5	50	Ma
Toro	Toro	6	50	Ma
Torpedo	Pyramid	6	52	Ma
Churchill	Churchill	7	48	Ma

Unlike the sweated leaves in most maduro wrappers, here is a natural maduro from the Talanga Valley in Honduras, using the uppermost priming of the Talanga Cubano tobacco plant. This is a full-bodied cigar in limited quantities, first offered in 2001 in a pressed shape and available in boxes of 25.

AUGUSTO REYES
Handmade in Santiago, Dominican Republic.

CRIOLLO:

Wrapper: Ecuador   *Binder: Dom. Rep.*   *Filler: Dom. Rep.*

EPICUR:

Wrapper: Ecuador   *Binder: Dom. Rep.*   *Wrapper: Dom. Rep.*

HANDMADE CIGARS: BRAND LISTINGS

NATIVO:

Wrapper: Dom. Rep.   Binder: Dom. Rep.   Wrapper: Dom. Rep.

Shape	Name	Lgth	Ring	Wrapper
	Criollo:			
Toro	Gordo	6¼	58	CC
Churchill	Churchill	7	48	CC
Toro	Toro	6	52	CC
Robusto	Robusto	5	50	CC
Corona	Lonsdale	5¾	40	CC
	Epicur:			
Perfecto	Perfecto Grande	6¼	54	CM
Perfecto	Perfecto Pequeño	5⅛	54	CM
Torpedo	Torpedo	6	50	CM
Robusto	Especiales	4¾	51	CM
Petit Corona	Coffee Break	4	44	CM
	Nativo:			
Double Corona	Presidente	7	50	CM
Grand Corona	Toro	6	46	CM
Robusto	Robusto	5	50	CM
Corona	Corona	5½	44	CM
Lonsdale	Lancero	6¾	40	CM

Well known for making cigars for others, Augusto Reyes decided to make his own brand in 2006. It comes in three styles: the medium-bodied Criollo (red band), the medium-bodied and smooth Epicur (blue band) and the medium-to-full-bodied Nativo (purple band). All are offered in boxes of 24.

AURORA 1495 SERIES

Handmade in Santiago, Dominican Republic.

Wrapper: Ecuador   Binder: Dom. Rep.   Filler: Dom. Rep., Nicaragua, Peru

Shape	Name	Lgth	Ring	Wrapper
Corona	Corona	5¼	43	CC
Robusto	Robusto	5	50	CC
Torpedo	Belicoso	6¼	52	CC
Double Corona	Churchill	7	50	CC
Toro	Sumo Toro	6	58	CC

This is a medium-to-full-bodied cigar created to celebrate the 510th anniversary of the founding of the city of Santiago in the Dominican Republic. Introduced in 2005, it's offered in boxes of 25, except for the Sumo Toro (20).

A special "Connoisseur Selection" was introduced in 2007, offering the Robusto with four different wrappers: Brazilian, Cameroon, Connecticut and Dominican-grown Corojo, so you can taste the difference for yourself!

AURORA BARREL AGED ★*New*★
Handmade in Santiago, Dominican Republic.

Wrapper: Dom. Rep.   *Binder: Dom. Rep.*   *Filler: Dom. Rep., Nicaragua*

Shape	Name	Lgth	Ring	Wrapper
Corona	No. 4	5¾	43	Os
Robusto	Robusto	5	50	Os
Double Corona	Churchill	7½	50	Os
Torpedo	Belicoso	6¼	52	Os

Introduced in 2007, the tobaccos in this blend have been aged for four years in cedar barrels for an extra-rich taste. It's medium-bodied, however, and offered in boxes of 25.

AURORA CIEN AÑOS
Handmade in Santiago, Dominican Republic.

Wrapper: Dom. Rep.   *Binder: Dom. Rep.*   *Filler: Dom. Rep.*

Shape	Name	Lgth	Ring	Wrapper
Corona	Corona	5¼	43	CM
Robusto	Robusto	5	50	CM

| Torpedo | Belicoso | 6¼ | 52 | CM |
| Double Corona | Churchill | 7 | 50 | CM |

Here is a celebration of the first cigar factory in the Dominican Republic, the La Aurora factory opened in 1903. This limited-edition brand debuted in late 2003, with only 400,000 cigars to be produced in total. It's a medium-to-full blend offered in elegant boxes of 25.

AURORA PREFERIDOS
Handmade in Santiago, Dominican Republic.
Wrapper: Brazil, Cameroon, Dom. Rep., Ecuador, USA/Connecticut
Binder: Dom. Rep.   Filler: Brazil, Cameroon, Dom. Rep.

Shape	Name		Lgth	Ring	Wrapper
	Cameroon line:				
Perfecto	No. 1		6	58	CM
Perfecto	No. 2		5	54	CM
Perfecto	No. 3		4	50	CM
Robusto	Robusto		5	50	CM
Perfecto	Platinum Tubes	*(tubed)*	5	54	CM
	Maduro line:				
Perfecto	Ruby Edition Tubes	*(tubed)*	5	54	Ma
Perfecto	No. 1		6	58	Ma
Perfecto	No. 2		5	54	Ma
Perfecto	No. 3		4	50	Ma
	Connecticut line:				
Perfecto	Sapphire Tubes	*(tubed)*	5	54	CC
Perfecto	No. 1		6	58	CC
Perfecto	No. 2		5	54	CC
	Corojo line:				
Perfecto	Gold Tubes	*(tubed)*	5	54	CM

Perfecto	Corojo No. 1	6	58	CM
Perfecto	Corojo No. 2	5	54	CM
	Emerald line:			
Perfecto	Emerald No. 1	6	58	Co
Perfecto	Emerald No. 2	5	54	Co
Perfecto	Emerald Edition *(tubed)*	5	54	Co
Robusto	Robusto	5	50	Co

The spectacular Preferidos 1903 Edition was introduced as a series of perfectos which reprises the shapes made by Don Eduardo Leon Jimenes at the opening of the La Aurora factory in 1903. Introduced in 1998, these are full-bodied cigars, mostly offered in the old perfecto shape that truly brings a little bit of the start of the 20th Century to smokers at the dawn of the 21st Century. All of the lines use a Dominican-grown binder and Brazilian, Cameroon and Dominican fillers, except for the Cameroon and Maduro lines (Dominican filler only) and the Emerald (Dominican and Nicaraguan filler). The Cameroon and Maduro (Brazil) series are medium-to-full in body while the Connecticut and Corojo lines are full-bodied. The Corojo series was introduced in 2003, Connecticut in 2004 and Emerald (Ecuador wrapper) in 2006. All lines are offered in boxes of 25 except for the tubed shapes (24s).

AVALON ★*New*★
Handmade in Esteli, Nicaragua and Miami, Florida, USA.

HAINT SERIES:
Wrapper: Brazil, Ecuador, USA/Connecticut

Binder: Dom. Rep.   Filler: Dom. Rep., Honduras, Nicaragua

JUKE SERIES :
Wrapper: Costa Rica, Ecuador, USA/Connecticut

Binder: Ecuador   Filler: Dom. Rep., Nicaragua

MASTERS SERIES:
Wrapper: Brazil, Cameroon

Binder: Dom. Rep.   Filler: Dom. Rep., Honduras, Nicaragua

Shape	Name	Lgth	Ring	Wrapper
	Haint Series:			

Robusto	Raw Head	5	52	Ma
Slim Panatela	Bloody Bones	6½	28	CC
Double Corona	Sack-A-Billy	7	60	Os
Long Corona	Gris Gris	6	44	CC
Pyramid	High John Root	6	60	Dual
	Juke Series:			
Robusto	Blue 5x50	5	50	Ma
Torpedo	Blue 6x54T	6	54	Ma
Long Corona	Blue 6x44	6	44	Ma
Double Corona	Red 7x52	7	52	CC
Grand Corona	Red 6x46	6	46	CC
Robusto	Red 5x48	5	48	CC
Double Corona	Ebony 7x50	7	50	CC
Torpedo	Ebony 4.5x54T	4½	54	CC
	Masters Series:			
Toro	Pinetop 6.5x52	6½	52	CM
Toro	Pinetop 5.75x48	5¾	48	CM
Double Corona	Pinetop 7x52	7	52	CM
Robusto	Pinetop 5.5x60	5½	60	CM
Torpedo	Pinetop 6.5x54	6½	54	CM
Robusto	Honeyboy 5x50	5	50	CC
Perfecto	Honeyboy 4.5x38	4½	38	CC
Toro	Honeyboy 6x60	6	60	CC
Long Panatela	Honeyboy 7x38	7	38	CC
Corona Extra	Blind Mississippi 5.25x46	5¼	46	Ma
Robusto	Blind Mississippi 5x50	5	50	Ma
Toro	Blind Mississippi 6x52	6	52	Ma

| Double Corona | Blind Mississippi 7x52 | 7 | 52 | Ma |
| Lonsdale | Blind Mississippi 6.5x44 | 6½ | 44 | Ma |

This complicated series was conceived in 2006 and delivered to national distribution in 2007 with the Haint Series scheduled to debut in 2008. The Haint Series (made in Miami) is flavored with each shape having a different style, ranging from floral to sweet to spicy to tart, featuring Brazilian maduro, Ecuadorian natural and Connecticut wrappers or both the Brazilian and Connecticut leaves on the High John Root.

The Juke Series is made in Nicaragua in three styles: Blue, full-bodied with a Costa Rican maduro wrapper; Red, medium in body with an Ecuadorian natural-shade wrapper and Ebony, mild with a Connecticut Shade wrapper.

The Masters Series is made in Miami in three styles as well: Pinetop, full-bodied with a Cameroon wrapper; Honeyboy, with a light Cameroon wrapper and a medium-to-full body and Blind Mississippi, featuring a Brazilian maduro wrapper and a medium body. The Masters Series cigars are offered in boxes of 20.

AVO
Handmade in Santiago, Dominican Republic.

Wrapper: USA/Connecticut   Binder: Dom. Rep.   Filler: Dom. Rep.

Shape	Name		Lgth	Ring	Wrapper
Toro	Avo No. 2	*(tube available)*	6	50	Co-Ma
Double Corona	Avo No. 3	*(tube available)*	7½	50	Co-Ma
Grand Corona	Avo No. 5	*(tube available)*	6⅞	46	Co
Robusto	Avo No. 9	*(tube available)*	4¾	48	Co-Ma
Pyramid	Piramides	*(tube available)*	7	54	Co-Ma
Torpedo	Belicoso		6	48	Ma
Robusto	Robusto	*(tube available)*	5	50	Co-Ma
Small Panatela	Puritos		4	30	Co

The perfectly-balanced marriage of five different tobaccos, mostly from the Cibao Valley of the Dominican Republic, gives the Avo line — created by Lebanese-born composer Avo Uvezian and introduced in 1987 — a rich flavor in a mild-bodied cigar. The maduro editions appeared in 2000 and wrap the same interior blend with a Connecticut Broadleaf wrapper for a mild-to-medium-bodied flavor. All shapes are available in boxes of 25, but the tubed cigars are offered in 20s and some shapes are offered in packs of four or five.

The Avo line has become well known for its limited-edition cigars, which started in 2001:

2001:	Avo 75	(7 x 50 in boxes of 10)
2002:	Avo 22	(5⅞ x 50 unbanded perfectos in boxes of 19 or 22)
2003:	Avo 77	(6½ x 50 in boxes of 14)
2004:	Avo Legacy	(5¾ x 48 in boxes of 12)
2005:	Avo LE5	(5⅝ x 52 unbanded in boxes of 20)
2006:	Avo 80	(6 x 52 perfecto in boxes of 24)
2007:	Avo LE7	(5⅝ x 48 unbanded in boxes of 20)

All featured Ecuadorian-grown wrappers and Dominican-grown binder and filler leaves. The Avo LE7 was made in a limited edition of 7,000 boxes (140,000 cigars) worldwide, with 4,000 boxes (80,000) for U.S. distribution.

AVO 787 ★*New*★
Handmade in Santiago, Dominican Republic.

Wrapper: Ecuador　　　*Binder: Dom. Rep.*　　　*Filler: Dom. Rep.*

Shape	Name	Lgth	Ring	Wrapper
Perfecto	Perfecto	5⅞	50	CM
Robusto	Robusto	5¼	52	CM
Toro	Toro	6	54	CM

This medium-bodied cigar was carefully blended to offer a rich taste featuring a Connecticut-seed, sun-grown wrapper from Ecuador and a Dominican San Vicente binder. Introduced to considerable fanfare in 2007, it's offered in boxes of 22.

AVO SIGNATURE SERIES
Handmade in Santiago, Dominican Republic.

Wrapper: Ecuador　　　*Binder: Dom. Rep.*　　　*Filler: Dom. Rep.*

HANDMADE CIGARS: BRAND LISTINGS

Shape	Name	Lgth	Ring	Wrapper
Robusto	Robusto	5	52	CM
Double Corona	Double Corona	7	50	CM
Long Corona	Lonsdale	6¼	43	CM
Torpedo	Belicoso	6	48	CM
Petit Corona	Small Corona	4½	43	CM

The Avo Signature Series appeared in 2001 and features the blend used for the famed 75th Anniversary cigar. It has a full-bodied flavor with a sun-grown Ecuadorian wrapper, available only in boxes of 10.

Avo XO
Handmade in Santiago, Dominican Republic.

Wrapper: Ecuador   *Binder: Dom. Rep.*   *Filler: Dom. Rep.*

Shape	Name		Lgth	Ring	Wrapper
Churchill	Maestoso	*(tube available)*	7	48	CC
Robusto	Intermezzo	*(tube available)*	5½	50	CC
Long Corona	Preludio	*(tube available)*	6	40	CC
Panatela	Serenata		5¾	38	CC
Petit Corona	Notturno	*(tube available)*	5	42	CC
Small Panatela	Presto		5	31	CC
Small Panatela	Allegro		4½	34	CC

The XO Series was introduced in the early 1990s and offers a medium-bodied blend of six tobaccos, using a Dominican-grown, Havana-seed binder with the Ecuadorian-grown, Connecticut-seed wrapper. The Serenata and Presto are available only in the XO Assortment Box packing.

B LINE
Handmade in Esteli, Nicaragua.

Wrapper: Ecuador   *Binder: USA/Connecticut*   *Filler: Nicaragua*

Shape	Name	Lgth	Ring	Wrapper
Torpedo	B1	6	50	CM

Robusto	B2	5	52	CM
Robusto	B3	5	50	CM
Robusto	B4	4½	52	CM

Created by Tony Borhani of Bahia fame in 2000, this blend offers a Sumatra-seed wrapper, Connecticut Broadleaf binder and Nicaraguan filler for a medium-bodied taste that is offered in 20s. Production was moved from Costa Rica to Nicaragua in 2001.

BACCARAT "THE GAME" HAVANA SELECTION
Handmade in Danli, Honduras.

Wrapper: Honduras　　　　　Binder: Honduras　　　　　Filler: Honduras

Shape	Name	Lgth	Ring	Wrapper
Small Panatela	Bonitas	4½	32	CC
Churchill	Churchill	7	48	DC-CC-Ma
Long Corona	Luchadores	6	44	CC
Lonsdale	No. 1	7	44	CC
Panatela	Panatela	6⅛	38	CC
Corona	Petit Corona	5½	44	CC
Small Panatela	Platinum	4¾	32	CC
Torpedo	Belicoso	6⅛	54	CC-Ma
Toro	Toro	6	50	CC
Pyramid	Polo	7½	52	CC
Robusto	Rothschild	5	50	DC-CC-Ma
Double Corona	Double Corona	7½	50	CC-Ma
Giant	King	8½	52	CC-Ma
Small Panatela	Connies	4	32	CC

This brand was formally introduced in 1978, but dates back as far as 1871 when it was supervised by Carl Upmann. The mild body produced by the blending of the Havana-seed fillers and binder and Connecticut-seed wrapper are sweetened by the use of a special sealing gum in the cigar's cap. It's offered in boxes of 25 in most sizes.

HANDMADE CIGARS: BRAND LISTINGS

BACCARAT SUMATRA
Handmade in Danli, Honduras.

Wrapper: Honduras   Binder: Mexico   Filler: Honduras

Shape	Name	Lgth	Ring	Wrapper
Lonsdale	No. 1	7	44	CM
Corona	Corona	5½	44	CM
Churchill	Double Corona	7	48	CM
Giant	Presidente	8½	52	CM
Robusto	Rothschild	5	50	CM
Toro	Toro	6	50	CM

This is a special edition of the mild-bodied Baccarat line with a Sumatra-seed wrapper created for Famous Smoke Shop in 2006. It's offered in bundles of 25.

BACCARAT VINTAGE
Handmade in Danli, Honduras.

Wrapper: Cameroon   Binder: Honduras   Filler: Honduras

Shape	Name		Lgth	Ring	Wrapper
Lonsdale	Brillante	(tubed)	6½	44	CM

This is a special-edition cigar made for Great Discovery's of Houston, Texas. Introduced in 2005, it's medium-to-full in body and offered in boxes of 20.

BACCHUS
Handmade in Santiago, Dominican Republic.

Wrapper: Brazil, Indonesia   Binder: Dom. Rep.   Filler: Dom. Rep.

Shape	Name	Lgth	Ring	Wrapper
Double Corona	Churchill	7	50	CM-Ma
Toro	Toro	6	50	CM-Ma
Lonsdale	Lonsdale	6½	44	CM-Ma
Robusto	Robusto	5	50	CM-Ma
Torpedo	Torpedo	6½	52	CM-Ma

HANDMADE CIGARS: BRAND LISTINGS

This brand was introduced in 1999. It features a Sumatra (natural) or Brazilian (maduro) wrapper and Olor binder for a mild-to-medium-bodied (natural) or medium-bodied (maduro) taste. It is offered in boxes of 25.

BAHIA GOLD
Handmade in Esteli, Nicaragua.

Wrapper: Ecuador *Binder: Dom. Rep.* *Filler: Dom. Rep.*

Shape	Name		Lgth	Ring	Wrapper
Churchill	Churchill		6⅞	48	CM-Ma
Torpedo	No. 2		6½	54	CM-Ma
Robusto	Robusto	*(tube available)*	5	50	CM-Ma
Toro	No. 3		6½	48	CM
Corona	No. 4		5½	42	CM
Short Panatela	No. 5		4½	38	CM

The Tabacalera Tambor in Costa Rica was the creation point for this 1997-introduced series of full-bodied cigars. Production migrated in 2001 from Costa Rica to Nicaragua. This series uses a Sumatra-seed wrapper from Ecuador and Dominican binder and filler. All of the finished cigars are aged for 12 months following rolling to ensure the perfect marriage of flavors for the smoker. All sizes are offered in boxes of 20.

BAHIA GOLD WHITE LABEL
Handmade in Esteli, Nicaragua.

Wrapper: Ecuador *Binder: Nicaragua* *Filler: Nicaragua*

Shape	Name	Lgth	Ring	Wrapper
Churchill	Churchill	6⅞	48	CC
Robusto	Robusto	5	50	CC

Tony Borhani's White Label blend was introduced in 2002. It offers a medium-bodied smoke featuring aged Ecuadorian-grown, Sumatra-seed, sixth-priming wrapper leaf. Only 200 boxes of 20 (4,000 cigars total) are produced monthly.

BAHIA ICON ★*New*★
Handmade in Esteli, Nicaragua.

Wrapper: Nicaragua *Binder: Nicaragua* *Filler: Nicaragua*

Shape	Name	Lgth	Ring	Wrapper
Robusto	Gran Robusto	5	56	CM
Toro	Gran Toro	6½	58	CM
Torpedo	No. 2	6½	52	CM
Perfecto	Salomon	7½	58	CM

The Icon is a new style of cigar from Tony Borhani, introduced in 2007. It's full-bodied, with six-year-old leaf from Jalapa for the wrapper and 12-year-aged leaf from the Condega and Jalapa regions used for filler.

BAHIA INSIGNIAS
Handmade in Esteli, Nicaragua.

Wrapper: Ecuador　　　　*Binder: Costa Rica*　　　　*Filler: Costa Rica*

Shape	Name	Lgth	Ring	Wrapper
Toro	Gran Corona	6½	54	CM
Churchill	Presidente	6⅞	48	CM
Robusto	Gran Robusto	5	55	CM
Petit Corona	Longsdale	4¾	44	CM

Designed as a 10th anniversary cigar from Tony Borhani, Insignias are full-bodied with a Sumatra-seed wrapper. Introduced in 2006, they're offered in boxes of 20.

BAHIA MADURO RED LABEL
Handmade in Esteli, Nicaragua.

Wrapper: USA/Connecticut　　*Binder: Nicaragua*　　　*Filler: Nicaragua*

Shape	Name	Lgth	Ring	Wrapper
Double Corona	Corona Gigantes	7	54	Ma
Torpedo	No. 2	6½	54	Ma
Robusto	Panchos	5½	52	Ma
Robusto	Robustos	5	50	Ma

This is a 1997-introduced, full-bodied cigar, with powerful Nicaraguan binder and filler and the classic Connecticut Broadleaf wrapper. Initial production of this cigar was at the Tabacalera Tambor in Costa Rica, but was relocated to Nicaragua in mid-2001.

BAHIA TRINIDAD
Handmade in Esteli, Nicaragua.

Wrapper: Nicaragua   *Binder: Nicaragua*   *Filler: Nicaragua*

Shape	Name	Lgth	Ring	Wrapper
Torpedo	No. 2	6½	54	CC
Robusto	Panchos	5½	52	CC
Robusto	Robustos	5	50	CC
Churchill	Churchill	6⅞	48	CC

Bahia Trinidads were introduced in 1997, but the blend was changed in 2002. This is now a medium-to-full-bodied smoke, featuring a Nicaraguan-grown Criollo 98 wrapper. Once rolled, Bahia Trinidads are aged for an additional 120 days to ensure perfect draw and the brand's signature flavor. Production shifted from Costa Rica to Nicaragua in mid-2001.

BAHIBA
Handmade, with mixed filler, in Nassau, Bahamas.

Wrapper: Ecuador   *Binder: Indonesia*   *Filler: Honduras, Nicaragua*

Shape	Name	Lgth	Ring	Wrapper
Churchill	Churchill	7	48	CC
Panatela	Corona	6	38	CC
Toro	Double Robusto	6	50	CC
Pyramid	Pyramid	6	52	CC

This is a medium-strength cigar from the makers of Graycliff, using mixed filler, available without cellophane in boxes of 25.

BAHIBA RESERVE PARADISO
Handmade, with mixed filler, in Nassau, Bahamas.

Wrapper: Indonesia   *Binder: Indonesia*
Filler: Brazil, Dom. Rep., Ecuador, Honduras, Nicaragua

Shape	Name	Lgth	Ring	Wrapper
Churchill	Churchill	7	48	CC
Toro	Double Robusto	6	50	CC
Pyramid	Pyramid	6	52	CC

This is a medium-strength, extra-aged blend introduced in 2002 which uses mixed filler, available without cellophane in boxes of 25.

BALMORAL ROYAL SELECTION
Handmade in San Pedro de Macoris, Dominican Republic.

Wrapper: Ecuador, Brazil   Binder: Dom. Rep.   Filler: Brazil, Dom. Rep.

Shape	Name		Lgth	Ring	Wrapper
Churchill	Churchill		7	48	CC-Ma
Torpedo	Torpedo		6¼	52	CC-Ma
Lonsdale	Lonsdale		6½	42	CC-Ma
Long Corona	Corona	(tube available)	6	42	CC-Ma
Robusto	Robusto		5	48	CC-Ma
Panatela	Panatela		5½	37	CC-Ma

Long a respected machine-made brand, this handmade version is mild in body with a Connecticut-seed wrapper or medium in body with the Brazilian-grown maduro wrapper. Distributed by the Arango Cigar Co., you can find it in individual cellophane sleeves in packs of 5 (Panatela and Torpedo only) or boxes of 25.

BANCES
Handmade in Cofradia, Honduras.

Wrapper: Ecuador, USA/Connecticut   Binder: Honduras
Filler: Dominican Republic, Honduras and Nicaragua

Shape	Name	Lgth	Ring	Wrapper
Corona	Brevas	5½	43	CM-Ma
Lonsdale	Cazadores	6¼	44	CM-Ma

Bances cigars are made in Honduras under the same supervision as the famous Hoyo de Monterrey and Punch lines. This is a true value cigar, with the same great qualities of its more famous sister lines.

HANDMADE CIGARS: BRAND LISTINGS

BANDIDOS ★*New*★
Handmade in Danli, Honduras.

Wrapper: Indonesia   Binder: none   Filler: Honduras, Nicaragua

Shape	Name	Lgth	Ring	Wrapper
Small Panatela	Cheroot	4¾	32	CM

Made by hand, this is a mild-to-medium-bodied cigar with a Sumatra wrapper and no binder. Distributed by Meier & Dutch, it is offered in boxes of 60.

BATTLEGROUND
Handmade in Santiago, Dominican Republic.

Wrapper: Cameroon, USA/Connecticut   Binder: Dom. Rep.
Filler: Dominican Republic, Honduras, Nicaragua, USA/Louisiana

Shape	Name	Lgth	Ring	Wrapper
Churchill	North/Grant	7	48	CC-CM-Ma
Torpedo	North/Custer	6	52	CC-CM-Ma
Robusto	North/Chamberlain	5	50	CC-CM-Ma
Torpedo	North/Sickles	4	40	CC-CM-Ma
Toro	North/Sherman	6	50	CC-CM-Ma
Toro	South/Lee	6	50	CC-CM-Ma
Churchill	South/Stuart	7	48	CC-CM-Ma
Torpedo	South/Cleburne or Forrest	6	52	CC-CM-Ma
Robusto	South/Stonewall	5	50	CC-CM-Ma
Torpedo	South/Pickett	4	40	CC-CM-Ma
Robusto	South/Foot Soldier	5	50	CC-Ma
Toro	South/Foot Soldier	6	50	CC-Ma
Churchill	South/Foot Soldier	7	48	CC-Ma

This unique series, made by MATASA, was introduced in 2002 by the Battleground Seegar Company. The Battlefield series salutes the American Civil War and incorporates great artwork of the featured historical figures in paintings by Ken Hendricksen. It is mild in the Shade series with a Connecticut wrapper and Dominican binder and filler; the blend is medium-bodied with a Cameroon

HANDMADE CIGARS: BRAND LISTINGS

wrapper, Dominican binder and Honduran filler and the Maduro is full-bodied with Connecticut wrapper, Dominican binder and a blend of Honduran and Nicaraguan filler. Most shapes are offered in boxes of 24 (Sickles and Pickett in 30s) with the Foot Soldier group also offered in boxes of 45.

A Battleground Vintage series, aged for one year, debuted in 2007. Either the Toro (Sherman or Lee) or Torpedo (Custer, Forrest or Cleburne) sizes are available in boxes of eight, 16, 24 or 50.

BAUTISMO DE FUEGO
Handmade, with mixed filler, in Esteli, Nicaragua.

Wrapper: Nicaragua   Binder: Nicaragua   Filler: Nicaragua

Shape	Name	Lgth	Ring	Wrapper
Double Corona	Presidente	7½	52	CM-Ma
Churchill	Churchill	7	48	CM-Ma
Lonsdale	Fumas	6½	44	CM-Ma
Toro	Toro	6	50	CM-Ma
Robusto	Rothchild	4½	50	CM-Ma
Corona	Corona	5½	42	CM-Ma
Torpedo	Torpedo	6	54	CM-Ma

The TESA Cigar Co. offers this blend, which is considered mild in body. It was introduced in 2004 and offered in bundles of 25.

BAUZA
Handmade in Santiago, Dominican Republic.

Wrapper: Ecuador   Binder: Dom. Rep   Filler: Dom. Rep.

Shape	Name	Lgth	Ring	Wrapper
Churchill	Casa Grande	6¾	48	CC
Double Corona	Fabuloso	7½	50	CC
Corona	Grecos	5½	42	CC
Lonsdale	Jaguar	6½	42	CC
Lonsdale	Medalla d'Oro No. 1	6⅞	44	CC

Short Panatela	Petit Corona	5	38	CC
Pyramid	Pyramid	5½	55	CC
Robusto	Robusto	5½	50	CC

Introduced in 1980, these medium-to-full-bodied cigars are high in quality and high in value, offered in boxes of 25. Enveloped in Ecuadorian wrappers, eight sizes are offered, all made by the artisans of the Tabacalera A. Fuente.

BAYAMO SUPERIORES ★Returns★
Handmade in Danli, Honduras.

Wrapper: Ecuador   Binder: Mexico   Filler: Colombia, Dom. Rep., Nicaragua

Shape	Name	Lgth	Ring	Wrapper
Torpedo	Belicoso	6¼	50	CC
Double Corona	Churchill	7½	50	CC
Lonsdale	Lonsdale	6½	44	CC
Torpedo	Perfeccion	7	48	CC
Robusto	Robusto	5	50	Ma
Robusto	Robusto	5½	50	CC

Originally introduced in 2000, this brand left the market in 2006 and returned in 2007. It's mild-to-medium in body and offered in boxes of 25.

BELINDA
Handmade in Cofradia, Honduras.

Wrapper: Ecuador, USA/Connecticut   Binder: Honduras   Filler: Dom. Rep., Honduras

Shape	Name	Lgth	Ring	Wrapper
Long Corona	Spanish Twist	6¼	43	CM-Ma
	Cedar-wrapped:			
Toro	Exquisito	6	50	CM
Double Corona	Prominente	7	50	CM
Churchill	No. 1835	7¼	46	CM
Grand Corona	Cubanos	5⅝	46	CM

HANDMADE CIGARS: BRAND LISTINGS

| Robusto | Epicure No. 5 | 5 | 50 | CM |
| Grand Corona | Ammo Cabinet | 6¼ | 45 | CM-Ma |

This old Cuban brand has been successfully re-introduced in 1994 as a medium-bodied cigar wrapped in sun-grown Ecuadorian (Sumatra seeds) or Connecticut Broadleaf (maduro) leaves. It is expertly made and presented in all-cedar boxes that continue the aging process. Intermittently available is the amazing Ammo Chest, an actual ammunition box lined with cedar and containing 105 cigars.

BELINDA BLACK
Handmade in Cofradia, Honduras.

Wrapper: USA/Connecticut   Binder: Honduras   Filler: Dom. Rep., Honduras

Shape	Name	Lgth	Ring	Wrapper
Churchill	No. 1835	7¼	46	Ma
Long Corona	Crystal Jar Humidore	6⅛	43	Ma
Grand Corona	Cubanos	5⅝	46	Ma
Robusto	Epicure No. 5	5	50	Ma
Toro	Exquisito	6	50	Ma
Double Corona	Prominente	7	50	Ma

This blend from Cigars by Santa Clara was introduced in 2003 with a medium-to-full body, featuring a Connecticut Medio Tiempo wrapper, offered in boxes of 20.

BELMORE CLASICO
Handmade in Santiago, Dominican Republic.

Wrapper: USA/Connecticut   Binder: Dom. Rep.   Filler: Dom. Rep., Nicaragua

Shape	Name		Lgth	Ring	Wrapper
Robusto	Robusto		5	50	CC
Churchill	Churchill	(tubed)	7	48	CC
Torpedo	Torpeditos		5	46	CC
Toro	Matador		6	50	CC
Double Corona	Caribe		7½	50	CC
Perfecto	Perfecto No. 2		4	50	CC

Torpedo	Torpedo	6⅛	52	CC

This series, also known as "Charles Fairmorn Belmore," was introduced in 1991, is produced in Santiago de los Caballeros in the Dominican Republic and uses only the smoothest Connecticut wrappers. These cigars are of medium body and are offered in boxes of 10.

BELMORE CAMEROON SELECTION
Handmade in Santiago, Dominican Republic.

Wrapper: Cameroon   Binder: Dom. Rep.   Filler: Dom. Rep.

Shape	Name	Lgth	Ring	Wrapper
Corona	Corona	5½	44	CM
Torpedo	Petit Torpedo	5	46	CM
Torpedo	Small Torpedo	5½	48	CM
Torpedo	Torpedo	6	50	CM
Robusto	Robusto	5	50	CM
Churchill	Churchill	7	48	CM

This line was introduced to the U.S. in 2005, with a medium-to-full-bodied flavor in boxes of 10.

BELMORE COLORADO ★New★
Handmade in Santiago, Dominican Republic.

Wrapper: Nicaragua   Binder: Dom. Rep.   Filler: Dom. Rep., Nicaragua

Shape	Name	Lgth	Ring	Wrapper
Robusto	Robusto	5	50	CM
Torpedo	Belicoso	6⅛	52	CM
Robusto	Gordo	5¼	54	CM

Introduced in 2007, this is a medium-to-full-bodied blend, offered in boxes of 10.

BELMORE E.R.P. SELECTION
Handmade in Santiago, Dominican Republic.

Wrapper: Ecuador   Binder: Dom. Rep.   Filler: Dom. Rep.

| Toro | Toro | 6 | 50 | CC |
| Torpedo | Torpedo | 6¼ | 52 | CC |

The Cobre series was introduced, along with the darker *Rojo*, in 2003. The *Cobre* (copper) Black Pearl is medium-to-full in body with an Ecuadorian-grown, Connecticut-seed wrapper, available in cabinets of 20.

BLACK PEARL CONGA ★*Returns*★
Handmade in Danli, Honduras.

Wrapper: Brazil   *Binder: Indonesia*   *Filler: Nicaragua*

Shape	Name	Lgth	Ring	Wrapper
Toro	Toro	6	50	Ma

Returned to distribution in 2007, this is a unique cigar with a mild body, offered in drums of 20.

BLACK PEARL GRAN D
BY LA PERLA HABANA
Handmade in Dali, Honduras.

Wrapper: Mexico   *Binder: Nicaragua*   *Filler: Dom. Rep., Honduras, Nicaragua*

Shape	Name	Lgth	Ring	Wrapper
Robusto	Gran Robusto	5¼	52	Ma
Torpedo	Gran Belicoso	5½	52	Ma

This was the first of the Black Pearl blends to be introduced, in 2000, bur revised in 2006. Now made in Honduras, it's full-bodied with a Mexican-grown, San Andres maduro wrapper, offered in cabinets of 20.

BLACK PEARL MORADO ★*New*★
Handmade in Esteli, Nicaragua.

Wrapper: Cameroon   *Binder: Nicaragua*   *Filler: Nicaragua*

Shape	Name	Lgth	Ring	Wrapper
Robusto	Robusto	4¾	52	CM
Toro	Toro	6	50	CM
Torpedo	Torpedo	6¼	52	CM

Introduced in 2007, "morado" means purple in Spanish and represents royalty, so why shouldn't this be the "king" of the Black Pearl blends? It's full-bodied with an elegant Cameroon wrapper, offered in cabinets of 20.

BLACK PEARL ROJO
BY LA PERLA HABANA
Handmade in Esteli, Nicaragua.

Wrapper: Nicaragua　　　　Binder: Nicaragua　　　　　Filler: Nicaragua

Shape	Name	Lgth	Ring	Wrapper
Robusto	Robusto	4¾	52	CM
Toro	Toro	6	50	CM
Churchill	Churchill	7¼	48	CM
Torpedo	Torpedo	6¼	52	CM
Toro	Supertoro	6	56	CM

Much appreciated for its depth of flavor, the Rojo was introduced in 2003. Compared with its sibling *Cobre*, it has a darker, Nicaraguan-grown wrapper and binder and a full-bodied flavor, offered in cabinets of 20.

BLAIR　★*Returns*★
Handmade in Guayaquil, Ecuador.

Wrapper: Ecuador　　　　Binder: Ecuador　　　　　Filler: Ecuador

Shape	Name	Lgth	Ring	Wrapper
Toro	Gordo Rosado	6	54	CC
Robusto	Robusto Rosado	5	50	CC
Toro	Toro Grande	6½	52	CC
Torpedo	Torpedo Rosado	6½	50	CC

James Norman, Ltd. re-introduced this brand from the Cigar Boom days once again in 2007. It's full-bodied and offered in bundles of 25.

BLANTON'S　★*New*★
Handmade in Lawrenceburg, Kentucky, USA.

Wrapper: USA/Connecticut　　　Binder: Dom. Rep.　　　Filler: Colombia, Dom. Rep.

Shape	Name	Lgth	Ring	Wrapper
Robusto	Blanton's Single Barrel Bourbon Whiskey *(tubed)*	5	50	CC

Introduced by the Kentucky Gentleman Cigar Co. in 2007, this is a unique cigar that uses tobacco which has been aged in Bourbon barrels! Offered in one size, this is a medium-to-full-bodied cigar in boxes of three, 10 or 25.

BLUE TRAIN
Handmade in Santiago, Dominican Republic.

Wrapper: Ecuador 　　　*Binder: Dom. Rep.* 　　　*Filler: Dom. Rep.*

Shape	Name	Lgth	Ring	Wrapper
Churchill	Churchill	6¾	46	CM
Toro	Toro	6	50	CM
Robusto	Robusto	5	50	CM
Robusto	Rothschild	4½	50	CM
Corona	Corona	5½	42	CM
Torpedo	Torpedo	6	54	CM

Here is a medium-bodied cigar distributed by Alliance Cigar, featuring a Connecticut-seed wrapper. It's available in bundles of 25.

BLUNTVILLE   ★*New*★
Handmade in Esteli, Nicaragua.

Wrapper: Nicaragua 　　*Binder: Nicaragua* 　　*Filler: Nicaragua*

Shape	Name	Lgth	Ring	Wrapper
Small Panatela	BluntVille	4	34	DC-CM

Introduced in late 2006, this is a small flavored cigar offered in single packs and boxes of 25 in Candela Honey, Sweet and Vanilla.

BOCK Y CA. EDICION DE ORO   ★*New*★
Handmade in Esteli, Nicaragua.

Wrapper: Ecuador 　　　*Binder: Nicaragua* 　　　*Filler: Nicaragua*

HANDMADE CIGARS: BRAND LISTINGS

Shape	Name	Lgth	Ring	Wrapper
Corona Extra	Corona	5⅝	45	CC
Churchill	Double Corona	7	48	CC
Lonsdale	Lonsdale	6½	44	CC
Robusto	Robusto	4½	50	CC
Toro	Robusto Largo	6	50	CC

Altadis U.S.A. introduced this line in 2007, named for one of the giants of the cigar trade in Cuba in the late 19th and early 20th centuries – Gustave Bock – who brand was one of the most prestigious. It's medium to full in body featuring a Sumatra-seed wrapper, offered in boxes of 20 or bundles of 25 at a value price.

BOHEMIAN
Handmade in Santiago, Dominican Republic.
Wrapper: Brazil   Binder: Dom. Rep.   Filler: Brazil, Dom. Rep.

Shape	Name	Lgth	Ring	Wrapper
Toro	Big Sur	6	70	Ma
Toro	Greenwich Village	6	60	Ma
Toro	Ginsburg	6	50	Ma
Robusto	North Beach	5	52	Ma
Robusto	Whitman	4	48	Ma

Sure, it's wild! It's got a rat-tail top and unfinished foot on all shapes. It's a full-bodied cigar with a Brazilian maduro wrapper (white label), Olor binder and Brazilian and Dominican filler leaves, introduced in 2000. You can enjoy them in boxes of 10 (Big Sur, G. Village), or 20 (Ginsburg, North Beach, Whitman).

BOHEMIAN BLACK
Handmade in Santiago, Dominican Republic.
Wrapper: Brazil   Binder: Dom. Rep.   Filler: Brazil, Dom. Rep., Nicaragua

Shape	Name	Lgth	Ring	Wrapper
Toro	Big Sur	6	70	Os
Toro	Ginsburg	6	50	Os

Toro	Greenwich Village	6	60	Os
Robusto	North Beach	5	52	Os

This Victor Sinclair-created blend is full-bodied with a jet-black wrapper, offered in boxes of 10 (Big Sur, Greenwich Village) or 20 (Ginsburg, North Beach).

BOHEMIAN BUDDHA
Handmade in Santiago, Dominican Republic.

Wrapper: Ecuador   *Binder: Ecuador*   *Filler: Brazil, Dom. Rep., Nicaragua*

Shape	*Name*	*Lgth*	*Ring*	*Wrapper*
Toro	Greenwich Village	6	60	CC
Robusto	North Beach	5	52	CC
Robusto	Whitman	4	48	CC
Slim Panatela	Vesuvio	5½	34	CC

This brand was introduced in 2003 as Bohemian Bamboo by Victor Sinclair Cigars to offer a medium-bodied, somewhat spicy taste. The name changed in 2005, but it still features an uncut foot on all shapes and a Connecticut-seed wrapper. The Greenwich Village is offered in 10s, the North Beach and Whitman in 20s and the Vesuvios in 50s.

BOHEMIAN RED
Handmade in Santiago, Dominican Republic.

Wrapper: Brazil   *Binder: Dom. Rep.*   *Filler: Brazil, Dom. Rep.*

Shape	*Name*	*Lgth*	*Ring*	*Wrapper*
Toro	Greenwich Village	6	60	Ma
Toro	Ginsburg	6	50	Ma
Robusto	North Beach	5	52	Ma

This is another Victor Sinclair creation, introduced in 2002. The Bohemian Red series (red label) with a Brazilian-grown Corojo wrapper offers a full-bodied flavor in the fourth edition of this series. You can enjoy them in boxes of 10 (Greenwich Village) or 20 (Ginsburg, North Beach).

HANDMADE CIGARS: BRAND LISTINGS

BOLIVAR
Handmade in Santiago, Dominican Republic.

Wrapper: Honduras   Binder: USA/Connecticut   Filler: Dom. Rep., Nicaragua

Shape	Name		Lgth	Ring	Wrapper
Toro	Toro		6	52	CM
Double Corona	Churchill		7	49	CM
Toro	Gigante		6	60	CM
Grand Corona	Lonsdale		6½	45	CM
Robusto	Robusto	(glass tube)	5½	50	CM

General Cigar introduced its new blend for Bolivar in mid-2005 as the most powerful in their entire line-up. Full-bodied, it features a San Agustin Ligero wrapper and filler leaves from the Dominican Republic and the Nicaraguan island of Ometepe. It's offered in boxes of 25 except for the Robustos, available in boxes of eight.

BOLIVAR COFRADIA
Handmade in Cofradia, Honduras.
Wrapper: Ecuador, USA/Connecticut

Binder: Ecuador, USA/Connecticut   Filler: Honduras, Nicaragua

Shape	Name	Lgth	Ring	Wrapper
Torpedo	Belicoso Fino	6¼	50	CM
Grand Corona	Cuban Corona	5⅝	46	CM
Corona	Corona	5½	43	CM
Churchill	Double Corona	6⅞	48	CM
Toro	Delmonico	6⅛	50	CM
Short Panatela	Palmita	5	38	CM
Short Panatela	Petit Bolivar	4½	35	CM-Ma
Lonsdale	No. 1	7	42	CM
Robusto	No. 554 Cabinet	5	54	CM-Ma
Toro	No. 654 Cabinet	6	54	CM-Ma
Double Corona	No. 754 Cabinet	7¼	54	CM-Ma

Grand Corona	Library Edition: "Sonnets from the Portuguese"	6¼	45	CM
Grand Corona	Library Edition: "The Scarlet Letter"	6¼	45	Ma
	Sun-Ripened Oscuro Series:			
Double Corona	Size A	7¼	49	Ma
Corona	Size C	5¾	42	Ma

Formerly known as Bolivar Fuerte, this brand was introduced in 2000. It is made in Honduras and offers a full-bodied taste with a Sumatra-seed wrapper and Connecticut Broadleaf binder. The newer maduro-wrapped shapes use a Connecticut Broadleaf wrapper and an Ecuadorian binder. Try them in boxes of 25 except for the tubos and Library Editions, offered in 20s.

BONAPARTE
Handmade in Santiago, Dominican Republic.

Wrapper: USA/Connecticut   Binder: Dom. Rep.   Filler: Dom. Rep.

Shape	Name	Lgth	Ring	Wrapper
Lonsdale	Lonsdale	6½	44	CC
Robusto	Robusto	5	50	CC-Ma
Toro	Toro	6	50	CC-Ma
Double Corona	Presidente	7½	50	CC

F&K Cigar of St. Louis introduced this salute to the famed French Emperor in 2002, adding maduro-wrapped shapes in 2006. It offers a mild flavor in bundles of 25.

BONILLA
Handmade in Rochester, New York, USA.

Wrapper: Brazil, Indonesia, Nicaragua, USA/Connecticut

Binder: Dominican Republic   Filler: Dominican Republic

This six-size blend was introduced in 2004 and is medium in body. It is offered in boxes of 25 in a choice of wrappers: Brazilian maduro, Sumatra, Nicaraguan Criollo and Connecticut.

HANDMADE CIGARS: BRAND LISTINGS

BOQUILLA
Handmade in Union City, New Jersey, USA.
Wrapper: Dominican Republic, Mexico, USA/Connecticut
Binder: Mexico   *Filler: Dominican Republic*

This cigar is made by a small factory of the same name. These are medium-to-full bodied cigars offered in 11 sizes in both natural and maduro wrappers, available in 25s.

BRETON COROJO VINTAGE
Handmade in Santiago, Dominican Republic.
Wrapper: Dom. Rep.   *Binder: Dom. Rep.*   *Filler: Dom. Rep.*

Shape	Name	Lgth	Ring	Wrapper
Corona Extra	Magnum 46	5⅝	46	CM
Long Panatela	Lancero	7½	38	CM
Petit Corona	Corvette	4½	40	CM
Double Corona	Monarca	7½	50	CM
Robusto	Robusto	5½	50	CM
Lonsdale	No. 1	6½	42	CM
Torpedo	No. 2	6⅛	52	CM

Introduced in 1999, this is a medium-to-full-bodied brand, offered in all-cedar boxes of 25 for all sizes except the Lancero (12s).

BRETON LEGEND SERIES
Handmade in Santiago, Dominican Republic.
Wrapper: Indonesia   *Binder: Dom. Rep.*   *Filler: Dom. Rep.*

Shape	Name	Lgth	Ring	Wrapper
Giant	Churchill	8	50	Ma
Grand Corona	Doble Corona	6½	46	Ma
Robusto	Robusto	5½	50	Ma
Long Corona	Lonsdale	6	44	Ma
Torpedo	Torpedo	6½	52	Ma

HANDMADE CIGARS: BRAND LISTINGS

Here is a medium-bodied cigar with a Sumatra maduro wrapper, offered in boxes of 25.

BREVE
Handmade in Navarette, Dominican Republic.

Wrapper: Indonesia   *Binder: Dom. Rep.*   *Filler: Dom. Rep., Nicaragua*

Shape	Name	Lgth	Ring	Wrapper
Perfecto	Figurado No. 2	4	50	CM

This is a full-bodied cigar made by Emilio Reyes and introduced by Eden's Gate Cigars in 2006 and offered in packs of five or a box of 25.

THE BRICK
Handmade in Danli, Honduras.

Wrapper: Ecuador   *Binder: Honduras*   *Filler: Honduras*

Shape	Name	Lgth	Ring	Wrapper
Robusto	Robusto	5½	60	CC
Double Corona	Churchill	7	56	CC
Torpedo	Torpedo	6½	54	CC

Here is a top-quality bundled cigar from the famous Toraño factory in Honduras, introduced in 2001. It offers a medium-bodied flavor in bundles of 25.

BRITTANIA
Handmade in Santiago, Dominican Republic.

Wrapper: USA/Connecticut   *Binder: Indonesia*   *Filler: Dom. Rep., Mexico, Nicaragua*

Shape	Name	Lgth	Ring	Wrapper
Perfecto	Perfecto No. 2	5	40	CC
Grand Corona	Cetro	6	46	CC
Torpedo	Torpedo	6⅛	52	CC
Giant	Viajantes	8½	52	CC
Small Panatela	Bonita	4½	30	CC

Is it a salute to Great Britain . . . or Britney Spears? In any case, this blend was introduced by Exclusive Cigars in 2006 and is mild in body, with a sweetened tip. All sizes are offered in boxes of 20.

HANDMADE CIGARS: BRAND LISTINGS

BRITTANIA RESERVE ★New★
Handmade in Santiago, Dominican Republic.

Wrapper: Ecuador   *Binder: Mexico*   *Filler: Dom. Rep., Indonesia, Nicaragua*

Shape	Name	Lgth	Ring	Wrapper
Perfecto	Perfecto No. 2	5	40	CC
Toro	Matador	6½	56	CC
Robusto	Robusto	5½	52	CC
Toro	Toro	6	50	CC
Torpedo	Torpedo	6⅛	52	CC
Double Corona	Churchill	7	50	CC

Exclusive Cigars debuted this medium-bodied blend in 2007. It features a Connecticut Shade wrapper and is offered in boxes of 20.

BROCATUS ★New★
Handmade in Santiago, Dominican Republic.

Wrapper: Ecuador   *Binder: Dom. Rep.*   *Filler: Dom. Rep.*

Shape	Name	Lgth	Ring	Wrapper
Robusto	Robusto	5	50	CM
Torpedo	Torpedo	6½	52	CM
Double Corona	Churchill	7	50	CM

Meier & Dutch introduced this brand to national distribution in 2007. It's mild in body with a Sumatra-seed wrapper, available in boxes of 25.

BUCANERO CANON CUBANO
Handmade in Esteli, Nicaragua.

Wrapper: Nicaragua, USA/Connecticut   *Binder: Costa Rica, Indonesia*
Filler: Costa Rica, Honduras, Italy, Nicaragua, USA/Connecticut

Shape	Name	Lgth	Ring	Wrapper
Robusto	Natural	5½	60	CM
Robusto	Maduro	5½	60	Ma

HANDMADE CIGARS: BRAND LISTINGS

These fat robustos use different blends. The Natural, introduced in 2005, has a Connecticut Shade wrapper, Sumatra binder and Nicaragua and Connecticut filler for a medium-to-full body. The Maduro debuted in 2007 and has a Nicaraguan Habano wrapper, Costa Rican binder and a blend of Costa Rican, Honduran, Italian and Nicaraguan filler for a full-bodied flavor.

BUCANERO EL CAPITAN
Handmade in Esteli, Nicaragua.

Wrapper: Costa Rica   Binder: Nicaragua   Filler: Dom. Rep., Nicaragua

Shape	Name	Lgth	Ring	Wrapper
Toro	El Capitan	6	50	Ma

This blend of the Bucanero brand was introduced in 2001. It's box-pressed and features a mild-to-medium-bodied taste. It is offered in boxes of 12.

BUCANERO FULL SAIL
Handmade in Esteli, Nicaragua.

Wrapper: Costa Rica   Binder: Nicaragua   Filler: Dom. Rep., Nicaragua

Shape	Name	Lgth	Ring	Wrapper
Toro	Toro	6	50	Ma
Torpedo	Belicoso Petite	5	54	Ma

This brand was introduced in 2002, offering a powerful, full-bodied flavor in a box-pressed format of 12 cigars per box for the Toro and 14 for the Petite.

BUCANERO PEG LEG
Handmade in Esteli, Nicaragua.

Wrapper: Costa Rica   Binder: Nicaragua   Filler: Dom. Rep., Nicaragua

Shape	Name	Lgth	Ring	Wrapper
Torpedo	Belicoso Petite	5	54	Ma

The Peg Leg was introduced in 2001 and offers a box-pressed, medium-bodied smoke in all-wood boxes of 14.

BUCANERO SALSA
Handmade in Esteli, Nicaragua.

Wrapper: Nicaragua   Binder: Indonesia   Filler: Dom. Rep., Nicaragua

HANDMADE CIGARS: BRAND LISTINGS

Shape	Name	Lgth	Ring	Wrapper
Toro	Belicoso	6	50	Ma

Introduced in 2003, this is an extra-full-bodied smoke with a Habano Criollo wrapper and box pressed in boxes of 12.

BUCANERO TEXAS STAR
Handmade in Esteli, Nicaragua.

Wrapper: Costa Rica   Binder: Nicaragua   Filler: Dom. Rep., Nicaragua

Shape	Name	Lgth	Ring	Wrapper
Toro	Toro	6	50	Ma

This brand was also introduced in 2000 and offers a medium-bodied smoke in a box-pressed format of 12.

BUCANERO WINDJAMMER AND CLASICO
Handmade in Esteli, Nicaragua.
Wrapper: Ecuador, USA/Connecticut

Binder: Dom. Rep., Nicaragua   Filler: Dom. Rep., Nicaragua

Shape	Name	Lgth	Ring	Wrapper
Torpedo	Belicoso	6	54	CC-Ma
Robusto	Robusto	5	50	CC-Ma

Created in 1995, this is a mild-bodied brand in the Windjammer style (natural wrapper), with an Ecuador-grown, Sumatra-seed wrapper and a Dominican binder. The Clasico (maduro) line was introduced in 1996 and is medium-bodied with a Connecticut Broadleaf wrapper and Nicaraguan maduro binder. Both are offered in top-hinged all-cedar boxes of 20.

BUCANERO "Z"
Handmade in Esteli, Nicaragua.

Wrapper: Ecuador   Binder: Dom. Rep.   Filler: Dom. Rep., Nicaragua

Shape	Name	Lgth	Ring	Wrapper
Toro	Toro	6	50	Ma
Churchill	Churchill	6⅞	48	Ma

This is a medium-to-full-bodied blend introduced in 2003, with a Sumatra-seed wrapper. It's offered in a box-pressed format with a spicy finish in boxes of 12.

BULLDOG
Handmade in Santiago, Dominican Republic.

Wrapper: USA/Connecticut   *Binder: Dom. Rep.*   *Filler: Dom. Rep.*

Introduced in 1996, this medium-bodied, three-size cigar line will not bark or bite! It's sure to become man's best friend in bundles of 25.

BUNDELO BY BUCANERO
Handmade in Esteli, Nicaragua.

CAMEROON:

Wrapper: Cameroon   *Binder: Nicaragua*   *Filler: Honduras, Nicaragua*

HAVANA ROSE:

Wrapper: Nicaragua   *Binder: Nicaragua*   *Filler: Nicaragua*

LA NOCHE:

Wrapper: Indonesia   *Binder: Nicaragua*   *Filler: Nicaragua*

ZIA:
Wrapper: Indonesia
Binder: Dom. Rep.   *Filler: Costa Rica, Dom. Rep., Honduras, Nicaragua*

Shape	Name	Lgth	Ring	Wrapper
	Cameroon:			
Robusto	Robusto	5	50	CM
Corona	Corona	5½	44	CM
Torpedo	Belicoso	6	54	CM
	Havana Rose:			
Toro	Canon	6	60	CC
Double Corona	Gigante	7	54	CC
Giant	Presidente	8	50	CC
	La Noche:			
Robusto	Robusto	5	50	CM
Churchill	Churchill	6⅞	48	CM
Torpedo	Belicoso	6	54	CM

	Zia:			
Robusto	Robusto	5	50	CM
Churchill	Churchill	6⅞	48	CM
Belicoso	Belicoso	6	54	CM

Here is a full line of bundled cigars from Bucanero, introduced in 2006. The
Cameroon line is double box pressed with a mild-to-medium-bodied taste, as is
the Havana Rose group, with a Nicaraguan Rosado wrapper. The La Noche and
Zia blends are both mild-to-medium, with the La Noche featuring a Javan
wrapper and the Zia a Sumatra-grown wrapper. All are offered in bundles of 20.

BUSTILLO
Handmade in Tampa, Florida, USA.
Wrapper: Honduras   *Binder: Honduras*   *Filler: Honduras*

Made by the Cammarata Cigar Co., this brand offers a full-bodied taste in two
sizes, one named for Academy Award-winning film director Francis Ford
Coppola.

BUTERA "LA PENNA"
Handmade in La Romana, Dominican Republic.
Wrapper: USA/Connecticut   Binder: Indonesia   Filler: Brazil, Dom. Rep., Honduras

Shape	Name	Lgth	Ring	Wrapper
Robusto	X	5	52	CM
Toro	EX	6	52	CM
Double Corona	EXL	6¾	52	CM

This is a limited-production version of the Butera line, offering a very full body
with a Connecticut Broadleaf wrapper in boxes of 20.

BUTERA ROYAL VINTAGE
Handmade in La Romana, Dominican Republic.
Wrapper: USA/Connecticut   Binder: Indonesia   Filler: Dom. Rep.

Shape	Name	Lgth	Ring	Wrapper
Robusto	Bravo Corto	4½	50	CC
Lonsdale	Cedro Fino	6½	44	CC

HANDMADE CIGARS: BRAND LISTINGS

Toro	Dorado 652		6	52	CC
Churchill	Capo Grande		7½	48	CC
Corona	Fumo Dolce		5½	44	CC
Panatela	Mira Bella		6¾	38	CC
Toro	Cornetta No. 1		6	52	CC
Petit Corona	Poca Bella		4	44	CC
Small Panatela	Piccolina		4	32	CC
Toro	Cappello A	(tubed)	6½	48	CC
Robusto	Cappello B	(tubed)	5	50	CC

Introduced in 1993, Butera Royal Vintage are true-blended, premium cigars handmade in the Dominican Republic by "first-row" cigar makers. Six distinctive whole-leaf tobaccos from three different countries are blended, including four specific types of long-filler leaves from the rarest Dominican crops. Every cigar is well-aged to maturity in cabinets of fine Spanish cedar and packaged in beautiful Mahogany chests of 20, except for the Cappello sizes, Cornetta No. 1 and Piccolinas, offered in boxes of 10. The spicy, flavorful blend is considered medium in body.

BUTERA VINTAGE MADURO
Handmade in La Romana, Dominican Republic.

Wrapper: USA/Connecticut   *Binder: Indonesia*   *Filler: Brazil, Dom. Rep.*

Shape	Name	Lgth	Ring	Wrapper
Robusto	No. 550	5	50	Ma
Toro	No. 650	6	50	Ma
Double Corona	No. 750	7	50	Ma
Long Corona	No. 644	6	44	Ma
Petit Corona	No. 444	4	44	Ma

This 1998-introduced brand is available only to selected dealers. It offers a smooth, medium-to-full-bodied taste in the Butera style, offered in boxes of 20.

BUTERA VINTAGE SELECT
Handmade in La Romana, Dominican Republic.

Wrapper: Brazil   *Binder: Dom. Rep.*   *Filler: Dom. Rep.*

Shape	Name	Lgth	Ring	Wrapper
Toro	Toro	6	52	CM
Churchill	Churchill	7½	48	CM
Robusto	Robusto	4½	50	CM
Corona	Corona	5½	44	CM
Torpedo	Belicoso	6	50	CM

Introduced in 2005, this is a full-bodied edition of the Butera brand, offered in boxes of 20 for all shapes except the Belicoso, in 10s.

C.A.O. L'ANNIVERSAIRE 1968-1998
Handmade in Esteli, Nicaragua.

L'*ANNIVERSAIRE 1968-1998 CAMEROON:*
Wrapper: Cameroon   *Binder: Nicaragua*   *Filler: Nicaragua*

L'*ANNIVERSAIRE 1968-1998 MADURO:*
Wrapper: USA/Connecticut   *Binder: Ecuador*   *Filler: Dom. Rep., Nicaragua*

Shape	Name		Lgth	Ring	Wrapper
Corona	Corona		5½	42	CM-Ma
Robusto	Robusto		5	50	CM-Ma
Churchill	Churchill		6⅞	48	CM-Ma
Torpedo	Belicoso		6	54	CM-Ma
Robusto	Toro		5½	55	CM-Ma
Perfecto	Tubo I	*(tubed)*	5½	46	CM-Ma
Perfecto	Tubo II	*(tubed)*	7	50	CM-Ma
Small Panatela	Petite Cigarillo		4	30	CM-Ma
Robusto	Rothschild		4½	50	CM-Ma
	L'Anniversaire Maduro only:				
Perfecto	10th Anniversary		6	50	Ma
	Trois Damant series:				
Grand Corona	Corona		5¾	46	CC-CM-Ma

Toro	Magnum	6	52	CC-CM-Ma

Developed in honor of the 30th anniversary of the C.A.O. brand in 1998, the maduro shapes are offered with a medium-to-full body and exquisite construction. The Cameroon series was introduced in 1999. Both styles are box-pressed (except for the Rothschild) and presented in boxes of 20, except for the Petit Cigarillo and 10th Anniversary, offered in tins or boxes of 10. The 10th Anniversary maduro cigar salutes a decade of the L'Anniversaire brand and was introduced in 2007.

A new and exciting line of tubed cigars in squared aluminum tubes debuted in 2001. The Box Pressed Tubos series features two shapes in each of the L'Anniversaire blends and each tube includes an individual bar code! The Trois Damant series is produced for Cigars by Santa Clara.

C.A.O. AMERICA ★*New*★
Handmade in Esteli, Nicaragua.
Wrapper: USA/Connecticut
Binder: Brazil   *Filler: Dom. Rep., Italy, Nicaragua, USA/Connecticut*

Shape	Name	Lgth	Ring	Wrapper
Robusto	Potomac	5	56	Stripe
Torpedo	Monument	6¼	54	Stripe
Toro	Landmark	6	60	Stripe

Two Connecticut wrappers create a pin-stripe effect on this unique cigar, introduced in 2007. A dark maduro Broadleaf covers most of the outside of the cigar, but a Connecticut Shade leaf peeks out underneath all the way around. The blend is full-bodied and the American is offered in dramatic boxes of 20 that features a fold-out top.

C.A.O. BLACK
Handmade in Esteli, Nicaragua.
Wrapper: Ecuador   *Binder: Nicaragua*   *Filler: Honduras, Mexico, Nicaragua*

Shape	Name	Lgth	Ring	Wrapper
Robusto	Storm	5	50	CC
Long Corona	Mosaic	6	42	CC
Toro	Bengal	6	50	CC

| Torpedo | Gothic | 6 | 52 | CC |
| Double Corona | Frontier | 7 | 50 | CC |

Distributed by Meier & Dutch, this blend appeared in national distribution in 2006. It offers a medium-to-full body with a Connecticut-seed wrapper in a limited-production run. All sizes are offered in elegant clamshell boxes of 20 with a unique black-and-white spatter design.

C.A.O. BLACK VR   ★*New*★
Handmade in Danli, Honduras.

Wrapper: Brazil   *Binder: Brazil*   *Filler: Mexico, Nicaragua*

Shape	Name	Lgth	Ring	Wrapper
Petit Corona	Mural	4½	44	Ma
Robusto	Totem	5	50	Ma
Toro	Moby	6	50	Ma
Torpedo	Cathedral	6	52	Ma
Double Corona	Convergence	7	50	Ma

Meier & Dutch debuted this version of the C.A.O. Black line in 2007. It features a Brazilian Arapiraca maduro wrapper and is medium-to-full in body. You can try it in boxes of 20.

C.A.O. "BRATALIA"
Handmade in Danli, Honduras.

Wrapper: Brazil, Honduras   *Binder: Nicaragua*   *Filler: Nicaragua*

Shape	Name	Lgth	Ring	Wrapper
Perfecto	Bratalia Perfecto Duo	6¾	55	Stripe

This is a wild salute to the champions of soccer: Brazil, winner of the World Cup in 2002 and Italy, winner in 2006. The combination "Bratalia" Perfecto Duo is a striped masterpiece, using the Honduran-grown Habano wrapper from the Italia and the Brazilian wrapper from the Brazilia line! It's offered in a special set of ten cigars in a special humidor.

HANDMADE CIGARS: BRAND LISTINGS

C.A.O. BRAZILIA
Handmade in Danli, Honduras.

Wrapper: Brazil   *Binder: Nicaragua*   *Filler: Nicaragua*

Shape	Name		Lgth	Ring	Wrapper
Robusto	Gol!		5	56	CM
Corona Extra	Piranha		4½	46	CM
Short Panatela	Cariocas		4	38	CM
Toro	Lambada		6	50	CM
Torpedo	Samba		6¼	54	CM
Double Corona	Ipanema		6⅞	50	CM
Toro	Amazon		6	60	CM
Perfecto	Anaconda		8	58	CM
Cigarillo	Mini		5	20	CM
Toro	Chango	*(tubed)*	6½	50	CM
Robusto	Box-Press		5½	55	CM

Here is a full-bodied, powerful blend of tobaccos introduced in 2001. With larger ring gauges for full enjoyment of the blend, Brazilias are offered uncellophaned in Brazil-green-colored boxes of 20 (Cariocas in tins of 10, Minis in 20 and Chango in boxes of five). An "Anaconda" size (8 x 58 perfecto) was introduced as a limited edition in 2004 only with production limited to 70,000; production was resumed on this shape in 2007.

C.A.O. CRIOLLO
Handmade in Esteli, Nicaragua.

Wrapper: Nicaragua   *Binder: Nicaragua*   *Filler: Nicaragua*

Shape	Name	Lgth	Ring	Wrapper
Short Panatela	Pampas	4	38	CM
Robusto	Pato	4⅞	50	CM
Grand Corona	Mancha	5⅝	46	CM
Toro	Bomba	6	50	CM
Toro	Conquistador	6⅛	52	CM

C.A.O. introduced this medium-bodied brand in mid-2002 featuring a Criollo wrapper. Each box of 20 has a unique lid that opens from the middle! The Pampas are offered in tins of 10.

C.A.O. Cx2
Handmade in Esteli, Nicaragua.

Wrapper: Cameroon *Binder: Cameroon* *Filler: Colombia, Nicaragua*

Shape	Name	Lgth	Ring	Wrapper
Torpedo	Beli	7	56	CM
Robusto	Rob	5	52	CM
Toro	Toro	6	54	CM

Introduced in 2005, this medium-bodied blend features both Cameroon wrapper and binder for a unique taste. They're offered in boxes of 20.

C.A.O. FLAVOURS
Handmade in Santiago, Dominican Republic.
Wrapper: Cameroon, Ecuador

Binder: Dom. Rep., Nicaragua *Filler: Dom. Rep., Nicaragua*

Shape	Name		Lgth	Ring	Wrapper
Petit Corona	Petite Corona		4	40	CC-CM
Corona	Corona		5¼	42	CC-CM
Small Panatela	Cigarillos		4	30	CC-CM
Robusto	Robusto		5	48	CM
	Bella Vanilla, Eileen's Dream, KarmaSutra Splash and Moontrance addition:				
Small Panatela	Tubo	*(tubed)*	4¾	30	CM
	Moontrance additions:				
Short Panatela	Small Cigar		4	38	CM
Torpedo	Torpedo		6¼	50	CM

C.A.O. has united its flavored cigars in a single series with four primary sizes, offered in 25s for the Petite Corona, 20s for the Corona and in tins of ten for the Cigarillo. The "Gold Honey" edition is made in Nicaragua, showcasing a

HANDMADE CIGARS: BRAND LISTINGS

Connecticut-seed Ecuadorian wrapper, Nicaraguan interior leaves and orange blossom honey from Florida. The "Bella Vanilla" and "Moontrance" series are made in the Dominican Republic with Cameroon wrappers and Dominican binder and filler. All have a mild and flavorful taste, with the "Bella Vanilla" incorporating vanilla beans from Madagascar and exotic fruit and bourbon vanilla extracts in the "Moontrance" blend. Two special sizes were added to the Moontrance line in 2004, including a tubed size, and another in 2007 (Small Cigar).

Introduced in 2003, the "Eileen's Dream" and "EarthNectar" series offer new flavors infused into the Cameroon wrappers and Dominican interior leaves. The former is a combination of Irish Cream and white chocolate truffles, while EarthNectar salutes the Tuscany region of Italy with a mixture of toasted almonds, cocoa, honey and raisins combined with Chianti. The "KarmaSutra Splash" introduced in 2004 features a Cameroon wrapper and Dominican binder and filler and combines the flavors of Hawaiian mango and chocolate mint ice cream!

C.A.O. GOLD LABEL
Handmade in Esteli, Nicaragua.

Wrapper: Brazil, Ecuador   *Binder: Nicaragua*   *Filler: Nicaragua*

Shape	Name	Lgth	Ring	Wrapper
Short Panatela	Gold Karats	4	38	Co
Cigarillo	Gold Mini	5	20	Co
Corona	Corona	5½	42	Co-Ma
Lonsdale	Lonsdale	6½	44	Co
Robusto	Robusto *(glass tube avail.)*	5	50	Co-Ma
Toro	Corona Gorda	6½	50	Co-Ma
Churchill	Churchill	7	48	Co-Ma
Torpedo	Torpedo *(glass tube avail.)*	6¼	52	Co-Ma
Double Corona	Double Corona	7½	54	Co-Ma
Perfecto	Perfecto	6	60	Co
Toro	Aurum *(tubed)*	6½	50	Co

Introduced in 1996, this brand features a Connecticut Shade-seed wrapper and a mild-to-medium taste. Box-pressed, these cigars are offered in boxes of 25, with the Robusto and Torpedo sizes also offered in glass tubes in boxes of 10. The Perfecto is a 2007 extension of the Tenth Anniversary size that was a limited edition of 100,000 cigars offered in 2006 in boxes of 10.

The Gold Maduro line was introduced in 2007 in six shapes, utilizing a Brazilian-grown maduro wrapper for a medium-bodied taste.

C.A.O. ITALIA
Handmade in Danli, Honduras.

Wrapper: Honduras　　　　　*Binder: Honduras*　　　*Filler: Italy, Nicaragua, Peru*

Shape	Name		Lgth	Ring	Wrapper
Robusto	Ciao		5	56	CM
Torpedo	Gondola		6¼	54	CM
Toro	Piazza		6	60	CM
Corona Extra	Novella		4½	46	CM
Short Panatela	Picollos		4	38	CM
Toro	Positano		6	50	CM
Toro	Largo	*(tubed)*	6½	50	CM

Here is a darkly-dressed, full-bodied cigar introduced in 2004. It features Italian-grown tobacco from the Benevenuto region in the filler, rarely-used in Caribbean-made cigars. They are presented in colorful, wood cabinets of 20, 25 (Novella only), five (Largo) or tins of 10 (Picollos).

C.A.O. Mx2
Handmade in Danli, Honduras.
Wrapper: USA/Connecticut

Binder: Brazil　　　　　*Filler: Dom. Rep., Honduras, Nicaragua, Peru*

Shape	Name	Lgth	Ring	Wrapper
Robusto	Rob	5	52	Ma
Toro	Toro	6	54	Ma
Torpedo	Beli	7	56	Ma
Short Panatela	Dagger	4	38	Ma
Toro	Gordo	6	60	Ma

Introduced in 2003, here is a unique blend focusing on two maduro leaves for the wrapper (Connecticut Broadleaf) and binder (Brazil). The results, when combined with a four-nation filler recipe, is a sweet, medium-to-full-bodied taste, offered on four larger sizes in boxes of 20. The Dagger is offered in a tin of five.

C.A.O. "THE SOPRANOS" EDITION
Handmade in Esteli, Nicaragua.

Wrapper: Brazil   Binder: Honduras   Filler: Colombia, Dom. Rep., Nicaragua

Shape	Name	Lgth	Ring	Wrapper
Robusto	Associate	5	52	CM
Toro	Solider	6	54	CM
Double Corona	Boss	7	56	CM
Toro	Tony Soprano Signature	6½	60	CM

Officially licensed by HBO, "The Sopranos" Edition debuted in 2005 and offers a full-bodied taste with a Brazilian Mata Fina wrapper. All shapes are offered uncellophaned in boxes of 20. The Tony Soprano Signature shape is a limited edition of 72,000 cigars offered in 2006.

To commemorate the final episode of the show in 2007, a special "C.A.O. The Sopranos Limited Edition" was created containing five cigars. Two were shaped like a baseball bat, two like a whisk broom with an 86 ring gauge at the end (commemorating the 86 episodes) and one like a champagne bottle. A total of 2,000 boxes were made (10,000 cigars total).

C.A.O. VISION
Handmade in Santiago, Dominican Republic.

Wrapper: Dom. Rep.   Binder: Dom. Rep.   Filler: Brazil, Dom. Rep., Nicaragua

Shape	Name	Lgth	Ring	Wrapper
Robusto	Catalyst	5	50	CM
Toro	Epiphany	6	50	CM
Torpedo	Prana	6¼	52	CM

Vision is the first Dominican-made cigar from C.A.O. and debuted in mid-2006. It offers a medium-to-full-bodied smoke featuring Dominican-grown tobacco in all three elements (Dominican Corojo filler!) and is presented in a unique "Sensi-Box" humidors of 20 cigars each that maintain a constant humidity of 68-72%.

HANDMADE CIGARS: BRAND LISTINGS

C.E. BECK Y CA.
Handmade in Esteli, Nicaragua.

Wrapper: Cameroon   *Binder: Nicaragua*   *Filler: Nicaragua*

Shape	Name	Lgth	Ring	Wrapper
Toro	El Jefe	6	60	CM
Pyramid	Sombrero	5½	60	CM
Torpedo	Ranchero	6	54	CM
Double Corona	Charro	7	52	CM
Toro	Buckaroo	6	52	CM
Robusto	Rodeo	5	52	CM

The Tabacalera Esteli created this brand in 2005, offering a mild-to-medium-bodied taste. It's offered in boxes of 25.

CABAIGUAN
Handmade in Miami, Florida, USA.

Wrapper: Ecuador   *Binder: Nicaragua*   *Filler: Nicaragua*

Shape	Name	Lgth	Ring	Wrapper
Grand Corona	Coronas Extra	5⅝	46	CC
Robusto	Robustos Extra	5¼	50	CC
Churchill	Imperiales	7	47	CC
Torpedo	Belicoso Finos	5½	52	CC
Small Panatela	Petit Cabaiguan	4½	32	CC
Toro	Guapos	5⅝	54	CC

Introduced in 2005, this is a mild-to-medium-bodied blend with a Connecticut-seed wrapper, offered in boxes of 24. The Guapos was added in 2007 and is available in boxes of 20.

CABALLEROS
Handmade in Santiago, Dominican Republic.

Wrapper: USA/Connecticut   *Binder: Dom. Rep.*   *Filler: Dom. Rep.*

HANDMADE CIGARS: BRAND LISTINGS

Shape	Name	Lgth	Ring	Wrapper
Double Corona	Churchill	7	50	CC
Robusto	Rothschild	5	50	CC
Churchill	Double Corona	6¾	48	CC
Corona	Corona	5¾	43	CC
Corona	Petit Corona	5½	42	CC
Torpedo	Belicoso	4½	50	CC

Introduced in 1993, these are mild-to-medium bodied cigars with much flavor, produced with long filler and made completely by hand. Imported from the Dominican Republic, Caballeros cigars are offered in individual cellophane sleeves inside cedar boxes of 25.

CABALLEROS VINTAGE SERIES
Handmade in Danli, Honduras.

Wrapper: USA/Connecticut   Binder: Honduras   Filler: Honduras, Nicaragua

Shape	Name	Lgth	Ring	Wrapper
Robusto	Rothchild	5	50	CC
Toro	Toro	6	54	CC

This medium-to-full-bodied blend was introduced in 2004 by James Norman Ltd. It's offered in a box-pressed format in boxes of 20.

CABAÑAS Y CARBAJAL
Handmade in Esteli, Nicaragua.
Wrapper: Ecuador, USA/Connecticut

Binder: Nicaragua   Filler: Dominican Republic, Nicaragua

Shape	Name	Lgth	Ring	Wrapper
Lonsdale	Lonsdale	6½	43	CM-Ma
Churchill	Churchill	7	48	CM-Ma
Double Corona	Inmenso	7¼	54	CM-Ma
Cigarillo	Joyitas	3⅝	24	CM

HANDMADE CIGARS: BRAND LISTINGS

Sharing the name of one of the oldest Cuban brands of them all, this version is made in Nicaragua for Cigars by Santa Clara. This edition is medium in body, introduced in 2005 with a Sumatra-seed natural or Connecticut Broadleaf maduro wrapper. It's offered in elegant upright boxes of 23 (Lonsdale only), 24 or 40 (Joyitas).

CABO CLASSIC
Handmade in Santiago, Dominican Republic.
Wrapper: Brazil, Dominican Republic, Ecuador   Binder: Dom. Rep.   Filler: Dom. Rep.

Shape	Name	Lgth	Ring	Wrapper
Torpedo	Torpedo	6½	52	CC-CM-Ma
Double Corona	Churchill	7	50	CC-CM-Ma
Toro	Toro Grande	6	54	CC-CM-Ma

Introduced in 2005, this is a mild-to-medium-bodied blend with a choice of wrapper: Brazilian maduro, Connecticut-seed (from Ecuador) or Cameroon-seed from the Dominican Republic. All are offered in bundles of 25.

CABO ROJO
Handmade in Santiago, Dominican Republic.
Wrapper: Indonesia   Binder: Indonesia   Filler: Dom. Rep.

Shape	Name	Lgth	Ring	Wrapper
Corona	Corona	5¾	43	CM
Churchill	Churchill	7	48	CM
Lonsdale	Lonsdale	7	43	CM
Robusto	Robusto	4¾	52	CM
Toro	Toro	6	50	CM

SACS Cigars offers this medium-to-full-bodied blend, presented in bundles of 25.

CACIQUE MIAMI
Handmade in Esteli, Nicaragua.
Wrapper: Nicaragua   Binder: Nicaragua   Filler: Nicaragua

Shape	Name	Lgth	Ring	Wrapper
Robusto	Robusto	5	52	CM

Toro	Toro	6	52	CM
Torpedo	Torpedo	6¼	52	CM
Double Corona	Churchill	7	50	CM

This blend comes from the Tabacalera Tropical, introduced in 2004. It features a medium-to-full-bodied taste with a sun-grown Corojo wrapper. It's an excellent value, offered in boxes of 25.

CAFÉ LIBERTAD ★New★
Handmade in Esteli, Nicaragua.
Wrapper: Mexico, USA/Connecticut   Binder: Nicaragua   Filler: Dom. Rep., Nicaragua

Shape	Name	Lgth	Ring	Wrapper
Torpedo	Belicoso Especial	5	52	CM-Ma
Robusto	Robusto Especial	5	54	CM-Ma
Toro	Toro Especial	6	50	CM-Ma
Corona Extra	Short Corona Especial	4¼	46	CM-Ma

Drew Estates introduced this blend in late 2007. It's infused with Fair trade-harvested coffees from Nicaragua and offers a choice of a Mexican natural or Connecticut Broadleaf maduro wrapper. It's medium in body and offered in boxes of 24.

CALLISTO
Handmade in Danli, Honduras.
Wrapper: Honduras   Binder: Honduras   Filler: Honduras

Shape	Name	Lgth	Ring	Wrapper
Long Corona	Lonsdale	6	44	CM
Robusto	Robusto	5	50	CM
Toro	Toro	6	50	CM
Double Corona	Presidente	7½	50	CM

This all-Honduran cigar debuted in 1999. It offers a medium-bodied taste and is available in bundles of 25.

CAMACHO COROJO
Handmade in Danli, Honduras.

Wrapper: Honduras   Binder: Honduras   Filler: Honduras

Shape	Name	Lgth	Ring	Wrapper
Torpedo	Figurado	6⅛	54	CM-Ma
Churchill	Churchill *(tubes available)*	7	48	CM-Ma
Toro	Toro	6	50	CM-Ma
Lonsdale	Cetros	6½	44	CM-Ma
Robusto	Monarca *(tubes available)*	5	50	DC-CM-Ma
Corona	Nacionales	5½	44	CM-Ma
Panatela	Petit	5½	38	CM-Ma
Pyramid	Diadema	8	60	CM-Ma
Toro	Gigante	6½	54	CM-Ma
Small Panatela	Machitos	4	32	CM
	Diploma Series:			
Robusto	Diploma	5	50	CM-Ma
Perfecto	11/18	6	54	CM-Ma
Perfecto	07/05	6	52	CM-Ma
	Great Discovery's series:			
Toro	Discovery Toro *(tubed)*	6	50	CM

Talk about puros! Here's a blend made completely from the Corojo variety of tobacco, all grown in the Jamastran Valley of Honduras. Introduced in 2000, the blend offers a powerful, sensational full-bodied flavor and is elegantly presented with brown bands with gold trim in all-cedar boxes of 20 except for the trumpet-shaped Diadema, offered in 10s and the Machitos, in tins of eight. The Diploma series, comprised of the Diploma, 11/18 and 07/05 sizes, is available with special bands in boxes of 18. Maduro wrappers, also grown in Honduras, became available on almost all sizes in 2006. Previously, a Mexican-grown maduro leaf had been used on two sizes.

A special 10th Anniversary Series of the Camacho Corojo was created in 2007.

HANDMADE CIGARS: BRAND LISTINGS

Box-pressed and medium-to-full in body, it's offered with a green band in boxes of 21 in five sizes: 4½ x50, 5x46, 6x60, 11/18 and Torpedo (6⅛x54).

CAMACHO COYOLAR PURO
Handmade in Danli, Honduras.

Wrapper: Honduras   Binder: Honduras   Filler: Honduras

Shape	Name	Lgth	Ring	Wrapper
Perfecto	Perfecto No. 1	4½	50	CM
Robusto	Rothschild	4½	50	CM
Torpedo	Torpedo	6	54	CM
Toro	Super Toro	6½	52	CM
Toro	Titan	6	60	CM

Here is an ultra-full-bodied blend introduced by Camacho Cigars in 2005. It was named in a contest won by Rod Mitchell of Chicago, Illinois for his name saluting the farm (Coyolar) in which the wrapper was grown. It has an black band with gold trim and lettering and is offered in all-black boxes of 25.

CAMACHO HAVANA
Handmade in Danli, Honduras.

Wrapper: Honduras   Binder: Honduras   Filler: Honduras

Shape	Name	Lgth	Ring	Wrapper
Churchill	Churchill	7	48	CM
Toro	Toro	6	50	CM
Robusto	Monarca	5	50	CM
Lonsdale	Cetros	6½	44	CM
Corona	Nacionales	5½	44	CM
Corona	Petit	5½	42	CM
Pyramid	Diadema	8	60	CM
Toro	Gigante	6	54	CM
Giant	H1	8½	52	CM
Robusto	H2	4½	50	CM

Petit Corona	H3	4¼	44	CM

This outstanding medium-bodied brand was originated in the 1960s and first produced in Nicaragua before moving production to Honduras. The band was redesigned in 2007 and is bright yellow with gold lettering and trim. It offers connoisseurs a wide range of sizes and features Criollo wrapper leaf from the Jamastran Valley of Honduras combined with Corojo binder and filler. The H Series was introduced in 2002 and offers extra aging to three sizes.

CAMACHO LIBERTY
Handmade in Danli, Honduras.

Wrapper: Honduras *Binder: Honduras* *Filler: Honduras*

Shape	Name	Lgth	Ring	Wrapper
Toro	11/18 for 2007	6	56	Stripe

The sixth edition of the limited-edition Liberty series features a "barber pole" wrapper style with Corojo and Maduro wrappers. It's medium in body but rich in flavor and is offered tissue-wrapped in individual coffins inside 2,000 chests of 20. The history:

2002:	Liberty Corona	(5½ x 44 in boxes of 10)
	Liberty Churchill	(7 x 48 in boxes of 10)
	Liberty Rothschild	(5 x 50 in boxes of 10)
	Liberty Toro	(6 x 50 in boxes of 10)
	Liberty Torpedo	(7 x 54 torpedo in boxes of 10)
2003:	Liberty	(8 x 52 torpedo in boxes of 20)
2004:	Liberty 11/18	(6 x 56 perfecto in boxes of 20)
	Liberty Amendm't XII	(8 x 54 torpedo in boxes of 20)
2005:	Liberty 11/18	(6 x 52 perfecto in boxes of 20)
2006:	Liberty 11/18	(6 x 52 perfecto in boxes of 20)
2007:	Liberty 11/18	(6 x 56 in boxes of 20)

A total of 25,000 cigars were made for the 2002 edition; 20,000 for the 2003 cigar; 30,000 of each shape in 2004 (60,000 total) and 40,000 for 2005-07.

CAMACHO NEGRO
Handmade in Danli, Honduras.

Wrapper: Mexico *Binder: Honduras* *Filler: Honduras*

HANDMADE CIGARS: BRAND LISTINGS

Shape	Name	Lgth	Ring	Wrapper
Double Corona	Churchill	7	50	Ma
Robusto	Robusto	5	50	Ma
Toro	Robusto Larga	6	50	Ma

Made by Tabacos Rancho Jamastran for Cigars by Santa Clara and introduced in 2005, this is a full-bodied blend. It's now offered with a Mexican maduro wrapper in a spectacular humidor box of 25.

CAMACHO SELECT
Handmade in Danli, Honduras.

Wrapper: Cameroon · *Binder: Honduras* · *Filler: Honduras*

Shape	Name	Lgth	Ring	Wrapper
Torpedo	Torpedo	6⅛	54	CM
Toro	Churchill	6½	48	CM
Toro	Super Toro	5¾	52	CM
Robusto	Robusto	5	50	CM
Long Corona	Lonsdale	6	44	CM

Originally created by Julio Eiroa of Camacho Cigars as a holiday gift for selected retailers in 2005, the blend was so popular it had to be added to the line. Featuring a Cameroon wrapper, it's medium in body and offered in boxes of 24. You can recognize it by the band: red with a black center and gold lettering.

CAMACHO SLR
Handmade in Danli, Honduras.

Wrapper: Honduras · *Binder: Honduras* · *Filler: Honduras*

Shape	Name	Lgth	Ring	Wrapper
Torpedo	Torpedo	6	54	CM
Toro	Toro *(tubes available)*	6	50	CM
Toro	Gigante	6	54	CM
Churchill	Churchill *(tubes available)*	7	48	CM
Robusto	Rothschild *(tubes available)*	4½	50	CM

Corona	Corona	5½	44	CM
	Great Discovery's series:			
Toro	Discovery Toro *(tubed)*	6	50	CM

This is a very powerful, full-bodied and spicy blend labeled as "Special Limited Reserve" of Camacho from Camacho Cigars. It debuted in 2003 and is offered in boxes of 25 except for the tubed cigars, offered in 20s. You can recognize it by its red band with white lettering and gold trim.

CAMACHO SLR MADURO
Handmade in Danli, Honduras.

Wrapper: USA/Connecticut   *Binder: Honduras*   *Filler: Honduras*

Shape	Name	Lgth	Ring	Wrapper
Toro	Gigante	6¼	54	Ma
Perfecto	Perfecto No. 1	4½	50	Ma
Perfecto	Perfecto No. 2	5½	50	Ma
Torpedo	Figurado	6	54	Ma
Toro	Toro	6	50	Ma
Robusto	Rothschild *(tubes available)*	5	50	Ma

The Rothschild size had been a part of the Camacho SLR line, but the maduro-wrapped series was expanded in 2005. It's double-banded with a red body, white lettering and gold tri. The blend is full-bodied and offered in boxes of 25.

CAMACHO TRIPLE MADURO   ★*New*★
Handmade in Danli, Honduras.

Wrapper: Honduras   *Binder: Honduras*   *Filler: Honduras*

Shape	Name	Lgth	Ring	Wrapper
Robusto	50 x 4.5	4½	50	Ma
Toro	60 x 6	6	60	Ma
Torpedo	Torpedo	6⅛	54	Ma
Perfecto	11/18	6	54	Ma

After an enormous effort, here is an all-maduro cigar: wrapper, filler and binder, hence the name "Triple Maduro." Introduced in 2007, it's full-bodied and offered in boxes of 18 with a majestic silver band. A total of 300,000 cigars in total were made in the first production run.

CAMMARATA
Handmade in Tampa, Florida, USA.

Wrapper: Honduras, USA/Connecticut   Binder: Honduras   Filler: Honduras

Carmela Cammarata Varsalona (1907-2000) was the founder of this brand from the famed Ybor City section of Tampa. She rolled cigars nearly until her death, creating an estimated five million in her career of 80-plus years. Today, the Cammarata line-up includes six blends (nine shapes total) varying from medium-bodied to full-bodied. Most use natural-shade wrappers, but there are two blends using Honduran-grown maduro wrappers.

CAMPESINO   ★*New*★
Handmade, with short filler, in Danli, Honduras.

Wrapper: Honduras   Binder: Honduras   Filler: Honduras, Mexico

Shape	Name	Lgth	Ring	Wrapper
Toro	Toro	6	50	CM
Robusto	Robusto	5	50	CM
Cigarillo	Cigarillos Especiales	4	28	CM

Introduced by Tobacco Exchange in 2007, this is a mild blend using short-filler tobaccos. The Toro and Robusto are offered in boxes of five; the Cigarillos in a box of 50.

CANELA
Handmade in Santiago, Dominican Republic.

Wrapper: Indonesia   Binder: Dom. Rep.   Filler: Dom. Rep.

Canela is offered by The Cigar Shop of Erie, Pennsylvania, offering a mild-to-medium body in a flavored style of cinnamon in two sizes.

CANIMAO   ★*New*★
Handmade in Danli, Honduras and Miami, Florida, USA.

Wrapper: Ecuador   Binder: Ecuador   Filler: Dom. Rep., Honduras, Nicaragua

Shape	Name		Lgth	Ring	Wrapper
Churchill	Churchill	*(tube available)*	7	48	CC

Double Corona	Double Corona	7½	50	CC
Lonsdale	Corona	6½	42	CC
Torpedo	Torpedo	6⅛	52	CC
Robusto	Robusto	5	50	CC
Robusto	Legendarios	5	50	CM
Perfecto	Jibaros	5⅝	50	CC

Introduced by Atabey Tobacco in 2007, this is a medium-bodied blend produced in both Honduras and the U.S. The Legendario has a darker wrapper than the Robusto and is offered in boxes of 15. All other sizes are available on boxes of 25.

CAONAO
Handmade in Miami, Florida, USA.

Wrapper: USA/Connecticut   Binder: Ecuador   Filler: Dom. Rep., Mexico

Introduced in 1998, this is a full-bodied brand featuring a Connecticut wrapper. Produced in 10 sizes in both natural-shade and maduro wrappers, it is offered in individual cellophane sleeves in all-cedar boxes of 25.

CAPAS
Handmade in Tamboril, Dominican Republic.
Wrapper: Indonesia, Nicaragua, USA/Connecticut

Binder: Dominican Republic   *Filler: Dominican Republic*

Shape	Name	Lgth	Ring	Wrapper
Grand Corona	Corona	6	46	Stripe
Double Corona	Churchill	7	50	Stripe

Amazing! Here's a completely unique brand of two sizes, offered with a double wrapper ("Dos Capas") of Connecticut and Indonesian leaves or a triple wrapper ("Tres Capas") with a Nicaraguan candela leaf added! Introduced by Felipe Gregorio in 2004, the body is medium and the line is offered in boxes of 10.

CARBON COPY CUBANS
Handmade in Santiago, Dominican Republic.
Wrapper: Ecuador   Binder: Dom. Rep.   Filler: Dom. Rep.

Shape	Name	Lgth	Ring	Wrapper
Robusto	Robusto	5	50	CC
Toro	Toro	6	50	CC
Double Corona	Churchill	7	50	CC
Torpedo	Torpedo	6½	52	CC
Giant	Presidente	8	52	CC

Carbon Copy was introduced in 2002 and originally offered in three sizes in three different blends. The C Series offered today is a mild-to-medium-bodied smoke with a Rosado wrapper and Corojo binder, offered in bundles of 25.

CARBON COPY SHORTY'S   ★New★
Handmade in Santiago, Dominican Republic.

Wrapper: Cameroon   *Binder: Dom. Rep.*   *Filler: Dom. Rep.*

Shape	Name	Lgth	Ring	Wrapper
Perfecto	Shorty's	4	48	CM

This small perfecto was introduced by Vintage Enterprises in 2007 and has a medium body, offered in boxes of 24.

CARBON COPY WEDGE   ★New★
Handmade in Santiago, Dominican Republic.

Wrapper: Ecuador   *Binder: Indonesia*   *Filler: Dom. Rep.*

Shape	Name	Lgth	Ring	Wrapper
Robusto		4½	52	CC
Robusto		5½	52	CC
Toro		6½	52	CC

Introduced in 2007, this is a uniquely-shaped cigar with a flattened end at the head that can be opened without a cutter to make it easy to smoke! It features a medium-bodied taste and is offered in boxes of 25 in three unnamed sizes.

CARBONELL
Handmade in Santiago, Dominican Republic.

Wrapper: Indonesia   *Binder: Dom. Rep.*   *Filler: Dom. Rep.*

HANDMADE CIGARS: BRAND LISTINGS

Shape	Name	Lgth	Ring	Wrapper
Cigarillo	Palmaritos	4	28	CC
Small Panatela	Demi Tasse	5	30	CC
Panatela	Panatella	6	36	CC
Long Panatela	Panatella Grande	7½	38	CC
Corona	Palma Short	5½	42	CC
Lonsdale	Palma	6½	42	CC
Lonsdale	Palma Extra	7	42	CC
Lonsdale	Corona	6½	44	CC
Churchill	Churchill	6⅞	46	CC
Double Corona	Presidente	7½	50	CC
Robusto	Toro	5½	50	CC
Giant	Soberano	8½	52	CC
Giant	Gigante	10	58	CC
Torpedo	Piramide Breve	5½	56	CC
Torpedo	Piramide	7½	64	CC
Torpedo	Piramide Gigante	8	68	CC

Here is the largest-selling brand in the Dominican Republic, widely available in the United States beginning in 1996. Created in 1907, it is produced in Santiago and features an Indonesian wrapper. Carbonell cigars are mild with exquisite flavor, devoid of bitterness and are presented in boxes of 20.

CARLOS TORAÑO CAMEROON 1916
Handmade in Esteli, Nicaragua.

Wrapper: Cameroon   *Binder: Nicaragua*   *Filler: Honduras, Nicaragua*

Shape	Name	Lgth	Ring	Wrapper
Corona	Corona	5½	42	CM
Robusto	Robusto	5½	52	CM
Churchill	Churchill	7	48	CM
Torpedo	Torpedo	6½	54	CM

Introduced in 2003, this blend is medium-to-full in body and each cigar has a three-quarters cedar wrap. Offering sweet, earthy tones, it is offered in boxes of 25.

CARLOS TORAÑO CASA TORAÑO
Handmade in Danli, Honduras.

Wrapper: Ecuador   *Binder: Nicaragua*   *Filler: Honduras, Mexico, Nicaragua*

Shape	Name		Lgth	Ring	Wrapper
Robusto	Robusto		4¾	52	CC
Toro	Toro		6¼	50	CC
Churchill	Churchill		7	48	CC
Torpedo	Torpedo		6½	54	CC
Grand Corona	Tubos	(tubed)	6½	46	CC

This is a special blend, introduced in 2004. It's the commercial version of a Toraño house blend, with a mild-to-medium-bodied flavor. It's available to everyone now, in boxes of 25.

CARLOS TORAÑO CASA TORAÑO MADURO   ★*New*★
Handmade in Danli, Honduras.

Wrapper: USA/Connecticut   *Binder: Honduras*   *Filler: Honduras, Nicaragua*

Shape	Name	Lgth	Ring	Wrapper
Robusto	Robusto	4¾	52	Ma
Toro	Toro	6¼	50	Ma
Torpedo	Torpedo	6½	54	Ma
Long Panatela	Lancero	7	38	Ma

This version of the Casa Torano line was introduced in 2007 and features a Connecticut Broadleaf wrapper. It creates a medium-bodied taste, offered in boxes of 25. The Lancero has a special finishing touch: a pigtail head!

CARLOS TORAÑO EXODUS 1959
Handmade in Danli, Honduras.

Wrapper: Honduras   *Binder: Honduras*
Filler: Costa Rica, Dom. Rep., Honduras, Mexico, Nicaragua

HANDMADE CIGARS: BRAND LISTINGS

Shape	Name		Lgth	Ring	Wrapper
Torpedo	Torpedo		6½	54	CM
Toro	Toro		6	50	CM
Double Corona	Double Corona		7	50	CM
Robusto	Robusto		5	52	CM
Perfecto	Perfecto		5¾	50	CM
Grand Corona	Tubos	(tubed)	6½	46	CM
Small Panatela	Tins		4⅛	30	CM

A salute to the pre-Castro era in Cuba, where Carlos Toraño was born! This is a full-bodied, box-pressed brand introduced in 2001, offered in an elegant box of 24 cigars in three layers of eight cigars each.

CARLOS TORAÑO EXODUS 1959 SILVER SERIES
Handmade in Danli, Honduras.

Wrapper: Honduras   Binder: Costa Rica   Filler: Costa Rica, Honduras, Nicaragua

Shape	Name	Lgth	Ring	Wrapper
Robusto	Robusto Corto	4⅞	52	CM
Grand Corona	Corona Grande	6⅛	46	CM
Double Corona	Grand Churchill	7	50	CM
Torpedo	Torpedo Especial	6¼	52	CM

This is a second Toraño Exodus brand, introduced in 2002. This blend is full in body with a Honduran-grown Criollo wrapper from 1998.

CARLOS TORAÑO NICARAGUAN SELECTION
Handmade in Esteli, Nicaragua.

Wrapper: Ecuador   Binder: Nicaragua   Filler: Nicaragua

Shape	Name	Lgth	Ring	Wrapper
Toro	Double Corona	6¼	50	CM
Small Panatela	Carlin	4⅛	32	CM
Short Panatela	Palmita	4½	36	CM

Petit Corona	Coronita	4	40	CM
Petit Corona	Petit Corona	5	42	CM
Churchill	Churchill	7	48	CM
Robusto	Robusto	5	50	CM
Torpedo	Torpedo	6¼	52	CM
Perfecto	Perfecto	5¾	50	CM

Introduced in 1997, this is a box-pressed, medium-bodied cigar with the excellent construction and perfect draw that has become a trademark of the Toraño brands. It features a Sumatra-seed wrapper and is offered in individual cellophane sleeves in all-cedar cabinets of 25.

CARLOS TORAÑO NOVENTA
Handmade in Esteli, Nicaragua.

Wrapper: Nicaragua *Binder: Nicaragua* *Filler: Nicaragua*

Shape	Name	Lgth	Ring	Wrapper
Robusto	Santiago	5	50	CM
Toro	La Esperanza	6	52	CM
Torpedo	Latin	6½	54	CM

A salute to the 90th anniversary of Santiago Toraño's migration from Spain to Cuba, this blend was introduced in 2006. Toraño eventually become one of the largest tobacco growers in Cuba, but had to leave in 1960 when the tobacco industry was nationalized. This anniversary cigar is medium in body and offered in boxes of 25.

CARLOS TORAÑO RESERVA DECADENCIA ★*New*★
Handmade in Esteli, Nicaragua.
Wrapper: USA/Connecticut

Binder: Indonesia *Filler: Dom. Rep., Honduras, Nicaragua*

Shape	Name		Lgth	Ring	Wrapper
Robusto	Robusto	*(glass tube)*	5	50	CC
Churchill	Churchill	*(glass tube)*	7¼	48	CC

This unusual blend debuted in late 2007 as a collaboration between the Toraño family and Wilson Creek Winery of Temecula, California, producer of the Decadencia Chocolate Port. The blending process infuses the tobacco with the essence of the wine and the cigars are aged in the same French oak barrels that aged the wine. Both sizes are offered in boxes of 20.

CARLOS TORAÑO RESERVA SELECTA
Handmade in Danli, Honduras.

Wrapper: Costa Rica, USA/Connecticut
Binder: Indonesia
Filler: Dominican Republic, Honduras, Nicaragua

Shape	Name		Lgth	Ring	Wrapper
Petit Corona	Petit Corona	(glass tubes)	5	40	CC
Robusto	Robusto	(glass tubes)	5	50	CC-Ma
Churchill	Churchill	(glass tubes)	7¼	48	CC-Ma
Torpedo	Torpedo	(glass tubes)	6¼	52	CC-Ma
Small Panatela	Tins		4⅛	30	CC

Here is a magnificent cigar, offered in elegant glass tubes, double-banded and wrapped in cedar sleeves for the finest in smoking pleasure. Thanks to the Connecticut Shade or Costa Rican maduro wrappers, the Reserva Selecta has a medium-to-full-bodied taste with leaves aged from three to five years. Try one size or all in presentation boxes of 20, or in packs of five.

CARLOS TORAÑO SIGNATURE COLLECTION
Handmade in Santiago, Dominican Republic.

Wrapper: Brazil
Binder: USA/Connecticut
Filler: Dom. Rep., Nicaragua

Shape	Name	Lgth	Ring	Wrapper
Robusto	Robusto	5	52	Ma
Toro	Toro	6	50	Ma
Churchill	Churchill	7	48	Ma
Torpedo	Torpedo	6	52	Ma
Perfecto	Perfecto	5	51	Ma

This medium-bodied blend was introduced in 2000 and offers a sturdy Brazilian-grown maduro wrapper and Piloto Cubano filler leaves. It is spectacularly packaged in Spanish Cedar and offered in a unique 9-9-7 keepsake box. The

HANDMADE CIGARS: BRAND LISTINGS

Churchill is also offered in a box of 10.

CARNAVAL BY COJIMAR
Handmade in Tamboril, Dominican Republic.

Wrapper: Ecuador   Binder: Dom. Rep.   *Filler: Dom. Rep.*

Shape	Name	Lgth	Ring	Wrapper
Small Panatela	Tins	4	30	CC

This is a mild-bodied, flavored line that debuted in 2006. It's available in Conga (White Russiian), Merengue (pineapple & rum) or Rumba (tropical fruit) in tins of 10.

CARRINGTON
Handmade in Santo Domingo, Dominican Republic.

Wrapper: USA/Connecticut   Binder: Dom. Rep.   *Filler: Dom. Rep.*

Shape	Name	Lgth	Ring	Wrapper
Double Corona	No. 1	7½	50	Cl
Long Corona	No. 2	6	42	Cl
Long Panatela	No. 3	7	36	Cl
Corona	No. 4	5½	40	Cl
Churchill	No. 5	6⅞	46	Cl
Robusto	No. 6	4½	50	Cl-Ma
Toro	No. 7	6	50	Cl-Ma
Pyramid	No. 8	6⅞	60	Cl

Introduced in 1984, Carrington cigars offer a mild to medium (natural) or medium-to-full (maduro) taste, with a solid core of spice and a nice, toasty flavor. The wrapper is Connecticut Shade in natural or maduro, with Dominican filler and binder in all sizes. All are offered in boxes of 25.

CASA ANTERO
Handmade in Santiago, Dominican Republic.

Wrapper: Ecuador   Binder: Dom. Rep.   *Filler: Dom. Rep.*

Shape	Name	Lgth	Ring	Wrapper
Robusto	Rothschild	5	50	CC
Toro	Toro	6	50	CC

HANDMADE CIGARS: BRAND LISTINGS

Corona	Brevas	5¼	43	CC
Long Corona	No. 1	6¼	44	CC
Double Corona	Churchill	7	50	CC
Torpedo	Figurado	5¾	56	CC

This blend is available only to members of the Tobacconists' Association of America (TAA). It was introduced in 2004 and offers a mild taste in bundles of 25.

CASA BLANCA
Handmade in Santiago, Dominican Republic.

Wrapper: USA/Connecticut *Binder: Mexico* *Filler: Dom. Rep.*

Shape	Name	Lgth	Ring	Wrapper
Short Panatela	Bonita	4	36	CC
Corona	Corona	5½	42	CC
Toro	DeLuxe	6	50	CC-Ma
Robusto	Half Jeroboam	5	66	CC-Ma
Giant	Jeroboam	10	66	CC-Ma
Lonsdale	Lonsdale	6½	42	CC-Ma
Double Corona	Magnum	7	60	CC-Ma
Toro	Obsequio	6	49	CC-Ma
Panatela	Panetela	6	35	CC
Double Corona	President	7½	50	CC-Ma
Robusto	Robusto	5	50	CC-Ma
Small Panatela	Scepters	5	32	CC

This line, which means "White House" in English, offers an extremely mild taste in a variety of sizes. Particularly noteworthy are the giant 66-ring Half Jeroboam and Jeroboam, among the thickest straight-sided cigars offered on the U.S. market. Most sizes are offered in boxes of 25.

CASA BLANCA RESERVE
Handmade in Santiago, Dominican Republic.

Wrapper: Ecuador *Binder: Mexico* *Filler: Dom. Rep.*

Shape	Name	Lgth	Ring	Wrapper
Double Corona	No. 1	7½	50	CC
Toro	No. 2	6	50	CC
Lonsdale	No. 3	6½	42	CC
Corona	No. 4	5½	43	CC
Robusto	No. 5	5	50	CC

"The best of the best" is the idea behind this upgraded selection of Casa Blanca, the Reserve Collection. Introduced in 1996, this elegant, medium-bodied line is offered with a Sumatra-seed wrapper in all-cedar cabinets of 25 cigars each.

CASA BLANCA RESERVE CAMEROON
Handmade in Santiago, Dominican Republic.

Wrapper: Cameroon		Binder: Mexico			Filler: Dom. Rep.
Shape	Name	Lgth	Ring	Wrapper	
Double Corona	No. 1	7½	50	CM	
Toro	No. 2	6	50	CM	
Lonsdale	No. 3	6½	42	CM	
Corona	No. 4	5½	43	CM	
Robusto	No. 5	5	50	CM	

This is the third Casa Blanca brand, introduced in 2004. It is mild-to-medium in body and offered in boxes of 25.

CASA DE ORO
Handmade in Esteli, Nicaragua.
Wrapper: Ecuador, Nicaragua

Binder: Indonesia				Filler: Dom. Rep., Honduras, Nicaragua	
Shape	Name	Lgth	Ring	Wrapper	
Torpedo	Torpedo	6½	52	CC-Ma	
Toro	Toro	6	52	CC-Ma	

Introduced in 2006 by C. Concepts of Irvine, California, "House of Gold" offers

HANDMADE CIGARS: BRAND LISTINGS

CAST-AWAYS
Handmade in Santiago, Dominican Republic.

Wrapper: USA/Connecticut   *Binder: Dom. Rep.*   *Filler: Dom. Rep.*

Shape	Name	Lgth	Ring	Wrapper
Robusto	Robusto	5	50	CC-Ma
Perfecto	Perfecto	4¾	44	CC-Ma

The formal name is "The Original No. 231 Factory Straight Cast-Aways," introduced by MATASA in 2006. There is a choice of natural (Connecticut Shade) or maduro (Connecticut Broadleaf) wrappers in a medium-bodied, value brand offered in trays of 100.

CAVANA
Handmade in Yonkers, New York, USA.

Wrapper: Mexico   *Binder: Dom. Rep.*   *Filler: Honduras, Mexico*

Introduced in 1996, this blend offers a medium body and is in limited distribution. There are eight sizes, all offered in a choice of natural or maduro wrappers, most in air-tight cases of five. One size is available with vanilla flavoring.

CENTENARIO
Handmade in Tamboril, Dominican Republic.

Wrapper: Nicaragua   *Binder: Nicaragua*   *Filler: Nicaragua*

Shape	Name	Lgth	Ring	Wrapper
Churchill	Classic A	7	48	CM
Toro	Classic B	6	55	CM
Robusto	Classic C	5	52	CM
Long Corona	Classic D	6	44	CM
Torpedo	Classic T	6	54	CM

This is a full-bodied, powerful line of cigars made by Felipe Gregorio in Nicaragua beginning in 2001. Production moved to the Dominican Republic in 2007. All sizes are offered in boxes of 20.

CERDAN
Handmade in Santiago, Dominican Republic.

Wrapper: Ecuador   *Binder: Dom. Rep.*   *Filler: Dom. Rep.*

HANDMADE CIGARS: BRAND LISTINGS

Shape	Name	Lgth	Ring	Wrapper
Short Panatela	Perlas	3⅝	38	CC
Long Panatela	Gables	7½	38	CC
Long Panatela	Juan Carlos	7	36	CC
Lonsdale	Welles	6¼	42	CC
Long Corona	Chamberlain	6	44	CC
Corona	Napoleon	5¼	42	CC
Corona	Ejecutivos	5½	40	CC
Robusto	Ribo's	5	50	CC
Torpedo	Otto's	6⅛	52	CC
Churchill	Churchill	6⅞	46	CC
Double Corona	Don Juan	7½	50	CC

Produced under the supervision of veteran cigar maker Juan Cerdan Soto, this brand offers a variety of shapes and strengths. Most shapes are medium in body, using a Connecticut-seed wrapper, offered in boxes of 5, 10, 25 or 50 cigars.

CHAIRMAN'S CHOICE ★Returns★
Handmade in Danli, Honduras.

Wrapper: Nicaragua   Binder: Nicaragua   Filler: Nicaragua

Shape	Name	Lgth	Ring	Wrapper
Toro	V.P.	5¾	48	CM
Robusto	Director	5	52	CM
Double Corona	C.E.O.	7	50	CM

Lignum-2 of San Leandro, California brought this brand back to life in 2007. It's now a medium-to-full-bodied smoke with a spicy finish, offered in boxes of 20.

CHAMUCO
Handmade in Esteli, Nicaragua.

BLACK MAGIC:
Wrapper: Nicaragua   Binder: Mexico   Filler: Mexico, Nicaragua

HANDMADE CIGARS: BRAND LISTINGS

Grand Corona	Magnum 46	5⅝	46	CC
Robusto	Noble Habana	5¼	54	CC
Petit Corona	Small Club Corona	4	44	CC

Mild-to-medium in body, this elegant blend was introduced by Drew Estates in 2006. It features a Connecticut-seed, shade-grown wrapper that is offered in boxes of 25 for most sizes, but in eights for the Cristales and 32 for the Small Club Corona.

CHEAP BASTARD
Handmade in Santiago, Dominican Republic.

Wrapper: USA/Connecticut *Binder: Dom. Rep.* *Filler: Dom. Rep.*

Shape	Name	Lgth	Ring	Wrapper
Double Corona	Churchill	6¾	50	CC
Robusto	Robusto	5	50	CC
Torpedo	Belicoso	6	52	CC
Robusto	Gordo	5½	62	CC
Corona	Corona	5½	42	CC

Created by the late Shawn Brawner and continued by his wife Lisa, this is a mild blend that salutes customers of the Old Towne Smoke Shoppe in Temecula, California who asked for "cheap cigars." Introduced in 2005, they're offered (and pre-punched!) in boxes of 50 except for the Gordo, unpunched and boxed in 24s.

CHEVERE ICE CREAM FLAVORS
Handmade in Danli, Honduras.

Wrapper: Honduras *Binder: Honduras* *Filler: Honduras*

Shape	Name	Lgth	Ring	Wrapper
Cigarillo	Cigarillos	3¼	20	CM
Small Panatela	430	4¼	30	CM
Corona	Mantecado	5½	40	CM

This cigar was introduced in 2002. It offers a medium-to-full-bodied, sweet taste in Amaretto, Irish Cream, rum, Tiramisu and vanilla in the cigarillo size and vanilla in the 430 and Mantecado size. It is offered in boxes of 50 (Cigarillo), 25 (Mantecado) and five (430).

HANDMADE CIGARS: BRAND LISTINGS

CHUBBYS
Handmade in Santiago, Dominican Republic.

Wrapper: Dom. Rep., USA/Connecticut   Binder: Dom. Rep.   Filler: Dom. Rep.

Shape	Name	Lgth	Ring	Wrapper
Torpedo	Torpe Grande	7	56	CC-Ma
Double Corona	Chubby Long	7	60	CC-Ma
Toro	Chubby Short	6	60	CC-Ma
Double Corona	On Diet	7	54	CC-Ma
Robusto	Midget	4½	54	CC-Ma

This line of fat cigars was introduced in 2004 by the Crown David Int'l Cigar Co. It is mild to medium in body and offered in wood cabinets of 20 cigars each.

CIBAO
Handmade in Tamboril, Dominican Republic.

Wrapper: USA/Connecticut   Binder: Dom. Rep.   Filler: Dom. Rep.

Shape	Name	Lgth	Ring	Wrapper
Perfecto	Pequenos Perfecto	4	51	CC
Short Panatela	Selecto	5	38	CC
Petit Corona	Petite Corona	5	42	CC
Robusto	Robusto	5	50	CC
Long Corona	Lonsdale	6	44	CC
Toro	Toro	6	50	CC
Churchill	Churchill	6⅞	46	CC
Double Corona	Presidente	7½	50	CC
Torpedo	Torpedo	7	54	CC
Giant	Gigante	10	60	CC

Off the market in 2002, this brand returned in 2003. Introduced in 1997, it offers a mild-to-medium-bodied taste, available in boxes of 25, except for the Pequenos (also available in 10s) and the Gigante, packaged individually.

HANDMADE CIGARS: BRAND LISTINGS

CISSO 8TH ANNIVERSARY
Handmade in Santiago, Dominican Republic.
Wrapper: Indonesia, Nicaragua, USA/Connecticut
Binder: Dom. Rep.   *Filler: Brazil, Dom. Rep.*

This line was introduced in 2005 and is offered in three sizes and four wrapper choices: Connecticut, Criollo, maduro and Sumatra. It has a medium-to-full body and is sold in boxes of 25.

CISSO BOURBON ★*New*★
Handmade in Rochester, New York, USA.
Wrapper: Indonesia   *Binder: Dom. Rep.*   *Filler: Dom. Rep.*

Here is a full-bodied cigar which is seeped in Kentucky bourbon and offered in three sizes. All are available in boxes of 25.

CISSO GRANDE ★*New*★
Handmade in Rochester, New York, USA.
Wrapper: Brazil, Indonesia, USA/Connecticut   *Binder: Dom. Rep.*   *Filler: Dom. Rep.*

This is a medium-to-full-bodied cigar in two fatter sizes with a choice of wrappers, including a Brazilian maduro. All are available in boxes of 25.

CISSO SUPERIOR ★*Returns*★
Handmade in Rochester, New York, USA.
Wrapper: Indonesia, USA/Connecticut   *Binder: Dom. Rep.*   *Filler: Dom. Rep.*

This is a medium-bodied cigar offered in six sizes in a choice of wrappers. All sizes are available in boxes of 25.

CISSO WINE ★*Returns*★
Handmade in Rochester, New York, USA.
Wrapper: Indonesia   *Binder: Dom. Rep.*   *Filler: Dom. Rep.*

Here is a full-bodied cigar with is seeped in red wine and honey and offered in five sizes. All are available in boxes of 25.

CLEMENTINE
Handmade in Danli, Honduras.
Wrapper: Honduras   *Binder: Honduras*   *Filler: Honduras, Nicaragua*

HANDMADE CIGARS: BRAND LISTINGS

Shape	Name	Lgth	Ring	Wrapper
Long Corona	Coronas	6¼	44	CM-Ma
Double Corona	Churchills	7½	50	CM-Ma
Giant	Immensas	8	54	CM
Lonsdale	No. 1	7	44	CM-Ma
Corona	No. 4	5½	44	CM-Ma
Double Corona	Presidente	7½	50	CM-Ma
Robusto	Rothschild	5	50	CM-Ma
Toro	Toro	6	50	CM-Ma
Giant	Viajante	8½	52	CM

This is a long-filler, bundle cigar, introduced in 1991, offering a full-bodied taste. The name of the brand supposedly came from the favorite song of the buyers who were looking for tobacco on the backroads of Central America when the brand was introduced. Arrgh!

COCOA
Handmade in Santiago, Dominican Republic.
Wrapper: Dom. Rep.   *Binder: Dom. Rep.*   *Filler: Dom. Rep.*

Introduced in 1989, this is a medium-bodied blend made in two sizes, with a Sumatra-seed wrapper. It is offered in bundles of 25.

COHIBA
Handmade in Santiago, Dominican Republic.
Wrapper: Cameroon   *Binder: Indonesia*   *Filler: Dom. Rep.*

Shape	Name	Lgth	Ring	Wrapper
Double Corona	Churchill	7	49	CM
Lonsdale	Corona Especiales	6½	42	CM
Corona	Corona	5⅛	42	CM
Petit Corona	Corona Minor	4	42	CM
Corona	Crystal Corona *(glass tube)*	5½	42	CM
Grand Corona	Lonsdale Grande	6¼	47	CM

Cigarillo	Miniatures		3⅞	24	CM
Small Panatela	Pequeños		4⅛	36	CM
Robusto	Robusto		5	49	CM
Corona Extra	Robusto Fino		4¾	47	CM
Toro	Toro	(tubed)	6	50	CM
Pyramid	Triangulo		6	54	CM

This version, the so-called "Red Dot" Cohiba debuted in 1997. General Cigar had produced a three-size, unbanded Cohiba for 20 years, but this medium-to-full-bodied blend has more of everything, including sizes and taste. The Corona Especiale is finished with a twisted head and the Crystal Corona is packaged in a glass tube. The product of five years of research, it is offered in a beautiful mahogany box.

A lengthy battle between General Cigar and the Cuban cigar-marketing firm Cubatabaco over ownership of the Cohiba trademark in the U.S. finally ended in 2006. The U.S. District Court for the Southern District of New York ruled against General Cigar's ownership of the Cohiba trademark in 2004, but was overturned by the U.S. 2d Circuit Court of Appeals in February 2005. The U.S. Supreme Court declined to review the case, leaving General Cigar with the rights to the Cohiba name in the U.S.

COHIBA BLACK
Handmade in Santiago, Dominican Republic.

Wrapper: USA/Connecticut   Binder: Dom. Rep.   Filler: Dom. Rep., Mexico

Shape	Name		Lgth	Ring	Wrapper
Churchill	Churchill		7	49	Ma
Corona	Corona		5½	42	Ma
Short Panatela	Pequeno		4⅛	36	Ma
Robusto	Robusto	(glass tube)	5½	50	Ma
Toro	Supremo		6	54	Ma

Introduced in 2006, this is a full-bodied but quite accessible cigar which features a Connecticut Broadleaf wrapper and three-year-aged interior tobaccos. All sizes are offered in boxes of 25 except for the glass-tubed Robusto, in boxes of eight.

HANDMADE CIGARS: BRAND LISTINGS

COHIBA EXTRA VIGOROSO
Handmade in Santiago, Dominican Republic.

Wrapper: Ecuador　　　*Binder: USA/Connecticut*　　*Filler: Dom. Rep., Nicaragua*

Shape	Name	Lgth	Ring	Wrapper
Robusto	XV 550	5	50	CM
Grand Corona	XV 645	6	45	CM
Toro	XV 652	6	52	CM
Pyramid	XV 660	6	60	CM
Double Corona	XV 749	7	49	CM

This Cohiba debuted in 2001, now known as "XV." It offers a full-bodied flavor and a very rich taste, featuring a Sumatra-seed wrapper and Connecticut Broadleaf binder. It is available in boxes of 20.

COJIMAR
Handmade in Santo Domingo, Dominican Republic.

Wrapper: Ecuador　　　*Binder: Dom. Rep*　　　*Filler: Dom. Rep.*

Shape	Name	Lgth	Ring	Wrapper
Toro	Double Corona	6½	54	CC
Robusto	Robusto	5	50	CC
Torpedo	Torpedo	6	50	CC
Corona	Señoras	5½	42	CC
Petit Corona	Senora Cafe	5	42	CC
Petit Corona	On The Go *(tube available)*	5	42	CC
Small Panatela	Señoritas	5	30	CC
Small Panatela	Carnaval	4	30	CC
Cigarillo	Solos	4	28	CC
Cigarillo	Minis	3½	26	CC
Cigarillo	Cigarillos	3½	26	CC

This cigar debuted in 1996. It now offers a range of popular sizes in a mild-bodied, flavored style, all finished with a sugared tip! The Double Coronas and

Robustos are offered in Chocolate Mint, Cognac and vanilla. Torpedos are available in vanilla only, but the Senoras come in cherry, chocolate, Cognac, mango, vanilla, rum and Sambuca flavors while the Senoritas come in all of those flavors plus honey and peach. The Solos come in Amaretto, cherry, chocolate, honey, peach, rum, Sambuca and vanilla. The Cigarillos are offered in coconut, Cognac and vanilla. Most sizes are available in boxes of 25, with the On The Go tubes and Carnaval offered in 10s.

COLBA 1492 ★New★
Handmade in Miami, Florida, USA.
Wrapper: Dom. Rep., Ecuador, Mexico
Binder: Honduras   Filler: Dom. Rep., Ecuador, Honduras, Nicaragua, Panama

Shape	Name	Lgth	Ring	Wrapper
Robusto	Guama	5	50	CC-CM-Ma
Corona Extra	Nucay	5½	46	CC-CM-Ma
Toro	Yahatuey	6	50	CC-CM-Ma
Short Panatela	Guarina	5	38	CC-CM-Ma
Torpedo	Canoa	6¼	52	CC-CM-Ma
Double Corona	Tuba	7	50	CC-CM-Ma
Double Corona	Cacique	7½	50	CC-CM-Ma
Perfecto	Cabanacan	6½	52	CC-CM-Ma
Torpedo	Taino	6¼	56	CC-CM-Ma
Giant	Siboney	8	56	CC-CM-Ma

This unique blend was created by Maxoly of Miami, Florida in 2007. It features a remarkable choice of wrappers, including Connecticut-seed leaf from Ecaudor, Dominican-grown and Mexican maduro and a choice of fillers which constantly changes. That makes the cigars anywhere from mild-to-medium to full in body, offered in a choice of boxes (of 10, 12, 20 or 25), cylinders (5, 7, 8 or 10) and fabulous Catauro baskets made of Yagua (palm leaves) with 5, 7, 8 or 10 cigars inside, in the way cigars used to be sold on the street of Miami, Tampa and Havana in the early part of the 20th Century.

A special series called the Colba Gem Collection, designed by Jackie Sarracino, offers bands with a small stone attached: Guama has a diamond; Nucay has amethyst; Yahatuey has a ruby; Canoa has topaz; Tuba has an emerald and Cacique has a sapphire!

HANDMADE CIGARS: BRAND LISTINGS

COLINAS ★*New*★
Handmade, with medium filler, in San Jose, Costa Rica.

Wrapper: Costa Rica   *Binder: Costa Rica*   *Filler: Costa Rica*

Shape	Name	Lgth	Ring	Wrapper
Double Corona	Churchill	7	52	CM
Long Corona	Corona	6¼	44	CM
Toro	Gordo	6	62	CM
Robusto	Robusto	5	50	CM
Small Panatela	Senoritas	4½	32	CM
Petit Corona	Petit	5	42	CM

Introduced to the U.S. market in 2007, this is the medium-filler line from the Tabacos de la Cordillera in Costa Rica. Like its sister brands, all of the tobacco is from ancestral seeds of Cuban tobacco strains of the 1940s and 1950s. The body is medium and all sizes except the Gordo (15) are offered in boxes of 25.

CONCH REPUBLIC
Handmade in Danli, Honduras and Key West, Florida, USA.

Wrapper: Ecuador, Honduras   *Binder: Dom. Rep.*   *Filler: Dom. Rep., Honduras*

Shape	Name	Lgth	Ring	Wrapper
Toro	Casino	6	48	Stripe
Double Corona	Churchill	7	50	CC-Ma
Slim Panatela	Cuba Libre	6	30	CC-Ma
Corona	Hemingway	5½	43	CC-Ma
Perfecto	King Conch	6½	54	CC-Ma
Small Panatela	Ninitos	4¾	32	CC-Ma
Long Panatela	Panatela	7	36	CC-Ma
Petit Corona	Petit Cuban	4½	42	CC-Ma
Pyramid	Piramide	6	55	CC-Ma
Giant	Presidente	8	52	CC-Ma
Robusto	Robusto	5	50	CC-Ma

Long Corona	Rothschild	6	44	CC-Ma
Lonsdale	The Best	7	44	CC-Ma
Toro	Toro	6	50	CC-Ma
Torpedo	Torpedo	6½	54	CC-Ma
	Made with mixed filler:			
Cigarillo	Cigarillo	4½	28	CC-Ma

Introduced in 1990, this brand is medium in body, with production moved primarily to Honduras in 2002 after originating in the Florida Keys. Take your choice of Ecuador-grown, Connecticut-seed wrappers or Honduran maduro wrappers, mostly in boxes of 25.

CONDEGA COROJO 1999
Handmade in Esteli, Nicaragua.

Wrapper: Nicaragua *Binder: Nicaragua* *Filler: Nicaragua*

Shape	*Name*	*Lgth*	*Ring*	*Wrapper*
Robusto	Robusto	5	52	CM
Toro	Toro	6	52	CM
Torpedo	Torpedo	6½	54	CM
Double Corona	Churchill	7	50	CM

The Tabacalera Tropical debuted this full-bodied blend in 2004. It has a fresh finish and is available in boxes of 20.

COPACABANA
Handmade in Esteli, Nicaragua.

Wrapper: Nicaragua *Binder: Nicaragua* *Filler: Nicaragua*

Shape	*Name*	*Lgth*	*Ring*	*Wrapper*
Short Panatela	Chico	4⅛	38	CM
Churchill	Churchill	7	48	CM
Petit Corona	Corona Elegante	4⅜	44	Ma
Perfecto	Figurado	4¾	51	CM
Robusto	Robusto	5	50	CM-Ma

HANDMADE CIGARS: BRAND LISTINGS

| Toro | Toro | 6 | 50 | CM-Ma |
| Torpedo | Torpedo | 6½ | 52 | CM |

Named for the famed nightspot, this is a medium-bodied Nicaraguan puro, introduced in 2003 by Harold Levinson Associates. Each size is presented in elegant wood boxes of 25.

COPPO
Handmade in Santiago, Dominican Republic.
Wrapper: Indonesia   *Binder: Dom. Rep.*   *Filler: Dom. Rep.*

This blend debuted in 2002 and offers a medium body in six sizes. It is available in bundles of 25 cigars.

COPPO BLACK BEAUTIES
Handmade in Santiago, Dominican Republic.
Wrapper: Dom. Rep.   *Binder: Dom. Rep.*   *Filler: Dom. Rep.*

This brand was introduced in 1998 and features a box-pressed combination of all Dominican-grown leaves with a darkly shaded wrapper. It is medium-to-full in body, made in five sizes and presented in cedar boxes of 25 cigars each.

COPPO CUBANO
Handmade in Santiago, Dominican Republic.
Wrapper: Cameroon   *Binder: Dom. Rep.*   *Filler: Dom. Rep.*

Introduced in 2002 by Mike Coppotelli, this blend is medium to full in body and is offered in six sizes. You can enjoy them all in boxes of 25.

COPPO DOMINICAN
Handmade in Santiago, Dominican Republic.
Wrapper: Ecuador   *Binder: Dom. Rep.*   *Filler: Dom. Rep., Ecuador*

Introduced in 1999, this blend is medium-bodied, made in seven sizes and comes in a cedar box of 25.

COPPO FLAVORS
Handmade in Santiago, Dominican Republic.
Wrapper: Dom. Rep.   *Binder: Dom. Rep.*   *Filler: Dom. Rep.*

Take your choice of delicate bourbon or cognac flavors in this three-size, all glass-tubed line, first offered in 2002. It is medium in body and available in boxes of 10 or 25.

CORDOVA
Handmade in Santiago, Dominican Republic.

Wrapper: Indonesia   *Binder: Indonesia*   *Filler: Dom. Rep.*

Shape	Name	Lgth	Ring	Wrapper
Long Corona	Corona	6	44	CM
Cigarillo	Miniature	3½	24	CM

Cordova is made by MATASA and was introduced in 2005. The Corona is available in cherry, rum and vanilla, but the Miniatures are flavored with the tips sweetened with cane sugar and offered in Cappuccino, cherry, chocolate, honey, rum, vanilla, Russian Freedom, Hawaiian Volcano, Italian Sambuca and Samba do Rio. They're offered in bundles of 25 or tins of 10; the Coronas are offered in boxes of 25.

CORONADO
BY LA FLOR DOMINICANA
Handmade in Santiago, Dominican Republic.

Wrapper: Nicaragua   *Binder: Dom. Rep.*   *Filler: Dom. Rep.*

Shape	Name	Lgth	Ring	Wrapper
Grand Corona	Corona Especial	5⅞	47	CM
Toro	Toro	6	52	CM
Double Corona	Double Corona	7	50	CM
Double Corona	Double Toro	7	54	CM
Double Corona	Corona Gorda	7	60	CM

Litto Gomez debuted this full-bodied blend in 2006. It uses leaves from the very top of the tobacco plant – the corona – for wrapper and has binder and filler leaves from his Estancia La Flor de Palma in La Canela, Dominican Republic. All sizes are boxes in 24.

COSMO
Handmade in Danli, Honduras.

Wrapper: USA/Connecticut   *Binder: Honduras*   *Filler: Honduras*

HANDMADE CIGARS: BRAND LISTINGS

Shape	Name	Lgth	Ring	Wrapper
Perfecto	Perfecto	4½	49	Ma
Perfecto	FBT	5½	50	Ma
Perfecto	Fancy Tales	6½	48	Ma
Robusto	Bully	4½	54	Ma
Toro	Boss	6	54	Ma

Here is a throwback of a cigar, like they used to be at the dawn of the 20th Century! With a maduro wrapper and all perfecto shapes, this brand from the historic Topper Cigar Company is medium-to-full in flavor and uses 50-year-old molds to shape these cigars. The Bully has another old-school touch: a pigtail head. Introduced in 2004, all of the shapes are offered in elegant wood chests of 25.

COSTA ★*New*★
Handmade in Penonome, Panama.

Wrapper: Dom. Rep.   *Binder: Panama*   *Filler: Panama*

Shape	Name	Lgth	Ring	Wrapper
Double Corona	Toro	7⅞	70	CM
Churchill	Churchill	7	47	CM
Toro	Robustos XL	6⅛	50	CM
Robusto	Robustos	4⅞	50	CM
Double Corona	Diego	7⅛	56	CM
Torpedo	Piramides	6⅛	52	CM

This blend was created in 2001, but reached U.S. national distribution in 2007. It's medium in body and offered in boxes of 25 except for the Toro, in 4s.

COSTA BRAVA ★*New*★
Handmade in Santiago, Dominican Republic.

Wrapper: Ecuador   *Binder: Dom. Rep.*   *Filler: Dom. Rep.*

Shape	Name	Lgth	Ring	Wrapper
Long Corona	Corona	6	44	CC
Double Corona	El Grande	7¼	54	CC

HANDMADE CIGARS: BRAND LISTINGS

Robusto	Robusto	5	50	CC
Toro	Toro	6	50	CC
Torpedo	Torpedo	6½	54	CC

Introduced in national distribution in 2007, this is a mild-bodied blend, presented in bundles of 20.

COURVOISIER
Handmade in Navarette, Dominican Republic.

Wrapper: Cameroon, Indonesia   Binder: Dom. Rep.   *Filler: Dom. Rep.*

Shape	Name	Lgth	Ring	Wrapper
Corona	Cognac Seasoned (glass tube)	5½	42	CM
Cigarillo	Cigarillos	4	28	CM

Introduced in 2003, this is a companion to the Maker's Mark brand. It features a Sumatra wrapper, is mild and offered in three-packs and boxes of 25. The cigarillos, with a Cameroon wrapper, come in tins of ten.

CREDO
Handmade in Santiago, Dominican Republic.

Wrapper: USA/Connecticut   Binder: Dom. Rep., Mexico   *Filler: Dom. Rep.*

Shape	Name	Lgth	Ring	Wrapper
Slim Panatela	Jubilate	5	34	CC
Corona	Athanor	5¾	42	CC
Churchill	Magnificat	7	46	CC
Robusto	Arcane	5	50	CC
Double Corona	Pythagoras	7	50	CC

The Credo cigar line has been designed by the famous Belaubre family with a French flair. Their recipe produces a medium-to-full-bodied strength smoke that is very smooth. The Magnificat, Arcane and Pythagoras models utilize a Dominican binder, while the Jubilate and Anthanor include a Mexican binder. The finished product, created in 1993, is offered in beautiful, instantly-recognizable boxes of 25 with their transparent deep blue stain, imported from France.

HANDMADE CIGARS: BRAND LISTINGS

CREDO LIGAS
Handmade in Danli, Honduras.

Wrapper: Indonesia   Binder: Honduras   Filler: Honduras

Shape	Name	Lgth	Ring	Wrapper
Slim Panatela	No. 1 Demi-Tasse	5½	32	CM
Robusto	No. 2 Robusto	5	50	CM
Corona	No. 3 Corona	5¾	43	CM
Churchill	No. 4 Churchill	7	48	CM
Giant	No. 5 Double Corona	8½	52	CM

This newer line of the Credo brand was introduced in mid-1997, featuring leaves from the Jamastran Valley grown from Cuban seeds. It offers a full-bodied flavor in five popular shapes, and is offered in cellophane sleeves in colorfully-adorned boxes of 25 that feature the masks of comedy and tragedy.

CREME DE JAMAICA
Handmade in Santiago, Dominican Republic.

Wrapper: USA/Connecticut   Binder: Indonesia   Filler: Dom. Rep.

Shape	Name	Lgth	Ring	Wrapper
Torpedo	Belicoso	6	50	CC
Double Corona	Churchill	7½	49	CC
Corona	Corona	5¾	42	CC
Toro	Toro	6½	49	CC
Lonsdale	Lonsdale	6½	42	CC
Robusto	Robusto	4¾	49	CC
Small Panatela	Momentos	4⅛	36	CC

Here is a grand name in cigars resurrected in mid-1999 under the supervision of Famous Smoke Shop. It has a mild body with a Connecticut Shade wrapper, Besuki binder and Piloto Cubano filler leaves. You can enjoy it in boxes of 25, or the Momentos in tins of six.

HANDMADE CIGARS: BRAND LISTINGS

CREMOSA CUBANA ★*New*★
Handmade in Santiago, Dominican Republic.

Wrapper: Indonesia　　　　*Binder: Dom. Rep.*　　　*Filler: Dom. Rep., Nicaragua*

Shape	Name	Lgth	Ring	Wrapper
Robusto	Robusto	5	50	CM
Corona	Corona	5½	42	CM
Toro	Toro	6	50	CM
Double Corona	Churchill	7	50	CM

Meier & Dutch introduced this brand into national distribution in 2007. It's medium in body and offered in boxes of 25.

CRISPIN PATIÑO
Handmade in Cumana, Venezuela.

Wrapper: Honduras　　　　*Binder: Venezuela*　　　　*Filler: Venezuela*

Introduced to the U.S. market in 1996, this has been a popular Venezuelan brand since 1928. Full-bodied, it is produced by the Patiño family, which started making cigars in 1900. Two sizes (Robusto and Double Corona) are long-filler and made with aged leaves, while the other three sizes in the line use mixed filler.

CRISTO CUBANOS
Handmade in Santiago, Dominican Republic.

Wrapper: USA/Connecticut　　　*Binder: Cameroon*　　　*Filler: Honduras, Nicaragua*

This five-size brand was introduced by Specialty Cigars in 1998, with excellent construction and a medium-bodied taste that offers a marvelous flavor. Two shapes (Corona and Lonsdale) are offered with maduro wrappers.

CROWN FUMAS
Handmade, with sandwich filler, in Santiago, Dominican Republic.

Wrapper: Honduras　　　　*Binder: Honduras*　　　*Filler: Honduras, Nicaragua*

Shape	Name	Lgth	Ring	Wrapper
Churchill	Churchill	7	48	CM
Toro	Toro	6	50	CM
Torpedo	Torpedo	6½	50	CM

| Corona | Corona | 5½ | 44 | CM |

The Crown David Int'l Cigar Co. offers this medium-bodied blend with a Corojo wrapper.

CROWN VINTAGE
Handmade in Santiago, Dominican Republic.
Wrapper: Dom. Rep.　　　　*Binder: Dom. Rep.*　　　　*Filler: Dom. Rep.*

Shape	*Name*	*Lgth*	*Ring*	*Wrapper*
Double Corona	Churchill	7½	52	CM
Torpedo	Belicoso	6½	52	CM
Toro	Toro	6	50	CM

This all-Dominican cigar by the Crown David Int'l Cigar Co. is offered in limited numbers and is medium-to-full in body.

CSX
Handmade in Santiago, Dominican Republic.
Wrapper: Dom. Rep.　　　　*Binder: Dom. Rep.*　　　　*Filler: Dom. Rep.*

Shape	*Name*	*Lgth*	*Ring*	*Wrapper*
Double Corona	Presidente	7¼	52	CM
Torpedo	Belicoso	6½	52	CM
Toro	Toro	6	50	CM
Corona	Corona	5½	44	CM

This is an extra-full-bodied blend of all Dominican tobacco, with primarily Ligero Cubano leaves in the filler.

CU-AVANA
Handmade in Santiago, Dominican Republic.
Wrapper: Dom. Rep., USA/Connecticut　　　*Binder: Dom. Rep.*　*Filler: Dom. Rep.*

Shape	*Name*	*Lgth*	*Ring*	*Wrapper*
Robusto	Robusto	5	50	CC-Ma
Toro	Toro	6	50	CC-Ma

Torpedo	Belicoso	6	52	CC-Ma
Double Corona	Churchill	7	50	CC-Ma

A Cigar Boom brand resurrected from the dead by Meier & Dutch in 2006, this blend is made by MATASA. It offers a mild-to-medium-bodied flavor with a choice of a Dominican-grown, Connecticut-seed or Connecticut maduro wrapper in boxes of 20.

CUBA ALIADOS
Handmade in Danli, Honduras.

Wrapper: Nicaragua   *Binder: Nicaragua*   *Filler: Dom. Rep.*

Shape	Name	Lgth	Ring	Wrapper
Torpedo	Belicoso	6½	56	CM-Ma
Robusto	Lance	5½	64	CM-Ma
Corona Extra	Corona De Lux	6½	46	CM-Ma
Toro	Toro Extra	6	53	CM-Ma
Double Corona	Doble Corona	7½	53	CM-Ma
Corona	No. 4 Cubanito	5½	44	CM-Ma
Petit Corona	Crema Cubanita	5	43	CM-Ma
Lonsdale	Lonsdale	6½	43	CM-Ma
Toro	Regordo	6	60	CM-Ma
Robusto	Robusto	5	50	CM-Ma
Pyramid	Piramide No. 3	5	50	CM-Ma
Pyramid	Piramide No. 2	6½	56	CM-Ma

An old Cuban brand owned by Rolando Reyes, this blend was revised in 2005 but continues the medium-to-full-bodied heft of this brand. Reyes made the brand in Cuba in the 1940s, then in New Jersey and Miami after the Cuban Revolution and in Honduras since 1989. It was originally introduced in national distribution in 1993, left the market due to trademark issues, then returned in 1999. The blend was changed in 2000 and was changed again to feature a Nicaraguan-grown Corojo wrapper. It's offered in boxes of 20.

HANDMADE CIGARS: BRAND LISTINGS

CUBA ALIADOS ANNIVERSARY ★New★
Handmade in Danli, Honduras.

Wrapper: Ecuador, Nicaragua   Binder: Ecuador   Filler: Dom. Rep., Nicaragua

Shape	Name	Lgth	Ring	Wrapper
Toro	Power	6½	56	CC-CM
Perfecto	Diademas No. 3	5½	54	CC-CM
Toro	Magico	6	48	CC-CM
Robusto	Short	4	48	CC-CM

This cigar was introduced in 2007 and salutes more than a centennial of the Cuba Aliados brand, originated in Cuba. It's medium in body, using six-year-aged tobaccos, offered in boxes of 10 (Power, Diademas No. 3) or 20 (Magico, Short).

CUBA ALIADOS DOUBLE FUERTE SPECIAL EDITION
Handmade in Danli, Honduras.

Wrapper: Honduras   Binder: Nicaragua   Filler: Dom. Rep., Nicaragua

Shape	Name	Lgth	Ring	Wrapper
Toro	Toro Negro	6	53	Ma
Robusto	Rothschild Negro	5	50	Ma

This is a new blend for 2006, offering a full-bodied blend. It features a Corojo wrapper and is available in boxes of 20.

CUBADOM
Handmade, with mixed filler, in Las Vegas, Nevada, USA.

Wrapper: Mexico   Binder: Dom. Rep.   Filler: Colombia, Dom. Rep., Mexico

Shape	Name	Lgth	Ring	Wrapper
Double Corona	Palma Real	7½	50	Ma
Churchill	Cazador	7	46	Ma
Lonsdale	Cervantes	6½	44	Ma
Corona	Breva	5¼	42	Ma

This is a full-bodied brand from the Las Vegas Cigar Co. that debuted in 1998. It is available only with a Mexican maduro wrapper, in boxes of 25.

HANDMADE CIGARS: BRAND LISTINGS

CUBAN CIGAR FACTORY "TRADICIONALES"
Handmade in San Diego, California, USA.
Wrapper: Ecuador, USA/Connecticut

Binder: Ecuador

Filler: Honduras, Mexico, Nicaragua

Shape	Name	Lgth	Ring	Wrapper
Corona	Corona	5¾	42	CM-Ma
Lonsdale	El Cubano	6¾	44	CM-Ma
Robusto	Robusto	5	50	CM-Ma
Grand Corona	Havana	6	46	CM-Ma
Toro	Monterico	5½	52	CM-Ma
Double Corona	Cuban Round Largo	7¼	50	CM-Ma
Double Corona	Presidente	7¾	52	CM-Ma
Torpedo	Torpedo	7	56	CM-Ma

Here is a mild-to-medium-bodied cigar that you can see being made by hand by the Cuban Cigar Factory in San Diego's Gaslamp District! It features a Connecticut natural or Ecuadorian maduro wrapper and is offered in boxes of 25.

CUBAN CIGAR FACTORY "VANILLA SWEETS"
Handmade in San Diego, California, USA.

Wrapper: Indonesia   Binder: Ecuador

Filler: Honduras, Mexico, Nicaragua

Shape	Name	Lgth	Ring	Wrapper
Petit Corona	Petit Corona	5	42	CM
Corona Extra	Emperador	5½	46	CM
Toro	Corona Grande	6	50	CM

Here is a carefully-made, all long-filler, flavored cigar that starts with Cuban-seed filler leaves and cures them with pure vanilla and a taste of honey. The quality of the result is obvious and you can try them in boxes of 25.

CUBAN CIGAR FACTORY "VINTAGE"
Handmade in San Diego, California, USA.

Wrapper: USA/Connecticut   Binder: Ecuador   Filler: Dom. Rep., Honduras

HANDMADE CIGARS: BRAND LISTINGS

Shape	Name	Lgth	Ring	Wrapper
Corona	Corona	5¾	42	CM
Robusto	Robusto	5	50	CM
Double Corona	Cuban Round Largo	7¼	50	CM
Torpedo	Torpedo	7	56	CM

Introduced in 1998, this blend is aged for 18 months after rolling and has a medium-bodied flavor, offered in boxes of 25.

CUBAN CRAFTERS
Handmade in Esteli, Nicaragua.

Wrapper: Cameroon, Nicaragua   Binder: Nicaragua   Filler: Nicaragua

Shape	Name	Lgth	Ring	Wrapper
Toro	Chairman	6	60	CM
Pyramid	Campana	5½	60	CM
Torpedo	Torpedo	6	54	CM
Double Corona	Churchill	7	52	CM
Toro	Toro	6	52	CM
Robusto	Robusto	5	52	CM
Short Panatela	Corto	5	38	CM

Created by the Tabacalera Esteli in 2003, this is a full-bodied blend available with two different styles: Cameroon (all sizes) or the Cabinet Selection with a Nicaraguan wrapper leaf (no Corto). Both are finished with a pigtail top and offered in boxes of 25.

CUBAN DELIGHTS
BY VICTOR SINCLAIR

Handmade, with mixed filler, in Santiago, Dominican Republic.

Wrapper: Indonesia   Binder: Dom. Rep.   Filler: Dom. Rep.

Shape	Name	Lgth	Ring	Wrapper
Double Corona	Churchill	7	50	CM
Corona	Corona	5½	42	CM

HANDMADE CIGARS: BRAND LISTINGS

Robusto	Robusto	5	50	CM

This brand was introduced in 2000 and is available in both a natural version and a flavored edition. Made with sandwich filler, this is a medium-bodied blend. The Corona also comes as a flavored shape, in Amaretto, cherry, rum and vanilla. All of these shapes come in boxes of 50.

CUBAN HONEYS   ★*New*★
Handmade in Santiago, Dominican Republic.
Wrapper: Dom. Rep.   Binder: Dom. Rep.   Filler: Dom. Rep.

Shape	Name	Lgth	Ring	Wrapper
Corona	Corona	5½	42	CM

This is a flavored line, introduced by Meier & Dutch in 2007. It's mild and comes in Amaretto, cherry, honey, rum and vanilla, in boxes of 25.

CUBAN HONEYS
Handmade in the Dominican Republic.
Wrapper: Indonesia   Binder: Dom. Rep.   Filler: Dom. Rep.

This is a flavored cigar in one size (4 x 32), available in Amaretto, cherry, honey and vanilla. Offered by Texana Cigar, it is offered in tins of 10.

CUBAN LEAF
Handmade in Esteli, Nicaragua.
Wrapper: Nicaragua   Binder: Nicaragua   Filler: Nicaragua

Shape	Name	Lgth	Ring	Wrapper
Robusto	Rothschild	4½	50	CM
Toro	Toro	5¾	48	CM
Torpedo	Torpedo	6¼	52	CM

Tabacalera Tropical introduced this brand in 2005, blending it around its Connecticut-Criollo hybrid wrapper grown on its farms in the Jalapa Valley. It's a medium-bodied blend offered in bundles of 20 and boxes of 50.

CUBAN PLEASURES
Handmade in Santiago, Dominican Republic.
Wrapper: USA/Connecticut   Binder: Dom. Rep.   Filler: Brazil, Dom. Rep.

HANDMADE CIGARS: BRAND LISTINGS

Shape	Name	Lgth	Ring	Wrapper
Short Panatela	Petite Corona	5	36	CC

Here is a mild-to-medium-bodied, flavored cigar, introduced by the Habana Cuba Cigar Co. in 2002. The Petite Corona size is available in Caribbean Rum Punch, Piña Colada and Tropical Passion flavors.

CUBAN ROUNDS
Handmade in Esteli, Nicaragua.

Wrapper: Nicaragua　　　　*Binder: Nicaragua*　　　　*Filler: Nicaragua*

Shape	Name	Lgth	Ring	Wrapper
Churchill	Churchill	7	48	CM
Toro	Toro	6	50	CM
Robusto	Robusto	5	50	CM

Phillips & King introduced this brand in early 2006, offering a medium-to-full body in economical boxes of 40.

CUBAN SANDWICH
Handmade, with mixed filler, in Santiago, Dominican Republic.

Wrapper: Indonesia, USA/Connecticut

Binder: Dom. Rep.　　　　*Filler: Dom. Rep., Honduras, Mexico, Nicaragua*

Shape	Name	Lgth	Ring	Wrapper
Corona	Breva	5½	44	CC-Ma
Lonsdale	Cetros	6¾	44	CC-Ma
Double Corona	Churchill	7	50	CC-Ma
Toro	Toro	6	50	CC-Ma

Introduced in 1996, this is a modestly-priced, mixed-filler cigar from one of the Dominican Republic's finest factories. The long and short filler pieces make up the center of the "sandwich" formed by the binder and results in a pleasant, mild-to-medium-bodied smoke. It if offered in natural (Indonesia) and maduro (USA/Connecticut) wrapper shades in boxes or bundles of 25.

HANDMADE CIGARS: BRAND LISTINGS

CUBAN SANDWICH ★*New*★
Handmade, with mixed filler, in Esteli, Nicaragua.

Wrapper: Nicaragua Binder: Nicaragua Filler: Nicaragua

Shape	Name	Lgth	Ring	Wrapper
Churchill	Cazador	6¾	46	CM-Ma
Corona Extra	Cremas	5½	46	CM-Ma
Double Corona	Especiales	7½	50	CM-Ma
Torpedo	Torpedo	7	52	CM-Ma

Here's a medium-bodied, value-priced cigar made for Mike's Cigars, offered in boxes of 25.

CUBAN SELECTION
Handmade in Santiago, Dominican Republic.

Wrapper: Dom. Rep. Binder: Dom. Rep. Filler: Dom. Rep.

Shape	Name	Lgth	Ring	Wrapper
Toro	Toro	6	50	CC
Churchill	Churchill	7	48	CC
Torpedo	Torpedo	6⅛	52	CC
Giant	Viajantes	8½	52	CC
Toro	Matador	6½	56	CC

This is a mild blend introduced by Exclusive Cigars of Aurora, Illinois in 2006. It's offered in bundles of 20.

CUBAN STOCK CLASSIC
Handmade in Santiago, Dominican Republic.

Wrapper: Dom. Rep., USA/Connecticut Binder: Dom. Rep. Filler: Dom. Rep.

Shape	Name	Lgth	Ring	Wrapper
Double Corona	Presidente	7½	52	CC-Ma
Torpedo	Belicoso	6¼	52	CC-Ma
Toro	Toro	6	50	CC-Ma
Robusto	Robusto	5	50	CC-Ma

HANDMADE CIGARS: BRAND LISTINGS

Corona	Corona	5½	44	CC-Ma
Petit Corona	Petit	4	40	CC-Ma
Toro	Magnum	6	60	CC-Ma
Double Corona	Double Magnum	7	60	CC-Ma

This is a mild-bodied cigar (with a Connecticut Shade wrapper) introduced in 2004 by the Crown David Int'l Cigar Co., offered in boxes of 20. It is mild-to-medium-bodied with the Dominican-grown maduro wrap.

CUBAN STOCK RESERVE
Handmade in Santiago, Dominican Republic.
Wrapper: USA/Connecticut   Binder: Dom. Rep.   Filler: Dom. Rep.

Shape	Name	Lgth	Ring	Wrapper
Double Corona	Presidente	7¼	52	CC
Torpedo	Belicoso	6½	52	CC
Toro	Toro	6	50	CC
Robusto	Robusto	5½	52	CC

This is a medium-to-full-bodied blend with an aged Connecticut wrapper.

CUBAN STOCK ROYAL SELECTION
Handmade in Santiago, Dominican Republic.
Wrapper: Dom. Rep., USA/Connecticut   Binder: Dom. Rep.   Filler: Dom. Rep.

Shape	Name	Lgth	Ring	Wrapper
Double Corona	Churchill No. 1	7½	52	CC-Ma
Torpedo	Belicoso No. 2	6¼	52	CC-Ma
Toro	Toro	6	50	CC-Ma
Robusto	Robusto No. 3	5	50	CC-Ma
Corona	Corona No. 4	5½	44	CC-Ma
Perfecto	Perfecto	7	48	CC-Ma
Perfecto	Mini-Perfecto	6	48	CC-Ma
Petit Corona	Petit	4	40	CC-Ma

HANDMADE CIGARS: BRAND LISTINGS

Introduced by Crown David Int'l in 2004, the Royal Selection offers a choice of wrappers, from Connecticut Shade to Dominican-grown maduro. Depending on the wrapper, it's medium to full in body and offered in boxes of 20.

CUBAN TWIST
Handmade, with mixed filler, in Danli, Honduras.

Wrapper: Honduras *Binder: Nicaragua* *Filler: Honduras, Nicaragua*

Shape	Name	Lgth	Ring	Wrapper
Long Corona	No. 400	6	44	CM
Toro	No. 500	6	50	CM
Churchill	No. 600	7	46	CM

This is a mild-bodied brand which has been re-introduced by Indianhead to the U.S. market in 2000. It is offered in boxes of 25.

CUBITA
Handmade in Santiago, Dominican Republic.

Wrapper: Ecuador *Binder: Dom. Rep.* *Filler: Dom. Rep.*

Shape	Name		Lgth	Ring	Wrapper
Double Corona	No. 2000		7	50	CC
Corona	No. 500		5½	43	CC
Lonsdale	No. 8-9-8		6¾	43	CC
Panatela	No. 2	*(tubed)*	6¼	38	CC
Toro	No. 700		6	50	CC
Robusto	No. 545		4½	50	CC
Cigarillo	Mini Delicias		3¾	26	CC
Small Panatela	Delicias		5⅛	30	CC

Introduced in 1986, this is a medium-bodied cigar, with excellent construction and a Connecticut-seed wrapper. The brand uses only aged tobaccos and offers these cigars in beautiful cedar cases of 25 cigars each packed in the historic 8-9-8 layering to preserve their perfect roundness.

HANDMADE CIGARS: BRAND LISTINGS

CUBITA SPANISH MARKET SELECTION
Handmade in Santiago, Dominican Republic.

Wrapper: Honduras   *Binder: Dom. Rep.*   *Filler: Dom. Rep., Nicaragua*

Shape	Name	Lgth	Ring	Wrapper
Double Corona	Churchill	7¼	50	CM
Robusto	Robusto	5¼	52	CM
Perfecto	Gran Cubita	5	50	CM
Toro	Toro	6	50	CM
Cigarillo	Mini	3¾	26	CM

Here is a full-bodied blend with a Honduran Criollo wrapper, Dominican Olor binder and Piloto Cubano and Nicaraguan Ligero, introduced in 2002. It is offered in elegant boxes of 20.

CUESTA-REY CABINET SELECTION
Handmade in Santiago, Dominican Republic.
Wrapper: Cameroon, USA/Connecticut

Binder: Dominican Republic   *Filler: Dominican Republic*

Shape	Name	Lgth	Ring	Wrapper
Giant	No. 1	8½	52	CC-Ma
Robusto	No. 47	4¾	52	CC-Ma
Lonsdale	No. 95	6¼	42	CC-Ma
Double Corona	No. 898	7	49	CC-Ma
Lonsdale	No. 1884	6¾	44	CC-Ma

Backed by more than a century of experience in the manufacture of handmade cigars since 1884, the Cabinet Selection offers mild-to-medium body featuring a Connecticut Shade wrapper, except for the No. 95, which uses a Cameroon wrapper. Connecticut Broadleaf tobacco is used for all of the maduro wrappers. All models are offered in cabinets of 25, except for the No. 898 (20s) and No. 1 (15s).

CUESTA-REY CENTENARIO COLECCION
Handmade in Santiago, Dominican Republic.

Wrapper: USA/Connecticut   *Binder: Dom. Rep.*   *Filler: Dom. Rep.*

HANDMADE CIGARS: BRAND LISTINGS

Shape	Name		Lgth	Ring	Wrapper
Corona	Centenario No. 5		5½	43	CC-Ma
Toro	Centenario No. 60		6	50	CC-Ma
Churchill	Aristocrat	*(glass tube)*	7¼	48	CC-Ma
Robusto	Robusto No. 7		4½	50	CC-Ma
Pyramid	Pyramid No. 9		6¼	52	CC-Ma
Torpedo	Belicoso No. 11		4⅞	50	CC-Ma
Robusto	Milano		5½	48	CC
Long Panatela	Rivera	*(tubed)*	7	35	CC
Robusto	Tuscany	*(tubed)*	5	50	CC
Small Panatela	Cameo		4¼	32	CC

Manufactured at the Tabacalera A. Fuente, this is a bolder version of the original Cuesta-Rey series, with a medium-to-full-bodied taste, introduced in 2000. The filler blend is based on four-year-aged leaves of Piloto Cubano. Most sizes are offered in boxes of 10, but there are plenty of options: packs of 3 (Tuscany), of 4 (No. 9, No. 11), of 5 (No. 5) and even a can of 12 (Milano)!

CUESTA-REY CENTRO FINO SUNGROWN
Handmade in Santiago, Dominican Republic.

Wrapper: Ecuador   *Binder: Dom. Rep.*   *Filler: Dom. Rep.*

Shape	Name		Lgth	Ring	Wrapper
Double Corona	Churchill No. 1		7	49	CM
Robusto	Robusto No. 7		4½	50	CM
Torpedo	Belicoso No. 11		4⅞	50	CM
Toro	Centro Fino No. 60		6	50	CM
Pyramid	Pyramid No. 9		6¼	52	CM
Long Corona	Captiva	*(tubed)*	6⅛	42	CM
Robusto	Cortez		5½	48	CM
Toro	No. 55		6½	55	CM

Recognizing the preferences for more robust cigars, the J.C. Newman Cigar Co.

HANDMADE CIGARS: BRAND LISTINGS

created the strongest version yet for the Cuesta-Rey line in mid-2003. By using a wrapper leaf from the "centro fino" (center) of tobacco grown in the Quevedo region of Ecuador with heavier Dominican-grown ligero, the result is a medium-to-full-bodied blend which has met with wide excitement. The line has expanded and replaced the Centennial Collection, discontinued in 2003. All sizes are offered in boxes of 10, except for the Captiva, offered in 20s.

CUESTA-REY STANFORD'S CAMEROON RESERVE
Handmade in Santiago, Dominican Republic.

Wrapper: Cameroon   *Binder: Dom. Rep.*   *Filler: Dom. Rep.*

Shape	Name	Lgth	Ring	Wrapper
Pyramid	Pyramid No. 9	6¼	52	CM
Double Corona	Churchill No. 1	7	49	CM

The Tabacalera A. Fuente originally created this medium-to-full-bodied blend to celebrate the 40th anniversary of Stanford Newman's introduction of Cameroon wrapper on Cuesta-Rey cigars in 1963. A small number of the Pyramid No. 9s appeared in a special Cuesta-Rey humidor that appeared in 2004. In 2005, the Pyramid No. 9 was issued in 1,750 boxes of 20 (35,000 cigars total). In 2006, the Churchill No. 1 size was created, issued in 1,000 boxes of 20 (20,000 total), with each cigar wrapped in gold paper!

CUETO
Handmade in Esteli, Nicaragua.

Wrapper: Nicaragua   *Binder: Nicaragua*   *Filler: Nicaragua*

Shape	Name	Lgth	Ring	Wrapper
Robusto	Rothchild	4⅞	52	CC-Ma

This handmade, member of the F.D. Grave line was introduced in 2003. It's medium in body and offered in boxes of 32.

CUEVAS
Handmade in Cruz des Almas, Brazil.

Wrapper: Brazil   *Binder: Brazil*   *Filler: Brazil*

Shape	Name	Lgth	Ring	Wrapper
Torpedo	Belicoso	6	52	CM-Ma
Double Corona	Churchill	7½	50	CM-Ma

Corona	Corona	5½	44	CM-Ma
Robusto	Robusto	5	52	CM-Ma
Toro	Toro	6	50	CM-Ma

This is a mild blend, introduced to the U.S. market in 2003 by the H.J. Bailey Company. It is offered in boxes of 25.

CUEVAS HABANOS
Handmade in Villa Gonzalez, Dominican Republic.

Wrapper: Ecuador, Indonesia   Binder: Dom. Rep.   Filler: Dom. Rep.

Shape	Name	Lgth	Ring	Wrapper
Toro	Toro	6	50	CC-Ma
Robusto	Robusto	4¾	52	CC-Ma
Churchill	Churchill	7	48	CC-Ma
Torpedo	Torpedo	6¼	52	CC-Ma
Corona	Corona	5¾	43	CC-Ma
Lonsdale	Lonsdale	7	43	CC-Ma

Introduced in 2005, this is a medium-to-full-bodied blend with a choice of wrappers: Ecuadorian-grown (Connecticut seed) or Indonesian (maduro). Both are offered in boxes of 25.

CUMBRES GOLD   ★New★
Handmade in San Jose, Costa Rica.

Wrapper: Costa Rica   Binder: Costa Rica   Filler: Costa Rica

Shape	Name	Lgth	Ring	Wrapper
Double Corona	Churchill	7	52	CM
Long Corona	Corona	6¼	44	CM
Churchill	Doble Corona	7½	46	CM
Petit Corona	Petit	5	42	CM
Pyramid	Piramide	6	52	CM
Robusto	Robusto	5	50	CM

Small Panatela	Senoritas	4½	32	CM
Toro	Toro	6	52	CM
Torpedo	Torpedo	6	52	CM

Introduced to the U.S. market in 2007, all of the tobaccos for these cigars was grown from ancestral seeds of Cuban tobacco strains of the 1940s and 1950s at the Tabacos de la Cordillera in Costa Rica. The "Cumbres de Puriscal Gold" line is mild-to-medium in body, offered in boxes of 20 for most shapes, but 24 for the Senoritas and 25 for the Churchill and Robusto.

CUSANO 10

Handmade in Santiago, Dominican Republic.

Wrapper: Ecuador   *Binder: Mexico*

Filler: Dom. Rep., Honduras, USA/Connecticut

Shape	Name	Lgth	Ring	Wrapper
Petit Corona	Crown Corona	5	42	CC

Here is the 10th anniversary cigar from Cusano, introduced in 2004. It features a Cuban-seed wrapper and a Sumatra-seed binder. It's a limited-production blend that's medium-to-full in body and offered in individually serial numbered boxes of 10.

CUSANO 18

Handmade in Santiago, Dominican Republic.

Wrapper: USA/Connecticut   *Binder: Dom. Rep., USA/Connecticut*

Filler: Brazil, Dominican Republic

Shape	Name	Lgth	Ring	Wrapper
Robusto	Robusto	5	50	CC-Ma
Grand Corona	Toro	6½	46	CC-Ma
Double Corona	Churchill	7¼	50	CC-Ma
Toro	Gordo	6¼	54	CC-Ma

Here is a rarity, a limited-production cigar which features 18-year-old filler leaves from Tabadom, first offered in 2003. The natural-wrapped "Double Connecticut" blend is of medium body with Connecticut Shade leaves for both wrapper and binder and Dominican-grown filler. The "Paired Maduro" debuted in 2005 with a Connecticut Broadleaf maduro wrapper, Dominican binder and aged Dominican

Olor and Brazilian Mata Fina maduro filler. Of course, they're offered in boxes of 18.

CUSANO CC
Handmade in Santiago, Dominican Republic.

Wrapper: Ecuador   Binder: Dom. Rep.   Filler: Dom. Rep.

Shape	Name	Lgth	Ring	Wrapper
Robusto	Robusto	5	50	CM
Long Corona	Corona	6½	42	CM
Double Corona	Churchill	7½	50	CM
Torpedo	Torpedo	6	52	CM
Short Panatela	Café Robusto	5	36	CM

This bundled brand was introduced in 2002 and offers a full-bodied taste thanks to its sun-grown wrapper.

CUSANO COROJO '97
Handmade in Santiago, Dominican Republic.

Wrapper: Ecuador   Binder: Mexico   Filler: Dom. Rep.

Shape	Name	Lgth	Ring	Wrapper
Double Corona	Churchill	7	50	CM
Toro	Toro	6	50	CM
Robusto	Robusto	5	50	CM
Torpedo	Torpedo	6	52	CM

This brand debuted in 2004 and uses sun-grown Corojo wrapper leaf from the 1997 harvest. It is medium-to-full in body and available in boxes of 20.

CUSANO M1
Handmade in Santiago, Dominican Republic.

Wrapper: USA/Connecticut   Binder: Dom. Rep.   Filler: Dom. Rep.

Shape	Name	Lgth	Ring	Wrapper
Robusto	Robusto	5	50	CC
Lonsdale	Corona	6½	42	CC

Double Corona	Churchill	7½	50	CC
Torpedo	Torpedo	6	52	CC
Short Panatela	Café Robusto	5	36	CC

Here is a mild-bodied smoke, introduced in 2000. It is available in bundles of 20.

CUSANO MC

Handmade in Santiago, Dominican Republic.

Wrapper: USA/Connecticut   Binder: Dom. Rep.   Filler: Dom. Rep.

Shape	Name	Lgth	Ring	Wrapper
Robusto	Robusto	5	50	CC
Lonsdale	Corona	6½	42	CC
Double Corona	Churchill	7½	50	CC
Torpedo	Torpedo	6	52	CC
Short Panatela	Café Robusto	5	36	CC

This bundled brand debuted in 2001 and offers a medium-bodied taste with a pleasant aroma, offered in 20s.

CUSANO P1

Handmade in Santiago, Dominican Republic.

Wrapper: USA/Connecticut   Binder: Dom. Rep.   Filler: Dom. Rep.

Shape	Name	Lgth	Ring	Wrapper
Robusto	Robusto	5	50	CC
Lonsdale	Corona	6½	42	CC
Double Corona	Churchill	7½	50	CC
Torpedo	Torpedo	6	52	CC
Short Panatela	Café Robusto	5	36	CC

Introduced in 2000, this is a medium-to-full-bodied smoke, featuring a Connecticut Broadleaf wrapper. It is available in bundles of 20.

brand was developed to Mr. Marshall's personal standards. It offers a medium body, with three to four-year-old tobaccos.

DANIEL MARSHALL BLACK LABEL HONDURAN AGED
Handmade in Danli, Honduras.

Wrapper: Honduras   Binder: Mexico   Filler: Honduras, Nicaragua

Shape	Name	Lgth	Ring	Wrapper
Robusto	Robusto	5	50	CC
Double Corona	Churchill	7½	50	CC

Created in 1996, this cigar exhibits none of the harshness which sometimes accompanies Honduran-made cigars. It boasts a Connecticut Shade wrapper and has a medium-to-full body; it is presented in all-cedar boxes of 25.

DANIEL MARSHALL RED LABEL   ★*Returns*★
Handmade in Santiago, Dominican Republic.

Wrapper: Ecuador   Binder: Dom. Rep.   Filler: Dom. Rep.

Shape	Name	Lgth	Ring	Wrapper
Robusto	Robusto	5	50	CC
Long Corona	Corona	6	43	CC
Churchill	Churchill	7	48	CC

Introduced in 1999 and now back on the market after a short hiatus, this blends sports a Connecticut-seed wrapper helps to provide a medium-bodied flavor. Crafted to complement the Ambiente by D. Marshall Humidor series, Red Label cigars are offered in slide-top cedar boxes.

DANIEL MARSHALL WHITE LABEL DOMINICAN   ★*Returns*★
Handmade in Santiago, Dominican Republic.

Wrapper: Cameroon   Binder: Mexico   Filler: Dom. Rep.

Shape	Name	Lgth	Ring	Wrapper
Long Corona	Corona	6	44	CM

You cannot stop the expanding cigar empire of the energetic Daniel Marshall, you can only hope to contain him! Introduced in 1999 and re-introduced in 2007, this line offers a medium-bodied, spicy and sweet smoke in three popular sizes, offered in all-cedar boxes of 25.

DANLYS
Handmade in Danli, Honduras.

Wrapper: Honduras *Binder: Mexico* *Filler: Honduras, Mexico*

Shape	Name	Lgth	Ring	Wrapper
Double Corona	Churchill	7½	50	CM-Ma
Panatela	Panatela	6	38	CM
Giant	President/Viajante	8	54	CM-Ma
Toro	Toro	6	50	CM-Ma
Lonsdale	No. 1	7	43	CM-Ma
Petit Corona	No. 4	5	42	CM

This is a fairly old brand, dating from 1972 and named for the city of manufacture ("Danlis," get it?). It is medium-to-full in body and is offered in natural and maduro wrapper shades, in economical bundles of 25.

DAVIDOFF
Handmade in Santiago, Dominican Republic.

Wrapper: Ecuador, USA/Connecticut *Binder: Dom. Rep.* *Filler: Dom. Rep.*

Shape	Name	Lgth	Ring	Wrapper
Long Panatela	Classic No. 1	7½	38	CC
Panatela	Classic No. 2 *(tubes available)*	6	38	CC
Slim Panatela	Classic No. 3	5⅛	30	CC
Cigarillo	Ambassadrice	4½	26	CC
Small Panatela	Primeros	4⅛	34	CC
	Aniversario Series:			
Giant	Aniversario No. 1 *(tube available)*	8⅔	48	CC
Churchill	Aniversario No. 2	7	48	CC
Toro	Aniversario No. 3 *(tubed)*	6	50	CC
	Grand Cru Series:			
Lonsdale	Grand Cru No. 1	6⅛	43	CC

HANDMADE CIGARS: BRAND LISTINGS

Corona	Grand Cru No. 2	5⅝	43	CC
Petit Corona	Grand Cru No. 3	5	43	CC
Petit Corona	Grand Cru No. 4	4⅝	41	CC
Petit Corona	Grand Cru No. 5	4	41	CC
	Millennium Series:			
Robusto	Robusto *(tube available)*	5¼	50	CM
Long Corona	Lonsdale	6	43	CM
Toro	Churchill	6¾	48	CM
Petit Corona	Petit Corona	4½	41	CM
Torpedo	Piramides	6⅛	52	CM
Robusto	Short Robusto	4¼	52	CM
Toro	Toro	6	50	CM
	Special Series:			
Double Corona	Double "R"	7½	50	CC
Robusto	Special "R" *(tubes available)*	4⅞	50	CC
Pyramid	Special "T"	6	52	CC
Perfecto	Short Perfecto	4⅞	52	CC
Petit Corona	Entreacto	3½	43	CC
	Thousand Series:			
Small Panatela	1000	4⅝	34	CC
Petit Corona	2000 *(tubes available)*	5	43	CC
Slim Panatela	3000	7	33	CC
Long Corona	4000	6⅛	43	CC
Grand Corona	5000	5⅝	46	CC
Robusto	6000	5	48	CC
	Small cigars:			
Cigarillo	Exquisitos	3⅝	22	CM

A carefully controlled series of events leads to the production of a Davidoff cigar.

HANDMADE CIGARS: BRAND LISTINGS

This celebrated brand, first created in Cuba in 1946, requires tobaccos which have been aged up to four years and only the finest leaves are used in a factory which is solely dedicated to the creation of this brand. Introduced in November 1990, four different blends are used to create the five different Davidoff series: the large-sized, but mild and light Anniversarios; the mild, delicate and aromatic Nos. 1-2-3, Tubos, Primeros and Ambassadrice; the fuller-bodied, but still mild "Thousand" series; and the fullest-bodied Grand Cru and Special ranges, which share the same blend. All use the finest Connecticut-grown wrapper available.

The Millennium Blend debuted in 2001, offering a full-bodied taste in four elegant sizes. This group uses an Ecuadorian, sun-grown wrapper and has a double band. You can find them in packs of four or five, or in boxes of 10 (Churchill only), 20 (Tubos and Short Robusto) or 25. The Exquisito is a mild-to-medium-bodied smoke, with Ecuadorian wrappers and Dominican binder and fillers.

Davidoff has been deeply involved in the production of limited-edition cigars. It started in 1997 with the "535" celebrating the 10th anniversary of the company's store at 535 Madison Avenue in New York (6 x 50 toros in boxes of 20). In 2002, it began formal production of Davidoff Limited Editions:

2002:	Special 48 Special 53	(4¼ x 48 perfecto in boxes of 10) (4⅞ x 53 perfecto in boxes of 10)
2003:	Panetela Extra	(6¼ x 40 in boxes of 10)
2004:	Robusto Real <<Especiales 7>>	(5½ x 48 in boxes of 10)
2005:	Robusto Intenso	(5⅛ x 52 in boxes of 10)
2006:	Diademas Finas Robusto 100	(6¾ x 50 unbanded perfectos in boxes of 10) (5 x 50 in boxes of 8)
2007:	Puro Robusto	(5⅜ x 52 in boxes of 10)

The 2007 Puro Robusto is made from all-Dominican tobaccos and has a pigtail head. It offers a full aroma and a peppery taste.

A special, limited-production cigar called the Royal Salomones (an 8 1/4-inch by 57-ring perfecto) was introduced in late 2007 for sale only in Davidoff of Geneva shops. It's a full-bodied blend with an Ecuadorian wrapper and Dominican binder and fillers offered in chests of 50.

HANDMADE CIGARS: BRAND LISTINGS

DEFIANCE ★New★
Handmade in Danli, Honduras.

Wrapper: Nicaragua   Binder: Nicaragua   Filler: Honduras, Nicaragua

Shape	Name	Lgth	Ring	Wrapper
Toro	The Guardian	6½	52	CM
Grand Corona	The Sentry	6	46	CM
Torpedo	The Instigator	6	54	CM
Robusto	The Renegade	5	50	CM

Created in 2007, this brand is designed to satisfy a smoker's needs for both a quality cigar and political resistance to the anti-tobacco forces in the U.S. Xikar Corporation, which developed the band, is contributing five percent of the per-box wholesale value of Defiance cigars and accessories to state tobacco-rights coalitions quarterly. The cigars themselves are medium in body featuring Criollo wrappers and Corojo binder leaves.

DELICIOSO
Handmade in Santiago, Dominican Republic.

Wrapper: USA/Connecticut   Binder: Dom. Rep.   Filler: Dom. Rep.

Shape	Name	Lgth	Ring	Wrapper
Double Corona	Presidente	7	50	CC
Toro	Toro	6	50	CC
Robusto	Robusto	5	50	CC
Corona	Corona	5½	44	CC
Petit Corona	Petit	4	40	CC
Long Corona	Panatela	6	40	CC
Small Panatela	Cigarette	4½	32	CC
Cigarillo	Cigarillo	4	20	CC

This is a mild-to-medium-bodied flavored cigar, introduced in 2004 by the Crown David Int'l Cigar Co. It is available with cherry, chocolate, cinnamon or vanilla flavoring, in boxes of 25 for most sizes and in 10s for the Cigarette and Cigarillo.

HANDMADE CIGARS: BRAND LISTINGS

DELUXE
Handmade, with mixed filler, in Danli, Honduras.

Wrapper: Honduras   *Binder: Honduras*   *Filler: Honduras*

Shape	Name	Lgth	Ring	Wrapper
Churchill	Churchill Deluxe	7	48	CM
Robusto	Robusto Deluxe	5	50	CM

Introduced by Camacho Cigars in 2003, Deluxe is offered in two sizes, with a medium body, and presented in boxes of 50.

DIAMOND CROWN
Handmade in Santiago, Dominican Republic.

Wrapper: USA/Connecticut   *Binder: Dom. Rep.*   *Filler: Dom. Rep.*

Shape	Name	Lgth	Ring	Wrapper
Giant	Robusto No. 1	8½	54	CC
Double Corona	Robusto No. 2	7½	54	CC
Toro	Robusto No. 3	6½	54	CC
Robusto	Robusto No. 4	5½	54	CC
Robusto	Robusto No. 5	4½	54	CC
Perfecto	Figurado No. 6	6	64	CC
Torpedo	Pyramid No. 7	6¾	54	CC-Ma

This mild-bodied, almost all-54 ring series is an impossible-to-find, 1996-introduced product of the Tabacalera A. Fuente y Cia., made for the J.C. Newman Cigar Co. of Tampa, Florida. You can find these cigars in elegantly-appointed boxes of 15.

DIAMOND CROWN MAXIMUS
Handmade in Santiago, Dominican Republic.

Wrapper: Ecuador   *Binder: Dom. Rep.*   *Filler: Dom. Rep.*

Shape	Name	Lgth	Ring	Wrapper
Giant	No. 1 Double Corona	8	50	CM
Double Corona	No. 2 Churchill	7	50	CM
Pyramid	No. 3 Pyramid	6⅜	50	CM

Toro	No. 4 Toro	6	50	CM
Robusto	No. 5 Robusto	5	50	CM
Torpedo	No. 10 Double Belicoso	6¾	54	CM

This is a full-bodied complement to the original Diamond Crown line, featuring a dark, Ecuadorian-grown wrapper. Introduced by the J.C. Newman Cigar Co. in 2003, it offers a rich flavor in a limited-production brand, offered in boxes of 20.

In 2005, a special edition of Diamond Crown Maximus in the original perfecto shape made by company founder J.C. Newman in 1895 (5¼ x 54) was offered in a total of 2,500 cigars, in 250 specially-prepared humidors.

In 2006, a special "Stanford's 90th Diamond Crown Maximus" – a 7-inch by 48-ring Churchill – was produced to honor Stanford Newman's 90th birthday (June 12; he died later in the year). It featured a Cameroon wrapper and Dominican-grown binder and fillers; only 20,000 were produced, released in 1,000 boxes of 20 cigars each.

DIANA SILVIUS
Handmade in Santiago, Dominican Republic.

Wrapper: USA/Connecticut   Binder: Dom. Rep.   Filler: Dom. Rep.

Shape	Name	Lgth	Ring	Wrapper
Double Corona	Diana Churchill	7	50	CC
Robusto	Diana Robusto	4⅞	52	CC-Ma
Churchill	Diana 2000	6¾	46	CC
Lonsdale	Diana Corona	6½	42	CC

Introduced in 1990, this is a superb smoke which is medium in body and rich in flavor. The blend of four filler tobaccos produces a smooth finish that leaves a hint of sweetness on the palate. The maduro-wrapped Robusto, introduced in 2003, features Connecticut Broadleaf. Every one of these cigars is made by the master rollers of Tabacalera A. Fuente y Cia. and is offered in boxes of 25 with the Robusto also available in 10s.

DOMAINE AVO
Handmade in Santiago, Dominican Republic.

Wrapper: Ecuador   Binder: Dom. Rep.   Filler: Dom. Rep.

HANDMADE CIGARS: BRAND LISTINGS

Shape	Name	Lgth	Ring	Wrapper
Robusto	<10>	5⅛	50	CC
Perfecto	<20>	4⅝	50	CC
Churchill	<30>	6¾	48	CC
Torpedo	<40>	6	52	CC
Perfecto	<50>	6	54	CC
Petit Corona	<60>	5	43	CC
Small Panatela	Puritos	4	30	CC

The purple-banded Domaine Avo series was introduced in 1998 to celebrate ten years of Avo cigars with a full-bodied taste. It features a Connecticut-seed, Ecuadorian-grown wrapper and is offered in boxes of 25 and packs of four or five.

DOMINGOLD
Handmade in Santiago, Dominican Republic.
Wrapper: USA/Connecticut
Binder: Honduras   Filler: Brazil, Dominican Republic, Nicaragua

Shape	Name	Lgth	Ring	Wrapper
Toro	Toro	6	50	CC-Ma
Long Corona	Lonsdale	6½	42	CC-Ma
Robusto	Robusto	5	50	CC-Ma
Corona	Corona	5½	42	CC-Ma
Double Corona	Churchill	7	50	CC-Ma
Robusto	Phat	5	65	CC-Ma
Torpedo	Belicoso	6	52	CC
Torpedo	Torpedo	6½	52	CC-Ma

These bundles of 20 cigars are seconds of one of the finest cigar factories in the Dominican Republic. You'll be hard-pressed to tell the difference between these medium-strength cigars and their more-famous siblings. The natural-wrapped version uses the Cameroon wrapper, while the maduro edition features Connecticut Broadleaf. The Phat size is offered in a bundle of 10 only.

HANDMADE CIGARS: BRAND LISTINGS

DOMINICAN BUNDLES
Handmade in Santiago, Dominican Republic.
Wrapper: Indonesia, USA/Connecticut   Binder: Dom. Rep.   Filler: Dom. Rep.

Shape	Name	Lgth	Ring	Wrapper
Double Corona	Presidente	7¾	52	CC-CM-Ma
Double Corona	Churchill	6⅞	50	CC-CM-Ma
Toro	Regulares	6	50	CC-CM-Ma
Lonsdale	No. 1	6¾	44	CC-CM-Ma
Corona	No. 4	5½	44	CC-CM-Ma
Robusto	Rothschild	5	50	CC-CM-Ma
Small Panatela	Babies	4½	32	CC-CM-Ma
Giant	Gigante	8½	52	CC-CM-Ma
Toro	Double Magnum	6½	60	CC-CM-Ma
Torpedo	Torpedo	6	52	CC-CM-Ma
Panatela	Super Fino	6	35	CC-CM-Ma

Offered by Juan Sosa's Antillian Cigar Company, these are medium-bodied, value cigars available with a choice of Connecticut natural or maduro wrappers or Sumatra wrappers in bundles of 25.

DOMINICAN DELICIAS
Handmade in Santiago, Dominican Republic.
Wrapper: USA/Connecticut   Binder: Dom. Rep.   Filler: Dom. Rep.

Shape	Name	Lgth	Ring	Wrapper
Robusto	No. 550	5	50	CC
Lonsdale	No. 643	6½	43	CC
Toro	No. 650	6	50	CC
Double Corona	No. 750	7	50	CC

Here is a mild-to-medium-bodied product of the MATASA Factory offered by Mike's Cigars introduced in 2003. It's an excellent value and available in slide-top boxes of 25.

HANDMADE CIGARS: BRAND LISTINGS

DOMINICAN DELIGHTS
BY VICTOR SINCLAIR
Handmade in Santiago, Dominican Republic.

Wrapper: Indonesia   Binder: Indonesia   Filler: Dom. Rep.

Shape	Name	Lgth	Ring	Wrapper
Cigarillo	Miniature	4	28	CM

This is a mild cigar which is made by hand and is offered in flavored bundles of 25 or 50 in cherry, rum or vanilla.

DOMINICAN ESTATES
Handmade in Santiago, Dominican Republic.

Wrapper: USA/Connecticut   Binder: Dom. Rep.   Filler: Dom. Rep.

Shape	Name	Lgth	Ring	Wrapper
Toro	Corona Gorda	6	50	CC
Double Corona	Double Corona	7	50	CC
Corona	Full Corona	5½	43	CC
Lonsdale	Lonsdale	6½	43	CC
Robusto	Robusto	4½	50	CC

Distributed by Cigars by Santa Clara, these cigars are mild, thanks to their Connecticut (or Connecticut-seed grown in Ecuador) wrappers, and very well constructed for an easy draw, available in bundles of 10.

DOMINICAN ORIGINAL
Handmade in Santiago, Dominican Republic.

Wrapper: USA/Connecticut   Binder: Dom. Rep.   Filler: Dom. Rep.

Shape	Name	Lgth	Ring	Wrapper
Double Corona	Churchill	7	50	CC
Giant	Fat Tub	10	66	CC
Giant	King Kong	8½	52	CC
Lonsdale	No. 1	6¾	43	CC
Corona	No. 2	5¾	43	CC-Ma

Double Corona	Presidente	7½	50	CC
Robusto	Robusto	4½	50	CC
Toro	Toro	6	50	CC

From Mike's Cigars, the Connecticut wrapper and Dominican filler give these cigars a mild taste, and they are offered in bundle packs of 25.

DOMINICAN REPUBLIC GOLD
Handmade in Navarette, Dominican Republic.
Wrapper: Dom. Rep.   Binder: Dom. Rep.   Filler: Dom. Rep., Nicaragua

Shape	Name	Lgth	Ring	Wrapper
Robusto	Robusto	5	50	CM
Long Corona	Extra Corona	6	42	CM
Grand Corona	Corona	6	46	CM
Toro	Toro	6	50	CM
Pyramid	Piramide	6½	52	CM
Torpedo	Torpedo	6½	52	CM
Double Corona	Churchill	7	50	CM

Also known as D.R.G., this is a full-bodied cigar introduced in 2002. It is offered in boxes of 25.

DOMINICAN SANTIAGO SELECTION   ★New★
Handmade in Santiago, Dominican Republic.
Wrapper: Brazil, Ecuador   Binder: Dom. Rep.   Filler: Dom. Rep., Nicaragua

Shape	Name	Lgth	Ring	Wrapper
Corona	No. 4	5½	42	CC-Ma
Long Corona	Cetro	6¼	44	CC-Ma
Robusto	Robusto	5	50	CC-Ma
Toro	Toro	6	50	CC-Ma
Churchill	Churchill	7	48	CC-Ma
Double Corona	Presidente	7½	50	CC-Ma

HANDMADE CIGARS: BRAND LISTINGS

Giant	Viajante	8½	52	CC-Ma
Torpedo	Torpedo	6	52	CC-Ma

These blends are offered by the Charles Fairmorn Factory, with a mild-to-medium taste with a natural wrapper or medium-bodied with a maduro wrapper. All sizes are offered in bundles of 25.

DOMINICAN SWEETS
Handmade in Santiago, Dominican Republic.
Wrapper: USA/Connecticut   Binder: Dom. Rep.   Filler: Dom. Rep.

Shape	Name	Lgth	Ring	Wrapper
Small Panatela	Small	5	30	CC
Panatela	Medium	5½	36	CC
Long Corona	Large	6	42	CC

This DomRey Cigar brand was introduced in 2001 and is mild in flavor, with the taste of vanilla, cognac or rum. It is presented in bundles of 20.

DOMINICANO ★New★
Handmade in Santiago, Dominican Republic.
Wrapper: Indonesia   Binder: Dom. Rep.   Filler: Dom. Rep.

Shape	Name	Lgth	Ring	Wrapper
Short Panatela	D.R. Dominicano	5	38	CM

Offered by Obrigada USA in 2007, this is a medium-to-full-bodied cigar available in only one size and offered in packs of five.

DOMINICOS
Handmade in Santiago, Dominican Republic.
Wrapper: USA/Connecticut, Pennsylvania   Binder: Indonesia   Filler: Dom. Rep.

Shape	Name	Lgth	Ring	Wrapper
Robusto	Robusto	5	50	CC-Ma
Toro	Toro	6	50	CC-Ma
Churchill	Churchill	7	48	CC-Ma

HANDMADE CIGARS: BRAND LISTINGS

Giant	Presidente	8	52	CC-Ma
Torpedo	Torpedo	6¼	52	CC-Ma

This brand was introduced by Toraño Cigars in 1999 and offers a value-priced, hand-made cigar of mild-to-medium body. You can take your choice of wrapper from Connecticut (natural) or Pennsylvania (maduro) in bundles of 25.

DOMINIQUE
Handmade in Santiago, Dominican Republic.

Wrapper: USA/Connecticut   Binder: Dom. Rep.   Filler: Dom. Rep.

Shape	Name	Lgth	Ring	Wrapper
Giant	No. 52	8½	52	Cl-CC-Ma
Lonsdale	No. 74	7	43	Cl-CC-Ma
Grand Corona	Madison	6	46	Cl-CC-Ma
Corona	Nacionales	5½	42	CC-Ma
Double Corona	Pierce	6⅞	49	Cl-CC-Ma
Robusto	Toro	4½	50	CC-Ma

Inspired by the 1983 version of the 1963 hit song "Dominique," these bundles are of high quality and moderate pricing, offering a mild-to-medium-bodied flavor in bundled packages of 25 cigars each.

DON ANTONIO
Handmade in Santiago, Dominican Republic.

Wrapper: USA/Connecticut   Binder: Dom. Rep.   Filler: Dom. Rep., Nicaragua

Shape	Name		Lgth	Ring	Wrapper
Long Corona	Lonsdale	*(tubed)*	6¼	44	CC
Robusto	Robusto	*(tubed)*	5	50	CC
Churchill	Churchill	*(tubed)*	7	48	CC

From the Charles Fairmorn factory comes this 2005 edition of Don Antonio in tubes, all with a mild-bodied flavor, available in boxes of 10.

HANDMADE CIGARS: BRAND LISTINGS

DON BARRETO
Handmade in Esteli, Nicaragua.

Wrapper: Nicaragua *Binder: Nicaragua* *Filler: Nicaragua*

Shape	Name	Lgth	Ring	Wrapper
Robusto	Robusto Porto	4¾	50	CM
Grand Corona	Toro Flaco	6	46	CM
Torpedo	Torpedo	6	52	CM

Made by the Oliva Family in Nicaragua, it's medium-to-full in body with up to four year of aging. Offered by Famous Smoke Shop, it's available in boxes of 25.

DON CISSO ★*Returns*★
Handmade, with mixed filler, in Santiago, Dominican Republic.

Wrapper: Indonesia, USA/Connecticut *Binder: Dom. Rep.* *Filler: Dom. Rep.*

The Cigar Factory del Yaque uses sandwich filler for this cigar for a medium body. There are five sizes, all offered in boxes of 25.

DON DIEGO
Handmade in La Romana, Dominican Republic.

Wrapper: USA/Connecticut *Binder: Dom. Rep.* *Filler: Brazil, Dom. Rep.*

Shape	Name	Lgth	Ring	Wrapper
Small Panatela	Babies	5¼	33	CM
Petit Corona	Chicos	5¼	33	CC
Petit Corona	Coronas Major (tubed)	5½	44	CC
Corona	Coronas	5½	44	CC
Toro	Grande	6	52	CC
Lonsdale	Lonsdales	6⅝	44	CC
Short Panatela	No. 5 Elite	4½	38	CC
Double Corona	Churchill	7	54	CC
Robusto	Robusto	5	52	CC
	Machine-made, with short filler:			
Small Panatela	Preludes	4	30	CC

HANDMADE CIGARS: BRAND LISTINGS

Well-known for its mild-to-medium-bodied taste, Don Diego cigars are popular thanks to their consistency of construction, accessible strength and excellent value. The brand originated in 1964 in the Canary Islands, but production was moved to the Dominican Republic in 1982. The packaging was revised in 2007 with most shapes in boxes of 27 except for the Corona Major (box of 21), No. 5 Elite (five packs only), Preludes (tins of 10) and the Babies and Chicos (boxes of 60).

DON DIEGO ANIVERSARIO
Handmade in La Romana, Dominican Republic.

Wrapper: Ecuador   Binder: USA/Connecticut   Filler: Dom. Rep., Peru, Nicaragua

Shape	Name	Lgth	Ring	Wrapper
Lonsdale	No. 1	6⅝	44	CC
Torpedo	No. 2	6⅛	52	CC
Corona	No. 3	5½	44	CC
Robusto	Lord Rothchilde	5	52	CC
Double Corona	Prime Minister	7	54	CC
Toro	Toro	6	54	CC

Introduced in 2003, this is a medium-bodied blend introduced to commemorate the 40th anniversary of the brand. It is offered in elegant, varnished cases of 25 cigars each, featuring a smooth Sumatra-seed wrapper and Connecticut Broadleaf wrapper.

DON DOUGLAS CABINET SERIES
Handmade in Esteli, Nicaragua.

Wrapper: Ecuador   Binder: Dom. Rep.   Filler: Dom. Rep., Nicaragua

Shape	Name	Lgth	Ring	Wrapper
Robusto	Robusto	5	50	CC
Churchill	Churchill	6⅞	48	CC
Torpedo	Belicoso	6	54	CC

Introduced by Bucanero Cigars in 2003, this is a mild-to-medium-bodied series which honors the founder of the Tabacalera Tambor. It is offered with a Sumatra-seed wrapper in elegant wood boxes of 12.

HANDMADE CIGARS: BRAND LISTINGS

DON ELIAS ★*New*★
Handmade in Santiago, Dominican Republic.

Wrapper: Indonesia   Binder: Dom. Rep.   Filler: Dom. Rep.

Shape	Name	Lgth	Ring	Wrapper
Robusto	Robusto	5	50	CM
Grand Corona	Lonsdale	6	46	CM
Toro	Toro	6	52	CM
Double Corona	Churchill	7½	50	CM

Here is a medium-bodied cigar that has been on and off the market, but was introduced again by Meier & Dutch in 2007. It's available in boxes of 25.

DON ELIO'S ★*New*★
Handmade in Miami, Florida, USA.

Wrapper: Cameroon   Binder: Dom. Rep.   Filler: Dom. Rep., Nicaragua

Shape	Name	Lgth	Ring	Wrapper
Petit Corona	Petit Corona	4	42	CM
Robusto	Robusto	5	50	CM
Churchill	Churchill	7	48	CM
Torpedo	Torpedo	6	52	CM

From Little Havana in Miami comes this full-bodied blend, introduced in 2007. It's distributed by Robusto's Cigar Co. and offered in boxes of 25.

DON ELLIOTT
Handmade in Santiago, Dominican Republic.
Wrapper: Dom. Rep., Indonesia, USA/Connecticut
Binder: Dominican Republic   Filler: Dominican Republic

This is a one-size (6 x 50), medium-to-full-bodied cigar from the Cigar Factory del Yaque, introduced in 2004. It is offered in bundles of 25 in a choice of wrappers, including a Dominican maduro.

DON FELO
Handmade, with short filler, in Danli, Honduras.
Wrapper: Honduras   Binder: Honduras   Filler: Honduras

HANDMADE CIGARS: BRAND LISTINGS

Shape	Name	Lgth	Ring	Wrapper
Double Corona		7½	50	CM
Churchill		7	48	CM
Panatela		6⅛	38	CM
Robusto		5	50	CM
Corona		5½	44	CM
Small Panatela	Felito	4¾	32	CM
Cigarillo	Piccolino	3½	24	CM

This is a medium-bodied line offered by Camacho Cigars, offered with a Sumatra-seed wrapper but without shape names for most sizes in bundles of 25, boxes of 50 for the Piccolinos and 10s for the Felitos.

DON GONZALEZ ★New★
Handmade in Esteli, Nicaragua.

Wrapper: Nicaragua, USA/Connecticut   Binder: Nicaragua   Filler: Nicaragua

Shape	Name	Lgth	Ring	Wrapper
Robusto	Robusto	5	50	CC-Ma
Toro	Toro	6	50	CC-Ma
Double Corona	Churchill	7	50	CC-Ma
Torpedo	Torpedo	6½	54	CC-Ma

Offered with a choice of a Connecticut natural-shade or Nicaraguan maduro wrapper, this blend debuted in 2007. It's mild-to-medium with natural wrappers and medium-to-full-bodied in maduro. All sizes are offered in boxes of 20.

DON JACINTO
Handmade in Miami, Florida, USA.

Wrapper: USA/Connecticut   Binder: Ecuador   Filler: Dom. Rep., Mexico

The Caonao Cigar Factory introduced this three-shape, mild-to-medium-bodied brand in 2000. It is offered in bundles of 25 cigars with a choice of natural or maduro wrappers.

HANDMADE CIGARS: BRAND LISTINGS

DON JOSE
Handmade in Danli, Honduras.

Wrapper: Honduras *Binder: Honduras* *Filler: Honduras*

Shape	Name	Lgth	Ring	Wrapper
Giant	El Grandee	8½	52	CC-Ma
Double Corona	San Marco	7	50	CC-Ma
Toro	Turbo	6	50	CC-Ma
Long Corona	Granada	6	43	CC-Ma
Robusto	Valrico	4½	50	CC-Ma
Torpedo	Torpedo	6½	52	CC-Ma

Distributed by the J.C. Newman Cigar Co., these Honduran handmades provide a rich taste in both a natural and maduro wrapper. The tobaccos are all grown in Honduras of Cuban-seed origin and are offered in bundles of 20 cigars each.

DON KIKI LIMITED RESERVE
Handmade in Esteli, Nicaragua

Wrapper: Nicaragua BROWN LABEL: *Binder: Nicaragua* *Filler: Nicaragua*

Wrapper: Nicaragua GREEN LABEL: *Binder: Nicaragua* *Binder: Nicaragua*

Wrapper: Nicaragua RED LABEL: *Binder: Nicaragua* *Filler: Nicaragua*

Shape	Name	Lgth	Ring	Wrapper
	Brown Label:			
Torpedo	Torpedo	6	54	CM
Double Corona	Churchill	7	52	CM
Toro	Toro	6	52	CM
Perfecto	Figurado	4½	48	CM
	Green Label:			
Double Corona	Churchill	7	52	CM

Robusto	Robusto	5	50	CM
Toro	Toro	6	52	CM
Toro	Double Corona	6	48	CM
Corona	Corona	5½	44	CM
Torpedo	Torpedo	6½	54	CM
	Red Label:			
Double Corona	Churchill	7	52	CM
Torpedo	Torpedo	6½	54	CM
Toro	Toro	6	52	CM
Robusto	Robusto	5	52	CM
Corona	Corona	5½	44	CM
Toro	Double Corona	6	48	CM

Master blender Kiki Berger developed the original blend in 2003, but two were added in 2004. The Brown Label offers a full-bodied taste while the Green Label is medium-bodied and the Red Label is mild-to-medium, slightly spicy taste. The Brown Label is offered in boxes of 25, while the Red and Green Labels are available in bundles of 25.

DON KIKI VINTAGE SELECTION
Handmade in Esteli, Nicaragua.

Wrapper: USA/Connecticut   *Binder: Nicaragua*   *Filler: Nicaragua*

Shape	Name	Lgth	Ring	Wrapper
Torpedo	Torpedo	6½	54	CC
Double Corona	Churchill	7	50	CC
Toro	Double Corona	6	48	CC
Robusto	Robusto	5	54	CC

Cuban Crafters introduced this blend, named for Kiki Berger, in 2006. It's medium in body featuring a Connecticut Shade wrapper, available in boxes of 20.

HANDMADE CIGARS: BRAND LISTINGS

DON LINO
Handmade in Santiago, Dominican Republic.

Wrapper: USA/Connecticut   Binder: Dom. Rep.   Filler: Dom. Rep.

Shape	Name	Lgth	Ring	Wrapper
Double Corona	Churchill	7½	50	CC
Lonsdale	No. 1 *(glass tube available)*	6½	42	CC
Corona Extra	Toro	5½	46	CC
Robusto	Robusto	5½	50	CC
Torpedo	Belicoso	6¼	52	CC
Torpedo	Petit Belicoso	5	52	CC
Small Panatela	Epicure	5	34	CC
Robusto	Rothschild	4½	50	CC

Don Lino is now made in the Dominican Republic, having been previously produced in Honduras in 1990 and later in Nicaragua. A new blend, introduced in 1998, is mild-bodied in taste and has consistent smooth flavors. It is available in boxes of 25, except for the tubed No. 1, offered in 10s or in packs of 3.

DON LINO 1989   ★*New*★
Handmade in Santiago, Dominican Republic.

CONNECTICUT WRAPPER:
Wrapper: USA/Connecticut   Binder: Indonesia   Filler: Brazil, Cameroon, Dom. Rep.

MADURO BOX PRESSED:
Wrapper: Nicaragua   Binder: Indonesia   Filler: Colombia, Mexico, Nicaragua

Shape	Name	Lgth	Ring	Wrapper
Robusto	Robusto	5	50	CC-Ma
Double Corona	Churchill	7½	50	CC-Ma
Torpedo	Torpedo	6¼	52	CC-Ma

Miami Cigar Co. introduced this cigar in 2007, an update of an old blend. The Connecticut-wrapped style is medium in body while the maduros are full-bodied. All are offered in boxes of 20.

HANDMADE CIGARS: BRAND LISTINGS

DON LINO AFRICA
Handmade in Esteli, Nicaragua.

Wrapper: Nicaragua   *Binder: Nicaragua*
Filler: Cameroon, Dom. Rep., Mexico, Nicaragua

Shape	Name	Lgth	Ring	Wrapper
Lonsdale	Punda Milia (Zebra)	6½	44	CM
Robusto	Duma (Cheetah)	5	50	CM
Toro	Kifaro (Rhinoceros)	6¼	52	CM
Toro	Kiboko (Hippopotamus)	6½	58	CM
Corona Extra	Kuro (Water Buck Deer)	4	45	CM
Double Corona	Tembo (Elephant)	7½	50	CM

This blend was introduced in 2003 and then re-blended for 2004. It's medium-to-full-bodied, using aged tobacco and offered in boxes of 25, except for the Koboko (24) and Kuro, in tins of four and boxes of 50. The elegant artwork on the box are characteristic is the Maasi, the indigenous people of the African Savanna.

DON MACHO
Handmade in Danli, Honduras.

Wrapper: Honduras   *Binder: Honduras*   *Filler: Honduras*

Shape	Name	Lgth	Ring	Wrapper
Double Corona	Presidente	7½	50	CC
Churchill	Churchill	7	48	CC
Lonsdale	No. 1	7	44	CC
Robusto	Rothschild	5	50	CC
Long Corona	Lonsdale	6	43	CC
Corona	Corona	5½	44	CC
Panatela	Panetela	6	38	CC

This is a mild-bodied cigar from Camacho Cigars, with a Connecticut-seed wrapper and value pricing, offered in boxes of 25.

HANDMADE CIGARS: BRAND LISTINGS

DON MATEO
Handmade in Santa Rosa de Copan, Honduras.

Wrapper: Mexico   Binder: Mexico   Filler: Mexico, Nicaragua

Shape	Name	Lgth	Ring	Wrapper
Slim Panatela	No. 1	7	30	CC
Panatela	No. 2	6⅞	35	CC
Long Corona	No. 3	6	42	CC
Corona	No. 4	5½	44	CC
Lonsdale	No. 5	6⅝	44	CC
Churchill	No. 6	6⅞	48	CC
Robusto	No. 7	4¾	50	CC-Ma
Toro	No. 8	6¼	50	CC-Ma
Double Corona	No. 9	7½	50	CC-Ma
Giant	No. 10	8	52	CC-Ma
Toro	No. 11	6⅝	54	CC-Ma

A medium-bodied taste in a banded, bundled cigar is the promise of the well-made and modestly-priced Don Mateo line. Mexican wrapper – Sumatra-seed for the natural shade and Morron for the maduro – is used with Nicaraguan leaf for filler on the natural-wrapped shapes and Mexican Morron for the maduros. All shapes are offered in bundles of 25.

DON OTILIO
Handmade in Santiago, Dominican Republic.

Wrapper: Ecuador   Binder: Dom. Rep.   Filler: Dom. Rep., Honduras

Shape	Name	Lgth	Ring	Wrapper
Robusto	Robusto	5	50	CC
Grand Corona	Doble Corona	6½	46	CC
Long Corona	Lonsdale	6	44	CC

Introduced in 1996, this brand is named for a long-time tobacco grower in the Dominican Republic. Don Otilio is a mild-to-medium-bodied blend of Dominican and Honduran filler, Cuban-seed binder and an Ecuadorian-grown wrapper.

HANDMADE CIGARS: BRAND LISTINGS

DON PABLO
Handmade in Las Vegas, Nevada, USA.
Wrapper: Mexico, USA/Connecticut   Binder: Ecuador   Filler: Dom. Rep., Mexico

Shape	Name	Lgth	Ring	Wrapper
Slim Panatela	Pencil	7	32	CC
Slim Panatela	Panatela	7	34	CC
Lonsdale	Panatela Especial	7	40	CC-Ma
Corona	Corona	5¾	42	CC
Toro	Monterico	5¾	52	CC-Ma
Toro	Cuban Round	5¾	48	CC-Ma
Churchill	Imperial	6¾	46	CC-Ma
Double Corona	Cuban Round Largo	7½	50	CC-Ma
Giant	El Cubano	8½	52	CC
Torpedo	Torpedo	6¾	58	CC-Ma

These are mild-to-medium-bodied cigars of good quality, handmade in a storefront on the Las Vegas strip. Fully in keeping with its location, this small factory offers some gaudy specialties, including a vintage line featuring the Largo, Imperial and Monterico sizes made with five-year-aged tobaccos, aromatic cigars in the Corona and Panatela Especial sizes and the Largo and Monterico sizes cured with 20-year-old cognac. You can also have cigars cured with rum or brandy or sweetened for a modest charge!

DON PEPIN GARCIA – BLACK EDITION   ★*New*★
Handmade in Esteli, Nicaragua.
Wrapper: Nicaragua   Binder: Nicaragua   Filler: Nicaragua

Shape	Name	Lgth	Ring	Wrapper
Petit Corona	Perla 1952	4¼	40	CM
Panatela	Corona Especial 1977	5½	38	CM
Robusto	Robusto 1979	5	50	CM
Torpedo	Belicoso 1970	5	54	CM
Perfecto	Figurado 1973	6	60	CM
Toro	Toro 1950	6	52	CM

This blend is made at the Tabacalera Cubana in Nicaragua and was introduced to national distribution in 2006. It's medium-to-full in body with a Habano Rosado wrapper. It's packed in elegant boxes of 20.

DON PEPIN GARCIA – BLUE EDITION
Handmade in Miami, Florida, USA.

Wrapper: Nicaragua   *Binder: Nicaragua*   *Filler: Nicaragua*

Shape	Name	Lgth	Ring	Wrapper
Robusto	Invictos	5	50	CM
Toro	Generosos	6	50	CM
Double Corona	Delicias	7	50	CM
Torpedo	Imperiales	6⅛	52	CM
Double Corona	Magnates	7⅝	49	CM
Giant	Exclusivos	9¼	48	CM

Named for one of the legendary cigarmakers of Miami, this blend was introduced for national distribution in 2005. It's medium-bodied with a deep blue band, offered without cellophane in boxes of 25.

DON PEPIN GARCIA - SERIE JJ
Handmade in Miami, Florida, USA.

Wrapper: Nicaragua   *Binder: Nicaragua*   *Filler: Nicaragua*

Shape	Name	Lgth	Ring	Wrapper
Torpedo	Belicoso	5¾	52	CM
Toro	Sublime	6	54	CM
Robusto	Selectos	5	50	CM
Perfecto	Salomon	7¼	57	CM

Medium in body, this white-banded line debuted in 2005. It's offered without cellophane in boxes of 24 for the Belicoso, Selectos and Sublime and in a box of five for the Salomon.

DON PEPIN GARCIA – SERIE JJ MADURO   ★*New*★
Handmade in Esteli, Nicaragua.

Wrapper: Nicaragua   *Binder: Nicaragua*   *Filler: Nicaragua*

Shape	Name	Lgth	Ring	Wrapper
Torpedo	Belicoso	5¾	52	Ma
Toro	Sublime	6	54	Ma
Robusto	Selectos	5	50	Ma

Introduced in 2007, this all-maduro line is full-bodied and rich in flavor. All sizes are offered in elegant boxes of 24.

Don Priamo ★*Returns*★
Handmade in Navarette, Dominican Republic.
Wrapper: Indonesia, USA/Connecticut
Binder: Dominican Republic   Filler: Dominican Republic, Nicaragua

Shape	Name	Lgth	Ring	Wrapper
Double Corona	Churchill	7	50	CC-CM
Grand Corona	Corona	6	46	CC-CM
Long Corona	Extra Corona	6	42	CC-CM
Pyramid	Piramide	6⅛	52	CC-CM
Robusto	Robusto	5	50	CC-CM
Toro	Toro	6	50	CC-CM
Torpedo	Torpedo	6½	52	CC-CM

On and off the market, this edition of Don Priamo is offered by Eden's Gate Cigars. It is full-bodied and offered in boxes of 25.

Don Rafael
Handmade in Santiago, Dominican Republic.
Wrapper: Indonesia, USA/Connecticut   Binder: Dom. Rep.   Filler: Dom. Rep.

Shape	Name	Lgth	Ring	Wrapper
Long Corona	No. 27 Lonsdale	6	44	CC-Ma
Corona	No. 37 Corona	5½	42	CC-Ma
Robusto	No. 57 Robusto	5	50	CC-Ma
Double Corona	No. 67 Churchill	7½	50	CC-Ma

Toro	No. 77 Toro	6	50	CC-Ma

This Victor Sinclair-produced brand is mild but with lots of flavor with a choice of Connecticut natural or Indonesian-grown maduro wrappers in boxes of 25.

DON RAMON
Handmade in Esteli, Nicaragua.

Wrapper: Ecuador   *Binder: Nicaragua*   *Filler: Nicaragua*

Shape	Name	Lgth	Ring	Wrapper
Double Corona	Churchill	7	50	CM-Ma
Torpedo	Torpedo	6½	52	CM-Ma
Robusto	Robusto	5	50	CM-Ma
Toro	Toro	6	50	CM-Ma

Developed by the H.J. Bailey Company and introduced in 2003, this is a medium-bodied blend named for Raymond Roth, father of company president Allen Roth. Re-blended for 2005, it is offered in boxes of 25.

DON REX
Handmade, with short filler, in Danli, Honduras.

Wrapper: Honduras Binder: Indonesia Filler: Brazil, Dom. Rep., Honduras, Nicaragua

Shape	Name	Lgth	Ring	Wrapper
Lonsdale	Lonsdale	6½	44	CM
Robusto	Robusto	5½	50	CM
Toro	Toro	6	52	CM
Double Corona	Double Corona	7½	50	CM

This old brand was resurrected by U.S. Cigar Sales in 2003 and is now distributed by General Cigar. It now offers a medium-bodied flavor with short filler, offered in economical bundles of 20.

DON SEBASTIAN
Handmade in Santiago, Dominican Republic.

Wrapper: USA/Connecticut   *Binder: Dom. Rep.*   *Filler: Dom. Rep.*

HANDMADE CIGARS: BRAND LISTINGS

Shape	Name	Lgth	Ring	Wrapper
Double Corona	Churchill	7½	49	CC
Corona	Corona (tubes available)	5¾	42	CC
Lonsdale	Lonsdale	6½	42	CC
Robusto	Toro	5½	49	CC

This is a handmade cigar offered to the mass market by General Cigar Company. It's mild-to-medium in body and offered in boxes, and in packs of five.

DON TOMAS
Handmade in Danli, Honduras.

Wrapper: Indonesia   Binder: Colombia   Filler: Colombia, Dom. Rep., Mexico

Shape	Name	Lgth	Ring	Wrapper
Torpedo	G.D.I. Vintage Belicoso (tubed)	6½	46	CM

With the debut of the Don Tomas Clasico in 2005, the original, mild-to-medium-bodied blend is now manufactured solely for Great Discovery's of Houston, Texas.

DON TOMAS CAMEROON COLLECTION
Handmade in Danli, Honduras.

Wrapper: Cameroon   Binder: Dom. Rep.   Filler: Brazil, Dom. Rep., Mexico

Shape	Name	Lgth	Ring	Wrapper
Perfecto	Perfecto No. 1	4	48	CM
Perfecto	Perfecto No. 2	5	48	CM
Perfecto	Perfecto No. 3	6	48	CM
Perfecto	Perfecto No. 4	7	48	CM
Robusto	Robusto	5½	52	CM
Perfecto	Crystals (tubed)	7	48	CM
Double Corona	Double Corona	7½	52	CM
Robusto	Rothschild	4½	50	CM

HANDMADE CIGARS: BRAND LISTINGS

This edition of the Don Tomas line debuted in 2000. It offers a genuine, three-year-aged Cameroon wrapper with four-year-aged interior leaves for a medium-to-full-bodied taste that is available in boxes of 25 except for the Crystals (8s).

DON TOMAS CANDELA
Handmade in Danli, Honduras.

Wrapper: Honduras   Binder: Honduras   Filler: Colombia, Dom. Rep., Mexico

Shape	Name	Lgth	Ring	Wrapper
Churchill	Churchill	7	48	DC
Lonsdale	Cetro No. 2	6½	42	DC
Robusto	Robusto	5½	50	DC

This old blend was revived for 2002 by U.S. Tobacco after nearly two decades. Of course, it's mild, and available in old-style packaging in boxes of 25.

DON TOMAS CLASICO
Handmade in Danli, Honduras.

Wrapper: Honduras, USA/Connecticut
Binder: Honduras, USA/Connecticut   Filler: Honduras, Nicaragua

Shape	Name		Lgth	Ring	Wrapper
Robusto	Allegro	(tubed)	5½	50	CM-Ma
Lonsdale	Corona Grande	(tubed)	6½	44	CM
Double Corona	Presidente		7½	50	CM-Ma
Robusto	Robusto		5½	50	CM-Ma
Lonsdale	Cetro No. 2		6½	44	CM
Small Panatela	Coronitas		4⅛	32	CM
Robusto	Rothschild		4½	50	CM-Ma
	Great Discovery's series:				
Robusto	Crystal Allegro	(glass tube)	5	50	CM

Completely re-blended in 2005, the Clasico line offers full-bodied taste with Honduran wrapper and binder in the natural-wrapped shapes and Connecticut Broadleaf wrapper and Connecticut binder for the maduro shapes. All are presented in dressed-up boxes of 25 except for the Coronitas, offered in tins of

10 and the Allegro (20s). The Crystal Allegro is made specially for Great Discovery's of Houston, Texas and offered in boxes of 20.

DON TOMAS SPECIAL EDITION
Handmade in Danli, Honduras.
Wrapper: Honduras, USA/Connecticut

Binder: Mexico | | | Filler: Dom. Rep., Mexico, Nicaragua

Shape	Name	Lgth	Ring	Wrapper
	Famous Smoke Shop Connecticut series:			
Double Corona	No. 100	7½	50	CC
Lonsdale	No. 200	6½	44	CC
Robusto	No. 300	5	50	CC
Long Panatela	No. 400	7	36	CC
Corona Extra	No. 500	5½	46	CC
Toro	No. 600	6	52	CC
Corona	No. 700	5½	42	CC
	House of Oxford series:			
Robusto	Corojo 554	5	54	CM
Toro	Corojo 660	6	60	CM
Churchill	Corojo 748	7	48	CM
Torpedo	Piramide No. 2	6	52	CM

The traditional Special Edition was discontinued in 2005, but a special line made for Famous Smoke Shop with a Connecticut wrapper and the special House of Oxford Special Edition Corojo series (Honduran wrapper) that debuted in 2002 continue. The Connecticut version is mild-to-medium-bodied available in boxes of 25, while the Corojo offers a full-bodied smoke with each cigar wrapped in tissue in boxes of 20.

DON TOMAS SUN GROWN ★*New*★
Handmade in Danli, Honduras.

Wrapper: Honduras | Binder: Honduras | | | Filler: Honduras

Shape	Name	Lgth	Ring	Wrapper
Robusto	Rothschild	4½	50	CM

Robusto	Robusto	5½	50	CM
Double Corona	Presidente	7½	50	CM
Lonsdale	Cetro No. 2	6½	44	CM
Toto	Gigante	6	60	CM

Made up of only Honduran tobacco grown in the Jamastran Valley, this is a medium-to-full-bodied, mildly spicy cigar introduced in 2007. It's offered in boxes of 25.

DONA FLOR
Handmade in São Gonçalo de Campos, Brazil.

Wrapper: Brazil   *Binder: Brazil*   *Filler: Brazil*

Shape	Name	Lgth	Ring	Wrapper
Torpedo	Piramide	6½	52	CC-Ma
Double Corona	Double Corona	7½	50	CC-Ma
Lonsdale	Churchill	6½	44	CC-Ma
Corona	Corona	5½	44	CC-Ma
Robusto	Robusto	5	52	CC-Ma
Short Panatela	Petite Corona	4¼	38	CC-Ma
Robusto	Selecao	5	52	CC-Ma
Toro	6x60	6	60	CC-Ma

The largest-selling brand in Brazil was introduced in 1977. It came to the U.S. market in 2005, with a medium-body with a Connecticut-seed wrapper and medium-to-full in body with a maduro wrapper. It's offered in boxes of 20, 25 or five depending on size.

A limited-edition Reserve Series debuted in 2006. It's full-bodied and features a Mata Fina wrapper and Corojo binder and filler, available in the Piramide, Double Corona and Robusto sizes only.

DOUBLE HAPPINESS ★*New*★
Handmade in Santiago, Dominican Republic.

Wrapper: Ecuador   *Binder: Dom. Rep.*   *Filler: Dom. Rep.*

HANDMADE CIGARS: BRAND LISTINGS

Shape	Name	Lgth	Ring	Wrapper
Robusto	Robusto	5	50	CC
Corona	Corona	5¼	43	CC
Torpedo	Torpedo	6¼	52	CC
Churchill	Churchill	7	48	CC
Double Corona	Presidente	7½	50	CC

Double Happiness was introduced during the Cigar Boom as a wedding cigar originally made in the Philippines. It's long off the market, but was revived in a Dominican-made version in 2007 by Meier & Dutch. This version is mild, offered in boxes of 20.

DUNHILL
Handmade in La Romana, Dominican Republic.
Wrapper: USA/Connecticut   Binder: Dom. Rep.   Filler: Brazil, Dom. Rep.

Shape	Name		Lgth	Ring	Wrapper
Double Corona	Peravias		7	50	CI
Toro	Condados		6	48	CI
Lonsdale	Diamantes		6⅝	42	CI
Panatela	Samanas		6½	38	CI
Corona	Valverdes		5½	42	CI
Robusto	Altamiras	(tubed)	5	48	CI
Churchill	Cabreras	(tubed)	7	48	CI
Robusto	Romanos		4½	50	CI
Corona	Tabaras	(tubed)	5½	42	CI

Introduced in 1989, Dunhill's master cigar makers roll a special selection of Piloto Cubano and Olor tobaccos from the Cibao Valley of the Dominican Republic. Wrapping the blend in a Dominican binder, the bunch is then finished with the finest quality Connecticut shade-grown leaf from the Windsor Valley. Prior to final packaging, these cigars are aged in cedar-lined rooms to provide the final mellowing of their mild-to-medium-bodied flavor.

Toro	Churchill	6½	48	CC
Long Corona	Corona	6	44	CC
Double Corona	Double Corona	7½	50	CC
Churchill	Fumas	7	46	CC
Robusto	Robusto	5	50	CC
Torpedo	Torpedo	6	54	CC

Here is a short-filler, medium-bodied cigar from the Tabacalera Perdomo in Nicaragua. Introduced in 2002, it is an excellent value, offered in boxes of 25.

EL COLOSO ★New★
Handmade in Santiago, Dominican Republic.

Wrapper: USA/Connecticut   Binder: Dom. Rep.   Filler: Dom. Rep.

Shape	Name	Lgth	Ring	Wrapper
Toro	Coloso	6	60	CC
Giant	Grand Coloso	8	60	CC

This is a mild-bodied blend in two very large sizes, offered in bundles of 16. The label shows Atlas bearing the weight of the world.

EL CREDITO
Handmade in Santiago, Dominican Republic.

Wrapper: Ecuador   Binder: Dom. Rep.   Filler: Dom. Rep., Nicaragua

Shape	Name	Lgth	Ring	Wrapper
Lonsdale	Fumas	6¾	44	CC-Ma
Churchill	Super Habanero	7¼	46	CC-Ma
Torpedo	Belicoso	6¼	50	CC-Ma
Long Corona	Cetros	6¼	43	CC-Ma
Double Corona	Churchill	7	50	CC-Ma
Grand Corona	Corona Extra	6¼	46	CC-Ma
Lonsdale	Corona Grande	7¾	44	CC-Ma
Giant	Gigantes	9	49	CC-Ma

Double Corona	Imperials	7¾	49	CC-Ma
Double Corona	Monarch	7¼	54	CC-Ma
Corona	Nacionales	5½	43	CC-Ma
Lonsdale	No. 1	6¾	43	CC-Ma
Cigarillo	No. 3	7	28	CC
Slim Panatela	No. 4	6	32	CC
Long Panatela	Panetelas	7	37	CC-Ma
Robusto	Rothchild	5	50	CC-Ma
Giant	Senadores	8	52	CC-Ma
Toro	Small Churchill	6	52	CC-Ma
Petit Corona	Small Corona	4½	40	CC-Ma
Churchill	Supremos	7¼	48	CC-Ma
Torpedo	Torpedo Extra	7¼	60	CC-Ma

This is a bundled, medium-bodied brand from the El Credito factory in the Dominican Republic, offered in bundles of 25.

EL DUQUE COGNAC ★New★
Handmade in Santiago, Dominican Republic.

Wrapper: Indonesia   Binder: Dom. Rep.   Filler: Dom. Rep., Nicaragua

| Shape | Name | Lgth | Ring | Wrapper |
| Double Corona | Double Corona (glass tubes) | 7¾ | 50 | CM |

Introduced by Meier & Dutch in 2007, this is a medium-to-full-bodied cigar that's infused with Cognac for a smooth taste. It's offered in boxes of 25.

EL GUAJIRO
Handmade in Tenerife, the Canary Islands of Spain.

Wrapper: Indonesia   Binder: Spain   Filler: Brazil, Dom. Rep.

This is a medium-bodied brand in seven shapes from the Canary Islands, using locally-grown binder and filler and offered in packs of five and 10, in cellophaned bundles of 20 and in cedar boxes of 25. The two machine-made small cigars are available in chocolate and vanilla-flavored styles.

HANDMADE CIGARS: BRAND LISTINGS

EL LAGUITO
Handmade in Guayaquil, Ecuador.

Wrapper: Ecuador   *Binder: Ecuador*   *Filler: Ecuador*

Shape	Name	Lgth	Ring	Wrapper
Long Panatela	Lancero	7½	41	CM
Corona Extra	Generoso	5½	46	CM
Torpedo	Gran Laguito	6¾	52	CM

Puros de Armando Ramos introduced this blend in 2006, named for the famed El Laguito factory outside of Havana, Cuba. The cigars are mild-to-medium in body and offered in boxes of 10 and 25.

EL LEGEND-ARIO BY CAMACHO
Handmade in Danli, Honduras.

Wrapper: Honduras   *Binder: Honduras*   *Filler: Honduras*

Shape	Name	Lgth	Ring	Wrapper
Toro	Toro	6	50	CM-Ma
Torpedo	Figurado	6⅛	54	CM-Ma
Toro	Bertha	6	60	CM-Ma

Made of 100% Jamastran tobacco, this is actually three different series in one brand: (1) a natural-wrapped, medium-bodied blend introduced in 2005; (2) a Corojo-wrapped edition with a medium-to-full body introduced in 2006 and (3) a maduro-shade Corojo-wrapped version, also introduced in 2006. All are offered unbanded in presentation trays, of 100 for the natural-wrapped and in combination trays of 100 (with all three sizes) for the Corojo and Corojo Maduro styles.

EL MAS CARBON
Handmade in Frankfort, New York, USA.

Wrapper: Cameroon   *Binder: Ecuador*   *Filler: Ecuador, Venezuela*

Shape	Name	Lgth	Ring	Wrapper
Robusto	El Culo Sexy	5½	50	CM
Lonsdale	El Chulo	6½	44	CM
Corona Extra	Caliente	5	46	CM

This is part of the Lars Tetens line, with a full-bodied flavor. All sizes are offered in boxes of 30, which are decorated with reproductions of oil paintings by Tetens.

EL MEJOR ESPRESSO
Handmade in Esteli, Nicaragua.

Wrapper: Mexico   *Binder: Cameroon*   *Filler: Honduras, Nicaragua*

Shape	Name	Lgth	Ring	Wrapper
Toro	Toro	6	52	Ma
Robusto	Robusto	5	50	Ma
Double Corona	Churchill	7	50	Ma
Torpedo	Torpedo	6½	54	Ma

Introduced in 2006 as "El Mejor Maduro," this is a box-pressed, all-maduro line from Meier & Dutch. It's offered in boxes of 20.

EL ORIGINAL
Handmade in Key Largo, Florida, USA.
Wrapper: Ecuador, Mexico

Binder: Nicaragua   *Filler: Dom. Rep., Honduras, Nicaragua, Peru*

Shape	Name	Lgth	Ring	Wrapper
Robusto	Corona	5½	48	CC-Ma
Robusto	Robusto	5	50	CC-Ma
Toro	Toro	6	52	CC-Ma
Churchill	Churchill	7	48	CC-Ma
Long Panatela	Lancero	7	39	CC-Ma
Torpedo	Torpedo	6¼	54	CC-Ma
Double Corona	Presidente	7½	50	CC-Ma
Torpedo	Torpedo Gigante	7½	54	CC-Ma

This blend was introduced in 1999 and is full-bodied. It offers a choice of wrapper: natural from Ecuador or a Mexican maduro and is available in boxes of 25 or bundles of 50.

HANDMADE CIGARS: BRAND LISTINGS

EL PRIMER MONDO ★New★
Handmade in Esteli, Nicaragua.
Wrapper: Nicaragua

Binder: Nicaragua
Filler: Honduras, Nicaragua, Panama, Peru

Shape	Name	Lgth	Ring	Wrapper
Robusto	Robusto	5	52	CM-Ma
Toro	Toro	6	52	CM-Ma
Torpedo	Torpedo	6¼	52	CM-Ma
Toro	Sesenta	6¼	60	CM-Ma

This cigar was introduced in late 2006, in three styles: Habano Criollo Maduro and Connecticut Shade (both with Honduran, Nicaraguan and Peruvian filler) and Rosado Oscuro (Nicaraguan and Panamanian filler). The Habano Criollo Maduro and Robusto Oscuro are medium-to-full in body while the Connecticut style is mild-to-medium. All sizes comes in boxes of 20, with the Sesenta in 15s.

EL REY DE LOS HABANOS
Handmade in Miami, Florida, USA.

Wrapper: Nicaragua *Binder: Nicaragua* *Filler: Nicaragua*

Shape	Name	Lgth	Ring	Wrapper
Robusto	Robusto	5	50	CM
Toro	Toro	6	50	CM
Double Corona	Churchill	7	50	CM
Corona	Corona	5½	44	CM
Torpedo	Torpedo	6⅛	52	CM

Made at El Rey de los Habanos in Miami, this is a mild-bodied blend, introduced in national distribution in 2005. All sizes are offered without cellophane in solid, all-cedar boxes of 23 cigars each.

EL REY DEL MUNDO
Handmade in Cofradia, Honduras.

Wrapper: Ecuador, USA/Connecticut *Binder: Honduras* *Filler: Honduras*

HANDMADE CIGARS: BRAND LISTINGS

Shape	Name	Lgth	Ring	Wrapper
Double Corona	1848	7⅝	52	CM
Short Panatela	Bon Bons	4¼	36	CM
Small Panatela	Cafe au Lait-Café Noir	4½	35	CC-Ma
Lonsdale	Cedars	7	43	CM
Toro	Choix Supreme	6⅛	49	CM
Grand Corona	Corona	5⅝	45	CM
Churchill	Corona Inmensa	7¼	47	CM-Ma
Giant	Coronation	8½	52	CM
Double Corona	Double Corona Deluxe	7	49	CM
Cigarillo	Elegantes	5⅜	29	CC
Torpedo	Flor de Llaneza	6¼	54	CM-Ma
Pyramid	Flor de LaVonda	6½	50	CM-Ma
Double Corona	Flor del Mundo	7¼	54	CM
Petit Corona	Petit Lonsdale	4⅝	43	CM
Slim Panatela	Plantations	6½	30	CC
Grand Corona	Rectangulares	5⅝	45	CM-Ma
Toro	Reserva Salado Cabinet	6	54	CM
Robusto	Robusto	5	54	Ma
Toro	Robusto Larga	6	54	Ma
Double Corona	Robusto Suprema	7¼	54	Ma
Robusto	Robusto Zavalla	5	54	CM
Short Panatela	Reynitas	5	38	CC
Toro	Robusto en Vidrio (glass tube)	5⅝	50	CM
Robusto	Rothschilde	5	50	CM
Panatela	Tinos	5½	38	CM
Grand Corona	Library Edition:"Ivanhoe"	6¼	45	CM

HANDMADE CIGARS: BRAND LISTINGS

This name means "The King of the World" in Spanish and it lives up to its name with its excellent construction and medium-to-full-bodied flavor from the Honduran filler and binder and Sumatran-seed Ecuadorian wrapper. Launched in its current form in 1994, a total of 47 sizes were originally planned, of which 26 are currently in production. The "Lights" group (Bon Bons, Elegantes, Plantations, Reynitas, Café au Lait) is mild-to-medium in strength, with a Connecticut wrapper, Honduran binder and filler tobacco from the Dominican Republic. Most sizes are offered in boxes of 20.

EL REY DEL MUNDO OLIVADOS ★*New*★
Handmade in Cofradia, Honduras.

Wrapper: Ecuador   Binder: USA/Connecticut   Filler: Dom. Rep., Honduras, Nicaragua

Shape	Name	Lgth	Ring	Wrapper
Robusto	Chateaux R	5	54	CM
Toro	Chateaux E	6	52	CM
Torpedo	Chateaux T	6⅛	54	CM
Toro	Chateaux X	6	60	CM
Double Corona	Chateaux D	7¼	54	CM

Introduced in 2007 by Cuban Imports, this is a full-bodied edition of the El Rey del Mundo brand. It features a dark, Sumatra-seed wrapper and is offered in boxes of 20.

EL REY DEL MUNDO REAL
Handmade in Cofradia, Honduras.

Wrapper: Honduras   Binder: USA/Connecticut Filler: Dom. Rep., Honduras, Nicaragua

Shape	Name	Lgth	Ring	Wrapper
Grand Corona	6-4-6	6¼	46	CM
Toro	6-5-0	6¼	50	CM
Toro	6-5-4	6¼	54	CM

Introduced in 2006, this is a medium-to-full-bodied cigar with a spicy tone thanks in part to its San Agustin wrapper and Connecticut Broadleaf binder. It's offered only in boxes of 20.

HANDMADE CIGARS: BRAND LISTINGS

El Rico Habano
Handmade in Santiago, Dominican Republic.

Wrapper: Ecuador, USA/Connecticut   Binder: Nicaragua   Filler: Nicaragua

Shape	Name	Lgth	Ring	Wrapper
Churchill	Double Corona	7	48	CC
Grand Corona	Gran Corona	5¾	46	CC
Robusto	Habano Club	4⅞	48	CC
Toro	Corona Suprema	6	50	CC
Double Corona	Gran Habanero Deluxe	7½	54	Ma
Robusto	Rico Club	5½	54	CC-Ma
Torpedo	Torpedo	6	54	Ma

Although produced by Ernesto Carrillo's Miami-based El Credito Cigar Co. since the early 1990s, this version was introduced in 2001. It features a rich, full-bodied taste, featuring natural wrappers grown in Ecuador and maduro wrappers of Connecticut Broadleaf (the maduro-wrapped versions debuted in 2003). It is offered in cabinet boxes of 25, newly redesigned in 2005 after a 1960s El Rico band was found in the factory in Miami and inspired the revision.

El Sarare
Handmade in Caracas, Venezuela.

Wrapper: Ecuador, Indonesia   Binder: Venezuela   Filler: Venezuela

Mild in body, this brand was introduced in 1997. It is offered in four sizes in a choice of wrappers in boxes of 25.

El Sol
Handmade in Santiago, Dominican Republic.

Wrapper: Dom. Rep., USA/Connecticut   Binder: Dom. Rep. Filler: Dom. Rep.

Shape	Name	Lgth	Ring	Wrapper
	Dominicana Clasico:			
Corona	Brevas	5½	42	CC-Co-Ma
Lonsdale	Corona Imperial	6¼	43	DC-CC-Co-Ma
Grand Corona	Palma Imperial	6½	46	CC-Co-Ma

HANDMADE CIGARS: BRAND LISTINGS

Double Corona	Churchill	7	50	CC-Co-Ma
Double Corona	Emperador	7¾	50	CC-Co-Ma
Robusto	Rothschild	4½	50	CC-Co-Ma
Lonsdale	Londres Deluxe /short filler/	6½	43	CC-Ma
	Millennium Dominicana:			
Robusto	Robusto	5	50	CC
Corona	Corona	5½	42	CC-Ma
Pyramid	Pyramid	6	52	CC-Ma
Toro	Toro	6	52	CC-Ma
Lonsdale	Lonsdale	6½	44	CC
Double Corona	Double Corona	7½	50	CC
	Dominican Secretos:			
Robusto	No. 4	5½	50	CC

This brand dates back all the way to 1928! In its current form, it offers a mild smoke in most shapes, up to a medium-bodied maduro flavor and features a Connecticut-seed wrapper. The Clasicos and Millenniums are offered in boxes of 25 while the Secretos are available in bundles of 25.

EL TIANTE 23 SERIES
Handmade in Esteli, Nicaragua.

Wrapper: Nicaragua   Binder: Indonesia, Mexico   Filler: Mexico, Nicaragua

Shape	Name	Lgth	Ring	Wrapper
Torpedo	Belicoso	6	54	CM-Ma
Robusto	Robusto	5	50	CM-Ma
Double Corona	Churchill	7	50	CM-Ma

Named for the famed pitcher Luis Tiant, born in Cuba, who played for six teams over 19 years in the big leagues from 1964-1982, this is a mild blend with a natural wrapper (Indonesia binder, Nicaraguan filler) and medium-bodied with a maduro wrapper (Mexican binder, Mexican and Nicaraguan filler). All are offered in boxes of, naturally, 23.

EL TITAN DE BRONZE
Handmade in Miami, Florida USA.

Wrapper: Brazil, Indonesia, USA/Connecticut　　　　　　*Binder: Ecuador*
Filler: Dom. Rep., Nicaragua

Shape	Name	Lgth	Ring	Wrapper
Double Corona	Churchill	7½	50	CC-CM-Ma
Torpedo	Torpedo	6½	54	CC-CM-Ma
Torpedo	Torpedo Chico	4½	54	CC-CM-Ma
Lonsdale	No. 1	6½	44	CC-CM-Ma
Grand Corona	Gloria Habana	6¼	46	CC-CM-Ma
Toro	Corona	5¾	48	CC-CM-Ma
Robusto	Robusto	5	50	CC-CM-Ma
Perfecto	Hemingway No. 2	4	46	CC-CM-Ma
Corona	Cubanito	5½	44	CC-CM-Ma
Long Panatela	Panetela	7	38	CC-CM-Ma
Toro	No. 52	6	52	CC-CM-Ma
	Made with short filler:			
Grand Corona	El Titan	6½	46	Ma
Cigarillo	La Senorita	5	28	Ma

This mild-to-medium-bodied brand is offered in cellophane sleeves in boxes of 25. Three wrappers are available: a natural-shade Connecticut leaf, darker Indonesian leaf or Brazilian maduro.

EL TITAN DE BRONZE GRAN RESERVA   ★*New*★
Handmade in Miami, Florida, USA.
Wrapper: Brazil, Cameroon, Ecuador

Binder: Ecuador　　　　　　　　　　　　　　*Filler: Dom. Rep., Nicaragua*

Shape	Name	Lgth	Ring	Wrapper
Double Corona	Churchill	7½	50	CC-CM-Ma
Toro	Corona	5¾	48	CC-CM-Ma

Toro	No. 52	6	52	CC-CM-Ma
Torpedo	Torpedo Chico	4½	54	CC-CM-Ma
Robusto	Robusto	5	50	CC-CM-Ma
Torpedo	Torpedo	6½	54	CC-CM-Ma

Introduced in 2007, you have a choice of blend with an Ecuadorian Habano, Brazilian Maduro (both full-bodied) or Cameroon (medium-bodied) wrappers. All are offered uncellophaned in boxes of 25.

EL TROFEO HABANO

Handmade in Folsom and South Lake Tahoe, California, USA, and Tamboril, Dominican Republic.

Wrapper: Cameroon, Indonesia, Mexico, USA/Connecticut
Binder: Dominican Republic   *Filler: Dominican Republic*

Introduced in 1996, this is eight-size line offered in three styles: mild-to-medium-bodied with a Connecticut wrapper, medium-bodied with an Indonesian wrapper and medium-to-full in the Cameroon and maduro shade (grown in Mexico). The four-shape Seleccion Marquez line is full-bodied and offered in natural and maduro wrappers.

ELOGIO

Handmade in Esteli, Nicaragua.

Wrapper: Nicaragua   *Binder: Nicaragua*   *Filler: Nicaragua*

Introduced in 2003, this medium-bodied cigar began with two sizes, expanded in 2004 and now has six sizes. Two sizes come have maduro wrappers available and all are offered in boxes of 24.

EMILIO REYES

Handmade in Navarrete, Dominican Republic.

Wrapper: Indonesia, USA/Connecticut   Binder: Dom. Rep.   Filler: Dom. Rep.

Shape	Name	Lgth	Ring	Wrapper
Robusto	Robusto	5	50	CC-CM
Long Corona	Extra Corona	6	42	CC-CM
Grand Corona	Corona	6	46	CC-CM

Pyramid	Piramide	6⅛	52	CC-CM
Toro	Toro	6	50	CC-CM
Torpedo	Torpedo	6½	52	CC-CM
Double Corona	Churchill	7	50	CC-CM

Bearing the name of the respected cigar maker Emilio Reyes, this brand debuted in 2001, left the market in 2003 and returned in 2004. It offers a medium-to-full body with a choice of wrappers in a value-priced bundle of 25.

EMMO 500
Handmade in Santiago, Dominican Republic.

Wrapper: Cameroon   *Binder: Dom. Rep.*   *Filler: Dom. Rep.*

Shape	Name	Lgth	Ring	Wrapper
Corona	Interlagos	6½	42	CM
Churchill	Indianapolis	7	48	CM
Lonsdale	Silverstone	6¾	40	CM
Robusto	Monza	5	50	CM

Here is a special blend of the Fittipaldi brand, introduced in 2002. The Emmo500 celebrates four famous names in auto racing with a full-bodied, limited-edition series. The band is distinctive for the black-and-white checkered flag and is offered in boxes of 25.

EN EL PUNTO
Handmade in Santiago, Dominican Republic
and Rochester, New York, USA.

Wrapper: Dom. Rep.   *Binder: Nicaragua*   *Filler: Dom. Rep., Nicaragua*

This four-size line has been on and off the market since 2000. It offers a full-bodied taste with a maduro wrapper, available in boxes of 25.

ERIN GO BRAGH   ★*New*★
Handmade in Santiago, Dominican Republic.

Wrapper: USA/Connecticut   *Binder: Dom. Rep.*   *Filler: Dom. Rep.*

HANDMADE CIGARS: BRAND LISTINGS

Shape	Name		Lgth	Ring	Wrapper
Robusto	Robusto	(tubed)	5	50	Ma

This favored salute to Ireland debuted in 2007. The medium-to-full bodied blend is infused with Irish Whiskey for a subtle taste, offered in boxes of 15.

ESCUDO CUBANO
Handmade in Santiago, Dominican Republic.
Wrapper: Brazil, Indonesia   *Binder: Dom. Rep.*   *Filler: Dom. Rep., Nicaragua*

Shape	Name	Lgth	Ring	Wrapper
Toro	Toro	6	50	CM-Ma
Double Corona	Churchill	7	50	CM-Ma
Torpedo	Torpedo	6½	52	CM-Ma
Lonsdale	No. 1	6½	44	CM-Ma
Robusto	Robusto	5	50	CM-Ma

Introduced in 1996, this is a mild-to-medium (natural) or medium-bodied (maduro) blend of tobaccos, including a Sumatra or Brazilian (maduro) wrapper, combined with Nicaraguan-grown Piloto Cubano and Olor filler leaves. These cigars are presented in unique cedar boxes of 25, featuring a plexiglass top!

ESPADA DE ORO
Handmade in Danli, Honduras.
Wrapper: Indonesia   *Binder: Honduras*   *Filler: Honduras*

Shape	Name	Lgth	Ring	Wrapper
Double Corona	Monarch	7	52	Ma
Robusto	Rothschild	5	50	Ma

Created in 1992, this is a Honduran and Indonesian brand that offers a medium-bodied taste, thanks to a specially-selected blend of Cuban-seed tobaccos grown in Honduras. It is offered in specially-constructed boxes of 10 or 20 cigars each.

ESPECIALES SELECTOS DOMINICAN
Handmade in Santiago, Dominican Republic.
Wrapper: USA/Connecticut   *Binder: Dom. Rep.*   *Filler: Dom. Rep.*

HANDMADE CIGARS: BRAND LISTINGS

Shape	Name	Lgth	Ring	Wrapper
Double Corona	Churchill	6⅞	50	CC-Ma
Toro	Toro	6	50	CC-Ma
Lonsdale	Lonsdale	6¾	44	CC-Ma
Robusto	Robusto	5	50	CC-Ma
Corona	No. 4	5½	44	CC-Ma
Torpedo	Torpedo	6	52	CC-Ma

Introduced in 1998, this is a mild-to-medium-bodied blend from Juan Sosa's Antillian Cigar Company. This blend of U.S. and Dominican tobaccos is offered in open-faced cedar boxes of 25 with a choice of Connecticut wrappers in either natural shade or Connecticut Broadleaf in a maduro shade.

ESPLENDIDO

Handmade in Tamboril, Dominican Republic.

Wrapper: Cameroon, Indonesia, USA/Connecticut

Binder: Dominican Republic   Filler: Dominican Republic

Shape	Name		Lgth	Ring	Wrapper
Double Corona	Churchill	(tube avail.)	7	50	CM
Torpedo	Torpedo		6¼	50	CM-Ma
Toro	Toro Regular	(tube avail.)	5¾	50	CC-CM
Robusto	Toro Gordo		5	52	CM-Ma
Short Panatela	Petite		5	36	CM
Lonsdale	Lonsdale		6¾	44	CM
	Cognac Luxury series:				
Double Corona	Churchill	(tubed)	7	50	CM
Toro	Toro	(tubed)	5¾	50	CM

This brand was introduced to the U.S. market in 2003, offering two series: the standard line, with an Indonesian wrapper, except for the Toro Regular, also offered with a Connecticut wrapper; and the Cognac Luxury series, with a Cameroon wrapper, offered in glass tubes. These are mild cigars, presented elegantly in boxes of 25 for the standard line (20 for boxes of tubed Churchills or

Toro Connecticut-wrapped) and 20 for the Cognac Luxury line (also in 10s for the Churchill). The Petite and Lonsdale sizes come in flavors: chocolate, vanilla and rum.

ESTEBAN CARRERAS 1961 LIMITADA
Handmade in Santiago, Dominican Republic.

Wrapper: Cameroon   *Binder: Ecuador*   *Filler: Dom. Rep., Nicaragua*

Shape	Name	Lgth	Ring	Wrapper
Corona	Corona	5½	42	CM
Robusto	Robusto	5	50	CM
Toro	Gran Corona	6½	50	CM
Torpedo	Torpedo	6¼	52	CM

Craig Cunningham of Dana Point, California introduced this blend in 2006. It's medium in body with a long-aged Cameroon wrapper and Sumatra-seed binder, offered in boxes of 25.

ESTEBAN CARRERAS IMPRESSO CONNECTICUT
Handmade in Santiago, Dominican Republic.

Wrapper: USA/Connecticut   *Binder: Dom. Rep.*   *Filler: Dom. Rep., Nicaragua*

Shape	Name	Lgth	Ring	Wrapper
Robusto	Robusto	5	50	CC
Toro	Toro	6	50	CC
Churchill	Churchill	7	48	CC
Torpedo	Torpedo	6¼	52	CC

Introduced in 2005, this is a mild-to-medium-bodied blend made in the Dominican Republic with a Connecticut Shade wrapper. All sizes are offered in cedar chests of 20.

ESTEBAN CARRERAS VIGILANTE COROJO
Handmade in Danli, Honduras.

Wrapper: Nicaragua   *Binder: Nicaragua*   *Filler: Honduras, Nicaragua, Peru*

Shape	Name	Lgth	Ring	Wrapper
Robusto	Robusto Grande	5	52	CM
Corona	Petite Corona	5½	43	CM

Torpedo	Petite Belicoso	5½	52	CM
Toro	Toro Grande	6½	54	CM
Toro	Super Toro	6¼	58	CM

Introduced in 2005, the Corojo line is medium-to-full in body and is offered in a box of 25.

ESTEBAN CARRERAS VIGILANTE MADURO
Handmade in Danli, Honduras.

Wrapper: Costa Rica   *Binder: Nicaragua*   *Filler: Brazil, Honduras, Nicaragua*

Shape	Name	Lgth	Ring	Wrapper
Corona	Petite Corona	5½	43	Ma
Robusto	Robusto Grande	5	52	Ma
Torpedo	Petite Belicoso	5½	52	Ma
Toro	Toro Grande	6½	54	Ma
Toro	Super Toro	6¼	58	Ma

This medium-to-full-bodied blend was also introduced in 2005. It features a Costa Rican-grown, aged maduro wrapper with a three-nation interior blend. It's attractively presented in boxes of 25.

EVELIO
Handmade in Danli, Honduras.

Wrapper: Ecuador   *Binder: Nicaragua*   *Filler: Honduras, Mexico, Nicaragua*

Shape	Name	Lgth	Ring	Wrapper
Corona	Corona	5¾	42	CC
Churchill	Double Corona	7⅝	47	CC
Lonsdale	No. 1	7	44	CC
Robusto	Robusto	4¾	54	CC-Ma
Toro	Robusto Larga	6	54	CC-Ma
Pyramid	Torpedo	7	54	CC

The lifetime of expertise which resides in master roller Evelio Oviedo is the secret behind this brand, introduced in 1996. This is a full-bodied but smooth smoke, prepared in the same all-by-hand method that Oviedo knew from his days in Cuba at the H. Upmann factory in Havana. Evelio cigars are presented in all-cedar boxes of 25.

EVELIO NICARAGUAN SELECTION
Handmade in Esteli, Nicaragua.

Wrapper: Nicaragua   Binder: Nicaragua   Filler: Nicaragua

Shape	Name	Lgth	Ring	Wrapper
Torpedo	652	6	52	CM

Introduced in 2006, this is an all-Nicaraguan line from the House of Oxford which features a Habano Rosado wrapper. It's medium in body and offered in boxes of 25.

EXCALIBUR
BY HOYO DE MONTERREY
Handmade in Cofradia, Honduras.

Wrapper: USA/Connecticut   Binder: USA/Connecticut
Filler: Dominican Republic, Honduras, Nicaragua

Shape	Name		Lgth	Ring	Wrapper
Double Corona	No. I		7¼	54	CC-Ma
Churchill	No. II		6¾	47	CC-Ma
Toro	No. III		6⅛	48	CC-Ma
Grand Corona	No. IV		5⅝	46	CC-Ma
Grand Corona	No. V		6¼	45	CC-Ma
Panatela	No. VI		5½	38	CC-Ma
Petit Corona	No. VII		5	43	CC-Ma
Churchill	Banquets	(tubed)	6¾	48	CC
Giant	Emperor		8½	52	CC-Ma
Robusto	Epicures		5¼	50	CC-Ma
Toro	Prensado Oscuro		6⅛	48	Ma
Cigarillo	Miniatures		3	22	CC
Cigarillo	Cigarillo		4	24	CC

Grand Corona	Library Edition: "The Holy Grail"	6¼	45	CC

Excalibur cigars are handmade in Honduras and are the choicest cigars of the famous Hoyo de Monterrey line. All of the shapes are wrapped in beautiful Connecticut Shade wrappers, which gives each and every Excalibur cigar a robust, medium-to-full-bodied, but exquisitely smooth taste. Shapes I-VII are available in boxes of 20, as are the Epicures, the box-pressed Prensados, Minis and Cigarillos; the Banquets and Emperors are packed in 10s. The Library Edition is produced for Cigars by Santa Clara.

EXCALIBUR 1066
BY HOYO DE MONTERREY
Handmade in Cofradia, Honduras.
Wrapper: Cameroon, USA/Connecticut

Binder: USA/Connecticut   Filler: Dom. Rep., Honduras, Nicaragua

Shape	Name	Lgth	Ring	Wrapper
Robusto	Merlin	5¼	50	CM
Grand Corona	King Arthur	6¼	45	CM
Churchill	Galahad	6¾	47	CM
Double Corona	Lancelot	7¼	54	CM
Toro	Dark Knight I	5¾	54	CM
Toro	Dark Knight II	6½	52	CM
Robusto	Dark Knight III	4½	50	CM
Robusto	Dark Knight IV	5	52	CM

Named for the year of the Norman Conquest of England, this brand salutes King Arthur and three members of his court — even though it was William the Conqueror who led the Normans to victory in 1066. The final, full-bodied, blend was chosen by consumers (!) who voted at General Cigar's top retailers by selecting for one of two test cigars available at each shop. Once chosen, the final version of Excalibur 1066 made its debut in mid-2000 and is offered in all-cedar boxes of 20. The wrappers are from Cameroon for all shapes except the Dark Knights, which have Connecticut-grown, Havana-seed wrappers.

HANDMADE CIGARS: BRAND LISTINGS

EXCALIBUR ROYAL STERLING
Handmade in Cofradia, Honduras.

Wrapper: Honduras   *Binder: USA/Connecticut*
Filler: Dominican Republic, Honduras, Nicaragua

Shape	Name	Lgth	Ring	Wrapper
Robusto	Nobilis	5¼	50	CC
Double Corona	Fortis	7¼	54	CC
Toro	Fidelis	6⅛	48	CC
Robusto	Dignitas	5½	52	CC

General Cigar's Villazon division introduced this unique blend in 2004. It features a remarkably light Honduran, shade-grown leaf as the wrapper. Medium-to-full in body, it's a limited production line, offered in boxes of 20.

EXCELLENCE
Handmade in Tamboril, Dominican Republic.

Wrapper: Cameroon   *Binder: Dom. Rep.*   *Filler: Dom. Rep., Nicaragua*

Shape	Name	Lgth	Ring	Wrapper
Robusto	Boulevardier	4¾	50	CM

This is a brilliant, one-size brand introduced by Felipe Gregorio in 2004, however, the size was changed from the original six inches by 42 ring to 4 3/4 by 50 in 2007. The blend features a blend of aged filler leaves and a Cameroon wrapper with a medium body. Only 1,000 boxes will be produced annually and each box will hold 48 cigars.

EXHIBIT
Handmade in Santiago, Dominican Republic.

Wrapper: Nicaragua   *Binder: Nicaragua*   *Filler: Honduras, Nicaragua*

Shape	Name	Lgth	Ring	Wrapper
Double Corona	A	7¼	54	CM
Toro	B	6¼	54	CM
Torpedo	C	6½	50	CM
Robusto	D	4½	54	CM

Corona	E	5½	44	CM

The Crown David Int'l Cigar Co. offers this full-bodied cigar with just a touch of Honduran filler to complement the otherwise all-Nicaraguan blend.

EXILE
Handmade in Esteli, Nicaragua.

Wrapper: Ecuador, USA/Connecticut   Binder: Nicaragua   Filler: Nicaragua

Shape	Name	Lgth	Ring	Wrapper
Robusto	Robusto	5	50	CC-Ma
Pefecto	Perfection 1	5½	49	CC-Ma
Toro	Churchill	6¼	50	CC-Ma
Torpedo	Perfection 2	7	49	CC-Ma

Created by Cuban Imports in 2006, Exile offers a choice of an Ecuadorian Rosado or Connecticut Broadleaf maduro wrapper along with a full-bodied taste. Each cigar is wrapped in a reproduction of the front page of the February 4, 1962 issue of the *New York Daily Mirror*, announcing the imposition of the Cuban trade embargo by U.S. President John F. Kennedy. All sizes are offered in boxes of 24.

EXQUISITO
Handmade in Santiago, Dominican Republic.

Wrapper: USA/Connecticut   Binder: Dom. Rep.   Filler: Dom. Rep.

Shape	Name	Lgth	Ring	Wrapper
Perfecto	Long Perfecto	7	48	Ma-Stripe
Perfecto	Short Perfecto	4½	48	Ma-Stripe
Torpedo	Long Belicoso	6	52	Ma-Stripe
Torpedo	Mini Belicoso	5	52	Ma-Stripe
Torpedo	Torpesito	7	56	Ma-Stripe
Double Corona	Double Corona	7	54	Ma-Stripe
Toro	Toro	6	50	Ma-Stripe

This line was introduced by the Crown David Int'l Cigar Co. in 2004 and offers a medium-bodied taste with a Connecticut-grown maduro wrapper and a mild-to-medium-bodied flavor with its striped, Connecticut natural and maduro wrapper. It is offered in boxes of 20.

EXQUISITO LIMITADO
Handmade in Santiago, Dominican Republic.
Wrapper: Dom. Rep.   Binder: Dom. Rep.   Filler: Dom. Rep.

Shape	Name	Lgth	Ring	Wrapper
Double Corona	E1	7¼	52	CM
Toro	E2	6	50	CM
Torpedo	E3	6¼	52	CM
Perfecto	E4	7	48	CM
Perfecto	E5	4½	48	CM
Perfecto	EE	6½	56	CM

The Crown David Cigar Co. introduced this blend in 2006. It's mild-to-medium in body featuring all-Dominican-grown tobacco in boxes of 20.

F.D. GRAVE
Handmade in Danli, Honduras.
Wrapper: USA/Connecticut   Binder: USA/Connecticut   Filler: Honduras, Indonesia

Shape	Name	Lgth	Ring	Wrapper
Double Corona	Churchill	7¾	50	CM
Double Corona	Corona Grande	7	52	CM
Robusto	Robusto	5	50	CM

One of the most respected names in U.S. cigar history is back with an all-handmade line of exceptional quality, made in Honduras. Introduced in late 1995, the four-shape line is full-bodied in taste and offers a Connecticut Broadleaf wrapper and filler, to complement the Honduran and Indonesian fillers. The F.D. Grave Connecticut Select series is presented in all-wood cabinet boxes of 25.

FACTORY DIRECT
Handmade in Esteli, Nicaragua.
Wrapper: Nicaragua, USA/Connecticut   Binder: Nicaragua   Filler: Nicaragua

HANDMADE CIGARS: BRAND LISTINGS

Shape	Name	Lgth	Ring	Wrapper
Robusto	Robusto	5	50	CM-Ma
Toro	Toro	6	50	CM-Ma
Torpedo	Torpedo	6½	52	CM-Ma
Churchill	Churchill	7	48	CM-Ma

Tabacalera Tropical created this mild-to-medium-bodied brand with a choice of wrappers: Nicaragua-grown Corojo '99 and maduro and Connecticut-grown. All are offered in bundles of 25 and in trays of 75.

FACTORY DIRECT NICARAGUAN CIGARS
Handmade in Esteli, Nicaragua.

Wrapper: Nicaragua   *Binder: Nicaragua*   *Filler: Nicaragua*

Shape	Name	Lgth	Ring	Wrapper
Robusto	Robusto	4½	50	CM
Churchill	Churchill	7	48	CM
Torpedo	Torpedo	6½	54	CM-Ma
Toro	Jumbo	6	60	CM-Ma
Giant	Magnum	9	50	CM-Ma
Robusto	Super Fuerte Robusto	5	52	Ma
Toro	Toro	6	50	CM

The TESA Cigar Co. introduced this brand in 2003, with a mild-to-medium body, available in wheels of 50 for all sizes except the Magnum and bundles of nine for most sizes. The Torpedo and Jumbo sizes are available box-pressed.

FAIR EXCHANGE
Handmade in Santiago, Dominican Republic.

Wrapper: USA/Connecticut   *Binder: Dom. Rep.*   *Filler: Dom. Rep.*

Shape	Name	Lgth	Ring	Wrapper
Robusto	Robusto	5	50	CC
Grand Corona	Gran Corona	6	46	CC

Toro	Toro	6	50	CC
Double Corona	Churchill	7	50	CC
Torpedo	Torpedo	6½	50	CC

This inexpensive bundled brand was introduced in 2001. It offers a mild-bodied taste in bundles of 25.

FAMOUS DOMINICAN SELECTION NO. 1000
Handmade in Santiago, Dominican Republic.

Wrapper: Indonesia — *Binder: Dom. Rep.* — *Filler: Dom. Rep.*

Shape	Name	Lgth	Ring	Wrapper
Long Corona	Corona	6	44	CC
Toro	Toro	6	50	CC
Double Corona	Double Corona	7½	50	CC
Lonsdale	Lonsdale	6½	42	CC
Robusto	Robusto	5	52	CC
Torpedo	Torpedo	6	54	CC

Introduced by Famous Smoke Shop in 2005, this is a mild-to-medium-bodied blend with a Sumatra wrapper offered in bundles of 20.

FAMOUS DOMINICAN SELECTION NO. 2000   ★*New*★
Handmade in Santiago, Dominican Republic.

Wrapper: USA/Connecticut — *Binder: Dom. Rep.* — *Filler: Dom. Rep.*

Shape	Name	Lgth	Ring	Wrapper
Churchill	Churchill	7	48	CC
Corona	Corona	5¾	43	CC
Lonsdale	Lonsdale	7	43	CC
Robusto	Robusto	4¾	52	CC
Toro	Toro	6	50	CC

This blend was introduced in 2007 and is mild in body. It's offered in bundles of 20.

HANDMADE CIGARS: BRAND LISTINGS

FAMOUS DOMINICAN SELECTION NO. 3000 ★*New*★
Handmade in Santiago, Dominican Republic.

Wrapper: Nicaragua　　　　　Binder: Dom. Rep.　　　　　Filler: Dom. Rep.

Shape	Name	Lgth	Ring	Wrapper
Torpedo	Belicoso	6½	52	CM
Double Corona	Churchill	7	50	CM
Corona	Corona	5⅝	42	CM
Robusto	Robusto	5	50	CM

Here is a medium-bodied blend with was introduced in 2007. It's offered in bundles of 20.

FAMOUS DOMINICAN SELECTION NO. 4000 ★*New*★
Handmade in Santiago, Dominican Republic.

Wrapper: USA/Connecticut　　　　Binder: Dom. Rep.　　　　　Filler: Dom. Rep.

Shape	Name	Lgth	Ring	Wrapper
Double corona	Churchill	7¼	50	CC
Corona	Corona	5¼	44	CC
Corona Extra	Corona	5¼	46	Ma
Long Corona	Lonsdale	6¼	46	CC
Panatela	Panatela	5¾	36	CC
Robusto	Robusto	5	50	CC
Robusto	Robusto	5¾	52	Ma
Toro	Toro	6½	52	CC

This is a mild-bodied line utilizing Connecticut wrappers for both the natural and maduro-wrapped shapes. Introduced in 2007, it's offered in bundles of 25.

FAMOUS DOMINICAN SELECTION NO. 5000 ★*New*★
Handmade in Santiago, Dominican Republic.

Wrapper: Ecuador　　　　　Binder: Dom. Rep.　　　　　Filler: Dom. Rep.

Shape	Name	Lgth	Ring	Wrapper
Double Corona	Double Corona	7½	50	CC

Long Corona	Corona	6	44	CC
Long Corona	Lonsdale	6	42	CC
Robusto	Robusto	5	52	CC
Toro	Toro	6	50	CC
Torpedo	Torpedo	6	54	CC

Here's a mild-to-medium-bodied blend introduced in 2007. It's offered in a bundle of 20.

FAMOUS EXCLUSIVES
Handmade in Esteli, Nicaragua.

Wrapper: *Nicaragua*   Binder: *Nicaragua*   Filler: *Nicaragua*

Shape	Name	Lgth	Ring	Wrapper
Petit Corona	Buenos	4	42	CC-Ma
Corona Extra	Cattivos	5½	46	CC-Ma
Torpedo	Torpedo	6	54	Ma
Toro	Tucos	6	60	Ma

This is a medium-to-full-bodied series made of all Nicaraguan tobacco and offered in slide-top boxes of 10 (Torpedo/Tucos), 28 (Cattivos) and 40 (Buenos).

FAMOUS HONDURAN SELECTION 1000
Handmade in Danli, Honduras.

Wrapper: *USA/Connecticut*   Binder: *Honduras*   Filler: *Honduras*

Shape	Name	Lgth	Ring	Wrapper
Double Corona	Churchill	7½	50	CM
Robusto	Robusto	5	50	Ma

Mild-to-medium in body with a Connecticut wrapper, this line was introduced by Famous Smoke Shop in 2006 and re-blended in 2007. It's offered in value-packed bundles of 20.

FAMOUS HONDURAN SELECTION 2000
Handmade in Danli, Honduras.

Wrapper: *Ecuador*   Binder: *Dom. Rep.*   Filler: *Dom. Rep., Nicaragua*

HANDMADE CIGARS: BRAND LISTINGS

Shape	Name	Lgth	Ring	Wrapper
Petit Corona	Petit Corona	4½	44	CM
Robusto	Robusto	5½	50	CM
Toro	Toro	6½	52	CM

Famous Smoke Shop introduced this medium-bodied brand with a sun-grown wrapper in 2006. It's offered in bundles of 20.

FAMOUS HONDURAN SELECTION 3000   ★New★
Handmade in Danli, Honduras.

Wrapper: Honduras   Binder: Honduras   Filler: Honduras

Shape	Name	Lgth	Ring	Wrapper
Corona	Corona	5½	44	CM
Robusto	Robusto Grande	5½	52	CM

Famous Smoke Shop introduced this medium-bodied brand with all-Honduras tobacco in 2006. It's offered in bundles of 20.

FAMOUS NICARAGUAN SELECTION 1000
Handmade in Esteli, Nicaragua.

Wrapper: Indonesia   Binder: Nicaragua   Filler: Nicaragua

Shape	Name	Lgth	Ring	Wrapper
Double Corona	Churchill	7	50	CM-Ma
Lonsdale	Lonsdale	6½	44	CM
Giant	Presidente	8	52	CM
Corona	Corona	5¾	43	CM
Robusto	Robusto	5	50	CM-Ma
Toro	Toro	6	50	CM-Ma
Torpedo	Torpedo	6½	52	CM

Here is a medium-bodied blend introduced in 2006 by Famous Smoke Shop. It features a Sumatra wrapper and is offered in bundles of 20.

HANDMADE CIGARS: BRAND LISTINGS

FAMOUS NICARAGUAN SELECTION 2000
Handmade in Esteli, Nicaragua.

Wrapper: USA/Connecticut   *Binder: Nicaragua*   *Filler: Nicaragua*

Shape	Name	Lgth	Ring	Wrapper
Torpedo	Torpedo	6½	52	CC
Robusto	Robusto	5	50	CC
Toro	Toro	6	50	CC
Torpedo	Belicoso	7	54	CC
Double Corona	Churchill	7	50	CC

This is a mild-to-medium-bodied blend with a Connecticut Shade wrapper introduced in 2007. It's offered in bundles of 20.

FAMOUS NICARAGUAN SELECTION 3000
Handmade in Esteli, Nicaragua.

Wrapper: Ecuador   *Binder: Nicaragua*   *Filler: Nicaragua*

Shape	Name	Lgth	Ring	Wrapper
Toro	Grande Robusto	6	60	CM
Double Corona	Presidente	7	52	CM
Robusto	Robusto	5	54	CM
Toro	Toro	5½	54	CM
Torpedo	Torpedo	5½	54	CM

Introduced in 2005, this is a full-bodied cigar with an Ecuador-grown Habano 2000 wrapper. It's available in bundles of 20.

FAMOUS NICARAGUAN SELECTION 4000   ★*New*★
Handmade in Esteli, Nicaragua.
Wrapper: Indonesia, Nicaragua, USA/Connecticut

Binder: Nicaragua   *Filler: Nicaragua*

Shape	Name	Lgth	Ring	Wrapper
Double Corona	Double Corona	7½	50	CM
Lonsdale	Lonsdale	6½	42	CC-CM

Robusto	Robusto	5	50	CC-CM
Toro	Toro	6	50	CM
Torpedo	Torpedo	6½	54	CC-CM
Petit Corona	Petit	4	40	CM

Introduced in 2007, this is a full-bodied blend featuring Nicaraguan wrappers in all sizes, but also Connecticut wrappers on the Lonsdale, Robusto and Torpedo and an Indonesian wrapper on the Toro. All sizes are offered in bundles of 25.

FAMOUS NICARAGUAN COROJO
Handmade in Esteli, Nicaragua.

Wrapper: Nicaragua   *Binder: Nicaragua*   *Filler: Nicaragua*

Shape	Name	Lgth	Ring	Wrapper
Double Corona	Churchill	7	50	CM
Corona	Corona	5½	42	CM
Lonsdale	Lonsdale	6½	42	CM
Robusto	Robusto	5	52	CM
Toro	Toro	6	50	CM
Torpedo	Torpedo	6	52	CM

Here is a spicy, full-bodied cigar with a Corojo wrapper, introduced in 2005. It's offered in bundles of 25.

FELIPE II FUSION
Handmade in Tamboril, Dominican Republic.

Wrapper: Nicaragua   *Binder: Nicaragua*   *Filler: Nicaragua*

Shape	Name	Lgth	Ring	Wrapper
Churchill	F1	7	48	CM
Grand Corona	F2	6	46	CM
Robusto	F3	5	54	CM

This is an elegant blend introduced in 2000. It starts off calmly enough as a medium-bodied smoke, but develops more power throughout. The name comes from the technique of fermenting all of the leaves in the cigar in the same bales.

HANDMADE CIGARS: BRAND LISTINGS

Only 50,000 cigars of each shape are produced annually, offered in boxes of 20.
Production moved from Nicaragua to the Dominican Republic in 2007.

FELIPE GREGORIO 1957 SERIES ★*New*★
Handmade in Tamboril, Dominican Republic.

Wrapper: Costa Rica　　　　　*Binder: Dom. Rep.*　　　　　*Filler: Dom. Rep.*

Shape	Name	Lgth	Ring	Wrapper
Double Corona	Imperador	6¾	50	Os
Toro	Rex	6	55	Os
Torpedo	Majestic	6	52	Os
Robusto	Victory	5	52	Os
Corona Extra	Coloniales	4½	46	Os

Introduced in 2007, this is a full-bodied line that features a Costa Rican-grown
wrapper produced from ancient Cuban seeds. All sizes are box-pressed and are
offered without cellophane in boxes of 20.

FELIPE ART OF POWER ★*New*★
Handmade in Tamboril, Dominican Republic.

Wrapper: Costa Rica　　　　*Binder: Nicaragua*　　　*Filler: Dom. Rep., Nicaragua*

Shape	Name	Lgth	Ring	Wrapper
Perfecto	Antonius	5½	47	CM
Perfecto	Lord Byron	5¾	56	CM
Perfecto	Caesar	5½	57	CM
Perfecto	Goliath	6	60	CM

This line was introduced to feature the unique Costa Rican "Pelo de Oro"
wrapper and shares the Felipe Power interior blend. Introduced in 2007, all sizes
are uniquely-shaped (including an inverse perfecto!), are in limited production
and offered in boxes of 10.

FELIPE FELIPE
Handmade in Tamboril, Dominican Republic.

Wrapper: Brazil　　　　　*Binder: Dom. Rep.*　　　*Filler: Dom. Rep., Nicaragua*

HANDMADE CIGARS: BRAND LISTINGS

Shape	Name	Lgth	Ring	Wrapper
Robusto	Rothschild	4¾	50	Ma
Toro	Super Rothschild	6	60	Ma

Developed by Felipe Gregorio and introduced in 2005, this is a full-bodied cigar with a five-year-aged Brazilian Arapiraca wrapper, offered in 25s (Super) and 50s (Rothschild).

FELIPE FUMAS
Handmade, with sandwich filler, in Tamboril, Dominican Republic.

Wrapper: Indonesia   Binder: Dom. Rep.   Filler: Dom. Rep.

Shape	Name	Lgth	Ring	Wrapper
Long Corona	Fumas	6	44	CM

Introduced by Felipe Gregorio in 2005, this is a mild-to-medium-bodied cigar with a Sumatra wrapper, offered in bundles of 25.

FELIPE GREGORIO
Handmade in Tamboril, Dominican Republic.

Wrapper: Nicaragua   Binder: Nicaragua   Filler: Nicaragua

Shape	Name	Lgth	Ring	Wrapper
Torpedo	Belicoso	6½	54	CM
Toro	Mystic Knight	6½	55	CM
Corona	Sereno	5¾	42	CM
Robusto	Robusto	5	52	CM
Perfecto	Petit Perfecto	5	52	CM
Robusto	Fat Boy	3½	55	CM

Introduced in 1992, this brand emphasized Jamastram Valley leaves from Honduras, but the blend was changed to an all-Nicaraguan puro in 2000. The brand still offers a full-bodied, but mellow flavor with an elegant, sweet aroma. The Mystic Knights size uses an all-organic tobacco blend and is offered as a box-pressed shape and the line is offered in elegant cedar boxes. Production was moved from Nicaragua to the Dominican Republic in 2007.

HANDMADE CIGARS: BRAND LISTINGS

FELIPE GREGORIO 3 TIERRAS
Handmade in Tamboril, Dominican Republic.

Wrapper: Brazil   *Binder: Dom. Rep., Nicaragua*   *Filler: Dom. Rep., Nicaragua*

Shape	Name	Lgth	Ring	Wrapper
Small Panatela	Escopeta	4½	30	Ma
Cigarillo	Lupara	3½	26	Ma

Talk about unique! Introduced by Felipe Gregorio in 2005, this cigar features a maduro wrapper around two interior "cigars" so that it resembles a two-bore shotgun! It's full-bodied, with the interior rolls of either all-Dominican Piloto Cubano or Nicaraguan Habana 92, delivering three different tastes to the smoker!

FELIPE POWER
Handmade in Tamboril, Dominican Republic.

Wrapper: Costa Rica   *Binder: Nicaragua*   *Filler: Dom. Rep., Nicaragua*

Shape	Name	Lgth	Ring	Wrapper
Torpedo	Petit Torpedo	4½	50	CM
Perfecto	Leopard	5½	55	CM
Perfecto	Obus	6	60	CM
Robusto	Special R	5	52	CM
Robusto	Triple R	5½	55	CM
Torpedo	No. 2	6⅓	54	CM
Toro	Full Power	6	60	CM
Double Corona	Double C	7½	50	CM

Featuring a Costa Rican-grown wrapper using ancestral Cuban seeds from the Pelo de Oro variety, this is a full-bodied cigar with lots of flavor. The most unusual shape is the Leopard, a perfecto whose wrapper is marked with polka dots of Connecticut Shade tobacco! Marking the 15th anniversary of the Felipe Gregorio brand, the Felipe Power line is offered in boxes of 26.

FITTIPALDI
Handmade in Santiago, Dominican Republic.
Wrapper: Brazil, Cameroon, USA/Connecticut

Binder: Dominican Republic   *Filler: Dominican Republic*

HANDMADE CIGARS: BRAND LISTINGS

Shape	Name	Lgth	Ring	Wrapper
Torpedo	Torpedo	7	54	CC-CM-Ma
Toro	Toro	6	50	CC-CM-Ma
Robusto	Robusto	5	50	CC-CM-Ma
Churchill	Churchill	7	48	CC-CM-Ma
Long Corona	Corona	6	44	CC-CM-Ma
	Made with short filler:			
Cigarillo	Valentina	3⅜	22	CC

Revamped in 2002, this brand is owned by famous Brazilian racer Emerson Fittipaldi, winner of Formula 1 world championships in 1972 and 1974 and the Indianapolis 500 in 1989 and 1993. The band features the checkered flag, symbol of victory in racing and the cigars are produced by the Reyes family.

The Gold Series has a medium-to-full-bodied taste with either Connecticut or Brazilian maduro wrappers while the Silver Series has a medium-bodied blend of Dominican binders and fillers with a choice of Connecticut, Cameroon or Brazilian maduro wrappers. All are offered in boxes of 25.

The Valentina debuted in 2002 and features a Connecticut-seed wrapper grown in Ecuador, Indonesian binder and Dominican filler. The blend is mild and available in natural and flavored varieties: coffee, honey, cinnamon, "manderine," raspberry, cherry, rum and vanilla in tins of 13.

FITTIPALDI ANNIVERSARY EDITION
Handmade in Santiago, Dominican Republic.

Wrapper: Ecuador   *Binder: Dom. Rep.*   *Filler: Dom. Rep.*

Shape	Name		Lgth	Ring	Wrapper
Robusto	Robusto	*(tubed)*	5	50	CC

This is a special edition, introduced in 2005. It offers a medium body, featuring an Ecuadorian-grown, Connecticut-seed wrapper, available in boxes of 20.

FIRE
BY INDIAN TABAC
Handmade in Danli, Honduras.

Wrapper: Costa Rica   *Binder: Nicaragua*   *Filler: Honduras, Nicaragua*

HANDMADE CIGARS: BRAND LISTINGS

Shape	Name	Lgth	Ring	Wrapper
Petit Corona	Petite Corona	4	40	Ma
Robusto	Robusto	4¾	52	Ma
Toro	Toro	6	50	Ma
Lonsdale	Lonsdale	6½	44	Ma
Double Corona	Double Corona	7	49	Ma

Originally introduced by Rocky Patel's Indian Tabac, the Fire line is now distributed by Meier & Dutch. It's full in body and offered in boxes of 20.

FIVE STAR
Handmade in Santiago, Dominican Republic.
Wrapper: USA/Connecticut   Binder: Mexico   Filler: Dom. Rep.

Shape	Name	Lgth	Ring	Wrapper
Lonsdale	No. 100	6½	44	CC-Ma
Long Corona	No. 200	6	44	CC
Double Corona	No. 400	7	50	CC-Ma
Toro	No. 500	6	50	CC-Ma
Robusto	No. 700	5	50	CC-Ma
Giant	No. 800	8½	52	CC-Ma

Introduced in 1998, this is a quality, bundled cigar from MATASA, distributed by Cigars by Santa Clara, with a mild body and a smooth finish. An excellent value, this brand is offered in bundles of 20 in either a Connecticut (natural) or Connecticut Broadleaf (maduro) wrapper.

FIVE STAR 2000 ★*New*★
Handmade in Santiago, Dominican Republic.
Wrapper: Dom. Rep., USA/Connecticut   Binder: Dom. Rep.   Filler: Dom. Rep.

Shape	Name	Lgth	Ring	Wrapper
Grand Corona	Casa Grande	6¼	46	CM-Ma
Double Corona	Churchill	7	50	CM-Ma
Perfecto	Perfecto	5⅛	48	CM-Ma

| Robusto | Robusto | 5 | 50 | CM-Ma |
| Toro | Toro | 6 | 50 | CM-Ma |

Made by a different Dominican factory than the standard Five Star line, this is a mild blend offered with a choice of a Dominican natural or Connecticut Broadleaf wrapper in chests of 50.

THE FLAVA ★*New*★
Handmade in Frankfort, New York, USA.

Wrapper: Venezuela   *Binder: Venezuela*   *Filler: Dom. Rep.*

Shape	Name	Lgth	Ring	Wrapper
Petit Corona	Cocoa	5	42	CM
Cigarillo	Cocoa/Vanilla	3	28	CM

This is a flavored line from Lars Tetens, with a full body offered in two sizes and two flavors. The petit corona-sized Cocoa is offered in boxes of 20 and the mini-sized cigar is available in boxes of 80.

FLOR DE A. ALLONES
Handmade in Cofradia, Honduras.

Wrapper: Ecuador   *Binder: USA/Connecticut*   *Filler: Honduras, Nicaragua*

Shape	Name	Lgth	Ring	Wrapper
Torpedo	Belicoso	6⅛	50	CM
Short Panatela	Especiales No. 5	5¼	38	CM
Grand Corona	Favoritas	5⅝	46	CM
Toro	Maximo	6⅛	50	CM
Churchill	Prominente	6⅞	48	CM
Toro	Regordo	6	54	CM
Lonsdale	Allones No. 1	7	42	CM
Robusto	Allones no. 7	5	50	CM
Grand Corona	Library Edition: "Old Man and the Sea"	6¼	45	CM

HANDMADE CIGARS: BRAND LISTINGS

This old brand, Flor de Antonio Allones – who was the brother of Ramon Allones – returns in 2000 once again. The blend is spicy, full-bodied in strength with a Sumatra-seed wrapper, presented in cedar cabinets of 25.

FLOR DE CIELO
Handmade in Miami, Florida, USA.

Wrapper: USA/Connecticut   Binder: Nicaragua   Filler: Nicaragua

Shape	Name	Lgth	Ring	Wrapper
Double Corona	Churchill	7	50	CC
Perfecto	Salamon	7¼	60	CC

This is a limited-production cigar which is bunched in Esteli, Nicaragua and then finished with the application of the wrapper in Miami! It's medium-to-full in body, has a unique flowered head and is offered in boxes of 20 for the Churchill and 10 for the Salamon.

FLOR DE CONSUEGRA
Handmade in Cofradia, Honduras.
Wrapper: Ecuador or Honduras

Binder: Honduras   Filler: Dom. Rep., Honduras, Nicaragua

Shape	Name	Lgth	Ring	Wrapper
Robusto	No. 9 Rothschild	4½	50	CM-Ma
Double Corona	No. 14 Sultan	7¼	54	CM-Ma
Grand Corona	No. 15 Churchill	6¼	45	CM-Ma
Toro	No. 16 Governor	6⅛	50	CM-Ma
Grand Corona	No. 17 Superiore	5⅝	47	CC-Ma
Churchill	No. 18 Casa Grande	7¼	46	CM-Ma
Churchill	No. 25 Double Corona	6¾	48	CM-Ma
Corona	No. 26 Corona	5¼	44	CM
Robusto	No. 30 Robusto	5¼	50	CM-Ma
Robusto	No. 54 Epicure	5½	50	Ma
Robusto	No. 59	5	50	CM
Grand Corona	No. 69 Deluxe Corona	6¼	46	CM-Ma

Robusto	No. 72 Robusto	5	54	CC-Ma
Toro	No. 73 Principale	6	54	CC-Ma
Torpedo	No. 219 Connecticut	7	48	CC
Toro	No. 271	6	50	CM
Toro	No. 278	6	52	CM-Ma
Double Corona	No. 282	7	54	CM
Double Corona	No. 299 Connecticut	7½	52	CC
Robusto	No. 300	5	50	Ma
Short Panatela	No. 568	5	38	CM
Petit Corona	No. 604	5	40	CM

This cigar is essentially a seconds line for well-known brands such as Belinda and El Rey del Mundo. In these sizes, it is mostly medium-to-full-bodied, offered in three wrapper shades and in bundles of 25.

FLOR DE COPAN ★*Returns*★
Handmade in Danli, Honduras.

Wrapper: Costa Rica, Honduras   Binder: Honduras   Filler: Honduras, Nicaragua

Shape	Name	Lgth	Ring	Wrapper
Double Corona	Churchill	7	52	CM
Panatela	Cigarillo	5⅞	35	CM
Petit Corona	Corona I	5	42	CM
Corona	Corona II	5½	44	CM
Torpedo	Figurado	6	50	CM-Ma
Lonsdale	Lonsdale	6¾	44	CM
Slim Panatela	Petit Cigarillo	5⅛	30	CM-Ma
Petit Corona	Petit Corona I	5	44	CM
Petit Corona	Petit Corona II	4¾	42	CM
Robusto	Robusto I	5	50	CM-Ma
Robusto	Robusto II	5½	48	CM

Perfecto	Short Figurado	5¼	54	CM
Robusto	Short Robusto	4	54	CM
Toro	Toro I	6	50	CM
Toro	Toro II	6	48	Ma

Distributed by Cigars by Santa Clara, this is a medium-to-full-bodied offering of cigars made at Altadis U.S.A.'s La Flor de Copan factory in Honduras. All sizes are offered in bundles of 25.

FLOR DE DIOS
Handmade in Santiago, Dominican Republic.

Wrapper: Nicaragua *Binder: Nicaragua* *Filler: Nicaragua*

Introduced in 1997, this three-size brand from Specialty Cigars returned to the market in 2002, offering a medium-bodied taste in boxes of 25.

FLOR DE FILIPINAS
Handmade in Manila, the Philippines.

Wrapper: Indonesia *Binder: Philippines* *Filler: Philippines*

Shape	Name	Lgth	Ring	Wrapper
Churchill	Churchill	7	47	CM
Toro	Toro	6	52	CM
Double Corona	Double Corona	7½	52	CM
Robusto	Robusto	5	52	CM

This brand has been on and off the U.S. market for years since its introduction in 1993. In its current form, it offers a mild body, distributed by F&K Cigars of St. Louis.

FLOR DE FLORES BLUE & WHITE
Handmade in Esteli, Nicaragua.

Wrapper: Ecuador, USA/Connecticut *Binder: Nicaragua* *Filler: Nicaragua*

W & P Cigar Corporation offers this blend, which first debuted in 1997 as a Miami-made brand. Now made in Nicaragua, it offers a medium-to-full-bodied taste in five shapes, with a choice of Ecuadorian-grown Connecticut-seed,

HANDMADE CIGARS: BRAND LISTINGS

	Reserva Selecta (Black Label):			
Double Corona	Churchill	7	50	CC
Corona	No. 4	5½	44	CC
Toro	Extra Corona	6	50	CC
Lonsdale	No. 1	6½	44	CC
Robusto	Wavell	5½	50	CC
Torpedo	Torpedo	6¼	52	CC
	Sandwich:			
Churchill	Churchill	7	48	CM
Churchill	Fuma	7	46	CM
Lonsdale	Lonsdale	7	44	CM
Double Corona	Super Cazador	7½	50	CM
Torpedo	Torpedo	7	52	CM

This brand was created by Arnaldo Gonzalez in 1993 and was made in Hialeah, Florida during the Cigar Boom, but closed and then re-appeared as a brand made in Nicaragua. The new 15 Aniversario, medium-to-full-bodied Gold Label and natural-wrapped Reserva Selecta (Black Label) are made in Florida, but the others are made in Nicaragua.

The Habanique Reserva Selecta and Reserva Selecta (Red Label) are medium-to-full in body; the Green & White Label, Esmeralda and Sandwich are mild and the Reserva Selecta is full bodied. All sizes are offered in boxes or bundles (Sandwich) of 25.

The 15 Aniversario was introduced in 2007 and is made in Miami. It's a full-bodied, limited-edition cigar of 1,500 boxes of 20 only (30,000 cigars total).

FLOR DE HONDURAS
Handmade in Danli, Honduras.

Wrapper: Honduras   Binder: Honduras   Filler: Honduras

Shape	Name	Lgth	Ring	Wrapper
Robusto	No. 450	4½	50	CM
Lonsdale	No. 642	6½	42	CM

Toro	No. 650	6	50	CM
Double Corona	No. 654	6¾	54	CM
Double Corona	No. 750	7½	50	CM

This is an old brand which dates back to 1996. Distributed by Mike's Cigars, it offers a mild-to-medium-bodied taste in boxes of 25.

FLOR DE JARDIN
Handmade in Danli, Honduras.

Wrapper: Ecuador, Nicaragua   Binder: Nicaragua   Filler: Honduras, Nicaragua

Shape	Name	Lgth	Ring	Wrapper
Lonsdale	Corona	6½	42	CC
Churchill	Churchill	7	48	CC-Ma
Long Panatela	Lancero	7½	38	CC
Robusto	Robusto	5	50	CC-Ma
Torpedo	Torpedo	6⅛	52	CC-Ma
Petit Corona	Petit Corona	5	42	CC

Created by cigar enthusiast Mike Makens and introduced in 2005, this is a mild-to-medium-bodied blend with a Ecuador-grown wrapper and medium-bodied in the Nicaraguan-grown maduro wrapper.

FLOR DE JAVA
Handmade in Jampu, Indonesia.

Wrapper: Indonesia   Binder: Indonesia   Filler: Indonesia

Marketed in Europe since 1998 and introduced to the U.S. in 2002, this is a very mild blend in six shapes, featuring a Sumatra wrapper, Besuki binder and Javan filler. It's an excellent beginner's cigar that's offered in boxes of 25.

FLOR DE LOS REYES
Handmade in Navarette, Dominican Republic.

Wrapper: Indonesia   Binder: Dom. Rep.   Filler: Dom. Rep.

Shape	Name	Lgth	Ring	Wrapper
Robusto	Robusto	5	50	CM

Toro	Toro	6	50	CM
Long Corona	Extra Corona	6	42	CM
Grand Corona	Corona	6	46	CM
Pyramid	Piramide	6⅛	52	CM
Torpedo	Torpedo	6½	52	CM
Double Corona	Churchill	7	50	CM

This brand is part of the Emilio Reyes group and debuted in 2001. It is medium in body, with a Sumatra wrapper. It is presented in bundles of 25.

FLOR DE MEXICO
Handmade in San Andres Tuxtla, Mexico.

Wrapper: Mexico   Binder: Mexico   Filler: Mexico

Shape	Name	Lgth	Ring	Wrapper
Grand Corona	No. 1	6½	46	CM-Ma
Corona	No. 4	5½	44	CM-Ma
Double Corona	Churchill	7	50	CM-Ma
Toro	Toro	6	50	CM-Ma

The "flower of Mexico" is medium-to-full bodied, available in 25s.

FLOR DE MURIAS
Handmade in Santiago, Dominican Republic.

Wrapper: USA/Connecticut   Binder: Mexico   Filler: Dom. Rep., Mexico

Shape	Name	Lgth	Ring	Wrapper
Double Corona	1876	7½	50	CC-Ma
Robusto	Epicure	5½	50	CC-Ma
Lonsdale	Port Royale	6½	42	CC-Ma
Churchill	Sovereign	6¾	45	CC-Ma

Also known as "La Flor de Murias," this is an old Cuban brand, brought back into distribution by Cigars by Santa Clara. The blend is mild-to-medium in body and all shapes are offered in boxes of 20.

HANDMADE CIGARS: BRAND LISTINGS

FLOR DE OLIVA
Handmade in Esteli, Nicaragua.
Wrapper: Ecuador, Indonesia, Nicaragua, USA/Connecticut
Binder: Nicaragua
Filler: Nicaragua

Shape	Name	Lgth	Ring	Wrapper
Long Panatela		7	38	CM
Corona		5¾	43	CM
Lonsdale		6½	44	CM
Robusto		5	50	CM-Ma
Double Corona		7	50	CM-Ma
Toro		6	50	CM-Ma
Giant		8	52	CM
Torpedo	Petit Torpedo	5	52	CM
Torpedo	Torpedo	6½	52	CM-Ma
	Corojo Series:			
Robusto		5	50	CM
Toro		6	50	CM
Double Corona		7	50	CM
Torpedo	Torpedo	6½	52	CM
	Giants Series:			
Robusto		5	60	CM
Giant		8	60	CM
Giant		10	66	CM
	Gold Series:			
Robusto		5	50	CC
Toro		6	50	CC
Double Corona		7	50	CC
Torpedo	Torpedo	6½	52	CC

HANDMADE CIGARS: BRAND LISTINGS

There's something for everyone in this line, which was introduced in 1996! Although most of the shapes have no name, they are all very well made and offer a wide variety of taste. The standard line uses an Indonesian (Sumatra) natural or Connecticut maduro wrapper and has a medium-bodied strength, as does the Giants Series. The Gold line uses an Ecuadorian-grown, Connecticut-seed wrapper and is medium-bodied, while the Corojo uses a Nicaraguan-grown wrapper and has a medium-to-full-bodied taste. All are offered in bundles of 25 except for the Giants, in 8s.

FLOR DE SELVA
Handmade in Danli, Honduras.

Wrapper: USA/Connecticut	*Binder: Honduras*	*Filler: Honduras*

Maya Selva's dynamic brand has received rave reviews in Europe, but has been on and off the U.S. market since its introduction in 1995. Returned to the U.S. market in 2004 by Cigar Action Corporation, this blend is offered in five sizes and has a medium-to-full-bodied flavor, available in boxes of 25.

FLOR DEL CARIBE
Handmade in Danli, Honduras.
Wrapper: USA/Connecticut

Binder: Honduras	*Filler: Dominican Republic, Honduras, Nicaragua*

Shape	Name	Lgth	Ring	Wrapper
Double Corona	Hispaniola	7¼	54	Ma
Churchill	Antigua	6¾	48	Ma
Toro	Martinique	6¼	50	Ma
Robusto	Dominica	5	54	Ma
Grand Corona	Barbados	6½	45	Ma

This old brand returned to the market in 2002, thanks to the Arango Cigar Company. Presented in boxes of 25, the Antigua and Barbados shapes are square-pressed and the blend offers a full-bodied smoking experience, thanks to its Connecticut Broadleaf maduro wrapper.

FLOR DEL TODO
Handmade, with mixed filler, in Danli, Honduras.

Wrapper: Ecuador	*Binder: Ecuador*	*Filler: Brazil, Dom. Rep., Nicaragua*

HANDMADE CIGARS: BRAND LISTINGS

Shape	Name	Lgth	Ring	Wrapper
Corona Extra	No. 4 Especial	5½	45	CC-Ma
Torpedo	Torpedo I	5	54	CC-Ma
Torpedo	Torpedo II	6	54	CC-Ma
Toro	Toro Especial	6	53	CC-Ma
Double Corona	Churchill Grande	7¼	53	CC-Ma

Made by the Puros Indios factory, this is a "Cuban Sandwich"-style cigar introduced by Meier & Dutch in 2006. It's medium in body and offered in bundles of 20.

FLORENTINO
Handmade in Esteli, Nicaragua.

Wrapper: Nicaragua   *Binder: Nicaragua*   *Filler: Honduras, Nicaragua*

Shape	Name	Lgth	Ring	Wrapper
Giant	President	8½	52	CM
Churchill	Churchill	7	48	CM
Toro	Toro	6	50	CM
Robusto	Robusto	5	50	CM
Pyramid	Pyramide	7	50	CM

Introduced in 1999 by the Arango Cigar Co., this is a medium-to-full-bodied blend featuring a Habana 2000 wrapper grown in Nicaragua. You can enjoy them in bundles of 20.

FLOWER CITY CIGAR ★*Returns*★
Handmade in Rochester, New York, USA.

Wrapper: Indonesia   *Binder: Dom. Rep.*   *Filler: Dom. Rep.*

This is a medium-bodied blend from the Cigar Factory del Yaque, offered in three sizes in boxes of 25.

FONSECA
Handmade in Santiago, Dominican Republic.

Wrapper: Dom. Rep., USA/Connecticut   *Binder: Mexico*   *Filler: Dom. Rep.*

HANDMADE CIGARS: BRAND LISTINGS

Shape	Name		Lgth	Ring	Wrapper
Long Corona	8-9-8		6	43	Co-Ma
Grand Corona	7-9-9		6½	46	Co
Double Corona	10-10		7	50	Co-Ma
Robusto	5-50		5	50	Co-Ma
Petit Corona	2-2		4¼	40	Co-Ma
Small Panatela	Minis		4⅛	30	Co
Corona	Corona	(tubed)	5½	42	Co
Churchill	Churchill	(tubed)	7	48	Co
Toro	Toro Grande		6	56	Co
Pyramid	Triangular		5¼	56	Co-Ma
Toro	Toro		6	50	Co
	30th Anniversary Series:				
Perfecto	30th Anniv. Perfecto		5¾	54	Co
Toro	30th Anniv. Toro		6½	52	Co

One of the world's most famous names in Port is also a respected name in cigars. Medium in body, this refined, cabinet-selection brand debuted in 1962 and was re-introduced in its current blend in 1991. It is blended from the choicest tobaccos grown in the Cibao Valley of the Dominican Republic. The wrapper is outstanding Connecticut Shade (natural) or Connecticut Broadleaf (maduro) leaf. The Triangular shape is one of the hardest to make and offers a rich flavor, concentrated by its conical shape.

The 30th Anniversary Series cigars were introduced in 2005, with a Dominican Olor wrapper, Honduran binder and Dominican and Nicaraguan filler. The Perfectos are offered in boxes of 10 and the Toros in 20s.

FONSECA CEDAR
Handmade in Santiago, Dominican Republic.
Wrapper: Ecuador, USA/Connecticut   Binder: Dom. Rep.   Filler: Dom. Rep., Honduras

Shape	Name	Lgth	Ring	Wrapper
Panatela	No. 1	5¾	38	CC

Corona	No. 2	5¾	43	CC-Ma
Grand Corona	No. 3	5¾	46	CC-Ma
Robusto	No. 4	5¾	50	CC-Ma

Made for Cigars by Santa Clara, this blend was originally for the German market, but has been sold for some time in the U.S. It's medium-to-full in body and has plenty of spice. All sizes are cedar-sleeved and offered in boxes of 25.

FONSECA CUBANO LIMITADO
Handmade in Santiago, Dominican Republic.

Wrapper: Honduras   Binder: Dom. Rep.   Filler: Dom. Rep., Nicaragua

Shape	Name	Lgth	Ring	Wrapper
Torpedo	Belicoso	6½	52	CM
Toro	Toro Gordo	6½	56	CM
Toro	Toro	6	50	CM
Robusto	Robusto	5	50	CM
Petit Corona	Brevita	4¾	43	CM

This is a full-bodied blend that was introduced in 2006. All sizes are offered in cedar boxes of 24.

FONSECA HABANA SELECTION ★New★
Handmade in Santiago, Dominican Republic.

Wrapper: Nicaragua   Binder: Nicaragua   Filler: Dom. Rep.

Shape	Name	Lgth	Ring	Wrapper
Petit Corona	Cadetes	4½	44	CM
Robusto	Cosacos	5	48	CM
Long Corona	Delicias	6	43	CM
Toro	Invictos	6	50	CM
Double Corona	Selection No. 1	7	50	CM

This edition of the Fonseca line is made for Meier & Dutch. It debuted in 2007 and is full in body, offered in elegant boxes of 20.

HANDMADE CIGARS: BRAND LISTINGS

FONSECA PREDILECTOS
Handmade in Santiago, Dominican Republic.

Wrapper: Cameroon   Binder: USA/Connecticut   Filler: Dom. Rep., Nicaragua

Shape	Name	Lgth	Ring	Wrapper
Robusto	No. 100	5¼	52	CM
Toro	No. 200	6¼	54	CM
Double Corona	No. 300	7¼	50	CM

Here is a medium-bodied blend with lots of flavor, made by MATASA and introduced by Mike's Cigars in 2005. It's offered in elegant clamshell-style 5x5 boxes of 25 with each cigar resting comfortably in a cedar sleeve.

FONSECA SERIE "F"
Handmade in Santiago, Dominican Republic.

Wrapper: USA/Connecticut   Binder: Dom. Rep.   Filler: Dom. Rep., Nicaragua

Shape	Name	Lgth	Ring	Wrapper
Robusto	Robusto	5	52	CM
Petit Corona	Breva	4¾	43	CM
Toro	Toro	6	50	CM

Introduced in 2002, this is a medium-to-full-bodied version of the Fonseca brand, with a dark Connecticut wrapper, offered in elegant boxes of 25.

FONSECA SUN GROWN CEDAR
Handmade in Santiago, Dominican Republic.

Wrapper: USA/Connecticut   Binder: Dom. Rep.   Filler: Dom. Rep., Nicaragua, Peru

Shape	Name		Lgth	Ring	Wrapper
Lonsdale	No. 1 Lonsdale		6½	44	CM
Torpedo	No. 2 Belicoso		6¼	52	CM
Robusto	No. 3 Wavell		5½	52	CM
Torpedo	No. 4 Petit Belicoso		4¼	50	CM
Churchill	No. 5 Churchill	*(tubed)*	7	48	CM

Here is an elegant blend with a medium-bodied flavor, with each cigar encased in individual cedar sleeves. Introduced in 2001, the brand is offered in boxes of 20.

FONSECA VINTAGE COLLECTION
Handmade in Santiago, Dominican Republic.

Wrapper: Ecuador   *Binder: Dom. Rep.*   *Filler: Dom. Rep.*

Shape	Name		Lgth	Ring	Wrapper
Torpedo	Belicoso		6¼	52	CC
Double Corona	Churchill		7	50	CC
Long Corona	Cetros		6	43	CC
Robusto	Robusto		5	50	CC
Grand Corona	Lonsdale	(tubed)	6¾	45	CC
Torpedo	Petite Belicoso		4¼	40	CC

This brand was introduced in 1998 and offers a Connecticut-seed wrapper and a mild-to-medium-bodied taste. You can find this exquisitely-made range in five sizes and in boxes of 20 or 24.

FRANCO
Handmade in Santiago, Dominican Republic.

Wrapper: USA/Connecticut   *Binder: Dom. Rep.*   *Filler: Dom. Rep.*

Shape	Name	Lgth	Ring	Wrapper
Lonsdale	Condados	6½	44	CM
Corona	Eminentes	5½	42	CM
Long Panatela	Gourmets	7	38	CM
Double Corona	Magnums	7½	50	CM
Torpedo	Pyramids	7	52	CM
Robusto	Regios	5½	50	CM

This is another brand whose availability had been inconsistent until distributed by Mike's Cigars. It's a medium-bodied blend with excellent construction, offered in elegant boxes of 25.

FRANK VINCENT SIGNATURE   ★*New*★
Handmade in La Romana, Dominican Republic.

Wrapper: USA/Connecticut   *Binder: Dom. Rep.*   *Filler: Dom. Rep., Nicaragua*

HANDMADE CIGARS: BRAND LISTINGS

Shape	Name	Lgth	Ring	Wrapper
Double Corona	Churchill	7	50	CC
Corona	Cuban Corona	5½	44	CC
Lonsdale	No. 1	6½	44	CC
Robusto	Robusto	5	50	CC
Toro	Robusto Xtra	6	50	CC

Famed actor Frank Vincent – Phil Leotardo in "The Sopranos" – had his own cigar debut in 2007. It's mild to medium in body and all sizes are offered in packs of 15.

FRANK'S WAY
Handmade in Tamboril, Dominican Republic.

Wrapper: Ecuador   Binder: Dom. Rep.   Filler: Dom. Rep.

Shape	Name	Lgth	Ring	Wrapper
Double Corona	Churchill	7	50	CC
Torpedo	Belicoso	6	54	CC
Robusto	Robusto	5	50	CC

This is a mild-bodied blend introduced by Felipe Gregorio in 2005, as a salute to legendary singer Frank Sinatra (1915-1998). It's offered in elegant boxes of 20.

FREE CUBA   ★*New*★
Handmade in Santiago, Dominican Republic.

Wrapper: USA/Connecticut   Binder: Dom. Rep.   Filler: Dom. Rep.

Shape	Name	Lgth	Ring	Wrapper
Robusto	Robusto	5	50	CC
Toro	Toro	6	50	CC
Torpedo	Torpedo	6½	52	CC
Double Corona	Churchill	7¼	50	CC

This is a medium-bodied resurrection of a Cigar Boom brand by Meier & Dutch that debuted in 2007. It's offered in boxes of 25.

HANDMADE CIGARS: BRAND LISTINGS

FUEGO DEL DIOS ★New★
Handmade in Guayaquil, Ecuador.

Wrapper: Ecuador   Binder: Ecuador   Filler: Ecuador

Shape	Name	Lgth	Ring	Wrapper
Robusto	Robusto	5	50	CM
Toro	Toro	6	50	CM
Perfecto	Petite Perfecto	5	48	CM
Torpedo	Torpedo	6	54	CM
Toro	Super Toro	6	60	CM

Featuring an Ecuadorian-grown, Corojo-seed wrapper and Sumatra-seed binder, this is a medium-to-full-bodied blend introduced in 2007. The "fire of the gods" is offered in boxes of 20.

FUENTE AGED SELECTION
Handmade in Santiago, Dominican Republic.

Wrapper: Dom. Rep.   Binder: Dom. Rep.   Filler: Dom. Rep.

Shape	Name	Lgth	Ring	Wrapper
	Don Carlos Edicion de Aniversario:			
Robusto	2006 Robusto	5¼	50	CM
Robusto	2006 Double Robusto	5¾	52	CM
Toro	2006 Toro	6¼	48	CM
	Fuente Fuente Opus X Forbidden X:			
Robusto	Uno 2006	5¼	50	CM
Toro	Dos 2004	6¼	48	CM
Robusto	Tres 2006	5¾	52	CM

This is a special line produced in 2006 by the Tabacalera A. Fuente and distributed by Prometheus International of Commerce, California. The Don Carlos Edicion de Aniversario was created by Carlito Fuente to celebrate the 30-year anniversary of the Arturo Fuente Don Carlos line. A total of 3,000 cigars of size were made and sold in 100 humidors of 90 cigars each in 2006. A separate release of 800 boxes of 30 cigars each (24,000 cigars) was made in 2007.

HANDMADE CIGARS: BRAND LISTINGS

The Forbidden X line is a special edition of the regular Opus X brand and include two shapes made in 2006 and one made in 2004 and aged three years. These are sold in special boxes of four cigars; a total of 20,000 cigars were made (5,000 each of the Uno and Tres and 10,000 of the Dos). All are full in body.

A special box of Opus X 2004 Lancero (7 1/2 x 41) was also produced in 2006, with four cigars per box and a total of 2,500 boxes released.

FUENTE FUENTE OPUS X
Handmade in Santiago, Dominican Republic.

Wrapper: Dom. Rep.   Binder: Dom. Rep.   Filler: Dom. Rep.

Shape	Name	Lgth	Ring	Wrapper
Torpedo	Perfecxion No. 2	6⅜	52	CM
Double Corona	Double Corona	7⅝	49	CM
Grand Corona	Fuente Fuente	5⅝	46	CM
Churchill	Reserva d'Chateau	7	48	CM
Petit Corona	Perfecxion No. 5	4⅞	40	CM
Toro	Perfecxion X	6¼	48	CM
Panatela	Petit Lancero	6¼	39	CM
Robusto	Robusto	5¼	50	CM
Torpedo	Belicoso XXX	4⅝	49	CM
Petit Corona	Perfecxion No. 4 Series X	5⅛	43	CM
Giant	Perfecxion A	9¼	47	CM
Torpedo	Super Belicoso	5½	52	CM

This full-bodied brand was started in 1992 and introduced in 1996 and is scarcely available anywhere. A project of the Tabacalera A. Fuente y Cia., this brand features all-Dominican tobacco, including the new rosado wrapper leaf grown on the Fuente's own farm.

A special ten-year anniversary "Forbidden X" humidor was created by Prometheus Ltd. in 2002 and included 100 cigars in 11 oddball shapes and wrappers specially made for the occasion. These included the "848" (8 x 48), "952R" (5¾ x 50 pyramid), "BBMF" (6½ x 64 perfecto), "Bellicoso" (5½ x 49), "Lancero" (7½ x 41), "Round to Square Shape" (5⅝ x 54), "Tapered Head and

Flair Bottom" (5¼ x 45), "eXtasy" (5 x 55 perfecto) and maduro-wrapped versions of the Lancero, Churchill and Robusto.

A "Forbidden X" (7⅝ x 41) specialty size was made available in 2003 as part of a two-disc video set describing the development of the Fuente farm and the creation of the Opus X brand. A second specialty size – 6¼-inch by 49-ring – was created for a "Platinum Edition DVD" set in 2004. In 2006, a three-cigar "Journey to Chateau de la Fuente" set was issued with a Lancero, Reserva d'Chateau and Royal 8 (5 x 40).

An "Opus 22" collection created to raise funds for the Cigar Family Charitable Foundation was sold in 500 boxes in 2004, with 22 cigars in individual coffins. It included the Chili Pepper (5½ x 54) and the Forbidden X. The 2005 "Opus 22" was also issued in 500 boxes and included the Serie X X Square (5⅝ x 54), BBMF (6½ x 64), LBMF (4 x 48), Shark (5⅝ x 56), Double Robusto (5⅝ x 54), Chili Pepper and Forbidden X Lancero. The 2006 edition of 22 includes 500 boxes with three standard sizes and odd sizes including the Rising X (6½ x 64 perfecto) along with the Serie X X Square, Shark, Double Robusto, Lancero, BBMF, LBMF and Chili Pepper. The 2007 version of 500 boxes includes three standard sizes as well as the Rising X, SerieX X Square, BBMF and BBMF Maduro, LBMF, Shark, Chili Pepper, Forbidden X Lancero and Scorpio (5 3/4 x 48).

A set of collectible Opus X cigars in tins were issued in late 2006, with tins of three issued with the Perfecxion X, Robusto and Reserva d'Chateau sizes.

FUNDACION ANCESTRAL ★New★
Handmade in San Jose, Costa Rica.

Wrapper: Costa Rica   Binder: Costa Rica   Filler: Costa Rica

Shape	Name	Lgth	Ring	Wrapper
Double Corona	Churchill	7	52	CM
Long Corona	Corona	6¼	44	CM
Robusto	Robusto	5	50	CM
Torpedo	Torpedo	6	52	CM

From John Vogel's Tabacos de la Cordillera comes this unique program of cigars created from ancestral seeds of tobacco strains grown in Cuba in the 1940s and 1950s! The Fundacion Ancestral line includes three different series of cigars from three different seed stocks: Vuelta Abajo 1940 (medium in body), Pinar Del Rio

1941 (full) and Artemisa 1944 (mild). Each cigar is made solely from one of these tobacco types, specially grown in Costa Rice. All are offered in boxes of 25 of packs of five (six for the Corona).

FUNDADORES JAMAICA
Handmade in Kingston, Jamaica.

Wrapper: Ecuador, USA/Connecticut   *Binder: Mexico*
Filler: Dominican Republic, Jamaica, Mexico

Shape	Name	Lgth	Ring	Wrapper
Double Corona	Churchill	7½	49	CC-CM
Toro	Robusto Gorda	6	50	CC-CM
Lonsdale	Lonsdale	6½	42	CC-CM
Corona	Corona	5½	42	CC-CM
Robusto	Petit Robusto	4	50	CM

This brand is produced by the Barrington House of Kingston, Jamaica and offers mild, rich flavors in the Gold Label Cabinet Series with vintage leaf. Connecticut Shade or Connecticut-seed (grown in Ecuador) wrappers are offered in both a claro and colorado maduro shade. You can enjoy these elegant cigars in boxes of 25 or in a five-pack!

G.R. SPECIALS
Handmade in Danli, Honduras.

BLACK BY GUILLERMO RICO:
Wrapper: Nicaragua   *Binder: Nicaragua*   *Filler: Nicaragua*

RED BY GEORGE RICO:
Wrapper: Nicaragua   *Binder: Nicaragua*   *Filler: Costa Rica, Nicaragua*

Shape	Name	Lgth	Ring	Wrapper
Churchill	Churchill	7	48	CC-CM
Torpedo	Pyramid	6⅛	52	CC-CM
Long Corona	Corona	6	44	CC-CM
Toro	Gran Robusto	6	54	CC-CM

HANDMADE CIGARS: BRAND LISTINGS

Introduced in 2005 and re-blended in 2007, this is a medium-bodied cigar in the Black Blend and medium-to-full-bodied in the Red Blend. All sizes are offered in bundles of 20.

G2
Handmade in Nassau, the Bahamas.

Wrapper: Costa Rica   Binder: Nicaragua   Filler: Ecuador, Nicaragua, Philippines

Shape	Name	Lgth	Ring	Wrapper
Robusto	Robusto	5	50	CC
Torpedo	Torpedo	6	52	CC
Churchill	Churchill	7	48	CC

The G2 is unique thanks to its double binder, both from Nicaragua, helping to give it a medium-to-full body. It was introduced in 2005 and is offered in boxes of 25 or sampler packs of five.

GARO ANIVERSARIO
Handmade in Santiago, Dominican Republic.

Wrapper: Nicaragua   Binder: Indonesia   Filler: Dom. Rep., Nicaragua, Peru

Shape	Name	Lgth	Ring	Wrapper
Giant	Garo A	8	48	CM
Perfecto	Salomon	7	58	CM
Toro	Robusto G	6¼	54	CM
Torpedo	Belicoso	6¼	54	CM

Here is a full-bodied blend to salute the 10th anniversary of the Garo line, introduced in 2005. It blends seven different tobaccos, including a sun-grown Corojo wrapper, into a unique smoking experience, offered in elegant boxes of 20.

GARO BLUE
Handmade in Santiago, Dominican Republic.

Wrapper: USA/Connecticut   Binder: Dom. Rep.   Filler: Dom. Rep.

Shape	Name	Lgth	Ring	Wrapper
Double Corona	Presidente	7½	50	CC
Churchill	Churchill	7	48	CC

Toro	Opus	6	50	CC
Lonsdale	Numero Uno	7	43	CC
Robusto	Robusto	4¾	52	CC
Torpedo	Torpedo	6½	52	CC
Corona	Corona	5¾	43	CC
Long Panatela	Panetela	7	38	CC

First available in 1996, the Garo "Blue" line is made by hand in the Dominican Republic, offering a mild-to-medium body. It uses only Cuban-seed long filler, combined with a Dominican Olor binder and genuine Connecticut Shade-grown wrapper leaves. Even the band is elegant, employing the famous "Fleur de Lis" design. All shapes are offered in boxes of 12 or 25.

GARO LOS LECTORES
Handmade in Santiago, Dominican Republic.

Wrapper: Nicaragua   *Binder: Indonesia*   *Filler: Dom. Rep.*

Shape	Name	Lgth	Ring	Wrapper
Churchill	Churchill	7	48	CM
Double Corona	Double Corona	7½	54	CM
Torpedo	Torpedo	6½	52	CM
Robusto	Robusto	4¾	52	CM
Toro	Robusto "G"	6¼	54	CM
Perfecto	Salomon	7	58	CM

Introduced in 2003, this blend offers a full-bodied flavor. The wrapper is sun-grown and offered in elegant boxes of 25.

GARO MADURO
Handmade in Santiago, Dominican Republic.

Wrapper: Brazil   *Binder: Dom. Rep.*   *Filler: Dom. Rep.*

Shape	Name	Lgth	Ring	Wrapper
Torpedo	Baritone	4½	52	Ma
Toro	Alto	6	50	Ma

Torpedo	Tenor	5½	52	Ma
Torpedo	Soprano	6½	52	Ma

Here is a 1997-introduced, all-maduro line which offers a full-bodied smoke, thanks to its three-year-aged Brazilian wrapper. It is offered in boxes of 12 or 25.

GENERATIONS BY NESTOR
Handmade in Danli, Honduras.
Wrapper: Nicaragua, USA/Connecticut
Binder: Costa Rica, Indonesia   *Filler: Dom. Rep., Mexico, Nicaragua*

Shape	Name	Lgth	Ring	Wrapper
Double Corona	Abuelo	7	50	CM
Toro	Papa	6	52	CC
Robusto	Hijo	5	48	CC

Introduced in 2006 by the House of Oxford, this line offers three tastes in three different shapes created by Nestor Plasencia and Nestor Plasencia Jr.! The Abuelo is medium-to-full with a Nicaraguan wrapper and filler and Costa Rican binder. The Papa is medium-bodied with an Ecuadorian wrapper, Indonesian binder and Nicaraguan and Mexican filler. The Hijo is mild-to-medium in body, with an Ecuadorian wrapper, Indonesian binder and Dominican and Nicaraguan filler. All are packed in elegant black-wood boxes of 20.

GENUINE COUNTERFEIT! CUBAN
Handmade in Esteli, Nicaragua.
Wrapper: Ecuador   *Binder: Nicaragua*   *Filler: Honduras, Nicaragua*

Shape	Name	Lgth	Ring	Wrapper
Corona	Corona	5⅝	44	CM
Double Corona	Churchill	7	52	CM
Lonsdale	Lonsdale	6¾	42	CM
Perfecto	Perfecto	4¾	52	CM
Robusto	Robusto	5	50	CM
Toro	Toro	6	50	CM
Torpedo	Torpedo	6	54	CM

HANDMADE CIGARS: BRAND LISTINGS

This square-pressed brand was launched in 2000 by the Tabacalera Perdomo and offers an Ecuadorian Rosado wrapper with a medium-to-full-bodied, extra spicy taste. It is box-pressed and offered in 25s.

GENUINE COUNTERFEIT! PRE-EMBARGO CUBAN
Handmade in Esteli, Nicaragua.

Wrapper: Ecuador   *Binder: Ecuador*   *Filler: Honduras, Nicaragua*

Shape	Name	Lgth	Ring	Wrapper
Corona	Corona Major	5⅝	45	CM
Double Corona	Prominente	7	54	CM
Lonsdale	Palmas de España	6¾	43	CM
Perfecto	Gourmet Figurado	4¾	51	CM
Robusto	Epicure	5	51	CM
Toro	Corona Gorda	6	51	CM
Torpedo	Belicoso Figurado	6	55	CM

This Tabacalera Perdomo-made brand was launched in 2001 and offers an Ecuadorian Rosado wrapper with a medium-to-full-bodied taste. All sizes are presented uncellophaned in factory-style wheels of 50!

GENUINE COUNTERFEIT! PRE-EMBARGO CUBAN
EDICION LIMITADA 1958
Handmade in Esteli, Nicaragua.

Wrapper: Nicaragua   *Binder: Ecuador*   *Filler: Honduras, Nicaragua*

Shape	Name		Lgth	Ring	Wrapper
Grand Corona	Corona Extra		5⅝	45	Ma
Lonsdale	No. 1		6¾	43	Ma
Robusto	Hermoso		5	51	Ma
Robusto	Gordito	/perfecto tip/	4¾	54	Ma
Toro	Maximo		6	51	Ma
Double Corona	Rey del Rey		7	54	Ma
Torpedo	No. 2		6	55	Ma

| Lonsdale | Palma de Espana | 6¾ | 43 | Ma |

Introduced in 2005, this is not a limited edition! Made by the Tabacalera Perdomo and marketed by Cigars by Santa Clara, you can get all you want of this medium-to-full-bodied blend in cedar boxes of 50.

GEORGES RESERVE
Handmade in Esteli, Nicaragua.

Wrapper: Ecuador *Binder: Cameroon* *Filler: Nicaragua*

Shape	Name	Lgth	Ring	Wrapper
Robusto	Robusto	5	50	CC
Corona	Corona	5½	42	CC
Toro	Toro	6	54	CC
Torpedo	Torpedo	6⅛	52	CC
Lonsdale	Lonsdale	6½	44	CC
Churchill	Churchill	7	48	CC

Famous Smoke Shop introduced this blend in 2006. Who's George? No one will say, but this cigar is produced by the Oliva Cigar Co. and offers a mild-to-medium-bodied flavor in slide-top wood boxes of 25.

GILBERTO CUBANA
Handmade in Esteli, Nicaragua.

Wrapper: Ecuador, Panama *Binder: Nicaragua* *Filler: Nicaragua*

Shape	Name	Lgth	Ring	Wrapper
Giant	President	8	52	CC-Ma
Toro	Super Corona	6	50	CC-Ma
Double Corona	Churchill	7	50	CC-Ma
Robusto	Robusto	5	50	CC-Ma
Torpedo	Torpedo	6½	52	CC-Ma
Lonsdale	Corona	6½	44	CC-Ma
Torpedo	Petit Figurado	4½	46	CC
Perfecto	Perfecto	5¾	52	CC

Torpedo	Figurado	6½	60	CC
Giant	Puff Daddy	8	60	CC-Ma
Robusto	Half Jerobaum	5	60	CC-Ma
Giant	Gigante	10	66	CC-Ma

This brand started in 1999 and offers a mild-to-medium taste with an Ecuadorian wrapper or medium-to-full with a Connecticut Broadleaf (maduro) wrapper. It is offered in bundles of 25, except for the Puff Daddy, Half Jerobaum and Gigante sizes, offered in eights. The Corona size is also available flavored, in vanilla or strawberry.

GIOCONDA
Handmade in Danli, Honduras.

Wrapper: USA/Connecticut   *Binder: Honduras*
Filler: Dominican Republic, Honduras, Nicaragua

New life was given to this old brand by Vincent & Tampa Cigar Co.'s Mario Garrido. It is now made in Honduras and offers a medium-bodied blend, presented in four sizes in natural and maduro wrappers in boxes of 25. The four-shape bundle group features a Connecticut Broadleaf wrapper.

GISPERT
Handmade in Santa Rosa de Copan, Honduras.
Wrapper: Ecuador, Mexico

Binder: Honduras, Nicaragua   *Filler: Honduras, Nicaragua*

Shape	Name		Lgth	Ring	Wrapper
Corona	Corona	(glass tube avail.)	5½	44	CC-Ma
Lonsdale	Lonsdale		6½	44	CC-Ma
Robusto	Robusto		5	54	CC-Ma
Toro	Toro	(glass tube avail.)	6	50	CC-Ma
Torpedo	Belicoso		6⅛	52	CC-Ma
Double Corona	Churchill		7	54	CC-Ma

This old brand, originated in Cuba in the 19th Century, has been on and off the American market for years. It was re-introduced by Altadis USA in late 2003 with the square-pressed maduro version offered in 2005. It offers a medium-bodied taste in the natural version with a Connecticut-seed wrapper and Honduran binder and medium-to-full with the Mexican maduro wrapper and Nicaraguan binder. The natural-wrapped cigars are offered in boxes of 25 (20 for the tubed sizes), while the maduro series is available in boxes of 20.

GOD OF FIRE
Handmade in Santiago, Dominican Republic.

Wrapper: Cameroon, Ecuador   Binder: Dom. Rep.   *Filler: Dom. Rep.*

Shape	Name		Lgth	Ring	Wrapper
	God of Fire 2005:				
Robusto	Double Robusto by Carlito		5¾	52	CM
Churchill	Churchill by Carlito		7	48	CM
Robusto	Robusto by Don Carlos		5¼	50	CM
	God of Fire 2007:				
Torpedo	Piramide by Carlito		6⅝	52	CM
Robusto	Tubo by Carlito	(tubed)	5¾	52	CM

Here is a unique, limited-edition series created by the Tabacalera A. Fuente and distributed by Prometheus International. There are two blends, one from Carlos Fuente ("Don Carlos") with Ecuadorian-grown wrappers and the other from Carlos Fuente, Jr. ("Carlito") with Cameroon wrappers. Distribution:

2004:	*Issued from 2004-06:*	
	Churchill by Carlito	(7 x 48 in indiv. coffins and glass tubes)
	Piramides by Carlito	(6⅝ x 52 in individual coffins)
	Churchill by Don Carlos	(7 x 50 in individual coffins)
2005:	*Issued from 2005-07:*	
	Double Robusto by Carlito	(5¾ x 52 in indiv. coffins or boxes of 10)
	Churchill by Carlito	(7 x 48 in indiv. coffins or boxes of 10)
	Robusto by Don Carlos	(5¼ x 50 in indiv. coffins or boxes of 10)

The cigars issued from 2004-06 were offered in individual coffins in boxes of 10, or in specially-made Prometheus humidors. The 2007 Piramides were issued in boxes of 10; the Double Robusto was offered in boxes of eight.

THE GOOD, BAD & UGLY   ★*New*★
Handmade in Esteli, Nicaragua.

HANDMADE CIGARS: BRAND LISTINGS

Shape	Name	Lgth	Ring	Wrapper
Double Corona	Churchill	7	50	CM
Torpedo	Pyramid	6⅛	56	CM
Long Corona	Gran Corona	6	44	CM
Toro	Gran Robusto	6	54	CM
Robusto	Robusto	5	52	CM

Introduced in 2006, the "Three Centuries" blend of the Gran Habano line sports a white label and a full-bodied taste. It's offered in elegant clamshell boxes of 25.

GRAN HABANO V.L.
Handmade in Danli, Honduras.

Wrapper: Nicaragua   *Binder: Dom. Rep.*   *Filler: Costa Rica, Nicaragua*

Shape	Name	Lgth	Ring	Wrapper
Double Corona	Churchill	7	50	Ma
Torpedo	Pyramid	6⅛	52	Ma
Toro	Robusto	6	54	Ma

This "very limited" edition of Gran Habano was introduced in 2005 and is limited to a total production of 250,000. Easy to recognize by its silver-foil band, it's offered in an all-cedar box of 15.

GRANDE DE ESPANA   ★Returns★
Handmade in Santiago, Dominican Republic.

Wrapper: USA/Connecticut   *Binder: Dom. Rep.*   *Filler: Dom. Rep.*

Shape	Name	Lgth	Ring	Wrapper
Churchill	Corona Gigante	7	48	CC-Ma
Double Corona	Picadores	7	52	CC-Ma
Toro	Toro	6½	50	CC-Ma

Mild to medium in body, this line is offered in elegant boxes of 25.

GRASS
Handmade in Frankfort, New York, USA.

Wrapper: Cameroon   Binder: Cameroon   Filler: Dom. Rep., Ecuador, Mexico

Shape	Name	Lgth	Ring	Wrapper
Robusto	Big	5	62	Ma
Robusto	Medium	4	50	Ma
Toro	Enduring Freedom	6	60	CM
Petit Corona	Star of Cuba	4½	41	Ma

This is a part of the Lars Tetens line and is full-bodied, with the Big, Medium and Star of Cuba especially aromatic. The Enduring Freedom and Star of Cuba are offered in boxes of 30; Big in 10s and Medium in 20s.

GRAYCLIFF
Handmade in Nassau, the Bahamas.

Wrapper: Indonesia   Binder: Indonesia
Filler: Brazil, Dominican Republic, Honduras, Nicaragua

Shape	Name	Lgth	Ring	Wrapper
Giant	Big Bamboo	16	50	CM
Double Corona	Chairman	7¾	50	CM
Long Panatela	Elegante	7¼	38	CM
Churchill	Presidente	7	48	CM
Torpedo	Pirate	6	52	CM
Panatela	Corona	6	38	CM
Toro	PGX	6	50	CM
Robusto	PG	5¼	50	CM
Small Panatela	Gran Dame	5	33	CM
Cigarillo	Roberta	4¾	26	CM
Petit Corona	Taco	4½	44	CM

Enrico Garzaroli, the elegant owner of Graycliff — the first five-star restaurant in the Caribbean — wanted a great cigar to complement his cuisine. With the help of Avelino Lara, supervisor of the Cohiba brand in Havana for many years, he has it. Starting in 1997 with a single roller, there are now 16 rollers producing these red-labeled, medium-to-full-bodied cigars with gorgeous wrappers and a rich flavor. The Big Bamboo shape is available either straight-sided or in a torpedo format, both with an uncut foot.

GRAYCLIFF CHATEAU
Handmade in Nassau, the Bahamas.

Wrapper: Costa Rica   Binder: Ecuador   Filler: Costa Rica, Honduras, Nicaragua

Shape	Name	Lgth	Ring	Wrapper
Robusto	PG	5¼	50	CC
Torpedo	Pirate	6	52	CC
Churchill	Presidente	7	48	CC
Perfecto	Salomon	7⅛	48	CC
Torpedo	Scooter	4	30	CC

Introduced in 2005 and featuring a purple band, this is a full-bodied blend with a Costa Rican-grown wrapper grown mostly on the Graycliff farms. It's offered in boxes of 25 for most shapes, but 24 for the Salomon and 10 for the Scooter.

GRAYCLIFF CRYSTAL
Handmade in Nassau, the Bahamas.

Wrapper: Ecuador   Binder: Indonesia   Filler: Brazil, Greece, Honduras

Shape	Name	Lgth	Ring	Wrapper
Churchill	Presidente	7	48	CM
Pyramid	Pirate	6	52	CM
Robusto	PG	5¼	50	CM
Petit Corona	Taco	4½	44	CM

This brand was introduced in mid-2002 and offers an uninhibited, full-bodied, peppery blast to all who try it. It has a white label and is available in standard boxes of 25 or five, or in a special crystal box!

GRAYCLIFF EMERALD
Handmade in Nassau, the Bahamas.

Wrapper: Ecuador   Binder: Indonesia   Filler: Brazil, Greece, Honduras

HANDMADE CIGARS: BRAND LISTINGS

Shape	Name	Lgth	Ring	Wrapper
Churchill	Presidente	7	48	DC
Robusto	PG	5¼	50	DC
Torpedo	Pirate	6	52	DC
Cigarillo	Roberta	4¾	26	DC

Here is a unique, candela-wrapped, green-label cigar introduced in 2003. It offers a medium-bodied flavor in elegant boxes of 25 (Roberta in bundles of 25).

GRAYCLIFF ESPRESSO
Handmade in Nassau, the Bahamas.

Wrapper: Costa Rica   Binder: Costa Rica   Filler: Brazil, Costa Rica, Nicaragua

Shape	Name	Lgth	Ring	Wrapper
Churchill	President	7	48	Ma
Robusto	PG	5¼	50	Ma
Toro	Pirate	6	52	Ma

The Espresso line was introduced in 2004, offering a full-bodied flavor. Black-banded, it is offered in boxes of 25 or in amazing Crocodile-covered chests.

GRAYCLIFF PROFESIONALE
Handmade in Nassau, the Bahamas.

Wrapper: Indonesia   Binder: Indonesia   Filler: Brazil, Honduras, Nicaragua

Shape	Name	Lgth	Ring	Wrapper
Giant	Big Bamboo	16	50	CM
Double Corona	Chairman	7¾	50	CM
Churchill	Presidente	7	48	CM
Long Panatela	Elegante	7¼	38	CM
Pyramid	Pirate	6	52	CM
Toro	PGX	6	50	CM
Robusto	PG	5¼	50	CM
Panatela	Corona	6	38	CM

HANDMADE CIGARS: BRAND LISTINGS

This is the second Graycliff brand and best known as the "Blue Label." It has rich flavor and aroma with a full-bodied taste. It is offered in cedar packs and boxes of five or 25. The Big Bamboo is offered in both straight-sided and torpedo shapes, both with an uncut foot.

THE GRIFFIN'S
Handmade in Santiago, Dominican Republic.

Wrapper: Ecuador, USA/Connecticut   Binder: Dom. Rep.   Filler: Dom. Rep.

Shape	Name		Lgth	Ring	Wrapper
Lonsdale	No. 200		7	43	CC
Long Corona	No. 300	*(tube available)*	6¼	44	CC
Corona	No. 500		5	42	CC-Ma
Slim Panatela	Privilege		5	31	CC
Double Corona	Prestige		7½	50	CC
Robusto	Robusto	*(tube available)*	5	50	CC-Ma
Toro	Toro		6¼	52	CC-Ma
Pyramid	Piramides		5½	52	CC-Ma
Perfecto	Perfecto		4⅝	52	CC
Cigarillo	Griffinos		3⅜	20	CC
Robusto	Short Robusto		4¼	48	CC

The Griffin's was created in 1984 by Swiss nightclub impresario Bernard H. Grobet, who owned and operated the Griffin's Club. Word spread throughout Switzerland about the quality of his house cigar and it was introduced in the U.S. in 1989. The filler includes three different Cibao Valley tobaccos combined with a Dominican binder and Connecticut-seed wrapper to give it a mildly spicy, flavorful taste. The maduro-wrapped shapes debuted in 2000 and feature Connecticut Broadleaf for a more full-bodied flavor. All shapes are offered in boxes of 25, or in 20s for the tubed shapes. The Griffinos are available in tins of ten. Limited Editions of The Griffin's have also been produced:

2004:	Special XX Edition	(5¼ x 52 in boxes of 20)
2005:	Special XXI Edition	(5½ x 50 in glass tubes in boxes of 10)
2006:	Special XXII Edition	(5½ x 50 perfecto in glass tubes in boxes of 10)

2007:   Special XXIII Edition   (5⅜ x 52 in aluminum tubes in boxes of 10)

The 2007 Special XXIII Edition is medium-to-full-bodied, with an Ecuadorian-grown wrapper and Dominican binder and filler. Production was limited to just 7,500 boxes (75,000 cigars) for worldwide distribution.

THE GRIFFIN'S FUERTE
Handmade in Santiago, Dominican Republic.

Wrapper: Ecuador   *Binder: Dom. Rep.*   *Filler: Dom. Rep.*

Shape	Name	Lgth	Ring	Wrapper
Toro	Toro	6	50	CC
Petit Corona	Short Corona	4	43	CC
Robusto	Robusto	4¾	48	CC

The Griffin's Fuerte series debuted in 2002, offering a more powerful, full-bodied flavor in three sizes with an Ecuadorian-grown, Connecticut-seed wrapper. The extra punch of flavor comes from San Vicente and Ligero filler leaves and the distinctively double-banded Fuertes are available only in 10s.

GUANTANAMERA   ★New★
Handmade in Danli, Honduras.

Wrapper: Nicaragua   *Binder: Nicaragua*   *Filler: Honduras*

Shape	Name	Lgth	Ring	Wrapper
Double Corona	Double Corona	7½	50	CM
Churchill	Churchill	7	48	CM
Lonsdale	Longsdale	6½	42	CM
Toro	Toro	6	52	CM
Torpedo	Piramide	6⅛	52	CM
Corona	Corona Guajira	5½	42	CM
Robusto	Robusto	5	50	CM
Petit Corona	Petit Corona	5	42	CM

This brand was created in 1997 in Miami but entered national distribution in2007 as a Honduran-made cigar. It's medium-to-full in body with a Criollo '98 wrapper.

HANDMADE CIGARS: BRAND LISTINGS

SIGNATURE ANNIVERSARIO:

Wrapper: Nicaragua   *Binder:* Dom. Rep.   *Filler:* India, Peru

SPECIAL EDITIONS:

Wrapper: Cameroon, Ecuador, Nicaragua

Binder: Dom. Rep., Nicaragua   *Filler:* Nicaragua, Peru

SPECIAL EDITIONS – BEAST & TITAN:

Wrapper: Costa Rica   *Binder:* Nicaragua   *Filler:* Dom. Rep., Honduras

SPECIAL EDITIONS – CREST GROUP:

Wrapper: USA/Connecticut   *Binder:* Nicaragua   *Filler:* Nicaragua

SPECIAL EDITIONS – TINS:

Wrapper: Brazil   *Binder:* Brazil   *Filler:* India, Peru

STATUS:

Wrapper: USA/Connecticut   *Binder:* Dom. Rep.   *Filler:* Dom. Rep.

VINTAGE SHAGGY:

Wrapper: Dom. Rep.   *Binder:* Dom. Rep.   *Filler:* Dom. Rep., Nicaragua

Shape	Name	Lgth	Ring	Wrapper
	Avenger G5:			
Toro	Toro	6	50	CM
Torpedo	Torpedo	6	52	CM
	Black Dragon:			
Robusto	Robusto	4¼	52	Ma
Giant	Grand Especial	8½	52	Ma
Double Corona	Imperial Presidente	7	56	Ma
Double Corona	Special Edition Tubo *(tubed)*	7	52	Ma
	G3:			
Toro	Toro	6	50	CM
Cigarillo	Tins	3¼	24	CM
	Grand Reserve Selection:			
Double Corona	Churchill *(glass tubes)*	7½	52	CC-Ma

Toro	Robusto	(glass tubes)	6	50	CC
Torpedo	Torpedo	(glass tubes)	6½	53	CC-Ma
	His Majesty's Reserve:				
Double Corona	Churchill		7½	52	CM
	Marquesa:				
Toro	Robusto		6	52	CM
Double Corona	Churchill		7½	52	CM
Torpedo	Torpedo		6½	53	CM
Perfecto	Perfecto		5	56	CM
Toro	Rothschild		6	54	CM
	Master's Select series:				
Toro	Robusto No. 4		6	50	CM-Ma
Double Corona	Churchill No. 5		7½	52	CM
Torpedo	Torpedo No. 6		6½	53	CM-Ma
Double Corona	Presidente		7	54	CM
Toro	XO		6	60	CM-Ma
Toro	Double Corona		6	52	CM
Corona Extra	Corona Gorda		5¾	46	CM
Robusto	El Duke		4¾	60	CM
	Prestige:				
Double Corona	Churchill		7	52	CM
	Royal Salute series:				
Torpedo	Torpedo		6½	53	CM
	Signature Anniversario:				
Toro	Red Rothschild		6	55	CM
Toro	Black Rothschild		6	55	CM
	Status:				

Double Corona	Churchill	(glass tube)	7	50	CM
Torpedo	Torpedo	(glass tube)	6½	52	CM
	Special Editions:				
Double Corona	Crest L'Grand		7½	55	Ma
Double Corona	Crest Churchill		7	52	Ma
Torpedo	Crest Torpedo		6½	52	Ma
Toro	Beast		6½	58	CM
Toro	Titan		6¼	50	CM
Toro	Black Beauty		6½	58	CC
Double Corona	Grand Age		7½	54	CM
Double Corona	Warlord		7	55	CM
Cigarillo	Tins		3½	24	CM
	Vintage Shaggy series:				
Toro	Toro		6	50	CM
Double Corona	Churchill		7	52	CM
Torpedo	Torpedo		6½	53	CM
	G-Series Tins:				
Cigarillo	Blend nos. 8-44-85-224-967		3¼	24	CC-Ma
	K-Series Tins:				(machine-made)
Cigarillo	Flavors		3½	26	CM

The Gurkha brand has been around, in one form or another, since 1887. That's as long as the Gurkhas, a Nepalese tribe who fought for the British in World Wars I and II, have been around. The cigar brand started in 1989 and includes a constantly-changing variety of blends and strengths. Production moved from the Dominican Republic to Honduras in 2007.

The Avenger G-5 (introduced in 2007) is full in body and is offered in boxes of 20. The Black Dragon line, made in Honduras, was introduced in 2006 in a special edition of five 100-cigar chests priced at $115,000 each. A more down-to-earth version debuted in 2007, still with a full-bodied flavor. The G3 series was introduced in 2006 and is full in body.

HANDMADE CIGARS: BRAND LISTINGS

The Grand Reserve shows a mild-to-medium body in bronze wax-sealed glass tubes offered in a vertical wood display, with a Connecticut wrapper, all Dominican filler and a light finish thanks to a touch of Louis XIII Cognac. The newer maduro-wrapped shapes use Connecticut Broadleaf wrappers, a little Honduran filler and have a medium-to-full-bodied flavor.

His Majesty's Reserve is one of the most expensive cigars anywhere with a list price of $7,500 per box of 20 and is medium-to-full in body. The Marquesa line was introduced in 2007 and offers a full body while the Master's Select series also offers a full-bodied selection of elegant sizes with a Nicaraguan-grown Habana 2000 wrapper, available in numbered, varnished boxes of 25.

The Prestige line debuted in 2007 and is mild-to-medium in body, offered in boxes of 20. The Royal Salute was originally introduced in 1992, with a Connecticut Broadleaf wrapper and a medium-to-full body in boxes of 22. The Signature Anniversario also debuted in 2007 and has a medium body with a natural wrapper (Red) and full body in maduro (Black), presented in boxes of 48.

The Special Editions include five different blends. The Beast and Titan were introduced in 2005, both full-bodied and each limited to 1,000 boxes per year. The Crest editions started in 2007 and are full-bodied. The other three Special Editions include Black Beauty, a mild-to-medium blend with an Ecuadorian wrapper, Dominican binder and Nicaraguan filler (boxes of 25); Grand Age, medium-to-full in body with a Cameroon wrapper, Nicaraguan binder and Nicaraguan and Peruvian filler (50s), and Warlord, full-bodied, with a Nicaraguan wrapper and filler and Dominican binder (30s).

Status is a new line for 2007, with a medium body, offered in frosted glass tubes in chests of 30. The Vintage Shaggy line debuted in 2006 and is medium in body with an uncut foot.

Some lines are not currently in production, but will return in the future. These include the Gurkha Legend, introduced in 2003 with a full-bodied taste in three sizes, which is sold out until 2009.

The G-Series tinned cigars debuted in 2006 in five blends: Dark Blend No. 8 (Connecticut maduro wrapper, mild-to-medium-bodied), Havana Select Blend No. 85 (Nicaragua wrapper, medium), Classic Blend No. 44 (Connecticut wrapper, mild-to-medium), Natural Light Blend No. 225 (Connecticut wrapper, mild-to-medium) and Mild Light Blend No. 967 (Connecticut wrapper, mild), all in tins of 10.

The K-Series Tins were introduced in 2006 and are machine-made in the

HANDMADE CIGARS: BRAND LISTINGS

Dominican Republic, with an Indonesian wrapper. A dizzying array of flavors is available: Caffe Tabac, Chocolate, Exotic Orient, Orange Spice, Passion Fruit, Ancient Warrior, Tiramissu, Kiwi Vanilla, Passion Mint, Cognac, Classic Blend, Mango Cream and Dulce Vanilla, all in tins of seven.

GURKHA CENTURION ★*New*★
Handmade in Navarette, Dominican Republic.

Wrapper: USA/Connecticut   Binder: Cameroon   Filler: Dom. Rep.

Shape	Name	Lgth	Ring	Wrapper
Perfecto	Double Perfecto	6	60	CM

Meier & Dutch distributes this one-size blend, introduced in 2007. It's full-bodied and offered only in boxes of six.

GURKHA DOBLE MADURO ★*New*★
Handmade in Navarette, Dominican Republic.

Wrapper: Costa Rica   Binder: Indonesia   Filler: Dom. Rep., Honduras

Shape	Name	Lgth	Ring	Wrapper
Toro	Toro	6	52	Ma

Here is a mild-to-medium-bodied blend with a silky Costa Rican maduro wrapper. Distributed by Meier & Dutch, it's offered only in boxes of five.

GURKHA EAST INDIA ★*New*★
Handmade in Danli, Honduras.

Wrapper: Ecuador. USA/Connecticut   Binder: Dom. Rep.   Filler: Dom. Rep.

Shape	Name	Lgth	Ring	Wrapper
Double Corona	Churchill	7	50	CC-Ma

Cigars by Santa Clara distributes this line of full-bodied cigars, introduced in 2007. You have a choice of a Sumatra-seed wrapper from Ecuador or a Connecticut Broadleaf maduro wrapper in boxes of 20.

GURKHA EXPEDITION 1887
Handmade in Navarette, Dominican Republic.

Wrapper: Ecuador   Binder: Dom. Rep.   Filler: Dom. Rep.

HANDMADE CIGARS: BRAND LISTINGS

Shape	Name	Lgth	Ring	Wrapper
Robusto	Robusto	4¾	50	CC
Toro	Toro	6	50	CC
Torpedo	Torpedo	6	52	CC
Double Corona	Churchill	7	52	CC

Here is a mild-to-medium-bodied version of the Gurkha line, distributed by Meier & Dutch beginning in 2006. It features a Connecticut-seed wrapper and is offered in boxes of 24.

GURKHA PLATINUM ★New★
Handmade in Navarette, Dominican Republic.

Wrapper: Dom. Rep.   *Binder: Dom. Rep.*   *Filler: Dom. Rep.*

Shape	Name		Lgth	Ring	Wrapper
Torpedo	Torpedo	*(glass tubes)*	6½	53	Ma
Double Corona	Churchill	*(glass tubes)*	7½	52	Ma

A flavored line, also distributed by Meier & Dutch, the Platinum is limited in production to 6,000 cigars annually and is infused with Louis XIII Cognac. Available nationally in 2007, it's medium-to-full in body and offered in boxes of 30.

GURKHA REGENT ★New★
Handmade in Navarette, Dominican Republic.

Wrapper: Cameroon, Nicaragua   Binder: Indonesia   *Filler: Dom. Rep.*

Shape	Name	Lgth	Ring	Wrapper
Robusto	Robusto	4¾	52	CM
Toro	Toro	6	50	CM
Torpedo	Torpedo	6½	52	CM
Churchill	Churchill	7	48	CM
	Nepalese Warrior series:			
Toro	Toro	6	52	CM

This version of the Regent line features a Nicaraguan wrapper and a medium body, distributed by Meier & Dutch in boxes of 20. The special Nepalese Warrior edition has a Cameroon wrapper and is offered only in boxes of five.

H. UPMANN

Handmade in the La Romana, Dominican Republic.
Wrapper: Indonesia, USA/Connecticut
Binder: Dominican Republic   *Filler: Brazil, Dominican Republic*

Shape	Name	Lgth	Ring	Wrapper
Grand Corona	Churchills	5⅝	46	CM
Torpedo	Belicoso	6⅛	52	CM
Corona	Coronas	5½	44	CM
Toro	Coronas Bravas	6½	48	CM
Lonsdale	Lonsdales	6½	44	CM
Toro	Toro	6	50	CM
Robusto	No. 100 Robusto	5	50	CM-Ma
Corona Extra	No. 200 Petit Churchill	4½	46	CM
Petit Corona	No. 300 Petit Lonsdale	4½	44	CM
Petit Corona	Petit Coronas	5	44	CM
Petit Corona	Tubos Gold *(tubed)*	5	44	CM
Corona	Corona Major *(tubed)*	5½	44	CM
Churchill	Monarch *(tubed)*	7	46	CM
Robusto	Library Edition: "The Glory"	5	52	CM
	Machine-made with short-filler:			
Small Panatela	Aperitif	4	30	CM
Small Panatela	Demi Tasse	4½	33	CM
	Great Discovery Series:			
Toro	Grand Corona *(glass tube)*	6	48	CM
Lonsdale	Discovery Habanero	6⅝	42	CM
Petit Corona	Black Gold *(glass tube)*	5⅛	42	CM

Legendary is the only way to describe the H. Upmann brand, originated in Cuba

HANDMADE CIGARS: BRAND LISTINGS

in 1844. Today's Dominican-produced Upmann appeared in the U.S. for the first time in 1975 and combines a medium-bodied taste with first-class construction and a consistency which makes this brand a dependable favorite of smokers everywhere. Following the trend to thicker cigars, the ring gauge of the Corona and Lonsdale shapes was expanded from 42 to 44 in 2004.

Maduro wrappers were introduced in this brand in 1998; maduro-wrapped cigars use a Connecticut Broadleaf wrapper and incorporate Mexican-grown leaves into the filler. Most shapes are available in boxes of 25, with the Monarch available in boxes of 10. The small cigars are packed in tins of 10 (Aperitifs) and boxes of 60 (Demi-Tasse).

The Library Edition is produced for Cigars by Santa Clara. The Great Discovery Series is a special group of glass-tubed shapes produced for Great Discovery's of Houston, Texas beginning in 1998.

H. UPMANN CABINET SELECCION ★New★
Handmade in La Romana, Dominican Republic.

Wrapper: Ecuador   Binder: Nicaragua   Filler: Dom. Rep., Nicaragua

Shape	Name	Lgth	Ring	Wrapper
Double Corona	Churchill	7	54	CC
Torpedo	Belicoso	6⅛	52	CC
Toro	Toro	6	54	CC
Corona	Corona	5½	44	CC
Robusto	Robusto	5	52	CC

Altadis USA introduced this elegant blend in 2007, featuring a Connecticut-seed wrapper and offering a full-bodied taste. It's adorned with a white band and gold trim and offered in slide-top cabinets of 22 cigars each.

H. UPMANN CONNOISSEUR
Handmade in La Romana, Dominican Republic.

Wrapper: USA/Connecticut   Binder: Dom. Rep.   Filler: Dom. Rep.

Shape	Name	Lgth	Ring	Wrapper
Corona	No. 10	5¾	42	CM
Grand Corona	No. 20	5¾	47	CM

Lonsdale	No. 30	6¾	42	CM
Robusto	No. 40	5	50	CM
Toro	No. 50	6	50	CM
Churchill	No. 60	7	46	CM
Double Corona	No. 70	7	52	CM

This edition of the H. Upmann brand was introduced in 2000. It has a medium body and is offered in old-time, all-cedar cabinet boxes of 25.

H. UPMANN RESERVE
Handmade in La Romana, Dominican Republic.

Wrapper: Ecuador   Binder: USA/Connecticut   Filler: Dom. Rep., Nicaragua, Peru

Shape	Name	Lgth	Ring	Wrapper
Torpedo	No. 1	5	44	CC
Robusto	Lord Rothchilde	5	50	CC
Toro	Double Corona	6	50	CC
Double Corona	Sir Winston	7	50	CC
Torpedo	No. 2	6⅛	52	CC

This blend of the venerable H. Upmann brand was introduced by Altadis USA in late 2003. This is a full-bodied, box-pressed Upmann with a Sumatra-seed wrapper, offered in boxes of 25.

H. UPMANN SIGNATURE
Handmade in Santa Rosa de Copan, Honduras.

Wrapper: Mexico, Nicaragua   Binder: Nicaragua   Filler: Honduras, Nicaragua, Peru

Shape	Name	Lgth	Ring	Wrapper
Grand Corona	Super Corona	5⅝	45	CM-Ma
Robusto	Double Eagle	5½	50	CM-Ma
Toro	Magnum 50	6	50	CM-Ma
Double Corona	Monarca	7	54	CM-Ma

This Honduran-made Upmann was commissioned by Cuban Imports and offers a

medium-bodied taste with a choice of wrappers: Connecticut-seed grown in
Nicaragua or Mexican maduro. All are offered in boxes of 20.

H. UPMANN SPECIAL SELECTION
Handmade in La Romana, Dominican Republic.
Wrapper: Indonesia, USA/Connecticut   Binder: Dom. Rep.   Filler: Brazil, Dom. Rep.

Shape	Name	Lgth	Ring	Wrapper
Churchill	Crown Imperial	7	46	CM
Lonsdale	Special Polo	6⅝	42	CM
Toro	Souvenir	6	50	CM
Grand Corona	After Dinner	5⅝	46	CM
Robusto	Rothschilde	4½	50	CM-Ma
Corona	New Yorker	5½	44	CM

It's more Upmann magic, this time with medium body with Indonesian wrappers
on all shapes and a Connecticut Broadleaf maduro wrapper on one size. Each
cigar is wrapped in aromatic cedar sleeves and then packed in boxes of 25.

H. UPMANN SUPER FUERTE
Handmade in La Romana, Dominican Republic.
Wrapper: USA/Connecticut   Binder: Ecuador   Filler: Dom. Rep., Nicaragua, Peru

Shape	Name	Lgth	Ring	Wrapper
Torpedo	Belicoso	6⅛	54	Ma
Robusto	Robusto	5	55	Ma
Toro	Toro	6	55	Ma
Double Corona	Churchill	7	58	Ma

Here's a more powerful H. Upmann, with a Connecticut Broadleaf maduro
wrapper and a medium-to-full-bodied taste. Introduced in 2005 by Cigars by
Santa Clara, it's offered in boxes of 20.

H. UPMANN VINTAGE CAMEROON
Handmade in La Romana, Dominican Republic.
Wrapper: Cameroon   Binder: Nicaragua   Filler: Dom. Rep., Nicaragua, Peru

HANDMADE CIGARS: BRAND LISTINGS

Shape	Name	Lgth	Ring	Wrapper
Short Panatela	Pequenos	4½	38	CM
Petit Corona	Petite Corona	5	40	CM
Corona	Corona	5½	44	CM
Lonsdale	Lonsdale	6⅝	44	CM
Double Corona	Churchill	7	50	CM
Robusto	Robusto	5	52	CM
Torpedo	Belicoso	6⅛	52	CM
Toro	Toro	6	54	CM

Added to the H. Upmann line in late 2003, this is a full-bodied blend with a genuine Cameroon wrapper, offered in boxes of 25. Fans of the Upmann brand will remember that Cameroon wrappers were used on the original Dominican-produced Upmann line in 1975, providing a rich flavor once again.

HABANA CLASICO ★*New*★
Handmade, with short filler, in Danli, Honduras.

Wrapper: Honduras   *Binder: Honduras*   *Filler: Honduras, Mexico*

Shape	Name	Lgth	Ring	Wrapper
Robusto	Robusto	5	50	CM
Torpedo	Torpedo	6⅛	54	CM

Introduced in 2007, this is a mild blend introduced by Tobacco Exchange. Both sizes are offered in bundles of 25.

HABANA GOLD
Handmade in Danli, Honduras.

Wrapper: Ecuador   *Binder: Dom. Rep.*   *Filler: Dom. Rep., Nicaragua*

Shape	Name	Lgth	Ring	Wrapper
Lonsdale	Lonsdale	7	44	CC
Double Corona	Churchill	7½	50	CC
Robusto	Robusto	5	50	CC

HANDMADE CIGARS: BRAND LISTINGS

This brand debuted in the mid-1990s, but died as the cigar boom ended. Revived in 2001 by the House of Oxford and made in Honduras, the taste is mild-to-medium in body and you can enjoy this new series in boxes of 25.

HABANA REAL ★*New*★
Handmade in Danli, Honduras.

Wrapper: Ecuador, Mexico   Binder: Honduras   Filler: Honduras, Mexico

Shape	Name	Lgth	Ring	Wrapper
Double Corona	Corona	7½	49	CC-Ma
Double Corona	Churchill	7	50	CC-Ma
Robusto	Robusto	5	54	CC-Ma
Torpedo	Torpedo	6⅛	54	CC-Ma
Toro	Canon	6½	60	CC-Ma
Petit Corona	No. 4	5	42	CC-Ma
Lonsdale	Lancero	7½	40	CC-Ma
Culebras	Culebra	6	38	CC-Ma

Tobacco Exchange introduced this cigar in 2007, with a mild-to-medium body with a Ecuadorian wrapper and medium-to-full with a Mexican maduro wrapper. All sizes are offered in boxes of 25.

HABANOS PUROS
Handmade in Esteli, Nicaragua.

BLEND NO. 1:

Wrapper: Ecuador   Binder: Ecuador   Filler: Honduras, Nicaragua

BLEND NO. 2:

Wrapper: Indonesia   Binder: Ecuador   Filler: Ecuador, Nicaragua

BLEND NO. 3:

Wrapper: Ecuador   Binder: Nicaragua   Filler: Nicaragua

BLEND NO. 4:

Wrapper: Nicaragua   Binder: Mexico   Filler: Honduras, Mexico, Nicaragua

HANDMADE CIGARS: BRAND LISTINGS

BLEND NO. 5:

Wrapper: Cameroon   *Binder: Honduras*   *Filler: Mexico, Nicaragua*

BLEND NO. 6:

Wrapper: Nicaragua   *Binder: Nicaragua*   *Filler: Costa Rica, Mexico, Nicaragua*

Shape	Name	Lgth	Ring	Wrapper
Robusto	Robusto	5	50	CC-CM-Ma
Churchill	Churchill	7	48	CC-CM-Ma
Torpedo	Torpedo	6	52	CC-CM-Ma

Three sizes, six blends! Started as a mail-order brand in 2001, Habanos Puros is now in national distribution. Blend No. 1 (yellow box) is mild with a Connecticut-seed wrapper. Blend No. 2 (green) is mild-to-medium in body with a Sumatra-grown wrapper. Blend No. 3 (canary) is medium-bodied as is Blend No. 4 (red), with a sun-grown Corojo wrapper. Blend No. 5 (mustard) is also medium-to-full with a Cameroon wrapper. Blend No. 6 (burgundy) is full-bodied with an H2000 maduro wrapper. All six blends are presented in upright cartons of 20 cigars each.

HABANOS PUROS FUERTE

Handmade in Esteli, Nicaragua.

Wrapper: Nicaragua   *Binder: Nicaragua*   *Filler: Costa Rica, Nicaragua*

Shape	Name	Lgth	Ring	Wrapper
Petit Corona	No. 4	4½	42	CM
Robusto	Robusto	4⅞	50	CM
Robusto	Siglo	5½	54	CM
Toro	Churchill	6½	48	CM
Torpedo	No. 2	6⅛	52	CM
Pyramid	Piramides	6	56	CM
Toro	Magnum 58	6	58	CM
Toro	Magnum 60	6	60	CM

This blend was introduced in 2006 and offers a full-bodied taste. It is offered in boxes of 25.

HANDMADE CIGARS: BRAND LISTINGS

HABANOS PUROS SELECCION SUPREMA ★*New*★
Handmade in Esteli, Nicaragua.

Wrapper: Nicaragua　　　　　*Binder: Nicaragua*　　　　　*Filler: Nicaragua*

Shape	Name	Lgth	Ring	Wrapper
Robusto	Royal Coronas	4½	48	CM
Robusto	Robustos	4⅞	50	CM
Churchill	Esplendidos	7	48	CM
Toro	Siglos	6	52	CM
Double Corona	Double Coronas	7½	50	CM
Torpedo	Piramides	6⅛	52	CM
Toro	Double Robustos	6½	54	CM

Introduced in 2007, this is a full-bodied cigar line that features a Nicaraguan sun-grown Corojo wrapper. All sizes are offered in all-cedar boxes of 10.

HAMILTONS HOUSE SELECTION
Handmade in Santiago, Dominican Republic.

Wrapper: Indonesia　　　　　*Binder: Dom. Rep.*　　　　　*Filler: Dom. Rep.*

Shape	Name	Lgth	Ring	Wrapper
Double Corona	Double Corona	7	50	CM
Toro	Toro	6	50	CM
Long Corona	Corona	6	44	CM
Torpedo	Torpedo	6	54	CM
Robusto	Robusto	5	52	CM

Now distributed by Famous Smoke Shop, this is a mild-to-medium-bodied cigar with a Sumatra wrapper that was originally introduced by the permanently-tanned actor George Hamilton. It's offered in elegant boxes of 25.

HAPPY CUBA
Handmade in Frankfort, New York, USA.

Wrapper: Ecuador　　　　　　　　　　　　　　*Binder: Cameroon*
Filler: Brazil, Dominican Republic, Honduras, Jamaica

HANDMADE CIGARS: BRAND LISTINGS

HAVANA ESPECIAL
Handmade in San Diego, California, USA.

Wrapper: Nicaragua   *Binder: Nicaragua*   *Filler: Dom. Rep.*

Introduced in 1996, this is a medium-to-full-bodied blend, available in four sizes (No. 1, 6 x 46; No. 2, 5 x 50; No. 3, 5½ x 52; No. 4, 6 x 54 torpedo) with maduro wrappers for all shapes and natural wrappers for the nos. 2 and 3.

HAVANA HONEYS
Handmade in Santiago, Dominican Republic.

Wrapper: Indonesia   *Binder: Dom. Rep.*   *Filler: Dom. Rep.*

Shape	Name		Lgth	Ring	Wrapper
Corona	Del Sol	*(tube available)*	5½	42	CM
Torpedo	Bueno		7	36	CM
Short Panatela	Rio		5	36	CM
Small Panatela	Tin		4	30	CM
Cigarillo	Poco		3½	20	CM
	Little cigars:				
Cigarillo	Kings		3¼	20	CM
Cigarillo	100s		3⅞	20	CM

Introduced in 1998, all shapes are flavored with honey, blackberry, chocolate, peach, rum or vanilla, plus cherry in the Tin and Poco sizes. You can enjoy them in boxes of 10, 16, 20, 25, 50 or 60 depending on the shape. The little cigars are machine-made and also come with mint flavoring.

HAVANA RUM
Handmade in Santiago, Dominican Republic.

Wrapper: Dom. Rep.   *Binder: Dom. Rep.*   *Filler: Dom. Rep.*

Introduced in 1988, this is a medium-bodied cigar made in two sizes with a Sumatra-seed wrapper, offered in bundles or boxes of 25.

HAVANA SANDWICH   ★*New*★
Handmade, with mixed filler, in Esteli, Nicaragua.

Wrapper: Indonesia   *Binder: Nicaragua*   *Filler: Nicaragua, Peru*

HANDMADE CIGARS: BRAND LISTINGS

Shape	Name	Lgth	Ring	Wrapper
Double Corona	Super Cazador	7½	52	CM
Double Corona	Churchill	7	50	CM
Torpedo	Torpedo	7	52	CM
Robusto	Robusto	5	50	CM

Miura Premium Cigars makes this medium-bodied cigar using mixed filler, offered in bundles of 25.

HAVANA STAR
Handmade in Danli, Honduras.

Wrapper: Nicaragua   Binder: Honduras   Filler: Honduras, Nicaragua, Panama

Shape	Name	Lgth	Ring	Wrapper
Small Panatela	Chicos	4½	32	CM

This brand debuted in 1998 and offers a mild-to-medium-bodied taste. You can enjoy it in packs of five.

HAVANA SUN GROWN
Handmade in Santiago, Dominican Republic.

Wrapper: Ecuador   Binder: USA/Connecticut   Filler: Dom. Rep., Mexico, Peru

Shape	Name	Lgth	Ring	Wrapper
Long Corona	Corona	6⅛	43	CM
Robusto	Robusto	5¼	52	CM
Grand Corona	Toro	6	46	CM
Churchill	Churchill	7	48	CM
Torpedo	Torpedo	6½	52	CM
Toro	Grande	6	54	CM

Previously known as Occidental Havana Sun Grown, this blend is distributed by the Alec Bradley Cigar Co. and was developed in 2001 by Hendrik Kelner. It offers a full-bodied flavor featuring a sun-grown wrapper from Ecuador using hybrid seeds that marry characteristics of both Piloto Cubano and Connecticut tobaccos. It is offered in boxes of 20.

HANDMADE CIGARS: BRAND LISTINGS

HAVANA SUNRISE ★*New*★
Handmade in Danli, Honduras.

Wrapper: Ecuador   *Binder: Nicaragua*   *Filler: Honduras*

Shape	Name	Lgth	Ring	Wrapper
Double Corona	Churchill	7½	50	CC
Torpedo	Torpedo	6½	54	CC
Toro	Emperador	6¼	54	CC
Robusto	Robusto	5	50	CC
Churchill	Havana	7	48	CC
Long Corona	Corona	6	44	CC

The Inter-American Cigar Co. introduced this edition of Havana Sunrise in 2007.
It's mild-to-medium in body and is offered in boxes of 25.

HAVANA SWEETS
Handmade in La Romana, Dominican Republic.

Wrapper: Indonesia   *Binder: Nicaragua*   *Filler: Colombia, Dom. Rep.*

Shape	Name	Lgth	Ring	Wrapper
Petit Corona	Boxed sizes	5	42	CM
Small Panatela	Tinned sizes	4	30	CM

This flavored brand was introduced by Altadis USA in 2005. It is offered in two
sizes, both available in Honey, Honey Berry and Irish Cream flavors in boxes of
25 or tins of seven.

HEAVEN
Handmade in Santiago, Dominican Republic.

Wrapper: Indonesia   *Binder: Dom. Rep.*   *Filler: Dom. Rep.*

Shape	Name		Lgth	Ring	Wrapper
Corona Extra	Corona	*(tube available)*	5½	46	CC
Torpedo	Torpedo		6	50	CC
Small Panatela	Petite	*(tube available)*	5	30	CC
Cigarillo	Cherubs		3½	26	CC

HANDMADE CIGARS: BRAND LISTINGS

This is a 1996-introduced, flavored series introduced by Heather Phillips's Heavenly Cigar Co. It features a Sumatra wrapper and a five-point flavoring process. The Petite and Corona are offered in all 14 flavors: Heavenly Vanilla, Angel's Spice (cinnamon), Cupid's Cherry Cream, Raging Rum, Chocolate Thunder, Sgrawberry Bananna Bliss, Midnight Mocha Creme, Heather's Honey Nut, Aphrodite's Amaretto, Orange Dreamsicle, Grape Goddess, Mango-Licious, Mojito Madness and Celestial Cognac! The Torpedo and Cherubs are available in Heavenly Vanilla, Cupid's Cherry Cream, Raging Rum, Celestial Cognac and Heather's Honey Nut. You can enjoy them in 5-packs or in boxes of 10, 25 or 50 or bundles of 25.

HELIX
Handmade in Danli, Honduras.
Wrapper: USA/Connecticut

Binder: Honduras, Mexico   Filler: Brazil, Dom. Rep., Honduras, Mexico

Shape	Name		Lgth	Ring	Wrapper
Petit Corona	x542		5	42	CC
Robusto	x550		5	50	CC-Ma
Toro	x652		6	52	CC-Ma
Churchill	x748		7	48	CC-Ma
Torpedo	XP Pyramid		6	54	CC-Ma
Giant	Super 8		8	54	CC-Ma
Small Panatela	Esplendido		4⅛	32	CC
Lonsdale	Cylinder	*(tubed)*	6½	44	CC-Ma
Robusto	Tubular	*(tubed)*	5	50	CC-Ma

Introduced to a great response in 2002, this is an delicate, mild cigar featuring an elegant Connecticut Shade wrapper and Mexican binder, offered in an electric-blue box of 25. In 2003, the maduro line was added with a Broadleaf wrapper and Honduran binder. All sizes are offered in boxes of 25 except for the tubed shapes, in 20s and the Esplendido, available in tins of 10.

HELIX REMIX
Handmade in Santiago, Dominican Republic.

Wrapper: USA/Connecticut   Binder: Indonesia   Filler: Dom. Rep.

HANDMADE CIGARS: BRAND LISTINGS

Shape	Name	Lgth	Ring	Wrapper
Robusto	Robusto	5½	50	CC
Corona	Corona	5¼	44	CC
Short Panatela	Petite Corona	5	38	CC
Small Panatela	Esplendidos	4⅛	32	CC

Introduced in 2005 and made in the famed General Cigar Dominicana factory, this is the first flavored cigar made by General Cigar! Originally called Helix Infusion, it's aimed at younger smokers in their 20s and 30s who find mild-bodied, flavored cigars more accessible. The "original" Remix is accented with Amaretto and the Café Mocha line was added using a coffee liqueur (same sizes) in 2007. The larger shapes are offered in boxes of 25 while the Esplendidos are available in tins of 10.

HENRY CLAY
Handmade in La Romana, Dominican Republic.
Wrapper: USA/Connecticut   *Binder: Dom. Rep.*   *Filler: Dom. Rep.*

Shape	Name		Lgth	Ring	Wrapper
Corona	Brevas		5⅛	42	Ma
Corona Extra	Brevas a la Conserva		5⅝	46	Ma
Churchill	Brevas Finas		6½	48	Ma
Toro	Grande	*(tubed)*	6½	48	Ma
Robusto	Rothchilde		5	50	Ma
Toro	Toro		6	50	Ma

This flavorful, medium-to-full-bodied brand is named for the famous American politician of the same name (U.S. senator from Kentucky 1806-07, 1810-11, 1831-42, 1849-52; U.S. representative and Speaker of the House 1811-14, 1815-21, 1823-25; U.S. Secretary of State 1825-29). This brand originated in Cuba and was once one of the world's leading brands of Havana cigars. The Henry Clay factory from those long-ago days in Havana is still pictured on the brand's box. Most sizes are offered in boxes of 25 without cellophane (Brevas in 50s, Grandes in 10s), or 20 with cellophane (Brevas in 25s).

HANDMADE CIGARS: BRAND LISTINGS

HENRY CLAY HONDURAN
Handmade in Danli, Honduras.

Wrapper: Nicaragua   *Binder: Nicaragua*   *Filler: Honduras, Nicaragua, Peru*

Shape	Name	Lgth	Ring	Wrapper
Double Corona	Churchill	7	52	CM
Lonsdale	Dalias	6½	44	CM
Torpedo	Belicoso	6⅛	52	CM
Robusto	Hermoso	5	50	CM
Toro	Grandes	6	50	CM

This is a medium-to-full-bodied version of the Henry Clay band, distributed by Cigars by Santa Clara beginning in 2005. It's offered in elegant boxes of 20.

HIDALGO
Handmade, with mixed filler, in Colon, Panama.

Wrapper: Ecuador   *Binder: Mexico*   *Filler: Dom. Rep., Honduras, Panama*

Shape	Name	Lgth	Ring	Wrapper
Lonsdale	Cazadore	7	44	CC
Lonsdale	Fuma	7	44	Ma
Corona	Corona	5½	42	CC-Ma
Churchill	Double Corona	7	48	CC-Ma
Giant	Monarch	8½	52	CC-Ma

Offered by Arango Cigar Co., these medium-bodied cigars use mixed filler (long and short) and are offered in bundles of 20 cigars each.

HIGH MONK
Handmade in Esteli, Nicaragua.

Wrapper: Nicaragua   *Binder: Nicaragua*   *Filler: Nicaragua*

Shape	Name	Lgth	Ring	Wrapper
Toro	High Monk	6½	54	Ma

No word on whether this brand was inspired by a drugged monk, or one filled with religious zeal. The TESA Cigar Co. introduced this line in 2004 and it is offered in boxes of 24.

HANDMADE CIGARS: BRAND LISTINGS

HOJA BORICUA
Handmade in Mayaguez, Puerto Rico.

Wrapper: Indonesia   *Binder: Dom. Rep.*   *Filler: Puerto Rico*

Shape	Name	Lgth	Ring	Wrapper
Short Panatela	Panatela	5	38	CM
Corona	Petit Corona	5½	42	CM
Lonsdale	Lonsdale	7	44	CM
Grand Corona	Grand Corona	6	46	CM
Robusto	Robusto	5	50	CM
Toro	Toro	6	50	CM
Torpedo	Torpedo	6½	52	CM
Double Corona	Churchill	7	50	CM

Here is a premium cigar from Puerto Rico, offered by the JFC Tobacco Corporation. It was introduced in 2002 and is medium in body, offered in wood boxes of 25.

HOJA BORICUA GRAN RESERVA
Handmade in Mayaguez, Puerto Rico.

Wrapper: Nicaragua   *Binder: Nicaragua*   *Filler: Puerto Rico*

Shape	Name	Lgth	Ring	Wrapper
Double Corona	Churchill	7	50	CM
Torpedo	Torpedo	6½	52	CM
Toro	Toro	6	50	CM
Robusto	Robusto	5	50	CM
Grand Corona	Corona	6	46	CM

This is a full-bodied brand which was introduced in 2004, offered in boxes of 20 or 25.

HOJA DE FLORES
Handmade in Esteli, Nicaragua.

Wrapper: Nicaragua   *Binder: Nicaragua*   *Filler: Nicaragua*

HANDMADE CIGARS: BRAND LISTINGS

This blend was introduced in 2002 and re-blended for 2003, 2004 and again in 2005. Initially made in Panama, it is now made in Nicaragua, with a full body, in five sizes. It is offered in boxes of 25.

HOJA REAL
Handmade in San Andres Tuxtla, Mexico.

Wrapper: Mexico	*Binder: Mexico*	*Filler: Mexico*

This well-known, 13-size Mexican brand has been in and out of circulation in the U.S. over the past several years. The line is medium-to-full in body and features a Sumatra-seed wrapper. There are two extra-large sizes: the Aniversario (10 x 46) and the Grande Cedar (12 x 70). Most sizes are offered in packs of five or boxes of 25, with the Grande Cedar available individually and the Aniversario in boxes of ten.

HOJA REAL PLATINO
Handmade in San Andres Tuxtla, Mexico.

Wrapper: Mexico	*Binder: Mexico*	*Filler: Mexico*

This is a three-size line from Hoja Real, introduced in the U.S. in 2001. It offers a medium-bodied taste with a Sumatra-seed wrapper, presented in elegant gift packs of five cigars each.

HONEY DELIGHTS
BY VICTOR SINCLAIR
Handmade in Santiago, Dominican Republic.

Wrapper: Indonesia	*Binder: Dom. Rep.*	*Filler: Dom. Rep.*

Shape	Name	Lgth	Ring	Wrapper
Cigarillo	Tin Packs	4	28	CM

Introduced in 2000, this is a mild, flavored cigar in cherry, honey, rum and vanilla in the Tins size. Honey Delights are offered in handy ten-packs.

HOOKAH
Handmade in Esteli, Nicaragua.

Wrapper: Nicaragua	*Binder: Nicaragua*	*Filler: Nicaragua*

Shape	Name	Lgth	Ring	Wrapper
Petit Corona	Petit Corona	4	44	CM
Corona	Corona	5½	42	CM

Robusto	Robusto	5	50	CM

This mild blend was introduced by the Tabacalera Tropical in 2004 and is now distributed by Harold Levinson Associates. It's flavor-infused with Tahitian Vanilla or Melon flavors in boxes of 24.

HOYO DE HONDURAS
Handmade in Danli, Honduras.

Wrapper: Honduras   *Binder: Honduras*   *Filler: Honduras*

Shape	Name	Lgth	Ring	Wrapper
Lonsdale	No. 1	7	44	CM
Corona	No. 4	5½	44	CM
Double Corona	Churchill	7	50	CM
Long Corona	Corona	6¼	44	CM
Torpedo	Torpedo	7	50	CM
Robusto	Rothschild	5	50	CM
Toro	Toro	6	50	CM
Giant	Viajante	8	54	CM

Created in 1985, this is an all-Honduran, full-bodied cigar from the House of Oxford, offered in economical bundles of 25.

HOYO DE MONTERREY
Handmade in Cofradia, Honduras.

Wrapper: Ecuador, USA/Connecticut   *Binder: USA/Connecticut*
Filler: Dominican Republic, Honduras, Nicaragua

Shape	Name	Lgth	Ring	Wrapper
Corona	Cafe Royales	5⅝	43	CC
Grand Corona	Churchills	6¼	45	CC-Ma
Corona Extra	Coronas	5⅝	46	CC-Ma
Short Panatela	Demi-Tasse	4	39	CC
Churchill	Double Coronas	6¾	48	CC-Ma
Toro	Governors	6⅛	50	CC-Ma

HANDMADE CIGARS: BRAND LISTINGS

Slim Panatela	Largo Elegantes	7¼	34	CC-Ma
Cigarillo	Margaritas	5¼	29	CC
Small Panatela	Petit	4¾	31	CC
Giant	Presidents	8½	52	CC-Ma
Robusto	Rothschilds	4½	50	CC-Ma
Petit Corona	Sabrosos	5	40	CC-Ma
Double Corona	Sultans	7¼	54	CC-Ma
Corona	Super Hoyos	5½	44	CC-Ma
Long Corona	Tubos *(tubed)*	6¼	43	CC
Robusto	Robusto	5½	54	CC-Ma
Robusto	Estelo *(tubed)*	5	52	CC-Ma
Grand Corona	Library Edition: "Utopia"	6¼	45	CC
	Silver Bundles:			
Grand Corona	Majestic	6⅛	45	CM-Ma
Toro	No. 50 Exquisito	6	50	CM-Ma
Robusto	No. 450 Robusto	4½	50	CM-Ma
Double Corona	Executive	7	54	CM-Ma

This ancient brand began in Cuba but first appeared in a Honduran-manufactured blend in 1969. Hoyo de Monterrey cigars are medium-to-heavy in flavor. Handmade in Honduras, these are truly quality cigars with a large variety of sizes to give exceptional satisfaction to the smoker. The tobaccos are blended from four nations, including the Cuban-seed Honduran binder and Sumatra-seed wrappers from Ecuador. The maduro wrappers use only the finest Connecticut Broadleaf available, combined with Connecticut Shade binder. Most sizes are offered in boxes of 25, with tubed cigars in 20s.

The Library Edition and Silver Bundles series is made for Cigars by Santa Clara. The Silver Bundles is offered in four popular sizes, packed in an inexpensive foil bundle of 25.

HOYO DE MONTERREY DARK SUMATRA
Handmade in Cofradia, Honduras.
Wrapper: Ecuador   Binder: USA/Connecticut   Filler: Dom. Rep., Honduras, Nicaragua

HANDMADE CIGARS: BRAND LISTINGS

Shape	Name	Lgth	Ring	Wrapper
Toro	Media Noche	5¾	54	Os
Toro	Noche	6½	52	Os
Grand Corona	Ebano	6	45	Os
Robusto	Espresso	4½	50	Os

This is a full-bodied blend for Hoyo, introduced in 2002. Specially selected, extra-dark Ecuadorian-grown, Sumatra-seed leaves are used for the wrappers on these cigars, imparting a richer taste. Three shapes are offered in traditional boxes of 25, with the Espresso shape available in a box of 40.

HOYO DE TRADICION ★New★
Handmade in Cofradia, Honduras.
Wrapper: Honduras

Binder: USA/Connecticut   Filler: Dom. Rep., Honduras, Nicaragua

Shape	Name	Lgth	Ring	Wrapper
Robusto	Epicure	5¼	50	CM
Grand Corona	Corona	5¾	45	CM
Toro	Toro	6	52	CM
Toro	Toro Grande	6¼	54	CM

Introduced in 2007, this is a medium-bodied blend with features a Honduran Viso Rosado wrapper and Nicaraguan filler leaves from the volcanic island of Ometepe. It features a giant red-and-white band and is offered in boxes of 25.

HUGO CASSAR DIAMOND COLLECTION
Handmade in Esteli, Nicaragua.
Wrapper: Nicaragua   Binder: Nicaragua   Filler: Nicaragua

Shape	Name	Lgth	Ring	Wrapper
Churchill	Churchill	7	48	CM
Corona	Corona Gorda	5½	42	CM
Long Corona	Corona	6	44	CM
Toro	Toro	6	50	CM

Robusto	Robusto	5	50	CM

The Hugo Cassar Diamond Collection first emerged in 1996, but left the market at the end of the Cigar Boom. It was reintroduced as a Dominican-made in 2004, but is now made in Nicaragua with a mild-to-medium body in bundles of 20.

HUGO CASSAR DOMINICAN
Handmade in Santiago, Dominican Republic.

Wrapper: Dom. Rep.　　　*Binder: Dom. Rep.*　　　*Filler: Dom. Rep.*

Shape	Name	Lgth	Ring	Wrapper
Double Corona	Churchill	7	50	CM-Ma
Toro	Toro	6	50	CM-Ma
Toro	Toro Grande	6	54	CM-Ma
Torpedo	Torpedo	6½	52	CM-Ma
Robusto	Robusto	5	50	CM-Ma

This is a mild-bodied, all-Dominican cigar introduced in 2005. It's offered in bundles of 20.

HUMBERTO MENDOZA
Handmade in Manila, the Philippines.

Wrapper: Indonesia　　　*Binder: Indonesia*　　　*Filler: Philippines*

Shape	Name	Lgth	Ring	Wrapper
Robusto	Robusto	5	52	CM
Lonsdale	Corona Larga	7	42	CM
Double Corona	Double Corona	7½	52	CM
Corona	Corona	5½	42	CM
Churchill	Churchill	7	47	CM

This brand is a tribute to the respected Cuban tobacco grower Humberto Mendoza and offers is a mild blend of tobaccos featuring an Indonesian wrapper grown in Java. It is available in bundles of 25.

HANDMADE CIGARS: BRAND LISTINGS

HUZGAR ★New★
Handmade in Frankfort, New York, USA.

Wrapper: Cameroon *Binder: Honduras* *Filler: Dom. Rep.*

Shape	Name	Lgth	Ring	Wrapper
Giant Corona	Double Corona	8½	44	CM
Robusto	Robusto	5	50	CM
Long Corona	Corona	6	44	CM

Introduced in 2007, this is a medium-to-full-bodied blend with subtle, spicy tones. All sizes are offered in bundles of 50.

ILLUSIONE ★New★
Handmade in Danli, Honduras.

Wrapper: Nicaragua *Binder: Nicaragua* *Filler: Nicaragua*

Shape	Name	Lgth	Ring	Wrapper
Petit Corona	68	4	44	CM
Robusto	88	5	52	CM
Toro	CG:4	5⅝	48	CM
Long Corona	F9	6¼	44	CM
Torpedo	2	5¼	52	CM
Churchill	888	6¾	48	CM
Double Corona	4/2G	7½	49	CM
Perfecto	M7	6½	58	CM
Culebras	2/3	6½	33	CM
Giant	1	9¼	48	CM

Introduced in 2007, this is a medium-to-full-bodied blend with plenty of mystery added to its all-Nicaraguan blend. It uses a double binder in all sizes and is presented in mahogany cabinets of 25 cigars each in a 5x5 format.

IMPERIO CUBANO
Handmade in Santiago, Dominican Republic.

Wrapper: Cameroon *Binder: Dom. Rep.* *Filler: Dom. Rep.*

HANDMADE CIGARS: BRAND LISTINGS

Shape	Name	Lgth	Ring	Wrapper
Corona	Corona	5½	44	CM
Robusto	Robusto	5	50	CM
Toro	Toro	6	50	CM
Torpedo	Torpedo	6½	52	CM

This brand was made in Miami for many years by the Antillian Cigar Company, but production was transferred in 2004 to the Tabacalera A. Fuente in the Dominican Republic. Featuring a Cameroon wrapper, these are medium-to-full-bodied cigars, offered in boxes of 20.

INDIAN TABAC 10 YEAR ANNIVERSARY ★New★
Handmade in Danli, Honduras.

Wrapper: Nicaragua   Binder: Nicaragua   Filler: Nicaragua

Shape	Name	Lgth	Ring	Wrapper
Robusto	Robusto	5	50	CM
Lonsdale	Lonsdale	6½	44	CM
Toro	Toro	6½	52	CM
Torpedo	Torpedo	6½	52	CM

This full-bodied blend was introduced in 2007 with a Habano wrapper. It's offered in boxes of 20.

INDIAN TABAC ANNIVERSARY LIMITED RESERVE
Handmade in Danli, Honduras.

Wrapper: Ecuador   Binder: Mexico   Filler: Honduras, Nicaragua

Shape	Name	Lgth	Ring	Wrapper
Robusto	Bear	5	50	CC
Churchill	Buffalo	7	47	CC
Torpedo	Bison	6½	54	CC

Returned to distribution in 2006 by Meier & Dutch, this is a mild-bodied cigar with a Connecticut-seed wrapper. It's offered in boxes of 25.

HANDMADE CIGARS: BRAND LISTINGS

ISABELLA
Handmade, with mixed filler, in Santiago, Dominican Republic.
Wrapper: Indonesia   *Binder: Indonesia*   *Filler: Nicaragua*

Introduced in 1997, this is a medium-bodied cigar available in six sizes . . . but with character, thanks to its Sumatra wrapper. The Corona and Delicioso sizes are also available in a flavored style, in cognac, rum and vanilla.

ISLA DE CUBA   ★*New*★
Handmade in Santa Rosa de Copan, Honduras.
Wrapper: Ecuador, USA/Connecticut
Binder: Nicaragua, USA/Connecticut   *Filler: Dom. Rep., Nicaragua*

Shape	Name	Lgth	Ring	Wrapper
Corona	Corona	5½	44	CC-Ma
Robusto	Robusto	5	54	CC-Ma
Toro	Toro	6	54	CC-Ma
Torpedo	Belicoso	6⅛	52	CC-Ma
Double Corona	Churchill	7	52	CC-Ma

This line was introduced in 2007 and is medium in body with a Connecticut-seed wrapper from Ecuador and Nicaraguan binder. It's medium to full in body with a Connecticut Broadleaf maduro wrapper and binder, but all sizes are offered in boxes of 25.

ISLA DEL SOL   ★*New*★
Handmade, with medium filler, in Esteli, Nicaragua.
Wrapper: Indonesia   *Binder: Nicaragua*   *Filler: Dom. Rep., Nicaragua*

Shape	Name	Lgth	Ring	Wrapper
Petit Corona	Gran Corona	5	44	CM
Robusto	Robusto	5	52	CM
Toro	Toro	6	52	CM
Double Corona	Churchill	7	50	CM

Drew Estates introduced this line in 2007, which uses a Sumatra wrapper and is infused with Sumatra Mandheling bean coffee and has a sugared tip. It's value-priced and offered in boxes of 20.

HANDMADE CIGARS: BRAND LISTINGS

ISLA DEL SOL
Handmade, with short filler, in Esteli, Nicaragua.
Wrapper: Ecuador   Binder: Nicaragua   Filler: Dom. Rep., Honduras, Nicaragua

Shape	Name	Lgth	Ring	Wrapper
Double Corona	Churchill	7	50	CC
Toro	Epicure	6	50	CC
Robusto	Robusto	5	50	CC
Torpedo	Torpedo	6½	54	CC
Torpedo	Belicoso	5	54	CC

Alliance Cigar distributes this medium-bodied blend made by the Tabacalera Perdomo. It features a Sumatra-seed wrapper in bundles of 25.

ISLAND AMARETTO
Handmade, with medium filler, in Yogyakarta, Indonesia.
Wrapper: Indonesia   Binder: Indonesia   Filler: Brazil, Dom. Rep., Indonesia

Shape	Name	Lgth	Ring	Wrapper
Short Panatela	Bellissima	4½	36	CM
Petit Corona	Bella	4¾	42	CM
Lonsdale	Grand Bella	7	42	CM
	Machine-bunched:			
Cigarillo	Treasures	3⅝	20	CM

This is the original version of the highly aromatic Island Amaretto brand, with medium filler instead of long filler leaves. It has a medium-bodied taste and is offered in boxes of 25, except for the Treasures, available in 50s.

ISLAND COLLECTION
Hand-rolled, with medium filler, in Yogyakarta, Indonesia.
Wrapper: Indonesia   Binder: Indonesia   Filler: Dom. Rep.,Indonesia

Shape	Name	Lgth	Ring	Wrapper
Petit Corona	Corona	4¾	42	CM
Lonsdale	Grand Corona	7	42	CM

Short Panatela	Petite	4½	36	CM
Cigarillo	Treasure	3⅝	20	CM

Introduced in 1999, this medium-bodied, all-Indonesian blend includes a hint of sweetness and is available in natural and in flavored versions in Amaretto, rum, mint and vanilla. It is available in boxes of 25 (or 50 for Treasures) and in packs of three or five.

ISLAND DELIGHTS
Handmade in Tamboril, Dominican Republic.

Wrapper: Indonesia　　　　*Binder: Dom. Rep.*　　　　*Filler: Dom. Rep.*

Shape	*Name*	*Lgth*	*Ring*	*Wrapper*
Small Panatela		4¼	32	CM
Corona		5½	42	CM

There are seven flavors in two shapes: take your choice of Amaretto, cherry, chocolate, Piña Colada, strawberry, rum and vanilla. A product of the JM Tobacco Company, Island Delights are offered in boxes of 24 in the larger size and tins of 10 in the smaller.

J. FUEGO GRAN RESERVA　★*New*★
Handmade in Danli, Honduras.

COROJO NO. 1:
Wrapper: Honduras　　*Binder: Costa Rica*　　*Filler: Costa Rica, Honduras, Nicaragua*

NATURAL:
Wrapper: Nicaragua　　*Binder: Honduras*　　*Filler: Honduras, Nicaragua*

Shape	*Name*	*Lgth*	*Ring*	*Wrapper*
	Corojo No. 1:			
Corona Extra	Corona	4½	46	CM
Robusto	Robusto	5	52	CM
Torpedo	Belicoso	6	54	CM
Double Corona	Elegante	7½	50	CM
Toro	Grande	6½	58	CM

	Natural:			
Corona Extra	Corona	4½	46	CM
Robusto	Robusto	5	50	CM
Toro	Toro	6½	52	CM
Torpedo	Belicoso	6	54	CM
Churchill	Churchill	7	48	CM

Jesus Fuego introduced these lines in 2007. The Corojo No. 1 blend features a Honduran-grown Corojo wrapper, is medium-to-full in body and offered in boxes of 21. The medium-bodied Natural line is also offered in three-layer boxes of 21.

J.L. SALAZAR Y HERMANOS RESERVA ESPECIAL
Handmade in Esteli, Nicaragua.

Wrapper: Ecuador   Binder: Nicaragua   Filler: Nicaragua

Shape	Name	Lgth	Ring	Wrapper
Torpedo	Torpedo	6¼	54	CM
Double Corona	Churchill	7¼	52	CM
Toro	Toro	6	52	CM
Robusto	Robusto	5½	52	CM

This is a full-bodied blend from the Tabacalera Esteli, introduced in national distribution in 2003. It is offered in boxes of 25.

JACK'S RESERVE ★*New*★
Handmade, with mixed filler, in Esteli, Nicaragua.

Wrapper: Indonesia   Binder: Nicaragua   Filler: Dom. Rep., Honduras, Nicaragua

Shape	Name	Lgth	Ring	Wrapper
Robusto	Robusto	5	52	CM
Toro	Toro	6	52	CM
Double Corona	Churchill	7	52	CM

Made with sandwich filler and a Sumatra wrapper, this is a mild-bodied blend introduced in 2007. It's available in bundles of 20.

HANDMADE CIGARS: BRAND LISTINGS

JAMAICA BAY
Handmade in Kingston, Jamaica.

Wrapper: USA/Connecticut   *Binder: Jamaica*   *Filler: Jamaica*

Shape	Name	Lgth	Ring	Wrapper
Toro	No. 200	6	50	CC
Robusto	No. 300	5	50	CC

The Arango Cigar Company revived this old brand, now made by Barrington House Cigars in Jamaica, in 2006. It's mild in body and offered in bundles of 20.

JAMAICA HERITAGE
Handmade in Kingston, Jamaica.

Wrapper: USA/Connecticut   *Binder: Mexico*   *Filler: Dom. Rep., Jamaica, Mexico*

Shape	Name	Lgth	Ring	Wrapper
Petit Corona	Corona Fina	5	40	CC
Robusto	Robusto	5	50	CC
Grand Corona	Petit Churchill	6	45	CC
Corona	Corona	5½	42	CC

This old brand returned in 2006, with a mild-bodied flavor using aged Jamaican filler. It is offered in boxes of 25.

JERICHO
Handmade in Danli, Honduras.

Wrapper: Nicaragua   *Binder: Honduras*   *Filler: Honduras, Nicaragua*

Shape	Name	Lgth	Ring	Wrapper
Robusto	Robusto	5	50	CM
Lonsdale	Candela	6½	44	DC
Toro	Toro	6	50	CM
Torpedo	Figurado	6⅛	54	CM
Churchill	Churchill	7	48	CM

This is a new blend of the Jericho line introduced by Meier & Dutch in 2006. Still made by Camacho Cigars, this medium-to-full-bodied blend is offered in boxes of 20. The Candela size is lighter with a mild-to-medium body.

HANDMADE CIGARS: BRAND LISTINGS

JM'S DOMINICAN
Handmade in Santiago, Dominican Republic.
Wrapper: Indonesia, USA/Connecticut   Binder: Dom. Rep.   Filler: Dom. Rep.

Shape	Name	Lgth	Ring	Wrapper
Cigarillo	Petit	4¼	28	CM
Corona	Corona	5½	42	CC-CM-Ma
Robusto	Robusto	5	50	CC-CM-Ma
Toro	Toro	6	50	CC-CM-Ma
Double Corona	Churchill	6¾	50	CC-CM-Ma
Torpedo	Belicoso	6	52	CC-CM-Ma
Robusto	Gordo	5½	62	CC-CM-Ma
Double Corona	Gordo Grande	6¾	62	CC-CM-Ma

Introduced in 1999, this is a value-priced cigar from the JM Tobacco Company. It features a choice of a Connecticut shade (medium body), Indonesian (medium to full body) or maduro wrapper (Connecticut Broadleaf; no Petit or Gordo Grande), Cuban-seed fillers and is offered in boxes of 24 or 50 cigars.

JM'S DOMINICAN CLASSICS
Handmade in Santiago, Dominican Republic.
Wrapper: USA/Connecticut   Binder: Dom. Rep.   Filler: Dom. Rep.

Shape	Name	Lgth	Ring	Wrapper
Long Corona	Lonsdale	6	44	CC
Robusto	Robusto Grande	5½	50	CC
Double Corona	Churchill	6¾	50	CC
Torpedo	Figurado	6	52	CC

This is a medium-to-full-bodied blend, introduced in 2004. It's offered in boxes of 20.

JML 1902   ★*New*★
Handmade in Santiago, Dominican Republic.
Wrapper: USA/Pennsylvania   Binder: Dom. Rep.   Filler: Dom. Rep.

HANDMADE CIGARS: BRAND LISTINGS

black-tube Sweet T's are offered more flavors including Chocolate Mint Martini, Peach Whiskey, Rum & Cola and Strawberry Daiquiri.

JOSE BENITO
Handmade in Santiago, Dominican Republic.

Wrapper: Indonesia   *Binder: USA/Connecticut*   *Filler: Dom. Rep.*

Shape	Name	Lgth	Ring	Wrapper
Small Panatela	Chico	4¼	34	CM
Slim Panatela	Havanito	5	32	CM
Grand Corona	Corona Major	6½	46	CM
Long Corona	Lonsdale	6	43	CM
Toro	Magnum	6	50	CM
Robusto	Robusto	5	50	CM
Double Corona	Presidente	7	50	CM

This well-known brand returned to circulation in 2003, with a mild-to-medium body, an Indonesian wrapper and a value price in boxes of 25.

JOSE LLOPIS
Handmade in Colon, Panama.

Wrapper: Ecuador   *Binder: Mexico*   *Filler: Dom. Rep., Honduras, Panama*

Shape	Name	Lgth	Ring	Wrapper
Giant	Viajante	8½	52	CC-Ma
Churchill	Churchill	7	48	CC-Ma
Lonsdale	No. 1	7	43	CC-Ma
Lonsdale	No. 2	6½	43	CC-Ma
Corona	No. 4	5½	43	CC-Ma
Long Panatela	Palma Extra	7	36	CC-Ma
Robusto	Rothschild	4¾	50	CC-Ma
Double Corona	Soberano	7¼	52	CC-Ma

Introduced in 1984 by the Arango Cigar Co., this cigar is offered in bundles of 20 and is medium in strength; it should not be confused with its milder sibling brand, Jose Llopis Gold.

HANDMADE CIGARS: BRAND LISTINGS

JOSE LLOPIS GOLD
Handmade in Colon, Panama.

Wrapper: USA/Connecticut   Binder: Mexico   Filler: Dom. Rep., Honduras, Panama

Shape	Name	Lgth	Ring	Wrapper
Giant	Viajante	8½	52	CC-Ma
Churchill	Churchill	7	48	CC-Ma
Lonsdale	No. 1	7	43	CC-Ma
Lonsdale	No. 2	6½	43	CC-Ma
Long Panatela	Palma Extra	7	36	CC-Ma
Corona	No. 4	5½	43	CC-Ma
Robusto	Rothschild	4½	50	CC-Ma
Pyramid	Pyramide	7	50	CC-Ma

Created in 1989, this well-respected brand is all handmade and wrapped in Connecticut shade-grown leaves (natural) or Connecticut Broadleaf (maduro). All of its sizes are offered in cedar boxes of 25, except for the Pyramid (20), the Viajante (10) and a five-pack of the No. 2 is available. This mild-bodied cigar is distinctive for its gold band.

JOSE MARTI
Handmade in Esteli, Nicaragua.
Wrapper: Ecuador, USA/Connecticut

Binder: Honduras   *Filler: Dom. Rep., Honduras, Nicaragua*

Shape	Name	Lgth	Ring	Wrapper
Double Corona	Don Juan	7¼	54	CM
Lonsdale	Lonsdale	6½	44	CM
Churchill	Valentino	7	48	CM
Torpedo	Masaya Figurado	6¾	54	CM
Robusto	Magnum	5	52	CM
Pyramid	Trinidad Pyramide	7	48	CM
Short Panatela	Petit Lancero	4½	38	CM
Corona	Remedios	5½	44	CM

range and a choice of Ecuadorian natural or Panama-grown maduro wrappers (full-bodied). Made by hand in Honduras, these cigars are offered in all-wood boxes of 20.

JOYA DEL REY
Hand-rolled in Danli, Honduras.

Wrapper: USA/Connecticut Binder: Honduras Filler: Dom. Rep., Nicaragua

Shape	Name	Lgth	Ring	Wrapper
Robusto	Robusto Grande _(glass tube)_	4¾	50	CM
Corona	Corona Grande _(glass tube)_	5½	42	CM
Toro	Toro Grande _(glass tube)_	6	50	CM
Double Corona	Churchill Grande _(glass tube)_	7	49	CM

The translation of this brand name means "Gems of the King." This is a medium-bodied brand using Cuban-seed tobaccos for the binder and filler. Joya del Rey cigars are offered in all-cedar boxes of five, 12 and 20.

JOYA DE NICARAGUA
Handmade in Esteli, Nicaragua.

Wrapper: Nicaragua Binder: Nicaragua Filler: Nicaragua

Shape	Name	Lgth	Ring	Wrapper
Churchill	Churchill	6⅞	48	CC-Ma
Toro	Toro	6	50	CC-Ma
Lonsdale	No. 1	6⅝	44	CC-Ma
Torpedo	Torpedo	6	52	CC-Ma
Robusto	Consul	4½	52	CC-Ma

Always popular since its introduction in the 1963, this cigar was re-blended in 1996 and re-blended again to its original flavor in 2000. This flagship product of the Tabacos Puros de Nicaragua factory now sports a medium-bodied taste thanks to an Nicaraguan-grown, Havana-seed wrapper. These cigars are meticulously cured and skillfully rolled which makes them truly the "Jewel of Nicaragua."

HANDMADE CIGARS: BRAND LISTINGS

JOYA DE NICARAGUA ANTAÑO 1970
Handmade in Esteli, Nicaragua.

Wrapper: Nicaragua   Binder: Nicaragua   Filler: Nicaragua

Shape	Name	Lgth	Ring	Wrapper
Churchill	Churchill	6⅞	48	CM
Robusto	Consul	4½	52	CM
Petit Corona	Machito	4¾	42	CM
Torpedo	Gran Consul	4¾	60	CM
Robusto	Robusto Grande	5½	52	CM
Torpedo	Belicoso	6	54	CM
Toro	Magnum 660	6	60	CM
Perfecto	Perfecto	6¼	58	CM
Long Panatela	Lancero	7½	38	CM
	Gran Reserva:			
Torpedo	Belicoso	6	52	CM
Churchill	Gran Consul	6⅞	48	CM
Toro	Robusto Grande	6	50	CM

Here is a full-powered blend which was one of the hits of the Retail Tobacco Dealers of America trade show in 2002. It's offered in all-wood boxes of 20.

JOYA DE NICARAGUA CELEBRACION
Handmade in Esteli, Nicaragua.

Wrapper: Nicaragua   Binder: Nicaragua   Filler: Nicaragua

Shape	Name	Lgth	Ring	Wrapper
Torpedo	Torpedo	6	52	CM
Churchill	Churchill	6⅞	48	CM
Toro	Toro	6	50	CM
Robusto	Consul	4½	52	CM
Corona	Corona	5½	42	CM
Toro	Gordo	5½	60	CM

This is a lighter version of the Antaño series, full-bodied, introduced in 2004 by MATASA. It's offered in elegant wood boxes of 20.

JOYA DE NICARAGUA SERIE C ★New★
Handmade in Esteli, Nicaragua.

Wrapper: Ecuador   Binder: Nicaragua   Filler: Nicaragua

Shape	Name	Lgth	Ring	Wrapper
Torpedo	Belicoso	6	54	CC
Toro	Toro	6	50	CC
Robusto	Robusto	5	52	CC
Corona Extra	Corona Gorda	5¼	46	CC

Here is a medium-to-full-bodied cigar with an Ecuadorian-grown, Connecticut-seed wrapper that was introduced in 2007. It's offered in boxes of 20.

JUAN CLEMENTE
Handmade in Santiago, Dominican Republic.

Wrapper: USA/Connecticut   Binder: Dom. Rep.   Filler: Dom. Rep.

Shape	Name	Lgth	Ring	Wrapper
Long Corona	Classic Grand Corona (tubes available)	6	42	Co
Petit Corona	Classic Corona	5	42	Co
Churchill	Classic Churchill	6⅞	46	Co
Double Corona	Classic Double Corona	7½	52	Co
Robusto	Classic Rothschild	4⅞	50	Co

Sought after since 1982, this is the product of a small cigar factory that has only one, ultra-demanding client. The Juan Clemente Classic line offers a full, round, medium-bodied smoke with complex flavors and spices, in boxes of 24 in most sizes.

JUAN CLEMENTE CLUB SELECTION
Handmade in Santiago, Dominican Republic.

Wrapper: USA/Connecticut   Binder: Dom. Rep.   Filler: Dom. Rep.

HANDMADE CIGARS: BRAND LISTINGS

Shape	Name	Lgth	Ring	Wrapper
Toro	No. 1	6	50	Co
Corona Extra	No. 2	4½	46	Co
Lonsdale	No. 3	7	44	Co
Corona	No. 4	5¾	42	Co
Torpedo	No. 5 Obelisco	6	52	Co

The vintage "Club Selection" line from Juan Clemente is a more robust blend, with four years of aging that creates a rich, smooth character for an exquisite smoke. These remarkable cigars are always easy to spot, with the band stylishly attached at the foot!

JUAN CLEMENTE RESERVE
Handmade in Santiago, Dominican Republic.

Wrapper: USA/Connecticut   *Binder: Dom.Rep.*   *Filler: Dom.Rep.*

Shape	Name	Lgth	Ring	Wrapper
Corona	Royal Coronas	5½	42	CC
Robusto	Epicures	5½	50	CC
Grand Corona	Le Parisien	6½	46	CC
Perfecto	Concordes	4	50	CC

The Juan Clemente Reserve Series was introduced in 2001 and offers a medium-to-full-bodied taste in some larger sizes with a distinctive double band, in boxes of 24.

JUAN LOPEZ
Handmade in Esteli, Nicaragua.

Wrapper: Nicaragua   *Binder: Nicaragua*   *Filler: Nicaragua*

Shape	Name	Lgth	Ring	Wrapper
Grand Corona	Corona	5⅝	45	CM
Churchill	Corona Gordas	7	48	CM
Torpedo	Belicoso	6⅛	52	CM
Toro	Epicure No. 1	6	54	CM
Robusto	Epicure No. 2	5	54	CM

Double Corona	Titanias	7¼	54	CM

This is a still-produced, much-respected Cuban brand which debuted in an all-Nicaraguan blend in 2004. Made by Altadis USA, it offers a rich, full-bodied flavor which has impressed the critics. Square-pressed, it is elegantly banded and presented in boxes of 20.

JUAN Y RAMON
Handmade in Santiago, Dominican Republic.

Wrapper: USA/Connecticut   *Binder: Dom. Rep.*   *Filler: Dom. Rep.*

Shape	Name	Lgth	Ring	Wrapper
Double Corona	Churchill	7	50	CC-Ma
Long Corona	Corona	6	42	CC-Ma
Robusto	Rothschild	5	50	CC-Ma
Grand Corona	Suave	6½	46	CC-Ma
Toro	Toro	6	50	CC-Ma

Here was a brand left for dead during the Cigar Boom, but resurrected by the Famous Smoke Shop in 2004 as a mild, bundled brand available in natural or maduro wrappers in bundles of 25.

JUDGES CAVE
Handmade, with mixed filler, in Danli, Honduras.

Wrapper: USA/Connecticut   *Binder: Honduras*   *Filler: Honduras*

Shape	Name	Lgth	Ring	Wrapper
Robusto	Robusto	5	50	CC
Double Corona	Churchill	7	50	CC

This is a mild-to-medium-bodied addition to the F.D. Grave line, introduced in 2004. Both sizes are offered in boxes of 50.

JUST FOR RETAILERS ★*New*★
Handmade in Esteli, Nicaragua.

Wrapper: Nicaragua   *Binder: Nicaragua*   *Filler: Nicaragua*

Shape	Name	Lgth	Ring	Wrapper
Robusto	Robusto	5½	50	CM-Ma

Pyramid	Piramide	6¼	52	CM-Ma
Toro	Super Toro	6½	52	CM-Ma
Toro	Titan	6	60	CM-Ma

The "JFR" was introduced in 2005, but made national distribution in 2007. It's full-bodied and available with either a natural Corojo wrapper or a Habano Maduro wrapper. All are finished with a pigtail head and offered in boxes of 50.

KAHLUA
Handmade in Esteli, Nicaragua.
Wrapper: Cameroon, Indonesia, USA/Connecticut   Binder: Indonesia   Filler: Nicaragua

Shape	Name	Lgth	Ring	Wrapper
Petit Corona	Corona	5	42	CC
Small Panatela	Tin	4⅛	32	CC
Robusto	Robusto	5½	48	CC
Torpedo	Torpedo	6	54	CC
Small Panatela	Mudslide Tin	4⅛	32	CM
Small Panatela	White Russian Tin	4⅛	32	Ma
Small Panatela	Martini Tin	4⅛	32	CM
Short Panatela	Petit Corona	4	38	CM
Toro	Tubo *(tubed)*	6	50	CM

Introduced in 2003, this flavored series from General Cigar is made by the innovative Drew Estate factory in Esteli, Nicaragua. It offers a range of sizes and a variety of wrappers using the unique essence of Kahlua for a medium-bodied taste. Connecticut Shade wrappers are used for most sizes, but the Mudslide uses Cameroon, the Martini a Sumatra leaf and the White Russian has a maduro wrapper. The Corona, Torpedo and Robusto are offered in boxes of 24, the Tubo in 20s, the Petit Corona in 40s, and the tins in 50s.

KALUA SUNRISE
Handmade in Santiago, Dominican Republic.
Wrapper: Dom. Rep.   *Binder: Dom. Rep.*   *Filler: Dom. Rep.*

Introduced in 1988, this is a medium-bodied cigar with a Sumatra-seed wrapper, offered in two sizes in bundles or boxes of 25.

HANDMADE CIGARS: BRAND LISTINGS

KENTUCKY GENTLEMEN CIGAR ★*New*★
Handmade in Lawrenceburg, Kentucky, USA.
Wrapper: USA/Connecticut, USA/Kentucky
Binder: Dom. Rep.   Filler: Colombia, Dom. Rep., Mexico, Nicaragua

Shape	Name		Lgth	Ring	Wrapper
Robusto	Robusto	*(tube available)*	5	50	Dual
Torpedo	Twist	*(tube available)*	6⅛	52	Stripe
Churchill	Colonel	*(tube available)*	7	48	Ma
Churchill	Fire-Tipped Churchill	*(tube available)*	7	48	Dual

This unique series debuted in 2007. The Robusto and Fire-Tipped Churchill are finished with maduro ends of Kentucky tobacco! The filler varies by size also with Dominican leaves in all and added filler from Colombia (Robusto), Mexico (Colonel) and Nicaragua (Twist). All are medium to full in body and are offered in boxes of 10 or 24.

KEY WEST 1876
Handmade in Santiago, Dominican Republic.
Wrapper: USA/Connecticut   Binder: Dom. Rep.   Wrapper: Dom. Rep.

The "1876" offers a mild body thanks to its Connecticut wrapper and Dominican interior leaves. Produced in six sizes, it is available in boxes of 25.

KEY WEST EXTRA
Handmade in Santiago, Dominican Republic.
Wrapper: USA/Connecticut   Binder: Dom. Rep.   Filler: Dom. Rep.

This is a medium-bodied blend made in three maduro-wrapped sizes that was introduced in 2005.

KEY WEST HAVANA GOLD LABEL
Handmade in Santiago, Dominican Republic.
Wrapper: USA/Connecticut   Binder: Dom. Rep.   Wrapper: Dom. Rep.

Introduced in 1994, it's become a Key West tradition! It offers a mild-bodied flavor with a Connecticut wrapper in six sizes and is packed in boxes of 25.

HANDMADE CIGARS: BRAND LISTINGS

KICK ASS SWEET CIGARS
Handmade in Santiago, Dominican Republic.

Wrapper: USA/Connecticut   *Binder: Dom. Rep.*   *Filler: Dom. Rep.*

Shape	Name	Lgth	Ring	Wrapper
Robusto	Robusto	5	50	CM-Ma
Torpedo	Torpedo	6½	50	CM-Ma
Toro	Toro	6	50	CM-Ma
Double Corona	Churchill	7	50	CM-Ma

Introduced in 2001, this is now a sweetened cigar with a mild-to-medium-bodied flavor, available in 25s.

KING DAVID   ★*New*★
Handmade in Esteli, Nicaragua.

Wrapper: Nicaragua   *Binder: Nicaragua*   *Filler: Nicaragua*

Shape	Name	Lgth	Ring	Wrapper
Double Corona	Presidente	7½	54	CM
Torpedo	Pyramide	6½	54	CM
Robusto	Robusto	5½	52	CM
Toro	Toro	6½	52	CM

Although a previous edition of King David had been made in Nicaragua, this is an all-new version from Flor de Gonzalez, made for Mike's Cigars. Named for the ancient Hebrew king who united the 12 tribes of Israel, it's a mild-to-medium-bodied cigar offered in flip-top wooden boxes of 25.

KING DOMINICAN
Handmade in Santiago, Dominican Republic.

Wrapper: USA/Connecticut   *Binder: Honduras*   *Filler: Brazil, Dominican Republic*

Shape	Name	Lgth	Ring	Wrapper
Lonsdale	No. 1	6½	42	CC-Ma
Corona	No. 2	5½	42	CC-Ma
Toro	No. 4	6	50	CC-Ma

Short Panatela	No. 5	5	35	CC-Ma
Robusto	No. 6	4¾	50	CC-Ma
Giant	No. 7	8½	52	CC-Ma
Double Corona	No. 8	7	60	CC-Ma
Giant	No. 9	10	66	CC-Ma
Double Corona	No. 10	7½	49	CC-Ma
Robusto	No. 13	5	66	CC-Ma
Torpedo	Belicoso	6½	52	CC-Ma

A full, yet deliciously mild cigar, introduced in 1989. The natural-wrapped version has a smooth herbal character, while the maduro wrapper offers a rich earthiness. These delicate flavors and the line's smooth draw is as unique as its range in some of the largest-available ring gauges. All sizes are offered in bundles of 25, except for the No. 8 and No. 13 sizes, offered in 10s and the mammoth No. 9, in bundles of five.

KINGS CLUB
Handmade in Danli, Honduras.

Wrapper: Ecuador　　　*Binder: Honduras*　　　*Filler: Dom. Rep.*

Introduced in 1997, this four-size brand is named after great royals of the past like King Arthur, Louis XIV and King Philip. The cigars themselves are medium-bodied and feature a blend of Dominican-grown Piloto Cubano filler leaves. The Kings Club is offered in all-cedar boxes of 25.

KINKY FRIEDMAN　★*New*★
Handmade in Santiago, Dominican Republic.

Wrapper: Honduras　　　*Binder: Costa Rica*　　　*Filler: Honduras, Nicaragua*

Shape	Name	Lgth	Ring	Wrapper
Toro	The Governor	5¾	60	CM
Torpedo	Kinkycristo	6¼	54	CM
Toro	The Willie	6	48	CM
Torpedo	Texas Jewboy	6	56	CM
Toro	Utopian	6	52	CM

HANDMADE CIGARS: BRAND LISTINGS

The irrepressible Kinky Friedman – songwriter and political candidate, among other things – debuted his own cigar line in 2007. These are medium-bodied cigars with a hint of spice and a creamy finish. The Willie is finished with a pigtail head and shaggy foot. All sizes are offered in boxes of 20.

KRISTIAN JAMES
Handmade in Danli, Honduras.

Wrapper: Indonesia   *Binder: Honduras*   *Filler: Honduras, Nicaragua*

Shape	Name	Lgth	Ring	Wrapper
Double Corona	Churchill	7	50	CM
Corona	Cuatro	5½	42	CM
Robusto	Rothschild	5	50	CM
Torpedo	Misile	6	54	CM

This brand debuted in 1997 and offers a mild-to-medium-bodied blend of tobaccos from three nations. It is offered in boxes of 25.

KRISTOFF
Handmade in Santiago, Dominican Republic.

Wrapper: Brazil, Nicaragua   *Binder: Dom. Rep.*   *Filler: Dom. Rep., Nicaragua*

Shape	Name	Lgth	Ring	Wrapper
Torpedo	Torpedo	6⅛	52	CM-Ma
Churchill	Churchill	7	48	CM-Ma
Toro	Matador	6½	56	CM-Ma

Introduced by Exclusive Cigars in 2006, this is a mild-to-medium-bodied blend with a Nicaraguan Habano wrapper. Maduro-wrapped shapes (Brazilian wrapper) are medium-bodied and debuted in 2007. All sizes are offered in boxes of 20.

LA AROMA DE CUBA
Handmade in Santa Rosa de Copan, Honduras.

Wrapper: Honduras   *Binder: Honduras*   *Filler: Honduras, Nicaragua*

Shape	Name	Lgth	Ring	Wrapper
Petit Corona	Corona Minor	4½	44	CM

Corona	Corona		5½	44	CM
Lonsdale	Cetro		6½	44	CM
Churchill	Churchill		6¾	48	CM
Robusto	Robusto		5	54	CM
Pyramid	Pyramid		6⅛	50	CM
Toro	Monarch		6	50	CM
Double Corona	Double Corona		7½	52	CM
Toro	Marquis	(tubed)	5¾	48	CM
Toro	Immensa		5½	60	CM
Small Panatela	Interlude		4¼	34	CM

La Aroma de Cuba is a medium-bodied blend with a spicy finish and a specially-grown Cuban-seed wrapper. Introduced in 2002, the blend was developed over a three-year period before the line was introduced by Ashton Distributors. It is available in boxes of 25 for most sizes, in boxes of 20 for the Marquis and in tins of eight for the Interlude.

LA AURORA
Handmade in Santiago, Dominican Republic.
Wrapper: Brazil, Cameroon   Binder: Dom. Rep.   Filler: Brazil, Cameroon, Dom. Rep.

Shape	Name		Lgth	Ring	Wrapper
Corona	Aurora No. 4		5¼	43	CM-Ma
Torpedo	Belicoso		6¼	52	CM-Ma
Toro	Bristol Deluxe		6⅜	48	CM
Toro	Bristol Especiales		6⅜	48	CM-Ma
Long Corona	Cetros		6⅜	41	CM
Churchill	Churchill		7	47	Ma
Short Panatela	Coronas		5	38	CM
Long Corona	Cristal	(glass tubes)	6⅜	41	CM
Double Corona	Double Corona		7½	50	CM

Small Panatela	Finos		4	30	CM
Toro	Gran Corona		6½	50	CM
Panatela	Palmas Extra		6¾	35	CM
Torpedo	Petit Belicoso		5	52	CM
Short Panatela	Petit Coronas		4½	37	CM
Robusto	Robusto		5	50	CM-Ma
Robusto	Robusto Deluxe		5	50	CM
Short Panatela	Sublimes	(tubed)	5	38	CM

Respected since its introduction in 1903, La Aurora is a medium-bodied cigar offering a unique blend of all-Dominican fillers and binder, completed with a rare Cameroon wrapper for a soft, accessible taste. The 2001-introduced maduro wrappers are from Brazil and are combined with Brazilian, Cameroon and Dominican fillers for a medium (natural) or medium-to-full-bodied (maduro) taste. It's offered in boxes of 25.

A special-edition La Aurora – the Excepcionales – was created for sale in New York only in 2007. It's a 5 3/4-inch by 48-ring robusto made with all-Dominican tobacco plus some Nicaraguan filler, it's a medium-bodied cigar offered unbanded in cabinets of 50. A total of 5,000 cigars were made.

LA CAOBA EXTRA
Handmade in Esteli, Nicaragua.

Wrapper: Nicaragua   *Binder: Nicaragua*   *Filler: Nicaragua*

Shape	Name	Lgth	Ring	Wrapper
Torpedo	Belicoso	6¾	54	CM
Churchill	Churchill	7	48	CM
Giant	Esplendido	8½	52	CM
Double Corona	Gold Medal	7½	50	CM
Lonsdale	Preferidos	6½	42	CM
Robusto	Robusto	4½	50	CM
Toro	Toro	6	50	CM

HANDMADE CIGARS: BRAND LISTINGS

Here was a Cigar Boom that was dead and buried until re-energized by Oscar Boruchin of Mike's Cigars. The new blend, introduced in 2004, is medium to full in body and is offered in larger sizes in well-priced boxes of 25.

LA CAROLINA
Handmade in Esteli, Nicaragua.

Wrapper: Nicaragua   Binder: Nicaragua   Filler: Nicaragua

Shape	Name	Lgth	Ring	Wrapper
Torpedo	Capitan	6	54	CM
Pyramid	Campaña	5½	56	CM
Churchill	Churchill	7	48	CM
Robusto	Toro Oscuro	5½	52	Ma
Robusto	Gran Robusto	5½	50	CM
Perfecto	Torpito	4½	54	CM
Corona	Corona	5½	42	CM

The Tabacalera Esteli introduced this brand in 2005 as a successor to the departed Cupido brand. This is a medium-bodied blend using all-Nicaraguan leaves. Named for an old Cuban brand, it's offered in boxes of 25.

LA CAYA
Handmade in Tamboril, Dominican Republic.

Wrapper: Indonesia, Mexico, USA/Connecticut

Binder: Dominican Republic   Filler: Dominican Republic

Shape	Name	Lgth	Ring	Wrapper
	Ecuador and Maduro San Andres lines:			
Long corona	Corona	6	44	CC-Ma
Robusto	Robusto	5	50	CC-Ma
Toro	Toro	6	50	CC-Ma
Double Corona	Churchill	7	50	CC-Ma
Torpedo	Torpedo	6½	54	CC-Ma
	Cameroon, Fuerte and Maduro Brazil lines:			

Toro	Gordo	6	60	CM-Ma
Double Corona	Churchill	7	50	CM-Ma
Torpedo	Torpedo	6	52	CM-Ma
Robusto	Robusto	5	54	CM-Ma
Toro	Toro	6	54	CM-Ma

From the Tabacalera La Caya, this brand was introduced in 2002. There are five series now, all using Dominican-grown binder and filler but with five different wrappers: Ecuador-grown from Connecticut seed (offered in boxes of 25), Mexican-grown maduro (25s), Brazilian maduro (24s), La Caya Fuerte using a Pennsylvania Broadleaf wrapper (24s) and Cameroon (24). The natural-shade lines are medium-to-full-bodied taste and the maduro-wrapped versions are full in body.

LA CORONA

Handmade in Santa Rosa de Copan, Honduras.

Wrapper: Ecuador, USA/Connecticut   Binder: Honduras   Filler: Dom. Rep., Honduras

Shape	Name	Lgth	Ring	Wrapper
Panatela	Coronita	5⅝	38	CC
Corona	Corona Cubana	5¾	42	CC
Lonsdale	Corona Corona	6¾	42	CC
Perfecto	Perfecto	5	50	CC-Ma
Churchill	Coronations	7	46	CC
Perfecto	Perfecto X	6½	50	CC-Ma
Torpedo	Campana	6	54	CC-Ma

Here is a rich, medium-bodied cigar that is worthy of the La Corona tradition with a choice of Connecticut-seed or Connecticut-grown maduro wrappers. It is offered in decorated boxes of 20.

LA CORONA DOMINICAN

Handmade in La Romana, Dominican Republic.

Wrapper: USA/Connecticut   Binder: Dom. Rep.   Filler: Dom. Rep.

Shape	Name	Lgth	Ring	Wrapper
Robusto	Robusto	5	50	CC

Petit Corona	Corona	4½	43	CC

This is a mild-to-medium-bodied version of La Corona, offered in packs of five for the Corona and four for the Robusto.

LA EMINENCIA
Handmade in Danli, Honduras.

Wrapper: Ecuador   *Binder: Honduras*
Filler: Brazil, Dominican Republic, Honduras, Nicaragua

Vincent & Tampa's La Eminencia is made by hand in Honduras and by machine in Tampa, Florida. Originally developed as a domestic Cuban brand by Ramon Allones in the late 1800s, today's handmade blend is mild to medium-bodied, with natural and maduro wrappers available in the boxed (four shapes) and bundle-packed (10 shapes) sizes.

LA ESCEPCION
Handmade in Cofradia, Honduras.

Wrapper: Ecuador   *Binder: Honduras*   *Filler: Honduras, Nicaragua*

Shape	Name	Lgth	Ring	Wrapper
Toro	Baltasar	6	50	CM
Torpedo	Caspar	6⅛	54	CM
Toro	Melchior	6⅛	50	CM

This brand is renewed nearly every year as a new series is introduced. The Serie VI was introduced in 2006, with a medium-to-full body, offered in boxes of 10. These are true limited editions, with each series limited to 50,000 cigars per size (150,000 per Serie):

1999:	Serie I Dalias	(6¼ x 48 in boxes of 20)
	Serie I Monterreys	(7 x 48 in boxes of 20)
	Serie I Especiales	(7¼ x 54 in boxes of 20)
2001:	Serie II Dalias	(6¼ x 48 in boxes of 20)
	Serie II Monterreys	(7 x 48 in boxes of 20)
	Serie II Especiales	(7¼ x 54 in boxes of 20)
2002:	Serie III M. Zavalla	(6⅛ x 50 torpedo in boxes of 20)
	Serie III F. Llaneza	(6⅛ x 48 in boxes of 20)
	Serie III E. Martinez	(6⅛ x 54 torpedo in boxes of 20)

2003:	Serie IV Tapa Negra 42	(6¾ x 42 in boxes of 20)
	Serie IV Tape Negra 45	(6¾ x 45 in boxes of 20)
	Serie IV Tapa Negra 48	(6¾ x 48 in boxes of 20)
2005:	Serie V No. 48	(6¾ x 48 in boxes of 20)
	Serie V No. 50	(6⅛ x 50 in boxes of 20)
	Serie V No. 54	(6 x 54 in boxes of 20)
2006:	Serie VI Baltasar	(6 x 50 in boxes of 10)
	Serie VI Caspar	(6⅛ x 54 torpedo in boxes of 10)
	Serie VI Melchior	(6⅛ x 50 in boxes of 10)

LA FINCA
Handmade in Esteli, Nicaragua.

Wrapper: Nicaragua   *Binder: Nicaragua*   *Filler: Nicaragua*

Shape	Name		Lgth	Ring	Wrapper
Double Corona	Bolivares		7½	50	CM
Grand Corona	Cazadore	/mixed filler/	6½	45	CM
Corona	Corona		5½	42	CM
Toro	Ammo Box		6⅛	50	CM
Robusto	Fifty Four		5	54	CM-Ma
Torpedo	Figurado		6¾	54	CM
Corona Extra	Fuma Corta		5½	46	CM
Grand Corona	Fuma Larga		6½	46	CM
Giant	Gran Finca		8½	52	CM
Toro	Joya		6	50	CM-Ma
Pyramid	Pyramides		7	49	CM
Robusto	Robusto		4½	50	CM-Ma
Lonsdale	Romeo		6½	42	CM
Churchill	Valentino		7	48	CM-Ma

"The Farm" is a popularly-priced, medium-bodied cigar. La Finca shapes are offered in boxes of 25, except for the Cazadores and Fumas, offered in bundles of 25 . . . and the Ammo Box, in which 91 La Fincas are packed in an authentic (but cedar-lined) 30-caliber steel ammunition chest!

HANDMADE CIGARS: BRAND LISTINGS

LA FLOR DE ARMANDO MENDEZ
Handmade in Tampa, Florida, USA.

Wrapper: USA/Connecticut   *Binder: Honduras*   *Filler: Honduras*

This is a one-size (6 x 50), medium-bodied blend, offered in six-packs from the Cammarata Cigar Factory in the Ybor City section of Tampa, Florida.

LA FLOR DE YNCLAN
Handmade in Santiago, Dominican Republic.

Wrapper: Ecuador   *Binder: Indonesia*   *Filler: Dom. Rep., Nicaragua*

Shape	Name		Lgth	Ring	Wrapper
Long Panatela	Lancero		7½	38	CC
Churchill	Churchill	(tubed)	7	48	CC
Torpedo	Torpedo		6	52	CC
Robusto	Robusto		5	52	CC
Toro	Corona Gorda		6½	52	CC

This is a mild-bodied blend, introduced in 2005 named for a very old Cuban brand. The Lancero has a pigtail head and all sizes are offered in boxes of 25 and packs of five (three for the Churchill), except for the Corona Gorda, offered only as part of a sampler pack!

LA FLOR DEL CANEY
Handmade in Santiago, Dominican Republic.

Wrapper: Cameroon   *Binder: Indonesia*   *Filler: Dom. Rep.*

Shape	Name	Lgth	Ring	Wrapper
Double Corona	Churchill	7½	50	CM
Lonsdale	Lonsdale	6½	43	CM
Toro	Toro	6	50	CM
Corona	Corona	5½	43	CM
Perfecto, kinda	Bouquet	4¾	59	CM

This is another old Cuban brand, now made in the Dominican Republic and released in 2001 by Mike's Cigars. It offers a medium-to-full-bodied flavor and like all products of the famed MATASA factory, it is well very constructed, especially the unique Bouquet size, with its bulge in the middle. It is offered in all-cedar display boxes of 25.

LA FLOR DOMINICANA
Handmade in Santiago, Dominican Republic.

CAMEROON CABINET SERIES:

Wrapper: Cameroon   *Binder: Nicaragua*   *Filler: Dom. Rep., Nicaragua*

DOUBLE LIGERO:

Wrapper: Ecuador   *Binder: Dom. Rep.*   *Filler: Dom. Rep.*

LIGERO:

Wrapper: Ecuador   *Binder: Dom. Rep.*   *Filler: Dom. Rep.*

LIGERO MYSTERIO:

Wrapper: Nicaragua, USA/Connecticut   *Binder: Dom. Rep.*   *Filler: Dom. Rep.*

LIGERO OSCURO CABINET SERIES:

Wrapper: Ecuador   *Binder: Dom. Rep.*   *Filler: Dom. Rep.*

PREMIUM LINE:

Wrapper: USA/Connecticut   *Binder: Dom. Rep.*   *Filler: Dom. Rep.*

RESERVA ESPECIALE:

Wrapper: Ecuador   *Binder: Nicaragua*   *Filler: Dom. Rep.*

LITTLE CIGARS:
Wrapper: Cameroon, Ecuador, USA/Connecticut

Binder: Dominican Republic   *Filler: Dominican Republic*

Shape	Name	Lgth	Ring	Wrapper
	Premium Line:			
Churchill	Mambises	6⅞	48	CC
Robusto	Maceo	5	48	CC
Lonsdale	Alcalde	6½	44	CC
Corona	Insurrectos	5½	42	CC
Petit Corona	Macheteros	4	40	CC
Toro	No. 5	6¼	52	Ma

HANDMADE CIGARS: BRAND LISTINGS

Toro	No. 6		5¾	54	Ma
Corona	No. 7		5½	42	Ma
	Reserva Especial:				
Double Corona	Churchill		6⅞	49	CC
Robusto	Robusto		5	48	CC
Robusto	Belicoso		5½	52	CC
Pyramid	Figurado		6½	52	CC
Toro	No. 100	*(tubed)*	6½	49	CC
Long Corona	No. 200	*(tubed)*	6	44	CC
Perfecto	El Jocko		4½	54	CC-Ma
	Cameroon Cabinet Series:				
Lonsdale	No. 1		6½	44	CM
Robusto	No. 4		6¼	54	CM
Robusto	No. 5		5	50	CM
	Ligero:				
Toro	L300		5¾	50	CC-Ma
Toro	L400		5¾	54	CC-Ma
Toro	L500		5¾	60	CC-Ma
Torpedo	Torpedo		6	54	CC-Ma
	Double Ligero:				
Robusto	DL-600		5¼	52	CM
Robusto	DL-660		4⅝	60	CM
Toro	DL-700		6½	60	CM-Ma
Pyramid	Chisel		6	54	CM-Ma
Pyramid	Chisel Gorda		5½	48	CM
Pyramid	Chiselito		5	44	CM-Ma
Double Corona	Churchill Especiale		6⅞	49	CM

HANDMADE CIGARS: BRAND LISTINGS

Long Panatela	Lancero	7	38	CM
Giant	A	9	47	Os
	Ligero Mysterio:			
Perfecto	Ligero Mysterio	7	54	Dual
	Ligero Oscuro Cabinets:			
Petit Corona	L200 Cabinet	4⅞	40	Os
Robusto	L250 Cabinet	4¾	48	Os
Toro	L300 Cabinet	5¾	50	Os
Toro	L400 Cabinet	5¾	54	Os
Toro	L500 Cabinet	5¾	60	Os
	Little Cigars:			
Cigarillo	Daiquiri	3½	26	CC-Ma
Small Panatela	Mojito	4	30	CM

This much-respected line was introduced in 1994 and offer brilliantly-made cigars in a variety of blends. The Premium Line is mild-to-medium in body with natural wrappers while the maduro-wrapped shapes are medium-to-full. The Reserva Especial line is medium-to-full in all shapes; the Tubos series was introduced in 2001. The Cameroon Cabinets Series debuted in 2007 and is full-bodied.

The Ligero series was introduced in 2001 and is full-bodied, featuring a spectacular Ecuadorian-grown wrapper for all shapes. The Double Ligero was introduced in 2003 and is full in body with a special tapered head to allow an easy draw! The limited-edition "A" uses a unique, jet-black Sumatra-seed wrapper. The Ligero Oscuro Cabinets were introduced in 2007 and feature a jet-black Sumatra-seed wrapper from Ecuador.

The Ligero Mysterio 2006 was a perfecto with a Nicaraguan wrapper, with ends wrapped in Connecticut Broadleaf maduro! For 2007, the body is dark with an Ecuadorian oscuro wrapper and Ecuadorian Connecticut-seed ends, offered in gift-style packs of five.

The Little Cigars debuted in 2007 and are made by hand. The Daiquiris come in a choice of an Ecuadorian natural or Connecticut Broadleaf maduro wrapper while the Mojitos are wrapped with Cameroon leaf.

HANDMADE CIGARS: BRAND LISTINGS

LA FLORIDITA
Handmade in Esteli, Nicaragua.

Wrapper: USA/Connecticut   Binder: Dom. Rep.   Filler: Dom. Rep., Nicaragua

Shape	Name	Lgth	Ring	Wrapper
Torpedo	Belicoso	6	54	CC-Ma
Corona	Corona	5½	42	CC-Ma
Double Corona	Corona Gigante	7	54	CC-Ma
Lonsdale	Lonsdale	7	44	CC-Ma
Robusto	Pancho	5½	52	CC-Ma
Toro	Toro	6	50	CC-Ma

Originally made in Costa Rica, this brand is now made in Nicaragua for Famous Smoke Shop and you have a choice of a Connecticut-seed wrapper in either a natural or maduro shade and a medium-to-full body. It is available in bundles of 25.

LA FONTANA CONSIGLIERE
Handmade in Danli, Honduras.

Wrapper: Honduras   Binder: Honduras   Filler: Honduras

Shape	Name	Lgth	Ring	Wrapper
Perfecto	Part I	4¼	50	CC
Perfecto	Part II	5½	50	CC
Perfecto	Part III	6½	50	CC

Introduced in 2005, this is a tribute to longtime cigar executive Sal Fontana as well as a salute to the three parts of "The Godfather" feature film series. It features a Connecticut-seed wrapper and Corojo binder and filler, with a medium-to-full-bodied flavor in boxes of 20.

LA FONTANA VINTAGE
Handmade in Danli, Honduras.

Wrapper: Honduras   Binder: Honduras   Filler: Honduras

Shape	Name	Lgth	Ring	Wrapper
Corona	Verdi	5½	44	CC
Robusto	Galileo	5	50	CC

HANDMADE CIGARS: BRAND LISTINGS

Lonsdale	Puccini		6½	44	CC
Churchill	Da Vinci		7	48	CC
Double Corona	Michelangelo		7½	52	CC
Slim Panatela	Rossini		5½	32	CC
Pyramid	Mona Lisa		4¾	44	CC
Torpedo	Belicoso		6⅛	54	CC
Panatela	Dante		6⅛	38	CC
Lonsdale	Cristal	(tubed)	6½	43	CC

This is a medium-bodied blend with a sweet taste on the tip, which debuted in 1993. It is constructed of Honduran-grown tobaccos in the binder and a light Connecticut-seed wrapper. This creation of master blender Tino Argudin is offered in elegant 20-cigar boxes except for the Cristales, offered in 10s.

LA GLORIA CUBANA
Handmade in Miami, Florida, USA and Villa Gonzalez, Dom. Rep.
Wrapper: Ecuador, USA/Connecticut

Binder: Nicaragua
Filler: Dom. Rep., Nicaragua

Shape	Name	Lgth	Ring	Wrapper
Double Corona	Charlemagne	7¼	54	CC-Ma
Double Corona	Churchill	7	50	CC-Ma
Toro	Corona Gorda	6	52	CC-Ma
Giant Corona	Corona Extra Larga	7¾	44	CC-Ma
Giant	Crown Imperial	9	49	CC-Ma
Double Corona	Double Corona	7¾	49	CC-Ma
Churchill	Glorias Inmensas	7¼	48	CC-Ma
Churchill	Glorias en Cedros (tubed)	6¾	48	CC
Corona	Glorias	5½	43	CC-Ma
Grand Corona	Glorias Extra	6¼	46	CC-Ma
Small Panatela	Glorias Petit	4¼	32	CC-Ma
Lonsdale	Glorias en Crystal (glass tubes)	6¾	43	CC

Robusto	Hermoso	4½	48	CC-Ma
Long Corona	Medaille D'Or No. 2	6¼	43	CC-Ma
Lonsdale	Medaille D'Or No. 1	6¾	43	CC-Ma
Panatela	Medaille D'Or No. 4	6	32	CC-Ma
Cigarillo	Medaille D'Or No. 3	7	28	CC-Ma
Small Panatela	Minutos	4½	40	CC-Ma.
Long Panatela	Panatela De'Luxe	7	37	CC-Ma
Pyramid	Piramides	7¼	60	CC-Ma
Giant	Soberano	8	52	CC-Ma
Torpedo	Torpedo No. 1	6½	54	CC-Ma
Robusto	Wavell	5	50	CC-Ma
Robusto	Serie R No. 4	4⅞	52	CC-Ma
Robusto	Serie R No. 5	5½	54	CC-Ma
Robusto	Serie R No. 6	5⅞	60	CC-Ma
Double Corona	Serie R No. 7	7	58	CC-Ma
Torpedo	Serie R Belicoso	5¾	56	CC
Robusto	Serie R Robusto	5	56	CC
Lonsdale	Library Edition: "A Tale of Two Cities"	7	45	CC

This is a medium-bodied smoke of absolutely exquisite quality made in the El Credito factory in Miami, Florida (primarily for local sale only) and in a larger facility in Villa Gonzalez, Dominican Republic. Most sizes are offered in boxes of 25, except for the Crown Imperial and the Piramides (made only in Miami), which are offered in boxes of 10, the Glorias en Cedro (14s and 7s) and the Hermosos (30s). The maduro shapes utilize a Connecticut Broadleaf wrapper. The Library Edition is made for Cigars by Santa Clara.

The Serie R debuted in 1999 and offers a full-bodied flavor in both natural and maduro wrappers in boxes of 24. The Glorias en Crystal features a glass tube in boxes of 10 and was released in 2001. There is also an annual limited-edition Serie R:

HANDMADE CIGARS: BRAND LISTINGS

2003:	No. 6 Limitada	(6½ x 64 in boxes of 24)
2004:	No. 7 Limitada	(7¼ x 60 torpedo in boxes of 24)
2005:	Limitada 2005	(7¾ x 62 torpedo in 1,400 humidors of 30)
2006:	Figurado Gigante	(7¾ x 63 perfecto in 1,400 humidors of 30)
2007:	Especiale 2002	(7 x 58 available only in a tray of 20 in the 250 Serie R Limitada Retrospectivo humidors)

For 2007, a special "Retrospectivo" humidor was created with100 cigars: 20 from each Limitada group of 2003-04-05-06 and the never-before-released 2002 Limitada. Ten cigars with natural wrappers and ten in maduro wrappers were included in each year grouping. Only 250 humidors were produced. The Serie R Robusto was released in 2005 in special promotional packs of six only.

LA GLORIA CUBANA RESERVA FIGURADO
Handmade in Santiago, Dominican Republic.
Wrapper: Ecuador, USA/Connecticut

Binder: Nicaragua   Filler: Dom. Rep., Nicaragua

Shape	Name	Lgth	Ring	Wrapper
Pyramid	Piramides Clasicas	7¼	56	CC-Ma
Perfecto	Selectos de Lujos	7¼	54	CC-Ma
Perfecto	Flechas Especiales	6½	49	CC-Ma
Robusto	Felicias	4⅝	49	CC-Ma
Perfecto	Regalias Perfectos	6¼	57	CC-Ma

This group of figurados was developed by La Gloria Cubana master Ernesto Perez-Carrillo in 2004 and expanded (Felicias and Regalias) in 2005. It's a rich and spicy, medium-to-full-bodied blend, with the maduro-wrapped editions using Connecticut Broadleaf tobacco. All are offered in special mahogany boxes of 20.

LA HABANERA
Handmade in Santiago, Dominican Republic.

Wrapper: USA/Connecticut   Binder: Dom. Rep.   Filler: Dom. Rep.

Shape	Name	Lgth	Ring	Wrapper
Double Corona	Presidente	7½	50	CC
Churchill	Churchill	6⅞	46	CC

HANDMADE CIGARS: BRAND LISTINGS

Long Corona	Diplomaticos		6	44	CC
Robusto	Emperadores		5½	50	CC
Slim Panatela	Especiales		5	30	CC
Lonsdale	Cristal	(tubed)	6¾	42	CC
Long Corona	Alumino	(tubed)	6	42	CC
Cigarillo	Tin		3½	26	CC

La Habanera was introduced to the U.S. market in 2006. It's mild-to-medium and offered in boxes of 10, 20 or 25. The Tins are flavored and available in natural, cherry, rum and vanilla.

LA HARA
Handmade in Esteli, Nicaragua.
Wrapper: Brazil, Indonesia   *Binder: Nicaragua*   *Filler: Nicaragua*

Shape	Name	Lgth	Ring	Wrapper
Double Corona	Presidente	7½	54	CM-Ma
Churchill	Churchill	7	48	CM-Ma
Toro	Toro	6	50	CM-Ma
Robusto	Robusto	4½	50	CM-Ma

The TESA Cigar Co. offers this medium-to-full-bodied brand, introduced in 2004. It is available with either a Brazilian maduro or Indonesian natural wrapper in boxes of 24.

LA HERENCIA CUBANA
Handmade in Miami, Florida, USA.
Wrapper: Brazil, Ecuador, Indonesia
Binder: Ecuador   *Filler: Dom. Rep., Ecuador, Honduras, Nicaragua*

Shape	Name	Lgth	Ring	Wrapper
Torpedo	Torpedo Chico	4½	54	CC-CM-Ma
Double Corona	Churchill	7½	50	CC-CM-Ma
Toro	No. 52	6	52	CC-CM-Ma
Torpedo	Torpedo	6½	54	CC-CM-Ma

Robusto	Robusto	5	50	CC-CM-Ma
Robusto	Corona	5¾	48	CC-CM-Ma

This medium-to-full-bodied, hand-made cigar is offered without cellophane wrapping in boxes of 25. You can take your choice of a Brazilian maduro or Connecticut or Sumatran natural-shade wrapper.

LA HERENCIA DE CUBA ★New★
Handmade in Tampa, Florida, USA.

Wrapper: Ecuador   Binder: Ecuador, Indonesia   Filler: Colombia, Dom. Rep.

Shape	Name	Lgth	Ring	Wrapper
Robusto	Robusto	5	52	CM
Torpedo	Torpedo	6	52	CM
Double Corona	Churchill	7	50	CM
Perfecto	Kimbumbia	5	54	CM
Torpedo	Petit Torpedo	5	52	CM
Grand Corona	Corona	6	46	CM
Petit Corona	Mareva	5	42	CM
Toro	Don Roberto	6½	56	CM

Made in the famed Ybor City area of Tampa, this line was created in 2002, but entered national distribution in 2007. There are three blends: Yellow, with a mild-to-medium body (Robusto, Torpedo, Churchill only); White, with a medium-to-full body using an Ecuadorian binder and also an added touch of Nicaraguan leaf in the filler (all sizes except Corona and Mareva) and Black, which is mild and offered in the Robusto, Torpedo, Corona and Mareva sizes only. All sizes are offered in boxes of 25 (Yellow and White) or 24 (Black).

LA INTIMIDAD
Handmade, with short filler, in Danli, Honduras.

Wrapper: Honduras   Binder: Honduras   Filler: Honduras

Shape	Name	Lgth	Ring	Wrapper
Long Corona	Natural	6	42	CM
Long Corona	Maduro	6	42	Ma

Toro	Toro	6	50	CM
Torpedo	Torpedo	7	54	CM

Known simply as "La Pantera" since introduction in 1996, the Diamond Collection is a mellow, mild-to-medium bodied cigar, thanks to its Sumatra-seed wrapper, offered in wooden boxes of 25.

LA PANTERA SAPPHIRE COLLECTION
Handmade in Danli, Honduras.

Wrapper: Ecuador *Binder: Honduras* *Filler: Honduras, Nicaragua*

Shape	Name	Lgth	Ring	Wrapper
Corona	Cuatro	5½	42	CM
Robusto	Rothschild	5	50	CM

This is a stronger blend (blue label) than its sister brand, the Diamond Collection (black label). Spicier and more robust, this is a medium-bodied cigar which features aged tobaccos and is offered in cedar cabinets of 25.

LA PERLA HABANA CLASSIC
Handmade in Santiago, Dominican Republic.

Wrapper: Indonesia *Binder: Ecuador* *Filler: Dom. Rep., Honduras, Nicaragua*

Shape	Name	Lgth	Ring	Wrapper
Robusto	Robusto	4¾	52	CC
Torpedo	Torpedo	6¼	52	CC

Introduced in 1997, this exquisitely-made cigar has a medium body and a famous old Cuban name. This reincarnation of the "Pearl of Havana" offers a 1994-vintage Indonesian wrapper in elegant cabinets of 20.

LA PERLA HABANA MADURO
Handmade in Santiago, Dominican Republic.

Wrapper: Brazil *Binder: Nicaragua* *Filler: Dom. Rep., Mexico, Nicaragua*

Shape	Name	Lgth	Ring	Wrapper
Perfecto	Perfecto	5	51	Ma
Toro	Toro	6	50	Ma
Torpedo	Torpedo	6¼	52	Ma

The maduro-wrapped, full-bodied blend was introduced in 1999 and revised for 2006, now using a Brazilian-grown Arapiraca wrapper. It's available in cabinets of 20.

LA PLATA NICARAGUAN SELECTION
Handmade in Esteli, Nicaragua.

Wrapper: Ecuador   Binder: Nicaragua   Filler: Honduras, Nicaragua

Shape	Name	Lgth	Ring	Wrapper
Double Corona	Double Corona	7	50	CC
Torpedo	Torpedo	6¼	54	CC
Toro	Toro	6	50	CC
Robusto	Robusto	5	54	CC
Toro	Corona	5¾	48	CC

This is a medium-to-full-bodied blend for the venerable La Plata brand, this time from Nicaragua with a Connecticut-seed wrapper. It is offered in all-wood boxes of 20 and features artwork from social activist and artist Tom Ellis.

LA PLATA LIMITED EDITION VINTAGE FUERTE
Handmade in Condega, Nicaragua.

Wrapper: Nicaragua   Binder: Nicaragua   Filler: Nicaragua

Shape	Name	Lgth	Ring	Wrapper
Torpedo	Belicoso	4¾	42	CM
Robusto	Corona Gorda	5½	48	CM
Toro	Siglo VI	5¾	54	CM

Introduced in 2005, this is a full-bodied cigar with a Habano-seed wrapper. It's offered in boxes of 20.

LA PRIMADORA
Handmade in Danli, Honduras.

Wrapper: Honduras   Binder: Indonesia   Filler: Honduras, Nicaragua

Shape	Name	Lgth	Ring	Wrapper
Giant	Emperor	8½	50	CC-Ma
Toro	Solitaire	6	50	CC-Ma

HANDMADE CIGARS: BRAND LISTINGS

LA TRADICION CUBANA
Handmade in Santiago, Dominican Republic.

Wrapper: Ecuador   *Binder: Honduras*   *Filler: Dom. Rep., Nicaragua*

Shape	Name	Lgth	Ring	Wrapper
Double Corona	Churchill	7	50	CC
Long Corona	Corona	6	44	CC
Long Panatela	Lancero	7	38	CC
Robusto	Robusto	5	50	CC
Toro	Corona Gorda	6	50	CC
Torpedo	Torpedo	6½	54	CC
Torpedo	Petit Torpedo	5	54	CC
Petit Corona	Petit Corona	4½	44	CC
Giant	The Big One	12	192	CC

Introduced in 1995, this brand is made under the supervision of the ever-vigilant Luis Sanchez, with production moved to the Dominican Republic after a 2007 fire in the original Miami factory. Offered in boxes of 25, the blend has a medium-to-full body. The Big One expanded from 90 to 192 ring gauge in 2005 and has remained there. It's almost a full pound of tobacco!

LA UNICA
Handmade in Santiago, Dominican Republic.

Wrapper: USA/Connecticut   *Binder: Dom. Rep.*   *Filler: Dom. Rep.*

Shape	Name	Lgth	Ring	Wrapper
Giant	No. 100	8½	52	Cl-Ma
Double Corona	No. 200	7	49	Cl-Ma
Lonsdale	No. 300	6¾	44	Cl-Ma
Robusto	No. 400	4½	50	Cl-Ma
Corona	No. 500	5½	42	Cl-Ma
Toro	No. 600	6	50	Cl

Introduced in 1986, this brand has a mild flavor and aroma in a well-constructed cigar, with a natural or maduro wrapper. An excellent value, these cigars are packaged in bundles of 20 cigars until 2007, when the brand was switched to cabinets of 20.

LA UNICA CAMEROON SERIES
Handmade in Santiago, Dominican Republic.

Wrapper: Cameroon *Binder: Dom. Rep.* *Filler: Dom. Rep.*

Shape	Name	Lgth	Ring	Wrapper
Torpedo	Torpedo No. 1	5⅝	55	CM
Toro	Churchill No. 2	6½	50	CM
Torpedo	Belicoso No. 3	5	50	CM
Robusto	Robusto No. 4	4½	52	CM

The Cameroon wrapper gives this version of the La Unica blend a medium body in four popular shapes. Made at the famed Tabacalera A. Fuente, this cigar was introduced in mid-2000 and is presented in elegant cedar cabinets of 25.

LA VENCEDORA
Handmade in Esteli, Nicaragua.

Wrapper: Cameroon *CAMEROON SERIES:* *Binder: Nicaragua* *Filler: Nicaragua*

Wrapper: Ecuador *PIRAMIDES SERIES:* *Binder: Ecuador* *Filler: Dom. Rep., Nicaragua*

Shape	Name	Lgth	Ring	Wrapper
	Cameroon series:			
Panatela	Especial	6	38	CM
Lonsdale	Lonsdale	6½	44	CM
Torpedo	Piramides	6½	52	CM
Double Corona	Double Corona	7	50	CM
	Piramides series:			
Torpedo	Vitola A	7	54	CC
Torpedo	Vitola B	6½	54	CC
Torpedo	Vitola C	6	52	CC

HANDMADE CIGARS: BRAND LISTINGS

LAMB'S CLUB
Handmade in Santiago, Dominican Republic.

Wrapper: Cameroon   Binder: USA/Connecticut   Filler: Brazil, Dom. Rep.

Shape	Name	Lgth	Ring	Wrapper
Double Corona	Churchill	7	50	CC
Long Corona	Corona Extra	6½	43	CC
Toro	Toro	6	50	CC
Robusto	Rothschild	4¾	50	CC
Petit Corona	Chico	4½	40	CC

Lambs Club is a super-premium Dominican cigar, handmade by Manuel Quesada's MATASA factory and distributed by the Finck Cigar Co. of San Antonio, Texas. Its rich, flavorful character is derived from the finest Dominican Olor and Piloto tobaccos, now wrapped with Cameroon leaf for a medium-bodied taste. All sizes are offered in boxes of 25.

LARS TETENS GOLF
Handmade in Frankfort, New York, USA.

Wrapper: USA/Connecticut   Binder: Dom. Rep.   Filler: Dom. Rep., Mexico

Shape	Name	Lgth	Ring	Wrapper
Double Corona	Brassie	7	50	CC
Robusto	Mashie	5	50	CC
Corona Extra	Niblick	5	46	CC
Petit Corona	Ringer	4½	41	CC

This is a full-bodied line with a slow-burning blend. All sizes are offered in boxes of 30.

LARS TETENS PHAT CIGARS
Handmade in Frankfort, New York, USA.
Wrapper: Cameroon and USA/Connecticut

Binder: Dominican Republic   Filler: Dominican Republic, Mexico

Shape	Name	Lgth	Ring	Wrapper
Torpedo	Asadachi	6	60	CM
Double Corona	Brooklyn King	7	50	Ma

HANDMADE CIGARS: BRAND LISTINGS

Lonsdale	Sun Fook Ka	6½	44	CC
Corona	Royal	6	44	CM
Small Panatela	Brooklyn Mini	4	34	Ma
Robusto	Shorty	5¼	50	Cl-Ma

This brand, heavily scented with aromatic oils, was created in 1979 and introduced into national distribution in 1995. It's medium-to-full in body and packed in boxes of 30 which incorporate a re-sealable bag with a humidification sponge. Box labels reproduce paintings or photographs of or by Tetens himself.

LAS CABRILLAS
Handmade in Santa Rosa de Copan, Honduras.
Wrapper: USA/Connecticut, Mexico   Binder: Mexico   Filler: Mexico

Shape	Name	Lgth	Ring	Wrapper
Small Panatela	Pizarro	5½	32	CC
Double Corona	Maximilian	7	56	CC-Ma
Giant	Columbus	8¼	52	CC-Ma
Double Corona	Balboa	7½	54	CC-Ma
Double Corona	De Soto	6⅞	50	CC-Ma
Robusto	Cortez	4¾	50	CC-Ma
Lonsdale	Ponce de Leon	6⅝	44	CC-Ma
Churchill	Vasco de Gama	7	48	CC-Ma
Long Corona	Magellan	6	42	CC
	Great Discovery's series:			
Robusto	New World *(glass tube)*	5	50	CC

The explorers of the "New World" are saluted in this brand, which debuted in 1993 and offers a medium-bodied taste with a choice of a Connecticut natural or Mexican maduro wrapper. The line expanded in 1997 to include the Maximilian, a double corona, which is offered in boxes of 20, and the Vasco de Gama, which like the rest of the brand – except Columbus (10s) and Pizarro (60s) – is available in boxes of 25. The New World robusto is made specially for Great Discovery's Inc. of Houston, Texas.

HANDMADE CIGARS: BRAND LISTINGS

LAS FUMAS DE PUERTO RICO
Handmade, with short filler, in Mayaguez, Puerto Rico.

Wrapper: Indonesia   *Binder: Puerto Rico*   *Filler: Puerto Rico*

Shape	Name	Lgth	Ring	Wrapper
Corona Extra	Fumas de Puerto Rico	5	46	CM

Introduced in 2003, this is a mild, second cousin to the Hoja Boricua brand, handmade with short filler, offered in bundles of 25.

LAS MEMORIAS CUBANA
Handmade in Santiago, Dominican Republic.

Wrapper: Ecuador   *Binder: Honduras*   *Filler: Dom. Rep., Nicaragua*

Shape	Name	Lgth	Ring	Wrapper
Robusto	Gordos	5	64	CC
Toro	Especiales	6	64	CC
Toro	Especiales XXL	6½	96	CC
Torpedo	Campanas	6½	60	CC

This is a full-bodied blend introduced by the La Tradicion Cubana factory in 2003. Production was moved to the Dominican Republic in 2007 and all of the shapes are wrapped in cedar and offered in boxes of 10, except for the XXL.

LAS VEGAS CIGAR CO.
Handmade in Las Vegas, Nevada, USA.

Wrapper: Ecuador, Mexico   *Binder: Dom. Rep.*   *Filler: Dom. Rep., Mexico*

Shape	Name		Lgth	Ring	Wrapper
Double Corona	Churchill		7½	50	CI-Ma
Corona	Corona		5¾	42	CI-Ma
Lonsdale	Corona Largo		6¾	44	CI
Toro	El Rey Corto		5	62	CI-Ma
Giant	Excalibur		8¾	52	CI-Ma
Grand Corona	Fuma	(short filler)	6¾	46	CI
Corona	Montefino		5¾	52	CI-Ma

HANDMADE CIGARS: BRAND LISTINGS

Small Panatela	Nix	5	30	Cl
Panatela	Panatela	6¾	36	Cl
Robusto	Rothchild	4½	52	Cl-Ma
Lonsdale	Rum	6¾	44	Cl-Ma
Torpedo	Torpedo	7	60	Cl-Ma

You'll find this small factory on the famous Las Vegas Strip. The body varies from mild (Corona, Corona Largo) to heavy (Excalibur, El Rey), with the majority of the sizes rated as medium. All of the shapes are available sweetened, and vanilla flavoring is available in the Nix size only.

LAURATO ★New★
Handmade in Tampa, Florida, USA.

Wrapper: Ecuador *Binder: Ecuador* *Filler: Colombia, Dom. Rep., Nicaragua*

Shape	Name	Lgth	Ring	Wrapper
Robusto	Robusto	5	52	CC
Torpedo	Torpedo	6	52	CC

Created by Miami attorney Michael Laurato in 2007, this is a mild-to-medium-bodied blend made in the famed Ybor City section of Tampa. It's elegantly presented in solid-wood, slide-top cabinets of 25.

LAZO ★New★
Handmade in Villa Gonzalez, Dominican Republic.

Wrapper: Brazil, Ecuador *Binder: Indonesia* *Filler: Dom. Rep.*

Shape	Name	Lgth	Ring	Wrapper
Corona	Corona	5½	42	CC-Ma
Petit Corona	Corto	4	40	CC-Ma
Double Corona	Double Corona	7	50	CC-Ma
Giant	Giant	8	54	CC-Ma
Toro	Grande	6½	54	CC-Ma
Lonsdale	Lonsdale	6½	44	CC-Ma
Torpedo	Piramide	6	52	CC-Ma

HANDMADE CIGARS: BRAND LISTINGS

Robusto	Robusto	5	50	CC-Ma
Toro	Toro	6	52	CC-Ma
Torpedo	Torpedo	6¼	52	CC-Ma

Offered in two styles – the natural-wrapped Lazo Rojo and the maduro-wrapped Lazo Dorado – this is a medium-bodied blend available in boxes or bundles of 25.

LEGENDS ★*New*★

Handmade in Nassau, Bahamas; Santiago, Dominican Republic; Danli, Honduras and Esteli, Nicaragua.

LEGENDS BY CAMACHO:
Wrapper: Honduas   *Binder: Honduras*   *Filler: Honduras*

LEGENDS BY CUSANO:
Wrapper: USA/Connecticut   *Binder: Dom. Rep.*   *Filler: Dom. Rep.*

LEGENDS BY DREW ESTATE:
Wrapper: Ecuador   *Binder: Dom. Rep.*   *Filler: Nicaragua*

LEGENDS BY GRAYCLIFF:
Wrapper: Indonesia   *Binder: Indonesia*   *Filler: Brazil, Dom. Rep., Nicaragua*

LEGENDS BY LA AURORA:
Wrapper: Dom. Rep.   *Binder: Dom. Rep.*   *Filler: Dom. Rep.*

LEGENDS BY MATASA:
Wrapper: Ecuador   *Binder: Dom. Rep.*   *Filler: Dom. Rep.*

LEGENDS BY PEPIN GARCIA:
Wrapper: Nicaragua   *Binder: Nicaragua*   *Filler: Nicaragua*

LEGENDS BY PERDOMO:
Wrapper: Nicaragua   *Binder: Nicaragua*   *Filler: Nicaragua*

LEGENDS BY PUROS INDIOS:
Wrapper: Ecuador   *Binder: Ecuador*   *Filler: Dom. Rep., Honduras*

LEGENDS BY ROCKY PATEL:
Wrapper: Honduras   *Binder: Honduras*   *Filler: Honduras*

HANDMADE CIGARS: BRAND LISTINGS

Shape	Name	Lgth	Ring	Wrapper
Toro, Torpedo	Legends	5¾	54	CC-CM-Ma

Keith Meier at Cigars International started this series as a challenge between four makers to offer a special blend in one size. The list of makers has expanded to ten and the brand began national distribution in 2007. The Puros Indios blend (green band) is mild; the blends from Cusano (gray), La Aurora (black) and MATASA (blue) are mild-to-medium; the blends from Graycliff (purple), Perdomo (red) and rocky Patel (orange) are medium in body; the Camacho (white) and Pepin Garcia (yellow) blends are medium-to-full. All use natural wrappers except for the Perdomo, which has a maduro wrapper and is the only shaped cigar in the series. All are offered in boxes of 20.

LE GRAN FUMA ★New★
Handmade in Danli, Honduras.

Wrapper: Nicaragua   Binder: Nicaragua   Filler: Costa Rica, Nicaragua

Shape	Name	Lgth	Ring	Wrapper
Churchill	Churchill	7	48	CM
Toro	Toro	6	54	CM
Torpedo	Torpedo	6⅛	52	CM

Introduced in 2007 by the G.R. Tabacaleras Unidas (makers of Gran Habano), this value-priced blend has a medium-to-full body, available in boxes of 20.

LEMPIRA
Handmade in Esteli, Nicaragua.

Wrapper: Nicaragua   Binder: Nicaragua   Filler: Nicaragua

Shape	Name	Lgth	Ring	Wrapper
Robusto	Robusto	5	52	Ma
Toro	Toro	6	52	Ma
Torpedo	Torpedo	6½	54	Ma
Double Corona	Churchill	7	50	Ma

Tabacalera Tropical introduced this new blend in 2004 to an old name from the Cigar Boom. This yellow-banded version of Lempira is all new, with a full-bodied, spicy taste, offered in boxes of 20.

HANDMADE CIGARS: BRAND LISTINGS

Giant	Soberanos	8½	52	CM
Toro	Toro	6	50	CM
Robusto	Wavell	5	50	CC-Ma
Corona	Supreme Maduro 200	5¾	43	Ma
Lonsdale	Supreme Maduro 300	6¾	43	Ma
Toro	Supreme Maduro 400	6	50	Ma
Giant	Supreme Maduro 500	8	50	Ma

Introduced in 1989, this veteran handmade brand has earned a reputation for excellence in taste, construction and value. The wide range of shapes and mild-to-medium-bodied flavor makes it accessible to many smokers. A product of the MATASA factory, it is offered in colorful boxes of 25.

LICENCIADOS ANIVERSARIO ★New★
Handmade in Santiago, Dominican Republic.

Wrapper: Honduras   Binder: Dom. Rep.   Filler: Dom. Rep., Nicaragua

Shape	Name	Lgth	Ring	Wrapper
Robusto	Robusto	5	52	CM
Toro	Churchill	6½	56	CM

Mike's Cigars introduced this special-blend, medium-to-full-bodied cigar for the 2007 holiday season. Made by MATASA, it's offered in elegant boxes of 24.

LICENCIADOS CAMEROON
Handmade in Santiago, Dominican Republic.

Wrapper: Cameroon   Binder: Dom. Rep.   Filler: Dom. Rep.

Shape	Name	Lgth	Ring	Wrapper
Perfecto	Invincible	5	50	CM
Robusto	Robusto	4¾	56	CM
Toro	Toro	6	50	CM

This version of Licenciados, also made by MATASA, was introduced in 2002. This is a medium-to-full-bodied cigar with a Cameroon wrapper and bold taste. It is offered in boxes of 25.

HANDMADE CIGARS: BRAND LISTINGS

LIGA PRIVADA NO. 9 ★*New*★
Handmade in Esteli, Nicaragua.

Wrapper: USA/Connecticut   Binder: Brazil   Filler: Don. Rep., Honduras

Shape	Name	Lgth	Ring	Wrapper
Toro	Parejo Oscuro	6	52	Os

This single-size brand was introduced, with limited distribution, by Drew Estates in 2007. It features a Broadleaf wrapper with a full body. Only 80,000 cigars were made in the first production run.

LITTLE CIGAR FACTORY
Handmade in Massapequa, New York, USA.

Wrapper: Cameroon, USA/Conn.   Binder: Indonesia   Filler: Dom.Rep., Nicaragua

Shape	Name	Lgth	Ring	Wrapper
Churchill	Churchill	7	47	CC-CM-Ma
Long Corona	Corona	6	42	CC-CM-Ma
Torpedo	Pyramid	6	54	CC-CM-Ma
Torpedo	Pyramid Box Pressed	5	54	CC-CM-Ma
Robusto	Robusto	5	50	CC-CM-Ma
Toro	Toro	6	50	CC-CM-Ma
Robusto	Gordo	5	60	Ma-Stripe
Giant	Colossal	9	60	CC-CM-Ma
Giant	Double Corona	8	50	CC-CM-Ma
Torpedo	Torpedo	8	56	CC-CM-Ma
Petit Corona	Flavors	5	42	CM
Small Panatela	Hito	5	30	CC-CM-Ma
Petit Corona	Petit Corona	5	42	CC-CM-Ma
Giant	Presidente	8	56	CC-CM-Ma
Short Panatela	Short Story	4	36	CC-CM-Ma

Here is a multi-wrapper approach, introduced in 1997. Most are available in a choice of Sumatra, Connecticut Shade, Connecticut Broadleaf (maduro) and

HANDMADE CIGARS: BRAND LISTINGS

Cameroon wrappers. The flavored cigars are available in cherry, chocolate, Cognac, Piña Colada, rum and vanilla. These are mild-to-medium-bodied cigars, available in boxes of 25.

LITTO GOMEZ DIEZ
Handmade in Santiago, Dominican Republic.

Wrapper: Dom. Rep.	Binder: Dom. Rep.			Filler: Dom. Rep.

Shape	Name	Lgth	Ring	Wrapper
Pyramid	Chisel Puro	5½	54	CM
Toro	Lusitano	6	54	CM
Grand Corona	Americano	5¾	46	CM
Robusto	Cubano	5	50	CM
Petit Corona	Oriental	4⅞	40	CM

Here is an elegantly-made, full-bodied blend introduced in 2004 by Litto Gomez, creator of La Flor Dominicana. Each size is offered in a brilliant, six-sided box of 50 cigars each.

LONE WOLF
Handmade in Santiago, Dominican Republic.

	LOBO FUERTE:	
Wrapper: Nicaragua	Binder: Nicaragua	Filler: Nicaragua

	LOBO ROJO:	
Wrapper: Honduras	Binder: Dom. Rep.	Filler: Dom. Rep.

	SIGNATURE SELECT:	
Wrapper: Ecuador	Binder: Dom. Rep.	Filler: Dom. Rep.

	SUNGROWN:	
Wrapper: Indonesia	Binder: Dom. Rep.	Filler: Dom. Rep.

	WOLFPACK:	
Wrapper: Indonesia	Binder: Dom. Rep.	Filler: Dom. Rep.

Shape	Name	Lgth	Ring	Wrapper
	Lobo Rojo:			
Robusto	Robusto	5	50	CM

HANDMADE CIGARS: BRAND LISTINGS

Corona	Corona	5½	43	CM
Torpedo	Torpedo	6	54	CM
Double Corona	Churchill	7	50	CM
Torpedo	Petite Belicoso	4½	50	CM
Toro	Toro	6	50	CM
Long Corona	Lancero	7½	40	CM
	Signature Select:			
Corona	Corona	5½	43	CC
Robusto	Robusto	5	50	CC
Toro	Toro	6	50	CC
Torpedo	Petite Belicoso	4½	50	CC
Double Corona	Churchill	7	50	CC
Torpedo	Torpedo	5¾	54	CC
Long Corona	Lancero	7½	40	CC
	Lobo Fuerte:			
Corona	Corona	5½	43	CM
Robusto	Robusto	5	50	CM
Toro	Toro	6	50	CM
Torpedo	Torpedo	6	54	CM
Double Corona	Churchill	7	50	CM
Toro	Grande	6	60	CM
	Sun Grown:			
Toro	Robusto	6	50	CM
Toro	Toro	6½	50	CM
Torpedo	Torpedo	6	52	CM
Double Corona	Churchill	7	50	CM
	Wolfpack:			

Robusto	Robusto	5	50	CM
Corona	Corona	5½	42	CM
Torpedo	Torpedo	6	52	CM
Double Corona	Churchill	6¾	48	CM

Lone Wolf is a 1996-created brand developed by well-known film and television stars Jim Belushi and Chuck Norris and acquired in 2000 by David Weiss. The Signature Select blend is mild to medium in body, while the 2006-introduced Lobo Rojo features a Honduran-grown Corojo wrapper and is medium-to-full in body. The Lobo Fuerte is considered full-bodied, the Sun Grown series is medium-bodied and the Wolfpack is a bundled cigar, also of medium body. All styles are offered in boxes of 20, except for the Wolfpack, in bundles.

LOS BLANCOS PREMIERE SELECTION
Handmade in Esteli, Nicaragua.

CONNECTICUT SHADE:

Wrapper: Nicaragua	Binder: Honduras	Filler: Nicaragua

CRIOLLO:

Wrapper: Honduras	Binder: Honduras	Filler: Nicaragua

MADURO:

Wrapper: Nicaragua	Binder: Honduras	Filler: Nicaragua

SUMATRA:

Wrapper: Indonesia	Binder: Honduras	Filler: Nicaragua

Shape	Name		Lgth	Ring	Wrapper
Torpedo	Torpedo		6½	52	CC-CM-Ma
Double Corona	Double Corona		7	52	CC-CM-Ma
Churchill	Churchill	(tubed)	7	46	CC-CM-Ma
Toro	Toro		6	52	CC-CM-Ma
Robusto	Robusto		5	52	CC-CM-Ma
Corona	Corona		5½	44	CC-CM-Ma

Cesar and David Blanco created Los Blancos in 1998. Their four blends offer a mild-to-medium-bodied taste in a choice of four styles: Connecticut Shade (blue band), Criollo (green), Maduro (yellow) and Sumatra (red). All sizes are offered in boxes of 24.

LOS BLANCOS PRIMOS
Handmade in Esteli, Nicaragua.

Wrapper: Nicaragua   *Binder: Nicaragua*   *Filler: Honduras, Nicaragua, Peru*

Shape	Name	Lgth	Ring	Wrapper
Double Corona	Double Corona	7	52	CM-Ma
Torpedo	Torpedo	6½	52	CM-Ma
Toro	Toro	6	52	CM-Ma
Robusto	Robusto	5	52	CM-Ma

Introduced in 2006 and re-blended for 2007, you now have a choice of a Habano Criollo Rosado or Habano Criollo Maduro wrapper. Either way, it's medium in body and offered in value-priced bundles of 25.

LOS REYES UNIDOS
Handmade in Navarette, Dominican Republic.

Wrapper: Dom. Rep.   *Binder: Dom. Rep.*   *Filler: Dom. Rep., Nicaragua*

Shape	Name	Lgth	Ring	Wrapper
Torpedo	Torpedo	6½	52	CM
Long Corona	Extra Corona	6	42	CM
Double Corona	Churchill	7	50	CM
Grand Corona	Corona	6	46	CM
Robusto	Robusto	5	50	CM
Toro	Toro	6	50	CM
Pyramid	Piramide	6⅛	54	CM

This is an Emilio Reyes blend with a medium-to-full body, returned to distribution by Eden's Gate in 2006. It is offered in boxes of 25.

LUSITANIA
Handmade in Esteli, Nicaragua.

Wrapper: Nicaragua   *Binder: Nicaragua*   *Filler: Nicaragua*

Shape	Name	Lgth	Ring	Wrapper
Double Corona	Double Corona	7½	50	CM-Ma
Double Corona	Churchill	6⅞	50	CM-Ma
Lonsdale	Corona	6½	42	CM-Ma
Torpedo	Torpedo	6¼	54	CM-Ma
Toro	Toro	6½	54	CM-Ma
Robusto	Robusto	5	50	CM-Ma

Mike's Cigars of Miami developed this brand, initially made by MATASA and now by the Tabacalera Perdomo. This is a medium-bodied blend, offered in all-cedar boxes of 20.

M&R DOMINICAN
Handmade in Santiago, Dominican Republic.
Wrapper: Ecuador   *Binder: Dom. Rep.*   *Filler: Dom. Rep.*

Shape	Name	Lgth	Ring	Wrapper
Toro	Grande	6	60	CC
Toro	Toro	6	50	CC
Double Corona	Churchill	7	50	CC
Torpedo	Torpedo	6½	52	CC
Giant	Presidente	8	52	CC

This is a mild-bodied brand, introduced in 2003, with a Connecticut-seed wrapper. All are offered in economical bundles of 25.

M3
Handmade in Esteli, Nicaragua.
Wrapper: Nicaragua   *Binder: Nicaragua*   *Filler: Dom. Rep., Nicaragua*

Shape	Name	Lgth	Ring	Wrapper
Corona	Isabella	5½	42	CM
Robusto	Chepito	4½	50	CM
Toro	Carmen	6	50	CM

Churchill	Maritza	7	48	CM
Torpedo	Allison	6½	54	CM
Double Corona	Ana	7½	52	CM
Toro	Muncho	6	60	CM

This brand was introduced by the TESA Cigar Co. in 2004. It is mild in body with a Connecticut-seed wrapper and offered in boxes of 22.

MACABI
Handmade in Santiago, Dominican Republic.

Wrapper: USA/Connecticut   Binder: Mexico   Filler: Dom. Rep., Nicaragua

Shape	Name	Lgth	Ring	Wrapper
Double Corona	Super Corona	7¾	52	Co-Ma
Double Corona	Double Corona	6⅞	50	Co-Ma
Lonsdale	No. 1	6¾	44	Co-Ma
Torpedo	Belicoso Fino	6¼	52	Co-Ma
Toro	Corona Extra	6	50	Co-Ma
Corona	Media Corona	5½	44	Co-Ma
Robusto	Royal Corona	5	50	Co-Ma
Toro	Double Magnum	6½	60	Co-Ma
Giant	Gigantes	8½	52	Co-Ma
Petit Corona	Mini Corona	5	40	Co
Panatela	Corona Fina	6¾	38	Co

Introduced in 1995, this red-band brand – launched as the "pride of Miami" – has been made in Santiago, Dominican Republic beginning in 1997. Handmade in the centuries-old tradition and under the watchful eye of master cigar maker Juan Sosa, Macabi brings a mild-bodied flavor with a Connecticut-grown natural wrapper and medium body with a Connecticut Broadleaf maduro wrapper. Very smooth and slightly spicy, these gems are offered uncellophaned in slide-top boxes of 25 except for the Double Magnum and Gigantes (10s) and Mini Corona (20s).

MACABI CAMEROON RESERVE
Handmade in Santiago, Dominican Republic.

Wrapper: Cameroon   *Binder: Dom. Rep.*   *Filler: Dom. Rep.*

Shape	Name	Lgth	Ring	Wrapper
Corona	No. 10	5½	44	CM
Robusto	No. 20	5	50	CM
Toro	No. 30	6	50	CM
Torpedo	No. 40	6¼	52	CM

Juan Sosa introduced this new blend in 1999, with a spicy, medium-bodied flavor and featuring a Cameroon wrapper (white band). Originally made in Miami, it is now made at the Tabacalera A. Fuente and is offered in boxes of 25.

MACABI DELUXE
Handmade in Esteli, Nicaragua.

Wrapper: Nicaragua   *Binder: Nicaragua*   *Filler: Nicaragua*

Shape	Name	Lgth	Ring	Wrapper
Robusto	Double Robusto	5	54	CM
Toro	Toro	6	50	CM
Torpedo	Torpedo	6	52	CM
Double Corona	Churchill	7	50	CM
Giant	Soberano	8	50	CM

Here is a full-bodied blend (black band) from Juan Sosa, made in Nicaragua and introduced in 2002. The wrapper is Habano Corojo and the cigars are box-pressed and presented in elegant mahogany boxes of 20.

MACANUDO
Handmade in Santiago, Dominican Republic

Wrapper: USA/Connecticut   *Binder: Mexico*   *Filler: Dom. Rep., Mexico*

Shape	Name	Lgth	Ring	Wrapper
Churchill	8-9-8	7	45	CI
Small Panatela	Ascot	4⅛	32	CI

HANDMADE CIGARS: BRAND LISTINGS

Lonsdale	Baron de Rothschild	6½	42	DC-Cl
Short Panatela	Caviar	4	36	Cl
Slim Panatela	Claybourne	6	31	DC-Cl
Short Panatela	Court _(tubed)_	4⅛	36	Cl
Robusto	Crystal _(glass tube)_	5½	50	Cl
Perfecto	Diplomat	4½	60	Cl
Giant	Duke of Wellington	8½	47	Cl
Robusto	Duke of York	5¼	54	Cl
Torpedo	Duke of Windsor	6	50	Cl
Corona	Duke of Devon	5½	42	DC-Cl
Corona	Hampton Court _(tubed)_	5½	42	Cl
Robusto	Hyde Park	5½	49	Cl
Robusto	Lords	4¾	49	Cl
Pyramid	Majesty	6	54	Cl
Cigarillo	Miniature	3¾	24	Cl
Short Panatela	Petit Corona	5	38	Cl
Long Panatela	Portofino _(tubed)_	7	34	Cl
Double Corona	Prince Philip	7½	49	DC-Cl
Giant	Prince of Wales	8	52	Cl
Toro	Thames _(tubed)_	6	50	Cl
Grand Corona	Trump	6½	45	Cl
Toro	Tudor	6	52	Cl
Lonsdale	Library Edition: "The Good Earth"	7	45	CC

Introduced by General Cigar in its current form in the United States in 1971, this is an exceptionally consistent cigar, made with Connecticut Shade wrappers that have been aged for at least three years. The cigar has a silky feel to the hand and has a taste which is only found in a Macanudo. Most sizes are offered in boxes of 25, except for the Ascots (tins of 10), Crystal (box of 8), Caviar (50), Court (30), Duke of Wellington (13), Miniature (8), Thames (20) and Prince Philip

HANDMADE CIGARS: BRAND LISTINGS

(10). Although originally developed and made for many years in Jamaica, all Macanudo production finally shifted to the Dominican Republic in October 2000. The Library Edition is made for Cigars by Santa Clara.

MACANUDO GOLD LABEL
Handmade in Santiago, Dominican Republic.

Wrapper: USA/Connecticut   Binder: Mexico   Filler: Dom. Rep., Mexico

Shape	Name		Lgth	Ring	Wrapper
Robusto	Duke of York		5¼	54	CI
Corona	Hampton Court	(tubed)	5½	42	CI
Toro	Tudor		6	52	CI
Torpedo	Shakespeare		6½	45	CI
Robusto	Somerset		5	54	CI
Double Corona	Lord Nelson		7	49	CI
Robusto	Crystal	(glass tube)	5½	50	CI

Introduced in late 2002, the Gold Label is a limited-edition line using Connecticut-grown wrapper leaves from the first and second primings to provide a lighter and sweeter taste than on the standard Macanudo "Café" line. Most sizes are in boxes of 25, but the Crystals are offered in a box of eight.

MACANUDO MADURO
Handmade in Santiago, Dominican Republic.

Wrapper: USA/Connecticut   Binder: Mexico   Filler: Dom. Rep., Mexico

Shape	Name		Lgth	Ring	Wrapper
Small Panatela	Ascot		4⅛	32	Ma
Robusto	Crystal	(glass tube)	5½	50	Ma
Corona	Duke of Devon		5½	42	Ma
Lonsdale	Baron de Rothschild		6½	42	Ma
Double Corona	Prince Philip		7½	49	Ma
Perfecto	Diplomat		4½	60	Ma
Corona	Hampton Court	(tubed)	5½	42	Ma
Robusto	Hyde Park		5½	49	Ma

HANDMADE CIGARS: BRAND LISTINGS

Although Macanudo had certain shapes with maduro wrappers previously, this specially-blended, all-maduro line was introduced in 1999 and offers a full-bodied, smooth taste in the most popular shapes. Each is offered in boxes of 25 cigars, except for the Ascot and Prince Philip, offered in 10s and the Crystals, in a box of eight.

MACANUDO ROBUST
Handmade in Santiago, Dominican Republic.
Wrapper: USA/Connecticut

Binder: USA/Connecticut   *Filler: Dom. Rep., Honduras, Nicaragua*

Shape	Name		Lgth	Ring	Wrapper
Small Panatela	Ascot		4⅛	32	CM
Double Corona	Prince Philip		7½	49	CM
Lonsdale	Baron de Rothschild		6½	42	CM
Corona	Duke of Devon		5½	42	CM
Robusto	Hyde Park		5½	49	CM
Corona	Hampton Court	(tubed)	5½	42	CM
Short Panatela	Petit Corona		5	38	CM
Slim Panatela	Portofino	(tubed)	7	34	CM

Originally introduced in 1998, the blend was re-made for 2003, with a full-bodied flavor thanks to a dark Connecticut Shade wrapper and Connecticut Broadleaf wrapper. You can find it in boxes of 25, except for the Ascots and Prince Philip sizes, offered in 10s.

MACANUDO VINTAGE 2000
Handmade in Santiago, Dominican Republic
Wrapper: USA/Connecticut   *Binder: Mexico*   *Filler: Dom. Rep., Mexico*

Shape	Name		Lgth	Ring	Wrapper
Double Corona	I	(glass tube)	7½	49	CM
Lonsdale	II	(glass tube)	6½	43	CM
Robusto	VIII	(glass tube)	5½	50	CM
Toro	X	(glass tube)	6	54	CM

The Vintage Cabinet Selection cigars are each more than four years in the

HANDMADE CIGARS: BRAND LISTINGS

MARDO ★New★
Handmade in Esteli, Nicaragua.

Wrapper: Ecuador   Binder: Nicaragua   Filler: Nicaragua

Shape	Name	Lgth	Ring	Wrapper
Torpedo	Torpedo	6½	54	CM
Robusto	Robusto	5	50	CM

Introduced in 2007, this is a mild-bodied cigar that features an Ecuadorian Rosado wrapper. It's offered in boxes of 24 or bundles of 25.

MARIA GUERRERO
Handmade in Santa Rosa de Copan, Honduras.

Wrapper: Cameroon   Binder: Nicaragua   Filler: Honduras, Nicaragua, Peru

Shape	Name	Lgth	Ring	Wrapper
Petit Corona	No. 444	4	44	CM
Short Panatela	Bonitas	4½	38	CM
Corona	Corona	5½	44	CM
Torpedo	Belicoso	6⅛	52	CM
Robusto	Robusto	5	54	CM
Toro	Toro	6	56	CM

This is an old Cuban brand which was named for the famous Spanish singer and which ceased production in 1985. Introduced to the U.S. market by Altadis USA in 2004, it is a medium-to-full-bodied blend featuring a Cameroon wrapper and presented in boxes of 25.

MARIA MANCINI
Handmade in Cofradia, Honduras.

Wrapper: Costa Rica, Nicaragua   Binder: Honduras   Filler: Nicaragua

Shape	Name	Lgth	Ring	Wrapper
Double Corona	Clemenceau	7½	50	CM-Ma
Corona	Corona Classico	5½	44	CM
Toro	Excellence	6	52	CM

Toro	Robusto Larga	6	50	CM-Ma
Robusto	De Gaulle	4¾	52	CM-Ma
Lonsdale	Grande	6½	44	CM
Lonsdale	Palma Delgado	6½	40	CM
Toro	Magic Mountain	6	54	CM-Ma

This is a square-pressed blend, featuring Cuban-seed tobaccos (and Costa Rican maduro wrappers) that produce a medium-to-full-flavored taste with an easy draw. It is offered in boxes of 20.

MAROMA
Handmade, with medium filler, in Danli, Honduras.

Wrapper: USA/Connecticut   Binder: Nicaragua   Filler: Honduras, Nicaragua

Shape	Name	Lgth	Ring	Wrapper
Churchill	Churchill	7	48	CC-Ma
Toro	Toro	6	50	CC-Ma
Corona	Corona	5½	42	CC-Ma
Lonsdale	Lonsdale	6½	44	CC-Ma
Robusto	Robusto	5	50	CC-Ma
Churchill	Fuma	7	46	CC

Introduced by Famous Smoke Shop, this is a mild-bodied blend with Connecticut natural and maduro wrappers, offered in very-well-priced boxes of 25.

MARTINEZ NEW YORK GOLD SERIES   ★*New*★
Handmade in New York, New York, USA.

Wrapper: Ecuador   Binder: Nicaragua   Filler: Dom. Rep., Honduras, Nicaragua

Shape	Name	Lgth	Ring	Wrapper
Churchill	Almirante	7	48	CM
Short Panatela	Bandito	4½	36	CM
Toro	Empire	6	54	CM
Double Corona	Fifth Avenue	7¼	54	CM

Robusto	La Patria	5	50	CM
Corona	Royal Corona	5½	44	CM
Toro	Toro	6	50	CM

Made in a small factory in New York since 1974, this line entered national distribution in 2007 courtesy of Cigars by Santa Clara. The Gold Series is medium-bodied and all sizes are offered in boxes of 20 except the Bandito (30).

MASTER BRADLEY'S PREMIUM DOMINICAN
Handmade in Santiago, Dominican Republic.

Wrapper: Indonesia   *Binder: Dom. Rep.*   *Filler: Dom. Rep.*

Shape	Name	Lgth	Ring	Wrapper
Long Corona	Breva	6	44	CC
Robusto	Toro	5	50	CC
Lonsdale	Churchill	7	44	CC

Introduced in 1997, here is a mild-to-medium-bodied, value-priced bundle of 20 cigars, each protected in an individual cellophane sleeve.

MATACAN
Handmade in San Andres Tuxtla, Mexico.

Wrapper: Mexico   *Binder: Mexico*   *Filler: Mexico, Nicaragua*

Shape	Name	Lgth	Ring	Wrapper
Double Corona	No. 1	7½	50	CC-Ma
Toro	No. 2	6	50	CC-Ma
Grand Corona	No. 3	6⅝	46	CC-Ma
Lonsdale	No. 4	6⅝	42	CC
Robusto	No. 7	4¾	50	CC
Giant	No. 8	8	52	CC-Ma
Double Corona	No. 10	6⅞	54	CC-Ma

Good value, good quality and a medium-bodied taste led by San Andres Valley tobaccos is the promise of Matacan, offered by Altadis USA in bundles of 20.

HANDMADE CIGARS: BRAND LISTINGS

MAYORGA
Handmade in Esteli, Nicaragua.

Wrapper: Costa Rica, Nicaragua   *Binder: Nicaragua*   *Filler: Nicaragua*

Shape	Name	Lgth	Ring	Wrapper
Robusto	Robusto	4¾	50	CM-Ma
Corona	Corona	5½	42	CM
Toro	Toro	6	50	CM-Ma
Churchill	Churchill	7	50	CM-Ma
Long Corona	Lonsdale	6	44	CM
Torpedo	Gordito	5	54	CM-Ma
Torpedo	Torpedo	6¾	52	CM-Ma
Toro	Crystal Rounds *(glass tubes)*	6	50	CM-Ma
	High Octane Series:			
Double Corona	Churchill Trios	7	50	CM-Ma
Robusto	Robusto Trios	4¾	50	CM-Ma
Toro	Toro Trios	6	50	CM-Ma
Grand Corona	Parejo Trios	5¾	46	CM-Ma

This medium-to-full-bodied, box-pressed brand was introduced in 1997 and is now produced by Cigars by Santa Clara. It offers a Nicaraguan shade-grown Habana 2000 wrapper, offered in all-cedar boxes of 25. The Parejo Trios is presented in a nine-comb triangular cabinet offering nine packs of three Parejos tied together! The newer Maduro blend features a Costa Rican wrapper and also presents a full-bodied flavor. The High Octane series was introduced in 2002 and is stronger than the standard blend.

MENDEZ Y LOPEZ
Handmade in Santiago, Dominican Republic.

Wrapper: Indonesia   *Binder: Dom. Rep.*   *Filler: Dom. Rep.*

Shape	Name	Lgth	Ring	Wrapper
Cigarillo	Palmaritos	4	28	CM
Small Panetela	Finos	5	30	CM

Corona	Favorito	5½	42	CM
Robusto	Robusto	5½	50	CM
Panatela	Panatela	6	36	CM
Lonsdale	Latinos	6½	42	CM
Lonsdale	Exclusivos	6½	44	CM
Churchill	Churchill	6⅞	46	CM
Lonsdale	Palma de Mayorca	7	42	CM
Long Panatela	Panatelas Extra	7½	38	CM
Double Corona	Presidentes	7½	50	CM
Giant	Soberanos	8½	52	CM
Giant	Viajante	10	58	CM
Pyramid	Piramide Breve	5½	56	CM
Pyramid	Piramide	7½	64	CM
Torpedo	Piramide Vajante	8	68	CM

This is a very old Cuban brand, now a mild-bodied brand with lots of shapes, including the stunning Piramide Gigante with its 68-ring diameter at the foot! It debuted in its present form in 1997 and is presented in boxes of 20.

MIKE DITKA
Handmade in Santiago, Dominican Republic.

Wrapper: Ecuador   Binder: Dom. Rep.   Filler: Dom. Rep., Honduras, Nicaragua

Shape	Name	Lgth	Ring	Wrapper
Double Corona	Churchill	7	50	CC
Toro	Double Corona	6	52	CC
Robusto	Robusto	5	50	CC
Torpedo	Torpedo	6½	54	CC

This is the cigar made for Mike Ditka's Restaurant in the Tremont Hotel in Chicago! Only in national distribution since 2003, it has a medium-to-full-bodied flavor with a Connecticut-seed wrapper. It's offered in all-cedar boxes of 24.

HANDMADE CIGARS: BRAND LISTINGS

MIKE'S 1950
Handmade in Santiago, Dominican Republic.

Wrapper: Honduras   *Binder: Honduras*   *Filler: Dom. Rep., Nicaragua*

Shape	Name	Lgth	Ring	Wrapper
Torpedo	Belicoso	6	52	CM
Double Corona	Churchill	7¼	54	CM
Lonsdale	Corona Larga	6½	44	CM
Robusto	Toro	5½	54	CM

Introduced in 2005, this cigar salutes the opening of Mike's Cigars by Mike Mersel in July 1950 in Miami Beach. Created by MATASA, it's medium-to-full in body, offered in boxes of 20.

MISTAKES   ★*New*★
Handmade, with mixed filler, in Santiago, Dominican Republic.

Wrapper: USA/Connecticut   *Binder: Dom. Rep.*   *Filler: Dom. Rep.*

Shape	Name	Lgth	Ring	Wrapper
Robusto	Robusto	5	50	CC
Lonsdale	Corona	6½	42	CC
Torpedo	Torpedo	6	50	CC
Double Corona	Churchill	7	50	CC

This is a mixed-fill blend introduced by Meier & Dutch in 2007. It's not a second, but a value cigar with a mild body that's offered in boxes of 20.

MISTER B
Handmade in Esteli, Nicaragua.

Wrapper: Ecuador, Nicaragua   *Binder: Ecuador*   *Filler: Nicaragua*

Shape	Name	Lgth	Ring	Wrapper
Long Corona	Lonsdale	6	43	DC-CC-Ma
Toro	Magnum	6⅛	50	DC-CC-Ma
Lonsdale	Original	7¼	45	DC-CM-Ma

Well known as a machine-made cigar, this brand was revamped as a handmade cigar in 2003. You have a choice of Ecuadorian-grown or Nicaraguan-grown wrapper and a mild-to-medium body. It's value priced and offered in bundles of 20 for less than a dollar a cigar!

MIURA DIRECTO DE FABRICA
Handmade in Esteli, Nicaragua.

Wrapper: Brazil, Ecuador, Panama   Binder: Nicaragua   Filler: Nicaragua, Panama

Shape	Name	Lgth	Ring	Wrapper
Toro	Supremo	6½	60	CC-CM-Ma
Torpedo	Magnum	7	62	CC-CM-Ma
Torpedo	Torpedo	6½	52	CC-CM-Ma
Perfecto	Figurado	6	60	CC-CM-Ma
Robusto	Robusto	5	50	CC-CM-Ma
Churchill	Churchill	7	48	CC-CM-Ma-Stripe
Torpedo	Torpedo Twister	7	52	Stripe
Perfecto	Figurado Twister	6	60	Stripe
Cigarillo	Mini-Habanos	3	22	CC

This is a medium-bodied brand introduced in 2004. It's offered with a choice of Brazilian maduro or Ecuadorian-grown, Connecticut-seed or Panamanian Rosado wrappers on most sizes. All sizes are offered unbanded and uncellophaned in boxes of 50 or 100.

MIURA DIRECTO DE FABRICA X-LIGERO
Handmade in Esteli, Nicaragua.

Wrapper: Nicaragua   Binder: Dom. Rep.   Filler: Panama

Shape	Name	Lgth	Ring	Wrapper
Toro	Buffallos	6¼	54	CM
Double Corona	Piramides	7	52	CM

Introduced in 2006, this is a full-bodied blend offered unbanded in five-level tray-filled boxes of 60.

HANDMADE CIGARS: BRAND LISTINGS

MIURA RESERVA SELECTA
Handmade in Esteli, Nicaragua.

Wrapper: Nicaragua   *Binder: Nicaragua*   *Filler: Panama, Peru*

Shape	Name	Lgth	Ring	Wrapper
Perfecto	Salomon	7⅓	60	CM
Churchill	Churchill	7	47	CM
Toro	Toro	6	54	CM
Robusto	Sublime	4½	54	CM

This is a medium-to-full-bodied blend with a Corojo wrapper. Introduced in 2006, it is offered in boxes of 24.

MJH   ★*New*★
Handmade in Guayaquil, Ecuador.

Wrapper: Ecuador   *Binder: Ecuador*   *Filler: Ecuador*

Shape	Name	Lgth	Ring	Wrapper
Robusto	Robusto Extra	5½	54	Ma
Double Corona	Churchill	7	54	Ma
Toro	Super Toro	6	60	Ma
Torpedo	Super Torpedo	6½	60	Ma

Marshall Holman designed this cigar and gave it his initials! Introduced in 2007, it's full-bodied and smooth, offered in boxes of 10.

MOCAMBO
Handmade in Danli, Honduras.

Wrapper: Ecuador, USA/Connecticut   Binder: Honduras   Filler: Honduras, Nicaragua

Shape	Name	Lgth	Ring	Wrapper
Short Panatela	Half Corona	3¾	36	CC-Ma
Cigarillo	Little Cigarillos	3¼	25	CC-Ma
Small Panatela	Senoritas	3½	30	CC-Ma
Cigarillo	Wilde Cigarillo	3½	27	CC-Ma
Cigarillo	Slim Panatela	5¾	24	CC-Ma

| Small Panatela | Wilde Havana | 3½ | 30 | CC-Ma |

Long known as an Irish-made cigarillo, now Mocambo is a handmade, Honduran brand, still in small sizes. The cigars have a medium body, a slightly unfinished look and are available in boxes of 25 or 50 with an Ecuadorian natural or Connecticut Broadleaf maduro wrapper.

MOMBACHO
Handmade in Esteli, Nicaragua.

Wrapper: Nicaragua   *Binder: Nicaragua*   *Filler: Nicaragua*

Shape	Name	Lgth	Ring	Wrapper
Torpedo	Belicoso	6¼	54	Os
Robusto	Robusto	5	54	Os
Toro	Corona Grande	6½	52	Os

This is a full-bodied blend introduced in 2004 and re-blended for even more power in 2005 by the Tabacalera Tropical. It features a powerful taste with three leaves of Esteli-grown ligero in the filler and a Corojo binder to compliment the jet-black Corojo '99 wrapper. It's available . . . if you dare . . . in boxes of 20.

MONTALVO   ★*New*★
Handmade in Kingston, Jamaica.

Wrapper: USA/Connecticut   *Binder: Mexico*   *Filler: Jamaica*

Shape	Name		Lgth	Ring	Wrapper
Double Corona	Dorchester		7½	49	CC
Toro	Stratford		6	50	CC
Torpedo	Triangulars		6	49	CC
Lonsdale	Yorkshire		6½	42	CC
Corona	Marvillas		5½	42	CC
Grand Corona	Tubulars	*(glass tubes)*	6	45	CC

This ancient Jamaican brand was re-introduced in 2007 by Barrington House International in two blends. The American market edition features a Jamaican filler and only 100,000 cigars were produced. The European version includes

Cuban-grown filler, but both have a full-bodied taste and are offered in boxes of 25 except for the Tubulars, in 10s.

MONTANA SPORT
Handmade in Guayaquil, Ecuador.

Wrapper: Ecuador   Binder: Ecuador   Filler: Ecuador

Shape	Name	Lgth	Ring	Wrapper
Robusto	Robusto	5	50	CM-Ma
Toro	Toro	6	50	CM-Ma
Churchill	Churchill	7	48	CM-Ma
Double Corona	Double Corona	7½	50	CM-Ma
Torpedo	Torpedo	5½	50	CM-Ma

Introduced in 2006, this blend offers a mild-to-medium-bodied taste with a natural wrapper or medium-bodied with a maduro wrapper, both of Sumatra seed. All sizes are offered in dress boxes of 25 adorned by a picture of Millie, the Spanish Spaniel of brand creator Robert White!

MONTE VERDE   ★New★
Handmade in Villa Gonzalez, Dominican Republic.

Wrapper: Ecuador   Binder: Indonesia   Filler: Dom. Rep.

Shape	Name	Lgth	Ring	Wrapper
Giant	Presidente	8	50	CC
Double Corona	Doble Corona	7½	50	CC
Double Corona	Giant	7	54	CC
Torpedo	Torpedo	6½	52	CC
Robusto	Robusto	5½	52	CC
Toro	Toro	6	50	CC
Churchill	Churchill	7	48	CC
Robusto	Rotschild	5	50	CC
Long Corona	Lonsdale	6	44	CC
Corona Extra	Corona	5½	46	CC

Robusto	Library Edition: "Jungle Book"	5	52	CM

Here is a unique version of Montecristo, created in 2003 for Cigars by Santa Clara. It offers a medium-to-full body with a rich flavor. The Kilimanjaro and Sublimation sizes are offered in 10s, the Afrique 444, Jambo, Jambo Jambo and Machame in boxes/tins of four, the Library Edition in 20s, the Safaris in 30s with the others available in boxes of 25.

MONTECRISTO CLASSIC COLLECTION
Handmade in La Romana, Dominican Republic.

Wrapper: USA/Connecticut   *Binder: Dom. Rep.*   *Filler: Dom. Rep.*

Shape	Name		Lgth	Ring	Wrapper
Small Panatela	Legends		4	30	CC
Petit Corona	No. 4		5	40	CC
Petit Corona	No. 5		4	40	CC
Corona	Especial No. 3		5½	44	CC
Corona	Tubo Especial	*(tubed)*	5½	44	CC
Lonsdale	Especial No. 1		6⅝	44	CC
Robusto	Robusto		5	52	CC
Toro	Toro		6	52	CC
Torpedo	No. 2		6⅛	52	CC
Double Corona	Churchill		7	54	CC
Corona	Tubo Especial	*(tubed)*	5½	44	CC
Robusto	Rothchilde	*(tubed)*	5	52	CC
Toro	El Conde	*(tubed)*	6	52	CC

Here is a specially-aged Montecristo, introduced in 2005 with a specially-selected Connecticut Shade wrapper. It offers a medium-to-full body packed in boxes of 20 in most sizes, although the Tubo Especial, Rothchilde and El Conde are in boxes of 10. Most sizes are also available in packs of three to seven.

MONTECRISTO CABINET SELECCION ★*New*★
Handmade in La Romana, Dominican Republic.

Wrapper: Ecuador   Binder: USA/Connecticut   Filler: Dom. Rep., Nicaragua, Peru

Shape	Name	Lgth	Ring	Wrapper
Double Corona	Churchill	7	54	CM
Torpedo	Belicoso	6⅛	52	CM
Toro	Toro	6	52	CM
Corona	Corona	5½	44	CM
Robusto	Robusto	5	52	CM

Here is a supreme example of quality in blending and construction, introduced in 2007. The Montecristo Cabinets use a Sumatra-seed wrapper and Connecticut Broadleaf binder to set a powerful tone in a limited-production cigar. It's offered in elegant, slide-top cabinets of 22.

MONTECRISTO CLUB CABINET SELECTION
Handmade in La Romana, Dominican Republic.

Wrapper: USA/Connecticut   Binder: Dom. Rep.   Filler: Brazil, Dom. Rep.

Shape	Name	Lgth	Ring	Wrapper
Corona	No. 10	5⅝	42	CC
Panatela	No. 20	6⅞	39	CC
Robusto	No. 30	5	50	CC
Lonsdale	No. 40	6¾	42	CC
Toro	No. 50	6	50	CC
Churchill	No. 60	7	46	CC
Double Corona	No. 70	7½	50	CC

This elegant presentation of a medium-bodied Montecristo features a Connecticut wrapper. Introduced in 2000, it offers the most popular sizes in traditional cedar cabinets of 25.

Short Panatela	Sabres	4½	38	CC

This version of Montecristo sports an elegant white label and was introduced in 2003. It offers a medium-bodied flavor with a Connecticut-seed wrapper, offered in boxes of 27 for all but the Court (15s), Prontos (7-pack) and Sabres (5-pack), but all shapes are also available in packs of three or four.

MONTECRUZ LITTLE CIGARS
Handmade in Esteli, Nicaragua.
Wrapper: Ecuador, USA/Connecticut
Binder: USA/Connecticut   *Filler: Dom. Rep., Nicaragua*

Shape	Name	Lgth	Ring	Wrapper
Short Panatela	Corona Chica	4½	36	CC-Ma
Small Panatela	Slim Corona	4½	32	CC-Ma
Cigarillo	Slim Panatela	4½	28	CC-Ma

Introduced in 2003, this is a medium-bodied small cigar line with a choice of an Ecuadorian, Sumatra-seed natural or Connecticut Broadleaf maduro wrapper in boxes of 24.

MONTECRUZ NEGRA CUBANA
Handmade in Esteli, Nicaragua.
Wrapper: Ecuador   *Binder: USA/Connecticut*   *Filler: Dom. Rep., Nicaragua*

Shape	Name	Lgth	Ring	Wrapper
Short Panatela	Chicos	4½	36	CM
Robusto	Robusto	4¾	50	CM
Panatela	Petite	5½	38	CM
Perfecto	Obsequio	5½	50	CM
Lonsdale	Lonsdale	6½	44	CM

This Montecruz debuted in 2002 with a full-bodied blend featuring a Sumatra-seed wrapper. It is offered in unique "Library Edition" boxes of 30 cigars each except for the Petite, offered in 40s.

HANDMADE CIGARS: BRAND LISTINGS

Montesino
Handmade in Santiago, Dominican Republic.

Wrapper: Ecuador, USA/Connecticut   *Binder: Dom. Rep.*   *Filler: Dom. Rep.*

Shape	Name	Lgth	Ring	Wrapper
Churchill	Gran Corona	6¾	48	CM-Ma
Lonsdale	No. 1	6⅞	43	CM-Ma
Long Corona	No. 2	6¼	44	CM-Ma
Corona	Diplomatico	5½	42	CM-Ma
Churchill	Napoleon Grande	7½	46	CM-Ma
Toro	Toro	6	50	CM-Ma
Robusto	Robusto	5	50	CM-Ma
	Sun Grown series:			
Torpedo	Belicoso No. 2	6	49	CM
Torpedo	Super Belicoso	6¾	54	CM
Torpedo	Belicoso Magnum	5¼	52	CM
Pyramid	Pyramid	6	52	CM

This well-known brand debuted in its current format in 1981 and is handmade in Santiago, Dominican Republic. Its quality of construction and full-bodied taste, combined with its modest cost, makes it an excellent value. The newer Sun Grown series features an Ecuadorian-grown wrapper. All sizes are offered in boxes of 25 except for the Pyramid, in 20s.

Montserrat II
Handmade in Esteli, Nicaragua.

Wrapper: Ecuador   *Binder: Indonesia*   *Filler: Nicaragua*

Introduced in 2005, this is a mild-bodied cigar, with a Connecticut-seed wrapper and Sumatra binder. It's offered in four standard sizes (Churchill, 7 x 50; Torpedo, 6 x 54; Corona, 6 x 50 and Robusto, 5 x 50) in boxes of 25.

Montserrat III
Handmade in Esteli, Nicaragua.

Wrapper: Indonesia   *Binder: Nicaragua*   *Filler: Nicaragua*

This is a medium-strength blend, introduced in 2005, featuring a Sumatra wrapper. It's offered in four standard sizes in boxes of 25.

MONTSERRAT IV
Handmade in Esteli, Nicaragua.

Wrapper: Nicaragua   *Binder: Indonesia*   *Filler: Nicaragua*

Introduced in 2006, this is a full-bodied, box-pressed, all-maduro blend with a purple band. It's offered in two sizes (Torpedo, 6 x 54; Corona, 6 x 50) in boxes of 25.

MONTSERRAT V
Handmade in Esteli, Nicaragua.

Wrapper: Nicaragua   *Binder: Nicaragua*   *Filler: Nicaragua*

Also introduced in 2005, this is a maduro-wrapped, all-Nicaraguan cigar with a medium-to-full body. It's offered in three sizes in boxes of 25.

MONTSERRAT FLAVORS
Handmade, with short filler, in Esteli, Nicaragua.

Wrapper: Indonesia   *Binder: Nicaragua*   *Filler: Nicaragua*

Here is a short-fill flavored brand, offered in one size (5½ x 44) in Coffee Liquor, Irish Cream, Pina Colada, cherry and vanilla in bundles of 20.

MONTSERRAT - LORENZO'S BLEND
Handmade in Esteli, Nicaragua.

Wrapper: Nicaragua   *Binder: Indonesia*   *Filler: Nicaragua*

The original blend of the Montserrat line, this is a medium-bodied blend with a Habano 2000 wrapper. It is offered in four sizes in boxes of 25.

MOORE & BODE
Handmade in Miami, Florida, USA.

Wrapper: USA/Connecticut   *Binder and Filler: Central & South American*

Shape	Name	Lgth	Ring	Wrapper
	Miami blend:			
Corona	Bishop	5	41	CI

Torpedo	Torpedo/Torpedo Extra	7	48	CC-CM
Torpedo	Belicoso	6¼	52	CC-CM
Pyramid	Piramide	6	52	CM
Pyramid	Piramide XP	6	54	CC-CM
Toro	Super 60	6	60	CC-CM

Introduced by Cigar Domain in 2007, this banded brand is a collection of overruns of all types from General Cigar factories in Danli and Cofradia, Honduras. It's offered in bundles of 20.

MR. DOMINIC ★Returns★
Handmade in Santiago, Dominican Republic.
Wrapper: USA/Connecticut   Binder: Dom. Rep.   Filler: Dom. Rep.

The Cigar Factory del Yaque makes this cigar in three sizes and a medium-bodied flavor. All sizes are offered in boxes of 25.

MURSULI
Handmade in Temple City, California, USA.
Wrapper: Honduras, Nicaragua   Binder: Honduras
Filler: Dominican Republic, Honduras

Blended by veteran cigar maker Oscar Mursuli, this line comes in 14 sizes with a choice of natural wrappers from Connecticut seed (grown in Nicaragua) or maduro-wrapped shapes on five sizes featuring leaves from Honduras. In maduro shade, this is a medium-to-full-bodied cigar, offered in boxes or bundles of 25 cigars each. The natural-wrapped shapes are mild-to-medium in strength. The Sweet Panatela is dipped in sugar syrup at the end only, while the Corona and Linda are also available in a sweetened style.

The Flavors style (6 x 36) is made with short-filler Dominican tobaccos and has an Indonesian wrapper and Honduran binder. It is mild and offered in Anise, Amaretto, chocolate, cherry, coffee, coconut, cinnamon, honey, mango, peach, rum, raspberry and vanilla.

MUSASHI
Handmade in Frankfort, New York, USA.
Wrapper: Cameroon, USA/Connecticut
Binder: Dominican Republic   Filler: Dominican Republic, Venezuela

Shape	Name	Lgth	Ring	Wrapper
Giant	Bass Master	8¼	52	Ma
Petit Corona	Sport	3	45	CM

This is a member of the Lars Tetens line, offering a full-bodied smoke. The actual blend was created by Tetens' friend Musashi Sonne in 1994. Both sizes are available in boxes of 30.

MYSTERIOSO
Handmade in Danli, Honduras.

Wrapper: USA/Connecticut   Binder: Ecuador
Filler: Costa Rica, Honduras, USA/Louisiana

Shape	Name	Lgth	Ring	Wrapper
Churchill	Dream	7	48	CC-Ma
Torpedo	Piramide	6¼	52	CC-Ma
Robusto	Enigma	5	50	CC-Ma

This blend was introduced in 2003 by the Battleground Seegar Co. of Hazardville, Connecticut. It's medium-bodied with a Connecticut Shade wrapper and full-bodied with a Connecticut Broadleaf maduro wrapper and Louisiana-grown Perique tobacco in the filler, available in boxes of 24.

NAT SHERMAN 489 ★New★
Handmade in Esteli, Nicaragua.

Wrapper: Ecuador   Binder: Nicaragua   Filler: Nicaragua

Shape	Name		Lgth	Ring	Wrapper
Grand Corona	Tubo No. 1	(tubed)	5⅝	47	CM
Toro	Tubo No. 2	(tubed)	6	52	CM

Introduced in 2007, this is a medium-to-full-bodied blend, offered with a Sumatra-seed wrapper. Both sizes are offered in boxes of five.

NAT SHERMAN 1400
Handmade in Esteli, Nicaragua.

Wrapper: Ecuador   Binder: Nicaragua   Filler: Nicaragua

HANDMADE CIGARS: BRAND LISTINGS

Shape	Name	Lgth	Ring	Wrapper
Lonsdale	Palma Grande	6½	44	CM-Ma
Churchill	Double Corona	7	48	CM-Ma

Named for the Broadway address of the Nat Sherman store in New York for more than 50 years, this is a medium-bodied blend with a Sumatra-seed wrapper introduced in 2005. It's offered in boxes of 14.

NAT SHERMAN HOST SELECTION
Handmade in Danli, Honduras.

Wrapper: USA/Connecticut   Binder: Honduras   Filler: Honduras

Shape	Name	Lgth	Ring	Wrapper
Small Panatela	Hudson	4⅞	32	CC
Corona	Hamilton	5½	42	CC
Lonsdale	Hunter	6	43	CC
Toro	Harrington	6	48	CC
Robusto	Hobart	5	50	CC
Torpedo	Hanover	5½	56	CC
Double Corona	Hampton	7	50	CC

Nat Sherman, "tobacconist to the world" for more than six decades, introduced its own lines of ultra-quality cigars to keep its legion of customers satisfied. Made by Ranchos Tabacos Jamastran, the Host Selection has a mild-to-medium body with a Connecticut wrapper and a sweet finish and a rustic aroma, offered in boxes of 25 except for the Hanover, in 20s.

NAT SHERMAN METROPOLITAN SELECTION
Handmade in Santiago, Dominican Republic.

Wrapper: USA/Connecticut   Binder: Dom. Rep.   Filler: Dom. Rep.

Shape	Name	Lgth	Ring	Wrapper
Corona	Anglers	5½	43	CC-Ma
Robusto	Union	4½	50	CC-Ma
Toro	University	6	50	CC-Ma

Torpedo	Explorers	6½	52	CC-Ma
Double Corona	Metropolitan	7	50	CC-Ma
Small Panatela	New York Smokes	5	32	CC
Short Panatela	Quickies	4	36	CC
Cigarillo	Cigarillo	3⅜	24	CC
Robusto	Bankers	5	66	CC-Ma

The 1995-introduced Metropolitan Selection offers a mild-to-medium-bodied flavor with a Connecticut Shade wrapper or the Connecticut Broadleaf maduro wrapper. The Smokes, Quickies and Bankers were added in 2005, the Cigarillos in 2006.

NAT SHERMAN OMERTA
Handmade in Esteli, Nicaragua.

Wrapper: Nicaragua   *Binder: Nicaragua*   *Filler: Nicaragua*

Shape	Name	Lgth	Ring	Wrapper
Torpedo	Omerta	6	54	CM

Using leaves grown solely on the La Joya Plantation owned by the Olivas, this full-bodied cigar was introduced in 2005. It's offered in a uniquely decorated box of six.

NAT SHERMAN SUAVE
Handmade in Santiago, Dominican Republic.

Wrapper: USA/Connecticut   *Binder: Dom. Rep.*   *Filler: Dom. Rep.*

Shape	Name	Lgth	Ring	Wrapper
Robusto	Dewitt Clinton	4½	50	CC
Toro	Harriman	6	50	CC
Corona	LaGuardia	5½	43	CC
Torpedo	Roosevelt	6	54	CC
Double Corona	Rockefeller	7½	50	CC

Named for great New Yorkers of the 19th and 20th Centuries, this mild-to-medium-bodied line was introduced in 2006. All sizes are offered in boxes of 25.

HANDMADE CIGARS: BRAND LISTINGS

NATIONAL BRAND
Handmade in Danli, Honduras.

Wrapper: Honduras *Binder: Honduras* *Filler: Honduras*

Shape	Name	Lgth	Ring	Wrapper
Giant	Imperial	8½	52	CC-Ma
Churchill	Churchill	7	48	CC-Ma
Long Corona	Lonsdale	6	43	CC-Ma
Corona	Corona	5½	42	CC
Robusto	Rothschild	5	50	CC-Ma
Toro	Toro	6	50	CC
Churchill	Soberanos	7	44	CC
Panatela	Royal Palm	6⅛	36	CC

First offered in 1978, this is a Honduran-produced cigar with all Honduran-grown tobacco, including a Connecticut-seed wrapper, offered in bundles of 25 cigars each. It is considered mild-to-medium in strength.

NATIONAL BRAND NICARAGUA
Handmade in Esteli, Nicaragua.

Wrapper: Honduras *Binder: Nicaragua* *Filler: Nicaragua*

Shape	Name	Lgth	Ring	Wrapper
Giant	Imperial	8½	52	CM
Torpedo	Figurado	6	54	CM
Churchill	Churchill	7	48	CM
Toro	Toro	6	50	CM
Robusto	Rothschild	5	50	CM
Robusto	Robusto Gordo	5	60	CM
Lonsdale	Cetros	6½	44	CM
Corona	Corona	5½	42	CM

Camacho Cigars introduced this full-bodied blend in 2004. It's offered in bundles of 25.

HANDMADE CIGARS: BRAND LISTINGS

NATIONAL BRAND SUNGROWN
Handmade in Danli, Honduras.

Wrapper: Honduras   Binder: Honduras   Filler: Honduras

Shape	Name	Lgth	Ring	Wrapper
Giant	Imperial	8½	52	CM
Churchill	Churchill	7	48	CM
Toro	Toro	6	50	CM
Robusto	Rothschild	5	50	CM
Corona	Corona	5½	42	CM

The Sun Grown edition was introduced in 2002, with a medium body. It's been well received and is offered in boxes of 20.

NATIVO
Handmade in Santiago, Dominican Republic.

Wrapper: Indonesia   Binder: Dom. Rep.   Filler: Dom. Rep.

Shape	Name	Lgth	Ring	Wrapper
Panatela	Cafe	5½	38	CM

This is a full-bodied blend with a Sumatra wrapper. It is hand-pressed and packed in bundles of 25.

NATURAL
Handmade in Esteli, Nicaragua.

Wrapper: Brazil, Cameroon, Indonesia, Mexico, USA/Connecticut   Binder: Nicaragua
Filler: Dom. Rep., Haiti, Honduras, Italy, Nicaragua, Syria, Turkey, USA/Louisiana

Shape	Name	Lgth	Ring	Wrapper
	12 Country Sweet Blend:			
Short Panatela	Jucy Lucy	3	38	CM
Robusto	Elixir 5-50 *(glass tube)*	5	50	CC
Perfecto	Egg	6	60	CC-Ma
	12 Country Cuban Blend:			
Torpedo	Dark Angel	6½	54	Ma

HANDMADE CIGARS: BRAND LISTINGS

Robusto	Root	5	55	Ma
Toro	Root Deluxe _(tubed)_	6	50	Ma
Petit Corona	Dirt	4	43	Ma
Torpedo	Dirt Torpedo	5	52	Ma
Culebras	Medusa	6	38	Ma
	10 Country Creamy Blend:			
Robusto	Clean Robusto	5	50	CM
	Meier & Dutch series:			
Torpedo	Pimp Sticks	6	52	CC

This brand was introduced in 2000 and re-organized in 2006, offering a wild variety of tobaccos and strengths from mild to full-bodied. There is a choice of wrappers in each blend, with maduro wrappers from Brazil or Connecticut. Most shapes are offered in stunning three-panel, fold-out, lacquered wood boxes of 24. The Pimp Sticks are made for Meier & Dutch Distributors.

NESTOR MIRANDA SPECIAL SELECTION ★New★
Handmade in Santiago, Dominican Republic.
Wrapper: Nicaragua   Binder: Nicaragua   Filler: Costa Rica, Nicaragua

Shape	Name	Lgth	Ring	Wrapper
Robusto	S.S. 5.5x54	5½	54	CM
Toro	S.S. 6x60	6	60	CM

Miami Cigar Co. introduced this brand, named for its founder, in 2007. It is medium in body and offered in boxes of 20.

NESTOR RESERVE EDITION 2000
Handmade in Danli, Honduras.
Wrapper: Nicaragua   Binder: Nicaragua   Filler: Honduras, Mexico, Nicaragua

Shape	Name	Lgth	Ring	Wrapper
Long Corona	Corona	6	43	CM-Ma
Churchill	Double Corona	7⅝	47	CM-Ma
Robusto	Robusto	4¾	54	CM-Ma

| Toro | Toro | 6 | 54 | CM-Ma |
| Torpedo | Torpedo | 7 | 50 | CM-Ma |

This blend was introduced in 2000, with an H2000 wrapper, by the House of Oxford and offers a full-bodied taste in boxes of 25.

NESTOR VINTAGE 1989
Handmade in Danli, Honduras.

Wrapper: Ecuador   *Binder: Honduras*   *Filler: Honduras, Nicaragua*

Shape	Name	Lgth	Ring	Wrapper
Robusto	454	4	54	CM-Ma
Toro	654	6	54	CM-Ma
Churchill	747	7⅝	47	CM-Ma

The House of Oxford's second generation of the Nestor 747 is the three-shape Vintage line, also a full-bodied cigar. However, this group uses 1989-vintage leaves and is presented in its original rounded shape in cedar cabinets of 50 cigars each (the 747 is also available in a box of 25). Each completed bunch of 50, tied with a silk ribbon, is aged for nine months after rolling to ensure that the aromas and flavors of the bunch have penetrated each of the cigars.

NICARAGUAN PRIMEROS
Handmade in Esteli, Nicaragua.

Wrapper: Indonesia, USA/Connecticut   *Binder: Nicaragua*   *Filler: Nicaragua*

Shape	Name	Lgth	Ring	Wrapper
Robusto	Parejos 5x	5	50	CC-CM-Ma
Toro	Parejos 6x	6	50	CC-CM-Ma
Double Corona	Parejos 7x	7	50	CC-CM-Ma
Torpedo	Figurados	6½	52	CC-CM-Ma

Introduced by El Sol Cigars in 2006, this blend offers a choice of Connecticut Shade, Indonesian Sumatra or Connecticut Broadleaf Maduro wrappers on all sizes. A Cameroon wrapper is available on the 7x. All sizes are offered in boxes of 25.

HANDMADE CIGARS: BRAND LISTINGS

NICARAO
Handmade in Esteli, Nicaragua.

Wrapper: Nicaragua *Binder: Nicaragua* *Filler: Nicaragua*

Shape	Name	Lgth	Ring	Wrapper
Petit Corona	Minuto	5	42	CM
Robusto	Robusto	5	52	CM
Torpedo	Piramides	6	52	CM
Double Corona	Julieta	7	50	CM

This version of Nicarao was created by the Tabacalera Tropical in 2004. The blend of medium-to-full in body using Corojo '99 leaves and offered in elegant boxes of 20.

NINO VASQUEZ
Handmade in Esteli, Nicaragua.

Wrapper: Nicaragua *Binder: Nicaragua* *Filler: Honduras, Nicaragua*

Shape	Name	Lgth	Ring	Wrapper
Double Corona	Gran Corona	7½	54	CM
Torpedo	Torpedo	6¼	52	CM
Churchill	Churchill	7	48	CM
Robusto	Robusto	5	50	CM
Long Corona	Corona	6¼	42	CM

This is a medium-to-full-bodied blend, first offered in 2002. It features a Corojo wrapper and is available in a humidifier-included box of 24.

NOMI
Handmade in Santiago, Dominican Republic.

Wrapper: Brazil *Binder: Dom. Rep.* *Filler: Dom. Rep.*

Shape	Name	Lgth	Ring	Wrapper
Double Corona	Presidente	7¼	52	Ma
Torpedo	Belicoso	6½	52	Ma
Corona	Corona	5½	44	Ma
Toro	Toro	6	50	Ma

The Crown David Int'l Cigar Co. offers this all-maduro line, with a medium-to-full-bodied flavor.

NORDING
Handmade in Danli, Honduras.

Wrapper: Costa Rica   Binder: Mexico   Filler: Honduras, Nicaragua

Shape	Name	Lgth	Ring	Wrapper
Torpedo	Torpedo	4	54	CM
Robusto	Robusto	5½	52	CM
Toro	Toro	6	58	CM

Developed by Rocky Patel for the celebrated pipe maker Erik Nording in 2006, this is a medium-bodied blend in the Robusto and Toro shapes, but the Torpedo is full-bodied. All shapes are offered in boxes of 25.

NU
BY COJIMAR
Handmade, with mixed filler, in Santiago, Dominican Republic.

Wrapper: Ecuador   Binder: Dom. Rep.   Filler: Dom. Rep.

Shape	Name	Lgth	Ring	Wrapper
Petit Corona	Sweet Tip	5	42	CC

This is a mild-bodied, flavored cigar with wild flavors like Midnite Trip (vanilla), Sunstar (orange and Tequila), DolceBanana (banana and passion fruit), KaffeCubano (coffee and Irish Cream) and ScarletMyth (grape with White Zinfandel) offered in wood, slide-top boxes of 25.

OCASO
Handmade in Santiago, Dominican Republic.

Wrapper: USA/Connecticut   Binder: Mexico   Filler: Dom. Rep.

Shape	Name	Lgth	Ring	Wrapper
Double Corona	Churchill	7½	50	CC
Toro	Toro	6½	48	CC
Lonsdale	Lonsdale	6½	43	CC
Robusto	Robusto	4¾	50	CC

HANDMADE CIGARS: BRAND LISTINGS

This brand is only available to members of the Tobacconists' Association of America. It is mild and offered in boxes of 25.

OCASO HONDURAN
Handmade in Cofradia, Honduras.

Wrapper: Ecuador   *Binder: USA/Connecticut*
Filler: Dominican Republic, Honduras, Nicaragua

Shape	Name	Lgth	Ring	Wrapper
Robusto	Robusto	5	54	CM
Toro	Robusto Larga	6⅛	50	CM
Double Corona	Robusto Suprema	7¼	54	CM

Made by Villazon & Co., this is a medium-to-full-bodied blend introduced in 2004. It's a TAA exclusive with a Sumatra-seed wrapper.

OCCIDENTAL RESERVE
Handmade in Santiago, Dominican Republic.

OCCIDENTAL RESERVE CONNECTICUT:
Wrapper: USA/Connecticut   Binder: USA/Connecticut   Filler: Dom. Rep., Indonesia

OCCIDENTAL RESERVE DOUBLE BROADLEAF MADURO:
Wrapper: Ecuador   Binder: USA/Connecticut   Filler: Dom. Rep., Indonesia

Shape	Name	Lgth	Ring	Wrapper
Torpedo	Torpedo	6	52	CC-Ma
Churchill	Churchill	7	48	CC-Ma
Toro	Toro	6	48	CC-Ma
Robusto	Robusto	4⅞	50	CC-Ma
Long Corona	Corona	6⅛	43	CC-Ma
Giant	Gigante	8½	52	CC

The Connecticut blend was introduced in 1999, as a mild blend offered by the Alec Bradley Cigar Company. The Double Maduro – featuring a Connecticut-seed wrapper and authentic Connecticut Broadleaf binder – was introduced in 2004 and also offers a mild-to-medium body. Both are an excellent value and presented in bundles of 25 (20 for the Gigante).

HANDMADE CIGARS: BRAND LISTINGS

OLD FASHIONED
Handmade in Santiago, Dom. Republic and Cofradia, Honduras.

DOMINICAN REPUBLIC:
Wrapper: Cameroon, USA/Connecticut   Binder: Mexico   Filler: Dom. Rep., Mexico

HONDURAS:
Wrapper: Ecuador, USA/Connecticut   Binder: Honduras, USA/Connecticut
Filler: Dominican Republic, Honduras, Nicaragua

Shape	Name	Lgth	Ring	Wrapper
	Made in the Dominican Republic:			
Small Panatela	Chico	4⅛	32	CC-CM
Lonsdale	No. 31	6½	42	CM
Corona	No. 32	5¾	43	CM
Short Panatela	No. 34	5	38	CM
Slim Panatela	No. 36	6	34	CM
Toro	No. 38	6¼	47	CM
Double Corona	No. 40	7½	49	CM
Robusto	No. 41	5½	49	CM
Slim Panatela	No. 350	7	34	CC
Short Panatela	No. 400	5	38	CC
Corona	No. 500	5½	42	CC-Ma
Robusto	No. 550	5½	49	CC-Ma
Lonsdale	No. 700	6½	42	CC-Ma
Double Corona	No. 749	7½	49	CC-Ma
	Made in Honduras:			
Toro	No. 1	6⅛	50	CM-Ma
Churchill	No. 2	6¾	48	CM-Ma
Robusto	No. 3	4½	50	CM-Ma
Grand Corona	No. 4	5¾	45	CM-Ma

Lonsdale	No. 5	6½	43	CM-Ma
Panatela	No. 6	5½	38	CM-Ma
Double Corona	No. 7	7¾	54	CM-Ma
Toro	No. 8	6½	54	CM-Ma

Here are Dominican-made seconds of Macanudo and Partagas, varying from mild to medium-to-full in strength. From Honduras, these are seconds of Hoyo de Monterey, Punch and like brands. A great value, they are offered in bundles of 20 or 25.

OLD POWDER KEG
Handmade in Hazardville, Connecticut, USA.

Wrapper: Nicaragua   Binder: USA/Connecticut   Filler: Nicaragua, USA/Louisiana

Shape	Name	Lgth	Ring	Wrapper
Churchill	Churchill	7	48	Ma
Torpedo	Torpedo	6	50	Ma
Robusto	Robusto	5	50	Ma

Introduced by the Battleground Seegar Company, the Old Powder Keg series is full-bodied and salutes Col. Augustus Hazard, who owned the Hazard Gun Powder Co. which blew up and ended the business, but left the town of Hazardville standing. It's a marvelous, richly-flavored three-nation blend offered in boxes of 24.

OLD SCHOOL
Handmade in Guayaquil, Ecuador.

Wrapper: Ecuador   Binder: Ecuador   Filler: Ecuador

Shape	Name	Lgth	Ring	Wrapper
Robusto	Pee Wee	5	50	CM
Torpedo	Campy	6	54	CM
Toro	Duke	6	60	CM

Marshall Holman introduced this salute, originally called "Brooklyn," to the Brooklyn Dodgers in 2006. The cigars are medium in body and salute the "Boys of Summer" from the great Dodger teams of the 1950s: shortstop Pee Wee

Torpedo	Torpedo	6½	52	CM
Short Panatela	Cigarillo	4	38	CM

Known as Oliva "O" Classic until renamed in 2006, this is a Nicaraguan puro, offering a medium-to-full-bodied flavor. It's offered in boxes of 20 for most shapes, packs of four or five in most shapes and in boxes of 10 for tubed shapes, 30 for the No. 4 and tins of five for the Cigarillo.

OLIVA SERIE O MADURO
Handmade in Esteli, Nicaragua.
Wrapper: USA/Connecticut   Binder: Nicaragua   Filler: Nicaragua

Shape	Name	Lgth	Ring	Wrapper
Robusto	Robusto	5	50	Ma
Robusto	Double Robusto	5	54	Ma
Double Corona	Churchill	7	50	Ma
Toro	Double Toro	6	60	Ma
Torpedo	Torpedo 652	6	52	Ma
Torpedo	Torpedo 754	7	54	Ma

The famous name of Oliva graces this brand, which debuted in 2001 as the Oliva "O" Maduro. It was renamed in 2006. With a Connecticut-grown maduro wrapper, it offers a medium-to-full-bodied flavor. All are presented in boxes of 20 except for the Double Toro (10).

OLIVA SPECIAL S
Handmade in Esteli, Nicaragua.
Wrapper: Ecuador   Binder: Nicaragua   Filler: Nicaragua

Shape	Name	Lgth	Ring	Wrapper
Petit Corona	No. 4	5	43	CC
Robusto	Robusto (tube available)	5	50	CC
Torpedo	Belicoso	5	52	CC
Grand Corona	Corona	6	46	CC
Perfecto	Diadema 646	6	46	CC

Toro	Toro *(tube available)*	6	50	CC
Torpedo	Torpedo	6	52	CC
Perfecto	Diadema 748 *(tube available)*	7	48	CC
Double Corona	Churchill	7	50	CC
Perfecto	Diadema 952	9	52	CC

Introduced in 2006, this is a full-bodied line with a sun-grown Ecuadorian wrapper. It's offered in boxes of 20 for most sizes, but in boxes of 10 for the tubed shapes and 30 for the No. 4.

OLIVA SERIE V ★New★
Handmade in Esteli, Nicaragua.

Wrapper: Nicaragua *Binder: Nicaragua* *Filler: Nicaragua*

Shape	Name	Lgth	Ring	Wrapper
Double Corona	Churchill Extra	7	52	CM
Long Panatela	Lancero	7	38	CM
Perfecto	Special V Figurado	6	60	CM
Toro	Double Corona	6	60	CM
Torpedo	Torpedo	6	56	CM
Torpedo	Belicoso	5	54	CM
Robusto	Double Robusto	5	54	CM

The Serie V features a high priming, sun-grown wrapper and Jalapa Valley ligero fillers for a full-bodied flavor. Introduced in 2007, it's presented in slide-top cabinets of 24 except for the Lancero, in 36s. A special size – a Culebras – is made only for special events.

OLIVEROS CLASSIC COLLECTION
Handmade in Santiago, Dominican Republic.

Wrapper: Brazil, Cameroon, Ecuador *Binder: Dom. Rep.* *Filler: Dom. Rep.*

Shape	Name	Lgth	Ring	Wrapper
Toro	Toro	5¾	50	CC-CM-Ma

HANDMADE CIGARS: BRAND LISTINGS

OLIVEROS KOPI LUWAK ★New★
Handmade in Santiago, Dominican Republic.

Wrapper: Brazil   Binder: Dom. Rep.   Filler: Dom. Rep.

Shape	Name	Lgth	Ring	Wrapper
Corona	Jambi	5½	42	Ma
Toro	Luwak	5¾	50	Ma

A flavored cigar featuring the unique taste of Kopi Luwak coffee grown in Sumatra, introduced in 2007. Mild to medium in body, it is infused with notes of coffee, java, mocha, cocoa beans and just a touch of vanilla, offered in boxes of 25.

OLIVEROS LTD
Handmade in Santiago, Dominican Republic.

Wrapper: Brazil   Binder: Dom. Rep.   Filler: Dom. Rep., Nicaragua, Peru

Shape	Name	Lgth	Ring	Wrapper
Robusto	Gran Robusto	5½	52	CM
Torpedo	Belicoso Fino	5½	50	CM

Introduced in 2006, this is a full-bodied, all-ligero line with a Brazilian Mata Fina wrapper. It's a limited edition, with only 2,000 boxes of 50 cigars each being produced for each size (200,000 cigars total).

OLIVEROS PLATINUM
Handmade in Santiago, Dominican Republic.

Wrapper: Brazil   Binder: Dom. Rep.   Filler: Dom. Rep.

Shape	Name	Lgth	Ring	Wrapper
Corona	Reyes Maduro	5½	42	Ma
Robusto	Toro Maduro	5¾	50	Ma

The Platinum Series was introduced in 2000. It offers a mild-to-medium-bodied flavor with a Brazilian maduro wrapper in a boxed-pressed format with a choice of either a Mocha Mint, sweet or vanilla fudge (!) finish.

HANDMADE CIGARS: BRAND LISTINGS

OLIVEROS XL
Handmade in Santiago, Dominican Republic.
Wrapper: Brazil, Dominican Republic
Binder: Dom. Rep., USA/Connecticut   *Filler: Dom. Rep., Honduras, Nicaragua*

Shape	Name	Lgth	Ring	Wrapper
Robusto	XL/52	5	52	CM-Ma
Toro	XL/55	6	55	CM-Ma
Toro	XL/60	5¾	60	CM-Ma
Torpedo	XL/B56	5	56	CM-Ma
Toro	XL/F56	6	56	CM-Ma
Double Corona	XL/55-7	7	55	Ma

The Habana Cuba Cigar Co. introduced this unrestrained, full-bodied powerhouse in 2004 with a Brazilian maduro wrapper, Connecticut maduro binder and three-nation filler blend. The Corojo version with a Dominican-grown wrapper, Dominican binder and Dominican and Nicaraguan filler debuted in 2005. Enjoy them – if you dare – in boxes of 20; the XL-55-7 is only offered in a giant humidor of 45.

OLOR
Handmade in Santiago, Dominican Republic.
Wrapper: USA/Connecticut   *Binder: Dom. Rep.*   *Filler: Dom. Rep.*

Shape	Name	Lgth	Ring	Wrapper
Robusto	Rothschild	4½	50	CC-Ma
Corona	Momento	5½	43	CC-Ma
Toro	Paco	6	50	CI-CC-Ma
Long Corona	Lonsdale	6¼	42	CC-Ma
Churchill	Colosos	7¼	48	CC-Ma
Short Panatela	Oloritos	4⅛	36	CC

This brand, introduced by Famous Smoke Shop in 1988, has won new friends among enthusiasts. Packed in slide-top cedar cabinets, these cigars are produced by General Cigar and are an excellent value and a smooth, mild-to-medium-bodied smoke in boxes of 25. The Oloritos are packed in fives.

OLOR FUERTE
Handmade in Cofradia, Honduras.

Wrapper: Honduras   Binder: Mexico   Filler: Brazil, Dom. Rep., Nicaragua

Shape	Name	Lgth	Ring	Wrapper
Corona	Corona	5½	42	CM
Torpedo	Belicoso	6	54	CM
Lonsdale	Lonsdale	6½	44	CM
Churchill	Churchill	7	48	CM
Toro	Magnum	6	60	CM
Robusto	Robusto	5	50	CM
Short Panatela	Poquitos	4⅛	36	CM

Here is a bolder version of the Olor line, featuring a Honduran Talanga Cubano wrapper and four-nation interior blend. Introduced in 2004, it offers a medium-to-full-bodied taste and is available in boxes of 25 (Poquitos in fives).

OLOR NICARAGUA
Handmade in Esteli, Nicaragua.

Wrapper: Ecuador   Binder: Nicaragua   Filler: Nicaragua

Shape	Name	Lgth	Ring	Wrapper
Robusto	Robusto	5	50	CM
Corona	Corona	5½	42	CM
Toro	Toro	6	50	CM
Lonsdale	Lonsdale	6½	44	CM
Double Corona	Churchill	7½	50	CM

Famous Smoke Shop introduced this version of Olor in 2006. It's full-bodied, made by the Oliva Cigar Company and offered in boxes of 25.

OLYMPIA
Handmade in Villa Gonzalez, Dominican Republic.

Wrapper: Indonesia   Binder: Dom. Rep.   Filler: Dom. Rep.

HANDMADE CIGARS: BRAND LISTINGS

Shape	Name	Lgth	Ring	Wrapper
Robusto	Robusto	4½	50	CM
Long Corona	Lonsdale	6	43	CM
Toro	Toro	6	50	CM
Churchill	Churchill	7	48	CM

This brand was introduced by Swisher International in 2002, offering a mild-to-medium-bodied taste, offered in boxes of 20.

OMAR ORTEZ ORIGINALS
Handmade in Esteli, Nicaragua.

Wrapper: Nicaragua — Binder: Nicaragua — Filler: Nicaragua

Shape	Name	Lgth	Ring	Wrapper
Torpedo	Belicoso	6⅛	52	CM
Robusto	Robusto	5	54	CM
Toro	Toro	6	54	CM

Named for a senior roller at the Nicaragua America Tobacco (NATSA) factory, this blend was introduced by Altadis USA in 2006. It's full-bodied and offered in rustic-styled wood boxes of 60 cigars each!

ONYX RESERVE
Handmade in La Romana, Dominican Republic.

Wrapper: USA/Connecticut — Binder: Nicaragua
Filler: Dominican Republic, Nicaragua, Peru

Shape	Name	Lgth	Ring	Wrapper
Petit Corona	No. 4	5	44	Ma
Cigarillo	Mini	3⅜	23	Ma
Small Panatela	Impulse	4	30	Ma
Lonsdale	Lonsdale	6⅝	44	Ma
Robusto	Robusto	5	50	Ma
Toro	Toro	6	50	Ma
Double Corona	Churchill	7	50	Ma

Torpedo	Mini Belicoso	5	52	Ma
Torpedo	No. 2 Belicoso	6⅛	52	Ma
Toro	Torbusto	5½	60	Ma

This second edition of the Onyx brand is medium-to-full-bodied and was introduced by Altadis USA in late 2000. It features box-pressed shapes (except for the Mini, Impulse, Churchill and Lonsdale) in elegant wooden boxes of 20 for most shapes, featuring a blackened Connecticut Broadleaf wrapper and three-nation filler blend. The Mini is offered in boxes of 40; the Impulse in tins of 10.

ONYX VINTAGE '97
Handmade in La Romana, Dominican Republic.

Wrapper: Mexico   *Binder: USA/Connecticut*   *Filler: Brazil, Nicaragua, Peru*

Shape	Name	Lgth	Ring	Wrapper
Toro	Black Prince	6	48	Ma
Robusto	Epicure	4½	50	Ma
Long Corona	Escepionale	6	42	Ma
Torpedo	Spanish Colonial	6	50	Ma

Among the best in the all-maduro field, this is a medium-bodied blend which features a 1997 San Andreas wrapper, available in boxes of 25.

OPTIMO CLASICO
Handmade in Santiago, Dominican Republic.

Wrapper: Indonesia   *Binder: USA/Connecticut*
Filler: Dominican Republic, Indonesia, Philippines

Shape	Name	Lgth	Ring	Wrapper
Robusto	No. I	4½	50	CM
Long Corona	No. II	6	43	CM
Toro	No. III	6	50	CM
Churchill	No. IV	7	48	CM
Giant	No. V	8	50	CM

HANDMADE CIGARS: BRAND LISTINGS

Once again, here is an Optimo handmade! Offered in five sizes, this version has a medium body and is offered in fairly-priced bundles of 20. The No. II size is offered in a flavored version in Amaretto, rum and vanilla flavors.

ORANGE LABEL
Handmade in Santiago, Dominican Republic.
Wrapper: Ecuador, USA/Connecticut

Binder: Dominican Republic   *Filler: Dominican Republic*

Shape	Name	Lgth	Ring	Wrapper
Double Corona	Churchill	7¼	52	CC-Ma
Torpedo	Belicoso	6½	52	CC-Ma
Toro	Toro	6	52	CC-Ma
Robusto	Robusto	5	52	CC-Ma
Lonsdale	Panatela	6½	40	CC-Ma
Petit Corona	Petit	4	40	CC-Ma
Corona	Corona	5½	44	CC-Ma

This is a mild-bodied cigar, introduced in 2004 by the Crown David Int'l Cigar Co. It features an Ecuadorian-grown natural or Connecticut-grown maduro wrapper in boxes of 25.

ORIGINAL CUBAN
Handmade, with mixed filler, in Esteli, Nicaragua.
Wrapper: Ecuador   *Binder: Dom. Rep.*   *Filler: Dom. Rep.*

Shape	Name	Lgth	Ring	Wrapper
Torpedo	Torpedo	6¼	52	CM
Double Corona	Churchill	7	50	CM
Robusto	Robusto	5	50	CM
Lonsdale	Corona	6¼	44	CM

This brand was introduced in 2005. It's made with mixed filler and offered in bundles of 25.

"ORIGINAL" CUBANS
Handmade in Santiago, Dominican Republic.

Wrapper: Ecuador   *Binder: Dom. Rep.*   *Filler: Dom. Rep.*

Shape	Name	Lgth	Ring	Wrapper
Robusto	Robusto	5	50	CC
Lonsdale	Corona	6½	42	CC
Torpedo	Belicoso	6	50	CC
Double Corona	Double Corona	7	50	CC

Here is a bundled, medium-bodied brand made by Tabadom for Meier & Dutch Distributors, introduced in 2006. It's offered in 20s.

ORIGINS ★*New*★
Handmade in Tamboril, Dominican Republic.

Wrapper: Brazil, Costa Rica, Indonesia, Mexico, Nicaragua, USA/Connecticut
Binder: Dominican Republic   *Filler: Dominican Republic*

Shape	Name	Lgth	Ring	Wrapper
	809 Series:			
Double Corona	Churchill	7	50	CM
Torpedo	Torpedo	6	54	CM
Robusto	Robusto	5	50	CM
Robusto	Toro	5½	54	CM
	203 Series:			
Double Corona	Churchill	7	50	CC
Torpedo	Torpedo	6	54	CC
Robusto	Robusto	5	50	CC
Robusto	Toro	5	50	CC
	505 Series:			
Double Corona	Churchill	7	50	CM
Torpedo	Torpedo	6	54	CM
Robusto	Robusto	5	50	CM

Robusto	Toro	5½	54	CM
	53-82 Series:			
Double Corona	Churchill	7	50	CC
Torpedo	Torpedo	6	54	CC
Robusto	Robusto	5	50	CC
Robusto	Toro	5	50	CC
	52 Series:			
Double Corona	Churchill	7	50	Ma
Torpedo	Torpedo	6	54	Ma
Robusto	Robusto	5	50	Ma
Robusto	Toro	5	50	Ma
	55 Series:			
Double Corona	Churchill	7	50	Ma
Torpedo	Torpedo	6	54	Ma
Robusto	Robusto	5	50	Ma
Robusto	Toro	5½	54	Ma

Felipe Gregorio created this series in 2007, with six different groups each named for the country code or area code of the wrapper! Thus, 203 salutes Connecticut (and a Connecticut Shade wrapper) and is mild in body; 505 is for Nicaragua (Habano '92 wrapper and full body); 52-83 is for Pinar del Rio in Cuba, the origin of the seeds for the Costa Rican-grown wrapper (medium body); 52 is for Mexico (full body, maduro wrapper); 55 is for Brazil (full body; Arapiraca wrapper) and 809 is for the Dominican Republic, where these cigars are made (Indonesian wrapper, medium body). All sizes are offered in boxes of 20.

ORO CUBANO ★*New*★

Handmade in Santiago, Dominican Republic.

Wrapper: Indonesia | *Binder: Dom. Rep.* | *Filler: Dom. Rep.*

Shape	*Name*	*Lgth*	*Ring*	*Wrapper*
Robusto	Robusto	5	50	CM
Toro	Toro	6	48	CM

Double Corona	Churchill	7	50	CM

Meier & Dutch introduced this brand for national distribution in 2007. It's mild and offered in boxes of 25.

OVER PRODUCTION

Handmade, with mixed filler, in Santiago, Dominican Republic.

Wrapper: USA/Connecticut   Binder: Dom. Rep.   Filler: Dom. Rep.

Shape	Name	Lgth	Ring	Wrapper
Double Corona	Churchill	7	50	Ma
Toro	Toro	6	50	Ma
Robusto	Robusto	5	50	Ma
Torpedo	Torpedo	6	52	Ma

This is a mild blend with mixed filler and a Connecticut Broadleaf wrapper, offered in bundles of 25. The label shows a husband getting ready for bed, while his wife holds their three screaming children!

OXFORD POST-EMBARGO SELECTION ★*New*★

Handmade in Santiago, Dominican Republic.

Wrapper: Indonesia   Binder: Mexico   Filler: Dom. Rep.

Shape	Name	Lgth	Ring	Wrapper
Double Corona	Churchill	7	50	CM
Toro	Toro	6	50	CM
Torpedo	Torpedo	6½	52	CM

The House of Oxford introduced this blend in 2007. It's medium in body and offered in value-packed trays of 100!

P. BELLO Y CIA.

Handmade in Villa Gonzalez, Dominican Republic.

Wrapper: Mexico, Nicaragua   Binder: Nicaragua   Filler: Dom. Rep., Nicaragua

This brand was originally introduced in 2000 and returned to the market in 2002, featuring a medium-to-full-bodied taste in the Linea D'Luxe (8 sizes) with a choice of a Habana 2000 wrapper or a Mexican maduro wrapper. The three-year-aged Linea Petaca (3 sizes) was introduced in 2005 and is full-bodied.

HANDMADE CIGARS: BRAND LISTINGS

PADILLA 1948 ★*New*★
Handmade in Miami, Florida, USA.

Wrapper: Nicaragua   *Binder:* Nicaragua   *Filler:* Nicaragua

Shape	Name	Lgth	Ring	Wrapper
Robusto	Robusto	5	50	CM
Churchill	Churchill	7	48	CM
Lonsdale	Lancero	6⅞	42	CM
Torpedo	Torpedo	6¼	52	CM

Made at El Rey de Los Habanos in Miami, this is a medium-to-full-bodied blend introduced in 2007. It features a Nicaraguan-grown Criollo wrapper and is offered in boxes of 20.

PADILLA HABANO
Handmade in Esteli, Nicaragua.

Wrapper: Nicaragua   *Binder:* Nicaragua   *Filler:* Nicaragua

Shape	Name	Lgth	Ring	Wrapper
Robusto	Robusto	5	50	CM
Churchill	Churchill	7	48	CM
Torpedo	Torpedo	6¼	52	CM

Introduced in 2005, this is an Oliva-made, medium-to-full-bodied blend featuring a Habano wrapper. It's offered in boxes of 20.

PADILLA MIAMI 8 & 11
Handmade in Miami, Florida, USA.

Wrapper: Nicaragua   *Binder:* Nicaragua   *Filler:* Nicaragua

Shape	Name	Lgth	Ring	Wrapper
Corona	Corona	5½	42	CM
Robusto	Robusto	5	50	CM
Perfecto	Salomon	7¼	57	CM
Churchill	Churchill	7	48	CM
Giant Corona	Lancero	7½	42	CM

Pyramid	Pyramide	6⅞	52	CM-Ma
Robusto	Exclusivo	5½	50	CM-Ma
Grand Corona	Monarca	6½	46	CM-Ma
Lonsdale	Superior	6½	42	CM-Ma
Long Corona	Corona	6	42	CM-Ma
Corona Extra	Principe	4½	46	CM-Ma
Toro	Imperial	6	54	CM-Ma
Torpedo	Torpedo	6	52	CM-Ma

The 1964 Anniversary Series was introduced to considerable acclaim in 1994 as a salute to the 30th anniversary of the Padron line. It offers a smooth flavor with four-year-aged tobaccos in both sun-grown and maduro wrapper shades. This is a limited-production series and all shapes are offered in boxes of 25, except for the Torpedo, offered in 20s. To assure customers of authenticity, a special band with individual numbering is attached to foil counterfeiters!

PADRON 1926 SERIES
Handmade in Esteli, Nicaragua.

Wrapper: Nicaragua   Binder: Nicaragua   Filler: Nicaragua

Shape	Name	Lgth	Ring	Wrapper
Double Corona	No. 1	6¾	54	CM-Ma
Torpedo	No. 2	5½	52	CM-Ma
Robusto	No. 6	4¾	50	CM-Ma
Robusto	No. 9	5¼	56	CM-Ma
Robusto	No. 35	4	48	CM-Ma
Torpedo	40th Anniversary	6½	54	CM-Ma
Perfecto	80 Years	6¾	54	Ma

Here is a salute to company founder Jose Padron's 75th birthday, introduced in 2002. Both sun-grown and maduro wrappers are available on this full-bodied, box-pressed cigar, featuring tobaccos aged for not less than five years. Limited to annual production of 100,000 cigars (a little more than 4,100 boxes of 24 cigars each), each cigar features a special double band with individual numbering to assure authenticity. The 40th Anniversary debuted in 2004 in boxes of 20 and the 80 Years in 2007 in boxes of eight.

PALMA REAL
Handmade in Tamboril, Dominican Republic.

Wrapper: Brazil, USA/Connecticut   Binder: Dom. Rep.   Filler: Dom. Rep.

Shape	Name	Lgth	Ring	Wrapper
Perfecto	Perfecto	4	52	CC-Ma
Robusto	Robusto	5	50	CC-Ma
Long Corona	Corona	6	44	CC-Ma
Toro	Toro	6	50	CC-Ma
Pyramid	Piramides	7	54	CC-Ma
Double Corona	Presidente	7½	50	CC-Ma

This is a mild-to-medium-bodied blend from Indianhead introduced in 2002. It's available with a choice of a Connecticut natural-shade wrapper or a Brazilian maduro, available in bundles of 25.

PALMA REAL ★New★
Handmade in Santiago, Dominican Republic.

Wrapper: Ecuador   Binder: Dom. Rep.   Filler: Dom. Rep.

Shape	Name	Lgth	Ring	Wrapper
Long Corona	Lonsdale	6	44	CC
Toro	Toro	6	50	CC
Torpedo	Torpedo	6½	52	CC
Double Corona	Presidente	7½	50	CC

Meier & Dutch distributes this brand, made at the La Aurora factory in the Dominican Republic. It's mild in body and offered in boxes of 25.

PALMAS PURO
Handmade in Santiago, Dominican Republic.

Wrapper: Brazil, Ecuador   Binder: Honduras   Filler: Dom. Rep., Nicaragua

Shape	Name	Lgth	Ring	Wrapper
Double Corona	Churchill	7	50	CC
Long Corona	Corona	6	44	CC

Petit Corona	Petit Corona	4½	44	CC
Torpedo	Petit Torpedo	5	54	CC
Robusto	Robusto	5	50	CC

Introduced in 2006, this is a medium-bodied blend which features an Ecuadorian-grown, Connecticut-seed natural or a Brazilian maduro wrapper. Both are offered in Boite Nature boxes of 25 or packs of five.

PARTAGAS
Handmade in Santiago, Dominican Republic.

Wrapper: Cameroon   *Binder: Mexico*   *Filler: Dom. Rep.*

Shape	Name	Lgth	Ring	Wrapper
Lonsdale	8-9-8	6⅞	44	CM
Grand Corona	Almirantes	6¼	47	CM
Torpedo	Aristocrat	6	50	CM
Double Corona	Fabuloso	7	52	CM
Lonsdale	Humitube (glass tubes)	6¾	43	CM
Cigarillo	Miniatures	3¾	24	CM
Robusto	Naturales	5½	50	CM-Ma
Grand Corona	No. 8 Maduro	6¼	48	Ma
Lonsdale	No. 1	6¾	43	CM-Ma
Corona	No. 2	5¾	43	CM
Giant	No. 9	8½	47	CM
Short Panatela	No. 4	5	38	CM
Panatela	No. 6	6	34	CM
Double Corona	No. 10	7½	49	CM-Ma
Toro	Padre (tubed)	6	50	CM
Small Panatela	Puritos	4⅛	32	CM
Robusto	Robusto	4½	49	CM
Long Corona	Sabroso (tubed)	5⅞	44	CM
Lonsdale	Library Edition: "Leviathan"	7	45	CM

HANDMADE CIGARS: BRAND LISTINGS

This famous brand, originated in 1845 and was one of Cuba's major brands through the time of the nationalization. In 1974, this version appeared, made in Jamaica. Production shifted to the Dominican Republic in 1978 and has been one of the most sought-after U.S. brands. It continues to use only the highest quality Cameroon wrappers which, combined with tobaccos from the Dominican Republic and Mexico, gives it a spicy, medium-to-full flavor. The Library Edition is made for Cigars by Santa Clara.

PARTAGAS 160 SIGNATURE SERIES
Handmade in Santiago, Dominican Republic.

Wrapper: Cameroon   *Binder: Mexico*   *Filler: Dom. Rep., Mexico*

Shape	Name		Lgth	Ring	Wrapper
Robusto	Robusto Minor		4½	48	CM
Robusto	Robusto		5	50	CM
Robusto	Robusto Major		5½	52	CM
Lonsdale	Crystal 160	*(glass tube)*	6¾	43	CM
Churchill	Cifuentes Especial		7	48	CM

The then-18-year-old tobacco used to make the famed Partagas 150 Signature Series in 1995 was ten years older when General Cigar decided to use the remainder to create a Partagas 160 series that debuted in 2006. Offered in boxes of 25 in three smaller sizes and in boxes of 10 for two larger shapes, it's full-bodied and offered in elegant wooden boxes.

PARTAGAS BLACK LABEL
Handmade in Santiago, Dominican Republic.

Wrapper: USA/Connecticut   *Binder: Dom. Rep.*   *Filler: Dom. Rep., Nicaragua*

Shape	Name		Lgth	Ring	Wrapper
Toro	Magnifico		6	54	Os
Robusto	Clasico		5¼	54	Os
Corona Extra	Corona		5½	45	Os
Toro	Gigante		6	60	Os
Robusto	Crystal	*(glass tube)*	5½	50	Os
Robusto	Bravo		4½	54	Os

Short Panatela	Prontos	4⅛	36	Os
Toro	Maximo	6	50	Os
Pyramid	Piramide	6	60	Os

This is a fairly new Partagas – a full-bodied blend introduced in 2001 – featuring a sun-grown Connecticut wrapper, La Vega Especial binder and ligero and Piloto Cubano filler leaves. You can find it in a striking black boxes of 20 for most shapes, but in boxes of 8 for the Crystals and packs of six for the Prontos.

PARTAGAS CIFUENTES WINTER BLEND
Handmade in Santiago, Dominican Republic.

Wrapper: Dom. Rep.   Binder: Dom. Rep.   Filler: Dom. Rep.

Shape	Name	Lgth	Ring	Wrapper
Robusto	Diciembre	5½	49	CM
Toro	Enero	6	54	CM
Grand Corona	Febrero	6½	45	CM

The third in General Cigar's series of seasonal blends, the Winter Blend for 2006-07 showcases all Dominican tobacco grown at General's farms. The wrapper and some filler leaves were grown in Mao in the Dominican Republic, while the binder comes from Jima and other fillers from La Vega. It's medium-to-full in body and like the Seasonal Blend Fall 2004 and Summer Blend 2005, is offered in boxes of 20.

PARTAGAS LIMITED RESERVE DECADAS
Handmade in Santiago, Dominican Republic.

Wrapper: Cameroon   Binder: Honduras   Filler: Dom. Rep., Nicaragua

Shape	Name	Lgth	Ring	Wrapper
Robusto	No. I	4½	49	CM
Robusto	No. II	5½	50	CM
Long Corona	No. III	6¼	43	CM
Double Corona	No. IV	7½	49	CM

Introduced in 2005, this is a full-bodied cigar which is named for the 10-year-old Cameroon wrapper leaf harvested in 1995. It also features rare filler leaves from the Nicaraguan island of Ometepe. It is offered in boxes of 20.

HANDMADE CIGARS: BRAND LISTINGS

PARTAGAS SERIE S
Handmade in Santiago, Dominican Republic.

Wrapper: Cameroon   Binder: Mexico   Filler: Dom. Rep.

Shape	Name	Lgth	Ring	Wrapper
Pyramid	Primero	6	60	CM
Torpedo	Preferido	6	52	CM
Perfecto	Perfecto	6	49	CM
Perfecto	Exquisito	7¼	54	CM
Perfecto	Esplendido	4½	60	CM

This series was introduced in 1999. It offers a medium-to-full-bodied taste in five traditional "figurado" shapes that are again of interest to today's enthusiasts. Each is offered in boxes of 25.

PARTAGAS SPANISH ROSADO
Handmade in Santiago, Dominican Republic.
Wrapper: Honduras

Binder: USA/Connecticut   Filler: Dom. Rep., Honduras, Mexico

Shape	Name		Lgth	Ring	Wrapper
Toro	Familia		6	54	CM
Toro	Gigante		6	60	CM
Robusto	San Agustin		5½	52	CM
Double Corona	Mitico		7	49	CM
Grand Corona	Ramon y Ramon		6½	45	CM
Robusto	Rojito		4½	50	CM
Corona	Sabroso	(tubed)	5⅝	44	CM
Short Panatela	Santiago		4⅛	36	CM

Introduced in 2003, this blend has a medium-to-full-bodied taste featuring a specially-grown Rosado wrapper from the San Agustin Valley in Honduras. Each of the shapes is offered in elegant boxes of 25 except for the Rojito, available in 40s, Santiago in 30s and the Sabroso, in 20s.

HANDMADE CIGARS: BRAND LISTINGS

PAUL GARMIRIAN 15TH ANNIVERSARY SERIES
Handmade in Santiago, Dominican Republic.

Wrapper: Nicaragua   Binder: Dom. Rep.   Filler: Dom. Rep.

Shape	Name	Lgth	Ring	Wrapper
Giant	Celebration	9	50	CM
Torpedo	Belicoso Extra	6¾	52	CM
Churchill	Churchill	7	48	CM
Toro	Connoisseur	6	52	CM
Robusto	Robusto	5	52	CM
Corona Extra	Corona Extra	5½	46	CM
Robusto	Short Robusto	4	50	CM
Corona	Corona	5½	42	CM
Petit Corona	No. 5	4	40	CM
Petit Corona	Bombones	3½	43⅓	CM

Here is a remarkably smooth, full-bodied blend to celebrate the 15th anniversary of the P.G. brand. It was originally issued with an Ecuadorian wrapper in the Belicoso Extra shape in 2006 in a limited-edition of only 15,000 cigars in 1,000 boxes of 15. It was expanded in 2006 with a Nicaraguan wrapper and offered in boxes of 25 for all but the Belicoso Extra (15/25/50) and Celebration (10).

PAUL GARMIRIAN ARTISAN'S SELECTION
Handmade in Santiago, Dominican Republic.

Wrapper: USA/Connecticut   Binder: Dom. Rep.   Filler: Dom. Rep.

Shape	Name	Lgth	Ring	Wrapper
Double Corona	No. 1	7½	50	CC
Toro	No. 2	6	50	CC
Robusto	No. 3	5	50	CC
Robusto	No. 4	5½	52	CC
Robusto	No. 5	5	52	CC
Churchill	No. 6	7	48	CC

Robusto	No. 7	4½	48	CC
Grand Corona	No. 8	6¼	46	CC
Corona	No. 9	5¼	42	CC

The Artisan's Selection was introduced in 1997 and is an expertly-constructed, mild-to-medium-bodied cigar, with a complex, Dominican-grown filler blend surrounded by a Connecticut Shade wrapper. It is noteworthy for its consistency and smoothness and is offered in cellophane sleeves inside cedar boxes of 25.

PAUL GARMIRIAN GOURMET SERIES
Handmade in Santiago, Dominican Republic.

Wrapper: USA/Connecticut *Binder: Dom. Rep.* *Filler: Dom. Rep.*

Shape	Name	Lgth	Ring	Wrapper
Giant	P.G. Celebration	9	50	CC
Double Corona	P.G. Double Corona	7⅝	50	CC
Torpedo	P.G. Belicoso	6¼	52	CC
Churchill	P.G. Churchill	7	48	CC
Long Panatela	P.G. No. 1	7½	38	CC
Grand Corona	P.G. Corona Grande	6½	46	CC
Torpedo	P.G. Belicoso Fino	5½	52	CC
Lonsdale	P.G. Lonsdale	6½	42	CC
Toro	P.G. Connoisseur	6	50	CC
Robusto	P.G. Epicure	5½	50	CC
Robusto	P.G. Robusto	5	50	CC
Robusto	P.G. No. 2	4¾	48	CC
Corona	P.G. Corona	5½	42	CC
Petit Corona	P.G. Petit Corona	5	43	CC
Short Panatela	P.G. Petit Bouquet	4½	38	CC
Petit Corona	P.G. No. 5	4	40	CC
Petit Corona	P.G. Bombones	3½	43⅓	CC
Panatela	P.G. Especial	5¾	38	CC

Torpedo	P.G. Torpedo	6¼	52	CC
Cigarillo	P.G. Joyitas	4½	26	CC
Robusto	P.G. Torito	4	50	CC

"Smooth, subtle, spicy and delicious." That's the response of many smokers who were delighted to enjoy a Dominican-produced cigar which has so many attributes of a high-quality Havana. The characteristics of the P.G. line include a scarce and richly-flavored medium-to-dark reddish-brown Colorado-colored Connecticut Shade wrappers which are the favorite of many connoisseurs, combined with Dominican binder and filler. The Especial shape is specially configured to be of interest to female smokers.

PAUL GARMIRIAN GOURMET SERIES II
Handmade in Santiago, Dominican Republic.
Wrapper: USA/Connecticut   *Binder: Dom. Rep.*   *Filler: Dom. Rep.*

Shape	Name	Lgth	Ring	Wrapper
Torpedo	Torpedo	6¼	52	CC
Torpedo	Belicoso Fino	5½	52	CC
Toro	Connoisseur	6	50	CC
Robusto	Robusto	5	50	CC

The Gourmet Series II was launched in 1999 in two shapes, offering a full-bodied smoke which is, at the same time, very smooth. It's offered in boxes of 25.

PAUL GARMIRIAN GOURMET SERIES MADURO
Handmade in Santiago, Dominican Republic.
Wrapper: USA/Connecticut   *Binder: Indonesia*   *Filler: Brazil, Dom. Rep.*

Shape	Name	Lgth	Ring	Wrapper
Giant	P.G. Celebration	9	50	Ma
Double Corona	P.G. Magnum	7	50	Ma
Torpedo	P.G. Belicoso	6¼	52	Ma
Grand Corona	P.G. Corona Grande	6½	46	Ma
Toro	P.G. Connoisseur	6	50	Ma
Robusto	P.G. Robusto	5	50	Ma

| Robusto | P.G. Torito | 4 | 50 | Ma |
| Petit Corona | P.G. Bombones | 3½ | 43⅓ | Ma |

The Maduro series, introduced in 2000, features a Connecticut Broadleaf wrapper, Indonesian binder and Brazilian and Dominican filler leaves. The result is a smooth smoke without any trace of acidity or harshness, offered in boxes of 25 except for the Celebration (10s).

PAUL GARMIRIAN GOURMET SERIES SOIREE ★*New*★
Handmade in Santiago, Dominican Republic.

Wrapper: Nicaragua   *Binder: Dom. Rep.*   *Filler: Dom. Rep.*

Shape	Name	Lgth	Ring	Wrapper
Torpedo	Belicoso	6¼	52	CM
Toro	Connoisseur	6	50	CM
Robusto	Robusto	5	50	CM

Here is a full-bodied, Corojo-wrapped blend from Paul Garmirian, introduced in 2007. It's the seventh P.G. blend and offers a smooth finish and rich taste in boxes of 25.

PAUL GARMIRIAN RESERVA EXCLUSIVA
Handmade in Santiago, Dominican Republic.

Wrapper: Ecuador   *Binder: Dom. Rep.*   *Filler: Dom. Rep., Ecuador*

Shape	Name	Lgth	Ring	Wrapper
Torpedo	Belicoso	6¼	52	CM
Churchill	Churchill	7	48	CM
Toro	Connoisseur	6	50	CM
Long Panatela	Gran Panatella	7½	40	CM
Robusto	Robusto	5	50	CM
Petit Corona	No. 5	4	40	CM
Corona Extra	Corona Extra	5½	46	CM
Corona	Corona	5½	42	CM
Robusto	Torito	4	50	CM

HANDMADE CIGARS: BRAND LISTINGS

Here is a Corojo-wrapped, mediuim-to-full-bodied cigar introduced in 2001 and expanded in 2002. It is offered in red wood cabinets of 25; some sizes are offered in boxes of 10 and the Torito in packs of three.

PELO DE ORO
Handmade in Tamboril, Dominican Republic.

Wrapper: Costa Rica   Binder: Dom. Rep.   Filler: Dom. Rep., Nicaragua

Shape	Name	Lgth	Ring	Wrapper
Robusto	Rothschild	5	50	CM
Petit Corona	Corona	5	42	CM
Grand Corona	Corona Gorda	5¾	46	CM
Perfecto	Perfecto	6	50	CM
Torpedo	Flechas	6	50	CM

Felipe Gregorio introduced this salute to a strain of old Cuban tobacco – "Golden Hair" or Pelo de Oro – used for the wrapper, in 2006. It's full-bodied and offered in old-style cedar cabinets of 50, except for the Flechas, which is finished with a head that looks like a paintbrush!

PERDOMO^2
Handmade in Esteli, Nicaragua.

Wrapper: Cameroon, Nicaragua   Binder: Nicaragua   Filler: Nicaragua

Shape	Name	Lgth	Ring	Wrapper
Torpedo	Milenario	6½	55	CM-Ma

The Tabacalera Perdomo introduced this box-pressed line in 1999 with a Cameroon (natural, red band) or Nicaragua (maduro, yellow band) wrapper and a full-bodied blend with all Nicaraguan binder and filler. Perdomo discontinued this line in 2007, but Meier & Dutch sells the Milenario in a round version without bands in bundles of 24 cigars each.

PERDOMO FRESCO
Handmade in Esteli, Nicaragua.

Wrapper: USA/Connecticut   Binder: Nicaragua   Filler: Dom. Rep., Nicaragua

Shape	Name	Lgth	Ring	Wrapper
Robusto	Robusto	5	50	CM-Ma

Double Corona	Churchill	7	50	CM-Ma
Toro	Toro	6	50	CM-Ma
Torpedo	Belicoso	5¾	54	CM-Ma

Introduced in 2002 by the Tabacalera Perdomo, the blend was revised in 2006. It features a Connecticut wrapper for a mild-to-medium body in either natural or maduro shades. All sizes are offered in bundles of 25 cigars.

PERDOMO HABANO ★New★
Handmade in Esteli, Nicaragua.

Wrapper: Nicaragua   Binder: Nicaragua   Filler: Nicaragua

Shape	Name	Lgth	Ring	Wrapper
Robusto	Robusto	5	52	CM-Ma
Robusto	Toro	5½	54	CM-Ma
Torpedo	Torpedo	6½	54	CM-Ma
Toro	Gordo	6	60	CM-Ma
Double Corona	Presidente	7	56	CM-Ma

Here is a full-bodied blend of tobaccos grown in the three major tobacco-growing regions of Nicaragua: Esteli, Condega and Jalapa. There's a choice of wrapper, with both a Corojo natural-shade and Nicaraguan-grown maduro available. Introduced in 2007, all sizes are presented in Spanish Cedar boxes of 20.

PERDOMO LOT 23
Handmade in Esteli, Nicaragua.

Wrapper: Nicaragua   Binder: Nicaragua   Filler: Nicaragua

Shape	Name	Lgth	Ring	Wrapper
Robusto	Robusto	5	50	CM-Ma
Toro	Toro	6	50	CM-Ma
Double Corona	Churchill	7	50	CM-Ma
Torpedo	Belicoso	5¾	54	CM-Ma

Introduced in 2006, this is a medium-to-full-bodied blend which features interior tobaccos grown on a single 103-acre lot near Esteli, Nicaragua. The crop was harvested in 2001 and aged until 2005 when it was rolled with Connecticut Shade wrappers. Nicaraguan natural-shade and maduro wrappers were used on all sizes starting in 2007. All sizes are offered in all-cedar boxes of 20.

PERDOMO RESERVE
Handmade in Esteli, Nicaragua.
Wrapper: Cameroon, Nicaragua, USA/Connecticut

Binder: Nicaragua   Filler: Nicaragua

Shape	Name		Lgth	Ring	Wrapper
Petit Corona	Petit Corona		4¾	44	CC-CM-Ma
Perfecto	Figurado		4¾	56	CC-CM-Ma
Robusto	Robusto		5	54	CC-CM-Ma
Toro	Epicure		6	54	CC-CM-Ma
Torpedo	Torpedo		7	54	CC-CM-Ma
Double Corona	Churchill		7	54	CC-CM-Ma
	Great Discovery's Series:				*(Champagne blend)*
Toro	CT	*(glass tube)*	6	50	CC

Formally named the La Tradicion Cabinet Series Perdomo Reserve, this line was introduced in 1998. It offers four different wrapper choices: Nicaraguan sun-grown White-label wrappers, the Gold-label "Champagne" series with Connecticut Shade wrappers; a Red-label-style with Nicaraguan-grown maduro wrappers (1999 introduction) and the Silver-label Cameroon wrapped edition (introduced in 2003). The result is a medium-to-full-bodied taste in the Champagne series and a full-bodied taste in the others, presented in the 8-9-8 format in Spanish Cedar cabinets of 25.

PERDOMO RESERVE LIMITED GOLF EDITION
Handmade in Esteli, Nicaragua.
Wrapper: USA/Connecticut   Binder: Nicaragua   Filler: Nicaragua

Shape	Name	Lgth	Ring	Wrapper
Petit Corona	Putter	4¾	44	CM
Perfecto	Fore!	4¾	56	CM
Robusto	Iron	5	54	CM

Toro	Eagle	6	54	CM
Torpedo	Birdie	6	54	CM
Double Corona	Double Eagle *(tube available)*	7	54	CM
Torpedo	Driver	7	54	CM
Giant	Hole in One	9	52	CM

Specially formulated for enjoyment on the course, this is a green-banded blend introduced in 2006. It's medium-to-full in body and offered in boxes of 25 for most sizes but boxes of 10 for the Double Eagle tubos and the Hole in One.

PERFECTO GARCIA

Handmade in Esteli, Nicaragua.

Wrapper: Ecuador, USA/Connecticut

Binder: Nicaragua *Filler: Dom. Rep., Honduras, Nicaragua*

Shape	Name	Lgth	Ring	Wrapper
Robusto	Waldorf	5	50	CC-Ma
Lonsdale	Ensign	6½	43	DC-CC
Grand Corona	Mayfair	5½	45	CC
Churchill	Churchill	7	48	CC
Toro	Magnum	6	50	CC-Ma
Torpedo	Belicoso	6	52	CC
Double Corona	1905	7¼	54	CC-Ma
Churchill	Brilliantes *(glass tubes)*	7	48	CC-Ma

First introduced at the turn of the 20th Century and a favorite for decades (especially in the Midwest), this famous brand was re-born in 1999 as a full-flavored, robust and smooth cigar. An excellent value in all of its sizes, it is presented with a choice of Ecuador-grown or Connecticut Broadleaf (maduro only) wrappers in protective cellophane sleeves and offered in mahogany boxes of 25 cigars each, except for the Brilliantes and Churchills, offered in glass tubes in boxes of 10.

HANDMADE CIGARS: BRAND LISTINGS

PERSONALES ★New★
Handmade in Santiago, Dominican Republic.

Wrapper: Ecuador *Binder: Dom. Rep.* *Filler: Dom. Rep., Nicaragua*

Shape	Name	Lgth	Ring	Wrapper
Robusto	Rothschild	5	50	CC-Ma
Toro	Matador	6	50	CC-Ma
Churchill	Churchill	7	48	CC-Ma
Torpedo	Torpedo	6⅛	52	CC-Ma

Introduced in 2007, Personales is a product of the Charles Fairmorn factory. It's mild-to-medium in body and is offered in cabinets of 25.

PETRUS
Handmade in Tamboril, Dominican Republic.

Wrapper: Nicaragua *Binder: Nicaragua* *Filler: Nicaragua*

Shape	Name		Lgth	Ring	Wrapper
Torpedo	Antonius		5	54	CC-Ma
Double Corona	Churchill	(tubed)	7	50	CC
Robusto	Rothschild		4¾	50	CC-Ma

Here is the original Petrus line introduced by Felipe Gregorio in 1996. Originally made in Honduras, production was moved to Nicaragua in 2005 and to the Dominican Republic in 2007. The blend is mild-to-medium in its Connecticut-seed, natural shade wrapper and medium-to-full-bodied in the "Oro Negro" version with a superb Connecticut-seed, sun-grown maduro wrapper around a blend of all-Nicaraguan-grown tobaccos.

PETRUS ETIQUETTE ROUGE
Handmade in Danli, Honduras.

Wrapper: Ecuador *Binder: Honduras* *Filler: Dom. Rep., Nicaragua*

Shape	Name	Lgth	Ring	Wrapper
Corona	Corona	5¾	44	CC
Churchill	Churchill	7	48	CC

This Felipe Gregorio brand has been on and off the market but returned in 2006. Now offered in two sizes, it's medium in body and available in boxes of 20.

PHEASANT HONDURAN SELECTION
Handmade in Danli, Honduras.

Wrapper: Ecuador, USA/Connecticut   Binder: Honduras   Filler: Dom. Rep., Honduras

Shape	Name	Lgth	Ring	Wrapper
Double Corona	Churchill	7	50	CC-Ma
Torpedo	Torpedo	6	50	CC-Ma
Robusto	Robusto	4¾	52	CC-Ma
Robusto	Rothschild	4½	48	CC-Ma
Robusto	Fast-Break	3¾	48	CC-Ma

Returning in 2002 after being off the market for a couple of years is Pheasant, introduced by R.D. Gomez, also the creator of an exquisite line of cigar cases and other leather accessories. The line was originally introduced in 1995 and offers a mild-to-medium taste with a Connecticut natural wrapper and a medium-bodied flavor with an Ecuadorian-grown maduro wrapper, available in boxes of 25, or 50 for the Fast-Break.

PHEASANT NICARAGUAN GRAN RESERVA
Handmade in Esteli, Nicaragua.

Wrapper: Nicaragua   Binder: Nicaragua   Filler: Nicaragua

Shape	Name	Lgth	Ring	Wrapper
Double Corona	Churchill	7	50	CM
Torpedo	Torpedo	6	50	CM
Robusto	Robusto	4¾	48	CM
Grand Corona	Corona	6	46	CM
Robusto	Fast Break	3¾	48	CM

Introduced in 2003, this puro is medium-to-full-bodied and offered in boxes of 20, except for the Fast Break, available in 40s.

HANDMADE CIGARS: BRAND LISTINGS

PHILLIPS & KING CUBAN REJECTS
Handmade, with sandwich filler, in Esteli, Nicaragua.

Wrapper: Nicaragua   Binder: Nicaragua   Filler: Nicaragua

Shape	Name	Lgth	Ring	Wrapper
Robusto	Robusto	5	50	CM-Ma
Churchill	Churchill	7	48	CM-Ma
Toro	Toro	6	50	CM-Ma

This line debuted in 2005, offering a medium-bodied, unbanded, value cigar in economical bundles or 10 or all-wood boxes of 50.

PHILLIPS & KING REJECTS
Handmade, with sandwich filler, in Santiago, Dominican Republic.

Wrapper: Dom. Rep.   Binder: Dom. Rep.   Filler: Dom. Rep.

Shape	Name	Lgth	Ring	Wrapper
Robusto	Robusto	5	50	CM-Ma
Churchill	Churchill	7	48	CM-Ma
Toro	Toro Grande	6	54	CM-Ma

Introduced in 2003 by Phillips & King, these are bargain-priced cigars, made by hand and offering a mild body. They are offered in wood boxes of 50.

PINTOR DINASTY ★New★
Handmade in Esteli, Nicaragua.

Wrapper: Nicaragua   Binder: Nicaragua   Filler: Nicaragua

Shape	Name	Lgth	Ring	Wrapper
Double Corona	Florentine	7	50	CM
Robusto	Ricardo	5	50	CM
Toro	Toro	6	50	CM
Torpedo	Torpedo	6½	54	CM

This line, made by Ricardo Pintor, was introduced in 2007 and is offered in a choice of wrappers: Nicaraguan-grown Corojo (medium to full in body) or Habana 2000 (medium body). It's offered in bundles of 20.

HANDMADE CIGARS: BRAND LISTINGS

PLASENCIA
Handmade in Esteli, Nicaragua.

Wrapper: Ecuador, Nicaragua   Binder: Nicaragua   Filler: Honduras, Nicaragua

Shape	Name		Lgth	Ring	Wrapper
Double Corona	Prominente		7½	50	CC
Torpedo	Belicoso		6¼	54	CC
Toro	Magnum		6	50	CC-Ma
Lonsdale	Longfellow		7⅛	42	CC
Lonsdale	Lonsdale		6¾	44	CC
Robusto	Robusto		4¾	52	CC-Ma
Toro	Opulencia	(glass tube)	6	50	CC-Ma
Petit Corona	T.K.O.		4	43	Ma

Here is a brand that celebrates the famous name of Plasencia — a name revered throughout the cigar world for the manufacture of outstanding cigars. These cigars are outstanding in their own right, with a Connecticut-seed natural or Nicaraguan maduro wrapper and a medium-bodied taste. They are offered in boxes of 25 except for the tubed Opulencia, available in 20s.

PLASENCIA RESERVA ORGANICA
Handmade in Esteli, Nicaragua.

Wrapper: Nicaragua   Binder: Nicaragua   Filler: Nicaragua

Shape	Name	Lgth	Ring	Wrapper
Robusto	Robusto	4¾	52	CM
Long Corona	Corona	6¼	44	CM
Toro	Toro	6	50	CM
Churchill	Churchill	7	48	CM

This is a completely organic cigar from Indianhead, blended from specially grown leaves, which combine for a medium-to-full-bodied flavor. Each cigar is cedar-wrapped and presented in boxes of 20.

PLASENCIA RESERVA ORGANICA EDICION LIMITADA 2001
Handmade in Esteli, Nicaragua.

Wrapper: Nicaragua   *Binder: Nicaragua*   *Filler: Nicaragua*

Shape	Name	Lgth	Ring	Wrapper
Churchill	Churchill	7	48	CM
Long Corona	Corona	6¼	44	CM
Torpedo	Piramide	6¼	52	CM
Toro	Toro	6	50	CM
Robusto	Robusto	4¾	52	CM

Composed of all organically-grown leaves, this is a medium-to-full-bodied blend created by Nestor Plasencia, Jr. and Famous Smoke Shop's Arthur Zaretsky in 2006. Only 15,000 cigars (200 boxes of each shape) were made, presented in boxes of 15.

PLAYBOY ★*New*★
Handmade in La Romana, Dominican Republic.

Wrapper: Ecuador   *Binder: USA/Connecticut*   *Filler: Dom. Rep., Nicaragua, Peru*

Shape	Name	Lgth	Ring	Wrapper
Torpedo	Belicoso	6⅛	52	CM
Churchill	Churchill	7	50	CM
Robusto	Robusto	5	52	CM
Toro	Toro	6	52	CM

A new blend and not related to the Playboy by Don Diego brand, Altadis USA debuted this cigar in 2007. It has a full-bodied flavor thanks to its Sumatra-seed wrapper and Broadleaf binder. It's offered in striking all-black boxes of 24 adorned with the Playboy rabbit logo on the top.

PLAYBOY
BY DON DIEGO
Handmade in La Romana, Dominican Republic.

Wrapper: USA/Connecticut   *Binder: Dom. Rep.*   *Filler: Dom. Rep.*

HANDMADE CIGARS: BRAND LISTINGS

Shape	Name	Lgth	Ring	Wrapper
Double Corona	Churchill	7	50	CC
Toro	Double Corona	6	52	CC
Toro	Gran Corona	6½	48	CC
Robusto	Robusto	5	50	CC
Lonsdale	Lonsdale	6⅝	44	CC

Here is the 1996-introduced brand named for the famous magazine and entertainment company, produced in cooperation with the famous Tabacalera de Garcia. The blend is medium in body and features a dark shade of Connecticut wrapper. The cigars are presented in elegant *boite nature* boxes of 25.

PLEIADES PARIS

Handmade in Santiago, Dominican Republic.

Wrapper: Ecuador, USA/Connecticut   Binder: Nicaragua Filler: Dom. Rep., Nicaragua

Shape	Name	Lgth	Ring	Wrapper
Double Corona	Charlemagne	7	54	CC
Lonsdale	Clemenceau	6⅝	44	CC
Robusto	DeGaulle	5	52	CC-Ma
Toro	Envoy	6	54	CC-Ma
Corona	Medaille d'Or	5½	44	CC

This brand was well known in the 1990s for its mild taste and elegant construction, but it exited the U.S. market in 2002. Revived by the giant Cigars by Santa Clara in 2004, this is a medium-bodied blend, offered in boxes of 25, with a choice of Ecuadorian natural or Connecticut maduro wrappers.

POR LARRAÑAGA

Handmade in La Romana, Dominican Republic.

Wrapper: USA/Connecticut   Binder: Dom. Rep.   Filler: Dom. Rep.

Shape	Name	Lgth	Ring	Wrapper
Lonsdale	Cetros	6⅞	42	CC
Toro	Toro	6	50	CC

Double Corona	Fabulosos	7	50	CC
Corona	Nacionales	5½	42	CC
Short Panatela	Petit Cetros en Cedro	5	38	CC
Pyramid	Pyramids	6	50	CC
Robusto	Robusto	5	50	CC

This is an ancient brand which first saw production in Cuba in 1834! Today's Dominican version is medium-bodied, offered in elegant boxes of 20.

POR LARRANAGA CABINET SELECCION ★*New*★
Handmade in Santa Rosa de Copan, Honduras.

Wrapper: Nicaragua　　　*Binder: Nicaragua*　　　*Filler: Honduras, Nicaragua*

Shape	Name	Lgth	Ring	Wrapper
Torpedo	Belicoso	6⅛	52	CM
Toro	Toro	6	56	CM
Grand Corona	Corona	5⅝	45	CM
Robusto	Robusto	5	54	CM
Petit Corona	No. 4	5	40	CM

Introduced in 2007, this is a special edition of the Por Larranaga brand with a full body and a Nicaraguan wrapper and binder. It's offered in elegant, slide-top cabinets of 22 cigars each.

POR LARRAÑAGA CUBAN GRADE
Handmade in Santa Rosa de Copan, Honduras.

Wrapper: Ecuador, Mexico　　　*Binder: Mexico*　　　*Filler: Dom. Rep., Honduras*

Shape	Name	Lgth	Ring	Wrapper
Petit Corona	Corona	4½	42	CC-Ma
Corona	Corona Gorda	5½	44	CC-Ma
Robusto	Robusto	5	50	CC-Ma
Toro	Toro	6	50	CC-Ma
Torpedo	Figurado	6⅛	52	CC-Ma
Double Corona	Double Corona	7	54	CC-Ma

HANDMADE CIGARS: BRAND LISTINGS

This is a special blend of Por Larrañaga for Cuban Imports, introduced in 2006. It's mild-to-medium in body with a choice of a Connecticut-seed natural or Mexican maduro wrapper, all in boxes of 20.

POR LARRAÑAGA HONDURAN BLEND
Handmade in Santa Rosa de Copan, Honduras.

Wrapper: Ecuador   *Binder: Honduras*   *Filler: Honduras*

Shape	Name	Lgth	Ring	Wrapper
Corona	Corona	5½	43	CC
Small Panatela	Coronitas	4½	32	CC
Robusto	Obsequio (perfecto tip)	5½	50	CC
Panatela	Petite Corona	5½	38	CC
Robusto	Robusto	4¾	50	CC

The blend was revised in 2003 for an old favorite, offering a mild-to-medium body. The Connecticut-seed wrapper is golden brown and all shapes are offered in boxes of 20, except for the Coronitas (24) and Petite Corona (30).

PORT ROYAL
Handmade, with mixed filler, in Danli, Honduras.

Wrapper: Indonesia   *Binder: Honduras*   *Filler: Honduras, Nicaragua, Panama*

Shape	Name	Lgth	Ring	Wrapper
Long Corona	Corona	6	44	CM
Double Corona	Churchill	7	50	CM
Robusto	Robusto	5	50	CM

This mixed-filler brand debuted in 1997. It uses sandwich filler and has a mild-to-medium-bodied taste, available in bundles of 15 or packs of five.

PORTO BELLO
Handmade in Santiago, Dominican Republic.

Wrapper: USA/Connecticut   *Binder: Mexico*   *Filler: Dom. Rep., Honduras*

Shape	Name	Lgth	Ring	Wrapper
Giant	No. 852	8½	52	CC
Double Corona	No. 750	7½	50	CC

HANDMADE CIGARS: BRAND LISTINGS

Churchill	No. 646	6⅞	46	CC
Toro	No. 650	6	50	CC
Lonsdale	No. 642	6¾	42	CC
Long Panatela	No. 736	7	36	CC
Long Panatela	No. 738	7½	38	CC
Corona	No. 542	5¾	42	CC
Robusto	No. 450	4½	50	CC
Pyramid	Piramide	7	50	CC

Created in 1988 for the House of Oxford, this is an economical, bundled brand which offers a mild taste in a handmade, all long-filler cigar – including a genuine Connecticut Shade wrapper!

PRECIOUS69.COM
Handmade in Frankfort, New York, USA.
Wrapper: Cameroon, Central African Republic

Binder: Ecuador   *Filler: Dominican Republic*

Shape	Name	Lgth	Ring	Wrapper
Toro	Mega Chunk	6½	50	CM
Petit Corona	Tone Jones	4	44	CM
Short Panatela	Irie	4	36	CM
Cigarillo	Burning Fingers	3	28	CM
	Machine-made:			
Small Panatela	Air Catcher	4	30	CM

This is a full-bodied member of the Lars Tetens line and is named after Tetens' band Precious69.com. Given Tetens' inventive approach to music, so are these cigars: open on both ends, so that a cutter is not required. But which end is the head and which is the foot? That question could give rise to another Tetens line: "Philosophy."

PREMIUM CUBAN
Handmade in Esteli, Nicaragua.

Wrapper: Nicaragua   *Binder: Nicaragua*   *Filler: Honduras, Nicaragua*

HANDMADE CIGARS: BRAND LISTINGS

Shape	Name	Lgth	Ring	Wrapper
Torpedo	Torpedo	6¼	52	CM
Churchill	Churchill	7	48	CM
Robusto	Robusto	5	50	CM
Long Corona	Corona	6¼	44	CM
Double Corona	Double Corona	7½	50	CM
Giant	Presidente	8	52	CM
Perfecto	Figurado	4½	46	CM

Premium Cuban is a full-bodied blend, featuring a Jalapa-grown wrapper. Introduced in 2005, it is offered in bundles of 25.

PREMIUM SELECTION
Handmade in Santiago, Dominican Republic.

Wrapper: Dom. Rep.   *Binder: Dom. Rep.*   *Filler: Dom. Rep.*

Shape	Name	Lgth	Ring	Wrapper
Corona	Corona	5½	44	CC-Ma
Robusto	Robusto	5	50	CC-Ma
Toro	Toro	6	50	CC-Ma
Churchill	Churchill	7	48	CC-Ma
Torpedo	Torpedo	6⅛	52	CC-Ma
Giant	Viajantes	8½	52	CC-Ma
Double Corona	Presidente	7½	50	CC-Ma
Toro	Matador	6½	56	CC-Ma

Offered by Exclusive Cigars of Aurora, Illinois, this is a mild-bodied blend which debuted in 2006. All of the tobacco comes from the Dominican Republic and all sizes are offered in bundles of 20.

PREMIUM VALUE
Handmade, with short filler, in Danli, Honduras.

Wrapper: Honduras   *Binder: Honduras*   *Filler: Honduras*

HANDMADE CIGARS: BRAND LISTINGS

Shape	Name	Lgth	Ring	Wrapper
Robusto	Robusto	4½	50	CC-Ma
Corona	Corona	5½	42	DC-CC-Ma
Toro	Toro	6	50	DC-CC-Ma
Churchill	Churchill	7	46	DC-CC-Ma

This is a unique brand introduced in 2002 by the Indianhead Cigar Co. and priced at about a dollar a cigar! Made with short filler, it offers a choice of candela, natural, maduro and flavored (sweet vanilla rum) versions in four sizes (natural and maduro only for the Robusto). You can enjoy them in boxes of 50.

PRIDA
Handmade, with short filler, in Santiago, Dominican Republic.
Wrapper: Ecuador   *Binder: Indonesia*   *Filler: Indonesia*

Shape	Name	Lgth	Ring	Wrapper
Corona	Corona	5¾	43	CC
Double Corona	Churchill	7	52	CC
Robusto	Robusto	4¾	52	CC

SACS Cigars of Davie, Florida offers this mild-to-medium-bodied blend, featuring a Connecticut-seed wrapper, in bundles of 20.

PRIDE OF JAMAICA
Handmade in Kingston, Jamaica.
Wrapper: Cameroon, USA/Connecticut
Binder: Cameroon, Mexico   *Filler: Dominican Republic, Jamaica, Mexico*

Shape	Name		Lgth	Ring	Wrapper
Double Corona	Churchill		7½	49	Ma
Toro	Magnum		6	50	Ma
Robusto	Robusto		4	50	Ma
Lonsdale	Rothschild		6½	42	Ma
Corona	Royal Corona		5½	42	CC-Ma
Grand Corona	Crystals	(glass tubes)	6	45	CC-Ma

HANDMADE CIGARS: BRAND LISTINGS

This famous brand – winner of several international awards – continues to be created daily in Kingston, Jamaica and offered in boxes of 25 much-respected cigars. Cameroon wrapper and binder is used to help give the mild, rich flavor for which Pride of Jamaica is so well known. The Royal Corona shape is also offered in a Connecticut Shade wrapper and Mexican binder. The Crystals are offered in boxes of 10 and feature a Mexican binder and Jamaican filler.

PRIMERO DE FABRICA
Handmade in Guayaquil, Ecuador.

Wrapper: Ecuador   *Binder: Ecuador*   *Filler: Ecuador*

Shape	Name	Lgth	Ring	Wrapper
Robusto	Robusto	5	50	CC-CM-Ma
Toro	Toro	6	50	CC-CM-Ma
Toro	Gran Toro	6	54	CC-CM-Ma
Churchill	Churchill	7	48	CC-CM-Ma
Double Corona	Double Corona	7½	50	CC-CM-Ma
Torpedo	Torpedo	5½	50	CC-CM-Ma
Toro	Toro Ex	6	60	CC-CM-Ma
Torpedo	Torpedo Ex	6	54	CC-CM-Ma

This blend was introduced in 2004 by Puros de Armando Ramos, offering three different wrappers: Corojo (with a mild-to-medium body), Rosado (medium) and maduro (medium to full). It's offered in bulk in boxes of 100.

PRIMO DE CUBA
Handmade in Danli, Honduras.

Wrapper: Honduras   *Binder: Honduras*   *Filler: Honduras*

Shape	Name	Lgth	Ring	Wrapper
Double Corona	Churchill	7	50	CM-Ma
Long Corona	Corona	6	44	CC-CM-Ma
Grand Corona	Corona Grande	6½	46	CC
Giant	General	8½	52	CM-Ma
Lonsdale	Lonsdale	7	44	CM-Ma

Double Corona	Presidente	7½	50	CM-Ma
Robusto	Rothschild	5	50	CM-Ma
Toro	Toro	6	50	CM-Ma

Mild-to-medium in body, this Nestor Plasencia-made brand was introduced in 2006 by Famous Smoke Shop. It's offered in bundles of 25.

PRIMO DEL REY
Handmade in La Romana, Dominican Republic.

Wrapper: Ecuador, Mexico   Binder: Nicaragua   Filler: Honduras, Nicaragua

Shape	Name	Lgth	Ring	Wrapper
Long Corona	Cazadores	6	44	Ma
Toro	Toro	6	50	CC
Toro	Toro	6	54	Ma
Corona	Corona en Tubo (tubed)	5½	44	CC
Lonsdale	Lonsdale	6½	44	CC
Robusto	Robusto	5	54	CC-Ma
Double Corona	Churchill	7	54	CC
Pyramid	Pyramid	6⅛	52	CC
	Cigars by Santa Clara series:			
Long Corona	Cazadore	6	43	Ma
Long Corona	No. 2	6¼	42	CC

Primo del Rey are first-quality cigars first produced in 1961. The blend was changed in 2003 (see below) and again in 2006; it now features a choice of a Connecticut-seed natural wrapper (mild in body) or a Mexican Morron maduro wrapper (medium body). All shapes are available in boxes of 20 (maduros and tubos) or 25 (others) except for the Cazadores, offered in 50s.

Cigars by Santa Clara still offers the 2003 blend in two shapes, featuring a mild-to-medium-bodied taste with a Brazilian natural or Mexican maduro wrapper.

HANDMADE CIGARS: BRAND LISTINGS

PRINCIPES

Handmade in Santiago, Dominican Republic.

Wrapper: Dom. Rep.   Binder: Dom. Rep.   Filler: Dom. Rep.

Shape	Name		Lgth	Ring	Wrapper
Short Panatela	Principes	*(tube available)*	5	38	CM

This is a bundled cigar from Miami Cigar & Co., available in boxes of 25 or flavored in tubes (vanilla or mint) in boxes of 20.

PRIVATE STOCK

Handmade in Santiago, Dominican Republic.

Wrapper: Ecuador, USA/Connecticut

Binder: Dominican Republic, Ecuador   Filler: Dominican Republic

Shape	Name	Lgth	Ring	Wrapper
	Long-filler:			
Double Corona	Private Stock No. 1	7¾	48	CC
Toro	Private Stock No. 2	6	48	CC-Ma
Panatela	Private Stock No. 4	5¾	38	CC
Corona	Private Stock No. 5	5¾	43	CC
Corona Extra	Private Stock No. 6	5¼	46	CC
Petit Corona	Private Stock No. 7 *(tube available)*	4¾	43	CC
Cigarillo	Private Stock No. 9	4⅝	26	CC
Petit Corona	Private Stock No. 10	4	40	CC
Robusto	Private Stock No. 11	4⅝	50	CC-Ma
Toro	Private Stock No. 14	6½	50	CC-Ma
	Medium filler:			
Toro	Private Stock Toro	6½	48	CC
Robusto	Private Stock Robusto	5⅛	50	CC
Panatela	Private Stock Panatela	5¾	38	CC
Long Corona	Private Stock Lonsdale	6	42	CC

Petit Corona	Private Stock Corona	5	42	CC
Double Corona	Private Stock Tubo No.1 (tubed)	6⅞	50	CC
Grand Corona	Private Stock Tubo No.2 (tubed)	6¼	46	CC

High standards of quality make the Private Stock label an excellent value for long-filler cigars with a mild-to-medium body featuring an Ecuador-grown, Connecticut-seed natural wrapper or Connecticut Broadleaf maduro wrapper (Dom. Rep. binder) in boxes of 25 (20 for the tubos). The medium-filler version (Connecticut wrapper, Ecuadorian binder) was introduced in 1999 and is offered in boxes of 20.

PRYME LIMITED EDITION GOLD SERIES
Handmade in Esteli, Nicaragua.

Wrapper: Ecuador
Binder: Mexico
Filler: Dominican Republic, Honduras, Mexico, Nicaragua

Shape	Name	Lgth	Ring	Wrapper
Robusto	100R	5¼	52	CC
Toro	200X	6⅛	50	CC
Churchill	300C	7	48	CC
Torpedo	400T	6⅜	52	CC

With a strictly limited production of 1,500 boxes per size, this full-bodied brand from the Alec Bradley Cigar Co. was introduced in 2004. It blends leaves from five nations into four thicker shapes with a Connecticut-seed wrapper into this "Gold Series Limited Edition." It is offered in boxes of 20.

PUCK
BY INDIAN TABAC
Handmade in Danli, Honduras.

Wrapper: Honduras
Binder: Nicaragua
Filler: Honduras, Nicaragua

Shape	Name	Lgth	Ring	Wrapper
Double Corona	Churchill	7½	50	CM
Lonsdale	No. 1	6½	44	CM

Toro	Toro	6	54	CM

Introduced in 2003 exclusively for the House of Oxford, this is a medium-to-full-bodied blend, available in boxes of 25. The playful character of Puck is brilliantly illustrated on the box.

PUEBLO DOMINICANO SERIE II ★*New*★
Handmade in Santiago, Dominican Republic.

Wrapper: Dom. Rep.   Binder: Dom. Rep.   Filler: Dom. Rep.

Shape	Name	Lgth	Ring	Wrapper
Torpedo	Belicoso No. 1	6¼	52	CC
Torpedo	Belicoso No. 2	5¾	52	
Torpedo	Belicoso No. 3	5	52	CC

Made at the La Aurora factory for Meier & Dutch Distributors, this is a medium-bodied cigar in a new blend for 2007, offered in boxes of 20. The Serie I was introduced in 2006.

PUERTO RICO 965
Handmade in Mayaguez, Puerto Rico.

Wrapper: Ecuador   Binder: Dom. Rep.   Filler: Puerto Rico

Shape	Name	Lgth	Ring	Wrapper
Toro	PR 965	6	50	CC

This is a mild or medium blend from JFC Tobacco, introduced in 2004. It's mild with an Ecuadorian, Connecticut-seed wrapper and offered in boxes of 20.

PUNCH
Handmade in Cofradia, Honduras.

Wrapper: Ecuador, USA/Connecticut   Binder: USA/Connecticut
Filler: Dominican Republic, Honduras, Nicaragua

Shape	Name		Lgth	Ring	Wrapper
Churchill	After Dinner		7¼	45	CM-Ma
Short Panatela	Bolo		4⅛	36	CM
Grand Corona	Cafe Royales	(tubed)	5⅝	45	CM-Ma

HANDMADE CIGARS: BRAND LISTINGS

Perfecto	Champion		4½	60	CM
Churchill	Double Coronas		6¾	48	CM-Ma
Corona	Elites		5¼	44	CM-Ma
Robusto	Gusto	(tubed)	5	52	CM-Ma
Slim Panatela	Largo Elegantes		7	32	CM-Ma
Petit Corona	London Club		5	40	CM-Ma
Lonsdale	Lonsdales		6½	43	CM-Ma
Robusto	Magnum		5¼	54	CM-Ma
Toro	Pitas		6⅛	50	CM-Ma
Giant	Presidents		8½	52	CM-Ma
Lonsdale	Punch		6¼	44	CM-Ma
Robusto	Rothschilds		4½	50	CM-Ma
Cigarillo	Slim Panatellas		4	28	CM
Grand Corona	Library Edition: "The Prince"	6¼	45	CM

Originated in Cuba in 1840, the world-famous Punch brand is handmade in Honduras since 1969 from Cuban-seed tobaccos grown in Honduras, Nicaragua and the Dominican Republic. This range offers a magnificent, easy smoke with unsurpassed, full-bodied taste and bouquet using Sumatra-seed, Ecuadorian-grown natural wrappers and Connecticut Broadleaf for the maduro-wrapped shapes. The Champion was introduced in a unique promotion in 2001, chosen by the vote of smokers in a nationwide "Heavyweight" promotion by a 58-42% margin against an alternate blend. Most sizes are offered in boxes of 25. The Library Edition is made for Cigars by Santa Clara.

PUNCH DELUXE
Handmade in Cofradia, Honduras.

Wrapper: Ecuador, USA/Connecticut Binder: USA/Connecticut
Filler: Dominican Republic, Honduras, Nicaragua

Shape	Name		Lgth	Ring	Wrapper
Double Corona	Chateau "L"		7¼	54	CM-Ma
Grand Corona	Chateau "M"		5¾	46	CM-Ma
Corona	Royal Coronation	(tubed)	5¼	44	CM-Ma

This is a special version of the regular Punch line with extra aging and a special band. The regular Punch line has a red band center with the words "Punch" and "Imported" in gold. The Deluxe line has a more subtle red band with "Punch" inside a shield over a white center spot with the letters "JG" inside. At the bottom of the band center is the name "Manuel Lopez" who owned the brand in Cuba from 1902-24. The Chateau L and M are offered in boxes of 25; the Royal Coronation in boxes of 30.

PUNCH GRAN CRU
Handmade in Cofradia, Honduras.

Wrapper: Ecuador, USA/Connecticut   *Binder: Ecuador*
Filler: Dominican Republic, Honduras, Nicaragua

Shape	Name		Lgth	Ring	Wrapper
Toro	Britania		6¼	50	CM
Double Corona	Diademas		7¼	54	CC
Churchill	Monarcas	(tubed)	6¾	48	CM
Giant	Prince Consorts		8½	52	CM-Ma
Robusto	Robustos		5¼	50	CC-Ma
Robusto	Superiores		5⅝	48	CM
Torpedo	No. II		6⅛	54	CM-Ma
Perfecto	Punchitos		4	50	CM

The Punch Gran Cru series is made from vintage tobaccos aged from 3-5 years under the supervision of Villazon & Co.'s master blenders. Grand Cru cigars are robust in taste, yet sweet with a marvelous bouquet, using Connecticut Shade wrappers, Ecuadorian binders and a three-nation filler blend. The distinctive red-centered band contains the words "Punch" and "Manuel Lopez" in gold, in and around a shield with a center white spot with the letters "JG," and a black rim around the bottom of the band.

PUNCH GRAN PURO
Handmade in Cofradia, Honduras.

Wrapper: Honduras   *Binder: Honduras*   *Filler: Honduras*

Shape	Name	Lgth	Ring	Wrapper
Robusto	Rancho	5½	54	CM
Toro	Sierra	6½	48	CM

production cigars anywhere.

A special, limited-edition "Viejo" line of 50,000 cigars (in boxes of 15) was introduced in 1999, offering four-year-aged Puros Indios cigars in the Presidente, Toro, Rothschild, No. 4 and Nacional shapes only.

PUROS INDIOS DOUBLE FUERTE SPECIAL EDITION
Handmade in Danli, Honduras.

Wrapper: Honduras   Binder: Dom. Rep.   Filler: Dom. Rep., Nicaragua

Shape	Name	Lgth	Ring	Wrapper
Toro	Cañones No. 1	6½	48	Ma
Robusto	Robusto	5	50	Ma

This "double strong" blend was introduced in 2005 and revised in 2006, offering full-bodied power. It features a Corojo wrapper and is available in boxes of 20.

PUROS INDIOS SPECIAL AGED
Handmade in Danli, Honduras.

Wrapper: Ecuador   Binder: Ecuador   Filler: Dom. Rep., Jamaica, Nicaragua

Shape	Name	Lgth	Ring	Wrapper
Torpedo	Piramide	6¾	64	CM-Ma

Made specially for Meier & Dutch Distributors, this is a full-bodied blend with up to eight years of aging! Limited in quantity, they're offered in packs of six.

PUROS NIRVANA
Handmade in Santiago, Dominican Republic.

Wrapper: Indonesia   Binder: USA/Connecticut   Filler: Dominican Republic

Shape	Name	Lgth	Ring	Wrapper
Torpedo	Torpedo	6½	52	CM
Double Corona	Churchill	7	52	CM
Robusto	Robusto	5	50	CM

Introduced in 2006, this is a medium-bodied blend from the Arango Cigar Company. It features a Sumatra wrapper, Broadleaf binder and three Dominican-grown filler tobaccos, available in boxes of 25.

HANDMADE CIGARS: BRAND LISTINGS

PUROS OF ST. JAMES
Handmade in Santiago, Dominican Republic.

Wrapper: Indonesia   Binder: USA/Connecticut   Filler: Dom. Rep.

Shape	Name	Lgth	Ring	Wrapper
Torpedo	Belicoso	6	52	CM
Double Corona	Churchill	7	50	CM
Lonsdale	Lonsdale	6½	44	CM
Robusto	Robusto	5	50	CM

This is a medium-bodied blend made by MATASA for Mike's Cigars and named for London's famous street of cigar merchants. Introduced in 2004, it's offered in bright red, slide-top cedar cabinets of 25.

QUADRADO ★New★
Handmade in Guayaquil, Ecuador.

Wrapper: Ecuador   Binder: Ecuador   Filler: Ecuador

Shape	Name	Lgth	Ring	Wrapper
Robusto	QRobusto	5	50	CM
Toro	QToro	6	50	CM
Torpedo	QTorpedo	5½	50	CM
Toro	QGordo	6	54	CM
Toro	QGrande	6½	60	CM

Puros de Armando Ramos introduced this cigar in 2007. It's box-pressed with a sun-grown wrapper and a medium-to-full body. It's offered in bundles of 20.

QUETZAL
Handmade in La Romana, Dominican Republic.

Wrapper: USA/Connecticut   Binder: Dom. Rep.   Filler: Dom. Rep.

Shape	Name	Lgth	Ring	Wrapper
Giant	No. 1	8	52	CC
Toro	No. 2	6	50	CC
Churchill	No. 3	7	48	CC

Lonsdale	No. 4	6¾	44	CC
Long Corona	No. 5	6	42	CC

Introduced in 1997, this brand is made up of Connecticut wrapper and Dominican interior leaves and offers a mild taste in bundles of 25 cigars each.

QUINTERO

Handmade in Santa Rosa de Copan, Honduras.

Wrapper: Honduras, Mexico   Binder: Nicaragua   Filler: Honduras, Nicaragua

Shape	Name	Lgth	Ring	Wrapper
Grand Corona	Corona	5⅝	45	CM-Ma
Churchill	Double Corona	7	48	Ma
Torpedo	Belicoso	6⅛	52	CM-Ma
Robusto	Robusto	5	54	CM-Ma
Toro	Toro	6	56	CM-Ma
Double Corona	Churchill	7¼	54	CM-Ma

Here is an old Cuban brand, reintroduced to the U.S. market by Altadis USA in 2005. With natural wrappers, it offers a medium-bodied taste, available in boxes of 20. The full-bodied, Mexican Morron maduro-wrapped shapes appeared in 2006, also offered in 20s. All shapes are box-pressed.

QUINTESSA

Handmade in Santa Rosa de Copan, Honduras.

Wrapper: Honduras   Binder: Nicaragua   Filler: Honduras, Nicaragua

Shape	Name	Lgth	Ring	Wrapper
Corona	Corona	5½	44	CM
Robusto	Robusto	5	54	CM
Toro	Toro	6	54	CM
Torpedo	Belicoso	6⅛	52	CM
Double Corona	Churchill	7	52	CM

Altadis USA Senior Vice President Jim Colucci was enjoying dinner and especially a glass of Quintessa wine in 2003 and three years later, introduced this line. It's medium-to-full in body, reasonably priced and offered in boxes of 25.

HANDMADE CIGARS: BRAND LISTINGS

QUISQUEYANA
Handmade in Tamboril, Dominican Republic and
New York, New York, USA.
Wrapper: Cameroon, Dominican Republic, Indonesia, USA/Connecticut
Binder: Dominican Republic   *Filler: Dominican Republic*

Quisqueyana is the present name for an old maker originally called Licey Cigars, founded by Luis Portes and Jose Flores in about 1901. The seven current blends debuted in 2002 and feature a Dominican binder and filler with different wrappers and blends for each series. The Reserve (1 shape) is medium-to-full in body. The Premium (4 shapes) is mild to medium with a Connecticut wrapper only. The Preferred (6 shapes) is mild with Connecticut wrap or full-bodied with a Dominican-grown wrapper. The Old Style (3 shapes) is full-bodied and has a Cameroon wrapper, the Original (4 shapes) is medium with a Connecticut wrapper leaf and the Magnum Q (3 shapes) is mild-to-medium and uses Connecticut aged wrappers.

This line includes several very large cigars, including the Old Style Grande (5 x 65 torpedo) and the entire Original series: Dona Rosa (7 x 65), Gigante (9 x 65) and Figurado (6 x 68 torpedo).

QUORUM
Handmade, with mixed filler, in Esteli, Nicaragua.
Wrapper: Nicaragua   *Binder: Nicaragua*   *Filler: Nicaragua*

Shape	Name	Lgth	Ring	Wrapper
Corona	Corona	5½	43	CM
Robusto	Robusto	4¾	50	CM
Toro	Toro	6	50	CM
Churchill	Churchill	7	48	CM
Torpedo	Torpedo	6	50	CM

This brand was introduced by the J.C. Newman Cigar Co. in 2002. It offers a medium-to-full-bodied taste in value-priced bundles of 20.

RAFAEL GONZALEZ
Handmade in Cofradia, Honduras.
Wrapper: USA/Connecticut   *Binder: USA/Connecticut*
Filler: Dominican Republic, Honduras, Nicaragua

HANDMADE CIGARS: BRAND LISTINGS

Shape	Name	Lgth	Ring	Wrapper
Double Corona	Churchill	7¼	54	CC
Grand Corona	Corona Extra	5⅝	46	CC
Churchill	Double Corona	6¾	48	CC
Lonsdale	Lonsdale	6½	43	CC
Robusto	Robusto	5½	50	CC
Toro	Toro	6⅛	50	CC
Short Panatela	Rafaelito	4⅛	36	CC

Here is one of the most honored names in Havana cigars, introduced by Famous Smoke Shop in a Honduran-made style beginning in 1999. This blend of a Connecticut wrapper, Connecticut Broadleaf binder and three-nation filler offers a medium-bodied taste. It is presented in the traditional Rafael Gonzalez-style box of 25 cigars each.

RAFAEL RAMOS ★New★
Handmade in Guayaquil, Ecuador.

Wrapper: Ecuador　　　　　Binder: Ecuador　　　　　Filler: Ecuador

Shape	Name	Lgth	Ring	Wrapper
Toro	Toro	6	50	CC-CM-Ma
Torpedo	Torpedo	6	50	CC-CM-Ma
Torpedo	Torpito	4½	50	CC-CM-Ma
Toro	Gordo	6	60	CC-CM-Ma

Puros de Armando Ramos introduced this blend, also known as "RR Doubles," in 2007. It's medium-to-full in body with a choice of wrapper shades, offered in boxes of 50.

RAMON ALLONES
Handmade in Santiago, Dominican Republic.

Wrapper: Dom. Rep.　　Binder: USA/Connecticut　　Filler: Dom. Rep., Nicaragua

Shape	Name	Lgth	Ring	Wrapper
Robusto	Gustoso	5	50	CM
Robusto	Maestro	5½	54	CM

| Grand Corona | Brioso | 6 | 45 | CM |
| Toro | Ultimo | 6½ | 49 | CM |

This brand originated in Cuba way back in 1837 and was made by the Partagas firm beginning in 1920. It appeared in a Dominican version in the 1970s and was completely revamped in 2001 with a La Vega Especial wrapper, a medium-to-full-bodied taste and available in boxes of 25.

RAMON ALLONES RESERVE ★New★
Handmade in Cofradia, Honduras.
Wrapper: Ecuador, USA/Connecticut
Binder: USA/Connecticut *Filler: Dominican Republic, Honduras, Nicaragua*

Shape	Name	Lgth	Ring	Wrapper
Lonsdale	Allones No. 1	7	43	CC
Torpedo	Allones No. 2	6¼	50	CC
Toro	Corona Gorda	6⅛	50	CC
Short Panatela	Corona Minor	5¼	38	CC
Grand Corona	Cuban Corona	5⅝	46	CC
Double Corona	Double Corona	6⅞	48	CC-Ma
Toro	Hermoso No. 1	6	54	CC-Ma
Robusto	Hermoso No. 2	5	50	CC-Ma
Grand Corona	Library Edition: "Chosen"	6¼	45	CC

Cigars by Santa Clara introduced this version of the Ramon Allones brand in 2007. It's medium to full in body, offered in solid cedar boxes of 20.

RANDELLO
Handmade in Danli, Honduras.
Wrapper: Honduras *Binder: Honduras* *Filler: Honduras*

Shape	Name	Lgth	Ring	Wrapper
Robusto	Robusto	5¼	54	CM
Toro	Toro	6¼	54	CM
Double Corona	Churchill	7	50	CM

HANDMADE CIGARS: BRAND LISTINGS

Torpedo	Belicoso	6½	54	CM

This line replaces the Randello X which debuted in 2003. The new, 2005-blended Randello is medium in body and offered in boxes of 20.

Rav ★New★
Handmade in Santiago, Dominican Republic.
Wrapper: Nicaragua, USA/Connecticut

Binder: Dom. Rep.   Filler: Dom. Rep., Nicaragua

Shape	Name	Lgth	Ring	Wrapper
Robusto	Robusto	5	48	CC-Ma
Toro	Corona Gorda	6	50	CC-Ma
Double Corona	Doble Corona	7	50	CC-Ma
Torpedo	Belicoso	6⅛	52	CC-Ma
Toro	Gran Corona	6½	54	CC-Ma

Take your choice of Connecticut-grown natural for a mild-to-medium-bodied taste in the Clasico line or Nicaraguan wrappers in the medium-bodied Viso-98 style in this brand, introduced in 2007. All sizes are offered in boxes of 20.

Red Head
Handmade in Esteli, Nicaragua.
Wrapper: Nicaragua   Binder: Nicaragua   Filler: Honduras, Nicaragua

Shape	Name	Lgth	Ring	Wrapper
Torpedo	Torpedo	6	52	CM
Churchill	Churchill	7	48	CM
Robusto	Robusto	5	50	CM
Cigarillo	Cigarillo	3¼	22	CM

Introduced in 2005, this is a value-priced, medium-bodied blend with a sun-grown wrapper. It's offered in boxes of 50.

Red Lion
Handmade in Santiago, Dominican Republic.
Wrapper: Brazil, Dom. Rep.   Binder: Dom. Rep.   Filler: Dom. Rep.

HANDMADE CIGARS: BRAND LISTINGS

Shape	Name	Lgth	Ring	Wrapper
Toro	Toro	6	60	CM-Ma
Perfecto	Maduro Figurado	4½	44	Ma

This is a medium-to-full-bodied blend, introduced by the Heavenly Cigar Co. It features a Dominican-grown Rosado or a Brazilian-grown maduro wrapper. The 6x60 shapes are offered in boxes or bundles of 15 while the figurado is offered in 25s.

REMEDIOS
Handmade in Esteli, Nicaragua.

Wrapper: USA/Connecticut   Binder: Mexico   Filler: Dom. Rep., Nicaragua

Shape	Name	Lgth	Ring	Wrapper
Toro	Corona Gorda	6⅛	50	CC-Ma
Double Corona	Clemenceau	7¼	54	CC-Ma
Grand Corona	Corona	5⅝	45	CC-Ma
Pyramid	Don Victor	6	54	CC-Ma
Robusto	Robusto	4½	50	CC-Ma

This is a high-quality blend, introduced in 1998. The combination of Connecticut wrapper (Broadleaf for maduro) and Mexican binder complement the blended filler to offer a medium-bodied smoke. The brand earned a gold medal in the 1998 Monde Selection in Brussels, Belgium.

REO
Handmade in Danli, Honduras.

Wrapper: Costa Rica   Binder: Nicaragua   Filler: Honduras, Nicaragua

Shape	Name	Lgth	Ring	Wrapper
Robusto	Robusto	5	52	CC
Torpedo	Torpedo	5¼	54	CC
Petit Corona	Corona	4½	44	CC
Toro	Chairman	6	58	CC

Introduced in 2005 by United Tobacco, this is a full-bodied cigar blended by Rocky Patel. It's offered with a gentle box-press in boxes of 20.

HANDMADE CIGARS: BRAND LISTINGS

REPEATER
Handmade, with mixed filler, in Danli, Honduras.

Wrapper: Honduras   Binder: Honduras   Filler: Honduras

Shape	Name	Lgth	Ring	Wrapper
Corona	Repeater 100	5½	43	CM
Long Corona	Repeater 200	6	43	CM
Lonsdale	Repeater 300	6½	43	CM
Lonsdale	Havana Twist	7	44	CM
Churchill	Churchill	7	48	CM
Robusto	Robusto	5	50	CM

This brand debuted in the late 1960s and utilizes medium-filler tobacco and a Sumatra wrapper to produce an enjoyable smoke of medium body. Some sizes are also available with vanilla flavoring.

REY MIGUEL   ★*New*★
Handmade in Miami, Florida, USA.

Wrapper: Ecuador   Binder: Nicaragua   Filler: Nicaragua

Shape	Name	Lgth	Ring	Wrapper
Double Corona	Churchill	7	50	CC
Grand Corona	Corona Gorda	5⅝	46	CC
Robusto	Robusto	5	50	CC
Toro	Toro	6	50	CC
Torpedo	Torpedo	6¼	52	CC

Made in Miami at El Rey de Los Habanos, this is a medium-bodied cigar with a Connecticut-seed wrapper. Created in 2006, it's offered in boxes of 25.

RIATA
Handmade in Danli, Honduras.

Wrapper: Mexico   Binder: Mexico   Filler: Honduras

Shape	Name	Lgth	Ring	Wrapper
Panatela	No. 200	6⅞	36	CM

Corona	No. 400	5½	44	CM
Lonsdale	No. 500	6⅝	44	CM
Toro	No. 600	6⅝	54	CM-Ma
Robusto	No. 700	4¾	50	CM-Ma
Toro	No. 800	6¼	50	CM-Ma
Double Corona	No. 900	7½	50	CM-Ma

Now back in circulation after a few years off, this is a medium-bodied blend of Riata, with a choice of natural-shade or maduro wrappers. You can enjoy either in bundles of 20.

RICHARD NIXON
Handmade in Frankfort, New York, USA.

Wrapper: Ecuador   Binder: Venezuela   Filler: Ecuador, Venezuela

Shape	Name	Lgth	Ring	Wrapper
Petit Corona	Milhous	4½	41	CM

This brand is part of the Lars Tetens line and salutes the 37th President of the United States, who served from 1969 until resigning in 1974. This is a full-bodied blend which underscores Tetens' admiration for one of the most remarkable men in the history of American politics, offered in boxes of 30.

RICOS DOMINICANOS
Handmade in Santiago, Dominican Republic.

Wrapper: USA/Connecticut   Binder: Honduras
Filler: Brazil, Dominican Republic, Nicaragua

Shape	Name	Lgth	Ring	Wrapper
Double Corona	Churchill	7	50	CC-Ma
Toro	Toro	6	50	CC-Ma
Corona	Breva	5½	44	CC-Ma
Lonsdale	Centro Largo	6¾	44	CC-Ma

This brand debuted in 1996 and offers a mild-to-medium bodied taste in either a natural or maduro (Broadleaf) wrapper. It has a rich aroma and, best of all, is an excellent value, offered in bundles of 20.

HANDMADE CIGARS: BRAND LISTINGS

RICOS DOMINICANOS BLACK LABEL
Handmade in Santiago, Dominican Republic.

Wrapper: Ecuador   *Binder: Honduras*   *Filler: Dom. Rep.*

Shape	Name	Lgth	Ring	Wrapper
Torpedo	Figurado EN	5¾	56	CC
Double Corona	Churchill EN	7	50	CC
Toro	Toro EN	6	50	CC
Lonsdale	No. 1 EN	6¾	44	CC
Robusto	Rothschild EN	5	50	CC
Corona	Breva EN	5¾	43	CC

This is a product of MATASA, with a medium body, offered in bundles of 20.

RIGOLETTO
Handmade in Santiago, Dominican Republic.

Wrapper: USA/Connecticut   *Binder: Dom. Rep.*   *Filler: Dom. Rep.*

Shape	Name	Lgth	Ring	Wrapper
Churchill	Black Magic	7½	46	CC-Ma
Lonsdale	Black Arrow	6¼	44	CC-Ma
Toro	Dominican Lights	6¼	48	CC-Ma
Robusto	Dominican Darks	5¼	50	CC-Ma

This brand, which debuted in 1905, is made by hand in the Dominican Republic using Connecticut Shade leaves for natural wrappers and Connecticut Broadleaf tobaccos for the maduro style. Medium in body, it's an underrated smoke, available in boxes of 25.

RIO DE CUBA
Handmade, with mixed filler, in Santiago, Dominican Republic.

Wrapper: Indonesia   *Binder: Indonesia*   *Filler: Nicaragua*

This is a flavorful, mixed-filler, medium-to-full-bodied cigar offered in five sizes. Try it in value-priced bundles of 25.

HANDMADE CIGARS: BRAND LISTINGS

RIO MAYOS
Handmade in Tarapoto, Peru.

Wrapper: Peru   Binder: Peru   Filler: Peru

Shape	Name	Lgth	Ring	Wrapper
Small Panatela	Rio Mayos	4½	30	CM

This is a medium-bodied blend offered by the Tabacalera Del Oriente, introduced in 2006. It's available in boxes of 50.

RITZ SQUARE
Handmade in Santiago, Dominican Republic.

Wrapper: Brazil, Indonesia   Binder: Dom. Rep.   Filler: Dom. Rep.

Shape	Name	Lgth	Ring	Wrapper
Double Corona	Churchill	7	50	CM-Ma
Toro	Corona Gorda	6	54	CM-Ma
Torpedo	Torpedo	6½	52	CM-Ma
Lonsdale	No. 1	6½	44	CM-Ma
Robusto	Robusto	5½	50	CM-Ma

This brand debuted in 2000 and is offered in both a natural-wrapped (Indonesian) and maduro-wrapped (Brazilian) version. It is a mild-to-medium (natural) or medium-bodied (maduro) smoke in a box-pressed format in boxes of 20.

ROCCO GAETANO D'ANGELO
Handmade in Tamboril, Dominican Republic.

Wrapper: Indonesia, USA/Connecticut   Binder: Dom. Rep.   Filler: Dom. Rep.

This 12-size brand was introduced in 2000 and features an Indonesian wrapper on most shapes or a Connecticut wrapper on four sizes (Rocco, Gaetano, Don D'Angelo Primo, D'Angelo). Two sizes (Tatone Carmine and Tatone Gino) have maduro wrappers. The curing of the tobacco is unique and based on root cellar concepts, imparting an aromatic quality. The blend is medium-bodied and is available in boxes of 25, with or without tubes. The five-shape Piccolino line was introduced in 2004 and is made with short filler.

| Toro | Toro | 6½ | 52 | CM |
| Torpedo | Torpedo | 6¼ | 52 | CM |

Famous Smoke Shop is the distributor for this line of what are essentially overruns and seconds of the Rocky Patel Sun Grown line. Full-bodied, they are offered in economical bundles of 20.

ROCKY PATEL FACTORY SELECTS COROJO & MADURO ★*New*★
Handmade in Danli, Honduras.

Wrapper: Nicaragua   *Binder: Nicaragua*   *Filler: Honduras, Nicaragua*

Shape	Name	Lgth	Ring	Wrapper
Torpedo	Mini Belicoso	5	48	CM-Ma
Toro	Toro	6	52	CM-Ma
Torpedo	Torpedo	6	52	CM-Ma

Cigar Domain introduced these full-bodied cigars in economical bundles of 20 in 2007.

ROCKY PATEL FUSION ★*New*★
Handmade in Danli, Honduras.

Wrapper: Ecuador   *Binder: USA/Connecticut*   *Filler: Dom. Rep., Nicaragua*

Shape	Name	Lgth	Ring	Wrapper
Robusto	Robusto	5½	50	CC
Torpedo	Torpedo	6¼	52	CC
Toro	Toro	6½	52	CC
Churchill	Churchill	7	48	CC

This blue-banded cigar is made for Meier & Dutch Distributors. It's an elegantly-styled, medium-bodied cigar that uses Connecticut wrapper leaves as the binder! It's available in boxes of 20.

ROCKY PATEL HONDURAN CLASSIC ★*New*★
Handmade in Danli, Honduras.

Wrapper: Nicaragua   *Binder: Honduras*   *Filler: Honduras, Nicaragua*

Shape	Name	Lgth	Ring	Wrapper
Robusto	Robusto	5½	54	CM-Ma
Toro	Toro	6½	52	CM-Ma
Torpedo	Torpedo	5	54	CM-Ma

Cigar Domain introduced this blend into national distribution beginning in 2007. It's full-bodied, with either a Corojo or maduro wrapper, in boxes of 20.

ROCKY PATEL JAVA
BY DREW ESTATE
Handmade in Esteli, Nicaragua.

Wrapper: Brazil, USA/Connecticut   Binder: Nicaragua   Filler: Nicaragua

Shape	Name		Lgth	Ring	Wrapper
Robusto	Robusto		5½	50	CC-Ma
Robusto	Wafe		5	54	CC-Ma
Petit Corona	Corona		5	42	CC-Ma
Toro	Toro	(tubed)	6	50	CC-Ma
Robusto	The 58		5	58	CC-Ma

Here is a flavored cigar, introduced in 2004. The line was expanded in 2006 to two series: Claro, with a Connecticut wrapper (mild-to-medium body) and Maduro, with a Brazilian wrapper (medium in body). All sizes are infused with coffee and mocha flavors in boxes of 24 except for the Wafe, offered in boxes of 40.

ROCKY PATEL OLDE WORLD RESERVE
Handmade in Danli, Honduras.

Wrapper: Costa Rica, Nicaragua   Binder: Nicaragua   Filler: Nicaragua

Shape	Name	Lgth	Ring	Wrapper
Robusto	Robusto	5½	54	CM-Ma
Torpedo	Torpedo	5	54	CM-Ma
Toro	Toro	6½	52	CM-Ma

HANDMADE CIGARS: BRAND LISTINGS

Churchill	Churchill (tubes available)	7	48	CI-CC-CM
Petit Corona	Petite Corona	4½	44	CI-CC-CM
Toro	Toro	6½	52	CI-CC-CM
Torpedo	Torpedo	6¼	52	CI-CC-CM
Short Panatela	Juniors	4	38	CI-CC-CM
Toro	Six by Sixty	6	60	CI-CC-CM
Perfecto	Perfecto	4	48	CI-CC-CM

The 1990 and 1992 Vintage lines were introduced in 2003. Both of these blends, created by Rocky Patel, feature special wrappers. The 1990 Vintage uses a Honduran Broadleaf wrapper for a full-bodied taste with a spicy flavor. The 1992 Vintage uses a Sumatra-seed leaf grown in Ecuador for the wrapper, yielding a milder spice and plenty of richness. Both are offered in boxes of 20, with the tubed models in glass tubes and the Juniors in boxes of 10.

The 1999 Vintage was introduced in 2006 and features a seven-year-old Connecticut wrapper. It's mild-to-medium in body, offered in boxes of 20.

ROLLER'S CHOICE
Handmade in Santiago, Dominican Republic.

Wrapper: USA/Connecticut   Binder: Mexico   Filler: Dom. Rep.

Shape	Name	Lgth	Ring	Wrapper
Double Corona	RC Double Corona	7	50	CC-Ma
Long Corona	RC Corona	6	43	CC
Grand Corona	RC Lonsdale	6½	46	CC-Ma
Robusto	RC Robusto	5	50	CC-Ma
Petit Corona	RC Pequeño	4¼	40	CC-Ma
Corona	RC Fino	5½	41	CC
Torpedo	RC Torpedo	5½	56	CC-Ma
Toro	RC Toro	6	50	CC
Corona	RC Cetro	5½	43	CC

While not as well known as some other brands, Roller's Choice was introduced in 1992 and is a well-constructed, mild-bodied cigar produced at MATASA, one of the Dominican Republic's most dependable factories. It is offered in boxes of 25 with a Connecticut Shade natural or Connecticut Broadleaf maduro wrapper.

ROLY
Handmade, with mixed filler, in Danli, Honduras.

Wrapper: Ecuador　　　　　　　　　　　　　　*Binder: Dominican Republic*
Filler: Brazil, Dom. Rep., Ecuador, Nicaragua

Shape	Name		Lgth	Ring	Wrapper
Double Corona	Churchill		7½	53	CM-Ma
Toro	Torpedo		6½	60	CM-Ma
Toro	Cetros		6	53	CM-Ma
Grand Corona	No. 2		6½	46	CM-Ma
Corona	No. 4		5½	44	CM-Ma
Robusto	Robusto		5	50	CM-Ma
Churchill	Cazadores	/short filler/	7½	47	CM-Ma
Grand Corona	Fumas	/short filler/	6½	46	CM-Ma

Here is a brilliantly constructed, medium-bodied cigar, available in a variety of shapes. Roly features a Sumatra-seed wrapper and Dominican binder and blended filler.

ROMEO Y JULIETA 1875
Handmade in La Romana, Dominican Republic.

Wrapper: Indonesia　　　　　*Binder: Dom. Rep.*　　　　　*Filler: Dom. Rep.*

Shape	Name		Lgth	Ring	Wrapper
Double Corona	Churchill	(tube available)	7	50	CM
Giant	Exhibicion No. 1		8½	52	CM
Toro	Exhibicion No. 3		6	50	CM
Robusto	Bully		5	50	CM
Lonsdale	Cedro Deluxe No. 1		6½	44	CM
Corona	Cedro Deluxe No. 2		5½	44	CM
Torpedo	Belicoso		6⅛	54	CM

HANDMADE CIGARS: BRAND LISTINGS

Double Corona	Deluxe No.1 (glass tube)	7	50	CM
Toro	Deluxe No.2 (glass tube)	6	50	CM
Corona	Romeo's Court (tubed)	5½	44	CM
Robusto	Rothchilde (tubed)	5	50	CM
Toro	Clemenceau (tubed)	6	50	CM
Torpedo	No. 2 (tubed)	6⅛	52	CM
Torpedo	Petite No. 2 (tubed)	5	52	CM
	Machine-made, with short filler:			
Small Panatela	Romeos	4	30	CM
Cigarillo	Petit Julietas	3⅝	23	CM
Cigarillo	Julietas	4⅞	28	CM
	Cigars by Santa Clara series:			
Toro	Dreams (glass tube)	6	50	CM
	Great Discovery's series:			
Toro	Lot 95 Series B	6	50	CM
	Zander-Greg series:			
Double Corona	La Ventana Churchill (glass tube)	7	50	CM
Toro	La Ventana Robusto (glass tube)	6	50	CM
Robusto	La Ventana Toro (glass tube)	5	50	CM

Here is the Dominican incarnation of one of the world's most famous brands, which originated in Cuba in the 19th Century. This blend features Dominican Olor binders and Dominican fillers and offers a medium-bodied taste. You can find it in boxes of 25 elegantly picturing Shakespeare's famous lovers, except for the tubed cigars, available in boxes of 10; the Exhibicion No. 1, offered in 20s and the small cigars, available in tins of 10 (Romeos) or 8 (Petit Julietas) and boxes of 10 (Julietas). Please note that the Exhibicion shapes are wrapped in cedar.

HANDMADE CIGARS: BRAND LISTINGS

ROMEO Y JULIETA ANIVERSARIO
Handmade in La Romana, Dominican Republic.

Wrapper: Ecuador   Binder: USA/Connecticut   Filler: Dom. Rep., Nicaragua, Peru

Shape	Name	Lgth	Ring	Wrapper
Robusto	Robusto	5	52	CM
Belicoso	No. 2	6⅛	52	CM
Corona	Corona	5½	44	CM
Double Corona	Churchill	7	54	CM
Toro	Toro	6	54	CM

This blend was introduced by Altadis USA in 2003 and offers a 130th anniversary salute to this most unique brand! Offered in lacquered boxes of 25, this is a full-bodied smoke with a highly-decorated black and gold band.

ROMEO Y JULIETA CABINET SELECCION ★*New*★
Handmade in La Romana, Dominican Republic.

Wrapper: Cameroon   Binder: Nicaragua   Filler: Dom. Rep., Nicaragua, Peru

Shape	Name	Lgth	Ring	Wrapper
Torpedo	Belicoso	6⅛	52	CM
Toro	Toro	6	54	CM
Corona	Corona	5½	44	CM
Robusto	Robusto	5	52	CM

The elite Cabinet Seleccion blend of Romeo y Julieta starts with a Cameroon wrapper and offers a medium-to-full-bodied blend. Introduced in 2007, it's specially banded in white with gold trim and packed in special, slide-top cainets of 22.

ROMEO Y JULIETA EDICION LIMITADA ★*New*★
Handmade in La Romana, Dominican Republic.

Wrapper: Mexico   Binder: Nicaragua   Filler: Honduras, Nicaragua

Shape	Name		Lgth	Ring	Wrapper
Torpedo	No. 2	*(tubed)*	6⅛	52	CM
Toro	Prominente	*(tubed)*	6	54	CM

Robusto	Rothchilde	(tubed)	5	54	CM

Billed as the "finest, rarest and most coveted Romeo y Julieta ever made," Altadis USA introduced this blend in 2007. It's a full-bodied cigar with a Corojo wrapper offered in intricate chests of 12. Every shape in the line is offered with a double band and in ruby-red aluminum tubes.

ROMEO Y JULIETA HABANA RESERVE ★New★
Handmade in Santa Rosa de Copan, Honduras.

Wrapper: Nicaragua   *Binder: Nicaragua*   *Filler: Honduras, Nicaragua*

Shape	Name	Lgth	Ring	Wrapper
Torpedo	Belicoso	6⅛	52	CM
Double Corona	Churchill	7	54	CM
Grand Corona	Corona	5⅝	45	CM
Robusto	Robusto	5	54	CM
Toro	Toro	6	56	CM

For the first time since the early 1990s, here is a Honduran-made Romeo! Introduced by Altadis USA in mid-2007, this is a full-bodied blend offered in traditionally-dressed boxes of 27.

ROMEO Y JULIETA RESERVA REAL
Handmade in La Romana, Dominican Republic.

Wrapper: Ecuador   *Binder: Nicaragua*   *Filler: Dom. Rep., Nicaragua*

Shape	Name	Lgth	Ring	Wrapper
Small Panatela	Minutos Petites	4	30	CC
Short Panatela	Lanceros	4½	38	CC
Corona	Corona	5½	44	CC
Lonsdale	Lonsdale	6⅝	44	CC
Double Corona	Churchill	7	50	CC
Robusto	Robusto	5	52	CC
Torpedo	No. 2	6⅛	52	CC
Robusto	Petite Robusto	4¼	54	CC

Toro	Toro		6	54	CC
Long Panatela	Porto Real	(tubed)	7	36	CC
Corona	Verona's Court	(tubed)	5½	44	CC
	Cabinet Selection:				
Corona	Corona	(glass tube)	5½	44	CC
Double Corona	Churchill		7	50	CC
Robusto	Robusto		5	50	CC
Toro	Toro		6	50	CC
	Ideal Tobacco series:				
Double Corona	Casino I	(glass tube)	7	50	CC
Toro	Casino II	(glass tube)	6	50	CC
Robusto	Casino III	(glass tube)	5	50	CC

Altadis USA introduced this blend in 2003, featuring a Connecticut-seed wrapper with a medium-bodied flavor. All of the cellophaned shapes are offered in 25s, except the Minutos Petities (7-packs) and the Lanceros (5s). The tubed shapes are available in 20s and the Petite Robusto is offered in a three-pack!

The Cabinet Selection was introduced by Harold Levinson Associates in 2005, also with a medium-bodied flavor.

ROMEO Y JULIETA RESERVE MADURO
Handmade in La Romana, Dominican Republic.
Wrapper: USA/Connecticut   Binder: Nicaragua   Filler: Dom. Rep., Nicaragua, Peru

Shape	Name	Lgth	Ring	Wrapper
Petit Corona	No. 4	5	44	Ma
Robusto	Petite Robusto	4¼	54	Ma
Lonsdale	Lonsdale	6⅝	44	Ma
Robusto	Robusto	5	50	Ma
Toro	Toro	6	50	Ma
Double Corona	Churchill	7	50	Ma

Torpedo	Mini Belicoso	5	52	Ma
Torpedo	Belicoso	6⅛	52	Ma
	Great Discovery's series:			
Robusto	Lot 96 Series B Maduro 10th Anniv. *(glass tubes)*	5	50	Ma

Introduced by Altadis USA in 2003, this blend features an earthy, medium-to-full-bodied flavor thanks to its blackened maduro wrapper and three-nation interior filler blend. The Mini-Belicoso and Belicoso shapes are box pressed. All shapes are offered in boxes of 25 with the Petite Robusto also offered in three-packs.

ROMEO Y JULIETA VIEJO ★*New*★
Handmade in La Romana, Dominican Republic.

Wrapper: Mexico   Binder: Nicaragua   Filler: Honduras, Nicaragua

Shape	Name	Lgth	Ring	Wrapper
Robusto	R	5	54	CM
Toro	E	6	54	CM
Torpedo	B	6⅛	52	CM
Double Corona	C	7	54	CM

This blend is made for Meier & Dutch Distributors and debuted in 2007. It has a gentle box press and is medium-to-full in body. It's available in boxes of 20.

ROMEO Y JULIETA VINTAGE
Handmade in La Romana, Dominican Republic.
Wrapper: Ecuador, USA/Connecticut

Binder: Ecuador, Mexico   Filler: Dom. Rep., Nicaragua, Peru

Shape	Name	Lgth	Ring	Wrapper
Long Corona	I	6	43	CC-Ma
Grand Corona	II	6	46	CC-Ma
Robusto	III	5	50	CC-Ma
Churchill	IV	7	48	CC-Ma
Double Corona	V	7½	50	CC-Ma

Pyramid	VI		6½	60	CC-Ma
Toro	VII		6	50	CC-Ma
Corona	Corona	(glass tube)	5½	44	CC
Toro	Toro	(glass tube)	6	50	CC
	Great Discovery's series:				
Churchill	Chavon River Edition Lot 21		7	48	CC

The Vintage line was introduced in 1993, but was revamped by Altadis USA in 2007. The natural-wrapped edition features an Ecuadorian-grown, Connecticut-seed wrapper, Mexican binder and Dominican filler for a mild-to-medium-bodied taste. The Corona, Toro and VII shapes were added in 2007, as was the medium-to-full-bodied maduro-wrapped blend, with a Connecticut Broadleaf wrapper, Ecuadorian binder and Dominican, Nicaraguan and Peruvian filler. All shapes are offered in boxes of 25 except for the no. VI (20s) and the tubed shapes (12s). The Great Discovery's edition is packed in boxes of 21.

ROSA CUBA

Handmade, with mixed filler, in Esteli, Nicaragua.

Wrapper: Ecuador   Binder: Nicaragua
Filler: Dominican Republic, Honduras, Nicaragua

Shape	Name	Lgth	Ring	Wrapper
Short Panatela	Angels	4½	38	CC
Corona	Flor de Rosa	5½	44	CC
Toro	Governor	6⅛	50	CC
Robusto	Herencia	4½	52	CC
Churchill	Mille Fleurs	6¾	48	CC
Grand Corona	Media Noche	6½	46	CC
Toro	Ortiz y Laboy	6½	52	CC
Lonsdale	Vargas	6½	44	CC

Introduced in 1996, this line offers a medium-bodied flavor with a magnificent Ecuador-grown, Sumatra-seed wrapper, in economical bundles of 20.

HANDMADE CIGARS: BRAND LISTINGS

ROUGH RIDER SWEETS
Handmade in Esteli, Nicaragua.

Wrapper: Nicaragua   *Binder: Nicaragua*   *Filler: Nicaragua*

Shape	Name	Lgth	Ring	Wrapper
Cheroot	Sweets	4½	38	CM

This rustic cigar was introduced by Indianhead in 2004. It has a clean-cut head and an uncut foot. A rarity, it's a handmade, all-tobacco cheroot, right out of a Spaghetti Western! It's offered in cedar boxes of 50 and packs of four in natural, Gold Dust Amaretto, Mud Slide Rum and Double Shot Whiskey.

ROXOR
Handmade in Esteli, Nicaragua.
Wrapper: Cameroon, Nicaragua, USA/Connecticut

Binder: Nicaragua   *Filler: Nicaragua*

Shape	Name	Lgth	Ring	Wrapper
Robusto	Robusto	5	54	CC-CM-Ma
Toro	Toro	6	54	CC-CM-Ma
Double Corona	Churchill	7	54	CC-CM-Ma
Torpedo	Torpedo	7	54	CC-CM-Ma

A medium-bodied cigar with a wild green-X band, introduced in 2005! It's offered with a choice of a Cameroon, Connecticut Shade or Nicaraguan-grown maduro wrapper, in clamshell boxes of 20.

ROYAL DOMINICAN   ★*New*★
Handmade in Tamboril, Dominican Republic.

Wrapper: Ecuador   *Binder: Dom. Rep.*   *Filler: Dom. Rep.*

Shape	Name	Lgth	Ring	Wrapper
Double Corona	Churchill	7	50	CC
Torpedo	Torpedo	5½	54	CC
Robusto	Robusto	5	50	CC

This blend was introduced by Felipe Gregorio in 2007. It has a medium-to-full body with an Ecuadorian-grown wrapper. All sizes are offered in boxes of 20.

ROYAL JAMAICA GOLD
Handmade in La Romana, Dominican Republic.

Wrapper: Nicaragua   Binder: Nicaragua   Filler: Honduras, Jamaica, Nicaragua

Shape	Name	Lgth	Ring	Wrapper
Petit Corona	Corona	5	44	CM
Grand Corona	Park Lane	6	47	CM
Short Panatela	Pirates	4½	38	CM
Robusto	Robusto	5	52	CM
Toro	Toro	6	52	CM
Torpedo	Belicoso	6⅛	52	CM
Double Corona	Churchill	7	54	CM

This is a totally new formulation of the Royal Jamaica brand, introduced by Altadis USA in 2004. It offers a medium-to-full-bodied taste and is elegantly presented in individual sleeves in boxes of 25.

ROYALES
Handmade in Santiago, Dominican Republic.

Wrapper: Indonesia   Binder: Brazil   Filler: Brazil, Dom. Rep.

Shape	Name		Lgth	Ring	Wrapper
Giant	No. 1		8½	52	CC
Double Corona	No. 2		7½	52	CC
Toro	No. 3		6	50	CC
Robusto	No. 4		5	50	CC
Lonsdale	No. 5		6⅝	44	CC
Long Corona	No. 6		6	42	CC
Petit Corona	No. 8		4½	44	CC
Toro	Glass Tube	*(glass tubes)*	6	50	CC
Slim Panatela	Babies		5¼	33	CC
Toro	6x60		6	60	CC

Introduced in 1992, Royales is a careful hand-blend of leaves, including a Java wrapper, that produces a mild cigar with a rich bouquet. All sizes are offered in 25s except for the Babies (60s) and tubed cigars (10s).

RUM RUNNER
Handmade in Yogyakarta, Indonesia.

Wrapper: Indonesia   *Binder: Indonesia*   *Filler: Brazil, Dom. Rep., Indonesia*

Shape	Name	Lgth	Ring	Wrapper
Perfecto	Cruzer	6	48	CM
Short Panatela	Wench	4½	36	CM
Petit Corona	Buccaneer	4¾	42	CM
Double Corona	Canon	7	50	CM
Lonsdale	Pirate	7	42	CM
	Machine-bunched:			
Cigarillo	Treasures	3⅝	20	CM

This is the original version of the Rum Runner, made in Indonesia. It has a medium body, is also made with medium filler and is offered in boxes of 25 for most sizes except for the Treasures, offered in 50s and the Canon, offered in 11.

RUY LOPEZ
Handmade, with short filler, in Danli, Honduras.

Wrapper: Ecuador   *Binder: Honduras*   *Filler: Dom. Rep., Honduras, Nicaragua*

This one-size (6 x 42) brand was machine-made for many years, but switched to handmade in 2002. It offers a medium-bodied taste in three flavors: Irish Cream, rum and vanilla. It is available in bundles of 25.

SABOR CUBANO
Handmade in Santiago, Dominican Republic

Wrapper: Brazil   *Binder: Honduras*   *Filler: Dom. Rep., Nicaragua*

Shape	Name	Lgth	Ring	Wrapper
Petit Corona	Coronita	4½	44	Ma
Torpedo	Petit Torpedo	5	54	Ma
Toro	Corona Gorda	6	52	Ma

Churchill	Grand Corona	7	48	Ma
Torpedo	Grand Torpedo	7	54	Ma
Robusto	Robusto	5	50	Ma
Long Corona	Corona	6	44	Ma

Here is another flavorful blend from Luis Sanchez at the Real Tabacalera Sanchez-Romay. Medium in body, this all-maduro line was introduced in 1997 and is offered in boxes of 20.

SABROSO
Handmade in Esteli, Nicaragua.

Wrapper: Ecuador *Binder: Nicaragua* *Filler: Nicaragua*

Shape	Name	Lgth	Ring	Wrapper
Robusto	Numero Uno	4¾	50	CC
Long Corona	Numero Dos	6	44	CC
Toro	Numero Tres	6	50	CC
Churchill	Numero Cuatro	7	48	CC
Giant	Numero Cinco	8½	52	CC

Introduced in 1996, this value-packed brand from Nicaragua offers a full-bodied taste and an excellent value. Sabroso cigars are packaged in bundles of 25.

ST. CROIX
Handmade, with mixed filler, in Santiago, Dominican Republic.

Wrapper: Dom. Rep. *Binder: Dom. Rep.* *Filler: Dom. Rep., Indonesia*

These are medium-bodied, flavored cigars, first offered in 1997. You can have your choice of Bing Cherry, Dutch Chocolate, French Vanilla, Rum Galleons, Liquorice Stix or Hazelnut in three different sizes in boxes of 26 or 50 (Cigarillos).

SAINT LUIS REY
Handmade in Santa Rosa de Copan, Honduras.

Wrapper: Mexico, Nicaragua *Binder: Nicaragua* *Filler: Honduras, Nicaragua, Peru*

Shape	Name	Lgth	Ring	Wrapper
Cigarillo	Luisitas	4⅞	24	CM-Ma
Short Panatela	No. 5	4½	38	CM

Corona	Corona	(glass tube avail.)	5½	44	CM
Toro	Double Corona		6½	48	CM
Toro	Toro		6	50	CM-Ma
Torpedo	Belicoso		6⅛	52	CM-Ma
Double Corona	Churchill		7	52	CM-Ma
Robusto	Rothchilde		5	54	CM-Ma
Robusto	Titan		5½	60	CM-Ma

This old Cuban brand was introduced in a Honduran version at *LE CIGAR NOIR - BEVERLY HILLS* on May 1, 1996. Re-blended for 2003 by Altadis USA, it is full-bodied but smooth on the draw. The Rothchilde was offered with a Mexican-grown maduro wrapper first and the other maduro-wrapped shapes were added in 2004. Most shapes are available in boxes of 25, except for the Rothchilde (offered in 25 or 50s), the Coronas en Tubo (20s) and the Luisitas (in 10s).

SAINT LUIS REY SERIE G
Handmade in Santa Rosa de Copan, Honduras.
Wrapper: Nicaragua, USA/Connecticut
Binder: Nicaragua, USA/Connecticut   *Filler: Honduras, Nicaragua*

Shape	Name	Lgth	Ring	Wrapper
Robusto	Short Robusto	4¼	54	CM-Ma
Robusto	Rothchilde	5	56	CM-Ma
Double Corona	Churchill	7	58	CM-Ma
Torpedo	Belicoso	6⅛	54	CM
Toro	No. 6	6	60	CM-Ma

The "SLR" Serie G was introduced in 2006, featuring a Connecticut Broadleaf maduro wrapper and binder and Nicaraguan filler for a smooth, medium-to-full-bodied taste. In 2007, the natural-wrapped shapes debuted, with Nicaraguan wrapper and binder and Honduran and Nicaraguan filler. The brand was originally offered in all-black boxes of 22, but are now in 25s.

SALUTE TO ARMS
Handmade in Esteli, Nicaragua.
Wrapper: Nicaragua   *Binder: Nicaragua*   *Filler: Nicaragua*

HANDMADE CIGARS: BRAND LISTINGS

Shape	Name	Lgth	Ring	Wrapper
Double Corona	Salute to Arms	7	50	CM

This unique brand is offered in your choice of U.S. Air Force, Army, Marines or Navy insignia boxes. The blend is of medium body, featuring a Sumatra-seed wrapper, offered in boxes of 25.

SAN CRISTOBAL ★New★
Handmade in Esteli, Nicaragua.

Wrapper: Nicaragua   Binder: Nicaragua   Filler: Nicaragua

Shape	Name	Lgth	Ring	Wrapper
Robusto	Clasico	5	50	Ma
Toro	Supremo	6	50	Ma
Grand Corona	Guajiro	6⅝	46	Ma
Torpedo	Fabuloso	6⅛	52	Ma
Double Corona	Monumento	7¼	49	Ma
Perfecto	Maestro	6	60	Ma

A stunning full-bodied blend introduced in 2007, San Cristobal is made for Ashton Distributors by Jose "Pepin" Garcia in Nicaragua. These cigars have a rich flavor and an extra-dark wrapper, offered in all-cedar chests of 22.

SAN MARTIN
Handmade in Tarapoto, Peru.

Wrapper: Peru   Binder: Peru   Filler: Peru

Shape	Name	Lgth	Ring	Wrapper
Churchill	Corona 1 Churchill	6¾	48	CM
Robusto	Corona Gorda	5	48	CM
Corona	Corona 4	5¼	42	CM
Panatela	Corona 5	6¾	38	CM
Perfecto	Perfecto	4	52	CM
Pyramid	Piramid	6	52	CM
Robusto	Robusto	4¾	52	CM

HANDMADE CIGARS: BRAND LISTINGS

SANTA ANA
Handmade in Santiago, Dominican Republic.

Wrapper: Dom. Rep.   *Binder: Dom. Rep.*   *Filler: Dom. Rep.*

Introduced in 1988, this is a vanilla-flavored, medium-bodied cigar with a Connecticut-seed wrapper, offered in two sizes in bundles or boxes of 25.

SANTA CRUZ
Handmade, with short filler, in Kingston, Jamaica.

Wrapper: USA/Connecticut   *Binder: Mexico*   *Filler: Dom. Rep., Jamaica, Mexico*

Shape	Name	Lgth	Ring	Wrapper
Petit Corona	Pirates	5	40	CC

Here is a mild cigar, introduced in 2003 by Barrington House International, offered in packs of five, available in two versions. The handmade edition (blue label) features a Connecticut wrapper and is all-tobacco, while a second version (red label) has a homogenized wrapper.

SANTA DAMIANA
Handmade in La Romana, Dominican Republic.

Wrapper: USA/Connecticut   *Binder: Dom. Rep.*   *Filler: Dom. Rep.*

Shape	Name	Lgth	Ring	Wrapper
Churchill	No. 100	6¾	48	CI
Corona Extra	No. 300	5½	46	CI
Robusto	No. 500	5	50	CI
Pyramid	No. 600	6	50	CI
Lonsdale	No. 700	6⅝	44	CI

Re-focused in 2003 on its original blend and shapes, this is a beautifully-finished cigar that defines what a "claro" wrapper looks like. Santa Damiana is a mild-to-medium-bodied smoke that originated in Cuba. Today's Dominican-manufactured Santa Damiana was introduced in 1992. All shapes are offered in cabinets of 25.

SANTA ROSA ★*Returns*★
Handmade in Santa Rosa de Copan, Honduras.

Wrapper: Ecuador   *Binder: Honduras*   *Filler: Honduras, Nicaragua*

HANDMADE CIGARS: BRAND LISTINGS

Shape	Name		Lgth	Ring	Wrapper
Double Corona	Churchill		7	50	CC
Corona	Corona		5½	44	CC
Belicoso	Pyramid		6⅛	52	CC
Robusto	Rothchilde		5	54	CC
Robusto	Sancho Panza		4¾	50	CC
Toro	Toro		6	50	CC
Toro	Tubo	(tubed)	6	48	CC

A favorite for many years as a mild-to-medium-bodied cigar, Santa Rosa returned to the U.S. market in 2007. It features a Connecticut-seed wrapper and is offered in boxes of 27.

SANTAMARIA
Handmade in Cumana, Venezuela.

Wrapper: Ecuador   *Binder: Venezuela*   *Filler: Venezuela*

Here is a medium-bodied brand from Venezuela, using two-year-old leaves. It offers a smooth taste in six sizes, presented in all-cedar boxes of 25.

SANTIAGO CABANA
Handmade in Key Largo, Florida, USA.
Wrapper: Ecuador, Mexico

Binder: Nicaragua   *Filler: Dom.Rep., Honduras, Nicaragua*

Shape	Name	Lgth	Ring	Wrapper
Robusto	Robusto	5	50	CC-Ma
Toro	Corona Gorda	6	52	CC-Ma
Churchill	Churchill	7	48	CC-Ma
Torpedo	Torpedo	6¼	54	CC-Ma

This brand must have nine lives. It has been on and off the market several times since its original introduction in the mid-1990s. This version has a choice of natural (Ecuadorian) or Mexican maduro wrapper, a medium-bodied taste and is offered in boxes of 25 or bundles of 50.

HANDMADE CIGARS: BRAND LISTINGS

SANTIAGO FUMAS

Handmade, with short filler, in Santiago, Dominican Republic.

Wrapper: Indonesia   Binder: Dom. Rep.   Filler: Dom. Rep.

Shape	Name	Lgth	Ring	Wrapper
Long Corona	Fumas	6	44	CM
Long Corona	Cazadores	6	44	CM
Churchill	Especiales	6⅜	48	CM
Robusto	Robusto	5	50	CM

This is a medium-bodied blend from Miami Cigar & Co. which features a Sumatra wrapper and is available in value-priced bundles of 25.

SANTIAGO SILK

Handmade in Villa Gonzalez, Dominican Republic.

Wrapper: Ecuador   Binder: Dom. Rep.   Filler: Dom. Rep.

Shape	Name	Lgth	Ring	Wrapper
Robusto	Robusto	4½	50	CC
Lonsdale	Lonsdale	6½	44	CC
Toro	Toro	6	50	CC
Churchill	Churchill	7	48	CC
Giant	Presidente	8	50	CC

Introduced in 1997, Santiago Silk has a medium-bodied flavor thanks to its Connecticut-seed wrapper. It's offered in individual cellophane sleeves in all-cedar boxes of 25.

SAVINELLI APERITIFS

Handmade in Santiago, Dominican Republic.

Wrapper: Brazil, USA/Connecticut   Binder: Dom. Rep.   Filler: Dom. Rep.

Shape	Name	Lgth	Ring	Wrapper
Small Panatela	Aperitif	4	30	CC-Ma

The small Apertif is made at the La Aurora factory and is available in ten-packs in six flavors: natural, maduro, honey, café, exotica and vanilla.

SAVINELLI EXTREMELY LIMITED RESERVE
Handmade in Santiago, Dominican Republic.

Wrapper: USA/Connecticut   Binder: Dom. Rep.   Filler: Dom. Rep.

Shape	Name	Lgth	Ring	Wrapper
Churchill	No. 1 Churchill	7¼	48	CC-Ma
Grand Corona	No. 2 Corona Extra	6⅝	46	CC
Long Corona	No. 3 Lonsdale	6¼	43	CC
Toro	No. 4 Double Corona	6	50	CC-Ma
Corona	No. 5 Xtraordinaire	5½	44	CC
Robusto	No. 6 Robusto	5	49	CC-Ma
Torpedo	No. 7 Belicoso	6	49	CC

"Extremely limited" is the key phrase in the name of this brand. Long famous for their high-quality pipes, the Savinelli tradition of craftsmanship is continued in this limited-distribution line of medium-bodied cigars introduced in 1995. All are made by the Tabacalera A. Fuente and offered in boxes of 25.

SAVINELLI FUERTE
Handmade in Esteli, Nicaragua.

Wrapper: Nicaragua   Binder: Nicaragua   Filler: Nicaragua

Shape	Name	Lgth	Ring	Wrapper
Corona	Corona S	5¾	44	CM
Robusto	Robusto	5	50	CM
Toro	Toro	6	50	CM
Robusto	Corona Gorda	5½	52	CM
Churchill	Churchill	6⅞	48	CM
Torpedo	Torpedo	6	52	CM

Introduced in 2004, this is a medium-to-full-bodied cigar with a Criollo wrapper grown in the Jalapa region. It's offered in elegant cabinets of 25.

SAVINELLI LIGA ESPECIAL
Handmade in Esteli, Nicaragua.

Wrapper: Nicaragua   Binder: Nicaragua   Filler: Nicaragua

HANDMADE CIGARS: BRAND LISTINGS

Shape	Name	Lgth	Ring	Wrapper
Robusto	Robusto	5	50	CM
Robusto	Corona Gorda	5½	52	CM
Torpedo	Torpedo	6	52	CM
Toro	Doble Corona	6½	54	CM

This is a Nicaraguan puro with a medium-to-full body, introduced in 2005. It's made by Tabacos Puros and offered in boxes of 20.

SAVINELLI NICARAGUA RESERVE
Handmade in Esteli, Nicaragua.

Wrapper: Nicaragua   *Binder: Nicaragua*   *Filler: Nicaragua*

Shape	Name	Lgth	Ring	Wrapper
Corona	Corona	5½	44	CM
Grand Corona	Corona Gorda	6⅝	46	CM
Robusto	Robusto	5	52	CM
Toro	Toro	6	50	CM
Double Corona	Churchill	7	52	CM
Torpedo	Torpedo	6½	54	CM

Here is a medium-bodied, box-pressed blend, introduced by Savinelli in 2002. It features a specially cross-bred Habana 2000 and Criollo wrapper and is offered in elegant slide-top boxes of 25.

SAVINELLI SPECIAL SELECTION
Handmade in Esteli, Nicaragua.

Wrapper: Ecuador   *Binder: Nicaragua*   *Filler: Nicaragua*

Shape	Name	Lgth	Ring	Wrapper
Torpedo	Robusto	5	52	CC
Torpedo	Toro	6	52	CC
Torpedo	Torpedo	6½	54	CC

The Tabacalera Oliva makes this medium-bodied, peppery cigar, introduced in 2005. All three sizes have torpedo-style heads and are offered in boxes of 20.

HANDMADE CIGARS: BRAND LISTINGS

SAVOY
Handmade, with sandwich filler, in Esteli, Nicaragua.

Wrapper: Ecuador, USA/Connecticut   Binder: Nicaragua   Filler: Nicaragua

Shape	Name	Lgth	Ring	Wrapper
Corona	Corona	5½	44	CC-Ma
Lonsdale	Corona Grande	6½	44	CC-Ma
Robusto	Robusto	5	50	CC-Ma
Toro	Toro	6	50	CC-Ma
Churchill	Churchill	7	48	CC-Ma
Torpedo	Torpedo	6	50	CC-Ma

This is a new blend under an old name, introduced in 2002 by Ashton Distributors. The wrapper is from Sumatra seed, with a medium body and all shapes are offered in boxes of 25. The maduro series, using a Connecticut Broadleaf wrapper, was introduced in 2005.

SCARFACE
Handmade in Santiago, Dominican Republic and Danli, Honduras.

SMALL CIGARS:

Wrapper: Indonesia   Binder: Dom. Rep.   Filler: Dom. Rep.

SAY HELLO TO MY LITTLE FRIEND:

Wrapper: Brazil, Ecuador   Binder: none   Filler: Costa Rica, Honduras, Peru

TONY MONTANA SERIES:
Wrapper: Brazil, Ecuador, Honduras

Binder: Honduras   Filler: Costa Rica, Honduras, Peru

Shape	Name	Lgth	Ring	Wrapper
Cigarillo	Mini	4	26	CM
Cigarillo	Cigarillo	3	20	CM
	Say Hello to My Little Friend:			
Cigarillo	Mini	4	28	CM-Ma

HANDMADE CIGARS: BRAND LISTINGS

	Tony Montana series:			
Robusto	5x52	5	52	CM
Double Corona	7x54	7	54	CM
Double Corona	The World is Yours	7	54	Triple

This started as a mild, handmade line of small cigars made in the Dominican Republic and introduced in 2006. It is themed after the famed 1983 film of the same name that starred Al Pacino. The Mini and Cigarillo are flavored, offered in Mango, Mocha Latte, rum and vanilla in both sizes.

The Say Hello to My Little Friend and Tony Montana Series were introduced in 2007 and are made in Honduras. The Tony Montana line has a choice of three styles based on the wrapper: "Power," with a Honduran Habano wrapper (medium body); "Money," with an Ecuadorian-grown, Sumatra-seed wrapper (mild) and "Respect," with a Brazilian maduro wrapper (full). The World Is Yours is an amazing cigar with all three wrappers on one cigar: Ecuadorian at the foot, Honduran in the center and Brazilian at the head! The 5x52 and 7x54 are offered in boxes of 30; The World Is Yours is available in cases of 18 individual coffins.

SCP
Handmade in Frankfort, New York, USA.
Wrapper: Cameroon   Binder: Cameroon   Filler: Brazil, Honduras, Jamaica, Nicaragua

Shape	Name	Lgth	Ring	Wrapper
Giant	Le Proxenete	8	46	Ma
Giant Corona	Exotique	8	40	Ma
Long Panatela	La Fume Fatale	8	36	Ma

This is a part of the Lars Tetens line and among the strongest of the Lars Tetens blends. All of the tobaccos are long aged and the blend is much more than the phrase "full-bodied" can imply. All are offered in three-packs.

SELECTO PURO DOMINICANO   ★New★
Handmade in Villa Gonzalez, Dominican Republic.
Wrapper: Dom. Rep.   Binder: Dom. Rep.   Filler: Dom. Rep., Nicaragua

Shape	Name	Lgth	Ring	Wrapper
Giant	Presidente	8	50	CC

HANDMADE CIGARS: BRAND LISTINGS

Double Corona	Doble Corona	7½	50	CC
Double Corona	Giant	7	54	CC
Torpedo	Torpedo	6½	52	CC
Robusto	Robusto	5½	52	CC
Toro	Toro	6	50	CC
Churchill	Churchill	7	48	CC
Robusto	Rothschild	5	50	CC
Long Corona	Lonsdale	6	44	CC
Long Panatela	Panatela	7	38	CC
Corona Extra	Corona	5½	46	CC

This was a Cigar Boom brand revived, with a new blend, in 2007. It is full-bodied and features a Dominican-grown wrapper. It's available in boxes of 25 for all sizes.

SEMPER FI
Handmade in Danli, Honduras.

Wrapper: Honduras   Binder: Honduras   Filler: Honduras, Nicaragua

Shape	Name	Lgth	Ring	Wrapper
Robusto	Robusto	5	50	CM
Toro	Toro	6	50	CM
Churchill	Churchill	7	48	CM
Torpedo	Figurado	6	54	CM

Made by Camacho Cigars and distributed by Alliance Cigar, this is a salute to the United States Marine Corps and its motto *Semper Fidelis* ("always faithful"), with a Connecticut-seed wrapper, offered in boxes of 25.

SEÑOR DAVID
Handmade in Santiago, Dominican Republic.

Wrapper: Indonesia   Binder: Indonesia   Filler: Dom. Rep., Nicaragua

This is a medium-to-full-bodied cigar made in three sizes, featuring Piloto Cubano filler leaves and a Sumatra-grown wrapper. It's offered in boxes of 25.

SERGIO MASTER ★New★
Handmade in Santiago, Dominican Republic.
Wrapper: Brazil, Indonesia, USA/Connecticut   Binder: Dom. Rep.   Filler: Dom. Rep.

The Cigar Factory del Yaque makes this medium-to-full-bodied blend with a
choice of Brazilian maduro, Connecticut or Sumatra wrappers. All four sizes are
offered in boxes of 25.

SHAGGYS
Handmade in Santiago, Dominican Republic.
Wrapper: Ecuador   Binder: Dom. Rep.   Filler: Cuba, Dom. Rep.

Shape	Name	Lgth	Ring	Wrapper
Double Corona	Shaggys	7½	52	CM

This brand was introduced in 2002, has an open foot and offers a messy, if
medium-bodied smoke, in boxes of 25.

SHAKESPEARE
Handmade in Santiago, Dominican Republic.
Wrapper: USA/Connecticut   Binder: Dom. Rep.   Filler: Dom. Rep.

Shape	Name	Lgth	Ring	Wrapper
Corona	Corona	5½	43	CC
Toro	Oxford	6	49	CC-Ma
Lonsdale	Lonsdale	6½	43	CC
Panatela	Palma	6⅞	39	CC
Slim Panatela	Panatela	6	32	CC
Double Corona	Stratford	7½	49	CC-Ma

This is an old brand name, brought back to life in 2006 by General Cigar and
distributed by Cigars by Santa Clara. It's mild in body and offers a choice of
Connecticut Shade or Broadleaf maduro wrappers in bundles of 20.

SHIRLEY TETENS RESERVE
Handmade in Frankfort, New York, USA.
Wrapper: USA/Connecticut   Binder: Ecuador   Filler: Dom. Rep., Ecuador

Shape	Name	Lgth	Ring	Wrapper
Double Coroba	Mother's Little Helper	7½	50	CM
Robusto	Mom	4½	50	CM
Petit Corona	Satisfaction	5	42	CM

This is a member of the Lars Tetens line and was created by Shirley Tetens (mother of Lars) in 1984-85. The overall flavor is mild and the blend has attained wide attention in Europe.

SIGLO 21
Handmade in Santiago, Dominican Republic.

Wrapper: USA/Connecticut   Binder: Dom. Rep.   Filler: Dom. Rep.

Shape	Name	Lgth	Ring	Wrapper
Robusto	No. 1	4½	50	CC
Lonsdale	No. 2	6½	44	CC
Toro	No. 3	6	50	CC
Churchill	No. 4	7	48	CC
Giant	No. 5	8	50	CC
Torpedo	No. 6	6¾	52	CC

Introduced in 1996 as a salute to the 21st century ("siglo" in Spanish). The cigars are medium-bodied, with excellent draw and a marvelous aroma. It is offered in elegant boxes of 25 cigars each.

SIGNATURE COLLECTION
Handmade in Esteli, Nicaragua.

Wrapper: Ecuador   Binder: Nicaragua   Filler: Nicaragua

Shape	Name	Lgth	Ring	Wrapper
Robusto	Robusto	5	50	CM
Perfecto	Diablo	5¾	54	CM
Torpedo	Torpedo	6	52	CM
Double Corona	Churchill	7	50	CM

styles, with a Connecticut Shade, Sumatran and Connecticut Broadleaf maduro wrapper. They're medium to medium-to-full in body, offered in boxes of 25.

SOLEDAD
Handmade in Danli, Honduras.

Wrapper: Ecuador　　　*Binder: Indonesia*　　*Filler: Honduras, Nicaragua*

Shape	Name	Lgth	Ring	Wrapper
Double Corona	Churchill	7	50	CC
Corona	Corona	5½	42	CC
Lonsdale	Lonsdale	6½	44	CC
Robusto	Robusto	4½	50	CC
Toro	Toro	6	50	CC

Famous Smoke Shop gave new life to this old name in cigars in 2004. This blend has a mild-to-medium body and features a Connecticut-seed wrapper in bundles of 25.

SOSA
Handmade in Santiago, Dominican Republic.

Wrapper: Ecuador, USA/Connecticut　　*Binder: Dom. Rep.*　　*Filler: Dom. Rep.*

Shape	Name	Lgth	Ring	Wrapper
Churchill	Churchill	7	49	CC-Ma
Robusto	Wavell	5	50	CC-Ma
Lonsdale	Lonsdale	6¾	43	CC
Corona	Brevas	5½	43	CC
Pyramid	Piramides	6½	54	CC-Ma
Panatela	Santa Fe	6	35	CC
Double Corona	Magnums	7¾	52	CC
Toro	Governor	6	50	CC-Ma

Juan Sosa is well known in the cigar trade for excellent products which are modestly priced. Originally made in Miami in 1964 and then in the Dominican Republic since 1974, this line bears his name and does it proud with a medium bodied-smoke and a choice of an Ecuadorian-grown Sumatra-seed wrapper or,

HANDMADE CIGARS: BRAND LISTINGS

for those who prefer maduro, a well-aged Connecticut Broadleaf. Sosa cigars are presented in slide-top cedar boxes of 25.

SOSA EXCLUSIVE SERIES
Handmade in Santiago, Dominican Republic.

Wrapper: Ecuador, Mexico   Binder: Dom. Rep.   Filler: Dom. Rep.

Shape	Name	Lgth	Ring	Wrapper
Corona	Cetro	5¾	44	CC-Ma
Petit Corona	Petit Cetro	4¼	40	CC-Ma
Toro	Gran Cetro	6	50	CC-Ma

Blended by Juan Sosa and introduced in 1999, you can choose from a Sumatra-seed wrapper grown in Ecuador or a maduro wrapper from Mexico. In either style, it's full-bodied, available in boxes of 25.

SOSA SUPER SELECTION
Handmade in Santiago, Dominican Republic.

Wrapper: Mexico   Binder: Dom. Rep.   Filler: Dom. Rep.

Shape	Name	Lgth	Ring	Wrapper
Torpedo	II	6¼	52	Ma
Corona	III	5¾	44	Ma
Robusto	V	5	50	Ma
Toro	VII	6	50	Ma
Double Corona	VIII	7	50	Ma

This "super selection" of the famous Sosa brand was introduced in 2000. It is offered in varnished, cedar-lined boxes of 24 without cellophane, offering a medium-bodied taste from the Tabacalera A. Fuente.

SPAG & CO.
Handmade in Santiago, Dominican Republic.

CALICO JACK – BLACK LABEL:

Wrapper: Indonesia   Binder: USA/Connecticut   Filler: Dom. Rep.

HANDMADE CIGARS: BRAND LISTINGS

CALICO JACK – BLACKBEARD:

Wrapper: Cameroon   *Binder: USA/Connecticut*   *Filler: Dom. Rep.*

CALICO JACK – RED LABEL:

Wrapper: USA/Connecticut   *Binder: USA/Connecticut*   *Filler: Dom. Rep.*

Shape	Name	Lgth	Ring	Wrapper
	Calico Jack - Black Label:			
Double Corona	Churchill	7	50	CM
Robusto	Robusto	5	52	CM
Torpedo	Torpedo	6	56	CM
Petit Corona	Petit Corona	4	40	CM
	Calico Jack - Red Label:			
Robusto	Robusto	5	54	CC
Torpedo	Torpedo	5½	58	CC
Petit Corona	Petit Corona	4	40	CC
	Blackbeard:			
Double Corona	Churchill	7	50	CM
Robusto	Robusto	5	52	CM
Torpedo	Torpedo	5½	58	CM
Toro	Toro	6	54	CM
Petit Corona	Petit Corona	4	40	CM

Introduced in 2006, this is a medium-to-full-bodied cigar in the Black Label style (skull & crossbones band) and medium-bodied in the Red Label (skull & crossbones) and Blackbeard (devil on the band). You can experience the pirate's brand in 8-9-8 boxes of 25 or bundles of 25 for the Petit Corona.

SPECIAL BLENDS BY H. KELNER
Handmade in Santiago, Dominican Republic.

Wrapper: Ecuador   *Binder: USA/Connecticut*   *Filler: Dom. Rep., Peru*

Shape	Name	Lgth	Ring	Wrapper
Petit Corona		4	41	CC

Torpedo		6	41	CC
Robusto		5	50	CC
Grand Corona		6	46	CC
Toro		6½	50	CC
Torpedo		5¾	52	CC
Double Corona		7¼	50	CC
Churchill		8	48	CC

Formerly known as "Kelner Seconds," these are now offered in bundles of 25 or bulks of 100 (starting in 2001) by the Alec Bradley Cigar Co. They are an excellent value with a mild-to-medium body.

SPIRIT OF CUBA
Handmade, with mixed filler, in Danli, Honduras.

Wrapper: Nicaragua, USA/Connecticut

Binder: Honduras, Nicaragua   Filler: Colombia, Honduras, Nicaragua

Shape	Name	Lgth	Ring	Wrapper
Robusto	Robusto	5	50	CC-CM
Churchill	Churchill	7	48	CC-CM

Here is a three-blend brand, introduced in 2003 by the Alec Bradley Cigar Co. It is available with a "Natural" wrapper (grown in Connecticut) and Honduran binder, a "Habano" wrapper (grown in Nicaragua, with a Nicaraguan binder) and a "Corojo" wrapper, also grown in Nicaragua, with a Honduran binder. The Habano blend is mild-to-medium in body and the Natural and Corojo blends are medium in body. All are made with sandwich filler, available in value-priced bundles (all three blends) or boxes (Natural and Habano blends) of 25.

STAG
Handmade, with mixed filler, in Danli, Honduras.

Wrapper: Honduras   Binder: Nicaragua   Filler: Honduras, Nicaragua

Shape	Name	Lgth	Ring	Wrapper
Slim Panatela	Panetela	6¼	34	CM
Corona	Corona	5¼	42	CM
Toro	Toro	6	50	CM

| Lonsdale | Lonsdale | 7 | 44 | CM |
| Giant | Gigante | 8½ | 52 | CM |

This is a mild-bodied blend, available in bargain-priced packs of ten.

STIXX ★*New*★
Handmade in Guayaquil, Ecuador.

Wrapper: Ecuador   *Binder: Ecuador*   *Filler: Ecuador*

Shape	Name	Lgth	Ring	Wrapper
Toro		6½	56	CM-Ma

Produced for Marshall Holman's Old School Cigars, this is a medium-bodied smoke with a Cameroon-seed wrapper or full-bodied with a maduro wrapper. It's offered in one size (no shape name) in boxes of 100.

STRADIVARIUS DE LOS MAESTROS ★*New*★
Handmade in Santiago, Dominican Republic.
Wrapper: USA/Connecticut

Binder: Dom. Rep.   *Filler: Dom. Rep., Mexico, Nicaragua*

Shape	Name	Lgth	Ring	Wrapper
Robusto	Robusto Major	5½	50	CC
Lonsdale	Lonsdale	6¾	43	CC
Double Corona	Churchill	7½	49	CC

When General Cigar's Daniel Nunez began putting away 100 or so bales of wrapper leaf 15 years ago, he wasn't sure how it would be used. But the 1992 wrapper he saved is the key to the Stradivarius de los Maestros line introduced in mid-2007. The 15-year-old Connecticut Shade wrapper is the key to the mild-to-medium-bodied taste of this ultra-premium cigar. Only 100,000 cigars will be produced for this brand annually and each year, a new (still 15 years old) wrapper will be employed. Each cigar is offered in an individually wax-sealed, wooden coffin inside boxes of 10.

SUAREZ GRAN RESERVE
Handmade in Santiago, Dominican Republic.
Wrapper: USA/Connecticut   *Binder: Dom. Rep.*   *Filler: Dom. Rep.*

HANDMADE CIGARS: BRAND LISTINGS

Shape	Name	Lgth	Ring	Wrapper
Robusto	Robusto	5	50	CC
Double Corona	Presidente	7½	52	CC
Grand Corona	Royal Corona	6½	46	CC
Long Panatela	Lonsdale	7	36	CC

This blend features a mild-bodied Connecticut wrapper in this carefully-produced brand. It is offered in boxes of 25 and smaller packs except for the Lonsdale, available in packs of six only.

SUMMUS ★New★
Handmade in Tamboril, Dominican Republic.

Wrapper: Mexico, USA/Connecticut   Binder: Dom. Rep.   Filler: Dom. Rep.

Shape	Name	Lgth	Ring	Wrapper
Robusto	Robusto	5	50	CC-Ma
Double Corona	Churchill	7	50	CC-Ma

This blend was created by childhood friends Felipe Gregorio and famed race driver Eddie Cheever, Jr. in two styles: Americano with a Connecticut wrapper (mild-to-medium body) and Latino, with a Mexican maduro wrapper (medium-to-full). Both debuted in 2007 and are offered in boxes of 10.

SUPERVISOR SELECTION ★New★
Handmade in Danli, Honduras.
Wrapper: Nicaragua

Binder: Costa Rica   Filler: Colombia, Honduras, Mexico, Nicaragua

Shape	Name	Lgth	Ring	Wrapper
Toro	Double Corona	6⅜	60	CM
Giant	President	9¼	50	CM
Robusto	Robusto	5	58	CM
Toro	Toro	6½	54	CM
Torpedo	Torpedo	7	58	CM

This medium-to-full-bodied blend comes from the Alec Bradley Cigar Co. It's offered in national distribution by Cigar Domain in boxes of 20.

TABACALERA PERDOMO ESTATE SELECCION VINTAGE 1991
Handmade in Esteli, Nicaragua.
Wrapper: Cameroon, Nicaragua, USA/Connecticut

Binder: Nicaragua   *Filler: Nicaragua*

Shape	Name		Lgth	Ring	Wrapper
Petit Corona	Imperio		5	44	CM-Ma
Toro	Epicure		6	54	CM-Ma
Robusto	Regente		5	54	CM-Ma
Double Corona	Aristocrata		7	54	CM-Ma
Toro	Prestigio		6½	54	CM-Ma
Toro	Nobleza	*(tubed)*	5⅝	48	CM
Toro	Maestro	*(tubed)*	6	54	CM

The "ESV 1991" is a limited-edition "white label" brand introduced in 2000 and featuring five-year-aged tobaccos and a choice of wrappers. It has a medium-bodied flavor with the Connecticut wrapper and medium-to-full-body in maduro. All are offered in mahogany boxes of 20. The tubed shapes, using Cameroon wrapper and vintage filler, appeared in 2005 and are offered in boxes of 10.

TABAMEX
Handmade in San Andres Tuxtla, Mexico.
Wrapper: USA/Connecticut   *Binder: Mexico*   *Filler: Mexico*

Shape	Name	Lgth	Ring	Wrapper
Giant	Presidente	8½	52	CM-Ma
Double Corona	Churchill	7½	50	CM-Ma
Lonsdale	Lonsdale	6⅝	42	CM-Ma
Toro	Toro	6	50	CM-Ma
Robusto	Robusto	5	50	CM-Ma
Robusto	Rothschild	4½	50	CM-Ma

This is a medium-bodied cigar offered by Famous Smoke Shop. It features a Connecticut wrapper and is available in bundles of 25.

HANDMADE CIGARS: BRAND LISTINGS

TABANTILLAS
Handmade in Santiago, Dominican Republic.

Wrapper: Ecuador, Indonesia *Binder: Dom. Rep.* *Filler: Dom. Rep.*

Shape	Name	Lgth	Ring	Wrapper
Giant	Gran Duque	8	50	CC
Robusto	Romeros	4½	52	CC-Ma
Churchill	1866	6¾	46	CC-Ma
Long Panatela	Havana Club	7¾	38	CC
Lonsdale	Reserva A	6¾	44	CC-Ma
Toro	Reserva B	6	48	CC-Ma
Double Corona	Reserva C	6¾	50	CC-Ma
Double Corona	Reserva D	7	50	CC-Ma

This brand initially appeared in 1996 and re-appeared in 1999 as a medium-bodied and spicy cigar, featuring a Javan natural-shade wrapper and an Ecuadorian-grown maduro wrapper. It is offered in boxes of 20 or 25.

TAINO CLASSICS
Handmade in Santiago, Dominican Republic.

Wrapper: Brazil, USA/Connecticut *Binder: Dom. Rep.* *Filler: Dom. Rep., Nicaragua*

Shape	Name	Lgth	Ring	Wrapper
Torpedo	Torpedo	6	52	CC-Ma
Double Corona	Churchill	7	50	CC-Ma
Toro	Toro Grande	6	54	CC-Ma

Here is a full-bodied blend, introduced in 2005 and made by members of the Taino indian tribe. It comes in either a Connecticut natural or Brazilian maduro wrapper in bundles of 25.

TAINO RESERVE
Handmade in Santiago, Dominican Republic.

Wrapper: Ecuador *Binder: Dom. Rep.* *Filler: Dom. Rep., Nicaragua*

Shape	Name	Lgth	Ring	Wrapper
Pyramid	Pyramid	6	58	CC

HANDMADE CIGARS: BRAND LISTINGS

Double Corona	Churchill	7	50	CC
Toro	Toro Grande	6	54	CC
Robusto	Robosto	5	52	CC
Grand Corona	Gran Corona	6	46	CC

This blend features a Connecticut-seed wrapper and a full-bodied taste. In was introduced in 2005 and offered in boxes of 24.

TAINO SWEETS
Handmade in Santiago, Dominican Republic.

Wrapper: Cameroon   *Binder: Dom. Rep.*   *Filler: Dom. Rep.*

Shape	*Name*	*Lgth*	*Ring*	*Wrapper*
Petit Corona	Sweets	5	42	CM
Small Panatela	Miniatures	4	32	CM

These are handmade, mild, flavored cigars offered in a choice of Cappuccino, cherry, chocolate, Hazelnut, Gran Marnier, rum, Sambuca and vanilla. The Miniatures are also offered in natural, but packed in coffee grounds!

TAINO XO
Handmade in Santiago, Dominican Republic.

Wrapper: Brazil   *Binder: Dom. Rep.*   *Filler: Dom. Rep., Nicaragua*

Shape	*Name*	*Lgth*	*Ring*	*Wrapper*
Toro	XO	6	60	Ma

Featuring a pigtail head, this is a full-bodied cigar. The tobacco is flavored with a mix of Black Sugar, cinnamon, molasses, red wine and rum that is fermented with yeast! It was introduced in 2005 and offered in boxes of 10.

TAMBOR DOMINICANO
Handmade, with mixed filler, in Santiago, Dominican Republic.
Wrapper: Brazil, Dominican Republic, Ecuador

Binder: Dominican Republic   *Filler: Dominican Republic*

Shape	*Name*	*Lgth*	*Ring*	*Wrapper*
Torpedo	Torpedo	6½	52	CC-CM-Ma

| Double Corona | Churchill | 7 | 50 | CC-CM-Ma |
| Toro | Toro Grande | 6 | 54 | CC-CM-Ma |

Take your choice of three different wrapper shades with a mild-to-medium strength in the Connecticut-seed wrapper (grown in Ecuador; white band), or medium-bodied with a Cameroon-seed wrapper grown in the Dominican Republic (red band) or a Brazilian maduro wrapper (black band). Introduced in 2005, all sizes are offered in bundles of 20.

TAMBORIL CONNECTICUT
Handmade in Tamboril, Dominican Republic.

Wrapper: USA/Connecticut   *Binder: Dom. Rep.*   *Filler: Dom. Rep.*

Shape	Name		Lgth	Ring	Wrapper
Lonsdale	Lonsdale		6½	42	CC
Long Corona	Corona		6	44	CC
Robusto	Robusto		5	52	CC
Churchill	Diablo	/perfecto tip/	7	47	CC
Double Corona	Double Corona		7½	50	CC
Torpedo	Torpedo		6	54	CC

This was a famed Cigar Boom brand resurrected by the original owner Abraham Shafir in 2005. It still offers a medium-bodied taste in this white-banded version, offered in boxes of 25.

TAMPA TROPICS
Handmade in Tampa, Florida, USA.

Wrapper: Cameroon   *Binder: Dom. Rep.*   *Filler: Dom. Rep., Nicaragua*

Produced in one size (6¼ x 52 torpedo) by the Cammarata Cigar Co. of Tampa, this blend offers a medium-bodied taste, in boxes of 25.

TATIANA
Handmade in Santiago, Dominican Republic.

Wrapper: Cameroon, Indonesia, Nicaragua   *Binder: Dom. Rep.   Filler: Dom. Rep.*

HANDMADE CIGARS: BRAND LISTINGS

Shape	Name	Lgth	Ring	Wrapper
Short Panatela	La Vita	5	38	CM
Long Corona	Classic *(tubes available)*	6	44	CM
Small Panatela	Dolce	5	30	CM
Small Panatela	Petites	4	30	CM
Cigarillo	Miniatures	3½	26	CM

This is a long-filler, medium-bodied, flavored brand from Miami Cigar & Co. featuring an Indonesian wrapper. It is available in either tins (Petite and Miniatures) or boxes of 25 or 50 in Amaretto, Cappuccino, cherry, cinnamon, chocolate, honey, Mandarin, rum, Tropical and vanilla depending on the size! The Miniatures are made with either a Cameroon (for flavors) or Nicaraguan (natural) wrapper. A special series of flavors was introduced in 2005 in the Petities and Classics sizes in Groovy Blue (berries, vanilla, Acacia Honey and Cognac), Night Cap (Marcona Almonds, vanilla, Café Arabica and Criollo Cocoa) and Waking Dream (vanilla cream, hazelnut and single-malt whiskey)!

TATUAJE
Handmade in Miami, Florida, USA.

Wrapper: Nicaragua   Binder: Nicaragua   Filler: Nicaragua

Shape	Name	Lgth	Ring	Wrapper
Corona	Noellas	5⅛	42	CM
Long Corona	Havana Cazadores	6⅜	43	CM
Robusto	Regios	5½	50	CM
Long Panatela	Especiales	7½	38	CM
Torpedo	Unicos	6⅛	52	CM
Double Corona	Tainos	7⅝	49	CM
Toro	Cojonu 2003	6½	52	CM
Robusto	Cojonu 2006	5½	52	CM
Robusto	Reserva J21	5	50	CM
Churchill	Reserva SW	7	47	CM
Giant	Reserva A Uno	9¼	47	CM

HANDMADE CIGARS: BRAND LISTINGS

Small Panatela	Petit Tatuaje	4½	32	CM
Pefecto	RC184 Ltd.	7¼	57	CM
Perfecto	RC 233 Ltd.	9⅛	55	CM
Toro	Gran Cojonu	6½	60	CM

This is a medium-to-full-bodied blend introduced by Pete Johnson in 2004 and made at El Rey de Los Habanos in Miami. It's perfectly constructed featuring a Nicaraguan Corojo wrapper and offered in elegant cedar boxes of 25, except for the Reserva A Uno, RC 184 and RC 233 (10s), Gran Cojonu (12s) and Petit Tatuaje (50).

TATUAJE HAVANA VI
Handmade in Miami, Florida, USA.

Wrapper: Nicaragua   Binder: Nicaragua   Filler: Nicaragua

Shape	Name	Lgth	Ring	Wrapper
Petit Corona	Angeles	4⅝	42	CM
Panatela	Victorias	6	38	CM
Grand Corona	Hermosos	5⅝	46	CM
Robusto	Nobles	5	50	CM
Torpedo	Aristas	6⅛	52	CM
Churchill	Almirantes	7	47	CM
Toro	Verocu 1 (West)	6¼	52	CM
Robusto	Verocu 2 (East)	5½	54	CM

Introduced in 2006, this is a medium-bodied blend produced at El Rey de Los Habanos in Miami. All sizes are offered in boxes of 24, except for the 2007-introduced regional issues Verocu 1 and 2, offered in 50s.

TATUAJE SERIES P
Handmade, with medium filler, in Miami, Florida, USA.

Wrapper: Nicaragua   Binder: Nicaragua   Filler: Nicaragua

Shape	Name	Lgth	Ring	Wrapper
Grand Corona	P1	5⅝	46	CM

Robusto	P2	5	50	CM
Toro	P3	6	50	CM
Churchill	P4	7	47	CM

Here is a medium-bodied Tatuaje blend, made with medium filler. Introduced in 2006, all sizes are offered in boxes of 31.

TAVIANO
Handmade in Santiago, Dominican Republic.
Wrapper: Cameroon   Binder: Dom. Rep.   Filler: Dominican Republic, Nicaragua

This is a medium-bodied, three-size blend introduced in 2003 by the Taviano Company of Tequesta, Florida. It features a Cameroon wrapper in elegant boxes of 25.

TE-AMO
Handmade in San Andres Tuxtla, Mexico.
Wrapper: Mexico   Binder: Mexico   Filler: Mexico

Shape	Name	Lgth	Ring	Wrapper
Lonsdale	No. 1 Relaxation	6⅝	44	CM
Long Corona	No. 2 Meditation	6	42	CM
Petit Corona	No. 4	5	42	CM
Giant	No. 6 CEO	8½	52	CM
Double Corona	No. 14 Churchill	7½	50	CM-Ma
Double Corona	No. 17 Presidente	7	50	CM
Toro	No. 19 Toro	6	50	CM-Ma
Robusto	Robusto	5½	54	CM-Ma

This very popular brand originated in the 1960s and is a product of the San Andres Valley, where all of the tobaccos for Te-Amo are grown. Considered to be medium-to-full-bodied in strength, the enthusiast has a choice of natural or maduro wrappers. Made in a wide variety of shapes and sizes, the range offered in the U.S. has been trimmed in recent years. All sizes are offered in boxes of 25 except for the C.E.O., in boxes of 10.

TE-AMO ANIVERSARIO
Handmade in San Andres Tuxtla, Mexico.

Wrapper: Mexico   Binder: Mexico   Filler: Dom. Rep., Mexico, Nicaragua

Shape	Name	Lgth	Ring	Wrapper
Grand Corona	Magnum 45	6½	45	CM
Toro	Toro	6	50	CM-Ma
Double Corona	Churchill	7½	50	CM
Robusto	Robusto	5	52	CM
Perfecto	Perfecto	5½	54	CM-Ma

This edition of the famous Te-Amo brand was introduced in 2000. It offers a Mexican-grown Habana 2000 wrapper and a medium-to-full-bodied taste in boxes of 25. The Toro and Perfecto shapes are offered in a box-pressed version, while the others are round.

TE-AMO WORLD SELECTION SERIES ★*New*★
Handmade in San Andres Tuxtla, Mexico.

DOMINICANA BLEND:

Wrapper: USA/Connecticut   Binder: Mexico   Filler: Dom. Rep., Mexico

HONDURAS BLEND:

Wrapper: Mexico   Binder: Mexico   Filler: Honduras, Mexico

NICARAGUA BLEND:

Wrapper: Mexico   Binder: Mexico   Filler: Nicaragua, Mexico

Shape	Name	Lgth	Ring	Wrapper
Double Corona	Churchill	7	54	CC-CM
Robusto	Robusto	5	54	CC-CM
Toro	Toro	6	54	CC-CM

Here is a bold experiment in flavor, introduced in 2007. The Dominicana Blend is medium in body with a Connecticut Shade wrapper, the Honduras Blend has a Corojo wrapper and is full-bodied and the Nicaragua Blend features a Criollo wrapper and is also full-bodied. The binder on all three blends is Mexican maduro and all three sizes in all three blends are offered in boxes of 15.

HANDMADE CIGARS: BRAND LISTINGS

TEXANA
Handmade in Esteli, Nicaragua.
Wrapper: Nicaragua, USA/Connecticut   *Binder: Nicaragua*   *Filler: Nicaragua*

Here is a brand which salutes the work of Robert Wooding Chappell, who grew tobacco in Texas in the middle of the 19th Century. There are three series: Texana (six shapes, introduced in 1997), mild-to-medium-bodied in flavor; the Drake (three shapes, all with Nicaraguan-grown maduro wrappers), full-bodied, and the Connecticut-wrapped Legend (three sizes), a mild smoke. You can try them in elegant wood boxes of 25.

THOMAS HINDS HONDURAN SELECTION
Handmade in Danli, Honduras.
Wrapper: Ecuador   *Binder: Honduras*   *Filler: Honduras*

Shape	Name	Lgth	Ring	Wrapper
Giant	Presidente	8½	52	CM
Double Corona	Churchill	7	49	CM
Torpedo	Torpedo	6	52	CM
Toro	Short Churchill	6	50	CM
Robusto	Robusto	5	50	CM
Corona	Corona	5½	42	CM

Introduced in the U.S. in 1994, Thomas Hinds Honduran Selection are premium, full-bodied cigars. The long-leaf filler and double binder are of Honduran origin, while the wrapper is a spicy Ecuadorian leaf. Look for it in cedar boxes of 25.

THOMAS HINDS NICARAGUAN SELECTION
Handmade in Esteli, Nicaragua.
Wrapper: Ecuador   *Binder: Nicaragua*   *Filler: Nicaragua*

Shape	Name	Lgth	Ring	Wrapper
Torpedo	Torpedo	6	52	CC-Ma
Double Corona	Churchill	7	49	CC-Ma
Toro	Short Churchill	6	50	CC-Ma
Corona	Corona	5½	42	CC-Ma
Robusto	Robusto	5	50	CC-Ma

HANDMADE CIGARS: BRAND LISTINGS

First offered in 1995, the Thomas Hinds Nicaraguan Selection showcases filler and binder tobaccos from the Jalapa region of Nicaragua. Easy to smoke thanks to top-quality construction, these cigars are elegantly packaged in handsome all-cedar boxes of 25. They are mild-to-medium-bodied in the natural shade wrappers and medium-bodied in the maduro shade wrappers.

TIA MARTIA
Handmade in Santiago, Dominican Republic.

Wrapper: Honduras   *Binder: Mexico*   *Filler: Dom. Rep., Honduras*

Shape	Name	Lgth	Ring	Wrapper
Lonsdale	No. 1	7	42	CM
Petit Corona	No. 4	5	42	CM
Double Corona	Churchill	7	50	CM
Double Corona	Presidente	7½	50	CM
Robusto	Robusto	5	50	CM
Toro	Toro	6	50	CM

Created in 1978 by the House of Oxford, this is a mild-to-medium blend of leaves from three nations, offered in value bundles of 25.

TIBURON
Handmade in Danli, Honduras.

Wrapper: Ecuador   *Binder: Indonesia*
Filler: Dominican Republic, Honduras, Nicaragua

Shape	Name	Lgth	Ring	Wrapper
Slim Panatela	Tiger Shark	6¼	33	CC
Long Corona	Great White	6	42	CC
Corona	Mako	5¼	42	CC
Churchill	Black Tip	7	48	CC
Giant	Hammerhead	8½	50	CC

Despite the fierce names of the shapes, these are mild-bodied cigars. They are offered in bundles of 25 cigars each.

HANDMADE CIGARS: BRAND LISTINGS

TIERRA DEL SOL
Handmade in Esteli, Nicaragua.

Wrapper: Nicaragua   Binder: Nicaragua   Filler: Nicaragua

Shape	Name	Lgth	Ring	Wrapper
Robusto	Robusto	5	50	CM-Ma
Lonsdale	Corona	6½	42	CM-Ma
Double Corona	Churchill	6¾	50	CM-Ma
Torpedo	Torpedo	6⅛	54	CM-Ma

The Tabacalera Perdomo makes this brand for Meier & Dutch Distributors. It's medium in body and offered in bundles of 20.

TOBACCONIST CHOICE ★New★
Handmade, with short filler, in Santiago, Dominican Republic.

Wrapper: USA/Connecticut   Binder: Indonesia   Filler: Dom. Rep.

Shape	Name	Lgth	Ring	Wrapper
Petit Corona	Flavors	5	40	CC

This is a flavored series from Battleground Cigar, offered in boxes of 30 in Rum Runner, Triple Cherry, Sweet Vanilla, Very Berry, Chocolate and Honey.

TOBACCONIST SERIES
Handmade in Santiago, Dominican Republic.
Wrapper: Brazil, Ecuador, Indonesia, USA/Connecticut

Binder: Dominican Republic   Filler: Dominican Republic

Shape	Name	Lgth	Ring	Wrapper
Double Corona	Churchill	7	50	CC-CM-Ma
Long Corona	Lonsdale	6	44	CC-CM-Ma
Robusto	Robusto	5	50	CC-CM-Ma
Torpedo	Torpedo	6½	52	CC-CM-Ma

The Victor Sinclair Cigar company developed this series, introduced in 2002, with a mild-to-medium-bodied taste. You have a choice of four wrappers: Ecuadorian Rosado, Connecticut, Sumatra or Brazilian maduro, all in boxes of 25.

HANDMADE CIGARS: BRAND LISTINGS

TONY ALVAREZ
Handmade in Esteli, Nicaragua.

Wrapper: Ecuador, Nicaragua   Binder: Nicaragua   Filler: Nicaragua

Shape	Name	Lgth	Ring	Wrapper
Torpedo	Torpedo	6	54	CC-CM
Double Corona	Churchill	7	50	CC-CM
Robusto	Robusto	5	50	CC-CM

Introduced in 2006, this is a mild-to-medium-bodied blend with the Ecuadorian wrapper or full-bodied with a Nicaraguan Habano wrapper. Either way, it's offered in bundles of 25.

TOPPER
Handmade, with medium filler, in Danli, Honduras.

Wrapper: USA/Connecticut   Binder: Honduras   Filler: Honduras

Shape	Name		Lgth	Ring	Wrapper
Petit Corona	Long T	/short filler/	4½	44	CM
Long Corona	Shorty	/short filler/	6	44	CM
	Topper Hand Made line:				
Torpedo	Belicoso		6	54	CC
Double Corona	Churchill		7	50	CC
Toro	Toro		6	50	CC
Robusto	Robusto		5	50	CC

The Danli line was introduced in 2002 by the venerable Topper Cigar Company. It offers a medium body with a Connecticut Broadleaf wrapper, available in boxes of 25. The Long T and Shorty were introduced in 2003 and are medium-bodied with short filler, sold in packs of four or five.

TORCEDOR
Handmade in Esteli, Nicaragua.

Wrapper: Nicaragua   Binder: Nicaragua   Filler: Honduras

Shape	Name	Lgth	Ring	Wrapper
Double Corona	Churchill	7	50	CM-Ma

HANDMADE CIGARS: BRAND LISTINGS

"Torcedor" means cigar roller in Spanish and this brand was originally introduced in 1996 as a mild cigar in large sizes by the House of Oxford. It has been re-blended with all-Nicaraguan tobaccos for 2004 and offers a medium body in boxes of 50.

TORRES
Handmade in Santiago, Dominican Republic.

TORRES FAMILY RESERVE:
Wrapper: Brazil, Dom. Rep.   *Binder: Honduras*   *Filler: Nicaragua*

TORRES REY CUBANO:
Wrapper: Dom. Rep.   *Binder: Nicaragua*   *Filler: Nicaragua*

TORRES UNICOS:
Wrapper: Brazil   *Binder: Honduras*   *Filler: Dom. Rep.*

TORRES VINTAGE RESERVE:
Wrapper: Nicaragua   *Binder: Mexico*   *Filler: Nicaragua*

TORRES COGNAC VINTAGE RESERVE:
Wrapper: Brazil   *Binder: Honduras*   *Filler: Dom. Rep.*

TORRES HONEY-WINE PRIMEROS:
Wrapper: Brazil   *Binder: Dom. Rep.*   *Filler: Dom. Rep.*

Shape	Name	Lgth	Ring	Wrapper
	Torres Family Reserve:			
Churchill	Churchill S	7	48	CM-Ma
Toro	Toro BC	6	50	CM-Ma
Torpedo	Belicoso T	6	52	CM-Ma
Robusto	Robusto No. 5	5	50	CM-Ma
	Torres Rey Cubano:			
Churchill	Churchill	7	48	Ma
Toro	Double Corona	6	50	Ma
Torpedo	Torpedo	6	52	Ma
Robusto	Robusto	5	50	Ma

Torpedo	Don Frank Figurado	5	50	Dual
Toro	Don Frank	6	50	Dual
	Torres Unicos:			
Double Corona	Churchill	7	50	Ma
Torpedo	Torpedo	6	54	Ma
Long Corona	Corona	6	44	Ma
Robusto	Robusto	5	50	Ma
	Torres Vintage Reseve:			
Double Corona	Churchill	7	50	CM
Toro	Toro	6	50	CM
Torpedo	Torpedo	6	52	CM
Robusto	Robusto	5	50	CM
	Cognac Vintage Reserve:			
Churchill	Churchill	7	48	Ma
Toro	Cognac No. 3	6	50	Ma
Robusto	Chateau Cognac	5	50	Ma
Torpedo	Cognac No. 2	6	54	Ma
	Honey-Wine Primeros:			
Churchill	Churchill	7	48	Ma
Long Corona	Corona	6	44	Ma
Robusto	Robusto	5	50	Ma

This brand started in 1996. The Family Reserve, Rey Cubano and the Unicos are medium in body, while the Vintage Reserve is medium-to-full and both flavored series are medium. All are offered in 25s.

TORRES & FAMILY
Handmade in Miami, Florida, USA.

Wrapper: USA/Connecticut   Binder: Ecuador   Filler: Dom. Rep., Mexico

HANDMADE CIGARS: BRAND LISTINGS

The Caonao Cigar Factory makes this four-size brand. It has a medium-bodied flavor with a Connecticut wrapper available in natural or maduro shades, offered in 25s.

TRADERS RESERVE
Handmade in Navarette, Dominican Republic.

Wrapper: USA/Connecticut   Binder: Dom. Rep.   Filler: Dom. Rep., Nicaragua

Shape	Name	Lgth	Ring	Wrapper
Robusto	Robusto	5	50	CC
Long Corona	Extra Corona	6	42	CC
Grand Corona	Corona	6	46	CC
Pyramid	Piramide	6⅛	52	CC
Toro	Toro	6	50	CC
Torpedo	Torpedo	6½	52	CC
Double Corona	Churchill	7	50	CC

This brand debuted in 2002, left the market and returned in 2004. It offers a full-bodied finish with a Connecticut natural wrapper. It is available in boxes of 25.

TREASURES OF COSTA RICA
Handmade in Tamarindo Beach, Costa Rica.

Wrapper: Costa Rica   Binder: Costa Rica   Filler: Costa Rica

Shape	Name	Lgth	Ring	Wrapper
Robusto	Robusto	5	50	CM
Torpedo	Belicoso	6	54	CM

This medium-bodied blend was introduced by Bucanero Cigars in 2004, but the Corinita offers full-bodied flavor. It's an elegant blend, presented in exotic chests of 16 cigars.

TRILOGY
Handmade in Danli, Honduras.

AUTHENTIC COROJO:

Wrapper: Nicaragua   Binder: Costa Rica
Filler: Dom. Rep., Honduras, Mexico, Nicaragua

EXOTIC MADURO :

Wrapper: Brazil *Binder: Indonesia* *Filler: Colombia, Nicaragua*

NATIVE CAMEROON:

Wrapper: Cameroon *Binder: Honduras* *Filler: Italy, Nicaragua*

Shape	Name	Lgth	Ring	Wrapper
Robusto	Robusto	5	50	CM-Ma
Double Corona	Churchill	7	50	CM-Ma
Torpedo	Torpedo	6⅛	52	CM-Ma

Here are three blends inside the same brand, introduced in 2002 by the Alec Bradley Cigar Company. The Authentic Corojo offers a medium-to-full-bodied flavor, while the Cameroon and maduro-wrapped lines are medium in body. From 2002-04, the cigars had a three-sided, triangular shape, changed to a round shape in 2005. All three are offered in elegantly-dressed boxes of 20.

TRINIDAD
Handmade in Santiago, Dominican Republic.
Wrapper: Ecuador, USA/Connecticut

Binder: Ecuador, USA/Connecticut *Filler: Dom. Rep., Nicaragua, Peru*

Shape	Name	Lgth	Ring	Wrapper
Torpedo	Belicoso	6⅛	52	CM
Torpedo	Mini Belicoso	5	52	CM
Double Corona	Churchill	7	50	CM
Toro	Toro	6	50	CM
Lonsdale	Lonsdale	6⅝	44	CM
Robusto	Robusto	5	50	CM
Petit Corona	Corona	5	44	CM
Long Panatela	Fundador	7½	40	CM
	Maduro-wrapped series:			
Short Panatela	Trini Petities	4	30	Ma
Robusto	Petite Robusto	4¼	54	Ma
Robusto	Robusto	5	55	Ma

Toro	Toro	6	55	Ma
Double Corona	Churchill	7	58	Ma
Torpedo	Belicoso	6⅛	54	Ma
	Maduro Cabinet Selection:			
Double Corona	Churchill	7	50	Ma
Petit Corona	Corona *(glass tube)*	5	44	Ma
Torpedo	Mini Belicoso	5	52	Ma
Robusto	Rothschild	5	55	Ma

This brand, then known as "TTT Trinidad" was first introduced to the U.S. market in late 1997. A lengthy trademark dispute was finally resolved in June 2001 in favor of Diego Trinidad, heir of the Trinidad trademarks for the territory of the United States, allowing further production of the brand, which was taken over by Altadis USA in 2002. The natural-wrapped blend offers a medium-to-full-bodied taste with a Sumatra-seed wrapper and Connecticut binder. Elegantly presented in cabinets of 20, it is designed to garner the same respect as its namesake, originally produced in pre-revolutionary Cuba.

The maduro-wrapped series debuted in 2004. This blend uses a Connecticut Broadleaf wrapper and an Indonesian-seed binder for a striking, full-bodied taste. All of the maduro-wrapped shapes are box-pressed and offered in boxes of 20 except for the Trini Petites (packs of 7) and Petite Robustos (in 3s and 20s).

The Maduro Cabinet Selection series is specially made for Harold Levinson Associates of Farmingdale, New York and debuted in 2007. It's uniquely presented in cabinets of 16!

In mid-2006, Altadis USA issued a set of 400 custom humidors to mark the 100th anniversary of the brand (actually in 2005) with a limited edition of 40,000 cigars featuring a Mexican-grown Corojo wrapper and Nicaraguan binder and filler. Each humidor included three sizes: 4¼ x 54 (33), 5 x 54 (33) and 6 x 54 (34).

TRINIDAD HABANA RESERVE ★*New*★
Handmade in Santa Rosa de Copan, Honduras.

Wrapper: Nicaragua   Binder: USA/Connecticut   Filler: Dom. Rep., Nicaragua

Shape	Name	Lgth	Ring	Wrapper
Robusto	Coloniales	5	50	CM

Toro	Robusto	6¼	50	CM
Perfecto	Perfecto	6	47	CM
Churchill	Sir Winston	7	48	CM

The Isla de Cuba Cigar Co. introduced this brand in late 2007. It features a Criollo '98 wrapper and is medium-to-full in body, offered in boxes of 25.

TRINIDAD Y CIA.
Handmade, with mixed filler, in Esteli, Nicaragua.

Wrapper: Ecuador   Binder: Honduras   Filler: Dom. Rep., Honduras, Nicaragua

Shape	Name	Lgth	Ring	Wrapper
Corona	Corona	5½	43	CM
Lonsdale	Corona Extra	6½	44	CM
Churchill	Double Corona	7	48	CM
Robusto	Robusto	4¾	50	CM
Toro	Toro	6	50	CM

This is a medium-bodied cigar with a Sumatra-seed wrapper and short filler, offered in value-priced bundles of 20.

TROPICAL DELIGHTS JUBILEE
Handmade, with short filler, in Danli, Honduras.

Wrapper: Honduras   Binder: Homogenized   Filler: Honduras, Nicaragua

Shape	Name	Lgth	Ring	Wrapper
Petit Corona	Jubilee	4½	42	CM

Introduced in 2005, this is a short-fill, mild, flavored brand with a homogenized binder and offered in natural, cherry, honey, rum and vanilla flavors in bundles of 25.

TROPICAL TREASURES
Handmade in Tamboril, Dominican Republic.

Wrapper: Indonesia   Binder: Indonesia   Filler: Dom. Rep.

HANDMADE CIGARS: BRAND LISTINGS

Shape	Name	Lgth	Ring	Wrapper
Petit Corona	Corona	5	42	CM

Introduced in 1998, this is a medium-bodied, flavored brand available in Almond Brandy, Cayman Chocolate, Columbian Coffee, French Cognac, Jamaican Sweets, Piña Colada, Spiced Rum, Sweet Cherry and West Indies Vanilla. You can try them in guaranteed-fresh, vacuum-sealed cans of 25.

TROYA
Handmade in Santiago, Dominican Republic.

Wrapper: Cameroon, USA/Connecticut   Binder: Dom. Rep.   Filler: Dom. Rep.

Shape	Name	Lgth	Ring	Wrapper
Torpedo	No. 81	6⅛	52	CM
Torpedo	No. 72	5	52	CM
Churchill	No. 63	7	50	CC
Lonsdale	No. 54	5¾	48	CC
Long Corona	No. 45	6¼	45	CC
Perfecto	No. 36	4	50	CM
Corona	No. 27	5½	42	CC

An old Cuban brand, Troya is a hand-crafted cigar of the highest quality, introduced in 1985. It had a medium body in a blend which was discontinued in 2003. A new blend which debuted in 2004 is mild, with a choice of Connecticut (Nos. 27, 45, 54 63) or Cameroon (Nos. 36, 72, 81) wrappers, offered in boxes of 24.

TROYA CLASICO   ★*New*★
Handmade in Esteli, Nicaragua.

Wrapper: Nicaragua   Binder: Nicaragua   Filler: Nicaragua

Shape	Name	Lgth	Ring	Wrapper
Robusto	XVIII	5	54	CM
Toro	LIV	6	52	CM
Churchill	LXIII	7	48	CM

HANDMADE CIGARS: BRAND LISTINGS

This is a medium-to-full-bodied cigar introduced by Lignum-2 in 2007 and made at Don Pepin Garcia's Tabacalera Cubana factory in Nicaragua. It features a Corojo wrapper and a combination of Corojo and Criollo filler tobaccos from the Jalapa Valley, offered in boxes of 20.

TROYA X-TRA
Handmade in Esteli, Nicaragua.

Wrapper: Nicaragua   Binder: Nicaragua   Filler: Nicaragua

Shape	Name	Lgth	Ring	Wrapper
Robusto	No. 18	5	52	CM
Grand Corona	No. 45	6¼	45	CM
Toro	No. 54	5¾	48	CM
Double Corona	No. 63	7	50	CM
Torpedo	No. 81	6⅛	52	CM

Here is a full-bodied version of the historic Troya brand, introduced in 2004, and distributed by Lignum-2. It features a Corojo wrapper and is offered in boxes of 24.

TWO-TONE
Handmade in Esteli, Nicaragua.

Wrapper: USA/Connecticut   Binder: Nicaragua   Filler: Nicaragua

Shape	Name	Lgth	Ring	Wrapper
Robusto	Robusto	5	50	Dual
Double Corona	Churchill	7	50	Dual

Here is a handmade edition of the venerable Muniemaker brand, introduced in 2005! It has both a Connecticut Shade and Broadleaf wrapper, which a medium-to-full-bodied taste, available in boxes of 24.

VALUE LINE DOMINICAN BLEND NO. 100
Handmade in Santiago, Dominican Republic.

Wrapper: USA/Connecticut   Binder: Dom. Rep.   Filler: Dom. Rep.

Shape	Name	Lgth	Ring	Wrapper
Corona	Corona	5½	42	CC

HANDMADE CIGARS: BRAND LISTINGS

VALUE LINE HONDURAN BLEND NO. 200
Handmade in Danli, Honduras.

Wrapper: Indonesia   Binder: Colombia   Filler: Colombia, Dom. Rep., Mexico

Shape	Name	Lgth	Ring	Wrapper
Double Corona	Churchill	7½	50	CM-Ma
Corona Extra	Corona	5½	46	CM
Toro	Corona Gorda	6	52	CM
Lonsdale	Lonsdale	6½	44	CM-Ma
Robusto	Rothschild	5½	50	CM-Ma

This is a mild-to-medium-bodied blend, introduced in 2004 by Famous Smoke Shop, offered in bundles of 20.

VALUE LINE HONDURAN BLEND NO. 300
Handmade in Danli, Honduras.

Wrapper: USA/Connecticut   Binder: Dom. Rep.   Filler: Dom. Rep., Nicaragua

Shape	Name	Lgth	Ring	Wrapper
Double Corona	Churchill	7½	52	CM
Corona	Corona	5½	42	CM
Churchill	Perfeccion	7	48	CM
Lonsdale	Lonsdale	6½	44	CM
Robusto	Robusto	5	52	CM

This is a mild-bodied blend introduced in 2004 by Famous Smoke Shop. Like its cousins, it is offered in economical bundles of 20.

VALUE LINE HONDURAN BLEND NO. 400
Handmade in Danli, Honduras.

Wrapper: Indonesia   Binder: Mexico   Filler: Dom. Rep., Mexico

Shape	Name	Lgth	Ring	Wrapper
Double Corona	Churchill	7½	52	CM
Churchill	Perfeccion	7	48	CM
Lonsdale	Lonsdale	6½	44	CM

Robusto	Robusto	5	52	CM

This is a medium-bodied blend introduced in 2004 by Famous Smoke Shop, also offered in bundles of 20.

VALUE LINE HONDURAN NO. 500 ★*New*★
Handmade in Danli, Honduras.

Wrapper: Nicaragua, USA/Connecticut   Binder: Honduras   Filler: Honduras

Shape	Name	Lgth	Ring	Wrapper
Churchill	Churchill	7	48	CC-CM-Ma
Double Corona	Double Corona	7	50	CC
Robusto	Double Robusto	5	60	CM-Ma
Torpedo	Grand Torpedo	7	60	Ma
Robusto	Robusto	5	50	CC-CM-Ma
Robusto	Robusto Extra	4¾	52	CM-Ma
Robusto	Rothschild	4½	48	CC-Ma
Robusto	Short Robusto	4¾	48	CC-Ma
Toro	Super Toro	6	60	CM-Ma
Toro	Toro	6	52	CM
Double Corona	Toro Extra Large	7	60	CM
Torpedo	Torpedo	6	52	Ma
Torpedo	Torpedo Minor	6	50	Ma

Take your choice of Connecticut, Habano or maduro wrappers in this medium-bodied blend introduced in 2007. It's offered in bundles of 20.

VALUE LINE NICARAGUAN BLEND NO. 300
Handmade in Esteli, Nicaragua.

Wrapper: Nicaragua   Binder: Nicaragua   Filler: Nicaragua

Shape	Name	Lgth	Ring	Wrapper
Double Corona	Churchill	7	50	CM
Lonsdale	Lonsdale	6½	44	CM

Robusto	Robusto	5	50	CM
Toro	Toro	6	50	CM
Torpedo	Torpedo	6	52	CM

Introduced in 2004 by Famous Smoke Shop and made at the Tabacalera Tropical, this is a medium-to-full-bodied blend featuring a Corojo wrapper. It is offered in economical bundles of 20.

VEGA FINA ★New★
Handmade in La Romana, Dominican Republic.

Wrapper: Ecuador   Binder: Indonesia   Filler: Colombia, Dom. Rep., Honduras

Shape	Name	Lgth	Ring	Wrapper
Double Corona	Churchill	7½	50	CC
Corona	Corona	5¾	43	CC
Lonsdale	Lonsdale	6½	43	CC
Petit Corona	No. 5	4	40	CC
Robusto	Robusto	5	50	CC
Toro	Toro	6	50	CC
Torpedo	Torpedo	6	50	CC

Altadis USA took one of its most popular cigars in Europe and began offering it as a value-priced selection on the American market in 2007. It features a Connecticut-seed wrapper and has a medium-bodied taste. All sizes are offered in boxes of 25.

VEGA REAL ★New★
Handmade in Santiago, Dominican Republic.

Wrapper: Dom. Rep.   Binder: Dom. Rep.   Filler: Dom. Rep.

Shape	Name		Lgth	Ring	Wrapper
Lonsdale	No. 1		6¾	42	CM
Long Corona	No. 2		6	42	CM
Corona	No. 3		5¾	42	CM
Lonsdale	Cristal	(glass tube)	6¾	42	CM

Long Corona	Aluminio	(tubed)	6	42	CM

Made by La Tabacalera, this is a Dominican puro with a full-bodied taste. It is offered in boxes of 10 or 20 or in packs of three.

VEGA TALANGA
Handmade in Danli, Honduras.

Wrapper: Honduras   Binder: Honduras   Filler: Honduras, Nicaragua

Shape	Name	Lgth	Ring	Wrapper
Toro	Tercio	6	54	CM
	Corojo series:			
Robusto	Rojo	5	50	CM
Perfecto	Oscuro	5½	62	CM
Torpedo	Azul	6	54	CM
Churchill	Blanco	7	48	CM

Introduced in 2002, the Tercio offers a medium-to-full-bodied taste. The full-bodied Corojo series debuted in 2003. The Rojo (red label) and Oscuro (black label) feature sun-grown wrappers, while the Azul (blue label) and Blanco (white label) use shade-grown wrappers. All are offered in boxes of 25.

VEGAS CUBANAS
Handmade in Miami, Florida, USA.

Wrapper: Nicaragua   Binder: Nicaragua   Filler: Nicaragua

Shape	Name	Lgth	Ring	Wrapper
Corona	Corona	5½	44	CM
Robusto	Invictos	5	50	CM
Toro	Generosos	6	50	CM
Double Corona	Delicias	7	50	CM
Torpedo	Imperiales	6⅛	52	CM
Double Corona	Magnates	7⅝	49	CM

Made at El Rey de Los Habanos in Miami, this is a mild-to-medium-bodied blend. Introduced for national distribution, it is offered uncellophaned in boxes of 25.

HANDMADE CIGARS: BRAND LISTINGS

VEGAS DE FONSECA
Handmade in Santiago, Dominican Republic.

Wrapper: Cameroon   *Binder: USA/Connecticut*   *Filler: Dom. Rep., Nicaragua*

Shape	Name	Lgth	Ring	Wrapper
Double Corona	Anteros	7	50	CM
Robusto	Sobrinos	5¼	50	CM
Long Corona	Vegas No. 2	6	43	CM
Petit Corona	Vegas Petite	4½	40	CM
Torpedo	Belicoso	6¼	52	CM
Toro	Toro	6	50	CM
Perfecto	Vegas No. 10	6	50	CM
Toro	Vegas No. 5	6¼	56	CM

This brand was introduced in 2000 and offers a exotic, box-pressed blend of Dominican and Nicaraguan filler leaves, surrounded by a Connecticut Broadleaf binder and an authentic Cameroon wrapper. It's a medium-bodied smoke, with excellent draw as you would expect from Manuel Quesada's MATASA factory. You can enjoy the "Farms of Fonseca" in boxes of 20.

VEGAS DE NICARAGUA
Handmade in Condega, Nicaragua.

Wrapper: Ecuador   *Binder: Indonesia*   *Filler: Dom. Rep., Nicaragua*

Shape	Name	Lgth	Ring	Wrapper
Churchill	Churchill	7	48	CM
Robusto	Robusto	4¾	50	CM
Corona Extra	Corona	5½	46	CM
Torpedo	Torpedo	6	50	CM

Distributed by Flor de Gonzalez, this is a medium-to-full-bodied blend introduced in 2006. It features a sun-grown wrapper and is offered in boxes of 25.

VEGAS DE TABACALERA ESTELI
Handmade in Esteli, Nicaragua.

Wrapper: Nicaragua   *Binder: Nicaragua*   *Filler: Nicaragua*

Shape	Name	Lgth	Ring	Wrapper
Torpedo	Torpedo	6½	54	CM
Double Corona	Churchill	7	52	CM
Toro	Toro	6	52	CM
Robusto	Robusto	5	52	CM

Here is a medium-bodied blend from the Tabacalera Esteli, introduced in 2003, offered in boxes of 25.

VENGEANCE
Handmade in Danli, Honduras.

Wrapper: Brazil　　　*Binder: Honduras*　　　*Filler: Dom. Rep., Honduras, Nicaragua*

Shape	Name	Lgth	Ring	Wrapper
Robusto	Robusto	5½	52	Ma
Toro	Toro	6	54	Ma
Torpedo	Torpedo	6½	52	Ma
Double Corona	Churchill	7	50	Ma

Introduced in 2006, this cigar was blended by Rocky Patel and offers a medium body. It's available in boxes of 20.

VERONA
Hand-rolled, with short filler, in Alexandria, Egypt.

Wrapper: Indonesia　　　*Binder: Indonesia*　　　*Filler: Dom. Rep., Honduras, Italy*

Shape	Name	Lgth	Ring	Wrapper
Cigarillo	Cigarillo	4	22	CM

This mild cigarillo was introduced in 2005. It is offered in tins of 10 in natural, vanilla, chocolate, coffee, cherry, coconut, Amaretto and creme caramel.

VIBE
Handmade in Danli, Honduras.

Wrapper: Honduras　　　*Binder: Nicaragua*　　　*Filler: Honduras, Nicaragua*

HANDMADE CIGARS: BRAND LISTINGS

Shape	Name	Lgth	Ring	Wrapper
Robusto	Robusto	5	52	CM
Torpedo	Torpedo	5¼	54	CM
Petit Corona	Corona	4½	44	CM
Toro	Chairman	6	58	CM

A full-bodied cigar introduced by United Tobacco in 2005, this blend (by Rocky Patel) features a Corojo wrapper. It's offered in boxes of 20.

VICTOR SINCLAIR
Handmade in Santiago, Dominican Republic.

Wrapper: USA/Connecticut   Binder: Dom. Rep.   Filler: Dom. Rep.

Shape	Name	Lgth	Ring	Wrapper
Double Corona	Churchill	7½	50	CC-Ma
Robusto	Robusto	5½	50	CC-Ma
Long Corona	Lonsdale	6	44	CC-Ma
Cigarillo	Tins	4	28	CC

Introduced in 1995, this handmade cigar features a Connecticut wrapper, but has also offered a maduro wrapper from Indonesia in the past. The blend is medium in body and offered in boxes of 25, except for the Tins (10s).

VICTOR SINCLAIR 10TH ANIVERSARIO
Handmade in Santiago, Dominican Republic.

Wrapper: Dom. Rep.   Binder: Dom. Rep.   Filler: Dom. Rep.

Shape	Name	Lgth	Ring	Wrapper
Churchill	Churchill	6¾	48	CM
Robusto	Robusto	5	48	CM
Toro	Toro	5¾	54	CM

Victor Sinclair Cigars introduced this blend in 2005, with a medium-to-full body, featuring a Corojo wrapper. It's offered in boxes of 20.

HANDMADE CIGARS: BRAND LISTINGS

VICTOR SINCLAIR LEGACY
Handmade in Santiago, Dominican Republic.

Wrapper: Brazil   Binder: Dom. Rep.   Filler: Dom. Rep.

Shape	Name	Lgth	Ring	Wrapper
Double Corona	Churchill	7	50	Ma
Perfecto	Figurado	4	50	Ma
Toro	Toro	5½	50	Ma
Torpedo	Torpedo	6½	52	Ma

This is a mild-to-medium-bodied blend introduced in 2005. It's box-pressed, offered in boxes of 20.

VICTOR SINCLAIR PRIMEROS
Handmade in Santiago, Dominican Republic.

Wrapper: Ecuador   Binder: Dom. Rep.   Filler: Dom. Rep., Nicaragua

Shape	Name	Lgth	Ring	Wrapper
Robusto	Robusto	5	50	CC
Double Corona	Churchill	7	50	CC

This is a medium-bodied blend introduced in 2004. It features a Connecticut-seed wrapper and is offered in boxes of 20.

VICTOR SINCLAIR SERIES 55 GRAND RESERVE BLUE
Handmade in Santiago, Dominican Republic.

Wrapper: USA/Connecticut   Binder: Dominican Republic
Filler: Brazil, Cameroon, Dominican Republic, Nicaragua

Shape	Name	Lgth	Ring	Wrapper
Robusto	Robusto	5	50	Os
Torpedo	Torpedo	6½	52	Os
Giant	Churchill	8	50	Os

Introduced in 2001, this is a full-bodied, five-tobacco blend all aged five years with a pitch-black Oscuro wrapper. Beginning in 2004, the 55 is presented in boxes of 20.

VICTOR SINCLAIR SERIES 55 GRAND RESERVE GREEN
Handmade in Santiago, Dominican Republic.

Wrapper: Ecuador   *Binder: Dominican Republic*
Filler: Brazil, Cameroon, Dominican Republic, Nicaragua

Shape	Name	Lgth	Ring	Wrapper
Robusto	Robusto	5	50	CM
Torpedo	Torpedo	6½	52	CM
Giant	Churchill	8	50	CM

Also introduced in 2001, this is a full-bodied, five-tobacco blend all aged five years with an Ecuadorian sun-grown wrapper. After being presented in boxes of 29, this series is offered in boxes of 20 beginning in 20.

VICTOR SINCLAIR SERIES 55 GRAND RESERVE RED
Handmade in Santiago, Dominican Republic.

Wrapper: Brazil   *Binder: Dominican Republic*
Filler: Brazil, Cameroon, Dominican Republic, Nicaragua

Shape	Name	Lgth	Ring	Wrapper
Robusto	Robusto	5	50	CM
Torpedo	Torpedo	6½	52	CM
Giant	Churchill	8	50	CM

Also introduced in 2001, this is a full-bodied, five-tobacco blend all aged five years with a Brazilian Corojo wrapper. It is presented in boxes of 20.

VICTOR SINCLAIR SERIES 55 GRAND RESERVE YELLOW
Handmade in Santiago, Dominican Republic.

Wrapper: Cameroon   *Binder: Dominican Republic*
Filler: Brazil, Cameroon, Dominican Republic, Nicaragua

Shape	Name	Lgth	Ring	Wrapper
Robusto	Robusto	5	50	CM
Giant	Churchill	8	50	CM
Torpedo	Torpedo	6½	52	CM

HANDMADE CIGARS: BRAND LISTINGS

This is a new version of the Series 55, introduced in 2004. This edition has a Cameroon wrapper, is full-bodied and is offered in boxes of 20.

VIEJA HACIENDA

Handmade, with mixed filler, in Tamboril, Dominican Republic.

Wrapper: USA/Connecticut   Binder: Dom. Rep.   Filler: Dom. Rep.

Shape	Name	Lgth	Ring	Wrapper
Robusto	Robusto	5	50	CC
Toro	Toro	5½	54	CC
Torpedo	Torpedo	6	54	CC
Double Corona	Churchill	7	50	CC

This brand was introduced by Felipe Gregorio in 2002. It is medium in body, with a Connecticut wrapper, available in red boxes of 25.

VIEJA TRADICION

Handmade in Danli, Honduras.

Wrapper: Costa Rica, USA/Connecticut

Binder: Honduras   Filler: Honduras, Nicaragua

Shape	Name	Lgth	Ring	Wrapper
Toro	Corona Gorda	6	52	CC-Ma
Robusto	Robusto	4¾	50	CC-Ma
Double Corona	Churchill	7	50	CC-Ma

Created by Swisher International in 2005, this is an old Plasencia family blend re-created in the 21st Century. It's full-bodied with a choice of Connecticut (natural) or Costa Rican (maduro) wrappers, offered in elegant boxes of 20.

VILLA DOMINICANA ★*New*★

Handmade in Santiago, Dominican Republic.

Wrapper: Ecuador   Binder: Mexican   Filler: Dom. Rep., Nicaragua

Shape	Name	Lgth	Ring	Wrapper
Robusto	Petite Robusto	4	50	CM
Robusto	Robusto	5	50	CM

| Toro | Corona Gorda | 6 | 50 | CM |
| Double Corona | Churchill | 7 | 50 | CM |

Villiger Stokkebye International introduced this blend in 2007, offering a value-priced, handmade cigar with a medium body and a Connecticut-seed wrapper. All sizes are offered in bundles of 25.

VILLA HAVANA
Handmade, with mixed filler, in Santiago, Dominican Republic.
Wrapper: Indonesia   *Binder: Indonesia*   *Filler: Dom. Rep., Honduras*

This brand was introduced in 1998 and offers a consistent draw with a medium-bodied taste in five sizes. You can find it in value-priced bundles of 25.

VOILA
Handmade in Santo Domingo, Dominican Republic.
Wrapper: Ecuador   *Binder: Dom. Rep.*   *Filler: Dom. Rep.*

This medium-bodied, three-size blend was introduced in 2004. It is offered in bundles of 25.

VIRTUOSO TORAÑO
Handmade in Esteli, Nicaragua.
Wrapper: Nicaragua   *Binder: Nicaragua*   *Filler: Honduras, Nicaragua, Panama*

Shape	Name	Lgth	Ring	Wrapper
Double Corona	Maestro	7	50	CM
Robusto	Encore	4¾	52	CM
Robusto	Forte	5½	56	CM
Torpedo	Crescendo	6½	54	CM

Initially made from 1995-2000, the Virtuoso returned in 2005. This blend features a wrapper grown at the Toraño's Pueblo Nuevo farm in Condega, Nicaragua and is mild-to-medium in body.

VISTA DE CUBA
Handmade in Santiago, Dominican Republic.
Wrapper: Ecuador   *Binder: Dom. Rep.*   *Filler: Dom. Rep., Nicaragua*

HANDMADE CIGARS: BRAND LISTINGS

Shape	Name	Lgth	Ring	Wrapper
Robusto	Robusto	5	50	CC
Toro	Toro	5¾	52	CC
Double Corona	Churchill	7	52	CC
Torpedo	Belicoso	6	56	CC

Uniquely co-owned by the Habana Cuba Cigar Co. and the independent cigar representatives who sell it, this is a mild-bodied blend introduced in 2005. It's offered in elegant boxes of 20.

VUELTABAJO
Handmade in Santiago, Dominican Republic.

Wrapper: Ecuador *Binder: Dom. Rep.* *Filler: Dom. Rep.*

Shape	Name	Lgth	Ring	Wrapper
Churchill	Churchill	7	48	CC
Lonsdale	Lonsdale	6½	44	CC
Robusto	Robusto	4¾	52	CC
Toro	Toro	6	50	CC

A winner during the Cigar Boom of the late 1990s, Toraño Cigars makes this mild-to-medium-bodied blend for Famous Smoke Shop, now in national distribution again. It's an excellent value in slide-top cedar boxes of 25.

W&D DOMINICAN
Handmade in Santiago, Dominican Republic.

Wrapper: Indonesia *Binder: Mexico* *Filler: Brazil, Dom. Rep., Mexico*

Shape	Name	Lgth	Ring	Wrapper
Churchill	Churchill	7	48	CC
Long Corona	Lonsdale	6¼	44	CC
Robusto	Robusto	5	50	CC
Toro	Toro	6	52	CC

This is a medium-bodied blend that has been on and off the market in recent years. All shapes are offered in bundles of 25.

HANDMADE CIGARS: BRAND LISTINGS

W&D HONDURAN
Handmade in Danli, Honduras.

Wrapper: Ecuador, Indonesia   Binder: Mexico   Filler: Dom.Rep., Mexico, Nicaragua

Shape	Name	Lgth	Ring	Wrapper
Lonsdale	Cetro	6½	44	CM-Ma
Double Corona	Presidente	7½	50	CM-Ma
Robusto	Robusto	5	50	CM-Ma

This is a medium-to-full-bodied blend offered in bundles of 25, featuring either an Ecuadorian-grown, Sumatra-seed or an Indonesian-grown wrapper.

WEST INDIES VANILLA
Handmade, with medium filler, in Yogyakarta, Indonesia.

Wrapper: Indonesia   Binder: Indonesia   Filler: Brazil, Dom. Rep., Indonesia

Shape	Name	Lgth	Ring	Wrapper
Perfecto	Cruzer	6	48	CM
Short Panatela	Carmelita	4½	36	CM
Petit Corona	Carmela	4¾	42	CM
Double Corona	Canon	7	50	CM
Lonsdale	Grand Carmela	7	42	CM
	Machine-bunched:			
Cigarillo	Treasures	3⅝	20	CM

This is a vanilla-flavored cigar originally introduced in 1995. The cigar is handmade, but with medium filler. It has a medium-bodied taste and is offered in boxes of 25, except for the Treasures, available in 50s and the Cruzer, available in 11s.

YUMURI 1492
Handmade in Navarette, Dominican Republic.

Wrapper: Brazil   Binder: Dom. Rep.   Filler: Dom. Rep.

Shape	Name	Lgth	Ring	Wrapper
Torpedo	Torpedo	6¼	52	CM
Churchill	Churchill	7	48	CM

Robusto	Robusto	4¾	52	CM
Toro	Toro	6	50	CM
Corona	Corona	5¾	43	CM

This is an old Cigar Boom brand, resurrected in 2005. It's medium in body, offered in boxes of 10 and 25.

Z-GAR ★*New*★
Handmade in Santa Rosa de Copan, Honduras.
Wrapper: Mexico, Nicaragua   Binder: Nicaragua   Filler: Honduras, Nicaragua

Shape	*Name*	*Lgth*	*Ring*	*Wrapper*
Cigarillo	Panetela	4⅞	26	CM-Ma

Made for Cigars by Santa Clara, this is a medium-bodied blend offered with a Nicaraguan H2000 wrapper or Mexican maduro wrapper. It's packed in boxes of 25.

ZELO DE CUBA
Handmade in Santiago, Dominican Republic.
Wrapper: Ecuador   Binder: Indonesia   Filler: Costa Rica, Honduras

Introduced in 1997, this is a full-bodied blend offered in five sizes in boxes of 25.

ZINO CLASSIC
Handmade in Santiago, Dominican Republic.
Wrapper: Ecuador   Binder: Honduras   Filler: Dom. Rep., Honduras

Shape	*Name*		*Lgth*	*Ring*	*Wrapper*
Long Corona	No. 1	*(tube available)*	6¼	44	CC
Panatela	No. 3		5¾	38	CC
Robusto	No. 6	*(tube available)*	5	50	CC
Short Panatela	No. 7	*(tubed)*	4⅝	34	CC
Churchill	No. 8	*(tubed)*	6⅞	48	CC
Double Corona	Double Corona		7½	52	CC

HANDMADE CIGARS: BRAND LISTINGS

This famous brand began in Honduras in 1975, but was finally discontinued in 2005. Instead, Zinos moved to the Dominican Republic in 2006, using mostly Honduran tobaccos but with a Connecticut-seed wrapper and a little Dominican filler leaf. The cigars are medium-to-full in body and offered in boxes of 20 for most sizes, but in 10s for the No. 8 and Double Corona.

ZINO PLATINUM CROWN
Handmade in Santiago, Dominican Republic.

Wrapper: Ecuador   *Binder: USA/Connecticut*   *Filler: Dom. Rep.*

Shape	Name	Lgth	Ring	Wrapper
Giant	Stretch	8¼	50	CC
Double Corona	Double Grande	7½	50	CC
Perfecto	Chubby Especial *(tube available)*	5⅞	61	CC
Toro	Barrel *(tube available)*	6	60	CC

A stunning introduction in 2003, this gorgeous and expensive brand features perfect construction, a Connecticut-seed wrapper and a full-bodied taste. The Barrel shape was introduced in 2004 and the Tubos in 2006. All sizes are offered in packs of three with the tubed cigars in boxes of 10.

ZINO PLATINUM SCEPTER
Handmade in Santiago, Dominican Republic.

Wrapper: Ecuador   *Binder: USA/Connecticut*   *Filler: Dom. Rep., Peru*

Shape	Name	Lgth	Ring	Wrapper
Robusto	Grand Master *(tube avail.)*	5½	52	CC
Perfecto	Chubby *(tube avail.)*	4⅞	54	CC
Torpedo	Stout	7	52	CC
Long Corona	Low Rider	6	43	CC
Petit Corona	Shorty	4½	43	CC
Perfecto	Bullet	4	48	CC
Small Panatela	XS	4	30	CC
Robusto	Pudge	4	50	CC
Robusto	Master Edition 2007	5	54	CC

Also introduced in 2003, this is a medium-bodied cigar with a Connecticut-seed wrapper that offers a slightly spicy smoke without bitterness and with splendid finish and class. The Grand Master, Chubby, Pudge and Stout are offered in boxes of 12, the Low Rider and Shorty are offered in boxes of 16, the Bullet in 14s and the XS in boxes of 10. The tubed cigars are available in boxes of 20.

The Master Edition 2007 is a special, double-banded production offered in large tins of 10.

4.
MACHINE-MADE CIGARS

This section provides the details on 90 brands of mass-market cigars, generally made by machine for distribution to the widest possible audience in drug stores, supermarkets and, of course, tobacco stores.

Each brand listing includes notes on country of manufacture, shapes, names, lengths, ring gauges and wrapper color *as supplied by the manufacturers and/or distributors of these brands.* Ring gauges for some cigarillos were not available.

Please note that while a cigar may be manufactured in one country, it may contain tobaccos from many nations. All brands utilize short-filler tobaccos unless otherwise noted.

Although manufacturers have recognized more than 70 shades of wrapper color, six major color classifications are used here. Their abbreviations include:

- ‣ DC = Double Claro: green, also known as "AMS" or Candela.
- ‣ Cl = Claro: a very light tan color.
- ‣ CC = Colorado Claro: a medium brown common to many cigars
- ‣ Co = Colorado: reddish-brown.
- ‣ CM = Colorado Maduro: dark brown.
- ‣ Ma = Maduro: very dark brown (also "double Maduro").
- ‣ Os = Oscuro, black.

Many manufacturers call their wrapper colors "Natural" or "English Market Selection." These colors cover a wide range of browns and we have generally grouped them in the "CC" range. Darker wrappers such as those from the Cameroons show up most often in the "CM" category.

Shape designations are based on our shape chart in section 1.03.

MACHINE-MADE CIGARS: BRAND LISTINGS

Careful readers will note the freedom with which manufacturers attach names of shapes to cigars which do not resemble that shape at all! For easier comparison, all lengths were rounded to the shortest eighth of an inch, although some manufacturers list sizes in 16ths or 32nds of an inch.

Readers who would like to see their favorite brand listed in the 2009 edition can call or write the compilers as noted after the Table of Contents.

1886
Machine-made in Cayey, Puerto Rico.

Shape	Name	Lgth	Ring	Wrapper
Corona	Queens	5⅝	42	CC

This one-shape brand features a Connecticut wrapper, around a sheet binder and a blend of short-filler tobaccos.

ALAMO SWEETS
Machine-made in San Antonio, Texas, USA.

Shape	Name	Lgth	Ring	Wrapper
Perfecto	Perfecto	4¾	46	CC-Ma
Cigarillo	Cigarillo	4⅜	29	CC-Ma

The Finck Cigar Company makes this sweetened cigar, which utilizes sheet wrapper and binder and Honduran filler tobacco for a mild taste. It's offered in boxes of 50.

ANTONIO Y CLEOPATRA
Machine-made in Cayey, Puerto Rico.

Shape	Name		Lgth	Ring	Wrapper
Cigarillo	Grenadier Whiffs		3⅝	23⅔	CM
Corona	Grenadier Tubos	*(tubed)*	5⅝	42½	CM
Cigarillo	Grenadier Minis		4½	28	CM
Slim Panatela	Grenadiers		6¼	33½	DC-CC-CM

| Panatela | Grenadier Panatela | 5⅝ | 35 | CM |
| Corona | Grenadier Coronas | 5⅝ | 42 | DC-CM |

This highly popular brand dates back to 1879. Today, it offers a fairly mild taste with Connecticut Broadleaf (for maduro), Connecticut Shade (some shapes) and Javan (most shapes) wrappers, sheet binders and Cuban-seed filler tobaccos. The Coronas are offered in honey and honey berry flavored versions.

ARANGO SPORTSMAN
Machine-made in Santiago, Dominican Republic.

Shape	Name		Lgth	Ring	Wrapper
Slim Panatela	No. 100		5¾	34	CC-Ma
Lonsdale	No. 200		6¼	42	CC-Ma
Churchill	No. 300		7	46	CC-Ma
Robusto	No. 350		5¾	48	CC-Ma
Churchill	No. 400		7½	48	CC-Ma
Lonsdale	Tubes	*(tubed)*	6½	42	CC-Ma
Cigarillo	Tens		4½	28	CC-Ma
Cigarillo	Little Cigars		4	20	CC

Popular since its introduction in 1984, this is a very mild and aromatic cigar, with a touch of vanilla flavoring. It offers an Ecuadorian wrapper, sheet binder and a filler blend of Dominican and Honduran tobaccos. Made in Tampa for many years, production shifted to the Dominican Republic in 2001.

BANKER'S CHOICE ★New★
Machine-made in Frankfort, Indiana, USA.

Shape	Name	Lgth	Ring	Wrapper
Corona Extra	Banker's Choice	5⅛	45	CC

Made by National Cigar, this is a mild-bodied cigar with a Connecticut Shade wrapper and short filler. It's offered in packs of five and boxes of 50.

MACHINE-MADE CIGARS: BRAND LISTINGS

BANCES
Machine-made in Santiago, Dominican Republic.

Shape	Name	Lgth	Ring	Wrapper
Churchill	Corona Immensa	6¾	48	CM-Ma
Robusto	Crowns	5¾	50	Ma
Panatela	El Prado	6¼	36	CM-Ma
Giant	Presidents	8½	52	CM-Ma
Long Corona	Palmas	6	42	CC-Ma
Panatela	Uniques	5½	38	CC-Ma

Bances is also a well-known handmade cigar. The machine-made style offers a Sumatra (natural) or Connecticut (maduro) wrapper, Connecticut binder and a blend of tobaccos from three nations in the filler. Only the Crowns shape uses a homogenized binder. You can find Bances in boxes of 25, but the Presidents are in 10s and the Cazadores and Uniques are in 50s.

BEN BEY
Machine-made in Frankfort, Indiana, USA.

Shape	Name		Lgth	Ring	Wrapper
Corona	Crystals	*(tubed)*	5⅝	44	CC

The Crystals are well named, as they are encased in a glass tube. The blend includes a Connecticut leaf wrapper, sheet binder and U.S. and Dominican tobaccos in the filler. Ben Beys are offered upright in specially-made cedar boxes of 50.

BLACK & MILD
Machine-made in King of Prussia, Pennsylvania, USA.

Shape	Name		Lgth	Ring	Wrapper
Small Panatela	Pipe-Tobacco Cigars *(tipped)*		5	30	Ma
Small Panatela	Fast Break		4	30	Ma
Cigarillo	Filter Tip	*(tipped)*	3⅞	20	Ma

Love the smell of pipe tobacco? Here's a cigar for you, with a pipe-tobacco filler and a homogenized wrapper and binder, offered in convenient five-packs.

MACHINE-MADE CIGARS: BRAND LISTINGS

Variations include an untipped version, an ultra-mild version and an apple, cream or wine-flavored style. The Fast Breaks size was introduced in 2006 and is available in non-flavored, mild and apple versions.

BLACK HAWK
Machine-made in Frankfort, Indiana, USA.

Shape	Name	Lgth	Ring	Wrapper
Corona Extra	Chief	5⅛	45	CM

The Chief has a medium body and uses a Pennsylvania leaf wrapper, a sheet binder and a blend of Dominican and U.S. tobaccos in the filler.

BLUNT WRAP LOADED
Machine-made in Santiago, Dominican Republic.

Shape	Name	Lgth	Ring	Wrapper
Small Panatela	Cigarillo	4½	30	CM
Petit Corona	Blunt	4½	40	CM

Introduced in 2006, this brand has a homogenized wrapper and binder and uses short-filler tobacco from Connecticut and the Dominican Republic. It's mild and offered in keep-fresh pouches in Apple, Blueberry, Grape, Peach, Strawberry and Sweet.

CANDLELIGHT
Machine-made in Dingelstadt, Germany.

Shape	Name	Lgth	Ring	Wrapper
Cigarillo	Mini	2⅞	20	CC-Ma
Small Panatela	Senorita	3¾	30	CC-Ma
Small Panatela	Corona Slim	4	30	CC-Ma
Short Panatela	Block Corona	4¾	38	CC-Ma
Panatela	Panatela Grande	6⅛	38	CC-Ma

All sizes are mild and use a Brazilian (maduro) or Sumatra (natural) wrapper, sheet binder and filler tobacco from Indonesia, Brazil and either the Dominican Republic or the United States. The Minis are finished with just a touch of vanilla aroma, and are available in Brazil, Sumatra, cherry and vanilla in tins of 10 or 20.

MACHINE-MADE CIGARS: BRAND LISTINGS

CARIBBEAN LINE
Machine-made in Yoe, Pennsylvania, USA.

Shape	Name	Lgth	Ring	Wrapper
Lonsdale	Casinos	6½	43	CC-Ma
Small Panatela	Petites	4	34	CC-Ma
Lonsdale	Rounds	7⅛	44	CC-Ma
Long Panatela	Royales	6½	35	CC-Ma

Available in fairly large sizes for mass-market cigars, this mild-bodied brand offers a natural leaf wrapper, has a sheet binder and a blend of short-filler tobaccos. All sizes are offered in wood boxes of 50.

CHARLES DENBY
Machine-made in Frankfort, Indiana, USA.

Shape	Name	Lgth	Ring	Wrapper
Corona	Invincible	5½	43	Cl

A Connecticut wrapper, sheet binders and a blended filler with American and Dominican tobaccos give this brand a medium body.

CHERRY BLEND
Machine-made in King of Prussia, Pennsylvania, USA.

Shape	Name		Lgth	Ring	Wrapper
Small Panatela	Pipe-Tobacco	*(tipped)*	5	30	Ma

The sweet smell of cherry is the appeal of this pipe-tobacco-filled cigar. Offered in packs of five, it has a homogenized wrapper and binder and a plastic tip for easy smoking.

CHEVERE SMALL CIGARS
Machine-made in Ballaghaderreen, Ireland.

Shape	Name	Lgth	Ring	Wrapper
Perfecto	Figurado	4	42	CM
Short Panatela	Half Corona	4⅛	37	CM-Ma

MACHINE-MADE CIGARS: BRAND LISTINGS

Cigarillo	Cigarillos	3⅛	23	CM-Ma
Small Panatela	Senoritas	3⅞	31	CM-Ma
Cigarillo	Tabaquitos	3½	20	CM
Cigarillo	Wilde Cigarillo	4	23	CM-Ma
Small Panatela	Wilde Havana	4⅛	31	CM-Ma

These little cigars medium in body and dry-cured, with a choice of Sumatra wrappers or maduro wrappers from Brazil. They are made by Villiger in Ireland and offered in boxes of 25 or 50 depending on size. The Cigarillos are offered in a flavored style in Honey Cream or vanilla.

CUBAN CLUB CLASSICS
BY HABANA GOLD
Machine-made, with 100% tobacco, in Ireland.

Introduced in 1998, this is an all-tobacco line in three sizes that features your choice of an Ecuadorian or Indonesian wrapper and Nicaraguan binder and short filler. The result is a mild smoke, offered in packs of five or eight.

CYRILLA
Machine-made in Santiago, Dominican Republic.

Shape	Name	Lgth	Ring	Wrapper
Long Corona	Nationals	6	42	CC-Ma
Churchill	Kings	7	46	CC-Ma
Churchill	Senators	7½	48	CC-Ma
Panatela	Slims	6½	36	CC-Ma

These are mild cigars, offered in bundles of 25 cigars each. They feature either an Ecuadorian (natural) wrapper or a Connecticut Broadleaf in the maduro shade, a sheet binder and filler tobaccos from the Dominican and Honduras.

DECISION MADURO
Machine-made in Tampa, Florida, USA.

Shape	Name	Lgth	Ring	Wrapper
Robusto	No. 250	5½	49	Ma

Grand Corona	No. 350	6¼	45	Ma
Corona	No. 450	5	44	Ma
Short Panatela	No. 550	5⅜	37	Ma

This brand has been around since 1935 and today offers a mild to medium smoke at a great value. The all-maduro series features a Connecticut Broadleaf wrapper, with a sheet binder and filler tobaccos from the Dominican Republic. Each size is available in economical bundles of 20.

DRY SLITZ

Machine-made in Yoe, Pennsylvania, USA.

Shape	*Name*	*Lgth*	*Ring*	*Wrapper*
Slim Panatela	Regular	5½	34	CC

This is a mild-bodied cigar with a homogenized wrapper, sheet binder and U.S. and Dominican tobaccos in the filler. The head of the cigar is finished with a small hole so that you can light it up without cutting!

DUTCH MASTERS

Machine-made in Cayey, Puerto Rico.

Shape	*Name*	*Lgth*	*Ring*	*Wrapper*
Petit Corona	Perfecto	4¾	44	CM
Panatela	Panatela	5½	36	CM
Slim Panatela	Cameroon Elite	6⅛	29½	CM
Corona	President	5⅝	40½	CM
Corona	Corona Sports	5⅝	42	CC
Corona	Corona Deluxe	5⅝	42	CM
Corona	Corona Maduro	5⅝	42	Ma
Corona	Honey Sports	5⅝	42	CM
	Dutch Masters Collection:			
Cigarillo	Cigarillo	4½	28	CC
Corona	Palmas	5⅝	42	CC

MACHINE-MADE CIGARS: BRAND LISTINGS

Remember the Dutch Masters television commercials of the 1960s, as the actors retired into the brand's trademark portrait at the end? The commercials are history, but the brand (introduced in 1911) continues to do well, offering a mild smoke in both manufactured and natural wrapper styles. The Corona Deluxe, Cameroon Elite and Corona Maduro shapes all feature natural leaf wrappers; all shapes have homogenized binders and a short-filler blend of Cuban-seed tobaccos. The Cigarillos and Palmas in the Dutch Masters Collection were introduced in 2002. The Cigarillos are offered in Cognac, chocolate, Honey Sports and vanilla, while the Palmas are available in honey, cognac and chocolate flavors. The Corona Sports shape was offered in a Gold & Honey and honey flavor in 2005.

EL MACCO
Machine-made in Frankfort, Indiana, USA.

Shape	Name	Lgth	Ring	Wrapper
Corona Extra	Puritano Dark	4¾	45	CM

This brand presents a medium-bodied taste and has a Pennsylvania leaf wrapper, a sheet binder and a blend of Dominican and U.S. tobacco in the filler.

EL PRODUCTO
Machine-made in Cayey, Puerto Rico.

Shape	Name		Lgth	Ring	Wrapper
Small Panatela	Little Coronas		4⅝	31	CC
Corona	Blunts		5⅝	40½	CC
Petit Corona	Bouquets		4¾	44	CC
Corona Extra	Puritano Finos		4⅞	46½	CC
Robusto	Favoritas		5	48½	CC
Robusto	Escepcionales		5⅛	52½	CC
Corona	Queens	(tubed)	5⅝	42	CC

Introduced in 1916, this was the smoke of choice (in the Queens size) for decades for the late comedian George Burns (1896-1996) and it continues to have many contemporary admirers. The many shapes are primarily clothed in manufactured wrappers; the Escepcionales and Queens feature a natural wrapper. All shapes use homogenized binders.

MACHINE-MADE CIGARS: BRAND LISTINGS

EL TRELLES
Machine-made in Jacksonville, Florida, USA.

Shape	Name	Lgth	Ring	Wrapper
Long Corona	Bankers	6	43	CC
Long Corona	Club House	6	41	Ma
Long Corona	Kings	6	41	CC
Pyramid	Tryangles Deluxe	5¼	45	CC

This is a very mild cigar, with a natural leaf wrapper from Connecticut (natural) or Mexico (maduro), sheet binder and a four-nation filler blend. El Trelles cigars are offered in convenient five-packs and by the box (of 50).

EL VERSO
Machine-made in Frankfort, Indiana, USA.

Shape	Name	Lgth	Ring	Wrapper
Grand Corona	Corona Extra Dark	5¾	47	CM
Corona Extra	Bouquet Dark	4¾	45	CM
Panatela	Commodore	6	36	CM
Corona Extra	Bouquet Light Leaf	4¾	45	Cl

The sunny graphics on the El Verso box herald a medium-bodied cigar with a Connecticut or Pennsylvania wrapper, either a Connecticut or sheet wrapper depending on the model, and American and Dominican filler.

EMERSON
Machine-made in Yoe, Pennsylvania, USA.

Shape	Name	Lgth	Ring	Wrapper
Petit Corona	Diplomat	4¾	42½	Cl

American and Dominican filler tobaccos are at the heart of this one-shape brand. It offers a medium body and has a homogenized wrapper and sheet binder.

EVERMORE
Machine-made, with 100% tobacco, in Frankfort, Indiana, USA.

MACHINE-MADE CIGARS: BRAND LISTINGS

Shape	Name	Lgth	Ring	Wrapper
Corona Extra	Original	4⅝	45	CI-CC-CM
Grand Corona	Corona Grande	5¾	47	CI-CM

This is an all-tobacco cigar, with a Connecticut leaf wrapper, Connecticut binder and a blend of American and Dominican tobaccos in the filler.

FARNAM DRIVE
Machine-made, with 100% tobacco, in Frankfort, Indiana, USA.

Shape	Name	Lgth	Ring	Wrapper
Corona Extra	Original	5⅛	45	CC-CC-Ma

This is an all-tobacco cigar that offers a medium-bodied taste and uses Connecticut leaves for the wrapper and binder and a blend of American and Dominican tobaccos in the filler.

FLORIDA QUEEN
Machine-made in Frankfort, Indiana, USA.

Shape	Name	Lgth	Ring	Wrapper
Petit Corona	Florida Queen	5	42½	CC

Here is a medium-bodied cigar, made up of American and Dominican filler tobaccos, a sheet binder and a genuine Wisconsin leaf wrapper.

GARCIA Y VEGA
Machine-made in Santiago, Dominican Republic

Shape	Name		Lgth	Ring	Wrapper
Petit Corona	Barons		4¾	41	CC
Petit Corona	Blunts		4¾	41	CC
Slim Panatela	Bravuras		5⅜	34	CC
Cigarillo	Chicos		4¼	27	CC
Cigarillo	Cigarillos		4¼	27	DC
Slim Panatela	Crystals No. 100	(tubed)	6⅜	34	CC
Long Corona	Crystals No. 200	(tubed)	6⅛	41	CC

MACHINE-MADE CIGARS: BRAND LISTINGS

Short Panatela	Delgado Panatela	5⅜	34	CC
Panatela	Elegantes	6⅜	34	DC
Corona	English Coronas *(tubed)*	5¼	41	CC
Panatela	Gallantes	6⅜	34	CC
Long Corona	Game Palma	6	42	DC-CM
Small Panatela	Game Cigarillos	4¾	30	CM
Long Corona	Gran Coronas *(tubed)*	6⅛	41	DC
Long Corona	Gran Premios *(tubed)*	6⅛	41	CC
Long Corona	Maduro Crystals *(tubed)*	6⅛	41	Ma
Cigarillo	Miniatures	4⅝	29	CC-Ma
Slim Panatela	Panatela Deluxe	5⅜	34	DC
Cigarillo	Pop's Crystals *(glass tubes)*	4⅝	29	CC
Corona	Presidente	5¾	41	CC
Petit Corona	Senators	4½	41	DC
Cigarillo	Whiffs	3¾	23	CC
Cigarillo	Whiffs Gold	3¾	23	CC
Long Corona	Maduro	6⅛	41	Ma

Since 1882, this brand has been a favorite all across the United States, enjoyed more than 300,000 times daily nationwide. The natural leaf wrapper comes from the Cameroon, Connecticut or Mexico and is combined with a sheet binder and a blend of filler tobaccos for the brand's characteristic mild taste. The Senators are offered in a sweet & mild flavor, as are the Cigarillos. The Miniatures are available in Vanilla Cordial and Rum Reserve. Garcia y Vega cigars are always fresh thanks to in-the-pack pouches or tubes and are offered in packs of 3, 4 or 5 cigars or in boxes of 30, 40 or 50.

The Game line was introduced in 2007 in two styles: Palma and Cigarillos. The Palmas come in Green, Honey and Vanilla while the Cigarillos are offered in Honey, Peach and Sweet.

GARGOYLE
Machine-made in Frankfort, Indiana, USA.

MACHINE-MADE CIGARS: BRAND LISTINGS

Shape	Name	Lgth	Ring	Wrapper
Panatela	Lanza	6	38	Cl

The cigar is not as ugly as the brand name might imply! It's actually a medium-bodied smoke with a Connecticut wrapper, sheet binder and a blend of American and Dominican filler.

GLADSTONE
Machine-made in Yoe, Pennsylvania, USA.

Shape	Name	Lgth	Ring	Wrapper
Perfecto	Perfecto	5	41	CC
Petit Corona	Blunts	5	43	CC

Just right for a short smoke are these small cigars, which are dipped for sweetness and offer a mild taste in packs of five and boxes of 50. The Blunts are offered in flavors: chocolate and vanilla.

GOLD & MILD
Machine-made in King of Prussia, Pennsylvania, USA.

Shape	Name		Lgth	Ring	Wrapper
Small Panatela	Pipe-Tobacco	*(tipped)*	5	30	CC

The gentle aroma of pipe tobacco is the appeal of this brand, which features a plastic tip for easy smoking and a homogenized wrapper and binder. It is offered in convenient five-packs.

HAUPTMANN'S
Machine-made in Frankfort, Indiana, USA.

Shape	Name	Lgth	Ring	Wrapper
Corona Extra	Perfecto	5⅛	45	Cl-CM
Corona	Broadleaf	5¼	43	CM
Corona	Corona	5¼	43	Cl
Panatela	Panatela	5¾	38	Cl-CM

This is a medium-bodied smoke, with a genuine Connecticut or Pennsylvania leaf wrapper, sheet binder and a blend of Dominican and U.S. tobaccos in the filler.

MACHINE-MADE CIGARS: BRAND LISTINGS

HAVANA BLEND
Machine-made, with 100% tobacco, in San Antonio, Texas, USA.

Shape	Name	Lgth	Ring	Wrapper
Churchill	Churchill	7	47	Ma
Petit Corona	Coronado	5	43	Ma
Corona	Delicado	5¾	43	Ma
Lonsdale	Doubloon	6½	42	Ma
Cigarillo	Palma Fina	6½	29	Ma
Short Panatela	Petit Corona	4¾	38	Ma
Robusto	Rothschild	5	50	Ma
Toro	Toro	6	50	Ma

This unique, all-tobacco brand features filler tobacco from the 1959 Cuban crop, combined with a Connecticut Broadleaf maduro wrapper. It has a medium-bodied taste and is offered in boxes of 25 or 50.

HAVANA BLEND SERIE SOMBRA
Machine-made, with 100% tobacco, in San Antonio, Texas, USA.

Shape	Name	Lgth	Ring	Wrapper
Lonsdale	Super Corona	6½	42	CC
Toro	Gran Corona	6¼	50	CC
Churchill	Double Corona	7	47	CC
Robusto	Five-Fifty	5	50	CC

This line was introduced in 2006. It is mild with a shade-grown Connecticut wrapper and filler tobaccos from Brazil, Nicaragua, Connecticut and a little pre-embargo Cuban filler. It's offered in boxes of 18 (Grand Corona only) and 25.

HOUSE OF WINDSOR
Machine-made in Yoe, Pennsylvania, USA.

Shape	Name	Lgth	Ring	Wrapper
Lonsdale	Palma	6½	43	DC

MACHINE-MADE CIGARS: BRAND LISTINGS

Here are the well-known products of the House of Windsor, offering a variety of sizes, mostly with the traditional Candela wrapper, grown in Honduras. These cigars feature natural leaf wrappers, sheet binders and short-fill tobaccos.

IBOLD
Machine-made in Frankfort, Indiana, USA.

Shape	Name	Lgth	Ring	Wrapper
Petit Corona	Blunt	4⅞	44	Cl-CM
Petit Corona	Black Pete	4⅞	44	CM
Robusto	Breva	5⅛	51	Cl-Ma
Panatela	Ideals	5⅞	38	Cl-CM
Short Panatela	Slims	5¼	35	Cl-CM
Cigarillo	Cigarillo	4¼	29	Ma

Manufactured by the National Cigar Corporation, this brand offers a medium-bodied taste thanks to its Pennsylvania (Connecticut on the cigarillo) leaf wrapper, sheet or Connecticut binder — depending on the shape — and the filler blend of U.S. and Dominican leaves.

J-R FAMOUS
Machine-made in Santiago, Dominican Republic.

Shape	Name	Lgth	Ring	Wrapper
Toro	Churchill	5¾	50	DC-CM-Ma
Panatela	Delicados	6	39	DC-CM-Ma
Long Corona	Plazas	6	42	DC-CM-Ma
Lonsdale	Presidents	7⅛	44	DC-CM-Ma

This is a mild-to-medium-bodied, highly popular cigar with a Sumatra-seed, Honduran-grown wrapper, sheet binder and Dominican and Honduran filler. The Delicados and Plazas shapes are offered in an aromatic blend. It is an excellent value and offered in boxes of 50.

JAMAICAN SMALLS
Machine-made in Mayaguez, Puerto Rico.

MACHINE-MADE CIGARS: BRAND LISTINGS

Shape	Name	Lgth	Ring	Wrapper
Small Panatela	Petit Vanilla	5	30	CM
Cigarillo	Jamaican Smalls	4	28	CM

The name is new (old: Nativo), but this is the same uniquely flavored cigar, with a Connecticut wrapper, sheet binder and flavored Puerto Rico filler. The Cigarillos are offered in Amaretto, Cognac, chocolate, vanilla, cherry and clove in boxes of 50. The Petit Vanillas are offered in boxes of 30.

JOHN HAY
Machine-made, with 100% tobacco, near York, Pennsylvania, USA.

Shape	Name	Lgth	Ring	Wrapper
Robusto	Cadet	5	49	CC-Ma
Grand Corona	Diplomat	6	46	CC-Ma

This brand goes back to 1882, when W.W. Stewart actually obtained permission from prominent American statesman John Hay – later Secretary of State – to issue a brand in his honor. The machine-made version is all tobacco, with a Lancaster County, Pennsylvania Broadleaf wrapper, Pennsylvania binder and a medium-filler blend from Connecticut, Maryland and Pennsylvania. There are four flavors available in the Diplomat size: cocoa, vanilla, Cognac and rum. This all-American cigar is offered in boxes of 50 or packs of five.

KEEP MOVING
Machine-made in Jacksonville, Florida, USA.

Shape	Name	Lgth	Ring	Wrapper
Petit Corona	Goodies	4½	41	CC

This one-size brand has a natural leaf wrapper, sheet binder and blends tobaccos of four nations in the filler. Look for Keep Moving in twin-packs, five-packs and in full boxes of 50.

KING EDWARD
Machine-made in Jacksonville, Florida, USA.

Shape	Name	Lgth	Ring	Wrapper
Corona	Invincible Deluxe	5¾	42	CC

MACHINE-MADE CIGARS: BRAND LISTINGS

Short Panatela	Panatela Deluxe		5¼	38	CC
Long Corona	Corona Deluxe		6	42	CC
Cigarillo	Cigarillo Deluxe		4¼	28½	CC
Petit Corona	Blunt		5	42	CC
Petit Corona	Imperial		5	40	CC
Panatela	Slim		5⅝	36	CC
Cigarillo	Specials		4⅜	28½	CC
Cigarillo	Tip Cigarillo	(tipped)	4⅞	28	CC
Cigarillo	Wood Tip Cigarillo	(tipped)	5½	29	CC
Cigarillo	Little Cigars		4⅜	29	CC

Britain's King Edward VII (1841-1910) is celebrated as the man who, with four words, revised the Victorian prohibition against tobacco soon after his ascension to the throne in 1901: "Gentlemen, you may smoke." This brand still bears his portrait and is now machine-made with a sheet wrapper and binder and a four-nation filler blend. The Deluxe shapes feature a natural leaf wrapper, while the Wood Tip Cigarillo is available in Sweet Cherry. Widely available in the U.S. and highly popular in England and 60 other countries, King Edward is offered in five-packs and boxes of 50. The Little Cigars are offered in packs of 20 in regular, cherry and ice menthol flavors.

LA FENDRICH ★Returns★
Machine-made in Frankfort, Indiana, USA.

Shape	Name	Lgth	Ring	Wrapper
Corona Extra	Favorita	5⅛	45	CC

This band returned to national distribution in 2007. Made by National Cigar, it features a Connecticut Shade wrapper and a medium-bodied taste. It's available in boxes of 50.

LORD BEACONSFIELD
Machine-made in Santiago, Dominican Republic.

Shape	Name	Lgth	Ring	Wrapper
Churchill	Rounds	7¼	46	CM-Ma

MACHINE-MADE CIGARS: BRAND LISTINGS

Slim Panatela	Lords	7	34	CM-Ma
Long Corona	Coronas Superba	6¼	42	CM-Ma
Panatela	Lindas	6½	36	CM-Ma
Corona	Cubanola	5½	44	CM-Ma
Churchill	Directors	7¾	46	CM-Ma

This is a veteran brand with a Sumatra wrapper and a three-nation, short filler blend, combined with a sheet binder for a mild taste. It is offered in boxes of 50 except for the Directors, offered in 25s.

LORD CLINTON
Machine-made in Yoe, Pennsylvania, USA.

Shape	Name	Lgth	Ring	Wrapper
Slim Panatela	Panatela	5¼	34	CC
Corona	Perfecto	5	42½	CI

The Panatela has a Connecticut wrapper, sheet binder and filler tobaccos from the Dominican Republic and the United States. It has a medium-bodied taste. The Perfecto has the same filler, but uses a sheet binder and wrapper.

MARK IV
Machine-made in Yoe, Pennsylvania, USA.

Shape	Name	Lgth	Ring	Wrapper
Lonsdale	Magnate	6½	43	DC

From the respected House of Windsor comes the Windsor & Mark line, which features natural leaf wrappers grown in Honduras, sheet binders and a filler blend of imported, short-filler, tobaccos. The Magnates are available in 3-packs.

MARSH
Machine-made in Frankfort, Indiana, USA.

Shape	Name	Lgth	Ring	Wrapper
Slim Panatela	Mountaineer	5½	34	CC-Ma
Panatela	Virginian	5½	37	CC-Ma

Panatela	Pioneer	5½	37	CC-Ma
Slim Panatela	Old Reliable	5½	33	Ma
Long Panatela	Deluxe	7	34	Ma
Long Panatela	Deluxe II	7	34	Ma
Long Panatela	Olde Style Stogies	7	34	Ma

This brand began back in 1840 and continues today as a popular mass-market cigar in many parts of the United States. All of the shapes are mild and all use either Wisconsin (most) or Pennsylvania-grown (Old Reliable) leaves for wrappers and sheet binders. Most of the shapes offer a U.S. and Dominican filler blend, except for the Old Reliable, which incorporates fire-cured Kentucky tobacco in its filler. The Deluxe and Old Style Stogies are finished with a pig-tail head. The heads of the Deluxe II shape are pre-drilled with holes to allow instant ignition without cutting.

MIAMI SUITES
Machine-made in Cayey, Puerto Rico.

Shape	Name	Lgth	Ring	Wrapper
Small Panatela	Miami Suites	4⅝	31	CM

Introduced in 1998, this cigar has a mild taste thanks to its Java wrapper. The line was changed with the shape enlarged from a cigarillo to a small panatela. Miami Suites have a homogenized binder and highly flavored short filler. It is offered in packs of six in Amaretto, Honey, Honey Berry, Irish Cream and Rum.

MIFLIN'S CHOICE
Machine-made in Frankfort, Indiana, USA.

Shape	Name		Lgth	Ring	Wrapper
Slim Panatela	Panatela	(tubed)	6⅜	32	CC-CM

This small cigar offers a choice of a Cameroon or Connecticut Shade wrapper, sheet binder and a blend of U.S. and Dominican tobaccos in the filler. It's offered in boxes of 20.

MOYA
Machine-made in Tampa, Florida, USA.

MACHINE-MADE CIGARS: BRAND LISTINGS

Shape	Name	Lgth	Ring	Wrapper
Robusto	Casadores	5½	48	CC-Ma
Grand Corona	Fumas	6	45	CC-Ma

This is a mild-bodied cigar featuring Domincan filler leaves available in inexpensive bundles of 25 cigars each.

MUNIEMAKER
Machine-made, with 100% tobacco,
in McSherrystown, Pennsylvania, USA.

Shape	Name	Lgth	Ring	Wrapper
Corona Extra	Regular	4½	47	Cl-CC-CM
Robusto	Straight	5⅛	48	CC
Grand Corona	Long	6	46	CC
Cheroot	Cheroot	5	33	CC
Robusto	Breva 100's	5⅛	48	CC-Ma
Slim Panatela	Panatela 100's	6	33	CC-Ma
Grand Corona	Palma 100's	6	46	CC-Ma
Perfecto	Perfecto 100's	5¼	52	CC-Ma
Corona Extra	Cueto	4⅞	45	Cl-CC
Corona Extra	Bouquet Special (tubed)	5⅛	46	CC-Ma
Corona Extra	Judges Cave	4½	47	Cl-CC-Ma

F.D. Grave began this line in 1884 with the goal of making "the best possible cigars at prices cigar lovers could afford." Now, F.D. Grave & Sons continues this tradition of all-tobacco, medium-to-full-bodied cigars, featuring Connecticut Broadleaf wrappers and binders around a core of U.S. tobaccos in the filler. The Perfecto 100s and Bouquet Specials are boxed in 25s, while most of the other shapes are available in boxes of 50. Handy packs of four and five cigars each are also available in most sizes.

MURIEL
Machine-made in McAdoo, Pennsylvania, USA
and Cayey, Puerto Rico.

MACHINE-MADE CIGARS: BRAND LISTINGS

Shape	*Name*	*Lgth*	*Ring*	*Wrapper*
Corona Extra	Magnum	4⅝	46½	CC
Small Panatela	Air Tips Regular *(tipped)*	5	30½	CC
Small Panatela	Air Tips Pipe Aroma *(tipped)*	5	30½	CC
Small Panatela	Air Tips Sweet *(tipped)*	5	30½	CC
Small Panatela	Flavored Tips *(tipped)*	5	30½	CC
Small Panatela	Coronella	4⅝	31	CC
Small Panatela	Coronella Sweet	4⅝	31	CC
	Muriel Sweets Little Cigars:			
Cigarillo	Black & Sweet	3⅞	20	CM
Cigarillo	Sweet & Mild	3⅞	20	CC
Cigarillo	Menthol	3⅞	20	CC

This famous brand features a manufactured wrapper and offer a variety of sizes for every smoker. The Coronella group includes all natural fillers, while the new Pipe Tobacco series includes pipe tobacco filler. All are made in Puerto Rico except for the Sweets, made in Pennsylvania. The Flavored Tips are offered in blackberry, chocolate and strawberry.

NAT CICCO'S ★*Returns*★

Machine-made in Santiago, Dominican Republic.

Shape	*Name*	*Lgth*	*Ring*	*Wrapper*
Churchill	Churchill Rejects	8	46	DC-CC-Ma
Long Corona	Plazas	6	42	DC-CC-Ma
Long Corona	Governor	6	42	CC
Robusto	Robusto Rejects	5½	49	DC-CC-Ma
Small Panatela	Jamaican Delights	5	34	CC-Ma
Lonsdale	Jamaican Palmas	6½	43	CC-Ma
Slim Panatela	Jamaican Regales	7⅛	34	CC-Ma
Long Panatela	Jamaican Rounds	7¼	36	CC-Ma

MACHINE-MADE CIGARS: BRAND LISTINGS

Here is the Nat Cicco series, in production again in 2007 after being on and off the market since the early 2000s. All are mild in body, featuring a Honduran wrapper, sheet binder and a mix of short-fill tobaccos. The Plaza line is offered in an Aromatic style. All sizes are offered in boxes of 50, except for the Governors (25).

No. 59 FACTORY THROW-OUTS
Machine-made in Tampa, Florida, USA.

Shape	Name	Lgth	Ring	Wrapper
Grand Corona	Factory Throw-Outs	6¼	45	CC

Inspired by the Stanford Newman, this cigar was introduced in 2006 and is made at the J.C. Newman Cigar Co. in Tampa. It features an Ecuadorian-grown wrapper, homogenized binder and short-filler and is offered in bundles of 20.

ODIN
Machine-made in Yoe, Pennsylvania, USA.

Shape	Name	Lgth	Ring	Wrapper
Petit Corona	Viking	4¾	42½	CC

The Odin Viking offers a medium-bodied taste, with tobaccos from the Dominican Republic and the United States in the filler. The wrapper is homogenized tobacco leaf and a sheet binder is used.

OPTIMO
Machine-made in Jacksonville, Florida, USA.

Shape	Name		Lgth	Ring	Wrapper
Long Corona	Admiral		6	41	DC-CC
Petit Corona	Blunt		4¾	42	CC
Slim Panatela	Brigadier	*(tubed)*	6¼	33	CC-Ma
Corona	Coronas	*(tubes available)*	5¼	42	CC-Ma
Long Corona	Palmas		6	41	Ma
Slim Panatela	Panatela		5¼	33	DC-CC
Petit Corona	Sports		4½	41	DC-CC
Cigarillo	Cigarillo		4⅜	28	DC

MACHINE-MADE CIGARS: BRAND LISTINGS

Optimo was, at one time, made of Cuban tobacco, but is today a mass-market favorite. It combines a natural leaf wrapper from Ecuador (candela), Connecticut (natural) or Mexico (maduro), a sheet binder and a four-nation filler blend, and is available in twin-packs, five-packs and, of course, full boxes of 50. The Coronas are available in rum flavor; the Blunts in peach and Icy Mint and the Cigarillos in Icy Mint, peach, grape and honey.

PALMA THROW-OUTS
Machine-made in Yoe, Pennsylvania, USA.

Shape	Name	Lgth	Ring	Wrapper
Lonsdale	Palma Throw-Outs	6½	43	Cl-CC-Ma

What an undeserving shape name! These are value-priced, machine-made seconds with a natural leaf wrapper, sheet binder and an imported, blended filler. Offered in packs of five and boxes of 50.

PEDRO IGLESIAS
Machine-made, with 100% tobacco, in Santiago, Dominican Republic.

Shape	Name	Lgth	Ring	Wrapper
Corona Extra	Crowns	5	45	CC-Ma
Long Corona	Regents	6	44	CC-Ma
Lonsdale	Lonsdales	6½	44	CC

This is an all-tobacco brand, featuring a Sumatra wrapper, Connecticut Broadleaf binder and a short-filler blend of tobaccos from three nations. All three shapes are offered in boxes of 50.

PHILLIES
Machine-made in Selma, Alabama, USA.

Shape	Name	Lgth	Ring	Wrapper
Corona	Perfecto	5¾	43	CC
Long Corona	Titan	6¼	44	CC
Long Corona	Titan Black	6¼	44	CC
Cigarillo	Black Max	5	27	CC

Petit Corona	Blunts		4⅞	41	CC
Short Panatela	Mini Blunt		4¼	37	CC
Slim Panatela	Panatella		5½	34	CC
Small Panatela	Mexicali Slim		4⅝	32	CC
Short Panatela	Phatz Cigarillos		4¼	36¾	CC
Corona	Sweets		5¾	43	CC
Small Panatela	Cheroot		5	32	CC
Cigarillo	Cigarillo	(tubes available)	4¼	27	CC
Cigarillo	Tips	(tipped)	4½	28	CC
Cigarillo	Tip Sweet	(tipped)	4½	28	CC

This well-known brand was created by Bayuk Cigar of Philadelphia and was trademarked way back in 1929. Phillies are constructed with a sheet wrapper and binder, with filler from Dominican and Honduran tobaccos, to provide its mild-bodied taste.

A wave of flavors appeared in 2002. Blunts are offered in banana, berry, chocolate aroma, coconut, Cognac, greene de menthe, honey, mango, Piña Colada, peach, Sambuca, sour apple, strawberry, watermelon and sweet vanilla. The Black Max shape, introduced in 2001, is available in mild, banana, chocolate, cinnamon, Honey Berry, peach, rum, strawberry and vanilla editions. The Cigarillos are featured in apricot, banana, berry, chocolate, cinnamon, coconut, Cognac, grape, honey, mango, peach, Piña Colada, sour apple, strawberry and watermelon with some flavors in tubes. The Mini Blunts are available in banana, peach, strawberry, sour apple and sweet. Mexicali Slims are offered in chocolate, Cognac and strawberry margarita. The Perfectos are available in strawberry. Titans are available in chocolate; Phatz Cigarillos are offered in peach flavor.

PRINCE ALBERT
Machine-made in King of Prussia, Pennsylvania, USA.

Shape	Name		Lgth	Ring	Wrapper
Small Panatela	Soft & Sweet Vanilla	(tipped)	5	30	CM
Small Panatela	Soft Cherry Vanilla	(tipped)	5	30	CM

MACHINE-MADE CIGARS: BRAND LISTINGS

These tipped cigars from John Middleton, Inc. are extremely mild and feature an all-pipe tobacco filler, aimed at providing pipe tobacco taste - and aroma - in cigar form.

R. G. DUN
Machine-made in Frankfort, Indiana, USA.

Shape	Name	Lgth	Ring	Wrapper
Petit Corona	Admiral	4¾	42½	CC
Petit Corona	Babies	4⅛	42	CC
Corona	Bouquet	5½	42½	CC
Slim Panatela	Youngfellow	5¼	34	CC

This is a medium-bodied cigar made by National Cigar. It offers a Connecticut, Wisconsin or Nicaraguan leaf wrapper, has a sheet binder and a blended filler of American and Dominican tobaccos.

RIGOLETTO
Machine-made in Tampa, Florida, USA.

Shape	Name		Lgth	Ring	Wrapper
Long Corona	Londonaire	(tubed)	6¼	44	CC-Ma
Corona Extra	Black Jack		5½	47	Ma
Long Corona	Black Lightning		6¼	44	Ma
Long Corona	Natural Coronas		6¼	41	CC
Long Corona	Palma Grande		6¼	41	CC
Long Corona	Natural Panatela		6¼	44	CC

This is a mild-to-medium brand produced in Tampa. First introduced in 1905, it features a Connecticut Broadleaf or Shade wrapper, a sheet binder and high-quality filler tobaccos from the Dominican Republic.

ROBERT BURNS
Machine-made in Santiago, Dominican Republic and Dothan, Alabama, USA.

MACHINE-MADE CIGARS: BRAND LISTINGS

Shape	Name		Lgth	Ring	Wrapper
Corona	Black Watch	(tubed)	5⅝	41	CC
Cigarillo	Cigarillo		4½	27	CC

The Black Watch model is made in Santiago, the Dominican Republic, with a Connecticut Shade wrapper, sheet binder and a multi-nation blend of filler tobaccos in three-packs and boxes of 30. The famous Cigarillos are made by Swedish Match in Dothan, Alabama with sheet wrappers and binders and blended filler, offered in five-packs and boxes of 50.

ROI TAN
Machine-made in Cayey, Puerto Rico.

Shape	Name	Lgth	Ring	Wrapper
Slim Panatela	Falcons	6¼	33½	CC

This famous old brand uses a manufactured wrapper and short-filler tobaccos for a mild taste in packs of five or boxes of 50.

ROSEDALE
Machine-made, with 100% tobacco, in Hartford, Connecticut, USA.

Shape	Name	Lgth	Ring	Wrapper
Perfecto	Perfecto	4⅞	48	CC-CM
Corona Extra	Londres	5¼	46	CM

Made continuously since the 1920s, Rosedale is a part of the Topper cigar group, made of 100% tobacco. The Connecticut Broadleaf wrapper (Shade wrapper also available on the Perfecto) surrounds a Connecticut binder and filler tobaccos from Brazil, the Dominican Republic and the U.S. It's offered in packs of 5 or boxes of 50.

ROYAL BLUNTS
Machine-made in Dothan, Alabama, USA.

Shape	Name	Lgth	Ring	Wrapper
Petit Corona	Blunts	4¾	41	CC
Cigarillo	Cigarillo	4⅝	29	CC

Introduced in 2004, this is a mild-bodied cigar with a homogenized wrapper and binder and U.S.-grown short-filler tobaccos. It's offered in many flavors: Cherry Vanilla, Wet Mango and Strawberry in packs of five, 25 or 50.

S.F.S.
Machine-made in Yoe, Pennsylvania, USA.

Shape	Name	Lgth	Ring	Wrapper
Panatela	Café Cubano	6½	35	CC
Panatela	Almond Liquer	6½	35	CC
Giant Corona	Churchill Rejects	8¼	43	DC-CC-Ma
Petit Corona	Robusto Rejects	5	43	DC-CC-Ma
Small Panatela	Cigarillo Rejects	4½	32	DC-CC

This is a flavored cigar with a natural wrapper, in two flavors in boxes of 50.

SAM HOUSTON
Machine-made in San Antonio, Texas, USA.

Shape	Name	Lgth	Ring	Wrapper
Toro	Grande	6	50	CC-CM-Ma
Long Corona	Corona	6	43	CC-CM-Ma
Perfecto	Perfecto	4¾	46	CC-Ma
Churchill	Churchill	7	47	CC-CM-Ma
Robusto	Rothschild	5	50	CC-Ma
Perfecto	Special Perfecto	4¾	46	CC-Ma
Cigarillo	Special Cigarillo	4⅜	29	CC-Ma

This salute to the "Father of Texas" and its first governor after independence (1836-38) is a mild blend of a Connecticut wrapper (all shapes), sheet binder and Brazilian, Honduran and Connecticut filler in the standard line. Three shapes also have an Indonesian wrapper available. The Special series features a sheet wrapper and binder and Brazilian and Honduran filler. All sizes are offered in value-priced boxes of 50.

MACHINE-MADE CIGARS: BRAND LISTINGS

SAN FELICE
Machine-made in Frankfort, Indiana, USA.

Shape	Name	Lgth	Ring	Wrapper
Petit Corona	Original	4¾	42½	CC

This brand has only one shape, but it's a popular corona thanks to its genuine Wisconsin wrapper. The filler is a blend of American and Dominican tobaccos, surrounded by a sheet binder.

SANTA FE
Machine-made in Jacksonville, Florida, USA.

Shape	Name	Lgth	Ring	Wrapper
Long Corona	Chiefs	6	42	CC
Long Corona	Fairmont	6	42	CC
Cigarillo	Little Cigars	3⅞	20	CC

This is a mild cigar, available in boxes of 25 for the larger sizes and packs of 20 for the Little Cigars. The Little Cigars are offered in Menthol, Mild, Peach, Mild Menthol, Strawberry and Grape flavors.

SUPRE SWEETS
Machine-made in McAdoo, Pennsylvania, USA
and Cayey, Puerto Rico.

Shape	Name		Lgth	Ring	Wrapper
Cigarillo	Tip Cigarillo	*(tipped)*	5⅛	27	CM
Cigarillo	Cigarillos		4¾	27½	CM
Petit Corona	Perfectos		4¾	42	CM
Cigarillo	Little Cigars		3⅞	20	CM

The Tip Cigarillo and Little Cigars are made in McAdoo, Pennsylvania, while the Perfectos and Cigarillos are produced in Puerto Rico. All styles feature a manufactured wrapper and binder around a short-filler center with just a hint of vanilla added.

MACHINE-MADE CIGARS: BRAND LISTINGS

SWEET-NUT
Machine-made in Tampa, Florida, USA.

Introduced in 1997, this is a mild, one-size (5⅝ x 30) line with features Dominican-grown filler and homogenized tobacco leaf binder and wrapper.

SWISHER SWEETS
Machine-made in Jacksonville, Florida, USA.

Shape	Name		Lgth	Ring	Wrapper
Petit Corona	Blunt		4⅞	42	CC
Toro	Blunt XL		6⅛	52	CC
Corona	Kings		5½	42	CC
Petit Corona	Perfecto		5	41	CC
Panatela	Slims		5⅜	36	CC
Cigarillo	Coronella		5	27½	CC
Small Panatela	Outlaw		4¾	32	CC
Long Corona	Giants		6⅛	44	CC
Cigarillo	Cigarillo		4⅜	28½	CC
Cigarillo	Mini Cigarillo		3½	20	CC
Cigarillo	Tip Cigarillo	*(tipped)*	4⅞	28	CC
Cigarillo	Wood Tip Cigarillo	*(tipped)*	4⅞	29	CC

Popular? Swisher Sweets are enjoyed everywhere, offering a mild, sweet taste with a manufactured wrapper and binder and a blend of filler tobaccos from four nations. The Outlaw is 100% tobacco and features a Honduran leaf wrapper; the King shape also features a natural leaf wrapper. The Cigarillo has an Ecuadorian wrapper and a four-nation filler blend. Flavors were introduced in 2002: the Blunts are available in grape, peach and strawberry; the Blunt XLs also in grape, peach and strawberry. The Outlaws are offered in Double Barrel Rum; the Cigarillos in chocolate, grape, peach, Tequila and strawberry, and the Tip Cigarillos are offered in cherry, grape and peach. The Mini Cigarillos are offered in grape, peach and strawberry. You can find this brand in thousands of locations, in familiar red five-packs and in boxes of 50.

MACHINE-MADE CIGARS: BRAND LISTINGS

TAMPA NUGGET
Machine-made in Tampa, Florida, USA.

Shape	Name		Lgth	Ring	Wrapper
Petit Corona	Sublime		4¾	43	CC
Petit Corona	Sublime Black		4¾	43	CC
Petit Corona	Blunt		5	43	CC
Panatela	Panatela		5½	36	CC
Cigarillo	Tip Sweet	*(tipped)*	5	28	CC

These "nuggets" incorporate sheet wrappers and binders with a blend of filler tobaccos from the Dominican Republic and Honduras for a mild and flavorful smoke.

TAMPA SWEET
Machine-made in Tampa, Florida, USA.

Shape	Name		Lgth	Ring	Wrapper
Petit Corona	Sweet Blunts		4⅞	43	CC
Petit Corona	Perfecto		4¾	43	CC
Small Panatela	Cheroot		4¾	31	CC
Cigarillo	Cigarillo		4⅜	29	CC
Cigarillo	Tip Cigarillo	*(tipped)*	5	28	CC

This brand features filler tobaccos from Colombia and Italy, surrounded by a homogenized wrapper and binder. The Cigarillos and Tip Cigarillos are offered in Honey Berry and strawberry.

TEXAS SWEETS
Machine-made, with 100% tobacco, in San Antonio, Texas, USA.

Shape	Name	Lgth	Ring	Wrapper
Lonsdale	Sisterdale	6½	42	CM
Robusto	China Grove	5	50	CM
Toro	Agua Dulce	6	50	CM
Churchill	La Grange	7	47	CM

| Small Panatela | Luchenbach | 4⅛ | 32 | CM |

This is an all-tobacco cigar with an Indonesian wrapper, Connecticut binder and Brazilian and Honduran short filler. It is flavored with rum and sweetness added. It is available in boxes of 25 except for the Luchenbach, in tins of 10.

TOPPER
Machine-made, with 100% tobacco,
in McSherrystown, Pennsylvania, USA.

Shape	Name	Lgth	Ring	Wrapper
Long Corona	Grande Corona	6	47	CC-Ma
Corona Extra	Breva	5½	46	CC-CM
Perfecto	Old Fashioned	4⅞	46	CC
Perfecto	Old Fashioned Extra Oscuro	4⅞	48	Ma
Corona	Ebony	5½	47	Ma

Since 1896, Topper cigars gave offered a mild, flavorful taste with excellent value. Each of these models is made up of 100% tobacco and is offered in handy packs of 4-5 cigars, or in colorful boxes of 50. All feature genuine USA/Connecticut wrappers and binders and short filler from the Dominican Republic and the United States.

TOPSTONE CONNECTICUT BROADLEAF
Machine-made, with 100% tobacco,
in Santiago, Dominican Republic.

Shape	Name	Lgth	Ring	Wrapper
Corona Extra	Extra Oscuro	5½	46	Ma
Corona Extra	Bouquet	5½	46	DC-CC-Ma
Corona Extra	Oscuro	5½	46	Ma
Grand Corona	Grande	5¾	46	Ma
Churchill	Directors	7¾	46	CC-Ma

These are well-known, 100% tobacco cigars formerly made in Tampa, Florida and featuring dark-cured Connecticut Broadleaf wrapper and binder and a three-nation short filler blend. The Directors are offered in boxes of 25, while the other shapes are available in four-packs or five-packs and in boxes of 50.

TRAVIS CLUB CLASSIC
Machine-made, with 100% tobacco, in San Antonio, Texas, USA.

Shape	Name	Lgth	Ring	Wrapper
Long Corona	Plaza (tubes available)	6	43	CC-Ma
Corona	Straight	5⅝	43	CC-Ma
Panatela	Panatella	5½	38	CC-Ma
Perfecto	Counsellor	5	50	CC-Ma
Robusto	Rothschild	4⅞	50	CC-Ma
Perfecto	Regalia	4¾	47	CC-Ma
Petit Corona	Sport Triangles	4¾	44	CC-Ma
Perfecto	Especiales	5⅛	55	CC-Ma
Perfecto	Senator	5⅛	52	CC-Ma
Corona	Corona	5⅝	43	CC-Ma
Churchill	Double Corona	7	47	CC-Ma
Toro	Magnum	6	50	CC-Ma
Small Panatela	Little Travis	4⅛	32	CC-Ma

This brand has been around since 1906 and is the flagship brand of the venerable Finck Cigar Company of San Antonio. Take your choice of a Connecticut wrapper in natural or maduro shades in packs of five or boxes of 25 or 50.

TRAVIS CLUB PREMIUM
Machine-made, with 100% tobacco, in San Antonio, Texas, USA.

Shape	Name	Lgth	Ring	Wrapper
Double Corona	Churchill	7	50	CC-Ma
Grand Corona	Corona Extra	6¼	46	CC-Ma
Toro	Toro	6	50	CC-Ma
Long Corona	Palma	6	43	CC-Ma

MACHINE-MADE CIGARS: BRAND LISTINGS

| Perfecto | Perfecto | 5¼ | 52 | CC-Ma |
| Robusto | Robusto | 5 | 50 | CC-Ma |

Here is a beautiful cigar which features all-tobacco, all-long-filler construction and a mild-bodied taste. The elegant wrappers are genuine Connecticut Shade, the binders are also Connecticut-grown and the filler is composed of leaves from the Dominican Republic and Brazil. Travis Club Premium cigars are presented in individual cellophane sleeves inside elegant, varnished wooden cabinets.

VILLA DE CUBA
Machine-made in Santiago, Dominican Republic.

Shape	Name	Lgth	Ring	Wrapper
Corona	Brevas	5¾	44	DC-CC-Ma
Long Corona	Majestics	6⅜	43	DC-CC-Ma
Giant Corona	Corona Grande	7¼	45	DC-CC-Ma

Choose a Sumatra or Connecticut Broadleaf (maduro) wrapper in this mild-bodied brand. It has a sheet binder and a three-nation blend of filler tobaccos.

VILLAZON DELUXE
Machine-made in Santiago, Dominican Republic.

Shape	Name	Lgth	Ring	Wrapper
Giant Corona	Chairman	7¾	43	CM-Ma
Lonsdale	Cetros	7⅛	44	CM-Ma
Lonsdale	Senators	6¾	44	CM-Ma

Here is a veteran brand which features a Sumatra (natural) or Connecticut (maduro) wrapper, sheet binder and a short-filler blend of tobaccos from three nations. It is offered in boxes of 50 except for the Chairman style, offered in 25s.

VILLAZON DELUXE AROMATICS
Machine-made in Santiago, Dominican Republic.

Shape	Name	Lgth	Ring	Wrapper
Long Corona	Commodores	6	42	CM
Slim Panatela	Panatella	5¾	34	CM

Similar to the regular Villazon Deluxe line, this brand is flavored with vanilla and features a Sumatra wrapper to complement the homogenized binder and three-nation filler blend. It is offered in boxes of 50.

WHITE OWL
Machine-made in Dothan, Alabama, USA.

Shape	Name		Lgth	Ring	Wrapper
Petit Corona	Blunt		4¾	41	CC
Petit Corona	Blunt Xtra		5	41	CC
Cigarillo	Coronetta		4⅝	29	CC
Short Panatela	Demi-Tip	(tipped)	5⅛	32	CC
Cigarillo	Miniatures		4⅝	29	CC
Slim Panatela	Panatela Deluxe		5¼	34	CC
Corona	Invincible		5⅜	41	CC
Corona	New Yorker		5⅝	41	CC
Slim Panatela	Ranger		6⅜	34	CC
Petit Corona	Sports		4¾	41	CC
Cigarillo	Cigarillo		4⅝	28	CC

This brand started way back in 1887. The line-up includes a sheet wrapper and binder around a five-nation blend of filler tobaccos and is offered in twin-packs, five-packs, six-packs or in boxes of 50. Flavored versions were added in 2002. The Miniatures are available in peach, strawberry and vanilla. The Sports shape is offered in blackberry, peach and vanilla while the Blunts are offered in sweet, grape, pineapple, watermelon and strawberry. The Blunts Xtra is available in Wild Apple, grape, peach, pineapple, vanilla and strawberry. The Cigarillos, introduced in 2005, are offered in sweet, watermelon, pineapple, grape and apple.

WM. ASCOT
Machine-made in Santiago, Dominican Republic.

Shape	Name	Lgth	Ring	Wrapper
Lonsdale	Palma	6¼	42	DC-CC-Ma
Slim Panatela	Panatela	5¾	34	DC-CC-Ma

Churchill	Churchill	7½	48	CC-Ma
Robusto	Robusto	5¾	48	CC-Ma

This is a very mild cigar, featuring an Ecuadorian wrapper, sheet binder and Dominican and Honduran filler tobaccos. The Palma is offered in a variety of wrapper shades in boxes of 25 and the Panatela is available in boxes of 50.

WILLIAM PENN
Machine-made in Dothan, Alabama, USA.

Shape	Name		Lgth	Ring	Wrapper
Cigarillo	Willow Tips	*(tipped)*	5	27	CC
Cigarillo	Braves		4⅝	29	CC
Perfecto	Perfecto		5⅜	41	CC
Slim Panatela	Panatela		5¼	34	CC

Introduced in 1924, William Penn cigars offer mild taste thanks to a multi-nation blend of filler tobaccos, surrounded by homogenized wrappers and binders. Made by Swedish Match, the brand is offered in five-packs and boxes of 50 in the larger sizes.

WOLF BROS.
Machine-made in Yoe, Pennsylvania, USA.

Shape	Name	Lgth	Ring	Wrapper
Small Panatela	Rum Crookettes	4½	32	CC
Small Panatela	Rum River Crookettes	4½	32	CC
Perfecto	Rum Crooks	5⅜	42	CC
Perfecto	Rum River Crooks	5⅜	42	CC
Perfecto	Sweet Vanilla Crooks	5⅜	42	CC

These well-known cigars are also produced by the House of Windsor. Most of these shapes offer an imported leaf wrapper, sheet binder and a blend of imported short filler tobaccos. Please note the well-known flavored rum and vanilla shapes.

MACHINE-MADE CIGARS: BRAND LISTINGS

Y.B.

Machine-made in Yoe, Pennsylvania, USA.

Shape	Name	Lgth	Ring	Wrapper
Petit Corona	Squires	5	42½	CC

This old brand includes only one size, but it offers a medium body thanks to filler tobaccos from the Dominican Republic and the United States and a sheet binder and wrapper.

ZINO

Machine-made, with 100% tobacco,
in the Netherlands and Switzerland.

Shape	Name	Lgth	Ring	Wrapper
	Made in the Netherlands:			
Cigarillo	Cigarillos Brasil	3½	20	CM
Cigarillo	Cigarillos Sumatra	3½	20	Co
Cigarillo	Red Mini	3½	20	Co
	Made in Switzerland:			
Corona Extra	Grand Classic Brasil	5½	46	CM
Slim Panatela	Relax Brasil	5¾	30	CM
Petit Corona	Classic Brasil	4¾	41	CM
Petit Corona	Classic Sumatra	4¾	41	Co
Corona Extra	Grand Classic Sumatra	5½	46	Co
Slim Panatela	Relax Sumatra	5¾	30	Co

Here are beautifully made, mild cigars which feature Brazilian or Sumatran wrappers, Java binders and Brazilian and Indonesian filler tobaccos, offering outstanding quality and value in all-tobacco cigarillos and small cigars. The cigarillos made in Holland also include French Burley tobacco in the filler blend.

5.
SMALL CIGARS

This section provides the details on 70 brands of small cigars, generally made by machine for distribution to the widest possible audience in drug stores, supermarkets and, of course, tobacco stores.

For the purposes of this listing, small cigar "brands" are limited to those whose lines are dominated by (i.e., 67 percent or more of the shapes are) cigarillo or cheroot-shaped cigars. In addition, handmade or mass-market brands that offer the cigarillo shape in their lines include:

Handmade brands (73):

Acid
Antelo
Bering
C.A.O. Brazilia
C.A.O. Gold Label
Cabanas y Carbajal
Campesino
Carbonnell
Casada
Chevere Ice Cream Flavors
Cohiba
Cojimar
Conch Republic
Cordova
Courvoisier
Cubita
Cubita Spanish Market Sel.
Davidoff
Delicioso
Dominican Delights
Don Felo
El Credito
El Rey del Mundo
El Titan de Bronze
Excalibur
Felipe Gregorio 3 Tierras
Fittipaldi
The Flava
Graycliff

Graycliff Emerald
The Griffin's
Gurkha
Harvill
Havana Honeys
Heaven
Honey Delights
Hoyo de Monterrey
Island Amaretto
Island Collection
JM's Dominican
La Flor Dominicana
La Gloria Cubana
La Habanera
Macanudo
Maker's Mark
Mendez y Lopez
Miura Directo de Fabrica
Mocambo
Montecristo
Montecruz Little Cigars
Nat Sherman Metro. Sel.
Onyx Reserve
Partagas
Paul Garmirian Gourmet
Precious69.com
Private Stock
Punch
Puritos
Quisqueyana

Red Head
Rocco Gaetano d'Angelo
Romeo y Julieta
Rum Runner
St. Croix
Saint Luis Rey
Sancho Panza
Scarface
Swisher Sweets Prem. Sel.
Tatiana
Verona
Victor Sinclair
West Indies Vanilla
Z-Gar

Machine-made (29):

Alamo Sweets
Antonio y Cleopatra
Arango Sportsman
Black & Mild
Candlelight
Chevere Small Cigars
Cuban Club Classics
Dutch Masters
Garcia y Vega
Havana Blend
Ibold
Jamaican Smalls
King Edward
Muniemaker

SMALL CIGARS: BRAND LISTINGS

Muriel	Sam Houston	Tampa Sweet
Optimo	Santa Fe	White Owl
Phillies	Supre Sweets	William Penn
Robert Burns	Swisher Sweets	Wolf Bros.
Royal Blunts	Tampa Nugget	Zino

Each brand listing includes notes on country of manufacture, shapes, names, lengths, ring gauges and wrapper color *as supplied by the manufacturers and/or distributors of these brands.* Ring gauges for some cigarillos were not available.

When comparing and considering cigars listed in this category, it may be worthwhile to remember the standard dimensions of mass-produced cigarettes: almost always 7.9 mm in diameter (20 ring gauge) with lengths of 85 mm (approx. 3¼ inches) or 100 mm (approx. 3⅞ inches).

Please note that while a cigar may be manufactured in one country, it may contain tobaccos from many nations. These cigars utilize short-filler tobaccos unless noted; many brands use homogenized (sheet) leaf for binders and/or filler.

Although manufacturers have recognized more than 70 shades of wrapper color, six major color groupings are used here. Their abbreviations include:

- ‣ DC = Double Claro: green, also known as "AMS" or Candela.
- ‣ Cl = Claro: a very light tan color.
- ‣ CC = Colorado Claro: a medium brown common to many cigars
- ‣ Co = Colorado: reddish-brown.
- ‣ CM = Colorado Maduro: dark brown.
- ‣ Ma = Maduro: very dark brown (also "double Maduro")
- ‣ Os = Oscuro: black.

Many manufacturers call their wrapper colors "Natural" or "English Market Selection." These colors cover a wide range of browns and we have generally grouped them in the "CC" range.

SMALL CIGARS: BRAND LISTINGS

Darker wrappers such as those from Cameroon show up most often in the "CM" category.

Readers who would like to see their favorite brand listed in the 2009 edition can call or write the compilers as noted after the Table of Contents.

AGIO
Machine-made in Geel, Belgium.

Shape	Name	Lgth	Ring	Wrapper
Cigarillo	Mehari's Java	3⅞	23	CC
Cigarillo	Mehari's Brasil	3⅞	23	Ma
Cigarillo	Mehari's Mild & Light (Ecuador)	3⅞	23	CI
Cigarillo	Mehari's Mild & Sweet (Orient)	3⅞	23	CM

Here is one of the famous brands in cigarillos, introduced in 1976, offering dry-cured cigarillos and small cigars for almost every taste. Most of the shapes use wrapper leaves from Java; the Mehari's Mild & Light uses a Connecticut wrapper; the Mehari's Brasil features a Brazilian-grown wrapper and the Mehari's Mild & Sweet wrapper is from the Cameroon. All use a sheet binder and a blend of mild tobaccos in the filler.

AL-CAPONE
Machine-made in Germany.

Shape	Name	Lgth	Ring	Wrapper
Cigarillo	Sweets	3¼	20	CC
Cigarillo	Sweets Filter	3¼	20	CC
Cigarillo	Slims	3¼	20	CC
Cigarillo	Pockets	2⅝	20	CC

These cigarillos are made by Dannemann, using Brazilian and Indonesian tobaccos and are offered in convenient packs of ten. The Sweets are flavored with Cognac and the Slims are rum-flavored.

SMALL CIGARS: BRAND LISTINGS

ALTERNATIVOS
Machine-made in Belgium.

Shape	Name	Lgth	Ring	Wrapper
Cigarillo	Blue (Vanilla)	3½	23	CC
Cigarillo	Red (Cherry)	3½	23	CC
Cigarillo	Gold (Rum)	3½	23	CC

This brand was originally introduced in 1994. It features Ecuadorian, Javan & Malawi tobaccos for a medium to full-bodied taste.

AMERICAN MADE
Machine-made in Mocksville, North Carolina, USA.

Shape	Name	Lgth	Ring	Wrapper
Cigarillo	Little Cigars	3⅞	20	CC

Introduced in 2006, this is a mild line offered in Full Flavor, Light & Mild, Cool Menthol, Sweet Peach, Vanilla and Tropical Coconut in packs of 20.

ANTONIO Y CLEOPATRA WISE GUYS
Machine-made in Santiago, Dominican Republic.

Shape	Name	Lgth	Ring	Wrapper
Cigarillo	Wise Guys	3⅝	24	DC-CM

This is an all-tobacco flavored small cigar, available in Cognac, Honey Berry and Irish Cream. Introduced in 2004, Wise Guys are offered in packs of two or 10.

ASHTON SMALL CIGARS
Machine-made, with 100% tobacco, in Geel, Belgium.

Shape	Name	Lgth	Ring	Wrapper
Cigarillo	Cigarillos	3¾	26	CC
Cigarillo	Mini Cigarillos	3¼	20	CC
Small Panatela	Senoritas	3½	30	CC

Introduced in 2003, this is a 100% tobacco line of small cigars with wrappers and binders from the Central African Republic for a medium-bodied taste. They are offered in boxes of 10 and 20.

SMALL CIGARS: BRAND LISTINGS

AVANTI
Machine-made, with 100% tobacco, in Scranton, Pennsylvania, USA.

Shape	Name	Lgth	Ring	Wrapper
Cheroot	Avanti	4½	34	Ma
Cheroot	Avanti Continental	5¾	34	Ma
Cheroot	Europa	5¾	34	Ma
Cheroot	Ipenema	5¾	34	Ma
Cheroot	Ramrod Deputy	4½	34	Ma
Cheroot	Ramrod Original	6½	34	Ma
Cheroot	Kentucky Cheroots	5¾	34	Ma

Here is an all-tobacco, dry-cured, medium-bodied line of cigars, famous since their introduction in 1972. The ingredients are simple: fire-cured tobaccos from at least three different crop years of the finest farms in Kentucky and Tennessee, all barn-cured for at least four months. The Avanti and Avanti Continental are flavored with Anisette; the Ramrod Deputy and Ramrod Original are Bourbon flavored.

The Europa, introduced in 1994, uses a Kentucky dark-fired wrapper and binder and a blend of Belgian and Italian dark-fired tobacco for the filler.

BACKWOODS
Machine-made, with 100% tobacco, in Cayey, Puerto Rico.

Shape	Name	Lgth	Ring	Wrapper
Cigarillo	Backwoods	4⅛	27	CC-Ma

This 100% tobacco brand offers a mild taste but a surprise in its unfinished, "open" end. It has a natural or blackened wrapper, no binder and a blend of short-filler tobaccos offered in Original, Black & Sweet Aromatic, Grape, Honey, Honey Berry, Sweet Aromatic and Wild Rum flavors. It is presented in foil packs of 8.

BEACH PALM ★*New*★
Machine-made in Suret, India.

Shape	Name	Lgth	Ring	Wrapper
Cigarillo	Little Cigars	3⅞	20	CM

SMALL CIGARS: BRAND LISTINGS

This line was introduced by A&T Tobacco Imports in 2007, with a homogenized wrapper and short filler. Flavors include Full, Mild, Menthol, vanilla, cherry, peach and sour apple. All are offered in packs of 20.

BETWEEN THE ACTS
Machine-made in Tampa, Florida, USA.

Shape	Name	Lgth	Ring	Wrapper
Cigarillo	Between the Acts	3⅛	20	CC

Between the acts of your favorite show you can enjoy this mild, flavorful smoke, made up of a sheet wrapper and binder and filler tobaccos from Indonesia and the United States. Offered in packs of 20.

BLACK AND BLUE
Machine-made in Tampa, Florida, USA.

Shape	Name		Lgth	Ring	Wrapper
Cigarillo	Platinum	*(tipped)*	5½	27	CM
Cigarillo	Gold Power	*(tipped)*	5½	27	CC

Introduced in 2005, this is a tipped little cigar using pipe tobacco filler and a sheet wrapper, offered in packs of 20.

BLACKSTONE
Machine-made in Jacksonville, Florida, USA.

Shape	Name		Lgth	Ring	Wrapper
Cigarillo	Tip Cigarillo	*(tipped)*	4⅞	28½	CC
Cigarillo	Little Cigar		3⅞	20	CC

Introduced in 1997, Blackstone has a pipe-tobacco filler surrounded by a homogenized wrapper. The Litle Cigars are available in cherry and vanilla flavors; the Tip Cigarillo in cherry, peach or vanilla.

BLUNT MASTER
Machine-made in Santiago, Dominican Republic.

Shape	Name	Lgth	Ring	Wrapper
Cigarillo	Blunt Master	4½	27	CM

SMALL CIGARS: BRAND LISTINGS

This is a mild, pre-sweetened cigar which is offered with a choice of a homogenized or Connecticut leaf wrapper, homogenized binder and has Dominican and Connecticut short-filler tobaccos. It was introduced in 2006.

CAPTAIN BLACK LITTLE CIGARS
Machine-made in Tucker, Georgia, USA.

Shape	Name	Lgth	Ring	Wrapper
Cigarillo	Filters	3⅞	20	CC
Cigarillo	Flavored	3⅞	20	CC

Featuring the famous taste of Captain Black pipe tobacco, these little gems offer a mild taste, with a sheet wrapper and a blend of Indonesian, Philippine and United States tobaccos. Flavors include Jamaican Sweets, Tahitian Sweet Cherry, Caribbean Peach Rum and Madagascar Vanilla. Available in packs of 20.

DANNEMANN
Machine-made in Germany and Switzerland.

Shape	Name	Lgth	Ring	Wrapper
	Made in Germany:			
Cigarillo	Moods *(filter tip available)*	2⅞	20	CC
Cigarillo	Sweets	3⅝	20	CC
Cigarillo	Speciale - Brazil	2⅞	25	Ma
Cigarillo	Speciale - Sumatra	2⅞	25	CC
Cigarillo	Speciale - Lights	2⅞	25	Cl
Cigarillo	Imperiale - Brazil	4¼	25	Ma
Cigarillo	Imperiale - Sumatra	4¼	25	CC
Cigarillo	Lonja - Brazil	5⅜	25	Ma
Cigarillo	Lonja - Sumatra	5⅜	25	CC
Cigarillo	Menor - Sumatra	3⅞	28	CC
Cigarillo	Pierrot - Brazil	3⅞	28	Ma
	Made in Switzerland:			
Slim Panatela	Lights - Sumatra	6	34	CC

Slim Panatela	Lights - Brazil	6	34	Ma
Corona Extra	Espada - Sumatra	5	45	CC
Corona Extra	Espada - Brazil	5	45	Ma

Geraldo Dannemann created this brand in 1873 and today, these famous all-tobacco, dry-cured cigarillos and small cigars feature primarily Sumatran and Brazilian tobaccos and are offered in a dizzying array of packs, tins and boxes of 25 for the small cigars.

DARK HORSE ★*New*★
Machine-made in Suret, India.

Shape	Name	Lgth	Ring	Wrapper
Cigarillo	Little Cigars	3⅞	20	CM

This line was introduced by A&T Tobacco Imports in 2007, with a homogenized wrapper and short-filler cigar tobaccos. The flavor styles include Full Flavor, Milds, Menthol, vanilla, cherry, peach and sour apple, all in packs of 10 or 20.

DAVIDOFF CIGARILLOS
Machine-made, with 100% tobacco,
in Denmark and the Netherlands.

Shape	Name	Lgth	Ring	Wrapper
	Made in Ny Kobing, Denmark:			
Cigarillo	Club Cigarillos	4	23	Co
Cigarillo	Mini Cigarillos	3½	20	CC
Cigarillo	Mini Cigarillos Light	3½	20	Co
	Made in Eersel, the Netherlands:			
Cigarillo	Demi-Tasse	4	22	CC
Cigarillo	Long Panatelas	5½	22	CC

These elegant cigars are all tobacco which use natural leaf and are dry-cured for smoothness. All feature a Sumatra wrapper, Java binder and filler tobaccos from Brazil and Indonesia.

SMALL CIGARS: BRAND LISTINGS

DJARUM SPICE ISLANDS ★New★
Machine-made in Indonesia.

Shape	Name	Lgth	Ring	Wrapper
Cigarillo	Cigarillo	3¾	24	CM

Phillips & King introduced this little cigar in 2007. It's exotic and spicy, with a taste of cloves and comes in packs of six.

DEAN'S LIL' CIGARS
Machine-made in Mocksville, North Carolina, USA.

Shape	Name	Lgth	Ring	Wrapper
Cigarillo	Dean's	3⅞	20	CM

This line debuted in 2004 and uses a homogenized wrapper and cigar tobacco in the filler. It's offered in Full Flavor, cherry, chocolate, rum, wild berry, Menthol, mild, peach and vanilla flavors in packs of 20.

DeNobili
Machine-made in Scranton, Pennsylvania, USA.

Shape	Name	Lgth	Ring	Wrapper
Cheroot	Popular	3½	34	Ma
Cheroot	Twin Pack	4	34	Ma
Cheroot	Economy	4	34	Ma
Cheroot	Kings	4½	34	Ma
Cheroot	Toscani	6½	34	Ma
Cheroot	Toscani Longs	6½	34	Ma

A wide variety of sizes marks this dry-cured, 100%-tobacco brand, which uses only dark-fired Kentucky and Tennessee tobaccos in its blend. A brand of distinction since 1896, the Denobili range is marked by a mellow, medium-bodied taste.

DOCKERS SWEET TIP
Machine-made in Santiago, Dominican Repubic.